AF623818

Western Political Thought

(From Bentham to Present Day)

Volume II

S.K. Sharma
Urmila Sharma

ATLANTIC
PUBLISHERS & DISTRIBUTORS (P) LTD

Published by

ATLANTIC

PUBLISHERS & DISTRIBUTORS (P) LTD

7/22, Ansari Road, Darya Ganj, New Delhi-110002
Phones : +91-11-40775252, 40775214, 23273880, 23275880
Fax: +91-11-23285873
Web: www.atlanticbooks.com
E-mail: orders@atlanticbooks.com

Copyright © Atlantic Publishers & Distributors (P) Ltd., 1998
Reprint 2003, 2006, 2013, 2017, 2020, 2021, 2022, 2023

All rights reserved. No part of this publication may be reproduced, stored in a retrieval system, transmitted or utilized in any form or by any means, electronic, mechanical, photocopying, recording or otherwise, without the prior permission of the copyright owner. Application for such permission should be addressed to the publisher.

Disclaimer

- The author and the publisher have taken every effort to the maximum of their skill, expertise and knowledge to provide correct material in the book. Even then if some mistakes persist in the content of the book, the publisher does not take responsibility for the same. The publisher shall have no liability to any person or entity with respect to any loss or damage caused, or alleged to have been caused directly or indirectly, by the information contained in this book.
- The author has fully tried to follow the copyright law. However, if any work is found to be similar, it is unintentional and the same should not be used as defamatory or to file legal suit against the author.
- If the readers find any mistakes, we shall be grateful to them for pointing out those to us so that these can be corrected in the next edition.
- All disputes are subject to the jurisdiction of Delhi courts only.

Printed & bound in India by Atlantic Print Services

Preface

Political thinkers, particularly in the nineteenth and twentieth century, have been searching for a harmonious formula for amicable relationship between the individual and state on the one hand and the state and international human community on the other. This effort was made from several directions: Utilitarianism, Idealism, Positivism, Socialism, Anarchism, Pluralism, Behaviouralism and the supporters of democracy. Political thinkers from Bentham to Marx and Marx to Bertrand Russell discussed human nature from the psychological and social standpoint, some emphasising psychological and some social aspects while exceptional few maintaining a more balanced view. In the individual-state relationship, while the individualists exclusively emphasised individual liberty, the Fascists and the Nazis gave total authority to the state. Few thinkers, including various shades of socialists, maintained a more balanced view. About the question of inter-state relationships while the Fascists and Nazis favoured conflict and war, contemporary thinkers including John Dewey and Bertrand Russell favoured fascism.

In controversies among various political thinkers: British, German, Russian, Italian, French and American, what strikes an impartial student of the nineteenth and twentieth century political thought is the fact that while every political thinker has had some special insight into political behaviour of human beings, most of them tended to exaggerate the partial truth into total and absolute principle. Political thought has today arrived at a more mature stage. The era of spectacular political thought is already over. The present serious student of political thought should keep his eye on the totality, the gestalt, the panorama, to arrive at a more balanced and integral view. This will require a collaboration of political science with other branches of humanities, particularly Psychology, Sociology and Economics. A sane political thought should be based on some psychological, social and economic facts and no less on ethics and spirituality. However, we should not expect a unanimous political thought ruling all over the world. Multiplicity in unity is the fundamental principle in all human affairs. This is particularly true in political thought.

This Volume II of Western Political Thought discusses various currents of Political Thought from Utilitarianism to Pluralism and Nazism. It includes political thinkers from Bentham to Bertrand Russell, from nineteenth century to Present day. While the subject matter has been derived from standard original works, it has been narrated in an analytical style and discussed from an integral standpoint. At the end of each chapter actual examination questions of various universities have been given so that the student may exercise for the examination. Among dozens of books by Indian and Western Authors on this subject, the present book claims to be more to the point, concise and providing answer to every question asked in various university examinations. Thus, the book has been prepared as an ideal textbook for post-graduate students of Political Science in all Indian Universities. Besides, it will serve as a ready reference book for the teachers.

However, suggestions are cordially invited from the indulgent readers for improvement in next edition.

S.K. SHARMA
URMILA SHARMA

Contents

1

Political Thought in 19th Century

According to Maxey "The nineteenth Century is beyond all comparison the most bewildering century of human experience. Old social values have lost their glamour and their place has been taken by new social values. Development of science and industry has completely changed the life and social environment of a man and therefore real change has occurred in our political thinking." Some of the changes were as follows :

1. Nation State the Centre of Modern Political Thought. Political thinking now revolves around the nation state. Hobbes and Bodin defended the absolute powers of the nation state. Hegel went a step further and said that the state is the march of God on earth. Burke, Locke, Rousseau and Montesquieu defended the constitutional or democratic state. Rousseau put emphasis on popular sovereignty and consequently on democracy.

2. American War of Independence. In 17th century America revolted against the British regime. She declared that !ife, liberty and pursuit of happiness are inherent rights of man bestowed by God or nature. This declaration of American independence is considered as the Magna Carta of liberalism.

3. French Revolution. French revolution went a step further. Liberty, equality and fraternity became the cry of the day, in whole of the world. It influenced the future course of history. It gave courage to public to oppose the Government. But reactionary thought gave rise to conflict between democracy and monarchy in which democracy and democratic ideas emerged triumphant. Industrial Revolution and scientific inventions changed the environment and living of the man. Scientific ideas gave a death blow to fatalism and superstitious thinking. The industrial revolution wiped out the existence of an independent individual artisan. Artisan class lost its former importance. A new class of industrial workers and of engineers and clerks etc. came into existence. As this new middle class became conscious of its rights, various ideologies came into existence.

4. Increase in Population and Urbanization. Asian civilization was rural, based on agriculture. Consequently, 19th century development of industry gave rise to industrial cities. Population rose by leaps and bounds. In 18th century the population of Europe and America was 18,76,93,000 and 60,00,000 respectively but gradually it became 60 crores and 24 crores respectively. In 18th century this ratio of urban population was 30% and 40% in England and America respectively, but now it became 75% and 50% respectively. In India, Calcutta, Bombay, Madras and Kanpur were merely villages but now their population became 108 lakhs, 98 lakhs, 45 lakhs and 22 lakhs respectively. Delhi's population is more than one crore. World population is more then 6500 crores and that of India 96 crores.

5. New Urban Problems. Rise of the new industrial cities gave rise to various new problems. Health, education, sanitation and maintenance of moral and family life and providing living wages to workers became the burning problems of the day.

6. Development of Transport and Communications. With the development of means of transport and communications, workers came in touch with one another and they began to exchange their ideas to solve their problems. This brought them in close contact with one another "Workers of whole world unite," became the cry of the day but fall of Soviet Union in 1991-92, gave set back to communist movement.

7. New Classes. Industrial revolution created new classes of manufacturers, shopkeepers, traders and administrators on the one hand and the workers on the other.

8. New Ideologies. Some thinkers like Herbert Spencer defended the polity of *laissez faire* which supported dominating class. On the other hand, Karl Marx developed the philosophy of communism or socialism to support the working class. Some thinkers like Bentham and Mill tried to reconcile the conflict by championing the cause of reforms to improve the lot of workers and general public on the basis of the greatest good of the greatest number.

9. Imperialism and Colonialism. Extreme nationalism and industrialisation forced powerful and industrialized countries to seek new markets and new places from where they may get raw materials. This tendency resulted in imperialism and colonialism. With the rise of national consciousness among the subject nations, this was replaced by new colonialism or by satellite system or by loans with strings.

10. Change in Intellectual Field. Darwin gave a new scientific outlook, an evolutionary theory of development and a theory of the survival of the fittest. This theory influenced Biology, Astronomy, Geology and Sociology. Political thinking was also affected. Spencer applied biology to political thinking. Later on, the psychological school of thought came into existence. According to Barker, "Psychology became the fashion of the day; if our forefathers used to think biologically we think psychologically." Later on political thought supporting capitalism, socialism and communism came into existence with various varieties such as fabianism, syndicalism and guild socialism etc.

DIFFERENT AND ANTAGONISTIC CONCEPTIONS

In 19th Century various schools of thought came into existence though no political philosophy dominated the political thought of whole century. Most of the political thoughts were mutually inconsistent. In Greek thought, City states dominated the political thought. During Roman empire, law dominated the political thinking. During medieval period, conflict between Church and the State dominated the political thought. But in nineteenth century antagonistic thoughts like individualism and absolutism, capitalism and communism came into existence. Some main political concepts were as follows :

1. Utilitarian Theory. Nineteenth century began with utilitarian thinking of Bentham and Mill. These thinkers championed the cause of reforms to improve the lot of general public. They pleaded for the greatest good of the greatest number.

2. Theory of the Historical Study of Law. Utilitarian thinkers produced legal thinkers like Jane Austin. Historical study of law became a dominating feature of the age. Scholars studied conceptions of Roman jurists, Bodin, Burke and Montesquieu to support their theories of law and constitution on historical basis.

3. Organic View of the State. Darwin's evolutionary theory gave impetus to compare the state with the human body. Following these footsteps, Spencer compared state with human body. He gave prominence to organic theory of the state. He drew his own conclusion and supported extreme individualism.

4. Utopian Socialism. With the development of industries and rise of working class, new problems and new thinking came into existence. Political thinkers were moved by the pathetic and pitiable conditions of the workers, their slum dwelling, their low wages and long working hours. Many thinkers applied themselves genuinely to find out the ways and means by which the condition of working class may be improved. Robert Oven, Saint Simon, Charles Fourier were most prominent among such thinkers. These thinkers however failed to find out a practical solution. So they were called visionaries. Thomas More wrote *Utopia* and so they were called utopian socialists.

5. Scientific Socialism. The utopian socialists failed to provide practical solutions for the problems of the day. Hence, a new scientific school of socialism came into existence under the leadership of Karl Marx and Engels. They pleaded that all history is the story of class war and exploitation of man by man. Rulers always exploited the ruled for their own benefit. Peace and prosperity can be gained only by wiping out the classes. There should be a classless society in which everybody will work according to his ability and get according to his needs. Ideas of Karl Marx dominated half of the mankind but nowhere communism has come into existence upto now. The conflict between capitalist countries and their supporters *versus* that of communist countries became burning problem of the day. Failure of communism in Soviet Union in 1991-92 gave it a set-back.

6. Idealism. Idealistic school of thought came into existence during 19th century. The German Philosopher Kant gave prominence to the idealistic thinking which reached to perfection in the hands of Hegel who supported absolutism by saying "State is the march of God on earth." Green liberalized it but Bosanquet again championed the cause of Hegel. Communists and fascists both borrowed their ideas from Hegelian philosophy interpreting it differently.

7. Doctrine of Sovereignty. With the advent of national states, the idea of sovereignty came into prominence. Jane Austin defined law as the conception of sovereign power. He said that "Law is the will of sovereign body which obliges a person or persons to a course of conduct."

8. Scientific or Psychological School. With the development of science, scientific ideas began to be applied to political thinking. Spencer applied evolutionary theory and biological conceptions to political thinking. Bagehot, Graham Wallas, McDougall etc. developed psychological school of thought.

Various schools of Political Thought developed during 19th century were generally antagonistic to one another. There was conflict between absolutism and democracy. Democracy and democratic ideas gradually emerged triumphant but 20th century witnessed the conflict of capitalistic and communistic thinking. Conflicts between individualism and state socialism are the dominating features and dominating problems of the modern times.

According to Francis W. Coker "Indeed, all schools of political thought — authoritarian or liberal, collectivistic or intellectualistic, conservative or reformist — agree that there is room somewhere for the fruitful use of human reason in choosing wise and avoiding unwise course of political action; all assume that man, by taking thought, can in some manner play an effective part in the mighty movement of human history."[1] The political thought of the nineteenth century or recent political thought, was an extension of the early modern political thought that covered the period of previous three centuries. Thus, recent political thought looks like a set of divergent ideas presenting the spectacle of a veritable 'Babel of promiscuous and largely unrelated concepts and doctrines'.[2]

REVISION OF LIBERALISM

The notion of liberalism found its modification and reinterpretation, even mutilation throughout the nineteenth century at the hands of eminent thinkers. The impact of Industrial Revolution continued to have its way in the domains of sociology and economics. Several schools arose to study the question of individual liberty *vis-a-vis* political authority from different, even opposite, standpoints. For example, while the individualists looked at the state as a necessary evil and justified the doctrine of the minimum possible area of state activity, the Collectivists dubbed the state as an agency of public welfare and defended the increasing area of its activity in the name of public welfare. However, both discarded abstract notions like those of law of nature or other assumptions of the age of reason.

1. Coker : *Recent Political Thought*, p. 30.
2. Maxey : *Political Philosophies*, p. 450.

Utilitarianism

(i) *Jeremy Bentham.* Jeremy Bentham, the founder of the English utilitarian tradition, ridiculed the notion of 'natural rights' as 'rhetorical nonsense upon stilts'. He justified the action of the individual as well as of the state on the maxim of 'utility'. Utility was substituted for conscience as the link between objective order and subjective will. Freedom was conceived more and more as a social utility. Happiness was conveniently discovered to coincide with moral duty and the moral problem was solved by denying its abstract existence. The function of the state was no longer conceived as the protection of man's natural rights but as the promotion of the greatest happiness of the greatest number."[3]

In the place of absolute standards of good and evil, Bentham substituted a relative ethical standard rooted in the principle of 'utility' that meant nothing else than the worldly satisfaction of the individual."[4] He advocated a number of reforms in the spheres of law, justice, prison houses, educational curriculum, electoral system and the like. Thus, it is commented that 'first, last and always Bentham is a reformer. But we must remember that he is a curious kind of reformer. Most reformers are perhaps too practical, too shortsighted; they cannot see the woods for the trees. But Bentham was so much preoccupied with his own definition of 'forest', and with various deductions from it that he did not see how little real woods are like his conception of them."[5]

(ii) *J.S. Mill.* John Stuart Mill advanced the doctrine of individual's sovereignty over himself, his own body and mind, and thereby shunned the case of state intervention until one were a nuisance to the freedom of others. He sanctioned the case of heavy taxation on 'unearned increments' accruing from 'socially-created values'. He went to the extent of defending the case of nationalisation of very important industries." He desired the state to over-step its sphere in this direction so as to enforce compulsory education to remove the ignorance of the citizens, release persons from the obligations of the contracts in perpetuity where the parties could not be competent judges of the effects of such obligations, make subject to public control all monopolies, limit working hours and regulate conditions of work, encourage scientific works, increase wages, levy taxes on economic rent, protect public health, introduce factory legislation, and launch insurance against illness, industrial accidents and indigence in old age. To a student of political thought such a shift in the stand of Mill looks quite puzzling. He may hold the view that reconciliation of the principle of *laissez faire* with that of socialism is an impossible task. However, the reason for this should be traced in his strong defence of competition and his equally strong disdain for the economic growth and expansion."[6]

The reinterpretation of liberalism at the hands of Mill was a result of his conscious as well as unconscious thinking. He realised that liberty for the

3. Hallowell : *Main Currents in Modern Political Thought*, p. 198.
4. M.J. Rendall : *An Introduction to Political Thought*, p. 330.
5. W.T. Jones : *Masters of Political Thought*, Vol. II, p. 368.
6. R.J. Halliday : *John Stuart Mill*, p. 108.

manufacturing class did not imply the same thing as for those belonging to the class of workers and toilers and thus a modification of the old philosophy of human action, if not an entirely new philosophy, was an urgent necessity if social progress was not to be checked by a social creed."[7]

(iii) *T.H. Green*. Green could well visualise the new social trend that had overtaken England in the later part of the last century. He gave a distinctly positive turn to the notion of liberty. It is evident from his own version of liberty that it is power 'to do or enjoy something', the element of worthiness to be determined by man's life in common with others. As Barker says: 'Liberty is, therefore, no negative absence of restraint, any more than beauty is the opposite of ugliness. It is a positive power of doing or enjoying something worth doing or enjoying."[8] The first Reform Act of 1832 and the second one of 1867 had democratised the character of the House of Commons and after the Chartist agitation of 1848 the legislation, as Prof. A.V. Dicey says, was passing from an individualist to a collectivist trend.[9] Thus, instead of feeling satisfied with mere emphasis on the negative area of state activity, Green frankly advocated the case of a welfare state determined to eradicate three gigantic social ills — ignorance, intemperance and pauperism.[10] Obviously, according to Green, the "state's characteristic function is that of removing external hindrances to the voluntary performance of good acts. In executing this task it has much more to do than defend the community from foreign attack and check traditional crimes and torts."[11]

(iv) *Herbert Spencer*. The individualistic line of argument found its reiteration in the scientific thought of Herbert Spencer. His argument relating to the province of government justified the concept of *laissez faire*. He subscribed to the doctrine of individualism while contributing his part to the organic theory of state. He argued that as uninterrupted evolution takes place in the world of nature, so should happen in the sphere of social development. The laws of biology and sociology confirm the fact of evolution. Hence, the state need not create obstruction in the way of social evolution. Spencer sought to justify the least possible scope of state activity on the basis of the biological laws of 'struggle for existence' and 'survival of the fittest'. It informed him to propound that "an individualistic policy for modern government could be proved to be right by the laws of both universal and organic evolution."[12]

The concept of *laissez faire* was so strongly advocated by the individualists like John S. Mill, Adam Smith and Herbert Spencer found its gradual erosion by a new trend that paved the way for the emergence of socialism. Bentham made an improvement upon earlier liberals like Locke; Mill revised Benthanism

7. E. Barker : *Political Thought in England* (1848-1914), p. 3.

8. *Ibid.*, p. 24.

9. *Ibid.*, p. 22.

10. Green : *Lectures on the Principles of Political Obligation*, p. 208.

11. Coker, *op. cit.*, p. 424.

12. *Ibid.*, p. 392.

and, finally, Green "gave Englishmen something more satisfying than Benthamism at a price they were prepared to pay, that he left liberalism as a faith instead of an interest, that he made individualism moral and social and idealism civilised and safe."[13]

DEFENCE OF DEMOCRACY

According to Coker, "Democracy is government by those who have a greater awareness of and a greater concern for the interest of all the members of the community. It has, therefore, been adopted to serve both freedom and happiness. Where government is controlled by the general body of citizens, it is least likely to establish unreasonable restraints upon individual conduct and most likely to be impartial in the determination and enforcement of whatever restrictions experience shows it is necessary to impose."[14]

The defence of democracy found its most outspoken form at the hands of John Stuart Mill. He appreciated the reform movement of democracy, and made some important suggestions for its better operation, Mill studied the case of democracy not only in the light of the principle of 'utility' or worldly happiness but also in the light of his own notion of 'liberty' that is the dearest possession of man. The whole treatment is based on the conviction that the representative government "is the only type that is conducive to the freedom and development of the moral and intellectual faculties in the individual, which a free society alone encourages."[15]

VARIETIES OF SOCIALISM

Shift in the trend of liberalism toward socialism of different sorts, created a sort of veritable Babel of largely varying concepts about the nature and form of a new and just social and economic order. It gave a message of hope for the exploited and oppressed sections of the community. Whether it was the mild socialism of some French and English socialists like Charles Fourier, St. Simon, William Thompson etc. also known by the nicknames of 'Christian' and 'Utopian' socialists or extreme socialism of Marx and Engels, the triumphant pace "meant a truceless war"; it also signified that "every society was divided into two armies engaged in that war, with the object on the one side of fastening and, on the other, of defeating the revolution which should inaugurate the final day."[16]

Prior to Karl Marx thinkers like William Thompson, Thomas Hodgskin, John Gray and John Francis Bray had set forth the doctrine that wage workers serving in the fields or factories were the real producers of wealth, most of which was taken away in a quite unjust manner by the community of the capitalists, traders and employers.[17] They suggested certain collectivistic schemes

13. C.L. Wayper : *Political Thought*, p. 193.

14. Coker, *op. cit.*, p. 11.

15. Frank Thakurdas : *The English Utilitarians and the Idealists*, p. 189.

16. Barker, *op. cit.*, p. 185.

17. See Max Beer : *History of British Socialism*, Vol. I, Part II, Ch. VII.

like state monopoly of the services of marketing and banking, a currency system based on time units of labour, voluntary co-operative societies in order either to ensure an exchange of goods on the basis of the quantities of labour employed in producing them or to secure generally an equitable distribution of wealth among those who create it."[18]

1. Christian or Utopian Socialism. The central theme of the arguments advanced by the Christian or Utopian socialists was to condemn the system of private property and unrestrained economic competition. They believed that changes could be achieved through appeals to the reason and good sense of the influential members of the community. They preferred the course of ushering in the new era of socialism by means of implementing the experiment of co-operative societies of communes in which the norms of justice, equality, brotherhood, benevolence and free association would replace the bad features of competition, coercion and class disharmony. Their basic doctrine received wide acceptability that if co-operation were substituted for competition as the mainspring of economic activity, most of the social evils would disappear.[19]

2. Fabianism. The English Fabians like George Bernard Shaw, Sidney Webb, Beatrice Webb, Harold Pease, William Clarke and some others took inspiration from the writings of Mill and repudiated what was said by Marx and Engels. Other leading English writers like David Ricardo and William Morris also influenced their thought. Founded in 1884, the Fabian Society brought out a collection of articles (*Fabian Essays*) in 1889 in which a distinctly anti-Marxian socialism was advocated. The goal of the English Fabians was 'the socialisation of the means of production, exchange and distribution, the whole to be controlled by a democratically organised state in the interest of the entire community.' They repudiated the idea of a bloody revolution and laid emphasis on the use of constitutional and democratic means. If the Marxists think in terms of the class war the Fabians do the same in terms of the solidarity of classes.[20]

3. Marxism. The most clear-cut and consistent form of socialism found its place in the works of Marx and Engels. It became a 'scientific' doctrine. It laid down the principles of social and economic change. Marx discovered the principles of social change and predicted the emergence of a new society. The basis of Marxism is the doctrine of class war which signifies that every society is ridden with the antagonism of classes and new social order takes place as a result of the struggle between these. Economics is the maker of history. The means of production, exchange and distribution of goods determine the character of a social stage and define relations between the owners of these means and those who are dependent upon them for the sake of their existence. On the basis of such an economic interpretation of history and the application of the law of dialectical materialism Marx predicted that the future society would signify the

18. Coker, *op. cit.*, pp. 17-18.

19. *Ibid.*, p. 18.

20. See R.C.K. Ensor : *Modern Socialism*, pp. xxxiii ff.

liquidation of the capitalist system in which the toilers would become the real masters in a classless and a stateless society. Marx is considered to be the first socialist writer whose work "can be termed scientific. He not only sketched the kind of society which he desired but spoke in detail about the stages through which it must evolve."[21]

The story of socialist thought hovers between the poles of Fabianism and Revisionism with their insistence on gradual development of society towards a new social order through democratic means, as well as Marxism with its emphasis on the importance of the economic factor in the progress of society and the part played by the class struggle in the fight to abolish class struggle. Some points common to both are like attainment of an economic order whose aim is service rather than profit, public in preference to private ownership of the principal means of production and distribution, elimination of waste, removal of gross inequalities of wealth, eradication of the insecurity of livelihood and establishment of the conditions of social justice.[22]

IDEALISM

In the recent political thought the thinkers of the school of Idealism tried to take state to mystical heights. The state was deified and the individual became a means. The state became a sacred, divine, mystical or metaphysical entity and the people were taught to exalt, glorify and adulate it, because it represented the realisation of the best and perfect condition of life. The result was that political theory reached very close to the world of ethics and metaphysics. Prof. J.W. Garner says: "Like ethics, political theory is concerned with what ought to be as well as with what actually is; the real nature of a thing is what the thing is when its growth is fully developed; the political philosophers, therefore, may very properly idealise the state and deal with it in its imaginary splendour and perfection."[23]

The idealist tradition was based on the assumption that man is a social and political creature by nature as well as necessity. Isolated from the life of his fellow beings the life of an individual is a life against nature. The real nature of the individuals can be developed only in society. Only by living in society a man can realise all that he has in him to be. He can develop his full self only by intercourse with his fellows by the realisation of social duties and the fulfilment of social obligations. Therefore, to the obvious benefits of security against violence and redress against injustice that the individual receives from the state, he owes it a debt of gratitude for its bestowal upon him of his own individuality in all its riches and with all its potentialities.[24] Thus, idealism maintains a close connection between ethics and politics and holds that no

---

21. C.E.M. Joad : *Modern Political Theory*, p. 41.
22. H.W. Laidler : *Social-Economic Movements*, p. 751.
23. Garner, *Political Science and Government*, p. 238.
24. Joad, *op. cit.*, p. 11.

political progress is possible apart from the application of the highest moral principles to our individual and social lives."[25]

Different trends of liberalism, socialism and idealism prevailed in the nineteenth century which demonstrated the need for new thinking in the light of changing social and economic conditions of the people. It also directed attention towards a plausible solution to the key issue of individual liberty *vis-a-vis* political authority. Other momentous issues involved the problems relating to the province of government, location of sovereignty, area of individual liberty, man's relationship with the society and the state. Answers to these were given by a host of eminent thinkers of England, Germany and France which contributed to the enrichment of the stock of political theory in various important ways.

Contemporary political thought should be studied not as basically different from but a continuation of the recent political thought. Trends in the recent political thought provide material for the political thought of the present century. To conclude with Coker, "In our political discussions today, when we seek some basic theoretical position to support or attack a proposed arrangement in governmental structure of policy, we still make use of criteria that were familiar in the writings of early nineteenth century. We argue variously as to the natural rights or the happiness of individual men. We deduce conclusion from conceptions of the nature of human society in general or the history of a particular political community. We consider the nature of man in terms now of his 'primitive' characteristic and now of his potentialities for development towards an 'ideal' to be attained in the future."[26]

QUESTIONS FOR EXERCISE

1. What were the conditions — intellectual, social, economic, religious and political etc. — which gave rise to the 19th century political thought?
2. What were the main concepts of the 19th Century political thought. State political thought of 19th Century.
3. The political thought of the 19th Century was as jumbled as its material and intellectual progress. Discuss.

25. E. Asirvatham : *Political Theory,* VI ed., p. 47.

26. Coker, *op. cit.*, p. 29.

2

Utilitarianism
Jeremy Bentham (1748—1832)

Utilitarian political philosophy is England's real contribution to European political thought. Both form the viewpoint of expediency as well as proper understanding of a philosophy. It is most imperative and unavoidable to study utilitarianism in contemporary social, economic, cultural and political philosophies. Political philosophies of Plato and Aristotle were the outcome of the conditions of Greek city states. Throughout middle ages either religion dominated politics or secular authority dominated papal authority. The philosophers like St. Augustine then represented their age.

Throughout 17th century political philosophers like Hobbes and Bodin defended absolutism. Locke stood for constitutional rule and Rousseau for popular sovereignty. Montesquieu propounded and expounded his theory of separation of powers for safeguarding individual freedom. All these philosophers were the product of their time and their philosophies equally influenced their age.

With its favourite slogan of liberty, equality and fraternity, French Revolution engulfed whole of Europe and immensely influenced political thought of the time. Burke tried to dilute the influence of French Revolution. In doing so he was supported by Hamilton and Madison in America who had otherwise supported the revolutionaries. Burke came forth with his famous conservativism and tried to undo the work of French Revolution forgetting that it was *fait accompli*. His conservativism only saved England from the onslaught of revolutionary tendencies.

Though Burke tried to undo the work of French Revolution yet the slogan of liberty, equality and fraternity, the keynote of this revolution, changed the very thinking of whole of Europe and England was no exception to that. They now began to think about mutual relationship of rulers and subjects and the extent of people's share in the administration. Through their writings Shelley, Baron and Burns also upheld this slogan. There was popular demand for individual liberty and removal of inequality and poverty of masses.

Utilitarian philosophy appeared as early as in 1872 when Richard Cumberland expressed utilitarian ideas in his treatise on *'Natural Law'*. Francis

Hutcheson gave this idea in a more concrete form by defining it as 'greatest good of the greatest number'. Priestley and Paby in England and Helvetius in France were among others who were forerunners of this school of thought. The credit of coining this term goes to Mill who used this word in one of his treatises.

BASIC PRINCIPLES OF UTILITARIANISM

1. Psychological Hedonism. Man weighs everything in terms of pleasure and pain. He always seeks pleasure. What gives him pleasure is good and what pains him is bad. In the words of Bentham, "Nature has placed mankind under the governance of two sovereign masters, pain and pleasure. It is for them to point out as to what we ought to do, as well as to determine what we shall do."

2. Pragmatism. Not idealism but fruits of action matter for the citizens. Davidson said that "We added to practical efforts to ameliorate the conditions of human life on national principles, and to raise the masses through effective state legislation."

3. Individualism. Utilitarians were liberals. Human beings have definite values. Their freedom consists in being free from everything but law. Law is essential for moral and material welfare of the subjects. Thus, utilitarians supported individualism.

4. Moral Standpoint. Utilitarians believed in moral values and judged everything from that viewpoint. It was most essential that the people should have high moral character and maximum moral development.

5. Inductive and Experimental Methods. Utilitarians used inductive and experimental methods of study. They were practical in their approach to every problem. They did not remain within the four walls of the lecture halls. They expounded their theories in the light of what was practical and actually happening in our day-do-day life. According to Metz, "It grew not so much from the closets of students or from lecture rooms as from the hard necessities of life and fluctuating daily struggle for co-existence."

6. Rejection of *Laissez Faire*. In so far as *laissez faire* is concerned the Utilitarians came to the conclusion that it was not in the collective interest of the society. Maxey has said, "As industrialisation proceeded, utilitarians found themselves increasingly convinced of the enlarged governmental interference in the domain of property and contract."

7. Men and Society Inseparable. Utilitarians believed that men and society are inseparable. They stressed the idea that man is an integral part of the society. Without society it shall not be possible for him to lead a happy and joyous life.

8. Associationism. Utilitarianism is close to associationism. To quote W.L. Davidson, "By Associationism is meant the attempt to explain philosophically the nature and formation of knowledge and find out units for sensation and exposition of principles according to which this formation is effected."

9. Greatest Good of the Greatest Number. Utilitarians stood for the greatest good of the greatest number of people. This could be obtained by promoting moral development of the people by looking after their progress and by uplifting them socially, economically and culturally and even mentally, morally and physically.

10. Government a Necessary Evil. Utilitarians believed that government was a necessary evil. It must be respected because without state authority man cannot make uninterrupted progress. State is essential for checking hindrances to the normal development and progress of the people.

11. Maximum Happiness of Maximum Number. The Utilitarians believed in the idea of happiness of maximum number of people. They were of the opinion that pleasure should not be the monopoly of only a section or class in the society but given to the greatest number of people. The existence of state could only be justified on how and to what extent the state promoted happiness. Bentham pointed out that the agency commanding authority on the subjects should promote happiness and pleasure and avoid pains.

12. Concept of Utility. Concept of utility is another basic principle of Utilitarian philosophy. It is the principle "which approves or disapproves of every action whatever, according to the tendency it appears to have to augment or diminish the happiness of the party whose interest is in question or, what is the same thing in other words to promote or oppose that happiness." An everlasting pleasure should be certain, durable and pure and should extend to all. Pleasure can be derived from wealth, health, power or benevolence, whereas backwardness, ill repute etc. can be the causes of pain. Causes of pain and pleasure can be simple as well as complex but it is difficult to generalise them because these differ from individual to individual.

13. State is Not Natural. Utilitarians were of the view that the state is not a natural necessity. It is a product of man's desire to satisfy his needs. The state should protect natural rights of the people.

14. Synthesis of Ethics and Politics. Utilitarians tried to combine ethics with politics. They felt that a state could not be devoid of ethical considerations. They believed that the state was not an end in itself but only means to an end.

Critical Estimate

1. Individualism. Utilitarians portrayed individualistic and not collective aspect of human life which was fundamentally undesirable and impracticable.

2. Expediency. Halvey has said that utilitarianism is nothing else but "an attempt to apply the principles of Newton to the affairs of politics and moral." The utilitarians have been charged to have sacrificed morality for the sake of expediency. The stress which this school of thought lays on quantitative pleasure has been denounced as derogatory to the dignity of mankind.

3. Oversimplification. The utilitarians have tried to oversimplify the whole philosophy and human nature which in fact is very complex and complicated. Of course everybody wants his own pleasure but he knows that his happiness will be problematic when others are there to enjoy with him.

4. Materialism. This philosophy is synonymous with materialism. It stands for nothing else but for pursuit of wealth and worldly happiness.

5. Fallacy of Aggregation. If happiness is the end of the state then state is not the agency which can promote collective happiness. There is nothing like collective pleasure, because happiness is always individualistic, both in nature and character.

6. Neglect of Organic State. Utilitarians have also been criticised for ignoring organic nature of the state. They have treated society only as a mathematical aggregate of its component members which is not correct.

7. Value of Ideals. Ideals are essential for advancement. But utilitarian philosophy does not care much for ideals. This is no indication of an advanced and progressive philosophy.

In spite of the above criticism the importance of this school of thought cannot be underestimated.

Appreciations

1. *Wayper*. "They were too coldly intellectual, too frigid and scholastic, and were not flattered by their view of mankind. But for long they were without serious competitors. Their great contemporaries, Rousseau, Kant, St. Simon and Marx were honoured in England : their critics at home were unconvincing. In consequence their influence was out of all proportions to their number."

2. *Prof. Dunning*. "English utilitarianism was one of the most potent forces in the intellectual life of all western Europe and of America as well."

3. *Maxey*. "The utilitarian philosophy is often described as the 19th century revival of the classical hedonism of Epicurus, which in truth it was but it was fruition also of critical realism of such scholars as Spinoza and Hume in the two preceding centuries."

JEREMY BENTHAM (1748-1832)

Bentham was born on February 15, 1748 in a family of rich lawyers in London. He was very intelligent. He learnt Latin at the age of three. He studied Voltaire when he was hardly six. He passed law but became a political thinker and writer. In 1776, he wrote *'Fragments on Govt.'* In 1789, he published *'Introduction to the Principle of Morals and Legislation'*. He wrote many other books such as *'The Defence of Usury'*, *'The Discourses on Civil and Penal Legistation'*, *'The Essay on Political Tactics'*, *'The Theory of Punishment and Rewards'*, *'The Treatise on Judicial Evidence'*. *'The Papers Upon Codification and Public Instruction'*, *'The Book of Fallacies'*, *'The Rational Evidence'* etc. He began as a Tory, but became Radical. He founded the school of Utilitarianism and brought many reforms. He died in 1832, when great reform took place. He was a great thinker and reformist.

Contemporary Situations

In the 19th century, British commerce and industry expanded phenomenally. Economically and politically, Britain became the most powerful nation in the world. Traditional legal and political system as well as the prevailing system of political ideas tended to distract the progress of British Industry and Commerce. It has been said that the "Britishers are conservative even in their revolutions." British philosophical radicals, whose leader was Bentham challenged the old order through the philosophy of utilitarianism. The political philosophy of Bentham was an effort to advance the cause of mercantile and manufacturing classes against the vested power of land owning classes and traditional institutions.

Meaning of Utility

Utility means usefulness. Utiliariansim is a philosophy in which ideas, institutions and acts are tested by their usefulness to the human beings who are affected by them. Usefulness means happiness of the people, and happiness is judged by the pleasure it brings to individuals. To each individual what gives him pleasure is good and what causes him pain is evil. The final test of everything is pleasure or pain that results from it. Even a person or institution is judged by the amount of pleasure it brings to other people compared with the pain it causes to some people. If an act of government brings more pleasure to a number of people then it is a good act. On the contrary, if it gives more pain than pleasure it is a bad act.

According to Bentham, utility is the criterion by which laws and institutions should be judged. The previous writers only described the laws of the country or the institutions. They could not say whether these were good or bad and, if they were bad, how they could be improved.

Bentham made Blackstone, the famous jurist, target of criticism, who in his commentaries had innovated the entire legal system of England, but had failed to evaluate the laws. In utilitarianism Bentham found the principle by which legal and political system could be adjudged and improved. But utilitarianism is not only a system of ethics, it is a theory of psychology. Individuals are moved to do that which brings them pleasure and to avoid that which brings them pain. In this way the law giver can influence the behaviour of the people because he may offer inducement of increased happiness to those who conform to the laws and inflict the deterrent punishment of pain upon those who would contravene the laws. Thus, the legislator should pass the laws which would promote happiness. As he has the power of awarding pleasures or inflicting pain through such laws he might also serve the ends that are in his private interest.

Jeremy Bentham coined the term utility and extensively used it in his philosophy. He gave utilitarian philosophy a systematic form. He put it on a scientific footing by making it a school of thought. Before him Hume and Priestley in England, Helvetius in France and Beccaria in Italy also used the term 'utility' but failed to put it on a scientific footing. Bentham used the term in a most scientific way. He himself confessed that he picked up the term from Priestley. He was so much impressed when he read the term 'greatest happiness of the greatest number of people' that he got an inner ecstasy. Wayper has quoted him to say that. "I cried out as it were in an inward ecstasy, like Archimedes at the discovery of the fundamental principles of hydrostatics, Eureka."

Gross Utilitarianism

1. Hedonism. Bentham started with the presumption that the cherished desire of every individual is to achieve pleasure and happiness. Man by nature is repulsive to miseries and pains. Everything in the society should be considered in terms of utility. Utility means maximum social pleasure and happiness. It is always in direct proportion to the pleasure. To avoid sorrow and dismay, according to Bentham, "Nature has placed mankind under the governance of two sovereign masters, pain and pleasure. It is for them alone to point out what we ought to do, as well to determine what we shall do. On the one hand, the standard of right and wrong, and on the other the chain of causes and affects are fastened to their throne. The principle of utility recognises this subjection and assumes it for the foundation of that system, the object of which is to rear the fabric of felicity by the hands of reason and law systems which attempt to question its deeds in sounds instead of senses, in caprice instead of reason, in darkness instead of light."

2. Utility. Thus, for Bentham everything was to be valued, adjudged and measured only in terms of pleasure and pain. He said, "The principle of utility consists in taking as our starting point, in every process of reasoning the calculus of comparative estimate of pains and pleasures and in not allowing any other idea to intervene. An adherent to the principle of utility holds virtue to be a good thing by reason only of the pleasures which result from the practice of it, he esteems vice to be a bad thing by reason only of the pains which follow in its train." Man should not only aim at his own pleasure, but at collective happiness of the greatest number of people.

3. Utility as Primary Criteria. Bentham was of the opinion that Utilitarianism is a philosophy in which everything ought to be tested in terms of utility and usefulness. Utility of all laws and actions of our legislators should be measured in terms of pains and pleasures which they give. Bentham said, "To seek pleasure and to shun pain is his sole aim, even at the moment when he is doing himself the greatest enjoyment or courting the most severe penalties. This maxim, unchangeable and irresistible, as it is, should become the chief study of the moralist and of the legislature. To these two motives the principle of utility subjects everything."

4. Calculus of Utility. Bentham was of the view that intensity, duration, certainty, proximity, fecundity and purity were some of the measuring rods for testing the extent of utility which an action ultimately gave. By frequency he meant the 'quality of its being followed by the pleasure of the same sort.' From purity he understood no threat to pleasure from any corner. For the purpose of utility, he felt that everybody was equal to the other, irrespective of his status and position in the society. Thus, he was an individualist. He did not contribute to the idea that traditionally existing institutions or ideas could not be challenged.

5. Four Sanctions. According to Bentham there are four sanctions regarding pains and pleasures:

(i) *Physical or Natural Sanction.* This implies those pleasures and pains which are not the product of any human efforts, but have been given by nature in the course of time.

(ii) *Moral Sanction.* This implies the sanction which is prompted by good-will or contempt at the hands of our fellow beings.

(iii) *Public Sanction.* This means legal sanction which is given to the individuals by the magistrates in exercise of their legal powers.

(iv) *Religious Sanctions.* This follows from religious doctrines.

6. Simple and Complex Pleasures. According to Bentham pleasures are simple or complex. Simple pleasures are in sense, wealth, skill, beauty, repute, power, piety, benevolence, malevolence, intellect, memory, imagination, hope, association and relief. Simple pains are in enmity, ill name, privation, memory, expectation and awkwardness. Man is governed under the yoke of these two masters namely pleasures and pains. Complex pleasures and pains arise out of these simple pains and pleasures in one form or the other.

Bentham was of the opinion that utility was something objective and not subjective in nature. For him such concepts as natural Justice and Law of Nature had no meaning.

7. Hedonistic Calculus. Every action should be judged on the basis of pleasure and pain. There were physical, religious, moral and political sanctions for pleasure. Utility must be clear and precise. It must have a single and sufficient account for motivation. It must be adjustable by means of a moral calculus. Bentham wanted to apply this principle on legislation also. Unity means share of people in legislation. Thus, democracy and not aristocracy is the ideal form of government.

Critical Evaluation

Bentham's theory of utility has been criticised on the following grounds:

1. Oversimplification. According to Bentham embracing pleasure and avoiding pain is the motivating and moving force behind all human activities. He has tried to classify pleasures and pains into simple and complex ones. He has put them all into a tabulated form. Here he is victim of oversimplification. The problem is not so simple as it appears to be or what he has made it look like. When put into actual practice and tested on hard and real complexities of life, the whole concept is bound to prove a broken reed.

2. Materialistic Theory. Bentham made his theory purely materialistic. His theory assigns no place to moral and immoral actions which a person is bound to perform in his day-to-day life. Murray has rightly observed, "If we take away conscience, as Bentham does, there is no such thing as a moral or immoral action though there may remain acts that are generally useful on the reverse. As there is no individual conscience, so there is no collective conscience."

3. Misunderstanding of Human Nature. According to Bentham human beings struggle for having maximum pleasure because according to him each pleasure must be followed by another successive pleasure. This is a very narrow outlook of human nature. This is rather sensual. Wise persons restrain desires rather than increasing them. They try to attain a stage of perfection where pleasure and pain have no meaning for them.

4. Underestimation of Society. Bentham has failed to understand the importance of society as a whole. He has laid stress only on individual pleasure. The basis of his theory is neither society nor state but the individual. He has forgotten that human beings are social animals and depend on society. He has also forgotten that individual without society is incomplete. As a realist he should have pleaded for collective rather than individual pleasure. Wayper has rightly said, "In his study of the individual he has left out both society and history. In refusing to consider the importance of history and society he ignored the strongest forces that have made what he is."

5. Inconsistent Theory. Bentham maintains that human beings struggle for their own individual pleasure. If that is true then how could they fight and care for social happiness. It is rather useless to expect from selfish individuals to act for a social action. It is difficult to reconcile egoism with altruism in his theory.

6. No Measuring Rod for Pleasure. Bentham has failed to provide any standard to judge whether pleasure has been achieved or not and to what extent. Without such a measuring rod the whole superstructure of this theory based on pleasure and pain is bound to collapse.

7. Impracticable Theory. Bentham has been criticised on the grounds that his theory sounds impracticable. It is well nigh impossible to give greatest hapiness to greatest number of people. In actual practice happiness is always the monopoly of those who are at the helm of affairs rather than those who are governed. It is confined to a few rather than to the greatest number of people. Even the socialist states cannot claim that they have given pleasure to greatest number of people.

8. Wrong System of Studying Political Institutions. Bentham tried to assess justification and soundness of political institutions in terms of happiness. Soundness of a political institution is directly and proportionately related to the pleasure which it gives to the people. He wanted to measure politics on the yard-stick of mathematics which is ridiculous. It cannot be denied that politics and mathematics are not related to each other and to measure one on the yardstick of the other is absolutely of no use.

9. Unanimity on Pleasure. The concept of pleasure differs from person to person and place to place. It has no unanimity and to give it a universal outlook is something which is not only impossible but impracticable as well.

10. Ambiguous Theory. In actual life there are actions which produce greatest happiness but not for greatest number of people and there are still other actions which though they give less happiness but give it to greatest number of people. Bentham has not suggested as to what course should be followed in such cases and which should be preferred especially when one and the same course might not produce greatest happiness for greatest number of people.

11. Ignored Habits. Even though Bentham makes us believe that the people always act under the influence of pleasure and pain but that is not always true. Many a time people become slave of evil habits and act under their influence without caring for the pains which would come to them out of these actions. Sometimes knowing well that his habits might bring him miseries in the long run a person still feels compelled to act contrary to his inner desire as is the case with all addicts to drugs or alochol.

12. Wrong Psychology. Bentham's theory makes people selfish and self centred. According to him every one cares for himself alone and not for anything else. This is neither the quality of good citizenship nor an indication of healthy society. His theory is based on wrong psychology.

13. Outdated Theory. According to Bentham, immediate pleasure is always to be preferred over deferred pleasures. When put into actual practice this idea is bound to lead to many difficulties. State spends mostly on projects which might not result in immediate benefits to the society but are meant for the succeeding generations. Such types of expenditures are most inevitable. These are indications of an advanced society. According to Bentham's theory, however, these are unwanted and not suited to modern times.

14. Stress on Quantity. By saying that maximum happiness of maximum number of people should be the aim of state, Bentham has laid stress on quantity. In every good philosophy, along with quantity, proper stress should also be laid on quality.

Thus Bentham's theory of utility as based on pleasure and pain theory is faulty and impracticable. Taken to its logical conclusion it is bound to indicate that Bentham had a narrow vision of the things. He tried to mould certain basic facts according to his own ideas and has not very much succeeded in that.

POLITICAL IMPLICATIONS OF BENTHAM'S UTILITARIANISM

1. Criteria of Utility. Bentham was the first to use the term 'utility' in a systematic way, with great minuteness and considerable details. His utilitarian philosophy had wide political implications. His straightforward statement challenging the then existing social and political institution had universal appeal.

2. Blow to Social Contract. His philosophy gave a severe blow to social contract theory. He said that the state was not the outcome of any contract but only because the people saw advancement in the state.

3. Challenge to State Supremacy. Bentham challenged the supremacy of state. This was of great political significance in those days. In most of the cases the state had no right to punish the subjects because people committed crimes due to defective laws passed by the legislators.

4. Individual Freedom. Another political implication of Bentham's philosophy was that he stood for individual freedom and demanded that the people must have a share in running their own administration. He thus stood for individual liberty in England when Spain and Turkey were establishing and strengthening their empire.

5. Democracy. Bentham's philosophy prescribed democracy and democratic institutions. It was a bold step in those days.

6. Re-examination of Institutions. Bentham's utilitarianism shook many of the age-old institutions from their very foundations. He very boldly said that the age of an institution was neither any guarantee nor proportionate to its utility. An institution should be judged from the purpose which it served and nothing else.

7. Political Reforms. Though it suffered from some drawbacks yet Bentham's philosophy was seriously studied. This in itself bears testimony to his influence. It was due to his efforts that Bill of Rights was passed in England. In the words of William Ebenstein, "He is the greatest single reformer in English History, particularly in the field of law. His main contribution to political science was not that he invented a new principle of political philosophy but that he steadily applied an empirical and critical method of investigation to concrete problems of government and administration.

8. Middle Class Social Philosophy. Bentham was a middle class social philosopher. The people of England are not extremists by nature. They are usually opposed to revolutions and radical social and political changes. Bentham was no exception to that. Throughout his political philosophy he did not preach revolution. He suggested only reforms. He wanted to reform the whole legal system. But he did not wish to outright replace it with a new order. Similarly, he wanted to reform the prisons. His love for democracy in itself proves that he always felt that there was room and scope for reforms. He did not condemn any of the legislative institutions. All that he suggested was that the legislators should behave nicely and realise their representative character. He suggested reforms in the state and never suggested that the sovereign or the state should be disobeyed.

POLITICAL THOUGHT OF BENTHAM

Natural Laws and Rights

Bentham was of the opinion that nature is a very vague term. The concepts of natural rights and natural laws are equally vague, uncertain and undependable. Accordingly, he did not believe in these theories. He, however, agreed with Hobbes that law is the command of sovereign and that state is the only source of law. Laws could be given by God and not by Nature. As laws were given by the sovereign, therefore, in every state there must be a supreme, undisputed and unquestionable sovereign authority to issue commands. The worth of laws always depended on the general obedience given to it and the utility which it promotes. Security, substance, equality and abundance were aims of a model law. People are punished mostly because of the mistakes of legislators who do not pass proper and healthy laws, sometimes even such laws are passed which are more respected in violation rather than in obedience.

The concept of natural Rights is simple nonsense. It has neither any existence nor value. The existence of 'Private Property' is justified.

As the state is sovereign and supreme authority it is exclusively responsible for giving laws. There is no justification in claiming natural rights. Natural rights are against state sovereignty and hence absolutely unjustified. The state is a contrivance. It is the foremost duty of legislators to see that the laws passed by them promote utility. The laws can be passed both by 'Natural Method' as well as 'Technical Method'. In the former case utility prevails whereas in the latter case 'procedure' comes to the front.

"Benthamism, shorn of its crudities, is simply humanism."[1] His primary concern was the welfare of the community. He had a living and practical interest in view and was not merely concerned with barren speculative theory.[2] Bentham described natural rights as "simple nonsense; natural and imprescriptible rights rhetorical nonsense — nonsense upon stilts." For the theory of natural rights he substituted the principle of utility.

Rejection of Contract Theory of State

In his the *Fragment on Government,* Bentham bitterly criticized Blackstone who praised the English law as a slow, natural growth in accordance with divine providence. "Bentham showed that it was a shamless tyranny, which worked only for the misery of the weak and poor, an elaborate mechanism for helping the educated and the powerful to keep down the ignorant and the oppressed."[3] He further attacked Blackstone for basing political obligation upon an original social contract. He argued that there was no such contract in the past and that, even if there was one, it did not bind the present generation. Nor would such a contract be regarded as a historical fact but merely as a logical concept. Every form of a contract theory of the state was rejected by Bentham.[4] Contract, consent, agreement furnish no basis for political rights and duties. The ultimate reason why men submit to the requirements of law and of government is, not that they or their ancestors have promised to do so, but that it is for their interest to do so. In Bentham's own well-known phrase, men obey the laws because "the probable mischiefs of obedience are less than the probable mischiefs of disobedience." Governments exist because they are believed to promote the happiness of those who live under them.

"The libraries of disquisition on the state of nature, with its iniquities or its blessedness according to the fancy of the writers; on the devious and complex process through which men emerged from the natural into the political state;

---

1. Brown, Ivor : *English Political Theory,* p. 102.
2. Davidson, W.L. : *Political Thought in England,* p. 48.
3. Brown, Ivor, : *op. cit.,* p. 102.
4. Fragment, Chap. I, Sec. XXXVI.

and on the survival of rights and duties from the earlier in the latter condition: all these were banned to peremptory worthlessness by the Benthamite formula."[5] The essence of the state, according to Bentham, was merely a habit of obedience. Such a dogma left no room for the history or the mystery which played so large a part in the political theory of the conservatives and the reactionaries.

The Utilitarian Theory of State

The utilitarian explanation of the state is an explanation in terms of an unlimited end, and in terms of the particular character of the state which differentiates it from man's other activities. A theory which maintains that the end of the state is the promotion of utility identifies the end of the state with the end of human life. Bentham and the utilitarians tell us that the state is the sole source of law, which is the most certain of the four 'sanctions', or overriding motives, which govern the lives of men. There are the physical sanction, which operates in the ordinary course of nature; the moral sanction, which arises from the general feeling of society; the religious sanction, which is applied by "the immediate hand of a superior invisible being, either in the present life or in a future"; and the political sanction, which operates through government and the necessity for which is the explanation of the state.

Thus, the state, for Bentham, is primarily a law-making body, a group of persons organized for the promotion and maintenance of happiness, and acting through law to that end. A law is the expression of a will in the form of a command. As law is the expression of a will, sovereignty can be predicated only of a being of which will can be predicated. Nature or reason or justice cannot be the supreme power in a state, because they cannot make law. As God and man are the only forms of existence possessing will; therefore law must emanate from one of them. The great task of law in the human world is to reconcile interests — "so to regulate the motive of self-interest that it shall operate, even against its will, towards the production of the greatest happiness." This it does by attaching artificial pains, or punishments, to certain actions of a particular kind which would not be conducive to the general happiness. It cannot concern itself with all actions which would not be conducive to the general happiness. Law in its very nature is limited, and its nature shows the bounds which any true state must set to its actions. Law should take cognizance of and turn into offences only those bad, adult, other-regarding actions whose punishment will increase the net balance of pleasure or decrease the net balance of pain. Morality must concern itself with all self-regarding actions, but they are beyond the province of law. "Legislation and morals," as Bentham puts it, "have the same centre but not the same circumference."

Law must be the command of a supreme authority. Bentham is prepared to admit the existence of civil society only when such an authority is habittually obeyed. His State is a sovereign State. Nothing it does, can be illegal. To speak of it as exceeding its authority is an abuse of language. This is true of the free state as well as of the most despotic of states.

5. Dunning, W.A., *A History of Political Theories* (From Rousseau to Spencer), p. 217.

Bentham set himself in direct antagonism to the predominant philosophy of the revolutionary and reforming parties of his day. He shared and applauded their confidence in written constitutions as guarantees of rational government, and in the simplification of legislation in every respect. But he regarded bills of rights, limitations upon the power to amend the constitution, and all other devices for restricting the supreme authority, as unsound in theory and worthless in practice. They rested largely for justification upon the idea that the distinction between free and despotic governments depended on the greater or less degree of power possessed by the supreme authority of the state. The ultimate sovereigns in all states possess precisely the same unlimited and undefined power. Whether any particular government is considered free or despotic depends on a variety of circumstances connected with the distribution and application of this power in its exercise.[6]

Democracy

In spite of his penchant for an unlimited sovereign power, Bentham had a strong liking for democracy. In his state all men have equal rights. All men have the right with all others to promote policy. All must be equal before the law. The state's most urgent tasks is to ensure a greater equalization of property. His perception that inequalities are inevitable did not blind him to the fact that too great inequalities are an insuperable obstacle on the road to the greatest happiness. He was perfectly right in recognizing, that a society which is without gross inequalities of fortune is happier than one which is not.

Conception of a Negative State

Though according to Bentham's principles the state can take far-reaching action so long as that will increase pleasure or decrease pain, his state is nevertheless fundamentally a negative one. It has no integral relation with the moral life of the citizen. It seeks to change him. It cannot help him to develop his character. It is not the state that moulds the citizens, it is the citizens that mould the state. State is a contrivance whereby man seeks to ensure happiness. The individual is prior to it. He is endowed with reason, the state, in no sense can be regarded as more real than he is himself.

Thus, Bentham's state is a trustee for the individual. It is a democratic state in full sense. The interests of the state are not superior to the interests of the individuals. Instead of extolling the English Constitution, Bentham, attacked it in right earnest. He pleaded for universal adult suffrage, subject to the test of ability to read. The object of all his proposals was "to secure the real and effective representation of the people" and to prevent political corruption. Bentham was eager that democracy should have its full sway. He recommended the equalizing of electoral districts, and the freedom of the press. He attacked the utility of the House of Lords and of monarchy on the ground that the interests of these institutions were not compatible with the interest of the people

6. *Fragment*, Chap. IV, Sec. XXIV.

at large. He believed that a single-chambered legislature, renewable every year, was most in accord with the democratic principles.

By means of his *Constitutional Code,* Bentham hoped to better "this wicked world by covering it over with Republics." Neither monarchy nor limited monarchy secures maximum happiness. "It is only when democracy rules that the interests of the governors and the governed become identical, for the greatest happiness of the greatest number is then the supreme end in view."[7]

The Purpose and Ends of Legislation

On the publication of his *Principles of Morals and Legislation* (1987), Bentham became a 'new Moses' of Legislation. Statesmen from different parts of the world looked to him for practical guidance. He was above parties and private interests, fully devoted to the common well-being. According to him, the ends of legislation are security, subsistence, abundance and equality. In simple language, the object is the good of the people. If laws are to be obeyed, it is necessary that legislation should carry the people along with it. Unwilling obedience and general dissatisfaction mean ultimate revolution. Bentham justified opposition to the state if that opposition would produce less pain than continued obedience. In that case, it is the individual's "duty and interest" to "enter into measures of resistance". This does not mean that Bentham allowed the individual to resist the state ordinarily and frequently. He allowed the use of 'the right to resist' only as a last resort and that too on the consideration of its utility. To avoid the chances of revolution, he advised the legislators that the reasons for legislation should be made plain and obvious to the people. People should be checked from pursuing their own selfish interests by means of fear and reward.

Practical Reforms

The practical reforms which Bentham advocated are summarized by Davidson, as follows: the reform of the corrupt and restricted parliamentary system; a thorough-going municipal reform; the humanization of the terribly cruel criminal law of the time; the improvement of prisons and prison management; the abolition of imprisonment for debt; the elimination of the usury laws; the repeal of religious test; the reform of the poor law; the suppression of 'sturdy beggars'; the utilization of able-bodied paupers; the training of pauper children; the establishment of a vast scheme of national education; the institution of 'frugality banks' (now known as savings banks) and friendly societies; the following of a code for merchant shipping; the protection of inventors; the encouragement of local courts; a comprehensive system of health legislation; the creation of the public prosecutors and of advocates for the poor; a thorough-going revision of hereditary rights; the supervision of scientific and philosophical foundation; and the recall of public officials.

Bentham wanted to devise systems and methods of legislation that would conform to and serve this great end. His services to ethical and juristic science

7. Dunning, W.L. : *op. cit.*, pp. 78-79.

were of the utmost value. With sublime confidence in the infallibility of his judgment he formulated codes of international law, constitutional law, civil law, and criminal law, which, embodied principles and suggestions that have not failed later generations. He was eager "to see justice administered, and happiness secured to the deserving and the oppressed."[8] He criticized existing laws and machinery for the execution of them. His object was primarily construction, and criticism was simply a means to this end.

Bentham realized that the laws of the day were in a chaotic condition. He took upon himself the task of codifying them, but no encouragement was given to him in his own country. Encouragement came, however, from foreign lands, particulary from France and Russia. Applying his utilitarian principles to the laws of these countries, he demonstrated how his theory would work in concrete instances.

Bentham had no patience with the unnecessary technicalities, redundancies, and obsolete phraseology fondly indulged in by framers of laws. Laws, must be expressed in plain and short easily-followed sentences. They should be put within the easy reach of those who are held responsible for obeying, them. Bentham criticized the mode of administering laws, which pressed most heavily on the poor. He condemned the dilatory methods of judges which involve unnecessary expenditure to the parties concerned, and the miscarriage of justice arising from the technicalities of law. With scant respect for the judge he heartily supported juries as a check on their despotism. "He insisted on individual responsibility in all judicial offices, and, as a corollary, advocated the propriety of only one judge to a tribunal; plurality of judges trying a case meant weakened responsibility in each."

Theory of Punishment and Prison Reforms

Bentham was much interested in the theory of punishment and prison reforms. The chief end of punishment was to prevent crime. It should not be merely vindictive. The pleasure of revenge should be given a minor place in the award of punishment. Punishment should be exactly suited to the purpose. It should be neither more nor less. It should secure the good of the community. If capital punishment was necessary for the safety and security of society, it was justifiable. Whether capital punishment was to be administered in cases other than murder, should be determined by considerations of utility, *i.e.*, their effect upon the general good. The execution of justice should be exhibited to the public eye so that prospective evil-doers seeing it would be frightened away from committing the crime.

Though Bentham's emphasis is on the different theory of punishment, this does not exclude the reformation of the criminal, which he regards as "a part of the calculation of the balance of consequences in meting out punishment." He believed that a great many criminals and evil-doers were capable of improvement and that they could be restored to society as useful and self-respecting members. He advocated many principal reforms for the reformation

8. *Ibid.*, p. 92.

of the criminal and for the teaching of industries while in confinement. He evolved a scheme known as 'Panopticon' for the systematic supervision of the daily life of the convicts. The prison buildings were to be arranged in a (semicircular) fashion so that the superintendent could have a view of all the cells from his residence. The scheme combined careful supervision and discipline with sympathy and improved environment. The criminals were to be taught useful trades and also given elementary education. Moral and religious training should be brought to bear upon them. On their discharge, they were to be provided with employment until they were able to regain the confidence of the public and stand on their own feet. Although many of these reforms did not come into being in Bentham's day, the "vast reforms of prisons and penitentiaries that have taken place since his day, and the institution of reformatories and industrial schools, derived impulse from him and have proceeded on the principle that he laid down."[9]

Bentham believed that punishment should fit the criminal and not the criminal the punishment. Punishment should be graded according to the nature of the crime, the previous character of the offender, his parentage, the circumstances in which the crime was committed, the motive of the criminal, and the kind of persons to whom the injury was done. Punishment was to be certain and impartial in its imposition. The only valid test of the adequacy of a punishment was its ability to secure public welfare.

Although Bentham's distinctive field was, however, that of ethics and jurisprudence. His distinctions in the various species of law contributed decisively to the elimination of ethical and juristic conceptions from the domain of the science of the state. He was keenly concerned to make a perfect job of his theory. The necessary advance in this direction was made by John Austin, a disciple of Bentham.

Contribution to Political Thought

Bentham's main task was to liberate political theory from medieval political vocabulary. He provided one of the most powerful of weapons against what William James used to call the 'Bitch Goddess'. He insisted that the state existed for man, not man for the state. He proclaimed that could the state be considered good where there were happy citizens. "The interest of the community then is what?" Bentham asked. And he answered, 'The sum of the interests of the several members who compose it." It applied an empirical and critical method of investigation to concrete problems of law and government. He extended the experimental method of reasoning from the physical branch to the moral. It denied the infallibility of the superior person who foists his own morality or type of happiness upon others. "Winnowing the grain from the chaff need not be such a dusty process as to blind Englishmen to the debt they owe to Jeremy Bentham."[10]

9. *Ibid.*, p. 11.
10. Wayper, C.L., *Political Thought*, Chap. II.

ESTIMATE OF BENTHAM

Bentham was one of the most important thinkers of utilitarian school of thought. His philosophy is studied very seriously even today. It is interesting to study different facts of his contribution.

1. As a Moral Philosopher. To Bentham conventional morality was irritating. Whether an action is good or bad should be judged from the happiness or utility, which it produced. If an action results in pains it is sure to be a bad action. An act of theft is not always bad. It could be good as well if it produced pleasure. It is surely bad, if the outcome of action is pain. Pleasures and pains were our sovereign master. These, however, proceed from physical, political, moral and religious sources. Temperance conserves health and pleasure and intemperance results in ill health and pain. Governmental legislation can result in bringing either pleasure or pain. Every praise of an action by the public morally encourages and thus gives pleasure, whereas condemning by the public results in pain. Coming to religious source when one performs duties towards God, he feels pleasure otherwise he is pained. Both pleasure and pain can be mathematically measured and arithmetically calculated. In estimating pleasure, intensity, duration, certainty, propinquity, remoteness, fecundity, purity and extent must be taken into consideration. Principles of pleasure were as certain as those of geometry. Pleasures and pains were both simple and complex. In the complex form these included wealth, skill, amity, good name, power, piety, benevolence, expectation and relief, whereas in simple forms are included pains of privation, nonsense, awakwardness, etc. All pleasures and pains differ in sensitivity and sensibility of pleasure and pains. These factors include health, strength, firmness of mind, sensibility, insanity, sex, age, rank, education etc. Correct utility of any political system could be determined only by a scientific process of evaluation of factors which are important considerations of weighing of pain and pleasure.

2. As a Political Philosopher. Bentham's political ideas are available in his '*Fragment on Government*'. He challenged the ideas of Blackstone in many respects. He did not agree with him that contract of any kind is the source of law. Theory of social contract is sheer nonsense. The people obeyed laws because the probable mischiefs of obedience are less than the probable mischiefs of resistance. The essence of a state is the habit of obedience of the people. As such, for all practical purposes, Bentham replaced contract theory with the doctrine of utility. As a political philosopher he was opposed to the doctrine of Natural Rights and did not favour French Declaration of Rights of Man. He said that if at all there are any rights for the people these should be liberty, property, security and resistance to oppression. Bentham was opposed to the concept of legal rights as man has no right by virtue of his humanity. Rights are only concessions which could be withdrawn at any time. There is no right which should not be abolished, if abolition of it is advantageous to the society. English constitution is far from satisfactory. The house of Lords and monarchy should be abolished. Bentham did not favour the idea of woman franchise. Republican form of government was the best for economy, efficiency and supremacy of people. If the government cannot promote greatest happiness of greatest number of people, it has no other jurisdiction to exist. Bentham was opposed to preference and privileges. He stood for free trade in economics.

Democracy is the best form of government. The government should be reposed in such persons who possess certain basic qualities as wisdom, goodness to discern, goodness to endeavour and knowledge to put intentions into action. According to Bentham, these are the natural foundations of sovereignty, and these are the requisites that ought to be found in every well constituted frame of government.

3. As a Reformer. Bentham believed that there is scope for reforms in British society, law and judicial procedure in law. He favoured condification of laws. A complicated procedure only served the lawyers and the poor were always in a disadvantageous position. He felt that at present justice was simply sold. He condemned delays by judges in giving justice. He was sore at the idea that the punishment was not proportionate to the crimes. He pleaded that the aim of punishment should be prevention of crimes.

As a political thinker Bentham has been assessed quite differently by various thinkers. According to some he was not at all a political philosopher, but merely a legal reformer. It has laso been said that he contributed nothing. His conception of utility which was the pivot of his political thought was faulty, impracticable and a borrowed one.

There is, however, another school of thought which feels that Bentham holds a very unique position in the European political thought. His influence on J.S. Mill was immense.

4. Practical Thinker. It has been said that Bentham did not contribute as a theorist, but as a realist and viewed things from a practical point of view. He was perhaps the first political thinker who pointed out glaring defects in English constitutional, legal and jail systems and stood for their reforms. As a practical thinker he preached that punishment should not be retaliatory but should aim at reforms. Though he was a radical thinker yet he did not suggest far reaching changes. He did not wish to suddenly upset the whole political system. One can appreciate his realism when one sees that with Bentham an area of stagnated legislation came to an and. According to Wayper, "They were as trenchant and vigourous and fearless in their attacks on aristocratic privileges as any new industrialist could desire..."

5. As a Legal Reformer. Bentham was one of those thinkers who condemned the theory of social contract and pleaded that the government should stand at the bar of public opinion. He elevated public opinion in an age in which preaching such a doctrine was considered a symbol of revolution. His government was not a mystery but was to be tested on the basis of utility. He was the first political thinker who boldly cried that the laws should be modified, complicated laws should be replaced by simple ones and the laws should be given wide publicity. Execution of laws should not only be simple and cheap but also quick. Sabine says: "Bentham's jurisprudence which was not only the greatest of his works but one of the most remarkable achievements of nineteenth century, consisted in the systematic application of point of view just sketched (promotion of happiness) to all branches of law, civil and criminal, and to the procedural law and the organisation of the judicial system." According to Gettell, "His confidence in his ability to create a system of laws guaranteed to promote the greatest good of the greatest number was unbounded."

6. Founder of Utilitarianism. Bentham's importance also lies in the fact that he was the founder of utilitarian school of thought. According to Maxey, "Here was a doctrine to rock the foundations of all accredited political theory." Sorley says: "Every concrete situation was analysed into its elements and these followed out into all its ramifications."

7. Forerunner of Marx. Bentham has been considered as the forerunner of Marx when he said that every problem required immediate investigation and that problems should have empirical approach. Some also give him credit for giving new words to English vocabulary.

8. As Educational Reformer. Wayper has drawn attention to another aspect of Bentham's philosophy namely that of education. He says, "Bentham's great interest in education too, deserves for him an honourable place in the list of the educational reformers of the country."

QUESTIONS FOR EXERCISE

1. "Utilitarianism is primarily an ethical theory based upon the phsychological theory known as Hedonism." Discuss.
2. "The state is essentially an organisation for the promotion of the greatest happiness of greatest number." Discuss this statement.
3. Assess influence of Utilitarianism on Social and Political reforms in England at that time. How far is it correct to call Bentham as an advocate of *lassiez-faire*?
4. Explain and criticise the basic principles of Bentham's utilitarianism and estimate the importance of Bentham in the history of political thought.
5. "Nature has placed mankind under the governance of two sovereign masters, pleasure and pain. It is for them alone to point out what we ought to do as well as to determine what we shall" — Bentham. Examine critically this criterion of legislation.
6. Bentham was "neither a moralist nor a philanthorophist, he was a legal philosopher and a reformer of the laws." Explain and discuss.
7. "Government is the Choice of Evils" — Bentham. Comment.
8. "In spite of shortcomings in his theory of utility, Bentham's contribution to political thought was enormous." Discuss this statement.

3

James Mill (1773-1836) and John Austin (1790-1859)

JAMES MILL (1773-1836)

James Mill was one of the staunchest followers of Benthamism. He imprinted the ideas of radicalism on this school of thought. According to Davidson, he was "the most strenuous and perhaps the ablest and most uncompromising disciple that Bentham had. He did incomparable service to the utilitarian cause, inasmuch as he brought to bear on the Benthamite teaching his keen psychological insight and application to it of the principles of Associationist School in which he was himself a master."

Political Ideas of James Mill

1. Law of Association. Mill followed inductive and experimental methods in his study. He believed in the 'Law of Association'. He described it in these words, "Our ideas spring up or exist in the order in which the sensations existed of which they are copies." In psychology and psychological associations frequency plays a great part, according to Mill.

2. Pleasure and Pain Theory. While dealing with 'Pleasure and Pain' Mill said that the 'utility' decides about morality and immorality. According to him not only the laws of morality but even many other laws could be measured on this yardstick. According to him, "This when applied by the community in its conjunct capacity, we call it law; when it is applied only by individuals in their individual capacity, we know it as the control of moral sentiments." To quote Davidson, "Pleasure and Pain, then, are of the essence of morality and moral approbation, praise and blame are applicable to man as a rational being who has the power of appreciating the consequences of actions in the light of an addition to or a diminution of the sum of pleasures."

3. Education. On education Mill had a secular outlook. He was against the introduction of religious education in schools. He pleaded that Bible should never be prescribed as a text-book for study. The education should be made widespread and available both to the high and the low. It should suit all pockets. It should be afforded by all. University of London was founded as a consequence of his efforts. Education should stand for "rendering the individual as much as possible an instrument of happiness, first to himself and next to other beings". Mill defined education as "The best employment of all the means which can be made use of, by man, for rendering the human mind to the greatest possible degree the cause of human happiness. Everything, therefore, which operated from the first germ of existence to the final extinction of life, in such a manner as to affect those qualities of the mind on which happiness in any degree depends, comes within the scope of present inquiry. "Education is a powerful weapon for moulding the people. It has immense influence on the individual as well as society as a whole. If education failed to achieve a particular end that could not be achieved by any other method, education should aim at giving happiness to all." Mill said: "As the happiness which is the end of education, depends upon the actions of the individidual, and as all the actions of men are produced by his feelings and thoughts, the business of education is, to make certain feelings or thoughts take place instead of others. The business of education, then is to work upon the mental successions". Mill was rather very much optimistic and aimed at making education impartial. Even today education is a great force and an effective weapon in changing the minds of the people and mobilising public opinion. Mill duly understood the value and importance of this weapon and wished to fully exploit that.

4. Government. Mill believed that by nature everyone attempts at securing his maximum happiness. In achieving this end he does not even mind encroaching upon the happiness of others. If given power, the people would use it for their selfish ends than for common good. In order to avoid this tendency it was essential that the government should restrain the individuals from encroaching upon the happiness of others. Since government also consisted of human beings, there is also danger that those in power might misuse their authority for their selfish ends, if not put under some restraints and checks. Mill saw that English governmental system was open to abuses and thus was not ideal. The ideal system is a representative form of government in which the people have authority to check the actions of legislators and keep an eye on their activities. Individual interest must conform to those of community and both must go hand in hand. People's represenatives in the House of Commons should be vested with more power. There should be frequent appeals to the electorates. Mill pleaded for adult suffrage at the age of 40 and also for those whose interests were not protected by any other institution, individual and organisation. Davidson has rightly said that "Mill's theory had far reaching and lasting consequences in British politics, appealing to practical politicians of the time and captivating the masses. In every way, he was the leader of the utilitarian radicals after Bentham, and the chief operative force, in affecting the practical reforms of the school."

5. Political Economy. Like Bentham, Mill was also influenced by Adam Smith's theory of *laissez faire*. In addition to Smith he was also influenced by Malthus. It was because of Ricardo's influence that he brought out his *'Element of Political Economy'*. He himself said that he introduced nothing new but gave systematic representation to the already existing thoughts. He believed that the growing population is prejudicial to 'utility'. He fully endorsed Malthusian doctrine which subsequently became the doctoring of his political philosophy. It has been said about his ideas on political economy that "These economic problems are set forth in admirable clearness and precision of statements and in a logical order that leaves nothing to be desired."

6. Jurisprudence. Mill had very broad and clear views about jurisprudence. He expressed them in *'Law of Nations'* in the *'Articles on Jurisprudence'*. He believed that the laws should be very accurately and clearly defined and that those acts which impair or destroy them should be ended by punishment. Suitable persons should be appointed to examine all questions relating to rights of the citizens and their violation by the authorities. Unrestrained authority is always prejudicial to liberty and as such those in authority should be put under check and control. Neither should there be unrestricted use of rights nor that of authority because both were injurious. Civil law should define rights and criminal law should suggest punishments. A code of procedure should discuss the duties of judges, their working conditions and salaries etc.

7. International Law. Mill had clear idea about international law. He fully understood that nations usually fought to preserve their independence and could not tolerate subordination. War was always on and so far nations have failed to end it. Since wars cannot be ended there is a very strong necessity of a codified law for governing the conduct of warring nations. Even the strongest nations could not ignore public opinion. All nations count and have their own place in the family of nations.

A code of law supervised and implemented by a tribunal was absolutely necessary for regulating international conduct. Mill compared individual behaviour with national conduct. He pleaded that like the interests of individuals the interests of nations were also motivated by the sense of occupancy, transfers and conquests and as such both should be treated more or less on the same footing.

Mill condemned piracy even in times of war. Under the influence of Adam Smith he stood for free traffic in times of war so far as individual property was concerned. The war should be immediately brought to an end as soon as the objects for waging war had been achieved.

8. International Tribunals. Mill supported the formation of tribunals for the administration of international law. These were bound to command international respect. Nations would automatically bow before their decisions provided these were impartial and of high standard, nature and significance. The decisions of the tribunal should be given very wide publicity. Public opinion should be so moulded that those nations which were not willing to refer their cases to such a tribunal should feel guilty and low in the world opinion. Even in cases where the parties were not willing to refer their cases to tribunal, decisions should be given for future guidance of those who had respect for public opinion and normally refer their cases to such tribunals.

9. Monarchy. Mill was not very much opposed to monarchy. According to him monarchy in itself is not bad, because usually the interests of the masses and the king could not be different. Monarchy however becomes bad only when a king submits himself to aristocracy.

10. House of Lords. In Mill's days House of Lords was a very powerful body. He wanted to reform it. He desired that powers of the Lords should be decreased, while those of Commons increased. He suggested, "Let it be enacted that if a bill, which has been passed by the House of Commons, and thrown out by the House of Lords, is renewed in the House of Commons in the next session of Parliament, and passed, but again thrown out by the House of Lords, it shall, if passed third time in the House of Commons, be law, without being again sent to the Lords."

JOHN AUSTIN (1790-1859)

1. Concept of Law : (i) *Definition.* According to Austin "Law....is an expression of will by determinate superior that a certain code of conduct came to pass failing which an evil will come upon those who deviate from that course."

(ii) *Positive Law and Positive Morality.* Law is positive in nature. It is given by a political superior to his subjects. It is the foremost duty of the people to obey and honour the commands of the sovereign. Their violation was punishable offence. Austin, however, distinguished between positive law and positive morality. He defined the positive morality as those laws which were given by the non-sovereign authorities or which were merely social commands and incorporated customs and conventions etc.

(iii) *International Law.* According to Austin international law is vague and negative mainly because there is no sovereign authority to enforce such laws.

(iv) *Types of Laws.* Austin further distinguished between positive laws, human laws and Divine laws. He also divided laws into 'Improper Laws,' 'Proper Laws' and 'Metaphorical Laws'. By improper Laws he understood social cusoms and traditions and also the laws dealing with international code of conduct, *i.e.* International Law. By Proper Laws he meant Divine Law, Civil Law and Laws of Association. Under the category of 'Metaphorical Laws' he placed laws relating to politics and economics.

(v) *Nature of Law.* Austin believed that law is the command of the superior. He also believed that law making is a conscious and deliberate process and not something which could be given to the people all of a sudden. Duguit has however criticised him by saying that law creates the state and not *vice versa.* For Austin laws are merely the expression of social necessity. In the words of Dunning, "He held that law making is a conscious and deliberate process, a conception that was later somewhat modified by Binding and adhering more recent representatives of the school in Germany."

2. Origin of State. Austin did not agree with social contract philosophers that the state is the result of any social contract. He agreed with Bentham that its commands were obeyed because the people derived more advantages by obeying the state commands rather than by disobeying them. The people by nature were habitual to obey the state. The state should aim at giving greatest happiness to greatest number of people. Austin did not agree with the idea that the individuals had rights against the state which were also binding on sovereign authority. He pleaded that all rights were the product of laws and created by it.

3. Concept of Soverignty : (i) *Classical Theory of Sovereignty.* Austin's greatest contribution to the political philosophy is his idea about sovereignty. He gave it a concrete and specific shape. Prior to Austin, Hobbes and Bodin made unsuccessful attempts to define sovereignty. It was for the first time that Austin gave it a very systematic definition. His definition is available in his book *'Lectures on Jurisprudence'* published in 1882. His theory is known as the classical theory about sovereignty. According to him, "If a determinate human superior not in the habit of obedience to a like superior, receives habitual obedience from the bulk of a given society, that determinate human superior is sovereign in that society and the society (including the superior) is a society political and independent."

(ii) *Characteristic Rights of Sovereign.* Thus, according to Austin, the characteristics of a sovereign are : (a) he should be determinate, (b) he should be human superior, (c) he should receive not casual but regular and habitual obedience from bulk of his subjects, and (d) he himself should not be in the habit of obeying commands from other similar superiors.

(iii) *Attributes of Sovereignty.* According to Austin the sovereign power must be unlimited and indivisible. Dividing of sovereignty was like killing and thus ultimately abolishing it. Sovereign is not only above all laws but is himself the source of all laws. The sovereign is inalienable and cannot alienate his authority to any other super authority.

4. Criticism of Austin's Conception of Sovereignty : (i) *Anti-democratic.* Austin believed that sovereign authority must be determinate which implies that the sovereignty could not vest in the people or class of people but only in a determinate individual. In other words, according to him, in democracies there was no sovereignty. Thus, he was anti-democratic and that way outdated. Among others this idea has been supported by Henry Maine.

(ii) *Concept of Determinate Superior.* Austin has been criticised for his concept of determinate human superior, as sovereign. On many occasions it is not possible to determine and locate sovereignty. Even in cases of limited monarchies it is difficult to say whether sovereignty vests in the monarch or in his councillors.

(iii) *Austin Believed that Sovereignty is Indivisible.* But today we find that this conception of sovereignty has fallen on thin ground. In federations, which are now the order of the day, the sovereign authority is clearly divided into two parts. It is partly vested in the centre and partly in units which join the federation.

(iv) *Inalienabiliy.* Austin believes that sovereign is 'inalienable'. This conception is wrong because today the sovereign authority is delegated not only to one person but to many who exercise powers on behalf of the sovereign. With the increase in work-load in every walk of administration this tendency of delegating the powers is increasing day by day.

(v) *Unlimited Power.* According to Austin power is unlimited. This is not correct because sovereign has his own limitations. National and International customs and conventions are great limitations on sovereign authority. Every state must enter into certain agreements and treaties concluded with other states, which become a limitation on the sovereign authority. International institutions like U.N.O. etc. are great limitations on this power.

(vi) *Habitual Obedience.* Austin believes that sovereign receives only habitual obedience. It means obedience is limited to the persons who are in the habit of obeying and is not ulimited in nature and character. According to Getell, "Nevertheless the legal theory of the complete external sovereignty or independence of state is not in accordance with the facts of present-day international life. The development of international good faith and complex inter-relation among states make it undesirable and in many cases impossible, for each state to be interpreter on international obligation or to fix standard of international conduct."

(vii) *Sovereign as Source of Law.* According to Austin what sovereign permits is law. The sovereign is the only source of all laws. This does not appear to be correct. The sovereign is not the only source of laws which we obey today. There are laws which are based on customs and conventions, or sanction or religion behind them. Even the most powerful sovereign dare not violate them.

(viii) *Criticism by Pluralists.* Austin has also been criticised by pluralists who ridicule his conception of unlimited and indivisible sovereignty. They believe that since society is divided, authority must also be divided. They support their argument by saying that in every society there are many associations and trade unions which command more respect than even the sovereign. According to L. Stephen, "As there is in nature, no such thing as a perfect circle or a completely rigid body, or a mechanical system in which there is notification, or a state of society in which men act simply with a view to gain, so there is in nature no such thing as an absolute sovereign."

(ix) *Ignores Customary Laws.* This thory ignores customary laws which have developed with the passage of time and which are the essence of human wisdom. Austin exaggerates human force and ignores history and historical facts. According to Garner, "It ignores the great body of customary laws which has grown up through usage and interpretation and which never had its source in the will of determinate human superior; but it errs in treating all laws as being merely commands and that it exaggerates the single element of force to the neglect of obvious historical facts with which Austin could not have been unacquainted."

(x) *Outdated.* It can be safely concluded that Austin's conception of sovereignty is purely and singularly outdated. It does not suit the convenience of modern definitions. However, it cannot be denied that the credit for giving a systematic definition of sovereignty goes only to Austin whose definition attracted the attention of his contemporaries and also of his followers and is respected even today.

5. Civil Liberty. According to Austin civil liberty is that kind of liberty which is given to the subjects by their sovereign. The sovereign is competent to increase or decrease the nature of such liberties provided he does not infringe the established customs and conventions. Austin believed that civil liberty must be based on 'utility'.

6. The Theory of Government. According to Austin, it is wrong to believe that the Governments come into existence after these are fully formed and mature. Governments grew with the passage of time. Their growth is linked with utility which a government provides. Therefore, it is not any contract in the utility which it provides to the masses which can give birth to state.

7. International Law. Austin believed that the law should be a written code of conduct. The laws should be specific and interpretable by the courts of laws. He did not believe in the concept and validity of international law since he believed in the legal concept of sovereignty. Such laws which had not been codified and which could not be enforced by the sovereign were not laws in the technical sense of the term. In the words of Dunning, "For those who, like the Austinians, demand that law be declared by a determinate human superior, international law could not be law, but only moral precepts which could bind the state sovereign only so long as he thought it convenient."

Estimates of Austin

(i) *Getell.* "Austin's idea did not receive approval from the jurists of his days but still his contribution to the conception of sovereignty and the support which he lent to Bentham have made him one of the top ranking political jurists of England."

(ii) *Garner.* "Austin's chief error consisted in unduly emphasising the purely legal aspects of sovereignty and in ignoring the facts and influences which lie at the back of the formal law, a very natural mistake for a lawyer to make. It may also be said that his theory is probably incapable of all states of society. But as a conception of the strict legal nature of the sovereignty, Austin's theory is, on the whole, clear and logical and much of criticism directed against it has been founded on misapprehension and misconception."

QUESTIONS FOR EXERCISE

1. "James did not give any new ideas in his political philosophy but simply regulated and upheld the philosophy given by Bentham." Discuss.
2. Discuss five essential liberties that were so eloquently described by Mill in his famous essay.

3. It has been said about Austin that "he separated the Theory of Sovereignty from its ethical and historical background and by a process of abstractions built up the science of positive law" — Gettell. Discuss.
4. Explain the contributions of Austin to the history of political thought.

4

John Stuart Mill (1806-1873)

John Stuart Mill, the eldest son of James Mill, was born in London on May 20, 1806. No child of James Mill underwent a more 'unusual and remarkable' boyhood than young John Stuart Mill. This fact has been admitted by J.S. Mill himself in his *Autobiography* (1873). J.S. Mill wrote his autobiography during the last five years of his life; most of the manuscript dates from 1870. Shortly after Mill's death the manuscript was edited and prepared for publication by his step-daughter Helen Taylor, who deleted a few passages where Mill referred to his father or his wife. Otherwise, it was printed as Mill left it still unfinished.

Two years after John's birth, his father came into contact with Jeremy Bentham. He was so much influenced by him that during the remainder of his life, he devoted his energy and talents to promoting the cause of utilitarian reform. Bentham's faithful disciple selected his son, John Stuart, "to be the legitimate heir of the Benthamite tradition."[1] Conforming to the dictates of his theory of the *tabula rasa*, James Mill set about to manufacture the perfect Utilitarian Mind by a process of rigidly targeted instruction.

Early Education

Mill's formal education was given under the direct tutelage of his determined parent. James Mill was an "exacting teacher of momentous subjects," and a stern and severe task master as well. John Stuart's education started with the study of Greek at an early age of three. At eight, he began the study of Latin, History and the Classics. In his fourteenth year there was an interlude for travel abroad. But while he spent the year living in France with the family of General Sir Samuel Bentham (Jeremy's brother), John's 'mental cultivation' continued without interruption. After his return to London, he read law, at the age of fifteen, with the Benthamite legalist, John Austin. His education also included earnest conversations with many distinguished members of the Benthamite circle who frequented Mill's residence. In the course of the daily drills, recitations, lectures and conversations, James Mill shaped as best he could his son's mind to suit the Benthamite image.

1. *John Stuart Mill — On Liberty*, ed. by Currin V. Shields, Introduction, p. vii (Liberal Arts Press, N.Y., 1956).

Professional Career

John Stuart's professional career began in 1823, when he was appointed as assistant to his father, the Examiner of Correspondence for the East India Company. He spent his entire professional life, a period of thirty-five years, in the employment of the East India Company. In 1856, he was promoted to the office of Chief Examiner, the post second in command in the home service to the Secretary. He held this office until the Company was dissolved by an Act of Parliament in 1858. Mill now declined an offer of a Government post, preferring instead to retire from the administrative service. In 1865, he was elected a member of the House of Commons for Westminster which he served three years, until his defeat for re-election. Mill devoted the last years of his life to his writings. Much of the time he lived in France with his step-daughter as a companion. Mill died on May 8, 1873 at Avignon, where he now lies buried in a tomb with his wife.

Literary Achievements

Mill's first great literary achievements may be found in the *Westminster Review,* whereby his pen he brought himself into a prominence that made him a real influence in philosophy and politics. The systematic expression of his political theory is to be found in his famous work *On Liberty* and in *Representative Government*. When these were published in 1859 and 1861 respectively, Mill had achieved great distinction as a philosopher. Through his famous *Political Economy* (1844) he became one of the most influential thinkers of the time.

In 1861 Mill wrote a series of articles for *Fraser's Magazine* (October-December, 1861) which were printed as a short treatise, *Utilitarianism,* published in 1863. In this work Mill drew his famous distinction between the quantity and quality of pleasure. By the time Mill concluded his exposition of utilitarianism, he had virtually abandoned every distinctive tenet of the Benthamite faith.

In 1865, two of Mill's lesser works were published : *An Examination of Sir William Hamilton's Philosophy,* and *Auguste Comte and Positivism*. Four years after, he published *The Subjection of Women* (1869), a fitting climax for his career as a writer of political essays. But after his death, several treatises of engrossing interest and high import saw the light. The first was the *Autobiography,* published in 1873. A sensation was aroused by the posthumous treatise, *Three Essays on Religion* were published in 1874. These two posthumous works marked a fitting close to a great career of scholarship and service. Green expressed his respect for him by echoing Gladstone's remark that Mill was a saintly man. He considered Mill to have been an 'extraordinary good man'.

EMPIRICAL METHOD

Mill's political philosophy was based on his principles of logic, formulated in his great work, *System of Logic : Ratiocinative and Inductive,* which he published in 1843. In the sixth book of his *System of Logic,* entitled *On the Logic of the Moral Sciences*, there are several lucid chapters on the logic of politics where he showed the need and urgency of the application of logical procedure to the phenomena of society and of government. The principles on which Mill proceeds in this book are those that he had expounded in the previous parts of his great treatise, especially in connection with Induction, which involves the deductive application of laws inductively obtained. The inductive process, according to him, consists in generalizing from experience, in discovering the causes of phenomena and ascertaining their laws, according to various experimental methods specifically formulated (agreement, difference, joint method of agreement and difference, residues and concomitant variations) and copiously exemplified, and in making application to new cases of the generalizations thus inductively reached and bringing them back to the facts of experience in order to have them verified and established. Mill rejected the method of arriving at truth purely on the basis of abstract thinking. He did not approve the method of those who try to formulate general principles either in the field of politics, or of economics, or of any social science, on the basis of specific experiences. His approach was highly empirical. The distinctive name by which he called his method was "The Physical or Concrete Deductive Method". It proceeds deductively, but by deduction from many, original premises, considering each effect as an aggregate result of many causes, operating sometimes through the same, sometimes through different agencies, or laws of human nature.

As age succeeds age, experience grows, and one generation of men differs from another. At any particular time, the circumstances of society determine its character. But the circumstances are in turn reacted on by the society and in no small degree are moulded by it. This throws the student of social science upon the study of history so that he may discover the law of human progress if possible. But the generalizations made from the facts and events of history are simply empirical laws of society, and need to be verified.

Mill applied his empirical method in explaining the validity of moral institutions. He demonstrated that many notions and principles in morals were merely common opinion and belief, mere sentiment or prejudice, untested by reason. On the other hand, what is valuable in morality is founded in experience and may be corroborated by it. Instead of basing moral ideas on intuition and holding them beyond the reach of human experience, Mill brought them into direct relation with experience and insisted on testing their validity thereby. On his detailed analysis, Mill found, that they ultimately derived their character from the pleasure-value of their consequences. Thus, Mill gave hedonistic colour to his thinking which runs through his later political writings.

Although pleasure is the ultimate test of moral value, Mill thought it essential to strengthen the utilitarian position by drawing a distinction between the different kinds of pleasure. He sought to establish the non-utilitarian proposition that some pleasures are of a higher quality than others. For Bentham and James Mill, pleasures differ only in quantity and one pleasure is as good in itself as another, as Bentham put it : "Quantity of pleasure being equal, push-pin is as good as poetry." On the contrary, J.S. Mill regarded it as quite compatible with the principle of utility to introduce the distinction between quantity and quality of pleasure, and to lay emphasis on quality. Pleasures are in themselves intrinsically different : there are higher and lower among them. The proof of this is appeal to intelligent people who have had experience of both : they are judges, and their testimony is decisive. In the words of Mill, "It is better to be a human being dissatisfied than a pig satisfied; better to be Socrates dissatisfied than a fool satisfied. And if the fool or the pig is of a different opinion, it is because they only know their own side of the question. The other party to the comparison knows both sides."

ALTERATIONS IN BENTHAMISM

Mill's assertion that pleasures differ not only in quantity but quality as well, is a truer reflection of human experience than Bentham's insistence to the contrary. However, Sidgwick, remarked that "if we are to be hedonists we must say that pleasures vary only in quantity, never in quality. Utilitarianism, must recognize no distinction between pleasures except a quantitative one.

However, in order to meet a challenge of the strong anti-hedonist movement of his day, Mill made use of the non-utilitarian argument that pleasures cannot be objectively measured. The felicific calculus is, absurd, and men have always relied upon the testimony of "those most competent to judge." "There is no other tribunal to be referred to even on the question of quantity. What means are there of determining which is the acutest of two pains or the intensest of two pleasurable sensations except the general suffrage of those who are familiar with both?"[2] Mill was, to quote Wayper, "of course right in maintaining the absurdity of the felicific calculus," but if it is once admitted that pleasures can no longer be measured objectively, a vital breach has been made in the well-known thesis of Utilitarianism.

Mill maintained the further non-utilitarian position by holding the view that not the principle of utility but the dignity of man is the final end of life. He approved of Humboldt's doctrine of 'self-realization'. "It really is of importance," he said, "not only what men do, but also what manner of men they are that do it." "What more or better can be said of any condition of human affairs," he asked, "than that it brings human beings themselves nearer to the best thing they can be?" Mill held that one pleasure is better than another if it promotes the sense of dignity in man. Thus, our criterion of goodness is no longer the principle of utility. The transformation of egoism into altruism is effected by the same process that turns a money-seeker into a miser. A man may begin by desiring money for the pleasure that it can procure him, but by and by he transfers his affections from the end to the means, and goes on amassing money for its own sake. So although pleasures to self is the ultimate explanation of human disinterestedness, self is forgotten gradually by the ethical

2. Wayper, C.L. : *Political Thought* (The English Universities Press Ltd., London, 1958), p. 111.

man in his earnest and devoted service to others, and his highest pleasure comes when he does not directly seek it. As such, his (man's) own happiness is found in doing good to his fellows or to other sentient creatures. Mill laid great stress on the Hedonistic paradox. Directly aiming at pleasure may fail to secure it. As Bain puts it, "Happiness is not gained by a point-blank aim; we must take a boomerang flight in some other line, and come back upon the target by an oblique or reflected movement." Thus, happiness, according to Mill, is to be found only indirectly "aiming at something else." This is to place moral ends above happiness, which becomes not indeed a state of pleasures but a state of mind which ensures when one pursues some moral end. Viewed from this viewpoint, the state becomes a moral institution with a moral end. Not utility but the promotion of virtue in the individual is what it must aim at.

Mill laid emphasis on the idea of moral obligation. Bentham had conceived of this as the product of the selfish desires and anticipation of men. Mill considered Bentham's view far too simple and naive. Fear, memory, self-esteem, he admitted, play their part in its composition, but so do love, sympathy, religious emotion and occasionally even self-abasement. Mill accepted the emotional basis of the state, but admited Green's contention that "public duties, and responsibilities cannot logically be derived from private rights and interests." He held that there is in mind or self or ego something more than what there is in matter. It is the characteristic of human mind that it presents itself not only in the form of a series of states, but it is also conscious of them. The ego or self is that which binds the states together, just as the thread holds the beads together in a necklace. This self-conscious state of human mind promotes the sense of dignity in man. Thus, Mill was against Bentham's idea of moral obligation being interpreted merely in terms of the principle of utility.

VIEWS ON GOVERNMENT

In spite of all his alterations in Benthamism, John Mill remained true to his utilitarian training. He viewed the government as an association of men, made by them for their social well-being. Human will and purpose are operative in the life or political institutions. A government functions at any particular time only so far as the people whom it controls are willing to accept it, and are able, as well as willing, to do what is necessary to keep it going and fulfilling its end. 'Social well-being' is the end of government. It means the possession of desirable qualities by a number of concrete human beings. It is not the perfect adjustment of the abstract relationships which make these men a society. The fostering of qualities as virtue and intelligence is the first criterion of good government. It is necessary for the moral development of the individuals. The machinery itself, only second in importance, the degree in which it is adapted to make the best use of such qualities as the individuals possess.[3]

3. *Representative Government*, Chap. II.

CONCEPT OF LIBERTY

Mill flatly rejected Comte's famous criteria of the happy society, 'order and progress', on metaphysical grounds. However, he often ascribed to a community attribute that cannot be readily predicted of a mere sum of human beings. These qualities must be the first consideration in any estimate of the social well-being. In his celebrated essay *On Liberty,* Mill set forth what must be the fundamental condition in the relation between the government and the individuals over whom it exercises authority.

In the opening passages of his essay, Mill posed a question : What are the limits of the collective authority of society over the individual? He set to explain 'a very simple principle' for determining the proper limits for individual and collective action. According to Mill, Interference is justified only by the need for 'self-protection' : to prevent harm to others. The thesis of his essay is :

> "....that the sole end for which mankind are warranted, individually or collectively, interfering with the freedom of action of any of their member, is self-protection — that the only purpose for which power can be rightfully exercised over any member of a civilized community, against his will, is to prevent harm to others. His own good, either physical or moral, is not a sufficient warrant. He cannot rightfully be compelled to do or forbear because it will be better for him to do so, because it will make him happier, because, in the opinions of others, to do so would be wise or even right. These are good reasons for remonstrating with him, or reasoning with him, or persuading him, of entreating him, but not for compelling him, or visiting him with any evil in case he does otherwise. To justify that, the conduct from which it is desired to deter him must be calculated to produce evil to someone else."[4]

Some collective interference in individual affairs is justified. An individual, said Mill, has duties as well as rights. He has duties to himself and to others. He has a duty to bear a fair share of society's burdens, and a duty not to injure others by his conduct. Society has jurisdiction over individual conduct, which affects the interests of others. When definite damage to others results from individual action, the case is taken out of the province of liberty and placed in that of law, because society has a right to protect its members from 'moral vices'.

Freedom of the Individual

Mill's doctrine, embodies a complete and systematic philosophy of individualism and *laissez-faire.* He emphasised the supreme importance of developing the individual in all the completeness of his being, so that his active and his intellectual nature might have their utmost scope and reach their highest efficiency. Without this general progress was impossible. Mill pleaded

4. *On Liberty,* Chap. I (Introductory).

that the individual should have the utmost freedom of thought, of speech and expression, and of action for development. Mill defended freedom of thought and expression, with Miltonian fervour and more than Milton's acumen.[5] He sustained individuality with the reasoning that William Von Humboldt had developed from different premises. He forcefully proclaimed that the repression of originality in thought and conduct, whether by law or by public opinion is fatal to the progress of the race. According to Mill, to discover to the world something which deeply concerns it, and of which it was previously ignorant, is "as important a service as human being can render to his fellow creatures, and in certain cases, as in those of early Christians, and of the Reformers, those who think with Dr. Johnson believe it to have been the most precious gift which could be bestowed on mankind."[6] The propounder of a new truth, according to Mill, should stand as stood, in the legislation of the Locrians, about 660 B.C., the proposer of a new law, with a halter round his neck, to be instantly tightened if the public assembly did not, on hearing his reasons, then and there adopt his proposition. People who defend this mode of treating benefactors cannot be supposed to set much value on the benefit. Mill believed that "this view of the subject is mostly confined to the sort of persons who think that new truths may have been desirable once, but that we have had enough of them now."

Self-regarding and Other-regarding Actions

Mill divided all actions into two categories — self-regarding actions and other-regarding actions. There should be no interference with self-regarding actions, but only with such other-regarding actions as produce positive, demonstrable harm to others. As a natural development of this position, Mill admitted that it is legitimate to oblige a man to bear his share in maintaining society. Conscription should not be regarded as an unwarranted infringement of liberty. One must not make himself a nuisance to other people. But if he refrains from molesting others in what concerns them, and merely acts according to his own inclination and judgment in things which concern himself, the same reasons which show that opinion should be free, prove also that he should be allowed, without molestation, to carry his opinions into practice, at his own cost. Individuality means that the individual's own nature and its development, must be the determining factor. If a man is not to be allowed to develop his own character at his own risk, then there is wanting one of the principal ingredients of human happiness and the chief ingredient of individual and social progress.

Kinds of Liberty

In the region of human liberty Mill includes the inward domain of consciousness, demanding liberty of conscience, liberty of thought and feeling, absolute freedom of opinion and sentiment and all subjects, practical or

5. *Political Theories from Luther to Montesquieu*, p. 244.

6. *On Liberty*, Chap. II.

speculative, scientific, moral, or theological. The liberty of expressing and publishing opinions belongs to that part of the conduct of an individual which concerns other people, practically inseparable from it. The principle requires liberty of tastes and pursuits, of framing the plan of our life to suit our own character, of doing as we like, subject to such consequences as may follow, without impediment from our fellow creatures so long as what we do "does not harm them, even though they should think our conduct foolish, perverse, or wrong." From this liberty of each individual follows the liberty within the same limits, "of combination among individuals; freedom to unite for any purpose not involving harm to others : the persons combining being supposed to be of full age and not forced or deceived."[7]

Mill wanted to promote the development of individual men and women, for all wise and noble things come, and must come, from individuals. There can be no self-development without liberty. Liberty is necessary for the happiness of society. Mill wrote in *On Liberty* : "No society in which these liberties are not, on the whole, respected, is free, whatever may be its form of government; and none is completely free in which they do not exist absolute and unqualified. The only freedom which deserves the name is that of pursuing our own good in our own way, so long as we do not attempt to deprive others of theirs or impede their efforts to obtain it. Each is the proper guardian of his own health, whether bodily or mental and spiritual. Mankind are greater gainers by suffering each other to live as seems good to themselves than by compelling each to live as seems good to the rest."[8]

The Problem of Social Ethics

The problem of social ethics according to Mill is to separate the legitimate sphere of individual liberty from that of collective authority. Mill did not value the freedom of other-regarding conduct as an end in itself. He stressed the value of liberty and urged its recognition. Individual freedom is justified, by a contribution to the general interest. Liberty is a valuable means to the more highly valued end of progress, in which every member of society has an interest.

Doctrine of Individual's Liberty of Conduct

Mill's doctrine of the individual's liberty of conduct may be summarized under three heads : (1) the advocacy of the due recognition of the place and importance of impulse and desire in man, as distinguished from intellect, thought in close connection with it — the "supreme need of amply acknowledging the active and energetic side of the individual's nature"; (2) insistence on the view that spontaneity or individuality is a necessary ingredient in happiness or human welfare; and (3) revolt against the conventionalities of society that hinder, or seem to hinder, the development and expression of individuality —

7. *On Liberty*, Chap. I.

8. *Ibid.*

against the despotism of social custom. Mill's conduct exemplified this revolt, and, he suffered in the public estimation. The independence that he claimed for himself, he demanded for every individual. He identified individual's energy with 'genius' or 'originality'. He forgot that energy, in certain cases, might be mere eccentricity which may not be strength, but weakness of character. He also did not sufficiently recognize that although a man's desires and impulses were indispensable to the development of his nature, they were not a sure guide to the proper outlet for this activity.

REPRESENTATIVE GOVERNMENT

In his *Representative Government* (1861), Mill discussed the form of government that would best apply the basic principles of liberty. That form of government is the best in which "the sovereignty, or supreme controlling power in the last resort, is vested in the entire aggregate of the community," every citizen not only having a voice in the expression of the sovereign will, but also, at least occasionally, an actual part in the discharge of some public function. The excellence of such a government is to be deduced from two principles : first, "that any task is done best by those whose rights and interests are immediately involved"; and second, "that the faculties of men — moral, intellectual and practical — are most developed and improved when they are in active exercise.[9]

Mill named it 'representative government', and made it conform strictly to its name by ascribing to it as its essential characteristic thus:

> "....that the whole people, or some numerous portion of them, exercise, through deputies periodically elected by themselves, the ultimate controlling power, which, in every constitution, must reside somewhere. This ultimate power they must possess in all its completeness. They must be masters, whenever they please, of all the operations of government."[10]

Mill apparently committed himself to the dogma of a determinate and absolute human sovereign combining the peculiarly ill-assorted thought of Austin and Blackstone. He separated himself from the French liberals like Guizot, who insisted that absolute power in any human depositary, even 'society' or the 'people', was incompatible with rational liberty. Mill had a definite horror of the tyrannical rule either of one person or of the society, working as a collective authority, over the individual. He knew that even his system of government has its weaknesses. The most dangerous of them is the exposure to the unjust domination of the numerical majority. An inevitable tendency of popular government toward 'collective mediocrity' enhances the peril from this source, so that power gravitates surely towards the less intelligent classes of the people. Hence, Mill supported the system of proportional representation, as the necessary complement of democratic government. The value of votes is not

---

9. *Representative Government,* Chap. III.

10. *Ibid.*, Chap. V.

always equal. Intelligence, education, and superior virtue count for more than ignorance, stupidity, and indifferent character. Hence, Mill advocated plurality of votes to the higher educated citizens. He even drew out a scheme and grouped citizens so as to show what classes should and what should not be allowed a plurality of votes on the basis of the classification according to mental culture and moral qualities. By introducing this system, Mill believed, the evils of extending the suffrage would be minimized, and the instructed minority would have a share in the government that would make always for progress. Under such a system the able man would be sure of coming to the position where the ability would tell for the common good, instead of remaining submerged beneath the surge of the mediocre and worse.[11]

Lord Lothian once told an Indian audience: "Democracy is not a gift to be conferred, but a habit to be acquired. It cannot succeed unless it produces a race of aristocrats — and an aristocrat I would define as one who puts more into life than he takes out of it." Mill was certain that democracy can produce aristocrats so defined. Men are made what they are by their education. By education Mill did not mean that which is exclusively concerned with books and academic studies. "The main branch of the education of human beings," he said, "is their habitual employment." Mill was an advocate of industrial as well as of political democracy. He believed, too, in education "in and through the exercise of social duties."

PROPORTIONAL REPRESENTATION

The principle, "every man to count for one; no man for more than one," is, Mill thought, a principle of false democracy. It implies the false belief that any man is as good as any other. Such a belief ignores the obvious differences of intelligence and virtue between men. It is "almost as detrimental to moral and intellectual excellence as any effect which most forms of government can produce." 'Exclusive Government by a Class' is false democracy. True democracy, on the contrary, will give weight and influence to all the different elements of society. It will give plural votes to capable persons. It will insist on proportional representations. It will also abolish the ballot since "people will give dishonest or mean votes from lucre, from malice, from pique, from personal rivalry, even from the interests of prejudices of class or sect, more readily in secret than in public." In a true democracy, Mill would grant suffrage to all adults of adequate age, conditioned by the fact that the voter is a tax-payer, not under legal disqualification. The suffrage was to be universal but graduated. If the power of voting were to reach the poorer classes the requirement that the voter should be a tax-payer necessitated the lowering of the amount of tax demanded. Although Mill did not discuss the question of Monarchy, he regarded second chamber as necessary for a true and successful democracy, which is not very satisfacotry from a practical viewpoint. In the second chamber will be especially represented those factors in the national life which will never be adequately

11. *Ibid.*, Chap. VII.

represented in an assembly popularly elected, so composed as to "incline it to oppose itself to the class interests of the majority, and qualify it to raise its voice with authority against their errors and weaknesses." True democracy should insist that representatives are true representatives and not mere delegates. It should not ignore the "radical distinction between controlling the business of government and actually doing it." It should realize that the true function of a parliament is not to administer but to watch and supervise the administration. And, lastly, it should be alive to the danger of majority tyranny, for it should know that "the silent sympathy of the majority may support on the scaffold the martyr of one man's tyranny; but if we would imagine the situation of a victim of the majority itself we must look to the annals of religious persecution for a parallel."[12]

In the development of British political thought John Stuart Mill was a pathetically symbolic figure. In his writings were reflected the intellectual cross-currents of the mid-nineteenth cnetury. Mill stood midway in a transition in British thought, not completed in his life-time. Born into the utilitarian movement Mill was a radical reformer in his youth. He agitated for the repeal of legislation which imposed restraints on the many members of British society for the benefit of the landed aristocracy. In his later years, however, Mill's enthusiasm for popular government declined, to the point of frank hostility toward democratic rule. He accounted for this shift in his thinking largely by the impression that Alexis de Tocqueville's 'remarkable work' made on him. Mill reviewed the first volume of *Democracy in America* when it appeared in 1835. He wrote a review of the second volume for the *Edinburgh Review,* Oct, 1840. Often in his writings Mill alluded to Tocqueville's views. In this report of the American experiment in democracy, what impressed Mill was the description of the 'weaknesses' and 'dangers' of popular rule. The basic problem in a system of popular government, Mill is to prevent the tyranny by a majority of the common people — "the uncultivated herd who now compose the labouring masses" — over a minority of exceptional individuals. Mill shared feeling with other middle-class Liberals of the nineteenth century.

MIDDLE-CLASS LIBERALISM

Mill's theory represents the best and the worst in liberalism. Out of utilitarianism there emerged two contrary traditions : the middle-class liberalism and the working-class socialism of the nineteenth-century. Both the individualist Herbert Spencer and the collectivist Robert Owen looked to the utilitarian creed for inspiration. But Mill's middle-class liberalism was a half-way house between the Radical reform of the Benthamites and the Fabian reform of the socialists. In his *Principles of Political Economy* Mill recognized that distribution was a matter of artificial arrangement which might be regulated by the state. He advocated taxation of the unearned increment of land. He laid the foundations which the Fabian party was destined to build. The essay *On Liberty* was a fine

12. *Ibid.*

indication of spiritual liberty and originality against restraints of legislation and of social opinion. But the trend towards something like State Socialism still remained. In his *Autobiography* Mill tells us that he looked forward to a time when "the division of the produce of labour ....will be made by concert on an acknowledged principle of justice." In his essay *On Utilitarianism* he abandoned the principle of self-interest and adopted the principle of self-sacrifice. "To serve the happiness of others by the absolute sacrifice of his own," was, he felt, "the highest virtue that can be found in man."

CONTRIBUTION OF J.S. MILL

J.S. Mill was the champion of individual liberty and very much valued democratic institutions. According to some, Mill contributed nothing new to Bentham's political philosophy but simply adjusted it to suit his times. They charge Mill with inconsistencies in philosophy. It is said that he was only an analyst and not a synthesizer of his analysis but in spite of all this Mill holds a very important place in English political system.

1. Improvement of Utilitarianism. Mill moulded and improved utilitarianism in such a fashion that it could face the challenge of the time and could survive in the face of all odds. Had Mill not appeared at the scene it would have been a different story altogether.

2. Franchise for Women. The credit for raising a voice for female suffrage goes to Mill. He was the first utilitarian to start for universal adult suffrage and not for manhood suffrage as was preached and propagated by his teacher Bentham.

3. Individualism. Before Mill Bentham had stood for individualism but his individual was an isolated entity struggling for his own pleasures and pains. The individual of Mill was thingking in terms of not external pleasures but only in terms of internal sanctions and conscience.

4. Democracy. Mill pleaded in those days when democracy has not got deep roots in the world. He was of the view that democratic outlook is a matter of habit and that the democratic system is much better than tough and rustic dictatorship. He appealed to people to realise the strength of vote. He appealed the votes to cast their votes very judiciously.

5. Liberty. Mill preached for liberty which was a bold step in those days. He did not like that the individual should be put in any way even under the control of their legislators. He stood for the combination of administrators and legislators.

6. Cause of Minorities. Mill supported minority representation. Though this was still a problem yet he made an attempt to solve it. He was a true and real supporter of democracy. Unless minorities are properly represented the whole system of democracy is bound to fail.

7. Upper House. Mill wanted to have proper use of Upper House by allotting them the functions of drafting the bills.

8. Qualitative Pleasure. Mill stood for qualitative instead of quantitative pleasure. The conception of quantitative pleasure had debased and degraded utilitarianism. By giving it qualitative conception, Mill raised the idea of utilitarianism and utility high in the eyes of people and political thinkers.

TRIBUTES

Following are some tributes to Mill's political Philosophy:

(i) *Lord Morley*. "For twenty years no one at all open to serious intellectual impressions has left Oxford without having undergone the influence of Mill's teachings."

(ii) *Prof. Maxey*. "Mill made penetrating comments on such matters as election methods, second chamber, executive organisation, local government, federal government, and the government of dependencies. On each of these subjects he was deeply provocative and made a contribution which modern student of government cannot afford to ignore."

(iii) *Davids*. "These views show Mill as a wise and practical legislator, fully alive to the dangers of popular government and animated by a strong sense of justice and by an earnest desire to put morality in its right place in the political legislation. His wisdom has had its effects, and even now appeal is constantly being made to Mill's teachings whenever progressive measures, affecting the character as well as the material interest of the nation, fail to be considered."

(iv) *John Bowle*. "And if the calibre of writers is to be judged by their effect on policy, Mill must rank high. As logician, economist and political philosopher he was regarded as a prophet in his own age."

(v) *Wayper*. "Dr. Ebenstein says that with the passage of time, "On Liberty" grows in stature and meaning because its predictions have come to life more realistically and more tragically than seemed possible in the middle of 19th Century, when belief in the progress of liberty was well nigh universal."

QUESTIONS FOR EXERCISE

1. "The worth of a state....is the worth of individuals composing it; and a state which dwarf its men....will find that with small men, no great thing can really be accomplished" — J.S. Mill. Comment.
2. "The only freedom that deserves the name is that of pursuing our good in our own way" — J.S. Mill. Comment.

5

Idealism : Immanuel Kant (1724-1804)

Utilitarianism failed to solve all the problems created by industrial revolution. It opposed the interference of Government in the name of economic and political freedom. In the words of Barker, "Not a modification of the old Benthamite premises, but a new philosophy was needed and that philosophy was provided by the idealistic school of which Green is the greatest representative." In the words of Hearnshaw, "It demanded reforms in the early days on the ground that if unuseful state restrictions and interferences were removed, the natural harmony of economic interests would ensure that all would be well." When those restrictions had been removed and *laissez faire* largely realized, utilitarianism was used to oppose any attempt to deal with the disharmonies of economic interest. It had done all that it could, but democracy was more alive than ever to these new problems to solve which some way had to be found, if democracy was to reconcile a true individualism with the new functions of the state. Carlyle criticised utilitarianism as each one for himself and devil take the hindmost.

IDEALISM IN POLITICAL PHILOSOPHY

There were germs of idealist thinking in the political philosophy of Plato and Aristotle. In modern age it began with Kant and Fichte but reached to its climax with George Wilhelm Friedrich Hegel. In England it was propunded by Thomas Hill Green, Bradely and Bosanquet, of which Green is mot famous.

Bosanquet has called it idealist theory of the state. Hobhouse has named it as metaphysical theory, Joad has called it Absolutist theory. Gettel calls it idealist ethical theory and others call it philosophical theory.

CHIEF CHARACTERISTICS OF IDEALISM

1. Universe Subsists within the Spirit or Mind. According to this philosophic theory, the entire world is fundamentally of the nature of spirit or mind, which accounts for its being called idealism.

2. Mechanistic Explanation of Universe is Inadequate. Idealists refuse to accept that the world or universe is susceptible to a mechanical explanation, or to believe that the processes of Nature can be explained on a mechanistic principle. For this reason the idealists are opposed to all deterministic thinking.

3. Teleological Explanation of Universe. Opposed to the mechanistic explanations of the universe the idealists turn to a teleological theory which holds that human life and natural processes have a common objective which both are simultaneously trying to achieve. They do not object to or reject science but for them the scientific explanation of the universe is not the last word on the subject. Their standpoint is best exemplified by the axiological attitude.

4. Synthesis between Man and Nature. It becomes inevitable for the idealists to believe that there is harmony between the natural processes and human activity. Both man and Nature are busy in working out a common destiny.

5. Man is Central to the Universe. Idealists are also humanists from this standpoint. They believe that man, being the ultimate in spiritual existent, is central to the universe. Human life has a universal and omniscient importance or value. And in man's ultimate good lies the final objective of the universe. It is in man that mind, the spiritual element underlying the entire universe, realises its essential and purest nature.

6. Special Attention to the Normative and Social Sciences. Opposed to the realists and the materialists, the spiritualists or idealists do not accept the scientific explanation of the universe, based on scientific laws. They prefer the assistance of the normative and the social sciences in their own scheme of the universe. Ethics, aesthetics and logic make up the three normative sciences while the chief among the social sciences are psychology and sociology. The idealistic explanation of the universe makes greater use of psychology, ethics, logic, aesthetics, etc., than of chemistry, physics, mathematics and the rest of the natural sciences. It is only natural for such an explanation to be completely opposed to the materialistic or naturalistic explanation of the universe.

7. Evaluative Explanation of the Universe. In other words, the idealists profess an evaluative explanation of the universe and of human life, which is what makes them idealist. It should be kept in mind that the term idealist does not imply the vague-minded dreamer or imaginative visionary. The idealist does not reject the assistance of the natural sciences in comprehending the universe but he does not accept such natural facts to make up all of human life. His consciousness comprehends the realization of truth, beauty and goodness in human life.

8. Conceptualism. In the field of epistemology the idealist is better called a conceptualist since he believes that the object has no existence apart from its concept. In professing this view the idealist propounds a theory completely at variance with the realist conception of the problem. He believes that the object and its qualities do not have any existence independent of the conception of them. Knowledge influences them. Knowledge of an object occurs not directly but indirectly, through the medium of thought. Objects are not public, since they change with the viewpoint from which they are observed. An object has no existence apart from the thought of it. Existence lies in being related to consciousness.

9. Universe is Knowable. The idealists hold that the universe can be known through the medium of reason or mind since both mind and the universe are invested with an identical spiritual element. Hegel goes so far as to establish an identity between mind and Nature by positing that mental categories coincide with stages in the development of the universe. Whatever the minor differences among them, all idealists hold that the universe is knowable.

10. Emphasis on the Mental or Spiritual Aspect of Universe. Another important characteristic of the idealist thought is that it emphasizes the mental or spiritual aspects of the universe without nullifying or completely rejecting materialistic explanation of it. It is this higher aspect which conveys some meaning to the lower or material aspect. And everywhere the lower can be explained in terms of the higher. The naturalists or materialists reverse this by explaining the higher in terms of the lower. Idealism opposes this process.

It is possible to derive political conception of the idealist position from the above elucidation.

IDEALISTIC THEORY OF STATE

The idealistic theory of state is also known as the absolute or metaphysical theory of state, because it presents an ideal picture of state as something divine and all powerful as God. It is difficult to establish it on the earth.

1. The Origin of Idealist Theory. The origin of the idealist theory can be traced back to Plato and Aristotle. Both the Greek philosophers regarded state as natural to man. It is only through the state that man can achieve his purpose of perfect and happy life. The state provides him with the proper environments for the fullest development of his personality. According to Aristotle, "State comes into existence for the sake of life and continues to exist for the sake of good life." The German idealists have been influenced by the philosophy of Rousseau from whom Hegel borrowed the idea of general will.

2. German Idealists. Like Plato and Aristotle, the idealists have laid a great emphasis on state. Some of the advocates of this theory regard the state as divine, omnipotent, infallible, absolute and just. The German idealist theory is a reaction against the eighteenth century naturalist rationalists, who regarded the state as the artificial device of man who consciously brought into existence to serve his needs and protect his rights. The German idealist philosophy considers the state as natural, original and organic. It is the source of individual rights. It is a manifestation of the general will which is independent of the will of individuals.

3. Hegel. According to Hegel, the state is an end in itself. It is a supreme means to good life. It is only in the state that man achieves the fullest development of his personality. State is like an individual who has his own will. It has achieved perfect development. The state is infallible. It can never do any wrong. Being source of individual rights man can have no rights against the state. It is the sacred duty of the individuals to obey the state. It is in the complete obedience to the state that man is most free. When man obeys the state, he obeys his best self.

4. Human Nature and Social Life. Idealism starts with a conception of human nature and interpretation of his social life. It distinguishes between specific voluntary acts of individual and his real will. It is the real will which reveals man's inner self and shows what he wants to be. Due to ignorance or under pressure of some physical need, he may act in a way that goes against his real will. An idealist perceives the part played by selfishness and narrow ambitions in the life of an individual but he pleads that behind his weakness there is something which is more constant and universal, more rational and spiritual. An institution is to be judged by the ideas and forces which bring it into existence. An idealist appraises the state by ideal standards, what it ought to be and not what it is.

5. Definition of State and its Theory. Hegel has defined the state. State is the march of God on earth. The individuals must worship it. Individuals are expected to sacrifice their all at the altar of state. Its commands must be obeyed. To disobey the state is to disobey God. There is no check on the authority of the state. The individuals have no right to revolt against it. If, as a result of revolution, another state comes into existence, it is the duty of individuals to pay their unquestioned allegiance to the new state and obey its command.

6. State as an End. According to the idealists state is not a means but an end in itself. It represents what is the best of the general will.

7. True Liberty is in Obeying the State. Liberty does not mean absence of restraint. It has a positive value. It is by carrying out one's duties and obligations to the state that one enjoys the perfect liberty. Man is most free when he perform such acts which do good to the society. The commands of the state are the outcome of the rational will. All the acts of the state are in the best interests of individuals. An individual does good to him and serve his own interest when he obeys the laws of state. In the words of Bradley, "Human liberty consists in discharging the obligation of one's status in society and finding one's place in social life."

8. Supreme Authority of the State. T.H. Green laid a great emphasis on the supreme authority of state. He did not visualise the existence of state apart from the lives of the individuals who compose it.

9. Will, not Force, is the Basis of the State. Will, not force, is the basis of the state. Force plays its own part in the existence of state and it helps to maintain peace. But it is not the only basis of state. People obey the law of the state not simply due to the fact that they fear its authority backed by force, but with the opportunities for full development. If force were the basis, the persons in authority would not submit to law of state. But we find that men in the military, in police also obey the state. Force may be necessary for the existence of state but it cannot sustain it. The authority of state lies in common consciousness of a common end. People are loyal to the state because they are convinced that it helps them to achieve the common end of peace and prosperity.

In most recent time, Nietzsche of Germany, idolised the state. Drawing upon the philosophy of Nietzsche, the military leaders of Germany inspired the

German people and prepared them for last two world wars. The great advocates of idealist theory were Kant, Hegel, Bradley, Green and Bosanquet.

10. Crticism of the Idealist Theory. The idealist theory of state has been subjected to severe criticism. The theory helps to curb the liberty of the individual. Individual is called upon to sacrifice his life and property for the sake of state whether good or bad. Following are the important criticisms of idealism:

(i) *Psychologically false*. The idealists believe that the state is a corporate body which has a will of its own which is distinct from the wills of the individuals. Psychologists, however, do not admit a common mind or will. The individuals have their own wills. A government may claim to be based on the general will of the people, so long as the latter support it.

(ii) *State is not omnipotent.* The theory is based on the false assumption that the state is universal and all powerful. But as yet there is no universal state. A state has a jurisdiction over a fixed area. In international sphere, a state does not enjoy unlimited power. It has to act under certain obligations and limitations imposed by the moral principles which guide the relations of one state to another. Even in internal sphere it is neither possible nor desirable that the state should have unlimited, unrestricted power. The power corrupts and absolute power corrupts absolutely. It sacrifices the liberty of the individual and curbs his personality. Hitler and Mussolini followed this theory and brought misery not only to their respective states of Germany and Italy but to whole of humanity.

(iii) *State as an end itself and not a means to an end.* The individuals exist for the sake of state. They can be sacrificed at its altar. This view cannot hold ground in the modern age of democracy. Of course, it is true that a man can develop his pesonality only as a member of the state. But it does not mean that he should merge his personality in the state and thus lose his individuality. On the other hand, state is an agency of the society which helps the individual to achieve his aim. As Aristotle said the state has come into existence for life and continues to exist for the sake of good life. Thus, state is not an end but a means for the achievement of an end. Its end is the happiness and well being of its members.

(iv) *Infallibility*. The idealists believe that the state is infallible and cannot do any wrong. Whenever there is any conflict between the state and the individual, the conduct of the state is always upheld and individual is invariably wrong. The proposition cannot be held as absolutely true. The state machinery is run by the human beings and to err is human. None but God is infallible. To exalt the state to the heights of God is to destroy the individual freedom altogether.

(v) *State cannot represent the real will of the individuals.* The idealists hold that the state has a mind and will which represents the real will of the individuals. As a matter of fact, there is no real will. If at all, the state represents the general will which may be the will of the majority or the will of the ruling class. Often, the real will is used as a garb to cover the tyrannical acts of the state. It is a device to present the arbitrary acts of the state as democratic.

(vi) *Identification of the state with society.* The idealists regard state and society as identical. But, as Maclver says, "To identify the social with the political is to be guilty of the grossest of all confusion which completely bars any understanding of either society or state." The state is the highest form of social organisation which holds the society together but it does not embrace all the social activities of man. The sphere of society is wider than that of state. Man's activities are not confined within the territorial limits of states, they cross its boundary. It is dangerous to equate the state with the society. It will invite and justify the state inferference in all the activities of man and curb his liberties.

(vii) *Wrong conception of liberty.* Idealist conception of liberty is wrong. It is absurd to say that man is not free when he obeys the laws of the state. The idealists believe that the state represents the real will of the individuals or that in obeying the will of the state, he obeys his own real will. As a matter of fact, the state has no will apart from the wills of the people. Individual is free only when he is able to follow the dictates of his own conscience. According to the idealists, an individual acts in ignorance if he disobeys the will of the state. He cannot differ from the state. He is under obligation to obey the laws and orders of the state. If this position is accepted, the individual will have no scope for development. It will destroy all the human values based on freedom and liberty of the individual.

(viii) *No Scope for international law of world government.* According to the idealist theory, the state is absolute and self-sufficient. It is the guardian of the whole moral world. An individual is bound to owe allegiance to the state alone and obey its laws. Beyond the frontiers of state, there does not exist any other authority. Idealist theory of the state stands in the way of international cooperation. The advance of science has brought the different states nearer to each other. Today, a man is not only a member of the state he lives in, he is a citizen of the world. He has got some international obligation as well. In the interest of world peace, he may have to criticise the act of his own state. Accepting the idealist view, Hitler tried to put the hands of clock back and brought misery to the whole world including Germany.

(ix) *Monistic conception of state is erroneous.* The idealists lay stress on the unity of state. But unity of state is unreal. State consists of a number of individuals. It is not an individual in itself. Man is not only a member of state, he has formed so many associations and their recognition by the society is breaking up the unity of state. Monistic theory of state does not hold much ground. Pluralistic theory of state is getting popular.

TWO KINDS OF IDEALISM

Idealism can be divided into extreme idealism and liberal or limited idealism. Main difference between these two schools of thought is that German school of thought led by Hegel made state omnipotent, and absolute and called it as "march of God on earth." On the other hand, English idealism led by Green did not consider state as absolute. it discarded the view that state is the end and individual is the means. It agreed with the importance of the state for the development of an individual. It discarded the view that state is omnipotent or absolute. They believed 'Will, not force, is the basis of state.'

Principles of Extreme Idealism

1. State is the highest development of man's personality. It is march of God on earth. Therefore, whatever is done by the state is moral and justifiable.

2. State is the end and individuals are the means. Without state individuals have no value. Whatever is good for the state, is also good for individual. Therefore, individual should obey the orders of the state. He should consider it his duty to carry out the orders of the state.

3. State is the embodiment of real will of the individuals. Real freedom of a man consists in obeying all orders of the state.

4. State is representative of highest virtue. It possesses its own personality distinct to individuals of which it is constituted. A man by carrying out its order thinks that he is carrying out his own real will and feels real freedom.

5. Extreme idealists sacrifice individual at the altar of state.

Principles of Liberal Idealism

1. Man is a social and political animal, he gets his value and importance only in society.

2. State is an ethical and moral institution. It should create the conditions for the highest development of man's personality. It is necessary for the moral development.

3. The aim of state is to develop full and free personality of man. Man depends on society for his development. According to Barker, "Instead of starting from a central individual, to whom the social system is supposed to be adjusted, the idealist starts from a central social system in which the individual must find his appointed orbit of duty."

4. The state and individual both are complimentary to one another.

5. The individual is in the same way part of the state as body's different organs are the parts of the body. State is the source of man's freedom and rights. Man is fully dependent on the state.

6. State is the friend and guide of an individual. State and individual both have similar aim *i.e.* full development of human personality. State control is for the welfare of the individual.

7. "Will, not force, is the basis of the state." But Idealists believe that political consciousness leads to the welfare of the state, our own welfare is also included in it. Green says that the state has risen owing to human consciousness of a common end. The state is sustained not by blind coercion, but coercion exercised according to law in the interests of the rights of the individual. The function of state is to create conditions to enable the individual to realise his pesonality. State must help to create social conditions in which there will be the fewest possible impediments in the way of each individual making the best

of himself. According to Green as Coker point out, "If a state fails persistently in serving the high moral purpose for which it exists namely making possible the self-realization of its citizen it loses its claims upon the allegiance of the latter, who then have rights against the state or at least against the government in which the state is then imperfectly actualised, and they may be justified in repudiating or resisting its commands."

Quotations Against Idealism

Some quotations as criticisms of Idealism are as follow :

1. *C.E.M. Joad.* "It is difficult to escape the conclusion that the attribution of real will to the individual which is necessarily in accord with general will in which it is submerged, is only a device for giving an appearance of justice and democracy to what otherwise appear the purely arbitrary and tyrannical acts of sovereign state."

2. *Barker.* "What the idealist does is not to construct an ideal, but to idealize the given data of imperfect society and to preach divine right of things as they are, their conception of what is real is rational is not correct."

3. *McGovern.* Hegel has proved to be forerunner of "morning star of the fascist theory of the state" and probably of other totalitarian theories.

4. *Wayper.* "Preaching the fulfilment of humanity, he has opened the floodgates wide to those surging tides of inhumanity that have threatened since he wrote to engulf the world. Ardent apostle of reason, he has done more than next to prepare the way for that age of unreason in which we live. The evil that he has done, has after him and is writ large on world today."

5. *Hobhouse.* The state is a great organisation. Its well being is something of larger and more permanent importance than that of any single citizen. Its scope is vast. Its services call for the extreme loyalty and sacrifice. All this is true. Yet when the states set up as an entity superior and indifferent to competent individuals, it becomes a false God, and its worship, the abomination of dissolution."

These criticisms apply to extreme idealist school led by Hegel and not on moderate idealists like Green who is an individualist and is logical and nearer to truth. Others are of opinion that idealism has been criticised because persons have failed to understand its real principles. Criticisms do not apply on Green's idealism.

IMMANUEL KANT (1724—1804)

Kant was born in 1724, and died in 1804. The history of his life is hard to write, in as much as he had neither life nor history, for he lived a mechanically ordered and old bachelor life in a quiet retired street of Konigsberg, an old town on the north-east border of Germany. His rising, coffee drinking, writing, reading, college lectures, eating, walking, all had fixed time. He passed 30 years of his life as a Professor. He was profoundly influenced by Rousseau. Some writers believe that Kant only gave new shape to the thought of Rousseau and Montesquieu.

Kant wrote many books, essays and articles. Most important of them are 1. *'Perpetual Peace', 1893 2, Critique.of Pure Reason 3. Critique of Practical Reason 4. First Metaphysical Principles of Theory of Law 5. The Natural Principles of the Political Order 6. The Principles of Political Right.*

POLITICAL IDEAS OF KANT

Kant propounded his ideas on 1. Moral freedom 2. State 3. Social contract 4. Sovereignty and law 5. Property 6. World peace.

Conception of Moral Freedom

According to Prof. Barker, Kant and Hegel both developed their political ideas supposing that the main virtue of man is moral freedom. They made this idea the central point of their thought. Kant interpreted freedom as the right to will, a self-imposed imperative of duty. He said that man being a thinking being, his conduct is controlled by some principles. He feels freedom by doing work according to some rules. Such freedom is moral freedom which is the distinctive feature of human being. It is a real freedom because a man works according to his inner call. It is categorical imperative of duty. Man remains free upto the time he works according to his inner conscience because he disciplines himself according to his inner call. If a man begins to work according to his bad ideas, he loses his freedom and becomes dependent. As per Barker, Kant interpreted freedom as the right to will, a self-imposed imperative duty.

Kant's conception of freedom is negative, limited and subjective. He followed individualistic ideas. He believed that the individual knows best what is beneficial for him. Therefore, man and not the state is the root of freedom. Being an intellectual person man is an end in himself. He cannot be made means of any other person.

Hegel's Criticism

Hegel criticised Kant's conception of freedom as negative because he held self-imposed duty and freedom as one and also it makes a man end in himself. It is subjective because it remains only in inner conscience and not in external sphere. But the main feature of Kant's freedom is inner conscience duty of an individual to obey the state. As such man becomes only a slave or tool for the welfare of the state.

Hegel's Criticism of Kantian Conception of Freedom

In Kant's philosophy free will of the individuals was uppermost. Every individual was an end in himself and none was to be considered as a means to an end. Kant was not prepared to sacrifice the liberty of the individuals on the altar of the state. Though the liberty of the individual was to be subordinated to the higher needs of social existence, Kant was not willing to abandon the liberty of the individuals.

Critics point out that Kant could not make up his mind as to whether he stood for the conception of "being left alone" or in the higher sense of providing opportunity for the development of man's higher faculties. According to Vaughan, Kant failed "because he hovered between the two entirely different conceptions of the state *i.e.* between individualism and idealism."

Hegel criticised Kant's conception of freedom as negative, limited and subjective. Barker is of the opinion that Hegel sketched positive and objective conception of freedom and as such his views about the state were different than those of Kant.

1. Negative. Hegel considered Kant's freedom as negative because it has no place for freedom of conduct as according to Kant freedom lies in inner moral will. He stated "To define freedom of Press as freedom to say and write is parallel to the assertion to do as we please." Thus, he was against freedom of Press.

2. Limited. Kan't concept of freedom is limited because it remains in the inner consciousness of man and does not come out of it while actually freedom can be realized only in society. As such Kant is individualistic.

3. Subjective. Kant's concept of freedom is subjective because it remains only as a consciousness of individual's mind.

According to Hegel the main element of man's freedom does not lie in the inner consciousness of man but in the social institutions. Hegel's freedom lies in outer world and as such it becomes social and positive. Hegel maintained that man can feel freedom only by taking part in social activities. According to Prof. Sabine, "The vital point of Hegelian conception of freedom is that civilization is not repressive of individual self-expression, that social forces are a medium in which the individual always moves and from which he derives the elements even of his individuality; that to be man at all requires participation in the life of communities; that education and culture are in general a medium of liberation."

Liberty is Possible Only in Social Life

Hegel's idea of freedom was based on the old Greek notion of an individual finding his true personality and his freedom in the state. Man has no inalienable rights. His freedom is a gift of state. The state not only allows but enlarges the freedom of the society. The state is "the actualisation of freedom." The social institutions and environments are the media through which an individual finds self-realization and freedom. There is little freedom of man or individual. An individual is really free when he is morally free. Kant's ideas are liberal and represent his modern outlook.

POLITICAL PHILOSOPHY OF IMMANUEL KANT

1. Rousseau's Doctrine of Moral Will. In the words of Heine, Immanuel Kant had 'neither life nor history for he lived a mechanically ordered and abstract old bachelor life, which marks the transition from the 18th century individualism and the philosophy of natural rights." The greatest contribution of Kant was his approach to politics from the viewpoint of morals. He considered political philosophy meaningless unless it was related to moral will. He adopted Rousseau's doctrine of moral will and made it the cornerstone of his philosophy. From Rousseau Kant learnt to respect human nature. Kant writes, "There was a time when I thought that this alone (a consuming thirst for knowledge and restless passion to advance it) could constitute the honour of mankind, and I despised the common man who knows nothing. Rousseau set me right. This blind prejudice vanished; I learnt to respect human nature and should consider myself far more useless than the ordinary working man if I did not believe that this view could give worth to all others to establish the rights of man."

2. Individualism and Socialism. The philosophy of Kant is individualistic. Every individual is an end in himself and none is to be considered as a means to an end. This did not mean that the individuals are to aim at their particular good. They were to aim only at a good of universal application. The will of the individual was free only to will rational objects. If it willed non-rational objects, it is not free in the real sense of the term. To quote Kant, "Nothing can possibly be conceived in the world or even out of it which can be called good without qualification except a good will." Kant had a great passion for the liberty of the individuals but at the same time he had also the idea of social good. He was not willing to abandon either of the two ideas, the individual good and the social good. As Vaughan says, "There is clearly a conflict in his mind between the claims of justice and the claims of individual freedom. He does not see his way fully to reconcile the two. He is too honest to sacrifice either."

3. Concept of Moral Freedom. Thus, the concept of moral freedom occupies a central place in the philosophy of Kant. According to him, besides, pure theoretical reason man has another faculty known as pure practical reason which tells him that there are certain things which he ought to do. It is the source of the convention that there is something universally binding on man as man. It is experience which brings him into contact with reality and assures him that God exists, that human will is free and that the soul is immortal. These are the propositions whose final validity can never be guaranteed by pure theoretical reason. It is this conception of 'ought' which raises man above the world of nature. The consciousness of 'ought' bound up, with the consciousness of freedom. According to Kant, our will is good only in so far as it is determined by the 'categorical imperative of duty'. The imperative of duty is categorial or unconditional *i.e.*, it must be obeyed independent of likes or dislikes. It is only by obeying the categorical imperative of duty that man becomes a member of the real world. In other words, the goodness of will lies in its being consciously determined by respect for the law of reason which is not imposed from without. Morality consists of doing what the moral reason prescribes as our duty. In order to be truly moral, an act should issue from the consciousness of duty and must not be dictated by considerations of personal interest or advantage. In short, according to Kant, moral freedom is the basic fact of human life; secondly, moral freedom consists in obeying the moral law of carrying out the 'categorical imperative of duty'. In order that the concept of 'Categorical Imperative of Duty' may not remain wholly formal and abstract; Kant deduces certain maxims from it which can be good guide to conduct to a great extent *e.g.* "Act so as to treat humanity, in the person or in that of anyone else, always as an end never as a means." In other words, the whole mankind is a great brotherhood.

4. Freedom of the Individual. Coming to the political ideas, Kant was a great individualist. He was not prepared to sacrifice the individual at the altar of the state. The state should not do anything which might interfere with the realisation of his true freedom by the individual. The moral freedom of the individual consists in obeying the categorical imperative of duty. This leaves little freedom for the individual.

5. State as Positive Good. Kant regards the state as an essential condition of moral freedom which exists "to promote the exercise of freedom in accordance with universal law; it is an instrument through which the voluntary actions of individual persons may be harmonised in accordance with the universal law of freedom". State, for Kant, thus becomes a positive good and not a necessary evil.

6. Social Contract for Freedom. Kant rejects the contractual theory as an account of the historical origin of the state. He, however, accepted the idea of social contract only to show that man can be compelled to obey the law which he did not accept of his own accord. By contract the people did not bring about a transition from a state of nature to an organised state. What they did was that they surrendered their eternal freedom in order to receive it immediately back as members of common wealth.

7. Conflict in Justice and Freedom. There is clearly a conflict in Kant's mind between the claims of justice and the claims of individual freedom. He did not see his way fully to reconcile the two. In one of his passages he rejected contract as a historical fact unequivocally; in another he accepted it as a mere idea, though a necessary idea; while still in another passage it is pronounced to be historically problematical and politically dangerous.

8. Emphasis on Rights and Duties of the Individual. Kant laid great emphasis on the rights and duties of an individual. There are certain rights founded on rational principles, which the Head of the state ought to respect. Such rights are rights to liberty and equality. But the enjoyment of rights does not imply individual caprice. Every right carries a corresponding duty.

9. More Emphasis. Kant put more emphasis on duties than on rights. Duty, according to him, was a matter of inner conscience.

10. No Right to Revolution. Kant did not give to the people the right to revolution. According to Vaughan, "Kant preached a stagnation which even Burke would have regarded as excessive." According to Kant, the overthrow and execution of sovereign was "an immoral and inexplicable sin like the sin against the Holy Ghost spoken of by theologians, which can never be forgiven in this world or in the next." If the people felt that their constitution is defective, the change could be brought about only by the sovereign itself, through reform, not by the people, through the revolution.

11. Forms of State and Government. According to Kant, there are three forms of state and two forms of government. The forms of the state are aristocracy, autocracy and democracy. The forms of the government are despotism and republican. According to Kant, the government which is not representative is not rational. The function of the representative may be performed by the king or the nobility or the elected deputies. It is true that the legislative power is with the people but the ruler of the people is the legislator. Kant does not assign any wide range to the state activity. He restricts its functions to the removal of obstacles to good life. According to him, "All that the state can do is to hinder hindrances to freedom; to establish a social condition of outward order in which truly moral acts may generally evolve kingdom of humanity." According to Barker, the attitude of Kant towards free state was on the whole 'somewhat misguiding and individualistic'.

12. Theory of Punishment. Kant did not accept the deterrent or the reformative theory of punishment. According to him, the primary object of punishment is punishment itself.

13. Property. Kant accepted the institution of property but did not favour its extreme individualistic view. The owner of property must not ignore the interests of his neighbours. The only justification of property lies in the necessities of man. Property is a derived right. The individual derived it from his sovereign 'the Lord of the land'.

14. Human Nature and World Peace. According to Kant, a state of peace cannot be expected from the nature of man for malevolence is deeply rooted therein. Within the state, the evils are mainly suppressed by law. In the external relations between the states it comes into the open unmasked. "Nowhere", says Kant, "does human nature present a less pleasant spectacle than in the relations of nations as a whole with one another." No state is for a moment safe from the other states. In respect of international justice it is based upon public laws to which every state must submit. The safeguarding of world peace ultimately depends upon the reactions of the citizens of the various states with each other, as well as their relations with other states, being regulated by law. Kant seems to postulate a world federation in which the individual states would be subject to the adjudication of the general collective will.

CRITICAL EVALUATION

1. Too Abstract. Kant's ideas have been criticised as being too abstract.

2. Freedom. Kant could not make up his mind as to whether he stood for freedom in the ordinary sense of the word or in the higher sense. According to Vaughan, Kant failed "because he hovered between the two entirely different conceptions of the state."

3. Different Opinions. William Humboldt described Kant's political writings as on the whole, not very important. Bertrand Russell has described him as 'mere misfortune'. To conclude in the words of Wright, "Philosophers since Hegel have differed in the importance which they have attached to the work of Kant and his immediate successors in Germany. Some find in Kant the central figure in the entire history of modern philosophy. He combined all that was the best in previous rationalism and empiricism, and an understanding of his thought is an indispensable preliminary to any serious philosophical undertaking. Others think that no philosopher of this period is as important as the great thinkers of the Renaissance and the Enlightenment. However, it is probably safe to say that since 1781 every philosopher of consequences has in some way or other, positively or negatively, consciously or unconsciously been indebted to Kant and his immediate successors."

QUESTIONS FOR EXERCISE

1. Elucidate the main tenets of the idealistic school of philosophy and name the thinkers who propounded it.
2. Prof. Maxey remarks that there was one group of 19th century political thinkers whose doctrines few understood at the time and few really understand that today, but whose influence on modern political thought has been enormous. Discuss.
3. "What the idealist does is not to construct an ideal but to idealize the given data of imperfect society, and preach the divine right of things as they are" — Barker. Examine critically the view implied in the above that idealism is a part of tactics of conservatism.
4. "The theory commonly spoken as idealism is in point of fact, as much suitable and dangerous enemy to the ideal than any brute denial of absolutism emanating from one-sided science." Do you agree with this statement of Hobhouse, if so, give reasons?
5. "Kant placed a conception of freedom which is negative, limited and subjective" — Barker. Discuss.
6. Kant's doctrine as to origin and nature of the state is merely Rousseau's put into the garb of Kantian terminology, his analysis of the government follows Montesquieu in like Manner" — Dunning. Elucidate and Discuss.

6

Georg Wilhelm Friedrich Hegel (1770—1831)

Born in the town of Stuttgart, Hegel acquired the knowledge of theology at Tubingen but left the institution calling it as 'deficient in philosophy'. For several years he served as a teacher in the cities of Bonn and Frankfurt, then as a professor in the Jena University, a newspaper editor and head of a gymnasium department in Nuremberg, till he occupied the important chair in Heidelberg University in 1816. More important than this is his career as a professor in Berlin University since 1818 which in a sense made him the 'official philosopher of his government'. In 1831 he died of cholera epidemic making the 'end of an epoch, the last fine effort of Germany's greatest age.'[1]

WORKS OF HEGEL

The works of Hegel are of a highly philosophical nature in which politics is dominated by logic and metaphysics. His political ideas are traceable in numerous lectures that he delivered at the university of Jena between 1804-06 in which he touched the issues of ethics, logic and metaphysics and thereby displayed his philosophy of nature and mind. These ideas assumed a form of their own in his *Philosophy of Mind* (1816) and the *Science of Logic* (1812-16). The thought of Hegel found a more precise and expansive formulation in the *Encyclopaedia of the Philosophical Sciences* first published in 1816. In his *Philosophical Sciences* he discussed logic and philosophy of nature and spirit.

In the field of political thought, Hegel's work *Outlines of the Philosophy of Right* (1821) is very important. It appeared as an elaboration of his earlier work titled *Philosophy of Spirit* containing his ideas on ethics and theory of state. The Berlin lectures of Hegel published separately as the *History of Philosophy, Philosophy of History* and *Philosophy of Fine Art and Religion* are an elaboration of third section of the *Encyclopaedia.* Hegel's methodology and the basic assumptions of philosophy are contained in his *Philosophy of Right,* about which Reyburn remarks that "it is intended to point out the way in which the principles of right realise mind and give it objectivity; and it is more

1. Will Durant, *The Story of Philosophy*, p. 295.

concerned to show how the infinite self-contained the whole mind which intrinsically comes to the light of day than to display the insufficiency of the whole field of right."[2]

Hegel puts his ideas in a very difficult language that is not easily intelligible to an average reader. It is also said that connecting bonds are missing in his works with the result that his political philosophy suffers from lack of intelligibility and flow of expression due to "an isolated study".[3] In his monograph titled *The Secret of Hegel,* Prof. J.H. Stirling feels nervous at the confirmation of endless jargons in the philosophical system of Hegel. He remarks that there is "a scrutiny of thought so profound that it is for the most part unintelligible".[4] The critics have wrongly interpreted the meaning of Hegel's philosophy. Perhaps Hegel himself would not have understood what he meant by it. But the truth is that when his philosophy "is stripped of its pretentious logical apparatus, Hegel is saying something both very old and very simple".[5]

DIALECTICAL IDEALISM

The political philosophy of Hegel shows influence of Aristotle, Rousseau, Kant and Fichte. Hegel's political philosophy answers to various political questions in a methodical manner. The questions are old and so are their answers. However, the only novel thing is the method adopted by Hegel while discussing them. The method of dialectics is as old as the Greeks, but Hegel applied it in a different way. The earlier Greek writers had used the term to describe the process by which one proposition was set over against another, and out of this confrontation a new proposition emerged, uniting the truth contained in each of the original ones. Hegel adopted the term dialectic to describe the movement of reason in human affairs as well as the strictly technical process by which truth is arrived at.

The Salient Features

1. Reason as Ultimate Reality. Like Fichte, Hegel believes that ultimate reality is 'Reason' or 'Spirit', but not matter. He describes it as 'Absolute Idea' or 'Reason' or 'Spirit' and contrary to the Kantian view, insists that there is nothing in the universe which the human mind cannot comprehend. In Hegelian philosophy again and again we come across such passages as the distinctive feature of human life is that it "is not swayed by blind impulses only, but is guided and controlled by ideas and it is ideas after all that rule the world."[6] This reason is dynamic. It is the principle of growth and development. The essence of reason which makes reality is self-consciousness. It has to pervade through several stages in an attempt to attain the highest form of self-consciousness of which it is capable. The fundamental premise of Hegel is that

2. See T.M. Knox (ed.), *Hegel's Philosophy of Right,* p. 242.
3. Frank Thakurdas, *German Political Idealism,* p. 212.
4. See Karl R. Popper, *The Open Society and Its Enemies,* Vol. II, p. 27.
5. Lancaster, *Masters of Political Thought,* Vol. III, p. 66.
6. Halder, *Neo-Hegelianism,* p. 333.

what is rational is real and what is real is rational. Everything that exists is the embodiment of reason. Permeating all mere appearance of a rational principle giving meaning to political institutions just as it gives harmony to the natural universe. The motivating power lies not in inert matter but in self-propelling thought which is independent of matter. By real or actual, Hegel does not mean the 'existing' but the force that really actuates the existing. Hegel says: "What is rational is actual and what is actual is rational. On this conviction, the plain man like the philosopher takes his stand, and from it philosophy starts in its study of the universe of mind as well as the universe of nature. If reflection, feeling, or whatever form subjective consciousness may take, looks upon the present as something vacuous and looks beyond it with the eyes of superior wisdom, it finds itself in a vacuum, and because it is actual only in the present, it is itself mere vacuity. If, on the other hand, the Idea passes for only an Idea, for something represented in an opinion, philosophy rejects such a view and shows that nothing is actual except the Idea. Once that is granted, the great thing is to apprehend in the show of the temporal and transient the substance which is immanent and the eternal which is present."[7]

2. Dialectic in Thought and Things. If reason motivates the law of dialectic, it becomes a law of logic denying and distinction not only between the thought and things but between the thought of different persons. Hegel does not mean by the dialectic the way in which opposite tendencies are adjusted in political life and history. He does not talk about the 'law of pendulum'. He does not say that historical changes proceed with the interaction of opposite forces. In his view, the dialectic constitutes a mechanism by which thought propels itself, or the way in which reason progressively embodies itself in the institutions. Wright rightly points out : "The dialectic begins with the most abstract conception of pure logic, that of mere being and terminates with the most concrete phases of thought, the philosophy of the Absolute Mind in its full comprehensiveness and concreteness."[8]

3. Three Stages. According to Hegel, there are three stages involved in the process by which reason moves through history and nature. These may be called the thesis, anti-thesis and synthesis. The thesis passes into its anti-thesis so that synthesis takes place. The synthesis however, becomes a new thesis. The process is repeated until all contradictions are resolved. Thus, no assertion is wholly true, and this is immediately seen to involve its opposite. Between these two attributes of truth and falseness, are aspects of the same assertion. The dialectic is self-propelling. Each new stage of synthesis represents a higher stage of growth or a still more true stage of evolution and this process continues to operate until the stage of final truth is reached.

4. Dialectical Social Development. Hegel examines the case of social development on the basis of dialectical methodology. He maintains that the family representing love is the thesis, the civil society representing competition

7. Hegel, *Philosophy of Right* (Translated from German into English by T.M. Knox), pp. 10-11.
8. Wright, *History of Modern Philosophy*, p. 328.

is its anti-thesis; and their synthesis lies in the nation-state which represents the elements of both love and competition. Family is Unity, the Civil Society is Particularity and the State is Universality. The tension between the unity of the family and the particularity of the civil society is resolved with the appearance of the state as the actuality of the universal order. Both the family and civil society are rational, since both are actual, but only the state is perfectly rational and perfectly ethical.

5. State as Embodiment of Reason. The state (nation) representing the synthesis of family and civil society, is a perfect embodiment of reason. Hobhouse says : "Just as in a simple religion the powers that be are ordained of God, so with the metaphysician who starts from the belief that the things are what they should be, the fabric of social life; and in particular the state system, is part of an order which is inherently rational and good, an order to which the lives of individuals are altogether subordinate."[9] The process of dialectic stops here, for the reconciliation has reached the stage of final truth. In the words of Hegel: "The ethical substance, as containing independent self-consciousness united with its concept, is the actual mind of a family and a nation. The concept of this idea has being only as mind, as something knowing itself, and actual because it is the objectification of itself, the movement running through the form of its movements. It is therefore (A) ethical mind in its nature or immediate phase — the Family. This substantiality loses its unity, passes over into divisions and into the phase of relation, *i.e.*, into (B) Civil Society — an association of members as self-subsistence, is only abstract. Their association is brought about by their needs, by the legal system — the means to security of person and property — and by an external organisation for attaining their particular and common interests. This external state (C) is brought back to and welded into unity in the Constitution of the State which is the end and the actuality of both the substantial universal order and public life devoted thereto."[10] Hegel has clothed the state with the tapestry of his system of dialectic. A good example of the loose and fanciful way in which the conception of opposites is used is thus put by Hegel : "The building of a house is, in the first instance, a subjective aim and design. On the other hand, we have, as means, the several substances required for the work — Iron, Wood, Stones. The elements are made use of in working up this material : fire to melt iron, wind to blow up the fire, water to set wheels in motion, in order to cut the wood, etc. The result is that the wind, which has helped to build the house, is shut by the house; so also are the violence of rains and floods, and the destructive powers of fire, so far as the house is made fireproof. The stones and beams obey the law of gravity, press downward, and so high walls are carried up. Thus, the elements are made use of in accordance with their nature, and yet to co-operate for a product by which their operation is limited. Thus, the passions of men are gratified; they develop themselves and their aims in accordance with their

9. Hobhouse, *The Metaphysical Theory of State*, p. 17.

10. Hegel, *Philosophy of Right*, paras 156-157.

natural tendencies and build up the edifice of human society; thus fortifying a position for Right and Order against themselves."[11] Thus, art is the thesis, religion is its anti-thesis, and philosophy represents their synthesis. So family is the thesis, civil society is its anti-thesis, and the nation-state exhibits their synthesis. The dialectical process begins from family and through civil society culminates in the nation-state.

The law of dialectical idealism lays down that idea is original, primary and self-operating. It also confirms the role of some Absolute Spirit in the making of history. Thus, Reason or Idea becomes inter-changeable with God. As Hegel himself says : "The Reason in most concrete form is God: governs the world the actual working of His government — the carrying out of plan is the history of the world. Philosophy strives to comprehend this plan for only that which has been developed as a result of it possesses a *bona fide* reality; that which does not accord with it is negative. Before the pure light of this divine idea — which is more than mere ideal — the phantoms of the world whose events are an incoherent concourse of fortuitous circumstances, utterly vanish. Philosophy wishes to discover the substantial purport, the real aspect of the reason in the comprehension of divine work."[12] In fine, history, according to Hegel, is the autobiography of God.[13]

Criticism of Dialectic

Hegelian system of dialectic has been subjected to denunciation by followers various trends of political philosophy. Some important criticisms are as follows:

1. Marxist Criticism. Marx borrowed heavily from Hegel, but he put the latter right side up. According to Marxism, the motivating force is not reason but matter. Contrary to Hegel, Marx insists that it is not the consciousness of man that motivates matter; it is the material factors that influence human consciousness. Marx thus retained the Hegelian method but rejected its contentions. In one of his letters to Dr. Ludwig Kugelmann, Marx wrote in 1868 thus: "Hegel's dialectic is the basic form of my dialectic, but only after it has been stripped of its mystical form and it is precisely this which distinguishes my method."

2. Defects of Rationalism. While Hegel's analysis is based on the premises of rationalism, modern school of psycho-analysis does not admit that the reason is the only or decisively motivating factor. While man is a rational creature, the elements of irrationality also influence his behaviour. He is less rational and more irrational as the non-rational factors like habit, sentiment, instinct, impulse etc. do play their part in governing the patterns of human behaviour. To quote Graham Wallas, human mind "acts like a harp, all of whose strings throb together; so that emotion, impulse, inference, are often simultaneous and inter-mingled aspects of a single mental experience".[14]

---

11. Hegel, *Philosophy of History*, p. 27.
12. Hegel, *Philosophy of History* (Translated from German into English by J. Siberee), p. 38.
13. Sidney Hook, *From Hegel to Marx*, p. 36.
14. Wallas, *Human Nature in Politics*, p. 99.

3. Flaws in Theory of Development. It has been pointed out that every kind of development does not take place in the way as the law of Hegelian dialectic tells us. Hegel treats social institutions in a process of evolution as a synthesis arisen out of their opposite elements of thesis and anti-thesis. But how can the state be taken as a final synthesis. What is the anti-thesis of the state and what is the future mechanism of dialectical process. Again, when the dialectic is extremely vague, how anti-thesis of art is the religion and how does philosophy represent their synthesis? In fact, the contradictions discovered by Hegel consist of so many sorts of different and opposite things that the dialectic "frequently loses its plausibility."[15]

According to Kelly, "Essentially, Hegel's weakness lay in two realms. He was perhaps unaware of their connection. The first weakness lay in his overt and daring conjugation of history and reason, in the claims he made for his secular providence of the will that had become mind, the mind had become will. Whatever history is, it is obviously not reason, no matter how reasonable the mind that perceives it, even if the mind is a creature of history. History is probably closer to Herder's variety of forms than to any idealist union of life and divinity created or imposed by conceptual apparatus. The second Hegelian weakness is his continued assertion of the European cultural claim."[16] To make the meaning of the second weakness more revealing, Kelly further says : "The religio-political synthesis or Eurocentric destiny within an ever-renewing and deepening system of speculation had been attacked by Strauss, Feuerbach, Bauer, Ruge and Marx. Their criticism exploded the cultural homogeneity of Europe by discovering masters and slaves where Hegel had thought to close the problem. Coercive transcendence, soon to be remitted to other continents, remained."[17]

CONCEPT OF FREEDOM

Positive Concept

Hegel's conception of freedom is very much different from that of Kant, while Kant treats it as a subjective and limited phenomenon, Hegel considers it to be positive and objective. Drawing inspiration from Rousseau, Hegel treats freedom as the essence of man; the distinctive quality of human life, the renunciation of which is tantamount to the renunciation of humanity itself. He writes: "The notion of freedom must not be taken in the sense of the casual free will of each individual but in the sense of the reasonable will, the will in and for itself."[18] Hegel's approach is quite different from other German idealists also who conceived it to be "an attribute or faculty of an individual person."[19] To Hegel man's freedom is associated with his life in society. It lies in obeying

15. Lancaster, *op. cit.*, p. 66.
16. Kelly, *Idealism, Political and History*, pp. 356-357.
17. *Ibid.*, p. 357.
18. Cf. Bosanquet, *The Philosophical Theory of State*, pp. 220-221.
19. Dunning, *op. cit.*, p. 155.

the dictates of self-imposed categorical imperative of duty. It is one aspect of pure abstract intelligence. The idea of the will, as a last abstraction, is the free will that wills the free will. In Hegel's own phrase, it "is eternal, universal, self-conscious, self-determining."[20]

As Herbert Marcuse observes: "Since man wishes to be judged in accordance with his own self-determined choices, he is free in relation to himself, whatever the external situation may impose upon him. No one can break in upon this inner conviction of mankind."[21]

Comprehensive Meaning

According to Hegel, freedom consists in transcending the limitations imposed on by our material and egoistic self and in realising the social aspects of our personality. The more we develop our rationality and spirituality, the more conscious we become of freedom in and around us. Hegel does not follow the line of John Stuart Mill in taking freedom as something of a negative character implying absence of restraints. Freedom does not signify the life of a man who has left this world like an ascetic. It is the positive power of an individual to determine his actions actively, deliberately and consciously and, for this reason, distinguishable with anything like whim or caprice or sentiment and the like. It is to be realised in relation to others, because relation to others is not merely a possibility but the necessity of mind, for it is by means of others and by means of sublation that mind preserves itself. Keeping it in view, Prof. Vaughan says that by freedom "is meant not the mere absence of external restraints : not the liberty of the individual to do what he wills with his own faculties and his own possessions, but the untrammelled development of man's powers, moral, intellectual and spiritual, according to the fundamental laws of our own nature."[22]

Influence of Rousseau

In his interpretation of freedom, Hegel is distinctly under the influence of Aristotle and Rousseau. He rejects the interpretation of Kant and insists that the freedom of a man cannot be conceived in isolation or in a self-imposed pattern of rational life. Freedom has a positive and an objective character : it expands itself and consists in the will to make one's outward self adequate to the measure of the fullness of his thinking self. Hence, when the will is free, objective, outwardly expressed, and creative, it manifests itself into three forms — law, inward morality and social ethics or *sittlechkeit* variously translated as social morality, ethical system, moral life and customary morality. Prof. Barker identifies *sittlechkeit* with social righteousness and says that it "is a spirit and habit of life expressed in the social opinion and enforced by the social conscience of a whole people; it is at one and the same time a mind of self-consciousness,

---

20. *Ibid.*, p. 156.

21. *Hegel and the Rise of Social Theory*, p. 206.

22. Vaughan, *Studies in the History of Political Philosophy*, Vol. II, p. 153.

because it is a spirit, and thing of external existence, because it is a visible system of habit and conduct."[23]

Law as Free Will

The first manifestation of will is law under which Hegel discusses the idea of personality, property and contract. All of them are the manifestations of free will. A living creature becomes a person only so far as he exercises free will to be a person. Material objects like property, are expression of man's free will and have no will of their own. A slave is no better than a property, since he lacks the free will to be free. Hegel judges laws and rights "not by a fixed standard, but with reference to various stages of culture and self-consciousness that history reveals."[24] But the second manifestation of will is the rules of inward morality. Here Hegel "discusses those aspects of self-determination in which the mere externality of law and the mere inwardness of morality are reconciled."[25]

As Lindsay puts it Hegel's philosophy of law is an immense advance on Kant and just because of that the abstractions of Kantian Ethics are really overcome in Hegel."[26]

Freedom in Nation-State

The final manifestation of will is the whole system of institutions and influences that make for righteousness in the nation-state. It includes law, custom, sentiment and moral will. It is the nation-state which represents social morality condensed in itself. The free will of the individual is fully raised in obeying customary morality of the community which is the working of a universal cause. It projects itself beyond itself and reaches the stage of perfection in so doing. It is the nation-state where man "has fully raised his outward self to the level of the inward self of thought : his free will has found its broadest expansion which its positive quality demands, and the highest expression which its objective character requires."[27]

Hegel exalts the nation-state with his interpretation of freedom. If state is the final embodiment of will, then no idea of force or contract can apply to it. The state must be envisaged not in terms of law or inward morality but as a custodian of social ethics. It is the highest expression of that social ethics at once precipitated in and enforced by social opinion which lies behind the life of the family, the political community itself. Barker observes : "That social morality is the product of a free will seeking to realise itself in a positive and objective form : and the state, as the highest expression and organ of social morality, is therefore also the product of that will — a product not in the sense

23. *Op. cit.*, p. 49.
24. *Ibid.*, p. 157.
25. *Ibid.*
26. A.D. Lindsay, *Kant*, p. 295.
27. Barker, *op. cit.*, p. 19.

of definite creation, at a given point of time, but in the sense of something gradually evolved, yet implicit all the time."[28]

Justification of State Absolutism

Thus, Hegel's conception of freedom leads to the justification of state absolutism. To quote Dewey : "Freedom is the consciousness of Freedom. Liberty of action has little to do with it. Obviously, it is only in this German idealistic system — particularly in the system of Hegel himself — that this has fully taken place. Meantime, when citizens of a state (especially of the state in which this philosophic insight has been achieved), take the laws of their state as their own ends and motives of action, they attain the best possible substitute for a reason which is its own object. They appropriate as their own personal reason the objective and absolute reason embodied perforce in law and custom".[29]

Criticism of Hegel's idea of Freedom

1. Paradoxical. Hegel's meaning of freedom is full of paradoxes. Choice is the essence of freedom and to deny its place is to deny freedom. To say that we are free only when we pursue our rational will embodied in the state and its institutions is to say that we have nothing like an independent choice. Hegel makes freedom absurd by holding that freedom is no freedom when it does not coincide with the good will. As Barker says, "Thus, may seem a facile reconciliation of the free moral will with the system of the state, achieved at the cost of the suppression of one of the factors and one of the impossible exaltation of the other."[30]

2. Conflicting Implications. Hegel's concept of freedom has some conspicuous implications in the realm of philosophy, logic and metaphysics, but it is not so in the world of politics which is full of diversities and conflicts. The fact of common good or general will may not be discovered so easily as visualised by Rousseau and Hegel to the extent that the individual may reconcile his will thereby and have the enjoyment of freedom. Naturally, for all practical purposes, individual's freedom would mean subordination to the will of the majority."[31] Hence, Prof. Berlin, accuses Hegel of doing an act of "monstrous impersonation".[32]

3. State Absolutism. Hegel's idea of freedom in the realm of politics signifies meek acceptance of the authority of the state. State and society become identifiable with each other. An attempt to ignore the distinction between the two "may lead to unlimited state regulation of life".[33]

---

28. *Ibid.*, pp. 19-20.

29. *Op. cit.*, p. 133.

30. Barker, *op. cit.*, p. 52.

31. See Bertrand de Jouvenel, *Sovereignty.*

32. See Isaiah Berlin, *Two Concepts of Liberty.*

33. Barker, *op. cit.*, p. 54.

4. Totalitarianism. The purpose of Hegel is to emphasise the absolute character of political authority. According to him, "The right of individual to become subjectively destined to freedom is fulfilled when they belong to an actual ethical order, because their conviction of their freedom finds its truth in such an objective order that they are actually in possession of their own essence or their own inner universality."[34] One finds here traces of a totalitarian system. The noted English sociologist Hobhouse condemns Hegelian interpretation for setting up the state as "a greater being, a spirit, a super-personal entity, in which individuals with their private consciences or claims of rights, their happiness or their misery, are merely subordinate elements."[35]

TOTALITARIAN THEORY OF STATE

Hegel's theory of state is characterised by absolutism, elitism and authoritarianism. The imperfect institution of the state is raised to the level of divinity, a mystic entity, an absolute idea on ethical substance. Then the same creation is identified with the imperfect state of Prussia, to justify its glory and majesty. This shows the influence of the ideas of Plato, Aristotle and Rousseau coupled with the events of national reaction against Napoleon Bonaparte after 1812.

State as Synthesis

The process of dialectic shows that the state is the final synthesis where are resolved the contradictions of family and civil society. Here the law of dialectic ceases in as much as the state represents a stage of final reconciliation. The civil society represents the anti-thesis of family, but both find their reconciliation in the nation-state. As society is different from family, so state is different from the civil society. The family rests on merely natural feelings of kindness, generosity and affection. While the civil bourgeois society stands for the economic and industrial world in which men appear as bread-earners. For the successful pursuits of their common interests, they demand police functions and administration of justice. The civil society is only an appearance within a larger system. It is only within the state proper that such a world as that of the bourgeois society could be conceivable. As Bosanquet puts it: "Its priority to the state is, like that of the family, the priority of comparative narrowness or simplicity, of dealing with fewer factors and representing human nature in a more special, though necessary, aspect."[36]

J.O'Malley makes the meaning of Hegel clear in these words : "Hegel uses the expression 'civil society' to designate that phase of human social life in which the needs and, therefore, the interests of the individual govern his relations with others. Thus understood, civil society is...the battlefield where

---

34. Hegel, *Philosophy of Right*, p. 158.

35. Hobhouse, *op. cit.*, p. 27.

36. Bosanquet, *The Philosophical Theory of State*, pp. 252-253.

everyone's individual private interest meets everyone else's...This is the sphere of economic life, whose regularities are expressed in the laws of political economy, and whose content is the pursuit of selfish ends."[37] He further says that the unity of social and political life "is effected within the modern state despite the apparent duality of civil and political life by means of an institutional framework whose principal features are (i) a monarch who comes to the throne by birth and thus independently of political factions, (ii) an extensive bureaucracy of salaried civil servants who constitute an estate or class whose aims are identical with those of the state itself, and (iii) an Assembly of States in which representatives of the crown and the executive power meet with representatives of the civil estates to deliberate and determine the way in which the aims of the state and of civil society shall be reconciled, and to translate their decisions into law".[38]

Based on Concept of Freedom

Hegel's conception of freedom justifies the case of state absolutism. The basis of the state is the free will of the individual. The objective and positive character of freedom creates law and rules of inward morality and finally manifests itself in the nation-state. Thus, the state maintains individual as a person and promotes his welfare and protects the minor groups of family and social life in which he partially seeks his welfare. It sustains social personality of the individual by carrying him away from an isolated to a social life. It teaches personality to transcend itself by giving its devotion to something beyond itself. Without the state man is nothing but a beast and a stupid and limited creature. Hegel says : "All the worth which the human being possesses — all spiritual reality — he possesses only through the state".[39] The individual realises freedom to the extent to which he identifies himself with the reason as manifested in the state and its institutions. The freedom of individual thus lies in willing the purposes of the state as his own. As the reason finally manifested in state is always right and the only way to secure freedom from bondage to the irrational impulses and desires lies in voluntary submission to the state. Analysing the meaning of Hegel, Wayper suggests that the state "is the school-master which brings him knowledge of the Spirit, of Absolute Reason. His real will impels him to identify himself with the Spirit. The spirit is embodied in the state. Therefore, it is the real will to obey the dictates of the state".[40]

Infallible Institution

The state is an infallible institution. It can do wrong. No plea of morality can frustrate or denounce its purpose. There is no standard of international law or external morality that might bind the jurisdiction of state activity. Hegel thus

---

37. J.O'Malley, "Introduction" to *Critique of Hegel's Philosophy of Right by Karl Marx*, p. xlviii.

38. *Ibid.*, xlviii.

39. Hegel, *Philosophy of History*, p. 39.

40. Wayper, *Political Thought*, p. 168.

repudiates the case of internationalism. There can be no ground, in theory or practice, for resisting state's decrees in the internal or external spheres. Its decrees are inspired by the real wills of those who obey him, even though they obey unwillingly. Rejecting the idea of super-national authority, Hegel writes: "The nation-state is mind in its substantive rationality and is therefore the absolute power on earth. It follows that every state is sovereign and autonomous against its neighbours ... There is no Praetor to judge between states; at least there may be an arbitrator, mediator, and even he exercises his functions contingently, *i.e.*, only in dependence on the particular wills of the disputants. It follows if the states disagree and their particular wills cannot be harmonised, the matter can only be settled by war."[41]

Admiration of War

Hegel admires war and denounces the idea of world peace. In an emergency the state may do as it pleases. As to what constitutes an emergency the state is to judge for itself. In theory at all times but in practice during war, the state may lawfully exercise complete authority over the lives of its citizens. The state of war reveals a nation's distinctive qualities and judges the glory and worth of a people. Hegal writes : "War has the higher significance that by its agency, the ethical health of peoples is preserved in their indifference to the stabilisation of finite institution; just as the blowing of winds preserves the sea from the foulness which would be the product of a prolonged, let alone, perpetual peace .. Sacrifice on behalf of the individuality of the state is the substantial tie between the state and all its members and so is a universal duty...."[42] Hegel believes that a state may, of course, sign treaties with another state, but because there "is no authority above the states and because the relations between them are governed not by universality but by contingency, these relations are continually shifting, and treatises, even if they purport to be binding in perpetuity, become in fact obsolete when the conditions which produced them change."[43]

Paradoxes in State Absolutism

Three somewhat paradoxical conclusions "follow from this doctrine of the absolutism of the state.

1. The state can never act unrepresentatively. Thus, the policeman who arrests the burglar and the magistrate who locks him up, are really expressing burglar's real will to be arrested and locked up, the policeman and the magistrate being the executive officials of a state which necessarily represents and expresses the real will of the burglar who is a member of it.

2. Importance of Relations. The relations which bind the individual to every other individual in the community, and also to the state as a whole, themselves form an integral part of the individual's persoanlity. He would not be what he is without them and he only is what he is because of them.

41. Hegel, *Philosophy of Right*, paras, 333-34.

42. *Ibid.*, paras 325-28.

43. Stace, *The Philosophy of Hegel*, p. 437.

3. The state contains within itself and represents the social morality of all its citizens. "Just as the personalities of all the individuals in the state are transcended and merged in the personality of the state, so the moral relations which each citizen has to each other citizen are merged in or transcended by the social morality which is vested in the state."[44]

Divinity of Nation-State

Hegel believes in the divinity of the nation-state. The state is glorified to the extent that it becomes a mystic entity. The state is a self-certain, absolute mind which acknowledges no abstract rules of good or bad, shameful or mean, crafty or deceptive. An idealise version of the *Republic* of Plato and that of *Social Contract* of Rousseau reappears when Hegel says : "In considering freedom, the starting point must not be individuality, the single self-consciousness, but only the essence of self-consciousness; for whether man knows it or not, this essence is extremely realised as a self-subsistent power in which single individuals are only moments. The march of God in the world, that is what the state is."[45] Again he says : "The state is the Divine Idea as it exists on Earth."[46]

Prussia an Ideal Nation-State

One peculiar aspect of Hegel's theory of state lies in the fact that he identifies his ideal state with the imperfect state of Prussia. Like Machiavelli, Hegel exalts his Prussian state simply to stand well with its rulers. His love for the motherland, his exile from the town of Jena, and his enthusiasm for the French Revolution all combined together to inculcate in him the conviction that only militant success would restore the prestige and self-respect of his nation. He says : "The German nation, under the influence of Christianity were the first to attain the consciousness that man, as man, is free; that it is the freedom of Spirit which constitutes the essence. The Eastern nations knew only that *one* is free, the Greek and Roman world only that *some* are free; while we know that all men absolutely (man as man) are free."[47] Keeping it in view, Dr. Lancaster says : "His views on state absolutism, moreover, reflected German experience — an experience through which he had himself lived — as well as the constitutional history of Germany on which he had a realistic grasp. In that history there had been no revolution to throw into relief the kinds of ideas of individual rights that had been important in both French and English history. In the Germanies there had been cultural nationalism, but this had not been accompanied by the sort of political unity long existent in Britain and France. Such a unity had to be imposed by force upon dozens of provincial populations and rulers."[48]

Thus, Hegel attempts to justify the absolute character of state authority.

44. Joad, *Modern Political Theory*, pp. 13-14.

45. Hegel, *op. cit.*, p. 36.

46. *Ibid.*, p. 279.

47. Hegel, *Philosophy of History*, paras 18-19.

48. *Op. cit.*, p. 46.

The state is not like an association of ordinary human beings; it is a Divine Idea or a mystic entity incapable of doing any wrong. It is infallible, supreme and omnipotent. It is entitled to secure every sacrifice which its interest may require of the individual. It is an end in itself, while the individual is the means who can be sacrificed at its altar. Every account of the nature of state is inadequate until it postulates that the individual "can utilise his potentialities as a man only by participating in the life of a great whole. And this greater whole is for Hegel, as it was for Plato and Aristotle, political society or the state."[49]

CRITICISM OF HEGEL'S THEORY OF STATE

1. Too philosophical, abstract and metaphysical. Hegel in very abstract terms attributes to the state a personality of its own distinct from that of the nation. He teaches us about its omnipotence, absolutism and divine character. The jargon of philosophcal language sacrifices the independence and autonomy of the individual at its all-embracing power. It denies to him the inalienable right of resistance but even the right to question the legitimacy or moral rightfulness of the authority or conduct of the state. The rationalism on the basis of which Hegel constructs the entire theory of state is beyond the understanding of a common man. Hegel does not deal with the things as they are and the state of which he conceives, resting on the free consent and cooperation of the moral will of every citizen, "may be laid up in heaven, but it is not established on earth."[50]

2. Repudiation of internationlism. Hegel's idealisation of war and his denunciation of world peace as well as his rejection of international law and world morality all are false and pernicious. Both Kant and Green advocated the cause of internationalism. But, Hegel has been worshipped as a prophet by the war-mongers. Hence, all peace-loving philosophers and statesmen have despised Hegel's philosophy.[51] Prof. Copleston treats it as 'an unpleasant feature of Hegel's political theory, and admires both Kant and Green for their support to the cause of federation of mankind.[52] A great internationalist Laski very rightly says : "The notion of an independent sovereign state is on the international side fatal to the well being of humanity. The way in which a state should live its life in relation to other states is clearly not a matter in which the state is entitled to be the sole judge. The common life of states is a matter for common agreement between states."[53]

3. Father of modern totalitarian ideologies. The idea of Hegel is a thorough-going defence of state absolutism much more sinister than that of Hobbes and Austin. The political theory of Hegel is distinctly inimical to individual freedom. Whenever a conflict occurs between the individual and the

49. F.C. Copleston, "Hegel" in Maurice Cranston (ed.), *Western Political Philosopher*, p. 66.

50. Barker, *op. cit.*, p. 91.

51. *Op. cit.*, p. 6.

52. Copleston, *op. cit.*, p. 97.

53. Laski, *A Grammar of Politics*, pp. 55-56.

state, the state must inevitably be right. Joad says: "The state exists for the individual; individuals do not exist for the state. Liberty has meaning only for the individual who compose the state. In other words, the state and the community are not ends in themselves."[54] Hobhouse calls it 'a false and wicked doctrine of the god-state'. He continues : "When we are taught to think of the world which we know as a good world, to think of its injustices, wrongs and miseries as necessary elements in a perfect ideal, then if we accept these arguments, our power of revolt is atrophied, our reasoning is hypnotised, our efforts to improve life and remedy wrong fade away into a passive acquiescence in things as they are; or still worse, into a slavish adulation of the Absolute in whose hands we are mere pawns."[55]

4. Identification of ideal state with the imperfect state of Prussia. Hegel idealises the data of his imperfect nation-state and preaches the divine right of the state. He presents a hopeless admixture of idealism and realism. It appears that the entire endeavour was made for the sake of glorifying the non-ideal state of Prussia. According to Lancaster, "When Hegel concerns himself with the concrete realities of politics, he abandons in effect his task as the philosopher of the universal and endows Prussia with the attributes logically belonging to the state abstractly considered."[56]

To conclude, the Hegelian theory of state is too abstract and philosophical a theoretical standpoint. From a practical angle of vision, it is a thorough-going defence of absolutism, elitism and authoritarianism. Ivor Brown says that, Hegel's doctrine means "spiritual servitude, bodily conscription, wars for national interests, and the devotion of human beings to Leviathan in peace and Moloch in war."[57]

CONCEPT OF GOVERNMENT

Hegel treats constitution as the complex of habits and responses produced by the generations living together under the same social and political institutions. The growth of civil society into statehood is marked by the increasing recognition that what the laws of the state command is rational. Public spirit and patriotism consist in the citizen's active consciousness that his needs are common needs, and in his indentification of the state as the supreme guarantor of those needs.

Sovereignty

According to Hegel, sovereignty belongs to the state as a whole. It does not reside in any one element. A sovereign is the monarch and the monarchical principle is present and active in every state. Sovereignty must be assigned scientifically to the monarch and not to the vague and indeterminate will of the people. As McGovern points out : "In short, Hegel's ideal form of government is a political pyramid with power centered at the top and gradually sinking

54. Joad, *op. cit.*, p. 18.
55. Hobhouse, *op. cit.*, p. 19.
56. Lancaster, *op. cit.*, p. 45.
57. Brown, *English Political Theory*, p. 145.

downwards, rather than rising from the bottom to the top. Or, to put the matter in other words, Hegel, like Carlyle, craved a social and political hierarchy, the many being guided and controlled by the few, and the few in turn being subordinated to one — the supreme head of the state."[58]

Constitution of the State

In his discussion of the constitution of the state, Hegel recognises three organs of government — legislative, executive and the crown. Hegel does not believe in the separation of powers, for each organ is not self-subsistent or hostile to the other. The whole is more real than the part, *i.e.*, one organ cannot be entrusted with all the powers. Hegel does not believe that one organ of government can have an independent character of its own. His dialectical interpretation curiously treats the legislature as the thesis, executive as the antithesis, and the crown representing the synthesis of the two.

The Weak Legislature

Hegel says that the authority of legislature is vested in the Estates Assemblies. But the legislature should consist of only those persons who have profound comprehension and insight. The legislature should be bicameral — one house composed of the land-owners and the other of the representatives chosen by professional and cultural associations. Hegel does not assign to the legislature the right of acting as a powerful check upon the executive. The legislature can neither appoint nor dismiss the executive, which is the sole concern of the monarch. The legislature is to act as an advisory body to the bureaucracy. About legislation, the legislature is to confine itself to proposing general rules to be given legal effect by the sovereign and detailed application by the body of civil servants. The executive function of the legislature is to serve as teachers to the people so that healthy public opinion is formulated and expressed. Thus, Hegel does not want to place legislature on a strong pedestal. The government should be conducted by the decrees of executive with a minimum of oversight by the legislature.

The Strong Executive

The executive occupies a very strong position in Hegel's theory of government. It consists of the permanent civil servants chosen for their demonstrated ability and serving in good behaviour. It represents the general will and reason of society. There may exist unions, corporations or other units of local administration, but the bureaucracy has the right to direct, control and superintend their activity. The civil service is not responsible to the legislature. Its organisation lies within the jurisdiction of monarch's authority. The highest civil servants have a deeper and more comprehensive insight into the nature of state's organisation and requirements. They are also more habituated to the business of government and have greater skill in it. They are able to do what is best even without the legislature. The laws should be proposed by the higher

58. McGovern : *From Luther to Hitler*, p. 321.

civil servants and the legislature should perform the functions of presenting such urgent needs of society as might have escaped their notice and calling their attention to public criticism likely to be directed to their administration of affairs. The law should take the form of general prescriptions, the detailed application of which should be made by the civil servants on their own responsibility subject to royal intervention in cases of abuse of authority.

Absolute Authority of the Monarch

The crown represents the synthesis of the legislature being the thesis and the executive being its anti-thesis. He becomes the sovereign holding absolute authority in his hands. The king makes the government coherent. Without him the people are like a formless mass and no longer a state. During emergencies the personal will of the ruler is decisive, while under ordinary circumstances government is to be carried out by the ministers and the bureaucracy. The king being sovereign stands at the apex. His authority is unlimited during the days of national emergency. Hegel says : "The sovereign is entrusted with the salvation of the state at the sacrifice of these particular authorities whose powers are valid at other times, and it is then that the ideality comes into its proper actuality."[59]

Critical Evaluation

Hegel's theory of government does not put the judiciary in a separate position. Like other French writers, he also builds his theory on the premises of duality theory according to which political organisation has only two organs — the legislature and the executive, judiciary being an adjunct of the latter. His theory stands for the justification of bourgeois aristocracy. He seeks to create a substitute for a part of the aristocratic governing class, a class recruited by birth and disposed to look upon office as private property. The whole system resembles neither the parliamentary nor the presidential models. It is a philosophical defence of the bourgeois civil service. Thus, Lancaster observes that Hegel "is pleading for a neutral civil service lifted above the sordid struggles of civil society and given dignity and moral authority by its responsibility to a monarch mystically conceived as the personification of the national culture and the national spirit. It was in many ways a noble conception, if in the end powerless in the face of the harsh relalities of bureaucratic power."[60]

CONTRIBUTION TO MODERN POLITICAL THOUGHT

Criticism of Hegel

In the history of political thought Hegel has been both denounced and lauded. A noted German philosopher and a contemporary of Hegel, Schopenhauer, says : "Hegel installed from above, by the powers that be, as the Certified Great Philosopher, was a flat-headed, insipid, nauseating, illiterate

59. Lancaster, *op. cit.*, p. 65.

60. *Ibid.*

charlatan who reached the pinnacles of audacity in scribbling together and dishing up the craziest mystifying nonsense. This nonsense has been noisily proclaimed as immortal wisdom by mercenary followers and readily accepted as such by all fools, who thus joined into a perfect chorus of denunciation as had never been heard before. The extensive field of spiritual influence with which Hegel was furnished by those in power has enabled him to achieve the intellectual corruption of a whole generation."[61] Caird remarks: "But the height of audacity in serving up pure nonsense, in stringing to other senseless and extravagant mazes of words, such as had previously been known only in mad houses, was finally reached in Hegel, and because the instrument of the most barefaced general mystification that has ever taken place, with a result which will appear fabulous to posterity, and will remain as a monument to German stupidity."[62] Prof. Popper concludes with a note of warning : "The Hegelian farce has done enough harm. We must stop it. We must speak — even at the price of soiling ourselves by touching this scandalous thing which, unfortunately without success, was so clearly exposed a hundred years ago."[63]

Admiration of Hegel

Hegel's admirers ranked him among one of the greatest philosophers of the world. His dialectical method sought to bridge up the gulf between reason, fact and value. It showed the way for Karl Marx. Several well-known thinkers like Marx, Schopenhauer, Nietzsche, Trietschke, Bernhardi, Droysen, Green, Bradley, Bosanquet and Savigny drew inspiration from Hegel in varying degrees. Out of the translation of his works in other languages, developed Hegelianism and Neo-Hegelianism. Augusto Vera, Benedotto Croce and Gentili popularised Hegelianism in Italy by emphasising the glorification of the nation-state. In America the influence of Hegel appeared on Morris, Palmer, Royce and John Dewey.

To quote John Dewey, "For a period Hegelian thought was almost supreme in Germany. Then its rule passed away almost as rapidly as it had been achieved. After various shiftings, the trend of philosophic thought was definitely 'Back to Kant'. Kant's greater sobriety, the sharp distinction he drew between the realm of phenomena and science and the ideal world, commended him after the unbridled pretensions of Hegelian absolutism. For more than a generation Hegel was spoken of with almost universal contempt. Nevertheless, his ideas loosed from the technical apparatus with which he surrounded them, persisted upon the historical disciplines. His influence was peculiarly deep and abiding. He fixed the pieces of Fichte and fastened them together with the pin of evolution. Since his days histories of philosophy or religion or institutions have all been treated as developments through necessary stages of an inner implicit idea or purpose according to an indwelling law. And an idea of a peculiar mission and destiny of German history has lost nothing in the operation.

---

61. *Ibid.*

62. Caird, *Hegel*, p. 18.

63. Popper, *op. cit.*, p. 273.

Exasperation which a bewildered world has sought since the beginning of the war to explain through the influence of a Darwinian struggle for existence and survival of the fittest, or through the influence of a Nietzschean philosophy of power, have their roots in the classic idealistic philosophy culminating in Hegel."[64]

Hegel's ideas served as an official philosophy. Bismarck carried out what Hegel and his students expressed and demanded. Till the days of Hitler, Hegel's political philosophy lived like a gospel truth in Germany. Hegel did great service to political thought by laying stress upon the significance of nation-state. By idealising the nature and character of political authority, he continued the tradition of Plato, Aristotle and Rousseau. Sabine admirably comments : "The philosophy of Hegel aimed at nothing less than a complete and systematic reconstruction of modern thought."[65]

Hegelian conception of state found adherents in other German writers and militarists like Nietzsche, Trietschke and Bernhardi who preached the nobility and indispensability of warfare, rejected internationalism and apotheosised the nation-state of Germany. Among them the name of Trietschke is more important who pronounced Hegel as 'the first real political personality among the German political philosophers' and idolised the Machiavellian dictum that the state is power. Other disciples laid stress on the self-assertive, aggressive and militant character of the state. These idealists even enjoined upon a strong and civilised state to impose its ideology upon the weak and backward states. Hence, the intellectual guilt of the first great war is attributed to the teachings of Hegel's disciples. J.W. Garner rightly says : "It is only fair to Hegel, however, to state that his philosophy was far less brutal and materialistic than that of Trietschke and that many of the latter's conclusions can hardly be said to have had anything in common with the Hegelian philosophy."[66]

QUESTIONS FOR EXERCISE

1. "The freedom of nature, the capacity of freedom is not actual freedom. For nothing short of state is the actualisation" — Hegel. Elucidate.
2. Barker says that in place of Kantian conception of freedom which he criticized as negative, limited and subjective, Hegel sketched a more positive and objective conception of freedom and a less individualistic conception of the state. Explain.
3. Describe Hegel's conception of freedom and show how it is more positive and objective than Kantian conception. Do you find anything objectionable about Hegelian conception of freedom.

---

64. Dewey, *op. cit.*, pp. 136-137.
65. G.H. Sabine, *History of Political Theory*, Ch. 31.
66. Garner, *Political Science and Government*, p. 234.

4. "Hegel in opposition to Kant sketched a more positive and objective conception of freedom and a less individualistic conception of the state" — Barker. Elucidate the above and describe the Hegelian conception of freedom and that of state. Also explain how the Hegelian conception of freedom is more positive and objective than Kantian conception.
5. "Nothing short of state is actualisation of Freedom" — Hegel. Explain.
6. "Hegel's philosophy is the very negation of democracy." How?
7. "The family as the immediate substantially of mind is specifically characterized by love which is mind's feeling of its own unity" — Hegel. Comment.
8. Examine the contribution of Hegel to Political thought. "Both Fascists and Marxists have built their political philosophy upon Hegelianism though curiously as a counterpart of one another." Explain and discuss.
9. "Hegel is father of totalitarian idealogies." Examine and discuss this statement carefully.
10. "State is the march of God on Earth." Examine Hegel's concept of state, individual and liberty.

7

Thomas Hill Green (1836—1882)

To any serious onlooker the assessment of the Victorian Age should appear a difficult task because the glow of its surface tends to conceal its undercurrent of troubles. On May 1, 1851, the worried Europe woke up to see the startling industrial progress of England as exhibited in the Crystal Palace Exhibition. The grimaces of the 'hungry forties' were gone on April 10, 1848, the Chartist Movement was skilfully quietened and the waves of the contemporary European revolt failed to reach the English shore with the result that amid the flurry of continental chaos the banner of England stood high fluttering the message of hope and promise.

The Crystal Palace Exhibition of 1851 was a glass-case witness to England's claim as the 'workship of the world". By that time the Iron Age in England was rapidly approaching its zenith and, thanks to the effort of George Stephenson of Tyneside, the Railway Age had brought its thrill of motion. In short, in England social and economic life was changing under the impact of scientific progress. One cannot deny the nest of material prosperity England secured since the "fifties to the credit of scientific and industrial advancement." But it is in this admission of fact that one may sense the real trouble of the Victorian era. Amid the cheer of material progress it was overlooked that the social belief had been darkened by a mood of doubt and scepticism.

In the first half of the 19th century the so-called discord between philosophy and religion, knowledge and faith had not grown poignant. In fact, in the early Victorian age popular excitement centred round the controversies between the side-issues of religion and not between philosophy and religion. The Oxford Movement which originated from an unmeaning ecclessiastical scare silently brought a religious revival. In the thirties and forties Tractarian brochures flooded England to cause a widespread storm of protest, and ultimately with the secession of Newman and his associates it had to breathe its last. But that this movement unknowingly pushed on a religious interest can be guessed from the picture of the time immediately following this movement. The Victorians were then regular both in private prayer and public worship. This lead in this line was given by the Royal family. Attendance in the church twice a day was not an uncommon feature of the family life. A concept of Christian fraternity was widely talked on even among the working classes. It was a sincere desire to heal the spiritual crisis of his age that inspired Thomas Hill Green to start his pen. The real need of the time was a new kind of philosophy which could avoid evangelical fads as well as materialistic scepticism and emphasize the essential greatness of men in the context of a religious temperament. The spirit of the age was waiting for a man who could come and say that philosophy on its part is seen to be the effort towards self-recognition of that spiritual life of the world, which fulfils itself in many ways but most completely in the Christian religion, and to be thus related to religion as the flower to the leaf."[1]

The philosophy which was roughly sketched by Coleridge and which occasionally lulled the imagination of J.S. Mill needed a man who would give it a comprehensive shape by his consistent thought. When in the Victorian England the spiritual view of life sadly sank down amid the torrents of material prosperity, Green a young student at Oxford, thundered : "In no depth of their debasement have men consented to confine the range of the mind within the limits of the fleshly tabernacle, which is the seat of its imprisonment."[2]

HERITAGE IN GREEN'S POLITICAL THOUGHT

1. Greek Heritage. Green was the founder of Neo-Hegelianism. He was very much influenced by Jowett Bentham who made him study Greek political philosophy. All English thinkers and politicians have been influenced by Greek political thinkers and Green was no exception to it. According to Barker, "Among the sources of his philosophy we must give the first place to the study of Greek classics...Generations of students have learned from Plato and Aristotle the lessons that man by the law of his being is a member of his political community; that the true state is a partnership in a life of virtue; that law is the expression of pure and passionless reason; that righteousness consists for each man in the fulfilment of his appointed function in the life and action of the community. The lessons have not been forgotten...."

2. German Heritage. German Idealists influenced Green in his concepts of political philosophy. From here he got the idea of philosophical theory of the state. To quote Barker again, "Another and more immediate influence is that of German philosophy. Green drew his inspiration from Kant and Hegel as well as from Plato and Aristotle. And in fact the philosophical theory of the state, of which Green and Bosanquet are the chief representatives, is a commentary and exposition, as expansion and modification, of the political philosophy first expounded in Germany at the end of eighteenth century and beginning of nineteenth century." Among German idealists it was from Kant that Green borrowed the idea that man could best realise himself in the state. He tried to be Kantian rather than Hegelian. He attempted to reconcile German Idealism with British Liberalism. He derived from Hegel the idea that the world was nothing but a single eternal activity. According to Gettell, "It should be noted, however, that Green never accepted the authoritarian elements of German

1. Green, T.H., *Works*, Vol. 3, p. 121.
2. Green, T.H., "College Essay on Loyalty", extracted from Nettleship's *Memoir*, p. 20.

Idealism. He stressed instead the social nature of man and the value of collective responsibility and well being through democratically controlled agents of Government. He viewed political theory as moral theory writ large and upheld the state as the indispensable champion of individual rights rather than as their enemy." Green followed Hegel in his metaphysical concepts. He accepted Kantian views in ethical and political fields.

3. British Heritage. Green was also influenced by the writings of Burke and Coleridge which represented reaction against Benthamite School of Thought.

BIOGRAPHY AND WRITINGS

Thomas Hill Green was born in Yorkshire on April 17, 1836. His father was a rector in Yorkshire where he lived for first fourteen years of his life. He studied at Rugby and Balliol College, Oxford. His whole life was spent at Oxford first as a tutor at Balliol College, later as a professor of moral philosophy. Green took an active interest in the affairs of the town. He was elected for Oxford Town Council and remained there for several years. In 1875, Green became the President of the Oxford Band of Hope Temperance Union. He died of Septicaemia in 1882 at an early age of fortysix but his ideas exercised great influence on modest idealist thinkers.

Among his most important works mention may be made of the following:

1. *Lectures on the Principle of Political Obligation.* These lectures were delivered by him in 1879-80 and published in 1882 after his death.

2. *Liberal Legislation and Freedom of Contract.* This lecture was delivered in 1880.

3. *Lectures on English Revolution.*

LIBERAL IDEALISM

"The singular contribution of T.H. Green to Political philosophy and to the development of the liberalism" says Gettel, "is to be found in his doctrine of positive freedom. What he conceived was a means of combining social responsibility with democratic freedom. And this in essence has become the present meaning of liberalism." The most solid statement of liberalism that Green ever made was in a lecture delivered in 1880 entitled, *'Liberal Legislation and Freedom of Contract'.* Green believed that human consciousness postulates freedom as the necessary condition of growth and development. In this connection it should be remembered that rights which constitute, the content of liberty postulated by human consciousness, demand the state for their satisfaction. "Human consciousness postulates liberty; liberty involves rights, rights demand the state." Green argued that the one thing in the world which had absolute value was the good will. The aim of human life was moral activity. The duty of the state is to remove all those obstacles or hindrances which come on his way and which obstruct the development of his personality.

During Green's day Herbert Spencer, the greatest champion of individualism, had carried the doctrine of state to the absurdities of logical limits. Spencer argued that the state should not undertake such activities as poor relief, public education or postal system. Green's answer to his kind of negativism was to assert the integral relationship of individual to the society. Following Rousseau and Kant, he held that individual personality could be realised only through the state and not apart from it. Against the conception of negative freedom Green set up a positive definition which defined : "As a positive power of capacity of doing or enjoying something worth doing or enjoying." "Freedom must therefore imply not merely a legal but an actual possibility, in view of existing circumstances of developing human capacities a genuinely increased power on the part of an individual to share in the good which a society has produced and enlarged ability to contribute to the common good."

Green maintains that if a person is incapable of using his faculties properly, then absence of restraint will not help him very much. Nobody stops him from doing what he would want to do, but if he is not equipped and trained to do something worthwhile this negative liberty of lack of external restraint is meaningless to him. The individual must be trained and equipped to do something that is good and worthwhile.

According to Green, "An individual can be said to be free only when he is in that state in which he shall have realised his ideal of himself, shall be at one with the law which he recognises as that which he ought to obey, shall have become all that he has in him to be and so fulfil the law of his being."

Green and Kant

Kant maintained that no man should be treated by others (or by himself) as merely a means but only as an end. In other words, every individual is an end in himself, and he should not be treated as a means to the interest of someone else. Green maintained that all this is very good, but how can we assure that men are not used merely as means for the interests of someone else? Green suggested that all the poor citizens should be fully educated and trained so that they may not be exploited, and freedom of contract may not be misused. It is the duty of society to equip each of its members with the training that would enable them to serve some useful function, to contribute something to common good.

Change in Liberal Ideas

According to Green human freedom consists in a positive power or capacity of doing or enjoying something worth doing or enjoying. Here Green introduced a change in liberal idea. The early liberals were concerned with removing restrictions and burdens on liberty of the individual by hereditary or non-democratic rulers. Green noticed that the individuals who were freed from the restraints imposed upon them by arbitrary Government were unable to make a constructive use of their freedom. They could be made to enter into unequal contracts or they led empty lives. People without proper education and training can make little positive contribution to social life. It is the duty of the society to provide education, whereas it is the duty of a citizen to use his talents for the betterment of society. Green also recognised the necessity for the Government to legislate for removing injustices and hindrances in the way of the highest development of its citizen so that he may enjoy positive freedom. In the words of Barker, "He begins from always clings to and finally ends in the Kantian doctrine of the free will in virtue of which man always wills himself as an end." Kant believed that freedom lies in obeying the inner conscience which can be achieved without the state but Green is of the opinion that freedom can only be attained within the state. Freedom is made possible by the state. The individual can achieve his freedom and moral development through the state. Green said, "Function of Government is to maintain conditions of life in which morality shall be possible and morality consists of self-imposed duties. Kant's freedom is limited and negative and remains in inner conscience but Green's freedom is positive and is possible in society by doing useful acts worth doing."

Differences with Hegel

Green also differs with Hegel in his conception of freedom. Both agree that freedom can only be possible within the state and believe in positive freedom. Hegel is of the opinion that the real freedom lies in obeying the state but Green believed that the individual enjoys freedom as a member of the state. Though each and every order of the state cannot be considered as synonymous to individual freedom, there is a difference between freedom and obedience of the state. Laws of an ideal state can be helpful to individual freedom but in actual states this cannot be true. Hegel failed to realize the difference between ideal and actual state. For the slaves of Athens, it cannot be said that every order of obedience to the state helped them in the realization of freedom. Green believed that the individual can feel freedom only following such laws which he considers helpful in the realisation of freedom. He cannot be said freely following autocratic or tyrannical laws against his will. In exceptional conditions he can oppose the immoral or tyrannical laws. Thus, Green believed in positive freedom in doing something or enjoying not only for self-satisfaction but for the welfare of the society. According to Green, "A man is free, when....he shall have realised the ideal of himself." Thus, Green has individualistic outlook and moderate idealism.

CONCEPT OF FREEDOM

According to Green freedom is a great blessing. The true end of citizenship could only be achieved on attaining freedom. It was necessary for self-realisation of citizens. According to Phyllis Doyle freedom could best be achieved in the state where the individual "shall be at one with the law which he recognises as that which he ought to obey : shall have come and that he has it in him to be, and so fulfil the law of his being." Barker says, "The state is a product of his consciousness. Human consciousness postulates liberty, liberty involves rights and rights demand state."

1. Freedom and State. From freedom Geen understood an environment in which one was permitted to make his own choice. He agreed with Hegel and

Kant that the state was conducive for freedom. He did not agree that without state freedom was not possible. Barker has expressed his ideas by saying that Liberty is, therefore, no negative absence of restraint, any more than beauty is the absence of ugliness. It is a positive power of doing something, not a freedom to do something of definite character, something which possesses the quality of being worth doing and not any and everything. In a free society its members are given freedom to contribute in the social good and have the capacity of doing or enjoying something in common with others. Green agreed with Kant that the state should perform the function of removing hindrances from the path of development of individual's personality. The state must not do anything which created obstacles in the path of individual's development.

2. Nature of Freedom. Green did not agree that freedom was in doing what one liked. That did not take into consideration the nature and object in which self-satisfaction is sought such as to prevent that self-satisfaction being found interfering with the realisation of the seeker's possibilities of this progress towards perfection, it is another thing when it contributes towards the end. Every one is free for having self-satisfaction but real freedom is possible only when that self-satisfaction was permissible under the rules. The social evil doers could get self-satisfaction but they are not free because their actions are not approved by the society. Green believed that everyone is free only to the extent to which he is in a position to control the impulses which drag him away from true self. A person becomes heteronomous as soon as he loses his self control. He would agree with Hegel that freedom found its highest expression in the state only. Gettell has remarked. "The singular contribution of T.H. Green to political philosophy and to the development of liberalism is to be found in his doctrine of positive freedom."

Sabine has also summed up Green's views on freedom in these words, "Freedom must, therefore, imply not merely but an actual possibility in view of existing circumstances, of developing human capacities, a genuinely increased owner on the part of an individual in the good which a society has produced, an enlarged ability to contribute to the common good. Freedom of contract may be a means to this end but it is not an end in itself." Barker says, "The one thing of the value is the goodwill....Liberty can only be liberty for this goodwill, it can only be liberty for the pursuit of the objects which such a will present to itself."

THEORY OF RIGHTS

1. Elements of Rights : (i) *Right to Freedom of Action.* This means to realise one's own capabilities. This right is collective and not isolated. It encourages others to contribute and participate in community welfare.

(ii) *Freedom of Individual Useless Without Society.* Without freedom of society the freedom of individual is of no use and in no way does it contribute to the individual freedom. To quote Green himself, "In analysing the nature of any right, we may conveniently look at it on two sides and consider it as on the one hand a claim of the individual, arising out of his rational nature, to the free exercise of some faculty, one the other, as a concession of claim in force...It is only a man's consciousness of having an object in common with others, a well being which is consciously his in being theirs and theirs in being his...There can be no reciprocal claim on the part of a man and animal each to exercise his powers unimpeded by the other, because there is no consciousness common to them. But a claim founded on such a common consciousness is already a claim conceded; already a claim to which reality is given by social recognition and thus implicitly a right."

2. Recognition of Right. Green believed that liberty involves rights. That right was a type of liberty of action. Rights were only personal and essential for self-perfection. Rights could only be claimed when these have been recognised by the society and also have social approval. All these were social rights and could only be preferred by society. There were no rights outside the society. According to Green, "The capacity on the part of an individual of conceiving a good as the same for himself and others, and of being determined to action by the conception, is the foundation of rights; and rights are conditions of that capacity being realised."

3. Natural Rights. Green believed that since rights were the product of society, they were not isolated. Hence, the theory of Natural Rights had no meaning in his philosophy. The people could not claim rights in the state of nature. Mill rejected the idea of social contract theory. He did not discard the phrase 'Natural Rights'. He reinterpreted that and gave that a different meaning. The Natural Rights were those which were to be possessed by all. These were necessary for their moral and rational development. According to Barker, "The ideal or natural rights, are broader or deeper than actual or legal rights, which are, at any given moment in any given state, the expression, necessarily partial and incomplete of the conception of natural rights attained by the state." Rights were recognised by the society to enable people to participate in the welfare of the community. To think of right against society is something inconceivable. Coker said, "Natural Rights are rights which should be enjoyed by a normally rational and moral man living in a rationally constitued society." Thus, naturai rights were the symbol of a perfect society. They had no pre-social standing.

Social recognition was actually recognition by moral consciousness of the society as a whole and not legal recognition. Natural rights had a direct bearing on morality rather than law because natural rights were necessary only for the moral development of mankind. Barker has said, "We cannot see that the rights of which Green speaks are relative to morality rather than law; and the recognition of which he speaks is recognition by common moral consciousness rather than by a legislature. The rights are relative to morality, in the sense that they are conditions of the attainment of moral end." Natural rights represent the morality and perfection of the state. Thus, every state should try to incorporate and embody natural rights. To quote Barker again, "On the one hand the rights of which Green speaks are so far related to law that they can be and are ultimately embodied in law; and they are so far related to morality that their value lies in their service to the moral end; and their source is to be found in the moral consciousness of the man. On the other hand, they are distinct from law, because actual rights embodied in the actual laws of a community never quite square with an ideal system; and they are distinct from morality; because they are enforceable...by external sanctions and morality is not, cannot be thus enforced."

THEORY OF PRIVATE PROPERTY

According to Green, if the people were to enjoy freedom of life it is essential that they must also have necessary conditions for its development. Property is essential for the free development of such a personality. According to Barker, "Property is a condition necessary for the free play of a capacity which can be exercised for the common benefit, it is the means for realising a will, which in possibility is a will directed to social good," Green did not hold extreme views about the retention of abolition of private property. He followed a middle course. He defended property in the form of capital but attacked landed property. Whereas capital provided wages for labourers and remained in circulation for the use of even the common man, landed property had no such utility. Green, however, believed that inequality of property might be regarded as the necessary price for free action. He admitted that if the institution of private property stood against the collective welfare of the society such an institution should be condemned in all respects. According to Barker, "Thus, any kind of property which realizes the will of one man at the expense of stopping the realization of the will of many, is instantly condemned."

Another problem which Green had to face was whether private property is wholly or partly responsible for the exploitation of the society and in creating proletariat class. Green held that only landed property is responsible for creating this class distinction. To quote Barker again, "It is thus to the system of landed property that Green seems inclined to assign the creation of a proletariat, neither holding nor acquiring property."

Criticism of the Theory

Green's conception of private property has been criticised on the following grounds :

1. Property not for Social Welfare. Green did not agree that property-owners should use private property for common social welfare. All that he pleaded was that it should be used for social good. In his 'Lectures' he himself says: "Whether anyone's will is actually and positively so directed, does not affect his claim to power. This power should be secured to the individual irrespective of the use which he actually makes of it, so long as he does not use it in a way that interferes with the exercise of like power by another, on the ground that its uncontrolled exercise is the condition of attainment by man of that free morality which is his highest good."

2. Inequality of Property. Green tried to defend inequality of property when he argued that different people have different wills and they should be allowed to develop their wills. This inequality has created class struggle and many other allied problems. It is a social evil.

3. Distinction in Capital and Property. On the one hand Green believed that private property is essential for the development of individuals and on the other hand he said that the society should not allow concentration of property. Green failed to reconcile this self-contradictory idea. Green's distinction between the capital and property is unique in character and it is difficult to follow and practise that in day-to-day life.

4. Self-Contradiction. Green's theory about private property is self-contradictory. On the one hand, he believed that every individual should be given full rights to have private property and concentration of wealth but on the other hand he believed that there should be no concentration as that was denial of social development.

5. Right to Wealth not Landed Property. Green believed that there should be freedom to hold private property in the form of wealth, but not in the form of landed property. This obviously is not understandable.

Summing up the discussion on Green's ideas about property, Barker says, "He would have the community assert the control it has hitherto failed to exert over the exercise of the rights of private property in land and he would urge that such control must be strict, since the thing controlled is so absolutely unique. On the other hand, he objects to the appropriation of unearned increment, by the state, on the ground that it could scarcely be attempted without grave detriment to individual initiative, which might otherwise be directed to the improvement of land and thereby to the service of society."

THEORY OF WAR

Green was not Hegelian in his ideas about war. He did not agree with Hegel that war is not only a necessity but always right. He believed that war is rather a cruel necessity. It is wrong action though often wars were waged to justify the rectifications of wrong actions of others. War is not the symbol of a perfect state but an indication of its imperfection. Perfection of states would lead to end of wars. The less the wars, the more were the chances of freer intercourse with other people and consequently more shall be the common interests and a common society. A common society is a step towards common international court.

No Justification for War

Green believed that since war denied free life, it could not be justified. Morally war is a wrong action. Green did not agree with those who said that right to free life is never denied to anybody but only to those who joined the ranks of army by themselves. He, on the other hand, believed that right to free life was a pious right and the people have no right whatsoever to surrender it even by themselves.

So-called Advantages of War

Green agreed that war has certain advantages namely that it develops spirit of heroism, patriotism and self-sacrifice. He, however, confessed that wars make people brutal and violate all human rights established in peace days. War was no solution for solving national or international problems. He did not believe that war is essential for the preservation of national integrity. In healthy nationalism there is no place of war.

War is an Evil

In every state the foremost right of individual is to demand right to life. War denied this right to the citizens. It was, therefore, wrong to think that war was in the interest of the people. A state which recognises or wages war can never be called a perfect state. War is an evil and should be treated so. In Green's words, "No state of war can make the destruction of man's life by man other than a wrong, although one wrong is not always chargeable upon all the parties to a war. There might be circumstances when war could be justified, but it must be accepted that war was a wrong act. Green did not agree with Hegel that war is in any way a necessity. No person has a right to kill any body or deprive him of his right to life. It was wrong to argue that killing of the people in the war is in any way justified. Wars could be eradicated. Wars are continuing on account of failure of the states in the performance of their duties properly. It is possible for the states to eradicate wars. In Green's words, "The more complete the organisation becomes, the more the motives and occasions of international conflicts tend to disappear, while the bonds of unity become stronger."

Criticism of Green's Theory

Green's theory of war has been criticised on following grounds :

1. Patriotism. Green's theory will kill a sense of patriotism among the people. The wars promote patriotism.

2. Wrong Diagnosis of War. It is wrong to believe that wars are the outcome of imperfection of state. There have been different causes for fighting wars and these have been differing from one age to the other.

3. Utopian Ideal. Green's pleading that wars should be eradicated from the society is utopian. There has been no society as yet which has not witnessed war. War is part of human society.

INDIVIDUAL AND SOCIETY

Green maintained that the individual obeyed the state because he realised that state acted for common good and for the welfare of all and also that will, not force, is the basis of state. Habitual obedience is rendered because of the will of the people. Green did not agree that any one could claim any rights against the society because society itself gave rights. Rights were given to the individuals for the welfare of the society. As such these were not above or beyond that society but within the society itself. Even though it was felt that laws were against the wishes of the people, none should try to violate them because it is just possible that those laws might be for common good. None should disobey the laws but everyone should try to get the laws constitutionally amended. No individual should try to disturb the existing order because such an attempt could result in social anarchy. Green said, "The common good must suffer more from resistance to a law or to the ordinance of a legal authority, than from the individual conformity to a particular law or ordinance that is bad, until its repeal can be repeated. It is thus the social duty of the individual to conform, and he can have no right that is against social duty."

Green believed that the individual has a right to arouse public opinion against unjust laws and in fact that is rather his duty. If the individual did not act in accordance with the wishes of the society he ought to be treated as an outlaw. It was the elementary duty of the state to see that it developed the instincts of the individual for social betterment.

STATE AND ASSOCIATIONS

1. Independence of Associations. Green discussed the relation of state with other associations like the family, church or trade union. According to him these associations have their existence in the state but are not the product of state activity. All these associations have their independent existence. They are essential for the individual as they were equally responsible for the development of their members.

2. Supremacy of State. Green was not a pluralist. He believed in the supremacy of state to the extent that a member enjoyed his rights not as a member of any association but because he was member of state. The state alone gives rights to the groups within it. Green, however, argued that the supremacy of state has certain limitations. The state should see that the associations are sustained. As soon as the state fails to perform this duty it is bound to lose its character and it practically ceases to exist.

3. Difference from Hegel. In his ideas about the state Green is closer to Aristotle than Plato. He is more Hegelian than Kantian. Like Hegel he wanted to give supremacy to the state. He differed from Hegel when he said that the state shall cease to exist if it did not preserve associations. In Hegel's philosophy societies get merged and absorbed in the state. In Green's philosophy these associations are esential for the very existence of state. Barker Says, "Because it (state) is the source of these adjustments, it must be the ultimate power. If it were not so, and if it were itself adjusted, it would not be such a source. But such finality, or if we like such sovereignty, must not be construed as irresponsibility. The state must not be concluded in vacuum or as an almighty Leviathan dwelling in solitude. It stands in relation to other states, and must adjust itself to those relations in the light of conception of a 'Universal brotherhood'. Here we touch one of the most distinctive of Green's conceptions, a conception which formed the theoretical justification of an attitude towards war that was already instinctive in his mind.

Political Philosophy

"Green", says Barker, "addressed himself to eliciting and explaining the presuppositions implicit in the contemporary life of the English state."[3] His credit lies in the fact that by his political philosophy, he gave a logical interpretation to the events of his time. In the earlier period utilitarians came with their well-knit theory, hammered hard and ultimately succeeded in injecting a spirit of individualism in the artery of administration. Individualistic attitude of the state developed in the wake of an organized philosophy. The collectivistic approach of the state developed, more under the influence of the necessity of facts, which needed a philosophy to rest on. Green's task was tc provide this philosophy of the collectivist state. As Laski says : "What the philosophy of the collectivist did was to provide the basis for understanding the necessity of the change. They prepared men to receive it...They established the canon of their age."[4]

COLLECTIVISM

Green's *Principles of Political Obligation* is an illustrative appendix of his *Prolegomena to Ethics*. His political philosophy was influenced less by this theoretician's concern for a coherence between his different shades of thought and more by his humanitarian outlook. His genuine distress at the sight of the poor, contributed largely to the development of his collectivism. He was a collectivist because he was a humanitarian and a true Christian who discovered moral responsibility of the state in arresting the danger of social calamity. As Bryce has pointed out, "He had the warmest interest in, and the strongest sympathy for, the humbler classes. No man had a truer love for social equality, or a higher sense of the dignity of simple human nature."[5] Because of this Christian love for the oppressed humanity he fe!t no contradiction in being both a collectivist and a liberal. He emphasized state-intervention but accepted the basic need of individual's right of free development.

Oxford Idealism

Green entered Oxford in 1855. His writing profusely contributed to the prestige of Oxford because with him, began its philosophical tradition. At a time when railways were changing the face of Britain, the only railroad permitted in Oxford was the ingenious contrivance in New College for circulating the port round the fireplace in the Senior Common Room."[6] In 1858, Green lamented : "I am almost ashamed to belong to a University which is in such a state of darkness."[7]

Oxford was ruffled by the Oxford Movement which actually placed an

3. Barker, Ernest, *Political Thought in England*, p. 22.
4. Laski, H.J., *The Leaders of Collectivist Thought, Ideas and Beliefs of the Victorians*, p. 420.
5. Bryce, James, *Contemporary Review*, May 1882.
6. Lindsay, D. and Washington, E.S., *A Portrait of Britain*, Chap. 9.
7. Nettleship, R.L., *Memoir*, p. 23.

insurmountable hurdle against the growth of philosophic thought. Drowned, as it was, in theological dogmas the Tractarian Movement cared little to comprehend the mind of the age. The aptitude for contemplation which is the real source of philosophy was cowed down amid the excitement of ecclesiastical controversy. So naturally philosophy could not have its nourishment. The Oxford Movement ultimately died down but it left back its leaven in the quadrangles of Oxford. The mood of theological discussion of the previous period was transformed into an ecclesiastical party spirit : theological debate was substituted by a crude form of platform intrigue and manoeuvre. The university came under the terrorism of an ecclesiastical Ring. So there was little of mental freedom necessary for contemplation. Memory-work being the most reliable means for winning these distinctions, they naturally felt no urge for a philosophical training. The young tutors, too, upon whom mainly rested the responsibility of teaching philosophy, were more interested in seeing their students come off with flying colours and so took pains to teach them methodical tactics out of their own experience. The burdensome syllabus of *Litterae Humaniores*, of which philosophical study was an appendage, put so heavy premium upon students' industry that they could really find no adequate time for a proper grasp of philosophical knowledge.

Benjamin Jowett appeared to usher in a new wave in Oxford. He translated three volumes of Plato in which his introduction and appendices contained more of philosophy than of mere commentary. It set in a true climate of philosophy in Oxford. But it was T.H. Green who came forward to complete the half-done task of his master. By his *Prolegomena to Ethics and Principles of Political Obligation*, he built up a positive philosophy which marked the beginning of a forceful philosophical movement ever remembered by posterity as the Oxford Idealism.

PHILOSOPHY OF STATE

Green was the firstman in the nineteenth century to construct a comprehensive philosophy of state. "He went straight," as David Ritchie relates, "from the declaration of the polls, when he was elected a town councillor, to lecture on *The Critique of Pure Reason*."[8] Green used his metaphysics as a necessary contrivance to come up to the field of political theory. He was both a philosopher and a practical reformer, both an idealist in philosophy and a liberal in politics.

1. State a Means to an End. Green's philosophy of the state was built up on a very sound and reasonable footing. In spite of his belief that the state was the embodiment of the Divine Spirit, he never considered the state an end in itself. It was a means to an end. That end was the full moral development of the individuals who compose it. Green's ethics made him to believe passionately with Kant that every man has a worth and dignity which forbids his exploitation for any purpose whatever. "The life of the nation," he insisted, "has no real existence except as the life of the individual composing it." "To speak of any

8. Ritchie, D.G., *The Principles of State Interference*, Chap. II, Section 1.

progress or improvement or development of a nation or society or mankind except as relative to some greater worth of persons," he wrote, "is to use words without meaning." In his context he regarded the functions of the state as being negative. According to him, the state cannot teach morality to men, nor can it make men moral, since morality consists in "the disinterested performance of self-imposed duties." State is to remove obstacles which prevent men from becoming moral. In order to remove obstacles the state must interfere to such an extent that what appears negative in form must soon appear most positive in content. "To any Athenian slave, who might be used to gratify a master's lust," Green wrote, "it would have been a mockery to speak of the state as a realization of freedom; and perhaps it would not be much less to speak of its as such to an untaught and underfed denizen of a London yard with gin-shops, on the right hand and on the left." It was for the state to see that the mental and physical malnutrition, together with the gin-shops, were removed. "To uphold the sanctity of contract," Green said, "is doubtless a prime business of government, but it is no less its business to provide against contracts being made which from the helplessness of one of the parties to them, instead of being a security for freedom, become an instrument of disguised oppression." Green's indignation at the moral degradation was of society expressed through his words : "We content ourselves with enacting that no man shall be used by other men as a means against his will, but we leave it to be pretty much a matter of chance whether or not he shall be qualified to fulfil any social function to contribute anything to the common good, and to do so freely." He would gladly have echoed Carlyle's statement "that no one should die ignorant who has the capacity of knowledge, that I call a tragedy, though it should happen, as by some computations it does, a thousand times a minute." If the state was to intervene to prevent that tragedy, its intervention was likely to be steady, constant, and far-reaching.

2. Negative Role of the State. The negative role which Green assigns to the state is nevertheless significant. He defines and limits state actions more than they could ever be defined and limited by the utilitarians. The State can do everything which will help. But it must do nothing which will hinder the free development of moral personality. The real function of government is to maintain the conditions of life in which morality shall be possible. The paternal government "does its best to make it impossible by narrowing the room for the self-imposition of duties and for the play of disinterested motives." Green, insisted that institutions exist for men, and not men for institutions.

Green did not idealize the state as Plato, Hegel and the subsequent English Idealists, Bradley and Bosanquet, did. On the contrary, Green tried to establish the importance of individual men and women. The state, according to him is not something more than the sum of the wills of its citizens.

3. The Will — the Real Basis of State. Green believed in the existence of the General Will. General Will is the real basis of the state. Legal sovereignty must reside in the supreme authority within the state. Behind this legal sovereign is the General Will, which really determines the habitual obedience of a people.

Men habitually obey only those institutions which represent the General Will. General Will means the will for the state, not the will of the state.

4. Against Monistic State. Green was fully conscious that there were states in which force was predominant. He had no liking for such states as they could not fulfil their ideal function. He rejected Rousseau's view that the General Will was entirely in abeyance in all existing states. He also rejected Hegel's view that the laws in all existing states were synonymous with the General Will. Unlike Hegel, Green tried to safeguard the individual against the monistic state. While for Hegel, Freedom is the voluntary identification of self with the laws of the state, according to Green, Freedom is the right of a man to make the best of himself. This is voluntary identification of self with the laws of the state.

5. Dream of an International Society. Green was also willing to admit the possibility of the state's supersession by other higher forms of society. "It is easy", he wrote "to conceive a better system than that of the great States of modern Europe with their national jealousies, rival armies, and hostile Tariffs." While acknowledging how far mankind is from realizing "the dream of an international court with authority resting on the consent of individual states," he believe, "that there is nothing in the intrinsic nature of a system of independent States incompatible with it, but that on the contrary every advance in the organization of mankind in states in the sense explained is a step towards it."

Green believed that good government may not always be popular government, and the dictatorship also may act according to the General Will. Thus, the seeds of authoritarianism are to be detected in Green's writings. But Green also loudly proclaimed that the best government can only be self-government. For the passive voluntary identification of self with an authoritarian state which Hegel demands, Green substituted an active participation in a democratic state which his individualism requires. Green, to quote Wayper, "the individualist, who judges State, Society, General Will by their worth for the development of individual morality and individual character, who so notably and so nobly dedicated himself, to social and political service in the city of Oxford, would not have been true to himself and he done less — and would certianly have made much less of an appeal than he did to Englishmen."[9]

6. Qualified Organic Theory of State. According to MacCunn, "If it be individualism to see in every political movement the fate of human beings and in every controversy over institutions the weal or woe of fellow citizens, then there are few more declared individualists in political philosophy than T.H. Green,"[10] Green refused to accept the Mechanistic theory of the state. Will, not force, is the true basis of the state. Green accepted the organic theory of the state only with many qualifications. He regarded the state as natural since man is necessarily a social animal. Freedom is not the absence of restraint but a

9. Wayper, C.L., *Political Thought*, Chap. III.

10. MacCunn, J., *Six Radical Thinkers*.

process of self-development by freely obeying laws and customs which a rational scheme of justice within the community. The state is essentially good, because it is indispensable to guide and enable men to understand their own moral obligations and to call upon the best in them. Green taught men to see that faith in their own moral development and faith in their fellow-men matters far more to them than any particular interest, they may have. In his distinction between outward acts and inward will, between what is better done even from the wrong motive and what is only valuable because of its motive, Green gave men a far sounder criterion whereby to judge state-action than did Mill with his doctrine of self-and-other-regarding actions. In doing so, Green gave the individual a far more effective protection against the undue exercise of the state's power than anything with which utilitarianism could provide him. Correcting and supplementing both utilitarianism and idealism, Green gave men a commonsense criterion which they could apply to states. Every state can be judged by its practical and ideal contents here and now. It is a good state if it contains the largest possible number of happy, moral human beings.

7. Individualism Tempered with Idealism. Green respected and admired Mill; but in the *Introduction to Hume* and in the *Prolegomena to Ethics,* as well as in the lectures on Mill's logic, his dissent from Mill's philosophy was made manifest. He pointed out the inadequacy of Mill's conception of cause. In the *Introduction to Hume* he made a somewhat contemptuous reference to the "juggle, which the modern popular logic performs with the word 'phenomenon';"[11] and from the ethical theory of utilitarianism his dissent was absolute and unqualified. He generously recognized the practical value of utilitarianism. This is the theory, he said, which has given the conscientious citizen in modern Europe "a vantage-ground for judging of the competing claims on his obedience, and enabled him to substitute a critical and intelligent for a blind and unquestioning conformity;"[12] and he pronounced that "there is no doubt that the theory of an ideal good, consisting in the greatest happiness and of the greatest number, as the end by reference to which the claim of all laws and powers and rules of action on our obedience is to be tested, has tended to improve human conduct and character."[13] But nevertheless Green rejected the idea of pleasure being the one true and moral action, and instead placed the *summum bonum* for man in "some perfection of human life, some realization of human capacities."[14]

POLITICAL OBLIGATION

The chief doctrine of Green's ethics was the mutuality of relationship between the individual and the society. He thought of the Government as the product of consent and not of force. Green was realistic enough to recognize

11. *Hume's Works,* i, 202.

12. *Prolegomena,* 361.

13. *Ibid.,* 363.

14. *Ibid.,* p. 390.

that as far as it is known to us most governments have originated by conquest of force rather than by the voluntary compact of their members. It is sovereignty that distinguished the state from all other associations. Sovereignty means that the state can compel its citizens to obey its laws and commands. The citizens render habitual obedience to them even when compliance with them appears irksome. In the absence of such habitual obedience the state and its sovereignty would cease to exist. The question arises "Why do people render this obedience to the laws enacted by the government? How is one to explain the phenomenon of political obligation? Various answers have been given to this most fundamental question in political science. Some are of the opinion that what keeps the mass of people into the path of habitual obedience to the authority of the government is their fear of punishment, the fear of police and law courts. According to them the state is based on and sustained by force. This view is not tenable. Force is only an element in the being of the state but not its sole basis; it may explain the fact of obedience in some case (and not in all) but not the duty of obedience. The relationship between the state and its members is more internal or organic than what mere force can account for. It is, therefore, wrong to find in the fear of punishment, the reason why people obey the laws of the state and respect its authority. Green says "The State...does not create rights but gives full reality to rights already existing."

The true explanation of political obligation of the habitual and willing obedience people render to their government was given by Green when he said that the state is based not on force but on will. According to Green, "Will is the basis of State. This means that the sovereign authority of the state is ultimately to be found in the common consciousness of a common end without which society is impossible. People agree to respect the authority of the state and its government because they realise that the state and government represent and embody the general will of all the members of the society. In obeying it they do not obey an alien master but their true or rational self. They obey it because there is the rational conviction that it makes the system of rights possible. It creates these conditions of well being which enable every citizen to realize his true rational self. They feel that it pursued a common good which includes their own welfare. This does not mean that every time an individual obeys the state law, he consciously reminds himself of the fact that the state represents the general will which includes his own. It means that when we reflect on the problem of political obligation, we find ourselves driven to postulate this elementary conception of a common good maintained by the state. It rises into clear consciousness only in reflective and thinking minds.

Resistance to Authority

Resistance to authority of the state is not justified except under special circumstances. Anyone who defies the laws of the Government interferes with that system of rights and liberty which is an essential condition to individual and social well being; and thereby with individual self-realisation. So long as the state remains true to its conception and represents the general will, resistance to its authority cannot be justified. But governments sometimes fail to embody the geneal will. They make laws in the interest of a section of the society only. They sometimes fail to recognize those rights which are essential for the development of the moral capacities of some individuals. Under such circumstances disobedience of its laws and resistance to its authority may be justified. But even in such cases disobedience is permissible only if it is resorted for the sake of the good of the society. It is never right to disobey the laws of the state merely for personal welfare. Before actually refusing to respect the authority of the government and rising into rebellion against it; all constitutional means of redressing grievances must be sought and tried. It is only when they have been tried and found wanting that rebellion becomes justifiable. In this connection it should be borne in mind that rebellion against the state means social chaos. It seriously disturbs the social order which is the condition precedent to every kind of progress. The whole should not be sacrificed for the part unless it has become absolutely imperative. Law, a man ought to obey, should be law of being or living according to nature.

In short the state is a manifestation of general will. According to Barker, State has a final moral value and is majestical. It is a moral being animated by a moral purpose. Force is not the basis of the state. Masses obey the state because it represents the general will. The state cannot remain constant and permanent without the consent of governed. Even despots and dictators have to bow before the general will. No state can permanently endure on the basis of force. To quote Baker if, "Society is so organized that every one's capability have free scope for their development, there is no need to resort to war displaying patriotism."

Evaluation

According to Wayper, Green gave Englishmen something more satisfying than Benthamism. His doctrine is positive in the sense that the ultimate purpose of the state is always positive. This is the liberation of human capacity for self determination towards a common good. We are all becoming socialists in the sense of accepting the state as the supreme and positive good, and in believing that its mission should be the promotion of common welfare in all aspects — social, economic and intellectual. The idealistic position can be defended on the ground that though the state can build social, political and economic institutions which would promote common good, provided they are used in the proper spirit by the citizens, it cannot secure that they shall be thus used by the people. The end of the individual is the fullest development of his personality. This no one can achieve for him, it must be his own concern. Good life is of such a personal character that the state cannot directly promote it. It can help a person to promote it himself. Though the idealistic view of the nature of the state activity rests on a sound basis it did not fully accord with the needs of modern state and falls short to the needs of socialistic pattern of society. According to Barker, "Green clings to the doctrine of free moral will. He is most liberal among idealists."

THEORY OF PUNISHMENT

Aim of Punishment

Green believed that the greatest restriction on state authority has been on the claim of the state to punish the individuals. The state should punish all those who violate established social rights of the citizens. Green, however, posed the question as to what the state should aim at while punishing the individuals and whether the punishment should be retributive, preventive or reformatory. According to Green the state should use force against anti-social elements and activities. It cannot use force in proportion to moral guilty of any individual because that is difficult to assess. The state also should not punish the individuals with a view to improving their morality as moral improvement is something internal. The external use of force cannot improve the moral actions of the people, which are solely and purely due to internal nature. Therefore, Green believed that the aim of punishment is neither retributive nor reformative but only preventive *i.e.*, deterrent. The state should aim at creating such conditions and environments in which anti-social elements, more particularly habitual law violators hesitated from committing the offence. It should create an atmosphere in which anti-social elements did not feel encouraged to hinder the moral development of law abiding citizens or restricting them from doing something which is worth doing or enjoying. The punishment is thus for the purpose of removing obstacles from the path of good citizens.

State's Right of Punishment

According to Green the right of the state to punish citizens is conditional. As such it is obligatory on the part of state to maintain an atmosphere for free life of the subjects. If the state is to be held responsible for the life of the citizens it must be given the right to punish those who hindered this free life. Thus, state's right of punishment is necessary if the system of rights and duties is to be established on sound footing in a society.

Moral Purpose of Punishment

According to Prof. Barker, "Punishment, like all state actions has a moral purpose and a moral quality. It is moral in the sense that its ultimate aim is to secure freedom of action for the moral will of every member of the community..." He further says that "Indeed punishment cannot in any full sense attain its proper purpose, which is the reassertion of the validity of rights, unless it produces some consciousness of that validity in the offender; and that consciousness to be effective must be due not to the mere feeling that there is external force behind the rights, but to further feeling that there is some higher and more internal sanction."

Effects of Punishment

Thus, according to Green, the effects of punishment were both direct and indirect. Directly the punishment is a force against anti-social forces. Indirectly it is "a shock which make possible the criminal's reformation of his own will."

BASIS OF STATE'S FORMATION

Will Not Force is the Basis

Green agreed with the Greek philosophers that by nature and necessity every individual is a political animal and as such is bound to obey the state. In this regard Green is near Plato and Aristotle rather than Locke and Rousseau. He believed that the Government is not the result of force but a product of mutual willingness of mankind. Force had its own part to play but it was the only factor which united people for the emergence of Government. In Green's words, "Even the most powerful and most despotic Government cannot hold a society together by sheer force; to that extent there was a limited truth in the old belief that Governments are not produced by consent." "Government," Green said, "depends on will and not on force; because the tie that binds human being to society is the compulsion of his nature and not the penalties of laws or the calculation of ulterior advantages."

Criticism of Social Contract

Green did not agree with Social Contract philosophers namely Hobbes, Locke and Rousseau that men enjoyed some rights before they joined the society. This theory cannot adjust the rights of the citizens with the authority of the state. According to Green the citizens had no rights prior to the formation of society. Common consciousness gave birth to rights and institutions. Man began to possess rights as a member of a civil society recognising common rights of others. Green called this common consciousness as a General Will. This General Will creates a system under which all obey the laws and maintain conditions necessary for their proper enforcement and their social customs. According to Green, "To ask why I am to submit to the power of the state is to ask to allow my life to be regulated in that complex of institutions without which I literally should not have a life to call my own, nor should he ask for a justification for what I am called on to do...I must be able to reckon on a certain freedom of action and acquisition for the attainment of those ends, and this can only be secured through common recognition of his freedom on the part of each other by members of a society, as being for a common good." Thus, the state is not the product of any contract but mutual willingness of its members. Green agreed with Rousseau that will not force made man obey laws and regulated the conduct of men in society. In the words of Barker, "...He is content to analyse and elucidate the pre-suppositions implicit in the actual life of existing states: he is content to show that fundamental premises of democracy that will, not force, is the basis of state, always and must be present in every state." Thus, Green was in a position to solve the great problem of adjusting the rights of men in the state of nature with the authority of civil state.

Common Good and Common Consciousness

Green realised that in every society the majority of citizens did not understand real meaning of common good or common consciousness. Even ordinary educated people usually had no clear idea of it. All the citizens in a state usually realised it in a very rudimentary form. If this idea had not existed in the minds of citizens the concept of common good would have fallen and thus the only uniting factor of state would have vanished. Since this idea was present in the minds of citizens that was the reason as to why the state was existing. The state shall collapse as soon as the citizens shall forget this. It was the most cherished duty of the state to develop this idea because it is essential both for the existence of the state and the development of individuals. According to Maxey, "Green's influence was all the more greater in that, while acknowledging the correctness of Hegel's view of the community, he idealised the state without defying it and identifying it with absolute right."

Need of Soverignty

Green believed that there must be a superior authority which should regulate the laws when necessary. Whether that authority is in General Will of determinate human superior is altogether a different problem. Unless there is a sovereign authority to get the laws obeyed, these were no better than morality. According to Green, "The sovereign should be regarded, not in abstraction as the 'wilder of coercive force, but in connection with the whole complex of institutions of political society. It is as their sustainer and thus as the agent of the general will, that the sovereign power must be presented to the minds of the people if it is to command habitual loyal obedience; and obedience will scarcely be habitual unless it is loyal, and not force."

KANT, HEGEL AND GREEN

(i) *Freedom*. Kant was an individualist. To him morality consisted in the disinterested performance of self-imposed duties. For him freedom was a right to self-impose an imperative for duty. Hegel, however, gave a broader and more and more positive objective view of freedom. According to Hegel, freedom must be positive. Green agreed with Kant that freedom consisted not in the absence of restraint but in obeying the laws of our own moral beings. For him freedom was something positive.

(ii) *Nature of State*. For Kant state is individualistic whereas for Hegel it is perfect life. According to Hegel state is the march of God on earth. Green, however, assigned only a negative function to the state namely that of hindering hindrance.

(iii) *War*. Kant was opposed to war. He suggested the formation of League of Nations to adjudicate general European will. For Hegel war is an evil but it cannot be avoided. Green, however, was of the view that war is neither necessary nor always justified. For Green war is a symbol of imperfect state. State perfection could be achieved only with the elimination of wars.

(iv) *Representative Government*. For Kant Representative system of Government is not good. So also is the case with Hegel who preferred constitutional monarchy over democracy. Green, however, stood for adult franchise and representative form of Government.

Hegelianism in Green

Green agreed with Hegel in so far as the concept of Divine Spirit is concerned. He believed that the ultimate consciousness of reality is God and that every individual is constituent of that system. He also said that individual is the reproduction of that Divine. Each and every individual is good for his true self. If there is anything to the contrary, that is primarily because there is no favourable environment. If favourable conditions are provided that goodself will give expression in every walk of life.

Kantianism in Green

Green agreed with Kant that there is free moral will. If there are any restrictions on the free will these are only self-imposed. He agreed with Kant that the state is not a necessary will but necessary good. It is needed to remove such hindrances which are on the path of individual and which do not allow him to express what is best in him. State is unavoidable in so far as moral perfection is concerned and as such it is ethically good as well. Green agreed with Kant that the state is required to guarantee rights of the people. As such the state is unavoidable in this respect as well.

Agreement with Kant

(i) *State as Source of Rights.* Green agreed with Kant that the state is the source and giver of all rights. There might be rights which the people enjoyed when states had not come into existence, but these are now guaranteed by the state as such. State is now responsible for their maintenance and upholding.

(ii) *Absolute Power of the State.* Green agreed with Kant that the state should possess absolute power. State should be considered supreme society over all other societies.

(iii) *Responsibility of the State.* It is the responsibility of the state to ensure that only such laws are passed which are according to common consciousness. In case laws of the state do not promote common good, the subjects have a right to disown such laws. For Green collective interests are always more important than individual laws and social welfare is even above. The people have not right to disobey the state except for the collective welfare of the state and society.

(iv) *Natural Law and Natural Rights.* Both Kant and Green did not agree with social contract theory about the origin of the state. Both, however, agreed that there were certain natural rights which always existed in some forms or the other. For Green natural law is the law which people should obey as moral personality whether or not the particular state in which they live enforces it or not. They also believe in the concept of natural rights, which the state should grant to the individuals for their moral betterment.

Difference From Kant

In spite of the above mentioned points of similarity between Kant and Green they differ from each other in following respects:

(i) *Effect of Action.* Whereas Kant did not bother about the effects of actions, Green had much concern about that. He believed that in effect every action must be considered and should in no way be ignored. An action is good, if the effect is good and *vice versa* equally holds good.

(ii) *Nature of Ethics.* Kant believed that ethics is static, whereas for Green it is evolutionary. According to Green what is ethically true today may not be so tomorrow.

Thus, Green was closer to Kant than Hegel, though he did not follow either intentionally. He is an original thinker. During the course of his philosophy if he came near to Kant than Hegel, that is a matter of chance.

CONTRIBUTION OF T.H. GREEN

1. Versatility. Green was influenced by various political philosophers in his philosophy. His philosophy was an attempt at adjustment of these different influences. As a true English thinker he loved traditions and wanted to adjust his ideas accordingly. He wanted to justify reforms of revolutionaries in a sober and moderate way. That was perhaps the reasons as to why Kant was more appealing to him than Hegel. He was more a Kantian than Hegelian. His political philosophy was well balanced and advanced. Various thinkers belonging to different schools of thought have interpreted his philosophy according to their convenience. This reflects the versatility of Green's philosophy.

2. Adjustment of Existing Ideas. One of Green's major contributions was that he adjusted the existing ideas in a manner which suited Englishmen who are not radicals but traditonalists. To quote Barker, "He has seized the philosophy of Greece and of Germany, and interpreted it for the Englishmen with a full measure of English caution and with a full reference to that deep sense of the liberty of the subjects and that deep distrust of reason of state which marks all Englishmen."

3. Made Liberalism a Faith. Green made libealism a faith, which was the need of the hour. Bentham had failed to give due place to liberalism in England. English people wanted to adopt liberalism but not at a very high cost. They were not willing to sacrifice their established customs, conventions and traditions. This odd job was skilfully accomplished by Green. According to Wayper. "Here thus Green's achievement is that he gave Englishmen something more satisfying than Benthamism, at a price they were prepared to pay, that he left liberalism a faith instead of an interest, that he made individualism moral and social and idealism civilised and safe."

4. Individualism. Green weighted individual, society and state in terms of individualism. He idealised the state as being the association of associations but did not make it Leviathan. By preaching that there were no pre-social rights of individuals and that rights were products of society and not against society, Green solved a very ticklish problem of right *versus* state. Barker said, "But the individual nevertheless remains the basis of all his thought. Green is not trammelled by any idealisation of the majesty of the state, he is more of an Aristotlean than a Platonist, more of a Kantian than a Hegelian."

5. State Activities. Green skilfully combined the negative and postive functions of the state. In principle he assigned negative functions to the state but in his treatment of the subject he assigned the state positive functions. Whereas Mill distinguished 'self regarding' and 'other-regarding' actions as the basis for state intervention, Green gave actions a realistic basis in the distinction of internal and external actions. The state is responsible for external actions only. Thus, Green gave a more concrete and realistic basis for state intervention, a task which Mill could not complete.

6. Moral Duty of the State. Green preached that the state has a moral duty of developing the social instinct of men. The more the social instincts were developed the more shall be the development of state.

7. Synthesis of Ethics and Politics. Thus, Green tried to combine morality with politics. There is no denial that if moral aspect of the state is developed many of our problems can be solved and the burden of the state might be considerably reduced. Phillips Doyle says, "Green's influence was all the greater in that while acknowledging the correctness of Hegel's view of the inseparability of the individual and the community, he idealized the state without identifying it with the absolute rights."

8. Expediency. Maxey has praised Mill's liberalism by saying that : "It was peculiar service of T.H. Green to inject into turbid conflux of ideologies, a liberal political philosophy in which social expediency was a dormant principle, a philosophy into which the concept of social expediency was raised to an ideal by the insistence of its author that expediency be determined by the moral obligation of the state to create an environment favourable to the full realisation of what is best in every individual."

9. Liberalism. "Green's liberalism ceased to imply any single and inviolable line of legislative policy and implied it, rather a combination of different line of policy to safeguard a variety of social interests, all accepted as contribution to general welfare."

CRITICISM OF T.H. GREEN

1. Critics point out that Green's theory that institutions are the embodiment of reason is dangerous. It may easily lead to the view that whatever is, is right.

2. His theory of sovereignty is not satisfactory. Green is of the view that sovereignty is supreme when supported by general will. According to Hobhouse, "In so far as it is will, it is not general and in so far as it is general, it is not will."

3. Green's view that in great men the bad is 'overruled' for good is not accepted. It is a reminder of the truth of Fredric, the Great's assertion that however bad the might used to attain a thing might be, there will always be found some philosopher to whitewash them.

4. Green's views about property are contradictory. He demanded land reform but did not find any danger in concentration of capital.

5. Green's approach is too much rational. His conception that individual works due to pure consciousness is unreal. Modern psychologists have proved that emotions and instincts play a major part.

6. It is difficult to defend his theory of natural rights.

7. It is difficult to agree with Green that war is always wrong. In case of wanton attack a country has sometimes no alternative except to defend itself.

ESTIMATE OF T.H. GREEN

1. *Barker.* "Green is not a searching idealist but a sober realist." "Green is not trammelled by any idealization of the majesty of the state; he is more of an Aristotlean than a Platonist and more of Kantian than a Hegelian."

2. *Maxey.* "Green represents a reaction not only against 13th Century rationalism, but also against certain interpretation of 19th century science."

"It was peculiar service of T.H. Green to inject into this turbid conflux of idealogies a liberal political philosophy in which social expediency was a dominant principle, a philosophy in which social expediency was raised to an ideal by the insistence of its author that expediency determined by the moral obligation of the state is to create an environment favourable to the full realisation of what is best in individual."

3. *Dr. Wayper.* "Here, this is Green's achievement that he gave Englishmen something more satisfactory than Bentham, at a price they were prepared to pay, that he left liberalism a faith instead of an interest, that he made individualism moral and social and idealism civilized and safe."

4. *Philips Doyle.* "Green's influence was all the greater in that while acknowledging the correctness of Hegel's view of the inseparability of the individuals and the community, he idealised the state without defying it and identified it with absolute rights."

5. *Sabine.* "What Green added to liberal theory was the conception of collective well being as a pre-condition of individual freedom and responsibility, consequently sound social policy justifies the protection of common interest such as public health or education or a decent standard of living no less than the protection of individual rights, such as private property."

"Full moral participation in a social life was for Green the highest form of self development and to create the possibility of such a participation was the end of liberal society." In truth however, Green was no Hegelian.

6. *Barker.* "Green is more Kantian than Hegelian and more Aristotlean than Platonist.

QUESTIONS FOR EXERCISE

1. Analyse briefly the elements of Greek, German and British heritage in Green's political thought.
2. Write a brief introductory note on liberal idealism of which main exponent is T.H. Green.

3. Give a brief account of the main tenets of Green's political thought.
4. "Human consciousnes postulates liberty, liberty involves rights, rights demand state" — Green. In the light of the above statement, show how T.H. Green explains the necessity of naturalness of state.
5. "Freedom consists in positive power or capacity to do or enjoy something worth doing or enjoying" — Green. Discuss.
6. 'In spite of his Hegelianism, Green remained a radical and an individualist.' Discuss this statement.
7. "Green's concept of liberty or freedom is positive, not freedom from but freedom for ...." Discuss.
8. Give a brief account of Green's Theory of Rights.
9. How far do you consider Green's formulation of the scope of state activity adequate to the needs of modern state?
10. Write short note on Green's Theory of Private Property.
11. Discuss briefly but clearly Green's views on war.
12. War is the attribute of an imperfect state? How does Green arrive at this conclusion? Do you agree with this view?
13. Discuss Green's views about (a) Individual and Society, and (b) State and Association.
14. "Human consciousness postulates liberty; liberty involves rights; rights demand the state" — Green. Elucidate and examine.
15. "The function of the government is to maintain conditions in which morality shall be possible. " Comment.
16. "The State does not create rights, but gives fuller reality to the rights already existing" — Green.
17. "Will, not force, is the basis of the State" — Green. Explain.
18. "It is commonly asked whether punishment according to its proper nature is retributive or preventive or reformatory. The true answer is that it is and should be all the three" — Green. Discus the statement.
19. What is the basis of State's formation according to Green? "Will, not Force, is the basis of the state" — Green. Comment on the above statement.
20. 'Green's revision of liberalism might be described as a revival of old concept of consent law which Bentham's criticism had expelled from utilitarianism." Discuss.
21. "If it be individualism to see in every political movement the fate of human beings and in every controversy over institutions the weal or woe of fellow citizens then there are few more declared individualists in political philosophy than T.H. Green" — MacCunn. Elucidate and discuss.
22. "Green is more Kantian than Hegelian." Discuss how and why of this statement?

8

F.H. Bradley (1846—1924) and B. Bosanquet (1848—1923)

FRANCIS HERBERT BRADLEY (1846-1924)

Bradley was the son of Dean of Westminster. He was a fellow of Martin College of Oxford. Bradley was a supporter of Hegelian idea. He wrote a book *"Ethical Studies"* in which on chapter "My station and its duties" is most important.

My Station and Its Duties

Bradley borrowed a great deal from Plato and Aristotle and also from Hegel. He maintained that what we call an individual man, is, what he is, becuase of and by virtue of community and communities are not mere names but something real. At birth the child is what he is in virtue of communities, he has something of civilized character, something of natural character which comes from human society. As he grows, the community in which he lives imposes itself in his being, in the language he learns and the social atmosphere he breathes, so that the constitution of his being implies relations of community in its every fibre. He is what he is by the fulfilment of self which consists in the fulfilment of those relations. These relations constitute his position or status, therefore we may say that his morality consists in fulfilment of his station and its duties. As man's life in the main is filled by his station in that system of wholes and this is partly by its laws and institutions and still more by its spirits, it gives him the life which he does live and ought to live. To be moral is to live in accordance with the moral traditions of one's country.

State a System of Whole

"It includes all communities which have any bearing on man. It is a moral organism, a systematic whole, formed by a common purpose of function. State organism has life and continuity of its own." Bradley supported ideas of Hegel in a modest manner.

Every part of the state organism has a spirit and consciousness of its own. Individuals like their full lives only so far as they qualify their specific field. "The breadth of my life is not measured by the multitude of my pursuits, not the space I take up amongst other man but by the feeling of the whole life which I honour as mine."

Criticism

Critics point out that there is nothing original in Bradley's ideas as these have been borrowed from Greek thinkers. His idea of state as a living being is contrary to facts. He failed to make distinction between state and society and gave too much power to state. His phrase "my station and my duties" can be interpreted to mean that man should remain satisfied with his lot. Such a view is reactionary and detrimental to the growth of humanity. It suits ruling elite class only.

Evaluation

In spite of all criticism Bradley pointed out the importance of society in shaping the character of man. He put emphasis on duty which he described in following words:

"Your turn may be to obey or command
just a obedience is as great as command."

His view of obedience in all circumstances is difficult to be sustained.

BERNARD BOSANQUET (1848-1923)

Bosanquet was born in 1848, the son of a Northumberland clergyman. He was a brilliant student of Harrow and Oxford. Green and Jowett had a great influence on him. Early in life, he became fellow of the University College, Oxford. He held the chair of Moral Philosophy at the St. Andrews University of Scotland. Most of his time was spent in independent study.

Bosanquet's Works

1. *Philosophical Theory of the State* (1899)
2. *Social and International Ideals* (1917)
3. *Logic* (1888)
4. *History of Aesthetic*
5. *The Value and Destiny of the Individual* (1913)

Hobhouse described Bosanquet as the most modern and faithful exponent of Hegel, but it is safe to say that although Bosanquet began with Rousseau and Green, he ended almost with Hegel and supported extreme idealism.

Actual and Real Will

Bosanquet speaks about the free moral will of the individual. Here he is inspired by Rousseau. He distinguished between the actual and real will of the individual. He said, "Man's true individuality is realised only through an expression of his real will, and the latter is essentially identical with the general will, which is realised only through the state." The rational or constant will of man from moment to moment as conscious individual is called actual will. On the other hand, the real will of the individual, which does not stand alone is linked with real will of other members in the society and it becomes general will. General Will is in the interests of common life of members of society. "The General will is expressed only when those participating direct themselves to the question : What is for the advantage of the whole association? Instead of the question what is for the advantage of myself, my friends or my party? The General Will is expressed then, only in decisions taken in a special way, or by people acting in a special frame of mind." Thus, the state embodies the general will.

BOSANQUET AND GREEN

Similarities

1. Need of the State. Both of them admitted the necesity of the state for the realisation of the higher life of man. However, while Green was individualistic, Bosanquet was prepared to subordinate the individual to the state.

2. Nature of the State. There is not much difference between Green and Bosanquet regarding the nature of the state and proper sphere of state action. Both of them believed that state is an ethical institution but it could not be used directly for promoting morality. The function of the state is to hinder hindrances to liberty.

3. Right to Rebel. Green supported the right of resistance in exceptional circumstances as he thought that the individual represented the social mind more adequately than the representatives of the state did. Bosanquet did not allow the individual a right of resistance on the ground that the orderly process of the state as organizer or rights and guardian of moral values were so important that "right of rebellion" may be almost nil.

4. Punishment. Regarding punishment both of them believed in the deterrent nature of punishment, but the views of Bosanquet were more positive than that of Green. He put emphasis on psychological aspect of problem. In short, the object of punishment according to him is not merely deterrent but also reformatory.

Differences

1. War. Green condemned war because it violated the right of every man to free life. But Bosanquet favoured war being a public act and "the state as such, certainly cannot be guilty of personal immorality."

2. Duties of the State. According to Bosanquet the state had a will and personality of its own and also aimed at moral responsibility to its citizens. To quote him again he says, " State is the guardian of moral interests and must be faithful to its duty."

3. State Authorities. Neither Bosanquet nor Green were in favour of absolute monarchy, both believed in representative parliamentarian type of Government, but Bosanquet tended towards Hegelianism and to a great extent to state absolutism.

4. Life and Better Life. According to Bosanquet, it is difficult to remove conflicts between the claims of mere life and better life as there is no organisation of humanity having common consciousness. The League of Nations (now U.N.O) was merely the means to make international law more effective, as such loyalty to the best life of community is desirable.

CONTRIBUTION TO POLITICAL THOUGHT

Bosanquet's political philosophy is available in his famous work *'Philosophical Theory of the State'*. About it Barker said, "In the light of a fuller experience and of fresh date he would sweep away some of the limitations which Green had hedged about his doctrine of the state as the organ for the realisation of free wills, and he would thus bring Green's philosophy to a point where it approaches close to, if it does not altogether blend with, the full Hegelian conception of the state."

1. Functions of the State. Bosanquent started with the idea that human beings without the state were imperfect. They required a community of mind or community which was pervaded over by a common mind — for their proper development, and for the growth of their fuller life. Bosanquent agreed with Rousseau that man without society was just an animal, not realising his responsibilities. Man developed and acted only in the society. Without community he was stupid. He did not agree with Hobbes and Locke that men by nature were isolated and that their perfection was only in becoming members of social institutions. Bosanquet agreed with Green that state was natural to man. State was one of the most important social institutions. Man's rational will was only that under which he acted in accordance with the wishes of society.

(i) *Negative Functions*. Bosanquet agreed with Green that the state should perform the negative function of removing the hindrances and not the positive function of reforming. The state should not apply external force but only moral system. Barker has said, "His conception of the nature and limits of state action is, like that of Green, negative. The state as such has force as the instrument and external things as the area and hindrance of hindrances to the human capacity as the function of the action which it can undertake. This principle, drawn from Kant, and identical with that adopted by Green, rests ultimately on the idea of the supreme and final value of the autonomy of the good will."

(ii) *Positive Functions*. Bosanquet agreed with Green that *prima facie* the state was allowed to perform negative functions but in actual practice it performed positive functions. The state should maintain external conditions necessary for the development of free will but should not direct free will. Bosanquet followed Hegel when he said that the state is responsible for developing the morality of individuals and should rather be moral in actions. State power is a mystery and should be treated with respect.

2. Rational and Irrational Wills. Like Rousseau Bosanquet distinguished between the rational and irrational wills of the individuals. The rational will which represented general will also represented common good. The state is a regulating force and co-ordinating agency. According to Bosanquet, if the individual has means to ascertain as to whether he is representing will of society and that the state is acting against common wishes, he may disobey the state and thus resist it.

3. Rights. According to Bosanquet the rights were nothing but the conditions which the state had secured for mutual adjustment of individuals. Barker has said, "The conditions which the state secures are rights and rights are, therefore, regarded by Bosanquet, as they are by Green, as concerned with the external conditions, are necessary for the free action of good will."

4. Nature of State. Bosanquet also believed that state is a political as well as social institution and he distinguished between the two. State is a social corporation which embodied and incorporated all institutions, organisations and bodies. "We also see it as a group of groups, a community of communities, embracing and sustaining the whole field of social co-operation." The state is a source of adjustment as well as it is a driving wheel. It is also an invigorating force which reminded all the individuals about the performance of their duties and suggested them to remove lethargy. Green himself says that "The state, as such, is limited to the office of maintaining external conditions of a good life, but the conditions cannot be conceived without reference to the life for which they exist and it is true, therefore, to say that the conception of the nation state involves at least an outline of the life to which, as a power, it is instrumental."

5. State Has Life. According to Bosanquet every institution and for that purpose even the state has life and does not depend on other living minds connected with it. The more the living minds are connected with the state the more generating and living the state will be. "All the institutions of a country so far as they are effective are not only products of thought and creations of mind, they are thought, and they are mind." According to him state is an institution. Since state represents life it is the ethical idea also. It represents common mind of all citizens. It is the common or more frankly speaking universal mind of the members.

6. Theory of Punishment. Bosanquet was to some extent nearing Green in his ideas about punishment. Punishment should aim to some extent at morality but it should not assume a positive character. Barker has said: "Thus, punishment may mean, not that henceforth I cease to have slips because I fear to experience a like shock again, but that henceforth I cease to have slips because I have come to my sense; have had my consciousness of the meaning of whole system of habits awakened; and have realised, in the light of such consciousness what my offending means."

7. Morality and State. Bosanquet differed from Green in his conception of morality. Green condemned war as an immoral act because it deprived individuals of the freedom of action and movement. He believed that the state as such could not be immoral because it is the custodian of our morality and moral actions. It is not bound by rights and standards of ethics. But the state is ultimately responsible for the actions of her agents and should see that the agents of the state were moral and right. Barker has pointed out that "Another view of this matter, to which some of us would rather cling, would emphasise far more strongly the responsibility of the state for its agents, and the responsibility of both the state and its agents at the bar of the civilized opinion."

8. Forms of Government. Bosanquet did not consider absolute monarchy to be the best form of Government. For him a Government which represents the will of the people and has representative character is best and ideal. The government should be given maximum power and authority. State, of course, represents the will of the people, but the people have a right to rebel against state under certain circumstances. This is so limited a right that it is practically non-existent.

9. Universal State. According to Bosanquet, an institution presupposes some common purpose in common minds. One individual does not form an association. At the same time large numbers of people without common ideal also do not form an association. Association or institution is an organisation which consisted of persons having common mind. The idea of mankind is quite common to all but still it differs from community to community and state to state. There could be no internationalism because the humanity is divided. Bosanquet agreed with Aristotle that religion is a uniting sentiment and can be one of the factors leading to internationalism. In a divided world of today internationalism is impossible but it is just a formula of common understanding and might even make internationalism a possibility.

10. State and Society. Bosanquet believed that the state is above society. It is state which regulated society and gave it a coherence. He also did not distinguish between legal and natural rights. He stressed that the state is sovereign and embodiment of general will. For him nation-state is supreme and above everything else. He had so much praise for the state that he believed that it in itself was embodiment of morality. He was of the view that the state created rights but was not itself bound by those rights. In his philosophy there is accordingly no provision for disobeying the authority of the state. The subjects have no right to challenge the authority of the state as the state is in itself the custodian of all rights.

CRITICAL ESTIMATE

1. Greatest idealist. Bosanquet was one of the interesting figures of the English political philosophy. J.A. Leighton called him, "the greatest of the idealists". This, however, is an overestimation.

2. Underestimated individualism. Bosanquet followed Green in his philosophy but without his liberalism. He developed Hegelianism to its full. Bosanquet has been criticised for raising the state to high ideals and thus subordinating individual to state.

3. State above ethics. Bosanquet's idea that the state did not know private morality and that it is above all ethics has been much criticised. His belief that international morality was not possible at this stage was also not desirable. If the state is above morality how could the subjects be moral?

4. Irresponsible State. Bosanquet has made the state irresponsible with the help of his philosophy. This is unacceptable to modern civilised societies.

5. State and Society. Bosanquet has wrongly identified state with the society, which is against the concept of individuality. It is undemocratic and it encourages slavish tendencies.

In spite of the above criticism there is no denying that without Bosanquet Hegelianism would have been incomplete. He gave fullest expression to the philosophy of Hegel.

CRITICISM OF IDEALISM

The idealist school of thought showed its influence both in Germany and England. Many of the important political philosophers and institutions were influenced by the teachings of these thinkers. However, this school of thought suffered from many drawbacks for which it has come under severe criticism. Some of the significant criticisms of this school of thought are the following:

1. Nature and Character of the State. The Idealists believe that the state is a moral organism. It is not the sum total of individuals composing it nor the aggregate of the people. It has certain qualities in aggregate which the members composing it do not possess. Today there is a general belief that the state is not moral but only a political institution. It has political and not moral obligations to discharge. If the state is considered as a moral organisation then the whole concept of political organisation is bound to collapse.

2. Identity of State and Society. The Idealists identify state with society. This implies that there is no place for society in the state. Society merges in the state. These philosophers have tried to idealise the state. However, the institutions like family, marriage etc. have always played important role in every state. Some of the institutions like the family existed even prior to the state. Some of the societies have wider and broader scope than the state itself. Therefore, merging of societies in the state is something fatal. It has come under severest criticism by pluralists who believe that the state is an association of associations. They are not willing to assign even a superior position to the state over any other association.

3. Made State Absolute. The Idealists have laid undue stress on the actions and activities of state. They have raised it above all legal and moral obligations. The state is the source of all laws. It is the custodian of individual's morality. This has been exploited by the Nazis and persons like Hitler and Missolini who used it for their own selfish ends.

4. Not Realists. Idealists do not deal with the things as they are. They are not realists in life. As Barker has said : "The state of which it conceives, resting on the free consent and co-operation of the moral will of every citizen, may be laid up in heaven, but it is not established on earth."

5. No Specific Place to Force. The Idealists preach that the state is obeyed because it has certain useful functions to perform. However, the very basis of state obedience is not exclusively force but also utility. It has some important functions to perform which are in the collective interests of individuals. This view of the individualists is rather fatal. We obey state for utility as well as because of the fact that force is also its integral part. One cannot say whether the state has acted for or against the wishes of a particular individual. As Laski has said: "I am asked to obey it only in so far as it is in actual fact promoting those purposes. It cannot be known whether it is promoting them except by examination of its operation; and if after conscious examination of them, I decide that it is not, my duty is obvious."

6. Narrow Outlook. The Idealist theory of the state has been criticised for its narrow outlook. For them 'nation-state' is the highest expression of state. They started with the idea of state more or less prevalent in the city-states, thus for them the nation-state was the ultimate form of state expression. It has become so narrow that it is difficult to adjust in it wider forms of state, the federations, internationalism, world federation, empires and commonwealth etc. To think of nation-state as the highest form of expression is to deny evolution of state which is anti-natural.

7. Too Intellectual. Idealist theory is too intellectual. The theory makes man a product of his conscious and not sub-conscious mind. However, the sub-conscious is as aware and forceful as conscious and to ignore anyone is something which will make human understanding imperfect. Sub-conscious is the emotional side of man and leaving emotion will be to build castles on sand.

8. Neglect of Purpose. According to social reformers and thinkers like Hobson, idealism stands for 'the static conservatism'. The greatest of the idealists, Hegel was conservative in his views about war and family. The idealists defended the institutions rather than the purpose for which they exist.

QUESTIONS FOR EXERCISE

1. Write a short note on the importance of political ideals of Francis Herbert Bradley?
2. Comment on the thesis that Bradley's presentation of the state is more Hegelian than Green's.
3. Discuss the main tenets of the political philosophy of F.H. Bradley.
4. Explain and discuss the political thought of George Bernard Bosanquet?
5. "Bosanquet gave a Hegelian turn to English idealism." Explain and bring out this distinction between state and society.
6. Explain briefly the points of difference between the German Idealist and the Oxford new Idealists, especially those between Green and Bosanquet.
7. "In constructing his own theory of the state, Bosanquet starts by a vindication of Rousseau." Comment.
8. J.A. Leighton has described Bosanquet as the greatest of the 'English Idealists'. How far do you subscribe to this view?
9. "The state is conceived as the operative criticism of all institutions...a working conception of life." Discuss.
10. Examine the contributions of Bernard Bosanquet to political thought.

9

Positivism : Auguste Comte (1798—1857)

Positivism has been characterised as 'scientific' for the simple reason that it sought to interpret human life in terms of natural sciences. Its representative thinker, Herbert Spencer, adopted a biological point of view in his study of society and state and thus contributed to what is also known by the name of biological school. To a good number of thinkers in England as well as elsewhere, it appeared that all human problems might be solved by a scientific methodology. Naturally appeal to science represented a new orientation and a new tendency standing for the possibility of mustering natural sciences into the service of social theory. This type of study "became so widespread in the last century that political science, for a time, seemed in danger of being wallowed by the natural sciences."

The positive method rejects all *a-priori* arguments; it rejects all abstract ideas: it rejects all absolute standards. It is inductive, concrete and relative. The mark of the positive thinker is to apply the methods and, so far as may be, the results of natural science to the investigation of the higher problems presented by the individual and political life of man. It is to build his conclusions upon the accumulated experience of the past as modified by observation of the changing circumstances of the present.

AUGUSTE COMTE (1798—1857)

Isidore Auguste Marie Francois Xavier Comte was born in Montellier of southern France on January 1, 1798. He died in 1857 A.D. Heralding the birth of a new science called sociology, his magnum opus *Cours de Philosophie Positive* was written during the period 1830-1842. In the words of Raymond Aron, "Auguste Comte may be considered as, first and foremost, the sociologist of human and social unity."[1]

Auguste Comte organised and classified the social thought prevailing before his times. Comte gave birth not only to a specific methodology of studying knowledge but also analyzed the evolution of human thinking and its various stages. The principle evolved by Comte in the study of human thinking presumes

---

1. Aron, Raymond, *Main Currents in Sociological Thoughts,* Part Ist, Pelican Books, 1965, p. 53.

gradual evolution and development in human thinking and is knows as the law of three stages of thinking.

THE LAW OF THREE STAGES

"Each of our leading conceptions," Comte said in *Politique Positive*, "each branch of our knowledge, passes successively through three different theoretical conditions; the theological or fictitious; the metaphysical or abstract; and the scientific or positive."[2] It is known as the law of three stages because, according to it, human thought has undergone three separate stages in its evolution and development. The main importance of this principle is that it provides the basis of sociological thinking.

According to Auguste Comte, human thinking has passed through the following three stages. There has been an evolution in the human thinking so that each succeeding stage is superior to and more evolved than the preceding stage :

(1) Theological or Fictitious stage,

(2) Metaphysical or Abstract stage,

(3) Positive or Scientific Stage.

Auguste Comte has explained his classification of human thinking into various stages as follows:

1. Theological or Fictitious Stage. According to Comte in this stage, "All theoretical conceptions, whether general or special bear a supernatural impress." This type of thinking is found among the primitive races and sometimes the thinking of children is also at this level. At this level of thinking there is a marked lack of logical and orderly thinking. The primitive man and children do not have the scientific outlook. Therefore, theological thinking is characterized by non-scientific or unscientific outlook. The main subject matter of theological thinking is natural events. The usual and unintelligible events of Nature tend man towards theological or fictitious interpretation of the events. Unable to discover the natural causes of the various happenings, the primitive man attributes them to imaginary or divine forces. The explanation of natural events in non-natural, divine or imaginary conditions is known as theological or fictitious thinking. For example, if we explain and understand the excess or deficiency of rain due to godly wrath, such a causal explanation would be in terms of theological or fictitious explanation. The theological thinking implies belief in an other-world wherein reside the divine forces which control the events in this world. Thus, it is clear that theological thinking implies a belief in divine and extra-terrestrial forces. Comte has classified the theological stage further into three loud stages. These are :

(1) Fetishism, (2) Polytheism, and (3) Monotheism.

(1) *Fetishism*. The first and primary stage in theological thinking is that of fetishism. Fetishism is a belief that there is some living spirit in the non-

2. Auguste Comte, *Politique Positive* (Paris, Cres, 1912), Four volumes, IV; p. 9.

living objects. This is also known as animism. As the very term animism signifies it means that the so-called inanimate objects are not dead and lifeless but are informed by a living spirit. The examples of fetishistic thinking can be seen from the widespread belief among rural people in India that some deity resides in trees. They are, therefore, seen to engage in the worship of trees etc.

(2) *Polytheism.* With the gradual development in human thinking there occurred a change in the form of thinking. The more evolved and developed a form other than that of fetishism known as polytheism. At this stage man had classified gods as well as natural and human forces. Each natural or human force has a presiding deity. Each god had some definite function and his scope and area of action was determined.

(3) *Monotheism.* The last and most developed form of theological thinking is seen manifested in monotheism. As the very term monotheism implies, at this level of human thinking a belief in one God had replaced the earlier belief in many gods. The monotheistic thinking symbolizes the victory of human intellect and reason over non-intellectual and irrational thinking. In monotheism it is believed that one God is supreme and that He is responsible for the maintenance of order and system in the world.

2. Metaphysical or Abstract Stage. The metaphysical or abstract thinking marks the second stage in the evolution of human. According to Comte each successive stage is an improvement upon the earlier stage. With the gradual improvement in human thinking the human problems also become more complex and intricate. The theological thinking was not adequate to tackle these efficiently. The appearance of conflicting and opposite forces in the world presented problems which could not be successfully tackled by monotheism. It was difficult to believe that the same God was responsible for primordial creation as well as destruction. A personal and concrete God could not account for the simultaneous creation and annihilation. In order to resolve this intellectual puzzle or riddle, metaphysical thinking was invented. Under metaphysical thinking, belief in an abstract transcendental entity or Absolute replaces the belief in personal concrete God. Under metaphysical thinking it is believed that an abstract power or force guides and determines the events in the world. Metaphysical thinking discards belief in concrete God.

3. Scientific or Positive Stage. After theological and metaphysical thinking comes the next stage known as scientific or positive stage. All metaphysical knowledge is based upon speculation and is at best inferential knowledge. There are no direct means to confirm the metaphysical knowledge. In the last analysis it is a matter of belief or temperament. The modern temper of man is such that it cannot remain satisfied with mere guesswork; it craves for positive knowledge which can be scientifically confirmed. The positive or scientific knowledge is based upon facts, and these facts are gathered by observation and experience. The observation and classification of facts are the beginning of the scientific knowledge. From the facts we generalize and draw conclusions. These conclusions, in turn, are subjected to verification and once verified these become eastablished laws, which can be relied upon in gathering and classifying the facts. The scientific thinking is thoroughly rational and in it there is no place for any belief or superstition.

Auguste Comte is of the opinion that all human thinking, before reaching the stage of positivism, must have passed through the two earlier stages of theological and metaphysical thinking. Even in scientific thinking some traces of types are to be usually found.

The above mentioned three stages are marked by Comte's three major works. The first stage, from 1820 to 1826, that of the *Opuscules*, the *Sommaire Appreciation de l'ensemble du passe moderne* and the *plan des travaux necessaries pour reorganiser la societe;* then the *Considerations sur le Powvoir Spirituel* and the *Considerations sur la Science et les Savants.* The second stage consists of the lectures of the *Course de Philosophie Positive* and the third stage, of the *System de Politique Positive.*

RELATION OF LEVELS OF THINKING TO SOCIAL ORGANISATION

Whereas Comte has tried to prove that there are various levels in human thinking, he has also tried to show that each of these is linked with a particular social organisation. According to Comte, social organisation in a particular society is correspondent to the stage of human thinking through which it happens to be passing. It is only with change in the level of human thinking that there occurs a change in the social organization. The types of social organizations obtaining at the various levels of human thinking are discussed briefly below:

1. Theological Stage and Social Organisation. In the theological condition of human thinking, the social organization was of a particular type. The particularity of social organization at this stage was that the social laws, political laws etc., were accepted as absolutely valid and nobody questioned their validity. The theory of divine rights of king was accepted. The king was accepted to be the representative of God; and, therefore, the law made by him could not be wrong. Most societies in the theological stage were ruled by monarchs and in some societies the king was considered to be a God on earth. The discipline was quite rigorous in these societies. The primary reason for the rigorous and martinet discipline was that the laws made by the king were considered to be divine and any violation of these was considered tantamount to disobedience of God's will. Therefore, no one easily dared to oppose and flaunt the laws of the society. Superstitions were rife in these societies.

2. Metaphysical Stage and Social Organisation. Under metaphysical stage of human thinking, social organization was of quite different type from the social organization under the theological stage. These societies were guided by some abstract principles. The political system also undergoes change and the power of the king becomes restricted. The constitutional system of government gets priority. The constitutional changes are gradual and there is a movement towards decentralisation of power leading ultimately to ushering in of democracy. Thus, under metaphysical stage some power passes into the hands of people.

3. Scientific Stage and Social Organisation: In the scientific stage the social and political laws are determined in a definite and well defined form. In these societies industry and technology predominates. The natural resources are harnessed for human good. The superstitions are mistrusted. Reason is demanded in every matter and the fear of divine wrath no longer prevails.

Our age is characterised by sense of crisis in culture. Like so many contemporary thinkers Comte believed that modern society was passing through a crisis. The crisis in society marks the death of the old sytem and the arrival of the new. The new system is led by those who wield spiritual power. They provide the model for the predominant way of thinking. They propound the ideas which serve as the basis of the new social order. In the modern age scientists wield the spiritual power which was formerly in the hands of the priests. The industrialists, on the other hand, are replacing the old military class. Social reform requires intellectual reform. Therefore, Comte suggested a synthesis of the sciences and the creation of positive politics in order to reorganise the society. In the words of Raymond Aron, "The result of this analysis of the contemporary crisis in terms of the opposition between the theological-military social type and the scientific-industrial social type is that Comte the reformer was not a theorist of revolution a la Marx nor a theorist of liberalism a la Montesquieu or Tocqueville; he was a theorist of positive science, and especially of the social science he calls sociology."[3]

According to Raymond Aron the early nineteenth century was characterised by the following features of industry:"[4]

1. Industry constitutes a scientific organization of labour. Instead of proceeding according to custom, production is organized with a view to maximum output.

2. As a result of the application of science to the organisation of labour, man is engaged in a tremendous development of his wealth and resources.

3. Industrial production implies concentration of workers in factories and suburbs. A new social phenomenon is developing: the existence of the working masses.

4. These concentrations of workers in industrial areas bring about an antagonism, whether latent or overt, between employees and employers, between proletariat and management or capitalists.

5. Whereas wealth, as a result of the scientific character of labour, continues to increase, there is also an increase in crises of overproduction, which seem to create poverty in the midst of abundance. Crisis of overproduction have an especially shocking quality, intolerable to the intelligence.

---

3. Aron Raymond, *Main Currents in Sociological Thought*, Part I, Pelican Books (1981), p. 65.
4. *Ibid.*, pp. 72-73.

6. The economic organization linked to the industrial and scientific aspect of labour is characterized by what is called free enterprise : profit-seeking on the part of management or merchants. Certain free-enterprise theorists even conclude that the condition of the increase of wealth is precisely unchecked profit-seeking and competition and that the less the state concerns itself with economic affairs, the more rapidly production and wealth will increase.

Of these, according to Comte, the first three are primary while the fourth is secondary. The essence of society is not free enterprise. It is a pathological element. In the industrial society, cherished by Comte the system is neither liberal nor socialist. The increase of wealth is consistent with the progress of society. Private ownership is necessary though no one has the right to use and abuse property. The present society is the ultimate in the progress of mankind. In the words of Francis Abraham and John Henry Morgan, "Comte believed that the new scientific-industrial society will become the society of all mankind. This is the ultimate stage in a series of successive transformations the human race goes through and each stage is decidedly superior to the previous one. The new system is built upon the destruction of the old, and, with evolution, come progress and the emancipation of the human mind."[5]

POSITIVISM

According to *The Concise Oxford Dictionary*, positivism means the philosophical system of Auguste Comte, recognising only positive facts in observable phenomena, and rejecting metaphysics and theism and religious system founded on this. Thus Comte was against all types of irrational elements in social thinking. "As long as man believes that social events were always exposed to disturbances by the accidental intervention of the legislator," Comte argued in his Positive Philosophy, "human or divine, no scientific provisions of them would be possible."[6] Comte developed the scientific method necessary for analysis of society.

CLASSIFICATION OF SCIENCES

From times immemorial thinkers have been trying to classify knowledge on one or the other basis. Early Greek thinkers had made a tripartite classification of knowledge. These were physics, ethics and politics. Later on, Bacon made the classification on the basis of the faculties of man namely, memory, imagination and reason. The science based upon memory is history and the science based upon imagination is poetry. The knowledge based upon reason is science of Physics, Chemistry etc. Comte classified knowledge on the basis of his observation of scientific or positive level of human thinking. The main aim of the classification of knowledge by Comte was to prepare the background and basis for the study of Sociology, a science invented by him. One the basis of this principle he also determined the methodology of sociology. Besides, this

5. Francis Abraham and John Henry Morgan, *Sociological Thought*, McMillan, 1985, p. 8.

6. Auguste Comte, *Positive Philosophy*, Trans, by Harriet Martineau (New York, Calvin Blanchard, 1838), Four Volumes, II, p. 14.

principle proved helpful in establishing the relation between sociology and other sciences. Indeed, by discovering some general principle, it is possible to establish relationship among various sciences.

COMTE'S PRINCIPLE OF CLASSIFICATION

Each science is concerned with some definite event or subject-matter, and these constitute the subject of its study. The class of a science is determined by these events. Comte also based his classification on this fact. He christened his principle of classification as the Law of Increasing Dependency. This principle has a special feature. In fact, the facts pertaining to different sciences differ in complexity. Some facts are simple while others complex, complex facts dependent upon the simple facts are general and are present everywhere. It is on this basis that Comte has classified various branches of knowledge. The science that is based upon complex facts is called a compelx science. The complex sciences are, in turn, based upon simple sciences. In order to study a complex science one has to study a simple science. Thus, each science is, in some measure, dependent upon some other science and by itself forms a basis of some other science. Thus, a complex science is based upon some simple science and in turn forms a basis of a more complex science. On this basis Comte has presented a serial order of sciences. In this serial order the most simple science is placed on the lowest tier followed upward by more and more complex sciences. Thus, the most complex science is placed on the top. This arrangement is of Increasing Dependency.

THE SERIAL ORDER OF CLASSIFICATION

In the arrangement made on the basis of the law of Increasing Dependency, Comte places Mathematics on the lowest wrung and the topmost wrung is occupied by Sociology. The hierarchy of this classification is as follows :

(1) Mathematics. (2) Astronomy, (3) Physics, (4) Chemistry (5) Biology, and (6) Sociology or Social Physics. From this classification it becomes plain that mathematics according to Comte, is the simplest science while Sociology is the most complex science. While Mathematics depends the least on other sciences, Biology is most dependent upon other sciences.

The social sciences are at the apex of the hierarchy for they enjoy "all the resources of the anterior sciences" and offer "the attributes of a completion of the positive method. All others are preparatory to it. Here alone can the general sense of natural law be decisively developed in the most difficult case of all."[7]

HOLISTIC APPROACH IN SOCIAL SCIENCES

In the words of Raymond Aron, "Science, as Comte conceives it, is not an adventure. It is not an endless and infinite quest. Science is a source of dogmas."[8] Comte believed that laws represent the essence of scientific truth.

---

7. *Ibid.*, pp. 383-84.

8. *Ibid.*, II. pp. 225-26.

The scientific laws however, cannot claim final truth. Science is pragmatic firstly, because it is the source of technological solutions and secondly because it has an educational value. Comte tried to unite the results and methods of sciences. He maintained that contemporary sciences are the expression of the positive spirit. The holistic approach is the natural direction of the progress of sciences. All sciences are the expression of the positive spirit. The holistic approach is the natural direction of the progress of sciences. All sciences progress towards the positive method. The sociology is the crowning glory of all sciences. The holistic approach starts with biology. Before it sciences such as mathematics, physics and chemistry were analytic. Biological approach, on the other hand, was holistic. It proceeded from the study of the organic wholes. Thus, science progressed from inorganic to organic sciences. To quote Auguste Comte, "In the inorganic sciences, the elements are much better known to us than the whole which they constitute; so that in that case we must proceed from the simple to the compund. But the reverse method is necessary in the study of man and society : man and society as a whole being better known to us, and more accessible subjects of study, than the parts which constitute them." Thus, Comte synthesises sciences to arrive at the supreme science of sociology. Sociology cannot explain social phenomena without reference to the total social context. An element of social entity can be understood only in the light of the whole social fabric. In the words of Comte, "There can be no scientific study of society either in its conditions or its movements, if it is separated into portions, and its divisions are studied apart."[9]

THE TRUE SCIENCE OF HUMANITY

According to Comte, "Man is to act by emotion and to think in order to act." Thus, man acts due to his feelings and evolution. These rather than reason rule the mind. Therefore, society should be governed by altruistic feelings. The scientific mind alone can govern feeling effectively. This control is constructive. The rationality of the human animal cannot guide man. Man cannot be positivist instinctively. He is easily governed by superstitions. He is not naturally scientific. In order to be scientific he must discover laws governing phenomena and take recourse to observation and experimentation. History is necessary so that human intelligence may attain its end vocation. Human society can progress only under the direction of sociology.

The evolution of society is in direct correlation to the progress of the human mind. Sociology marks the apex of the progress of human mind and in this too sociology of knowledge is the 'true science of human mind'. The mind is social as well as historical though it functions in a social matrix. Naturalistic science of society explains man's past development as well as his future. Science of sociology is the study of the totality of human intellect and its social actions in time. It is the convergence of mind, society and history. Later on, Comte maintained that sociology is the cumulative result of the activity of the

9. *Ibid.*, p. 225.

human mind. Comte's life-long mission was the establishment of the sociology as the abstract theoretical science of social phenomena, the culmination of all sciences. "Thus", he explained in *System of Positive Polity* "we already possess celestial physics (astronomy), terrestrial physics (geology and geography), mechanical and chemical physics (engineering and chemistry), vegetable physics (botany), animal physics (zoology). We still need one physical science — social physics (sociology) — in order to complete the natural sciences."[10] Within these rather highminded terms, Comte took in hand to define and circumscribe the parameters of the new science. He said, "I understand Social Physics to mean that science which occupies itself with the study of social phenomena, considered in the same light as astronomical, physical, chemical and physiological phenomena, that is to say, as being subject to natural and invariable laws, the discovery of which is the special object of its researchers."[11]

FATHER OF SOCIOLOGY

Auguste Comte is universally regarded as the founder of modern sociology. Indeed, the very term sociology for this particular discipline of knowledge was coined by him and the credit of nomenclature is due to him. Comte had named this science as Social Physics initially. The naming of this science as Social Physics was due to the belief of Auguste Comte that the methods and principles of this newly founded science should be as precise and definite as those of pure sciences. Later on Comte reduced the two term nomenclature of this science to a single term, sociology. In the hierarchy of sciences, Comte placed sociology at the highest rung. In conformity with his general principle Comte held that the study of sociology requires prior knowledge of the five sciences preceding it, namely, Mathematics, Astronomy, Physics, Chemistry, Biology and that the laws of Sociology were dependent upon the basic laws of these sciences. Sociology as yet is a new science, it is passing through its formative period. It has not as yet fully crossed the metaphysical level of human thinking and entered upon the scientific and positive stage though the direction of its march is perceptibly in this line. It would no doubt one day become a full-fledged science. Comte has a very wide conception of sociology. According to him all other social sciences are subsumed under it. He believed in a unified integral study of all social sciences taken together.

SOCIAL STATICS AND SOCIAL DYNAMICS

Tracing the central point of Comte's study Raymond Aron wrote, "To summarize, the point of departure of Comte's thought is a contemplation of the internal contradiction of the society of his age, the contradiction between the theological and military type and the scientific and industrial type. He began with the analysis of certain moment in history. Since this moment in history is characterized by the spread of scientific thinking and of industrial activity,

10. Auguste Comte, *System of Positive Polity* (New York, Burt Franklin, 1966), Four Vols., IV, p. 27.
11. *Ibid.*, p. 39.

Comte believed that the only way to put an end to the crisis is to create that system of scientific ideas which will govern the new social order, just as the system of theological ideas governed the social order of the past."[12] This desired system of scientific ideas is sociology. According to Comte sociology is a very wide discipline. In order to make an orderly study of the subject, Comte divided sociology into two divisions. These divisions were known as Social Statics and Social Dynamics. The social statics is concerned with the present structure of the society. It studies the current laws, rules and present condition of the society. In social statics is observed as to how the present social laws are affecting the society. It also does evaluation of the social structure. The social statics also studies the correlation between various social facts. To quote August Comte, "The statical study of sociology consists in the investigation of the laws of action and reaction of the different parts of the social system apart, for the occasion, from the fundamental movement which is always gradually modifying them."[13]

The other branch of sociology is known as Social dynamics. Under social dynamics we study as to how the processes of social changes are taking place. Social dynamics is the theory of social progress. A true science of humanity must find out both the laws of order and progress. While the laws of order are the concern of social statics, the laws of progress are discovered through social dynamics. In Vol. II of his *Positive Philosophy*, Comte wrote : "The distinction is between two aspects of theory. It corresponds with the double conception of order and progress; for order consists in a permanent harmony among the conditions of social existence, and progress consists in social development."[14] Sociology is the study of social systems and not the individuals. Individual is the study of psychology. Social statics analyses social structure at a given moment. This helps in the understanding of the nature of social order. Social dynamics describes the successive and necessary stages in the development of mind and society. The social dynamics is a science which tries to discover the laws and principles underlying social change and progress. It also tries to find out the conditions necessary to maintain the continuity of social progress. In order to study the history of social change and progress we have to study the rules and principles of social change in an historical perspective. The history reveals to us the ways in which social changes have taken place. In fact, social change augurs progress. By historical study of the problems of social change we can generalize certain laws and principles which are basic to all social change. On the basis of these generalizations we can make projection about future.

Social progress requires population increase and the growth of human mental abilities. It is observable in all the aspects of society — physical, moral, intellectual and political. The concept of dynamics includes the theory of progress,

12. Aron Raymond, *Main Currents in Sociological Thought*, Part, I, 1911, p. 69.

13. August Comte, *Positive Philosophy*, Vol. II, p. 219.

14. *Ibid*., p. 217.

the law of three stages and the evolutionary development of society. To quote Auguste Comte, "In short social dynamics studies the laws of succession, while social statics enquires into those of coexistence; so that the use of the first is to furnish the true service in regard to order, and this suitability to the needs of modern society is a strong confirmation of the philosophical character of such a combination."[15]

SOCIOLOGICAL METHOD

The most important contribution of Auguste Comte, however, is not the definition and demarcation of sociology but the methodology which it ought to pursue. He maintained that the positive science of society called sociology must pursue the method which was followed by mathematics, astronomy, physics, chemistry and biology. He insisted that the new science must be positive. Positive means pursuing scientific methods of analysis and prognosis. To quote Francis Abraham and John Henry Morgan, "Sociology must use the 'positive' method, which, for Comte, meant the subordination of concepts to facts and the acceptance of the idea that social phenomena are subject to general laws — social laws."[16] The social laws, however, by the very nature of social phenomena, are more complex and less rigid. The laws of sociology, therefore, are only probable and not certain. "The idea of treating social science," Comte explained in *System of Positive Polity*, "as an application of mathematics in order to give it a positive character had its source in the metaphysical prejudice that outside of mathematics there can be no real certainty." "This prejudice," he continues, "was natural at the period when all positive knowledge lay within the sphere of applied mathematics...But since the rise of the great positive sciences...such a prejudice is entirely inexcusable."[17]

The method of sociology includes observation as well as experimentation. Observation must be guided by a theory of social phenomena. Experimentation is controlled observation. In sociology experimentation involves the study of pathological cases. "Central to sociology," Comte once said, "is the comparison of the different coexisting states of human society on the various parts of the earth's surface...By this method," he explained, "the different stages of evolution may all be observed at once. These conventional methods of science — observation, experimentation and comparison — must be used in combination with the historical method." "The historical comparison of the consecutive states of humanity is not only the chief scientific device of the new political philosophy...it constitutes the substratum of the science, in whatever is essential to it."[18]

Again, sociology uses historical method in the study of human society. Every social phenomenon can be understood only in a social context. Emphasizing

15. *Ibid.*, Quoted from J.H. Abraham, *Origins and Growth of Sociology* (New York, Penguin Books, 1977), p. 111.
16. Francis Abrahm and John Henry Morgan, *Sociological Thought*, 1985, MacMillan, India, p. 15.
17. Comte, *System of Positive Polity*, IV, p. 52.
18. Comte, *Positive Philosophy*, II, p. 251.

the importance of historical analysis in the study of social phenomena, Comte said, "The chief phenomenon in society — the gradual and continuous influence of generations upon each other — would be disguised or unnoticed for want of the necessary key, *viz.*, historical analysis."[19] The sociological method is scientific since Comte calls sociology Social Physics. Its precision, however, is not mathematical since social phenomena are more complex and dynamic. This, however, does not diminish the importance of sociology nor the value of sociological method. As Comte pointed out, "We shall find that there is no chance of order and agreement but in subjecting social phenomena, like all others, to invariable natural laws, which shall, as a whole, prescribe for each period, with entire certainty, the limits and character of social action."[20]

SOCIAL STATICS OR SOCIAL STRUCTURE

In order to appreciate the views of Auguste Comte regarding sociology, it is necessary to understand his views regarding social structure. And in order to understand the social structure it is necessary to know the place of individual, family, state, religion and morality in society. The views of Comte on this issue are discussed below :

1. Individual in Social Structure. From the sociological point of view the views of Comte with regard to the place of an individual in a society are quite peculiar. He accepts individual as an abstract emotional entity only. Comte does not assign any place to individual in the development of society. "Men are bound together," Comte said in the second volume of *Positive Philosophy*, "by the very distributions of their occupations; and it is this distribution which causes the extent and growing complexity of the social organism."[21]

2. Family in Social Structure. According to Comte the individual is not a social unit. He regards family as a social unit. For purposes of sociology he regards family as the starting point in the society. In the opinion of Comte, family occupies a pivotal position in society and sociology. Family has been accepted as the starting point of society and the study of sociology begins from here. In the development of society, the family provides the base of progress and advance. From the growth of family emanates the growth of cities and state. According to Comte the family is based upon two main planks — Affection and Sympathy.

3. Place of State in Social Structure. In the scale of social development after family the state occupies the place of importance. A group of families residing together constitute a state. A group of families living in closeness to each other and sharing a common language constitute a society. Besides, a common land tract is also necessary for the state. For the development of state and society, cooperation is a *sine qua non.* Without cooperation among families there can be no development in either state or society. The cooperation found

---

19. *Ibid.*, p. 261.

20. *Ibid.*, Vol. I, p. 14.

21. *Ibid.*, Vol. II, p. 15.

in state and society is of a special type. This cooperation is in the form of division of labour and coordination of efforts. In division of labour the functions between various sections of society are determined. While doing this it is kept in mind that there is proper coordination of efforts. Comte's view of cooperation is a developed form of an affection and sympathy principle earlier elaborated by him. He said that "it is evident that not only most political institutions and social manners, on the one hand, and manners and ideas on the other, be always mutually connected; but further that this consolidated whole must always be connected by its nature, with the corresponding state of the integral development of humanity."[22]

With the development of the spirit of cooperation there comes into being in society two classes of people. The first are those who cooperate and the other class is constituted by people who arrange and supervise cooperation. The latter class gradually assumes the status of guides or controllers of the society. This controlling power gradually takes the form of state. This political or state authority rules over society on the basis of certain principles. According to Comte the basis of political authority is the feeling of religion and morality. It needs to be clearly emphasized here that the concepts of religion and morality held by Comte are quite different from the usual meaning attached to these concepts.

4. Religion and Morality in Social Structure. According to Comte religion and morality occupy important place in social structure. For social control both are excellent devices. According to Comte a social control established by law and state is bound to be ineffective. It will be artificial. The state of control is based upon fear and therefore lacks true spirit of allegiance. Contrary to this the social control based upon religion and morality is based upon conscience and love. It is true that in ancient time morality and religion were effective instruments of social control; but, however, Comte is not in favour of traditional religion. According to Comte the kind of religion suited to modern conditions is very different from the ancient religion. He calls the new religion to be Religion of Humanity. It is based upon humanism and rejects the deistic conception of Religion.

SOCIAL DYNAMICS OR SOCIAL PROGRESS

According to Comte there are three types of social progress. There are Physical Progress, Intellectual Progress and Moral Progress. Each of these will be discussed below :

(1) Physical Progress. The fundamental progress of mankind is the physical progress. In the absence of physical progress no other kind of progress is possible. By physical progress we understand any progress in outward living conditions namely, housing, agricultural, industrial production etc. For the social progress, physical progress provides the base. Physical progress is the first rung in the ladder of social progress.

---

22. *Ibid.*, p. 22.

(2) Intellectual Progress. In social progress, intellectual progress occupies a very important place. By intellectual progress alone we can understand the progresses of social cohesion and social disintegration and also the forces which lead to social disruption and disorder. Comte believed that if our intellect can be made to accept the importance of social cohesion, our selfish feelings will automatically turn into altruistic desires. The increase in feeling of altruism would, in turn, lead to great strides in social progress.

(3) Moral Progress. Though Comte generally attached highest importance to intellectual progress, he later on inclined towards moral progress. In his book *Positive Polity,* Comte attached great importance to moral progress.

A special reason is suggested for this change of outlook in Comte's thinking. He fell in intellectual love with a lady Clotide de Vaux in 1845. This left its emotional, intense and lasting impression on his mind. As a result of this he came to regard love and affection more valuable than intellectual powers. He remarked that we become tired of everything except loving. Thus, he began to regard the feeling element to be of higher value than the intellectual element. The great importance he came to attach to morality was a direct result of the more importance he attached to emotion in comparison with intellect. Deviating from his general philosophy, Comte began to regard morality to be the highest aim of man's development. He gave the name of religion of love of humanity to this new outlook.

RELIGION OF HUMANITY

In the beginning Comte attached great emphasis to intellect and science. He was a votary of reason and positivism. Later or there was change in his outlook and he began to attach more emphasis to religion and moraiity than to reason. In his book *Positive Polity* Comte clearly attaches more value to sentiment, religion and morality than to intellectualism. This shift in his outlook was a consequence of his new outlook and theory of Religion of Humanity.

Comte's Religion of Humanity was based upon morality and religion. It was not based upon belief in a Divine force. Indeed Comte was opposed to theological type of religion, and, according to him, God lived in the ignorance of man. The object or religious worship should be, according to Comte, mankind and not God In his religion of Humanity, Comte wanted a synthesis of the teachings of all the religions of all the world with regard to good conduct and fellowship among men. He wanted to rid religion of its theological excrescences. With this aim in view Comte established a society known as Positive Society. With the help of this society Comte wanted to raise the physical, intellectual and moral standard of people. He wanted that mankind should advance from self-interest toward altruism. Each man should develop in him consideration for other human beings and try to do good by them.

Comte was not in favour of traditional Christianity. He was of the opinion that Christianity employed the instruments of political pressure and tyranny in order to gain allegiance of people to Christian religion. Of course, Comte had incorporated the humanitarian principles of Christianity in his religion of humanity. Comte had made provision for the priests in his religion. The main difference between his priests and those of religion was that while religious priest used conversion to obtain allegiance of people, the humanitarian priests were to use persuasion only for practice of their religion. In the *Religion of Humanity* the will, the freedom and competence of the followers were stressed.

Comte's religion of humanity was criticized by various scholars variously. According to Christian scholars the religion of humanity was nothing more than a mixture of science and Catholic religion. According to others it was nothing but Catholicism minus Christianity. In fact, Comte's religion was primarily a code of morality.

CRITICAL EVALUATION

About the importance of Auguste Comte in the history of sociology, Raymond Aron has written, "In fact, all the theories which today emphasize the similarity of a great many institutions on both sides of the iron curtain, which reject the importance of the mechanisms of economic competition — all those theories which attempt to isolate the essential characteristics of industrial civilization — could rightly claim to derive from Auguste Comte. He is, as it were, the theorist of industrial society, this side of or outside of the doctrinal disputes between capitalists and socialists, between theorists of free enterprise and theorists of planning."[23] Even if this claim is not accepted, no one can deny Comte's important place in sociology as the founder of this valuable science. In the words of Francis Abraham and John Henry Morgan, "A scholar must not be judged strictly by his accomplishments in scientific discovery alone, as important as that judgement might be; he must also be assessed in the social and historical context within which his thought took place. Comte, while making naive mistakes and wrong decisions, nevertheless, set the stage for the development of one of the most important scientific adventures of modern man, *viz.*, the emergence of the social science of sociology."[24]

However, the following points of criticism may be raised in the social thought of Augste Comte:

1. It is questionable whether sociology can imitate the method pursued in mathematics and physics. Comte's calling sociology, social physics has certain limitations particularly in the light of the fact that he admits that the study of social phenomena can never hope to be as exact as the studies in physics.

2. The leading ideas of Comte's sociology may be useful but as Raymond Aron points out, "His detailed description of industrial society is often liable to ridicule."[25]

3. Comte's conception of industrial society is based upon the faith that wars are not more relevant to human society. History however, has not justified

23. Raymond Aron, *Main Currents in Sociological Thought*, Vol. I, 1965, p. 77.

24. Francis Abraham and John Henry Morgan, *Sociological Thought*, p. 20.

25. Auguste Comte, *Positive Philosophy*, Vol. II, p. 22.

the views of Auguste Comte. Even now the human society is facing war in so many countries.

4. Comte hailed the western society as leader of humanity's progress. This may not be acceptable to thinkers in other continents.

5. Comte's prediction that the European society will not conquer people of other races has not proved to be justified.

6. Comte maintained that philosophers and scientists had spiritual power to lead industrial society. This, however, has proved to be an utopian dream like Plato's ideal of the philosopher king.

7. Comte thought that the social scientists will wield the spiritual power over and above the temporal hierarchy. Spiritual power, however, is not at the apex .even now.

8. Comte maintained that in the scientific organisation of the industrial society, each individual will be given a position commensurate with his merits. This meritocracy has not been observed anywhere.

9. Comte declared that there cannot be true unity in a society when it is not governed by a body of ruling ideas. Unity of thought, however, has never been fully realised in the course of history.

10. According to Comte the crucial advances in the history of human mind could have been foreseen by a superior intelligence. This determinism leaves nothing for chance or accident.

11. According to Comte the factors of variation are three in number : race, climate and political action. This classification and limitation of factors of diversity in society is clearly not acceptable to other social thinkers.

12. Comte was systematically arbitrary in his treatment of family. He frequently confused traits of his own social organisation as universal traits of family.

13. The programme of social reconstruction outlined by Comte should be achieved itself according to his laws of positivist dynamics. This is far from being true.

In spite of the above mentioned criticism Auguste Comte will be hailed as the founder of the religion of humanity, a religion which alone may save the world from a future catastrophe. Pointing out the value of Comte's concept of religion of humanity Raymond Aron wrote, "If one insists on deriving a religion from sociology (which I do not), the only one that seems to me thinkable, were I forced to do so, is that of Auguste Comte, because it does not instruct us to love one society among others, which would be tribal fanaticism, or to love the social order of the future, which no one knows and in whose name one begins by exterminating all sceptics."[26]

---

26. Raymond Aron, *Main Currents in Sociological Thought*, p. 78.

THE IDEAL STATE

Comte rejected Platonic metaphysics though he reconstructed his ideal state in a Platonic manner. He rejected all metaphysical and abstract principles. He accepted only positive principles drawn by induction from the past and the present. Nevertheless he as a Platonist sought to reconstruct an ideal state, though in the light of his scientific principle. Again, though influenced by the medieval church more than by Plato, Comte drew distinction between the temporal and spiritual classes in Platonic manner. His ideal state represents a complex amalgam of Platonic approach and the scientific principles. To quote Barker, "His ideal state would have been one in which the spiritual class, a combination of savants, orthodox in science, expressive of reason and acting by persuasion rather than force, guided the course of affairs in the light of scientific principles."

SCIENTIFIC STUDY OF POLITICS

Comte made significant contributions to the field of sociology and thereby provided ample material to the 'scientific' study of politics. As Lencester has said, "We are now so accustomed to the scientific way of looking at social and political question that we are prone, perhaps because of his oddities, to underrate a man like Comte. If, however, we consider the state of opinion at the time he wrote, we get a more balanced estimate of the significance of his suggestions. It was only the rare thinker at that time who had shaken himself free from what Comte called the theological and metaphysical preconceptions and Comte was only one of those who did so most boldly." To quote Sabine, "What Comte contributed was not so much a new discovery as the hope that speculation might be replaced by science, that the concept of society might be analysed and its laws discovered by method that would conform to the cannons of empirical verification, and that relationship might be traced in detail between social institutions and human nature. Comte's philosophy was not a culmination but the beginning, the mid-point from which might be dated the whole vast effort to bring social studies within the sweep of modern science."

QUESTIONS FOR EXERCISE

1. Define Positivism, What are its advantages as a method of study?
2. Descibe the contribution of Auguste Comte's Positivism.

10

Biological Theory : Herbert Spencer (1820—1903)

Herbert Spencer was born on April 27,1820. He was the son of a teacher. Whatever education he received was as a private student. He took up engineering and at the age of 17, he became a trained engineer. Later on, he worked on the Editorial board of a magazine "Pilot". He was an Assistant Editor of *Economist*, where he came in contact with the great scholars like Eliot, Newman, Tyndall and Huxley. In 1853, he left the job and devoted himself to writing. Due to economic hardship, he could never marry. He suffered from indigestion and eye strain. His income improved later on due to popularity of his books. In 1898, he moved to Brighten and died in 1903. He was the greatest champion of individualism on biological basis. To quote Hearnshaw, "Spencer was not so much a man as an intellectual organism and his passage through this world was rather an existence than a life. He was all head and no heart; he never fell in love and never married."

Spencer's Writings

Spencer was a profilic writer. He wrote 18 large volumes. In the words of Sabine, "Spencer's synthetic philosophy was an astonishing system of 19th Century rationalism, covering the whole range of knowledge from physics to ethics worked out through 35 years and in 10 volumes and constructed with an important charge of plan between the prospectus and the concluding volume." Spencer's important writings are :

1. *Social Statics* (1850)
2. *The Proper Sphere of Government* (1852)
3. *Theory of Population* (1852)
4. *Art of Education* (1854)
5. *Education* (1861)
6. *The Social Organisation* (1860)
7. *Specialised Administration* (1871)
8. *Man or the State* (1864)
9. *Principles of Sociology*

10. *Sins of Legislation.*
11. *Descriptive Sociology.*
12. *Principles of Ethics* (1891)
13. *Essays* (Three volumes)
14. *Autobiography* (Three volumes).

Exponent of Scientific School

Herbert Spencer was the chief exponent of scientific school of thought. He tried to develop his philosophy on rational footing with a scientific approach. He was an ardent follower of the concept of 'Evolution'. He believed that the state should not take upon itself the duty of protecting the poor. If the state undertook this type of job that will mean denial of proper and legitimate right to those against whom the state was defending. Spencer did not believe in the institution of private property as that is against evolution and evolutionary tendencies. He tried to reconcile his individualism with evolutionary theory. Scientific school of thought did not like to merge social institutions in the state because these have done much more work than the state.

Influences on Spencer

1. Influence of English Radicalism. Spencer was influenced by English Radicalism. He was born in a family which was virtually non-conformist. It was from his childhood that he learnt to disobey the authority in all forms. He learnt to disobey the state when he came in contact with his uncle, Rev. Thomas Spencer, who was an advanced theologian. He began to believe that the Church was a growth and subject to change and adjustment to external conditions. It was in this period that Spencer came in touch with Joseph Struge of Birmingham who founded in 1841 a weekly named 'Non-Conformist' and subsequently joined 'Complete Suffrage Union'.

2. Influence of Thomas Hodgskin. Another great influence on Spencer was that of Thomas Hodgskin with whom he came in contact as sub-editor of 'Economist'. Thomas Hodgskin was essentially an anti-Benthamite Radical. He extended the philosophy of *Laisses Faire* both to Economics and Politics. In the words of Barker he believed that "the function of the Government was accordingly negative: it extended only to securing of a free field for the operation of laws; and human laws were as prejdicial as natural laws were the reverse. The ultimate goal and utopia of the nature was thus a state of anarchy, in which Government had disappeared and the sentiments of each were automatically adjusted in a spontaneous harmony with those of all."

3. Influence of German Idealism. Another factor which influenced Spencer was the German Idealism of Schelling and Schlegel. It was from German Idealism that he got the idea of life. He said, "Life is the cause of a universal evolution." In fact it is universal evolution for Spencer that he was even willing to include phenomena of a solar system in the idea of life. He started from universal evolution and subsequently came to biological evolution. It was under these influences that both nature and society were seen as living organic units which are bound to develop. This development is called the process of individuation.

4. Study of Natural Subjects. From the study of the Natural subjects, Spencer learnt the system of natural process and natural growth. He learnt to say goodbye to customs and conventions. As Barker has pointed out "....and thus Spencer came to 'social evolution' not from biology, and from any use of biological analogy, but from a sweeping view of universal evolution expressed in terms of physics : a view which included in its sweep both sociology and biology and indeed astronomy and geology also, as all alike parallel manifestations of the same law."

5. Role of Biology. In Spencer's political philosophy, biology had an important role to play. He based sociology on biology. He believed that external environments do influence the living beings from generation to generation. Living beings are to adapt and adjust themselves to new environments. This adaptation is a matter of equilibrium of forces and energies. It is the adjustment of living beings to environments. In the early stages the equilibrium was more indirect rather than direct. According to Spencer present equilibrium once attained, men would do what they ought to do and even Government would vanish like anything. The value of the society should be judged in the form of perfection which it attained. This idea of anarchy does not seem to be appealing. As Barker says: "Thus, his conception of evolution, just because it postulates a final end which is the standard of justice, is reconciled with his radical politics but just for that reason also his political theory goes askew, because it tends to a view of Government and social institutions as unjust and unjustifiable." To quote Sabine, "Spencer built upon utmost purely deductive system of philosophy, bringing social theories into relation to biological evolution and the supposed conclusion of the physical sciences, but he left the practical conclusions almost where they had been."

Spencer contributed a lot to different fields of social sciences like politics, economics, ethics, sociology and psychology. He used biological method so as to prove his contentions. However, the line of individualism runs through all his writings. As he had seen the rise and growth of utilitarianism at the hands of Bentham followed by James Stuart Mill and John Stuart Mill, he could not ignore the basic notion of the happiness of the individual. What makes him different from Mill is that he seeks to give a scientific orientation to social philosophy by bringing it into relationship with biology and sociology and, for this reason, with biological and social evolution.[1]

DEFENCE OF INDIVIDUAL FREEDOM

Spencer's *Social Statics* (1851) is an important work in defence of natural rights and individual freedom. He lays down the doctrine of the law of equal freedom whereby each individual desires to attain freedom limited only by the necessity of like freedoms for others so that the maximum amount of happiness

1. G.H. Sabine, *History of Political Theory*, IV Ed., p. 652.

may be attained by the maximum exercise of capacity. In his *Social Organism* (1860) he emphasises that society is like an organism, because 'it grows and is not made' and that it should be left to grow under the free play of social influence and not made. The state has no right to hinder the process of social development. His paper on *Administrative Nihilism* (1871) contains a partial explanation in favour of this point. A similar idea is contained in the *Principles of Sociology* whose first volume appeared in 1876. Here he affirms that if we want to comprehend social aggregate, we must understand the units of society. He seeks to prove that "the characteristics of the associated state must be the consequences of the inherent properties of the associated individuals. The individual may be regarded from two aspects, an outer and inner. In the former aspect, he is a being with a faculty that demands freedom as the condition of that adaptation to function which constitutes perfection; in the latter, he is a consciousness, endowed with an inherent sense of justice which makes him claim for himself, and with a sympathetic affection which makes him respect in others; the freedom his faculty requires."[2]

The line of individualistic argument is also traceable in *Man* Versus *State.* In it the idea of social contract is emphasised in a way different from that of Hobbes and Locke. The justification of the existence of political authority is sought in the protection and promotion of the happiness of the individual by the action of the state. If the state tries to give me more, which it can only do by taking more from me, in order to get the means for its gifts, it breaks the tacit agreement we have made. Once again, this emphasis becomes implicit that natural rights necessarily involve social contract whatever incidental or irrelevant mention of social organism may adorn the process of the argument."[3]

THEORY OF EVOLUTION

Spencer studied politics through biology and attempted synthesis of all scientific knowledge. He plunged into the sphere of metaphysics, ethics, theology, biology, psychology and sociology and claimed that he emerged with the supreme law of the universe in his grasp. He was also confident in asserting to have actually chalked out the boundary line between the knowable and the unknowable and thus correctly divined the basic laws of cosmology. He bequeathed to the posterity a larger understanding of the essential inter-relationship of formerly dissociated departments of knowledge. Metz observes that Spencer "abstracted, classified, generalised and moved forward to more and more abstract unifications until he had reached a point from where he could sum up the universe in a single formula."[4]

Spencer "used to explain the present constitution and condition not only of the starry universe, the planetary system, the face and figure of the earth, the flora and fauna of the world, together with the bodies of men, but also of

---

2. Barker, *Political Thought in England,* p. 83.

3. *Ibid.*, p. 87.

4. Rudolf Metz, *A Hundred Years of British Philosophy,* p. 102.

the minds of the men and the forms of human society. Indeed, the primary aim of the Synthetic Philosophy was precisely the solution on naturalistic and evolutionary lines of the problems of ethics and politics."[5]

Spencer thus believed in the theory of evolution. Confirming the conclusions of the biologists like Darwin, Huxley and Wallace, he turned to biology to amplify and sustain his philosophy. But he rejected the thesis of Weismann and believed in the inheritability of acquired characteristics. Likewise, he discarded the Darwinian thesis that selection takes place through accidental variation. He substituted it with the view that variation and adaptation are manifestations of purpose. Yet, he agreed with the Darwinian doctrines of the 'struggle for existence' and the 'survival of the fittest'. He always maintained the perfect reasonableness of inferring that structural adaptations are transmissible by heredity.

According to Spencer the perfect society will appear only when man has fully adjusted himself to his environment; when an equilibirium is reached between the individual organism and the social organism. Spencer postulated: "All evil results from the non-adaptation of constitution to conditions...Equally true is it that evil perpetually tends to disappear. In virtue of an essential principle of life, this non-adaptation of an organism to its conditions is ever being rectified, and modification of one or both continues until the adaptation is complete. Whatever possesses vitality from the elementary cell upto the man himself, inclusive, obeys this law."

Defence of *Laissez Faire*

1. The operation of the law of evolution should not be obstructed by state and government. The state should refrain from placing obstacles in the operation of this law. It is no business of the state to protect the weak and the unfit, for the ultimate result of shielding fools from folly would be to fill the world with fools. Let the social equilibrium be set up and for that let there be a struggle for existence entailing survival of the fittest. Any human species whose constitution is to be moulded into fitness for new condition of existence must be placed under those conditions. Spencer writes : "Only by the process of adaptation itself can be produced that character which makes social equilibrium spontaneous. And hence while his process is going on, an instrumentality must be employed, firstly, to bind men into the social state and secondly to check all conduct endangering the existence of the state. Such an instrumentality, we have in government."[6]

2. If the law of evolution were allowed to take its natural course, a state of static balance and perfection would come. The genuine adjustment of the individual with his surroundings would occur when there is a liberty of action to enable the individuals to learn by experience what is best to pursue. The accruing experience transmitted from one generation to another would inevitably

5. Hearnshaw, *The Social and Political Ideas of Some Representative Thinkers of the Victorian Age*, p. 80.

6. Spencer, *Social Statics*, pp. 126-127.

and necessarily mould human faculties into complete fitness for social life. In the presence of perfect equilibrium or in the absence of any antagonism between the individual and society the state would be unnecessary and superfluous, when the final state is reached.

Critical Evaluation

1. The principle of evolution and the hope for a perfect equilibrium are contradictions in terms. Modern science rejects the notion of a final equilibrium where the process of evolution stops. It believes that the evolution is a never-ending process wherein each adaptation creates new conditions calling for fresh adaptation. The evolution of human conduct can never attain a static repose. Its horizon always recedes and there is never a perfect and final adaptation. Each new adaptation suggests a new set of problems and leads to a newer sort of adaptation.

2. Ideal of the future is thoroughly utopian. By denouncing the existing social system Spencer adopts a medieval point of view which sees the producer and author of all evil and violence in all governments. Instead of holding fast to the idea that the social conditions of a given time are just and perfectly good, so far as they represent the best possible approximation to the ideal, Spencer is apt to set such social conditions over against his ideal and then to criticise them by his ideal standard as imperfect and unjust. If such a stage of evolution represents a state of equilibrium or adaptation, the present society does the same. But Spencer erroneously considers the social institutions unjust and unprofitable. His denunciation of the existing social system including the sphere of state activity and the hope for a final equilibrium cannot be reconciled with each other.

3. Criticism against defence of *laissez faire* on biological grounds. It is true that Darwinian principles of the struggle for existence and the survival of the fittest cannot be operative in a society of human beings. The modern conception of state activity demands protection of the down-trodden against the privileged. Spencer's defence of *laissez faire* on biological grounds added to the infamy of individualism. Joad says that it "implied a reversion to the ethics of barbarism, and not only discredited Individualism in the eyes of socially-minded men, but had particularly important consequences in the economic sphere."[7]

CONCEPT OF STATE AS SOCIAL ORGANISM

Spencer was one of the most powerful advocates of the organismic theory on the nature of state. The state is a real person, a living organism possessing organs which perform functions analogous to those of an animal or a plant. Spencer's doctrine of social organism represented an anti-thesis of the juridical theory which conceives the state as a legal fiction or a pure mental concept. His biological concept described the state in terms of a natural science. He

7. Joad, *Modern Political Theory*, p. 30.

views the individuals who compose it as akin to the cells of a plant or an animal. He postulated a relation of inter-dependence between the individuals. The society such as exists between the organs and parts of a biological organism and the whole structure.

Barker very finely defines the term organism thus : "When we speak of an organism we mean (1) a living structure composed of parts different in kind; (2) that those parts, by reason of their difference, are complimentary to one another and mutually dependent; (3) that the health of the whole consequently depends on the healthy discharge of each part of its own proper function. An organism thus possesses the correlative attributes of a high degree of differentiation and a high degree of integration; and 'organic unity' means unity in and through difference. Again, an organism just because it is a living structure and just because it works so subtly through the reciprocal functions of its parts, cannot be changed from without by any mechanical act. It grows; it grows from within by a development which affects all its parts simultaneously; and such growth is what is called organic growth."[8]

Spencer's doctrine of social organism manifested his belief in a parallelism between the individual and the social organisms. The elaborate analogy has the following main features :

1. Similar Processes. Both physiological and social organisms begin as germs, undergo a process of continuous growth and with growth the parts become more and more unlike and exhibit greater complexity of structure. The development happens from simple to complex, from homogeneous to heterogeneous, from indifferentiation to differentiation. As the lowest type of animal is all stomach, respiratory surface limb, so primitive society is all warrior, all hunter, all hut-builder, all tool-maker. As society grows in complexity, division of labour follows, that is, new organs with different functions appear corresponding to the different functions in the animal and in that fundamental trait they become alike.

2. Inter-dependence of Parts. There is a mutual dependence of parts in the case of both the organisms, the full performance of the functions of each member being essential to the health and preservation of the rest.

3. Replacements. The slow but consistent replacement of cell tissues and blood corpuscles in a natural organism, by which it is destroyed and reproduced, is paralleled by the processes in society by which it is permanently maintained, notwithstanding the death of component members.

4. Identical Systems. Spencer attributes to both the animal organism and the social organism a 'sustaining system' consisting of the alimentation in the former and production in the latter; a 'distributing system' consisting of the circulatory apparatus in the human body and a transportation system in the society; and a 'regulatory system' consisting of the nervous system in the animal, and of government and armies in the social organism. Murray explains

---

8. Barker : *Political Thought in England*, pp. 90-91.

the meaning of Spencer thus : "The workers, the men who form the soil, work the mines and factories, and workshops are the alimentary organs of a society, the wholesalers, retailers, bankers, railway and steamshipmen correspond to the vascular system of an organism. The professional men — doctors, lawyers, engineers, rulers, priests — the thinkers, in short, perform the functions of the brain and the nervous system."[9]

Difference Between Biological and Social Organism

Spencer accepted following points of extreme unlikeness between the biological and social organisms:

1. While the natural organism is concrete in structure as its units are bound together in close contact, the social organism is discrete as its units are free and more dispersed.

2. The social organism has no nervous sensorium. While in the animal organism sensorium is concentrated in a small part of the aggregate, in the social organism it is diffused throughout the aggregate. There is no social sensorium. Each individual member of a social organism is a separate centre of consciousness, and is capable of independent action and even of existence to a certain degree.

3. The social aggregate, though discrete, is still a living whole. Garner says: "Spencer's denial of the existence of a nerve sensorium in society was probably the result of his individualistic thinking. After his long argument in support of the organic theory of society, it seemed necessary to reconcile his biological theory with his doctrine of individualism by showing that, after all, there is a difference and that the parts are not dependent on the whole, as they are in the case of animal organism."[10]

Criticism of Spencer's Theory of Social Organism

1. Exaggeration. Spencer exaggerated the points of similarity between the natural and social organisms. As both differ largely from each other, to draw an elaborate analogy between the two is sheer exaggeration. There may be discovered some lines of analogy, but their extreme is misleading. In this connection, Barker rightly points out: "The state is not an organism; but it is like an organism. It is not an organism, because it is not a physical structure....The fact, however, remains that state is not an organism, because it is a self-determining system of minds which are themselves self-determining, and the whole analogy leads to confusion instead of clearness, unless we are clear about the terms of the comparison, and unless we are also clear that metaphor is not argument, and that a parallel between the state and the individual is not an explanation of this relation."[11]

2. Difference Between Society and Personality. Spencer sought to establish

9. Murray : *Social and Political Thought of the Nineteenth Century*, p. 21.

10. Garner, *op. cit.*, pp. 217-18.

11. Barker, *op. cit.*, pp. 91-92.

a reconciliation between the organic character of society and the atomistic character of individual personality. The more he laboured for the parallel, the more he forgot about the nature of proper relationship. For the sake of justifying his defence of *laissez faire* he made his entire analysis inconsistent. If the society is an organic whole, the individual cannot maintain its organic character. And if it is all done for the sake of a definite purpose such as *laissez faire*, the theory is not at all a theory of organism, but an essay on expediency. It is for the simple reason that in spite of doing such a great labour, Spencer "bows the social organism out of doors."[12]

3. Idea of organism does not coincide with theory of evolution. Keeping in view Spencer's principle of evolution, it may be said that the law demands continual adaptation to continually progressing state of conditions. The fact of the state of adaptation should not be ignored that in the study of parallelism between the social and physiological phenomena, Spencer was much more careful of the social organism and sometimes he picked up a feature of undifferentiated jelly fish and at others of a higher type of vertebrate.

4. Wrong Prophesy about Future. As a scientific thinker, Spencer ought to have suggested what the future stage of evolution would be and then what type of parallelism would eventually take place. Instead of doing this, he came out with a glowing prophesy that in future perfect equilibrium would take place.

DEFENCE OF NATURAL RIGHTS

Sanctity of Rights

Spencer affirmed faith in the dogma of natural rights. He asserted that as every individual consciously recognises the rights of others and feels bound to respect them and as natural rights alone ensure both happiness and freedom, the rights have a sacrosanct character and even the state cannot abrogate them. The primary function of the state is to find out means of securing these rights for the citizens, otherwise the individual may defy the authority of state for the sake of defending his rights. Thus, the theory of natural rights constitutes a solid core of Spencer's thought. It firmly reiterates his hostile attitude towards the state. As Barker says: "Natural rights are the sand of refuge in which the individual buries his head to escape a pursuing State."[13]

Equal Freedom

Spencer defined rights as nothing but artificial divisions of the general claim to exercise one's faculties. He called them natural, because they are pre-social and are inherent properties of the human constitution as divinely ordained. The fundamental thing in the world is the free exercise of individual capacity. In it alone lies the happiness ordained for man by nature. Spencer thus justified the law of equal freedom whereby each individual attains a freedom limited

12. *Ibid., op. cit.*, p. 118.
13. *Ibid.*, p. 109.

only by necessity of like freedom for others and whereby alone maximum happiness follows from the maximum exercise of this capacity.

Internal and External Freedom

Spencer studied individual freedom from two sides — internal and external. In the former, man is a being with a faculty which demands freedom as the condition of that adaptation to function which constitutes perfection. In the latter, man is consciousness endowed with an inherent sense of justice which makes him claim for himself, and with a sympathetic affection which fills in him respect for others, the freedom his faculty requires. In speaking of the external aspect, Spencer expressed his belief in the benevolence of nature and harmony of interests. His speaking of the internal aspect expressed his belief in the innate instinct of justice and in that sympathetic affection of this instinct termed beneficience which makes everyone spontaneously inclined to allow others to claim, and to support others in claiming what he defends himself.

Private and Public Rights

Then, Spencer's defence of natural rights suggests their two-fold classification — private and public.

1. The Private Rights. These are concerned with individual's life, family and property. The free exercise of faculties is a natural right. Property is also one of the elements of our nature. Right to property excludes the case of private ownership of land because it contravenes the law of equal freedom demanding èqual access to the land. Spencer emphasised the political freedom of the families. He attacked the subjection of women and children. He insisted that in an ideal system the family should disappear and the law of equal freedom should be extended to all men, women and children. This represents the withering away of coercion at the hands of males over females, and of the parents over their children.

2. The Public Rights. These are concerned with the state. Spencer calls the government a vicious and immoral institution, which most unnecessarily interferes with the free play of human faculties. The government is a necessary evil, for it has to maintain conditions ultimately leading to the stage of a perfect equilibrium. Yet it must justify its existence by interfering as little as possible. According to Spencer it can be done in three ways:

(i) The state must permit its citizens to abandon the benefits of citizenship by ignoring its burdens.

(ii) It must meet the demands of the law of equal freedom by admitting all the citizens to an equal share in its imposition of all the restraints.

(iii) It must try to delimit its scope of activity and concern itself only with three things — namely, protection, administration of the law of equal freedom, and the maintenance of natural rights.

Critical Evaluation

Spencer's defence of natural rights embodies an identification of science with morality. This natural rights become moral rights. He argues that if we look at the life of the individual on the assumption that it is worth living, we must conclude that the acts necessary for its maintenance are rights and the liberties. The presence of other fellow-beings demands that man must not claim any right of action which interferes with the rights of his fellows. If man thus abandons some of his claims and liberties the rest of his claims and liberties may be regarded as ethical rights. Spencer very clearly says that "to recognise and enforce the rights of the individuals is at the same time to recognise and enforce the conditions to a normal social life : there is one vital requirement for both."[14]

Criticism of Spencer's Defence of Natural Rights

1. Confused and self-contradictory. Spencer put property in the list of natural rights. The state must not interfere with the natural rights of the individual. And yet his law of equal freedom postulates public and national ownership of soil. When he recognised that such ownership of soil may and must be private property in its products because the producer has mixed his labour with the products and because he has hired the soil for a consideration for the community and has obtained a right which is valid as he has secured the consent of society before expending his labour. The phrase of social consent obviously destroys Spencer's whole defence. If a right so elementary as that of private property involves social recognition, it is difficult to see how rights can in their nature be pre-social or independent of social recognition.

2. It cuts across the earlier premises of the thought. Spencer's emphasis on the organic character of society in his theory of evolution and his belief in the natural rights implying an atomistic character of individual's personality are like two opposite poles. The conception of individual's personality are like two opposite poles. The conception of individual's natural rights cannot accord with the organic and evolutionary conception of the state. If society has an organic character, individual's rights are subject to the fact of social recognition. But Spencer's stress on the independent position of individual's personality is destructive of any reconciliation that might possibly be established. Barker correctly points out that Spencer's philosophy "consequently begins and ends as an incongruous mixture of natural rights any physiological metaphor."[15]

3. Under-rating of the significance of man's social existence by defending the case of natural rights. Bentham was right in calling natural rights 'rhetorical nonsense'. There can be no right independent of man's social existence. To say that natural rights are pre-social is to talk like a utopian philosopher. Green rightly visualised that there can be no possibility of rights existing in a pre-social stage. Rights are also co-relative with the duties. Laski insists: "He that

14. *Ibid.*, p. 105.

15. *Ibid.*, p. 71.

will not perform functions cannot enjoy rights any more than he who will not work ought to enjoy work."[16] Similarly, Hobhouse asserts: "Rights and duties, then, are conditions of social welfare, or as we define such welfare, of a life of harmony to this welfare, every member of the community stands in a double relation. He has his share in it. That is the sum of his rights. He has to contribute his share. That is, the sum of his duties."[17]

4. It confuses the scope of state activity. If the society has been in a stage of evolution and one day the stage of perfect equilibrium would arrive, naturally the state has to wither away. But Spencer's defence of natural rights wants the state to continue independently with the need to preserve and protect the individual and his rights, ultimately enforcing that free energy of faculty which was the instrument for obtaining complete individuation. The assertion that men entered into a sort of contract with each other to preserve their natural rights shows that the primary function of the state changed from a gradually slackening adjustment between individuals to the continual enforcement of these contracts. Thus, Doyle observes: "The conception of the state as a gradually evolving natural organism whose main function was to harmonise the individual parts into a living whole disappeared. In its stead, Spencer envisaged a mechanical contrivance made by men to preserve their individuality."[18]

ARDENT INDIVIDUALISM

The political ideas of Herbert Spencer present the most powerful defence of *laissez faire.* Like John Stuart Mill, he sets out with a frank denunciation of the ideal character of the state and calls it 'a necessary evil'. Yet his individualistic approach is much more subtle and ardent so much so that in the end individualism is replaced by a state of anarchy. The state is to help the advent of the stage of perfect equilibrium and then to make its necessity outlived. Thus, while Mill confined the scope of state activity to a minimum possible extent, Spencer seeks to do away with it in the age of final prefection and reaches the point of 'condoning complete anarchy'.[19] Elliot says: "Spencer was a man of immensely strong individual personality. There can be a little question that this was the basis of his doctrine of social freedom. He could not bear to have his liberty of thought and action curtailed in any kind of way. His personality was everywhere intruded and could suffer no limitations and live under no compulsion."[20]

Arguments in Favour

1. State Aggressor. Spencer begins with the assertion that the existence of the state is a result of man's inherent perversity and egoism and that in reality it is an aggressor rather than a protector. He argues: "Be it or be it not

16. Laski : *A Grammar of Politics,* p. 34.

17. Hobhouse : *The Elements of Social Justice,* p. 34.

18. Doyle : *A History of Political Thought,* p. 226.

19. *Ibid.,* p. 566.

20. Elliot : *Herbert Spencer,* p. 64.

true that man is shaped in iniquity and conceived in sin, it is unquestionably true that government is begotten of aggression and by aggression."[21] Analysing it, Barker says: "There is much aggression on freedom within the state as without the state, for the state is making its small aggressions daily."[22]

2. Darwinianism. Spencer's individualism draws support from the Darwinian principles of the struggle for existence and the survival of the fittest. In the social organism, those members who are not fit to play their part must be eliminated in the interest of the whole. It is not the business of political authority to perpetuate their weakness by making provisions for them. Each individual should be allowed to stand alone or fall according to his worth unaided by the props and support of the state. He should be left free to work out his own destiny without the guidance and tutelage of the government. Thus, by leaving each individual to do that for which he is best fitted, the strong and fit classes survive, the unfit elements are eliminated and thus the good of society is promoted.

3. Negative State Regulation. Emphasising the negatively regulative character of state activity, Spencer speaks against all legislation for the regulations of trade and commerce, sanitary arrangements, public education, poor relief, post offices, currency, public health and recreation etc. If the state happens to do anything in regard to these it violates the principle of legitimate intervention. It has to do nothing beyond the works of protection, administration of law and justice and rigid enforcement of contracts, for the liberty which a citizen "enjoys is to be measured, not by the nature of government machinery he lives under, whether representative or other, but by the relative paucity of the restraints it imposes on him."[23]

4. The Sins of Legislators. The approach has been reiterated in Spencer's monography on *The Sins of Legislators.* Spencer very rabidly denounced the heavy work of legislation. The statute books are full of errors, blunders and unhappy guesses. Spencer protested against the worship of the legislature and asserted that as the great political supersition of the past was the divine right of kings, that of the present is the divine right of parliaments. The divine right of parliament means only the divine right of the majority. Spencer argued that the majority has no right to be respected. The laws passed by the parliaments are not sacred in themselves. They may be challenged by the people over whom they intend to exercise coercion. Spencer's monograph reviews much of the unwise legislation of the past, dwells upon the evils which result from it, and concludes that because most of this type of legislation has been replaced or modified in the past, it ought never to have been enacted."[24]

5. Defence of Natural Rights. Spencer specifically warns that the state should not usurp the natural rights of the individual and, if it does, the individual

---

21. Spencer : *Man* Versus *State*, p. 54.
22. Barker, *op. cit.*, p. 87.
23. Spencer : *Man* Versus *State*, p. 54.
24. *Ibid.*, p. 95.

is authorised to rise in revolt. In this connection Spencer propounds the phrase of 'ignoring state'. His argument desires the individuals to shake off the burdens of citizenship. For the sake of equal freedom the individual can refuse to fulfil his social obligations. Hence, the government must meet the demands of the law of equal freedom by admitting all its citiens to an equal share in the enforcement of all restraints it imposes. The factor of dissent must be generalised by the state. As the state is to disappear in future, it should remain in existence for the sake of protecing natural rights alone and do nothing to overwhelm them. An individual can defy the power of state in defence of his own rights.

6. Anarchism. Spencer's individualism turns towards anarchism. When the state is merely instituted for the purpose of curbing the wicked propensities of the individual and protecting him from the fraud and violence of his fellow-beings, government can have no reason of its existence in the morally perfect conditions of society. The state is unjustified in doing whatever tends to produce the greatest happiness or which will subserve the general good. Spencer calls it by the name of governmental despotism, as there is no standard or test for determining what is expedient or what is for the general good except the opinions of the governors themselves. Thus, Spencer finds the government as incidental and existing until the conditions of voluntary outlawry are adopted by the individuals. He says: "As amongst Bushmen we find a state antecedent to government, so may there be one in which it shall have extinct."

Criticism

Spencer's assumption of *laissez faire* is wrong and untenable. The argument that the state is a necessary evil and that all restraints as such are wrong has not been borne out by the experience of mankind under the regime of political organisation. History shows that the progress of civilisation has been achieved to a very large extent by wisely directed state action. The state is definitely a positive good and a welfare agency. It is true that at times the end of the state has been perverted to the detriment of the public good, but this is no reason for condemning the state, as an evil. Seeley rightly says that to characterise each restraint as inherently evil in itself is to ignore the fundamental distinction between that which is useful and good and that which is bad."[25] Garner says: "Spencer's doctrine that the state exists only because crime exists, and that it would subserve no purpose in a society of morally perfect beings, cannot be accepted. The function of the state in the complex civilisation of today is not merely repressive, not simply negatively regulative; it has a higher task than that of restraints and punishment : the task of protecting, encouraging and fostering the common welfare."[26]

The scope of state activity cannot be limited to a particular minimum, because the state has to wither away. On the contrary, with the increasing complexity of modern civilisation the need for state action is growing. In comparatively recent years a strong reaction against the principle of *laissez*

25. Garner, *op. cit.*, p. 465.

26. *Ibid.*

faire has taken place owing largely to the conditions resulting from the growth of industrialism. Huxley rightly observes: "The higher the state of civilisation, the more completely do the actions of one member of the social body influence all the rest, and the less possible is it for any one man to do a wrong without interfering more or less with the freedom of all his fellow-citizens. So that even on the narrowest view of functions of the state it must be admitted to have wider powers than the advocates of police theory are disposed to admit."[27]

THE ARISTOTLE OF VICTORIAN ENGLAND

Spencer puts disparate elements together. Instead of starting from a single point like a deductive theorist or taking conclusions out of the given material like an empiricist, he draws inspiration from different sources and thus produces an incongruous mixtures in his political theory.

Similarly, Spencer's natural aptitude for engineering and the study of natural sciences filled in him a love for study of the principles of evolution. His study of the German Idealism of Schelling and Schlegel convinced him of the idea of life. But his hope in the final stage of anarchy and his insistence on the naturalness of rights does fit with his theories of social evolution and social organism. As Barker points out: "In Spencer this interpretation is confused. He did not really approach politics through science, without preconceptions drawn from other sources, and with the sole idea of eliciting the political lessons which science might teach. On the contrary, he was already charged with political preconceptions when he approached science, and sought to find in science examples or analogies to point out a moral already drawn and adorn a tale whose plot was already sketched. The fundamental confusion which he never surmounts is due to the fact that the *a priori* conceptions of individual rights with which he starts do not and cannot accord with the organic and evolutionary conception of the state which he attains through the use of natural science."[28]

On the whole, it is time that many of Spencer's doctrines have now outlived their usefulness, yet it is also true that to a very great extent he reflected the spirit of his age."[29] Spencer's various theories are certainly full of inconsistencies and confusion, but it is all due to existence of two different and incompatible systems in his political philosophy. In the field of political thought Spencer ranks as a great champion of individual liberty in an age of growing collectivism. He made an attempt to liberalise individual faculties to limit the functions of the state and to decentralise power. It is because the final political liberties "were not worth sacrificing to subordinate economic

---

27. *Ibid.*, p. 466. Likewise, Garner observes : "So long as men live in groups, they will have collective want which can be satisfied only through state organisation, and hence there is no reason for believing that necessity for the state will ever disappear, or that the role which it now plays in the life of human societies will ever diminish." *Ibid.*, p. 465.

28. Barker, *op. cit.*, p. 71.

29. Ebenstein : *Great Political Thinkers*, p. 600.

securities."[30] To conclude with Barker: "On the whole, Spencer suited England; and on the assumption that a nation deserves the political theory which it gets, we may say that England deserved Spencer."[31]

QUESTIONS FOR EXERCISE

1. "Spencer brought social theories into relation with biological evolution, but he left the practical conclusions almost where they had been." Comment on the above showing (a) how Spencer brought social theories into relation to biological evolution; and (b) how he left the practical conclusions where they had been.
2. To what extent was the application of biological doctrine of evolution as applied by Herbert Spencer to the social science detrimental to the political thesis of individualism of nineteenth century?
3. Barker says that the Philosophy of Herbert Spencer is an incongruous mixture of Natural Rights and Physiological metaphor.
4. "Herbert Spencer attempted to combine in his social philosophy an extreme form of collectivism with an extreme faith in *laissez faire*." Discuss.
5. The Philosophy of Spencer begins as well as ends with a queer mixture of Natural Rights and organic allegories of the state. Comment on the statement.
6. How does Herbert Spencer reconcile his theory of innate rights of the individual with the organic theory of the state?
7. "Every man has a freedom to do all that he wills provided he infringes not the equal freedom of any other man" — Spencer. Discuss.
8. How far did Spencer succeed in his defence of *laissez faire* on the basis of biology?
9. How did Herbert spencer reconcile his individualism with the belief in the doctrine of organism? Compare and contrast the individualism of Spencer with that of John Stuart Mill.
10. "Herbert Spencer attempted to combine in his social philosophy an extreme form of collectivism with an extreme faith in *laissez faire*." Discuss.

30. Catlin : *A History of Philosophers*, p. 411.

31. *Op. cit.*, p. 54.

11

Psychological Thought and Thinkers

BAGEHOT (1826—1877)

Psychological Problem

Bagehot was the first English political philosopher who made a real psychological approach to political problems. Plato's conception of the philosophical ruler was based on his assumptions about men's nature. Machiavelli thought of man as egoistic. Hobbes thought him of selfish and of quarrelsome nature and Locke thought him to be of peaceful nature. Bagehot did not start with assumptions, but made them the object of study. The problem which he tried to solve was "Assuming the truth of the doctrine of natural selction, how are we to account for the momentous transition from the brute level of the struggle for existence to the human level of social organisation and co-operation." To Bagehot this traditional problem was the key to all subsequent development of the human race.

Bagehot wrote *Physics and Politics,* published in 1867. According to Hearnshaw, it was "a sociological footnote to the doctrines of evolution, prevailing in sixties." But according to Barker, this is a book which should be termed as *Psychology and Politics* instead of *Physics and Politics.*

POLITICAL PHILOSOPHY

Spencer tried to introduce theory of evolution in political philosophy but to connect biology with the political science is improper. According to Barker, "Her (nature's) fittest are measured by no canon of absolute worth, but by the relative canon of adaptation to conditions and nature's first will be law in any scale of human values if the conditions prevelent are not law. Her (nature's) law are simple statement of cruel facts, her rights are simply brutal powers. To import moral rights of freedom or equality into this sphere is meaningless." Thus, political problems can be tackled in a psychological rather than biological way. Bagehot was the pioneer in this field.

Stages of Social Development

1. Preliminary stage. This was the stage of non-polity. In this stage man was a creature of strong emotions. He had no tradition and no foresight. This stage corresponds to Hobbes's state of nature. During this period unconscious education modified his nature. Men started organising themselves into groups under some sort of leadership.

2. The stage of fixed polity or fighting age. With the development of some sort of leadership emerged the second stage in the process of social development. In this stage persons having a common descent united together and lived in groups more easily than those descending from a different ancestor. Different groups started fighting. In struggle for existence between rival groups those who were more united and better disciplined had an advantage over those lacking these qualities. In the second stage man brings two qualities of representation and family, and being disciplined in these two qualities he comes to the third stage.

3. The stage of fixed polity or the age of discussion. In this stage those groups will be successful which are well organised and well disciplined and for this it is necesary that there should be common code of conduct, common language and common ideas. Thus, Bagehot supported national integration. Those will survive who are most organised and integrated and this can be achieved through the unity of religion and state. In the words of Sabine, "To gain that obedience, primary condition is the identification, not the union but the sameness of what we now called church and state...what is therefore requisite is a single government regulating the whole human life. No division of power is endurable without danger and probably without destruction; the priest must not teach one thing and the King another. King must be priest, and prophet King, the two must say the same thing because they are the same."

Bagehot based his philosophy on imitation. He is of the opinion that imitation plays a greater part than reason.

In early stage, the quantity and not quality was vital. It was ruled by despots. In the second stage those groups survived in the struggle that were compact, well organized and best disciplined. To quote Bagehot, "Unless you can make a strong co-operative bond your society will be conquered and killed out by some other society which had such a bond. He found group bond in social custom of the group. The despots continued in second stage but in the third and final stage an element of democratic rule was introduced in the government. The individuals were allowed to discuss public affairs among themselves.

The English Constitution

Published in 1869 this book contained important contribution of Bagehot to political philosophy. He introduced a new method as he believed that the proper method to understand a constitution was to relate it to life and view it as a living object. "One of the great merits of this book is that it broke away from the old tradition of looking at the British System of government from the legal point of view and concentrated on its actual working. In this book, he not only described constitution, but gave introduction to the political ideas prevailing these days." His said "King has right to be consulted, right to advise and right to warn."

Critical Estimate

Bagehot was the first philosopher who introduced psychology in the political thought of modern period. He recognised the value of symbolism as force determining political behaviour. He brought home the difference between the parliamentary and presidential type of Govt. According to Dicey, "Bagehot has brought more knowledge of life and originality of mind to the elucidation of theory and practice of English politics than any other man since Burke." Bryce said : "If Bagehot had lived to apply his method he might have exercised almost as great an influence as that was exercised in the middle of 18th century by Montesquieu."

With the development of Sociology and Psychology, a new school of Political Thought came into existence. As Barker remarked, "If our forefathers used to think biologically, we think psychologically."

WILLIAM MCDOUGALL (1871—1938)

Born in 1871, McDougall studied at Cambridge, London and Oxford and then at Harvard and Duke Universities. According to him human conduct is determined by instinct, while reason plays a secondary role.

His Works

1. *Introduction to Social Psychology*
2. *The Group Mind*
3. *Social Psychology*
4. *Outlines of Psychology*
5. *On Character.*

POLITICAL IDEAS

According to McDougall, Psychology is a science of human behaviour. Politics can be useful and realistic only with the help of psychology. For this one should take into account human emotions and instincts. Man is a bundle of emotions. Reason follows the emotions. About the importance of instincts McDougall writes, "Take away these instinctive dispositions with their powerful impulses and the organism would become incapable of activity of any kind, would be inert and motionless like a wonderful clock work whose main springs have been removed or steam engine, whose fire has been withdrawn. These impulses are the mental forces that maintain and shape all the life of individuals and societies and in them we are confronted with the central mystery of life, mind and will."

Definition of Instinct

Defining instinct, McDougall calls it, "An inherited or innate psychophysical disposition which determines its possessor to perceive, and to pay attention to, objects of a certain class, to experience an emotional excitement of a particular quality upon perceiving such an object, and to act in regard to it in a particular manner, or at least, to experience an impulse to such an action." As has been pointed out in the above definition, instinct generated behaviour tends to concentrate a person's attention on some particular objects. There are therefore three stages in instinctive action — Cognitive, Affective and Conative. With every instinct a particular emotional excitement is felt. The following are the instincts and the related emotions :

MAJOR INSTINCTS

	Instinct (1)	*Emotion* (2)
1.	Escape	Fear
2.	Repulsion	Disgust
3.	Curiosity	Wonder
4.	Pugnacity	Anger
5.	Self-Assertion	Positive Self-feeling
6.	Self-Abasement	Subjection
7.	Parental	Tender Emotion

Besides the above mentioned instincts, McDougall mentioned some more of them in which the related emotional feeling is not quite as obvious. They are as follows :

8.	Gregariousness	Loneliness
9.	Acquisitiveness	Feeling of Ownership
10.	Constructiveness	Feeling of Creativeness
11.	Food Seeking	Appetite
12.	Sex	Lust
13.	Appeal	Distress
14.	Laughter	Amusement

According to McDougall these instincts are affected by the intelligence. The variety in their expression is due to the intelligence of the human individual. With the exception of laughter all the other instincts are found both in human beings and animals. Among them, the acquired tendencies such as self-assertion, self-abasement, parental and gregariousness are not universal. Sex, escape, curiosity and laughter etc., are practically universal and innate. Food seeking tendencies are found in all animals because all of them seek food. Similarly, the constructive tendency is found in men as well as in animals. To acquisitiveness, the quality of universality cannot be attributed though it is found in quite a number of living beings. Calling for help in times of danger and seeking help has its own biological importance and is a tendency possessed by all creatures. As a result of this, members of the group or the family come to the assistance of the victim. The tendency to avoid an undesired and detested object and to feel a repulsion for it is obvious in almost all creatures.

Major instincts play a major part and provide all the primary motives necessary for the family, social grouping, and for war, religion and all other social activities. Instincts were not acquired by the individual, but were handed down to him by heredity.

McDougall did not agree with Bentham that all human actions could be interpreted in terms of self-interest. According to him actions of man are not governed by any unitary desire, but by the manifold and complex tendencies of his nature.

McDougll's book "*The Group Mind*" can be said a reincarnation of Plato's *Republic* but with new psychological outlook.

According to McDougall, organised social aggregate has a separate entity and distinct individuality of its own. As group has a mental system of its own with individual minds as units, the group mind develops laws of its own and acts as a substantial unit. To quote him again, "A society when it enjoys a long life and becomes highly organised, acquires a structure and quality which are largely independent of the qualities of the individual who enter into its composition and take part for a brief time in life."

McDougall believed that, the nation is a people or population which enjoys some degrees of political independence and possessed national mind of character. Its essence is psychic, its mental organisation gives it effective group life. It has a definite character different from any individual or all individual characters taken together. Homogeneity is necessary for such a mind. Following facts are necessary for homogeneity:

1. A common race.
2. Freedom of communication among members.
3. Eminent leaders.
4. A well defined common purpose.
5. Long continuity of existence.
6. Organisation of national mind.
7. National self-consciousness.
8. Emulation with other nations.

Idea of nations, according to McDougall, binds the individuals together. It is a sentiment and emulates affective aspects. In U.K., U.S.A. and France an approach was being made to reconcile individuality with collectivity and consequently the executive was subordinated to the legislature. The ideal organisation was that which permitted the best minds to exercise their greatest influence. Public opinion was the expression of moral judgement of the national mind as defined by its leaders. Thus, Mcdougall's irrationalism lead him to worship of a national state and towards aristocratic leadership.

Evaluation

McDougall enriched the study of political science by his psychological contribution. However, there is little similarity between him and Plato. But he can be credited to have introduced psychological ideas in political thought.

IMPACT OF PSYCHOLOGY

Spencer introduced biology and evolutionary theory in politics. Kar Zacheria discussed the chemistry, mechanics, psychology and biology of the state. Valagraf combined the psychic and biological conception of the state. Bluntschli insisted on the living and organic character of the state.

Upto the middle of 19th century, biology and its theory of evolution dominated the political thought. In the beginning of 20th century the social and political philosophers increasingly sought help of psychology. Psychological concepts like will and reason, customs and tradition, instinct and impulse, became current coins for social and political thinkers in their study of the causes and phenomena of social and political growth. Bagehot, Graham Wallas, Mc-Dougall, Norman Angel and Miss Follet became pioneer in this respect. According to Barker, psychology has become the fashion of the day. If our fathers thought biologically, we think psychologically. No political theory can be adequate or scientific which does not take proper consideration of human nature. For realisation of the solution of moral, industrial and educational problems, psychological approach is necessary. The psychological approach to political problems was made by Gabrial Trade (1843-1904). Emile Durkheim (1858-1917) in France and older psychologists led by Lester F. Ward in U.S.A.

Older political thinkers adopted Aristotle's psychology and its division of reason, passion and concupiscence. The systematic study of individual psychology is a recent growth. Formerly, Aristotle thought that passions cloud reason. Reason is marked by precise thinking, but human mind is liable to be corrupted by the influence of fewer faculties of which the second one is passion or emotion.

Modern psychologists Sigmund Freud, C.J. Jung and William Reich developed the psychology of the unconscious and of unity of mental functions. William James and John Dewey proved that the human organism acts as a unity and it is impossible to separate the organic, emotional and rational functions of the mind. This idea gave a death blow to the value of reason which previously dominated the political thought. Psychologists proved that men are guided more by passion than by reason.

While French revolutionaries tried to introduce the worship of reason, the British empiricists considered reason as a slave of passion. But even they thought that reason possesses an independent and self-subsistent existence. They hold this belief even now though it had been discarded in America and European continent.

Conclusions of Psychologists

1. As per old political thinkers, state embodied reason. They wanted to unleash reason to give it full scope but now psychologically, those ideas cannot be accepted. The psychologists showed the complexity of mind. It is difficult to predict how man would behave in particular circumstances. Psychologists also brought home the importance of propaganda and education as factors in politial control and importance of emotions, slogans and sentiments.

2. Psychologists are of the opinion that men generally did not act in a rational manner, but their thinking is determined by unconscious motives and instincts. Political leaders realised that they had to cater to the instincts and impulses of the people without surrendering to them. Their prejudices should be taken into account. Leaders of democratic countries follow double policy of catering the people's prejudices for their purposes. To make this duplicitous dealing successful, specialists in propaganda and persuasion are in great demand. Graham Wallas showed the importance of rational control and guidance to save from this unconscious motivation.

3. Psychologically man is never fully rational except in abstract matters. Reason and emotions go together. Emotional feelings, rational feelings and rational functions influence one another. Sentiments and passions guide the reasoning of a human being.

4. New political thought attempts to discuss actual political behaviour and phenomena to analyse them and to draw lessons from them. McDougall and Trotter were pioneer in this field.

Conclusions of Social Psychologists

1. Trotter. Man is a gregarious animal. The innate tendencies towards self-preservation, nutrition and reproduction are essentially egoistic but animal herd requires homogeneity of self to survive. So man brought the instinct of living in assembly with others from the prehuman state. In human group life, this instinct functions as intellectual process. Action in harmony with other is much more comfortable than action in opposition to them. Adherence to group ideas appears reasonable because mankind rationalizes the subconsciously derived ideas of social prominence. Emotions as well as ideas are fixed by the gregarious relationship to an overwhelming degree.

In politics whenever an idea or project, be it war or peace, can be identified with the accepted herd principles. External as well as internal relations in modern nation are guided by appeals to the group consciousness of its members.

2. Ross. American sociologist Ross shows a tendency to a greater emphasis on social facts and lesser emphasis on the individual or logical facts.

3. William Graham Sumner. He is of the opinion that man survives through group struggle like other animals.

4. Freud. According to Freud and his followers, the original nature of man consists of certain "egoistic impulses". These impulses are circumscribed by the assumed necessities of social life as expressed in folkways, mores and customs. Social norms clash with original tendencies. To avoid clashes the impulses are submerged by the automatic machanism of human mind reappearing in dreams and in various disguises. The neuroses and psychoses are a result of the incapacity of mind to make an effective expression of the impulses in the presence of social forces repressing them. Thus, the new dynamic psychology is of great value in explaining behavioural tendencies of man in society. Freud emphasized on importance of sex as a guiding factor in human life.

Desires and interests common to members of group can be rationalized first in the individual but when the form of rationalization is fixed by group acceptance when it returns to the individual stamped with the approach of the herd then it has all sanction that is needful to give the force of self-evident incontrovertible truth. Clever politicians ascertain the desires and offer "sound" reasons for their satisfaction.

5. Cooley, Lippman and Miss Follet. They made valuable contributions to the application of social psychology to political problems by way of indicating the difficulties of executing democracy in modern national states. The basic democratic ideas of justice, loyalty, sympathy, truth, freedom and lawfulness were developed in face to face relations. Lippman pleads that wrong or dubious information is dangerous. Man interprets all development with his inadequate mental apparatus, namely his stereotypes which he has developed. Reliable information may serve as the basis of an adequate and intelligent public opinion in a democratic society. Miss Follet urges for greater recognition to group life and activities while guarding against the dangers of localism by an effective federal system.

Social psychology can be applied only in social behaviour. Political behaviour is to be studied in group and not in its individual aspects. Both historical and statistical facts should be used for drawing conclusions. Thus, social psychology has brought many facts and valuable information which is helpful in political science.

Social psychologists have also thrown light on political pathology as of sick societies like fascism and Nazism which is treated as form of political and social sickness.

While psychological thinking dominated political thought now outside factors such as the social, physical environments, the economic conditions, climate and culture have to be taken into accounts as all these factors affect human mind. Among these factors economic factor is the most important. Today psychological approach has been superseded by the economic approach. The political thought of a man is influenced by his environment or work through which he earns his livelihood. Capitalism, socialism and communism all indicate importance of economics in politics as cash nexus rules the world.

QUESTIONS FOR EXERCISE

1. Give a critical analysis of the psychological ideas of Bagehot. How does he connect Psychology and Physics with Politics?
2. "A society when it enjoys a long life and becomes highly organised acquires a structure and qualities which are largely independent of the qualities of the individuals who enter into its composition and take part for a brief time in life" — McDougall. Explain.
3. "McDougall's irrationalism leads him to a worship of the national state, it also leads him to advocate aristocratic leadership and control of the state" — McGovern. Explain.

4. "Ever since Bagehot wrote *Physics and Politics*, Political theorists have turned social psychologists." Explain the importance of psychological approach to political problems in 20th century.
5. Discuss the strength and weakness of psychological approach to the problems of the state. To what extent has the psychological approach been superseded by the economic approach in recent political thought?
6. "If our fathers thought biologically, we think psychologically" — Barker. Explain.
7. What is the meaning of Barker's assertion that political philosophers of the present era approach political problems from the psychological point of view? How far is this approach correct or wrong? Is there any other point which has eclipsed in importance the psychological approach to political problems?

12

Graham Wallas (1856—1932)

Born in 1858 in a clergyman's family. Graham Wallas received his education at Shrewsbury School and Corpus Christi College, Oxford. He started as a school teacher, but later on became a famous scholar. He was partly instrumental in the foundation of the London School of Economics. He was appointed head of the department of Political Science in that School and taught for about 30 years. On his retirement, he was succeeded by Prof. Harold J. Laski. Wallas served for about twenty years on the Senate of the London University and made valuable contributions towards its administration. As a member of the London School Board, the London County Council and the Royal Commission on Civil Service, he showed his interest in practical politics.

Graham Wallas' important works are *Human Nature in Politics* (1908), *The Great Society* (1914) and *Our Social Heritage* (1921). All these sought to interpret political phenomenon in terms of psychological forces. According to Graham Wallas, politics is largely "a matter of subconscious processes of habit and instinct, suggestion and imitation," and only slightly of conscious reason. Although in his later writings, Wallas discussed the organization of thought and will, and gave more attention to the rational element in political psychology, his approach was anti-intellectual. In order to study politics in a psychological context Wallas emphasized the necessity of a new approach to the study of politics. He changed from the qualitative to the quantitative methods of argument. Rockow has rightly said, "While Professor McDougall is Platonic, Professor Graham Wallas is obviously an Aristotelian."[1]

Though Graham Wallas received a lot of help from books on psychology, he based his conclusions on material derived from his own experience as a teacher, administrator and practical politician, and also from the accounts of the thought processes of his students and friends in England and America. He says, "My main material has been derived from my experience, during more than 40 years, as a teacher and administrator, and from the accounts of their thought-processes given by poets and others who were not professed psychologists, by some of my students and by friends in England and America." Graham

1. *Contemporary Political Thought in England,* Chapter on G. Wallas.

pondered as to how far the knowledge accumulated by modern psychology could be made useful for the improvement of thought-processes for a working thinker.

QUANTITATIVE METHOD IN POLITICS

Wallas said that the people who follow the quantitative method in politics they will not face disappointment in their day-to-day affairs. Larger and more exact collections of detailed political facts were being accumulated every year. Whether carried on by permanent officials or Royal Commissions or Cabinet Ministers the intellectual work of preparing legislation took every year a more quantitative and less qualitative form.

According to Wallas, the method followed by the Commission on Poor Law of 1833-34 was in *a priori* form. It is admirably illustrated by indicating that labouring men will not exert themselves unless they are offered the alternative of starvation or rigorous confinement, though no attempt is made to estimate the proportion of the working population of England whose character and conduct is represented by such instance. The Poor Law Commission of 1905 was driven to new lines. It did not assume that human energy is dependent solely on the working of the human will in the presence of the ideas of pleasure and pain. It was forced to tabulate and consider innumerable quantitative observations relating to the very many factors affecting the will of paupers and possible paupers. After the commissions of 1834 and 1905, it was to be considered whether men voted best in areas where they kept up habits of political action in connection with parliamentary as well as municipal contests, and whether an election involving other points besides poor law administration was more likely to create interest among the electorate.

HUMAN NATURE IN POLITICS

On the basis of his keen observations of different political situations in England and elsewhere, Wallas concluded that "the study of politics is just now (1908) in a curiously unsatisfactory position."[2] The expectations aroused in the minds of thinking people had not been fulfilled. The actual working of democracy was due to defective political institutions, to restricted franchise and inadequate education. Wallas believed that enough attention had not been paid to the facts of human nature. His work was an attempt to interpret political phenomena in terms of psychological forces rather than in terms of form and structure. The fundamental forces considered were those of Intelligence, Love and Happiness. His work was suggestive rather than conclusive, but it inspired and stimulated further inquiry."[3]

According to Wallas the study of politics must not be separated from the study of human nature. His works were attempts at overcoming the separation between the two. The student of politics must deal with the full man who is

2. *Human Nature in Politics* (opening paragraph).

3. Lippmann, Walter, *Preface in Politics, Public Opinion,* and other works.

a creature "compact of emotions, impulses and instincts as well as conscious reason." If the political doctrines are based on the view of man as a rational being whose every act is the result of an intellectual process by which he "first thinks of some end which he desires and then calculates the means by which that end can be attained," he would have to leave aside his text-books and change his views while dealing with practical issues. Wallas asked his readers to do away with the intellectual fallacy, and overcome their "tendency to exaggerate the intellectuality of mankind." If a faithful record of all that an individual did and said in the course of a day were to be studied, we would find that a very small number of activities were a result of a deliberate search for the means of attaining ends. Most of them would be found to be half-conscious repetitions, under the influence of habit. Thus, politics must "legally be a matter of subconscious process of habit and instinct, suggestion and imitation" and "only in a slight degree the product of conscious reason." This is contrast to the rationalistic and collectivistic approaches of Hobhouse and Clifford. In *Human Nature in Politics* Graham Wallas suggests that reason has little to do with the whole process. The secret of politics, lies in man's suggestibility, his habits and emotions. The emotional or 'suggestive' power of the symbols my country, my party, my nation is the real basis on which politics rests and by which it operates.

Wallas described the most important of impulses and instincts, affection or love; fear and the desire for property, the fighting instinct and the instincts of suspicion, curiosity, and the desire to excel. Intelligence and the desire for happiness are also fundamental forces shaping human life. Graham Wallas was not an irrationalist. He did not exclude reason or intelligence completely from political life. He simply drew attention to the fundamental role played by subconscious factors. According to him, the "empirical art of politics consists largely in the creation of opinion by the deliberate exploitation of subconscious non-rational inference." In his later writings, he gave more attention to the rational element in the psychology of politics.

HUMAN POLITICAL BEHAVIOUR

According to Graham Wallas human political behaviour is influenced by psychological equipment and political environment which is subject to constant change. New political entities and new habits of thought and feeling come into existence and shape political behaviour. The national flag, national anthem and political parties are the chief political entities round which develop habits of thought and feeling, may have intellectual origins; but to the mass of people they are something more than bare ideas. They are 'emotion-charged and emotion-making names'. The appeal to emotions is the stock-in-trade of all skilled political leaders."[4] Emotions tend to associate themselves with certain political slogans, or with a party. "White Supremacy" in the Southern States, "The Party of Lincoln", "Jeffersonian Democracy", "The Grand Old Party",

4. *Human Nature in Politics*, Chap. II.

are all symbols which arouse in the appropriate hearer a complex of feeling and impulse which are sufficient for all practical purposes.

Graham Wallas indicated the manner in which party leaders are able to make an emotional appeal to the citizens through party symbols and shibboleths, reducing the critical capacity of the voters and making them easy victims of the party propaganda.[5] This most clearly manifest during elections. Each party coins a few slogans and makes them emotional symbols. Great efforts are made to create public opinion by a deliberate appeal to the emotional suggestibility of the people. Thus, elections become 'psychological orgies' and 'exercises in spell-binding.' "The party names and symbols, the party colours, placards and songs are all let loose on the suggestibility of the electorate."

VOTING BEHAVIOUR

According to Wallas that in politics men act under the immediate stimulus of affection and instinct. Affection and interest may be directed towards political entities. When people form inferences, results of their political actions, they do so, in a non-rational way not by a process of reasoning. Their minds act like a harp, "all of whose strings throb together; so that emotions, impulse, inference, are often simultaneous and intermingled aspects of a single mental experience." This non-rational character of man's mental processes is heightened when he act in excitement and as a part of a crowd. According to Wallas, so far as their mental and intellectual life is concerned, a great majority of people live under the conditions of a crowd. They substitute non-rational for rational inference. Urbanization has increased this tendency manifold. The radio, the press and the cinema do this work too well. The excitement caused everywhere during World War II and the manner in which President Roosevelt induced the people of the U.S.A. to enter it were excellent illustrations of the way in which suggestion and sympathetic excitement influence public opinion. Graham Wallas revealed the subtle and pervasive way in which public opinion is formed by non-rational processes.

According to Wallas, there was a great disparity between actual democracy and the intellectual assumptions of the eighteenth and nineteenth century philosophers of democracy. Politicians exploit names, images and symbols to secure the votes of the people. Voting for a particular party does not indicate that one has given it after an impartial examination of the whole problem. Votes are given as the name of a particular party arouses the sympathy of the voter. Sometimes clever posters do the trick. Elections are floods of mass suggestions. The electorate can be hypnotized by the popular press, drugged with advertisements, deafened by the boosting of the business candidates. It can be influenced by centralized mass suggestion, exercised through all the organs which form and control public opinion, into condoning and even encouraging a polity of hatred and passion of which each individual would be ashamed in his private capacity in his private capacity.

---

5. *Ibid.*

The arguments of Graham Wallas cut the ground from under the feet of the democrat. Education of the people is no remedy; Instead of minimizing the evil, it tends to maximize it. Elementary education given to the voter leaves him or her at the mercy of the clever manipulator of the public opinion.

Social Improvement from Social Invention

However, Graham Wallas was not anti-democrat. he did not advise the people to leave everything to the most intellectual persons. He argued that the best intellects may themselves be the victims of suggestion; leaving matters to them would not necessarily improve matters. Moreover, "government without consent is a complicated and ugly process." The remedy lies in the gradual extension of the sphere in which intelligence can play a greater role in politics. Man must increase the part to be played by reason in the management of his common business. Modern psychology must offer a much truer, though a more complex conception of human nature on which the politician can build. With the help of new quantitative methods, political thinkers would be able to state their problems more fully and answer them with greater accuracy than in the past. These tendencies may enable us to develop a new political science. Wallas "looks forward to improvement by education, and he looks forward to guidance rendered effective by a clearer perception of the impulses upon which men and women act. Perhaps, an election will become more and more the educational process for which he, like Mill, ardently hopes."[6] Wallas hoped that the name of Humanity might become charged with emotion and come to have as much emotional effect as the national flag, national anthem and party labels possessed at the present time. As a great optimist, he expected much in the way of social improvement from 'social invention'. He laid stress on deliberate plans of social control and direction. He attempted to give a more socialized content to the doctrines of political liberty and natural rights.

'SOCIAL EQUALITY' IN DEMOCRACY

Successful operation of democracy depends upon the acquisition and dissemination of knowledge, for efficient participation of individuals in group affairs, either directly or under the guidance of leaders. Lippmann, Lowell, Zueblin, Cooley, Dicey, Ellwood, Follett, Godkin, A.B. Hall, Mecklin and Wallas have given special attention to the subjects of public opinion and education. The works of Lippmann and Wallas particularly emphasized the unconscious factors that play a prominent part. They insisted that man's human nature must be considered as a factor in all discussion of political activity in a democracy.

Wallas saw that though the representative government constantly growing, but nowhere is it a complete success, Bentham's theory ignores the importance of the unconscious drives to behaviour without consideration of which the problems of democracy cannot be squarely met.[7] The success of democracy,

6. Murray, R.H. : *The History of Political Science from Plato to the Present*, New York (1929).

7. *Human Nature and Politics*, p. 22.

which include the idea of social equality,[8] demands that political faith be strengthened, combating the domination of the unconscious upon which the unscrupulous leaders can play to obtain their own ends.[9] Wallas advocated reform of the electoral systems so that an election would become the agency for forming an intelligent opinion. Wallas urged the social organization of thought as a method of attaining a more rational basis of behaviour.[10]

DOCTRINE OF LIBERTY

Wallas considered liberty highly essential for the successful working of democracy. Any socialized theory of liberty should provide, for the conscious and organized will to use them. Liberty is a positive as well as a negative concept. According to Wallas, the Periclean notion of liberty was far more helpful than the negative definitions of John Stuart Mill and Sidney Webb. He did not favour empty individualism of J.S. Mill. Whenever he discussed individual liberty, he remembered social needs.

POLITICAL REFORMS

Wallas considered the present working of government as burdensome and uncreative. He pointed out to the discrepancy between the structure and functions of government.[11] Present human mind has failed to develop proper forms of co-operative thought to keep pace with the governing complexity of social life. The committees, municipal councils and the House of Commons are not true to their purpose of group deliberation. Thinking is done in small groups of party leaders or of individual members, in correspondence and interviews between members and responsible officials. Any reform at improving the capacity for deliberation of democratic institutions must recognize the complexity of legislative problems and the existence of forms of impersonal means of communication. The House of Commons may be forced to diminish its membership. It may abolish the Committee of the Whole House. The Cabinet will have to rely on the work of committees. The size of the local bodies has to be reduced. The House of Lords must assume the nature of a Royal Commission.

According to Wallas, changes should be made in the civil service in order to increase the possibilities of creative thought on their part. They should be prevented from the spirit of narrow professionalism. The spirit of originality should be encouraged. If civil administration is to be humanized, great opportunities should be given to officials for creative thought. They should make public investigation of some public matters. They should made oral reports to parliamentary or cabinet committees. Their reports on the working of departments should be signed by them.

---

8. *Ibid.*, p. 231.
9. *Ibid.*, pp. 206 ff.
10. *Ibid.*, pp. 185 ff, *The Great Society*, Chap. XI.
11. *Ibid.*, Chap. VIII.

NATIONALITY AND INTERNATIONAL ORGANISATION

Graham Wallas devoted his attention to the problems of nationality and international organization. A great majority of sociologists agree that the sovereign national state cannot be regarded as the final stage in political evolution. Some form of international organization would eliminate national wars in a manner similar to that in which the national state has ended neighbourhood and sectional conflicts. In his latest book, *Our Social Heritage*, Wallas asserted that society and civilization cannot long endure unless some adequate method is found to avert the destructive wars of the modern era. Wallas made a number of suggestions about how to build up reaction patterns founded upon international co-operation rather than national egoism and rivalry.[12]

CONTRIBUTION TO POLITICAL THOUGHT

Graham Wallas was a great humanitarian, a democrat and a rationalist. According to him, democracy in practice may be pretty bad, but at least it is better than government by an irresponsible dictator or oligarchy, and the one or the few are apt to be as irrational as the many. Wallas was optimistic that mankind though normally irrational, may be trained or educated to act more or less rationally. Wallas' work is concerned with discovering effective methods of substituting rational control of social processes for the unreasoning group action of the herd within the democratic framework. Graham Wallas wielded great influence. His writings won for him a very high place in the literature of politics. Most of the books on politics make a reference to his works. His quantitative method is followed everywhere.

QUESTIONS FOR EXERCISE

1. Describe in brief the main political ideas of Graham Wallas.
2. Write an essay on impact or Psychology on Political Science with special reference to the contribution of Graham Wallas.
3. Describe briefly the psychological approach to political problems with special reference to Graham Wallas and add a short criticism.
4. "Wallas lays stress upon the fact that politics is only in a slight degree the product of conscious reason. He agrees that it is largely a matter of sub-conscious process, of habit and instinct, of suggestion and limitation. He believes that the art of politics largely consists in the creation of opinion by a deliberate appeal to non-rational inference and the emotional suggestion" — Gettle. Explain in the light of this statement the main ideas of Graham Wallas.

---

12. *Our Social Heritage*, Chapters IX-XII.

13

Rise of Socialism

Socialism is the economic organisation in society in which the society has the right over all physical means which are controlled by representatives of the society who are responsible to society, and all the members of society have a right to obtain the profit of results of such a production conducted on a socialist basis. As stated in the 11th impression of the Encyclopedia Brittanica, socialism is "that policy or theory which aims at securing by the action of central democratic authority a better distribution than now prevails."

DEFINITION OF SOCIALISM

Some of the more popular definitions of socialism are as follows :

1. *G.D.H. Cole*. "Socialism denotes a classless society in which economic activities are directly conducted under public auspices on a basis of public ownership of the means of production and democratic control of the uses to which capital and labour are to be applied."

2. *Hughan*. "Socialism is a political movement to abolish exploitation by means of collective ownership and democratic management of the basic instruments of production and distribution."

3. *Sellers*. "Socialism is a democratic government whose purpose is to secure an economic organisation of society which will give the maximum possible, at any time of justice and liberty."

The following are the main institutions of socialism :

1. State ownership. In socialism, the state owns the entire wealth of the country comprising land, industry, means of transport and communication, banks, etc. It is the state which arranges social amenities like education, sanitation, health, recreation, etc.

2. Equality of opportunity. Socialism provides everyone with equal opportunities for progressing. No distinctions based on sex, caste, race or class are made among them.

3. Maximum distribution of national income. The national income is distributed among the maximum number in socialist societies. This does not allow extreme inequality in the income of people.

DEMOCRATIC SOCIALISM

Individualism and the theory of *laissez faire* was most popular, before the dawn of socialism and its spread in the west. Democratic or collective socialism regards state as a welfare institution devoted to the common cause of mankind. For social democrats, state is an agency which stands for better means and methods of distribution. Among others this school of thought found patronage from Robert Owen, Sidney, Harold Laski and G.D.H. Cole.

Till the close of 19th century individualism remained on the forefront, when it received set back with the spread of socialism. Socialism changed the very approach to every political problem and opened a new era both in politics and political science. It was seriously studied both in the East as well as the West. Socialism as expounded by Marx was gradually modified by several political thinkers. Democratic socialism became quite popular in England.

The state was regarded as a necessary evil by individualists. It was to be tolerated because there was no escape out of it. The interference of the state in human development should be reduced to the minimum. Democratic socialists or collectivists believed that the state was a welfare agency. It aimed to promote common good and moral, intellectual and economic development of the people.

COLLECTIVISM

Objectives

The objectives of Democratic Socialism differ from country to country, however, following are the objectives which it will like to achieve.

1. Collective social interest. Narrow individual interest should be given a subordinate position over collective social interests.

2. Opposed to free trade. Collectivists are opposed to the idea of free trade. The trade should be so regulated that no individual is exploited and community welfare is promoted.

3. Cooperation rather than competition. There should be cooperation rather than competition in the society. All energies should be used for collective welfare rather than wastage.

4. Co-operation between employer and employee. There should be co-operation between the employer and the employee.

5. No concentration of wealth. Wealth should not be allowed to get concentrated in the hands of only few individuals.

6. Reduction of inequalities of wealth. Inequalities in wealth should be reduced by progressive means of taxation.

7. Community control on means of production. There should be community control over all means of production which should be used for collective good.

8. Freedom of life. Every individual should be left free to have his own way of life.

9. Rights guaranteed. Civil, political and economic rights should be guaranteed for all.

10. Freedom of religion. Every one should be permitted to follow his own faith.

11. Democracy. There should be democracy not only in political but in social and eocnomic fields as well.

12. Abolition of private property. Private property should be abolished as it is a common source of exploitation.

13. Social needs. Social needs should determine the quality and quantity of goods to be produced.

14. Public sector. Important services and industries should be brought under public control.

15. Motive of social service. Social service and not private profit should be the motive in so far as industry is concerned.

POLITICAL PHILOSOPHY OF SIDNEY WEBB

Sidney Webb joined Fabian School of Thought in 1885, a year after the formation of Fabian Society. He became one of the prominent and leading members of this new philosophy. He was assigned the task of writing '*Socialist Essay*' along with four other authors. He did full justice to the task. He was a moving figure of his party. He influenced the course of legislation of his times. Following was his political philosophy:

1. Historical progress of democracy. History demonstrates irresistible progress of democracy and continuous progress of socialism. Webb pleaded that aristocracy had given birth to extended suffrage and also to universal adult franchise. Introduction and development of democracy was testimony to the fact that the world was heading towards socialism.

2. Socialism. In the field of industry, Webb said that a transformation on socialistic lines was gradually coming and that socialism was bound to come. According to him joint stock and corporate enterprises were largely replacing individual management. Coker has expressed the philosophy of Webb by saying that, "The owners of property are, no longer, as they were under the domestic system of production, managers of the business to which they devote their property."

3. In favour of capitalism. As regards capitalist system, Webb agreed that capital was neither a theft nor an evil. It was not an institution which retarded national progress. It was only an agency for exploiting the poor and living on the profits earned by others. The capitalist was not the superintendent of industry. He was no longer an entrepreneur. He earned because he spent money and invested that in the business. He earns because he manages the affairs of business and takes pains in that.

4. Dangers of large scale industry. Webb was of the opinion that individual responsibility has been destroyed due to large scale business. It has also given a great set back to economic individualism. Large scale industry was a specific danger to democracy though it has the advantage of checking waste etc. The world was confronted with this serious problem.

5. Extensive state control. Webb favoured the idea of gradual extension of government control over industry which, for him, was the best solution of the problem. By extensive control the state shall be in a position to promote the welfare of the people and deliver the goods.

6. Revolution. As a Fabian, Webb was of the view that revolution was no solution to the problem and that such a step was bound to create social upheaval and disorder. In order to have orderly development it was essential that the changes should be gradually introduced so that there was no serious dislocation in existing social, economic and political set up.

7. State. Webb did not believe that the state was an instrument for the exploitation of the poor. It was not an agency which sided with one class to suppress the other. It was an effective and useful instrument, if at all there was any defect in the working of the state agency that should be improved by peaceful methods. The state should be completely utilised for collective welfare.

8. Democracy. Webb had faith in democratic set up. He did not agree with the idea that democratic devices have been set up to help the landed or propertied classes. Democratic institutions were the best agencies for the development of a nation. Democracy is the method for controlling state activities. If suffrage was properly exercised and used, the state could not misuse its authority. Webb stood for the promotion of democracy and democratic institutions.

9. Parliamentary form of government. Webb favoured parliamentary form of government. It should be solely and perfectly responsible to the people and the electorates.

10. His influence. Sidney was perhaps the only one person who considerably influenced national legislation during his life time. The labour Party of England is indebted to him for writing its constitution. He was also one of the cabinet minister in the first labour cabinet.

COLLECTIVISM OR STATE SOCIALISM

Collectivism is a form of socialism which rose as reaction against extreme individualism of 19th century. It is an imposing word to be set over against individualism. Its essence can be put in these words: "That the competitive system assures the happiness and comfort of the few at the expense of the suffering of many and that the society must be reconstituted in such a manner as to secure the general welfare and happiness."

Broadly, collectivism is a term for a trend in social development, a programme of economic reform, a theory of general welfare, and a utopian order for mankind, technically a general label for comprehensive schemes of authoritative control such as socialism, communism, syndicalism and Bolshevism; and specifically a name for the trend away from the extreme *laissez faire* of the 19th century. Collectivist principles can be found in the work of Edward Berstein in Germany. Jean Juares in France, Karl banting in Sweden and Edward Anseel. For improving social goods, as against the individual good advocated by individualists; for getting rid of evils of capitalism, private property and competition; Collectivist consider state as a positive good, which can be employed to serve the collective good. Collectivist firmly believe that the state action alone can remove exploitation and promote social welfare. According to Coker, "Collectivism is as vague a word as Individualism for the socialist doctrines of economic determinism labour created values and class war." He recognises that differences in wealth create divisions of the community into different and often opposing political groups. But he discredits the doctorine of a clear cut distinction of classes and continual antagonism between them.

COLLECTIVISM

Definition

1. *Prof. C.E.M. Joad.* "Collectivism is that form of social theory which through the actions of central democratic authority want a better distribution and in subordination there to a better production of wealth than is now possible."

2. *Encyclopaedia of Social Sciences.* "Collectivism is the imposing word to be set out against individualism. It is broadly a term for a trend in social development...a programme of economic reform, a theory of general welfare and utopian order for mankind; technically a general level for comprehensive scheme of authoritative control such as socialism, communism, syndicalism and specifically a name for the trend away from the extreme *laissez faire* of the 19th century."

Characteristics

1. Society for Collective Interests. Collectivism is a social theory as it aims at bringing into existence a new type of society. The present society is not based on sound economic principles. It protects the interests of only few individuals and as such should be changed. It should aim at bringing about a new type of society.

2. Central State. The collectivists stipulate a central state. The state will act for the welfare of all and not for few individuals or any particular section of society. It will not be a bureaucratic state.

3. Change Through Legislation. Legislative measures will be the only method for bringing about changes in the authority of the state. All changes will be brought about by democratic means and methods and not with the use of either violence or hatred. The use of force is condemned.

4. Anti-Capitalism. According to collectivists capitalist system has very much degenerated the means of production and distribution. The new society will change the whole system. Capitalist control over the means of production will end and means of production and distribution will be controlled by the society. It will be a system in which workers will take more and more interest in the work which they do. The work will increase both qualitatively and quantitatively. The profits will not go to few individuals but to the society as a whole. Wealth of the society will increase and will also be evenly distributed. The workers will get a share in profit in proportion to the functions which they will perform.

Collectivism is thus an evolutionary doctrine which aims at removing all the evils which capitalism is alleged to have introduced in the society. It seeks to wipe out from the society both starvation as well as poverty. All should work, when there is work to do.

Prof. Hearnshaw's Views

According to Prof. F.J.C. Hearnshaw following are the main objectives of collectivists :

1. Individual should be downgraded and community exalted.
2. Private enterprises should be extinct.
3. There should be expropriation of the landlords.
4. All competitions should be eliminated.
5. Capitalism should be brought to an end.
6. There should be equalisation of human conditions.

Hearnshaw was convinced that many social evils will come to an end if capitalism is brought to an end. There will be neither competition nor selfishness nor wastage. It will be a new society governed by the principle of unity, economic justice and social service. Work and worth of each individual will then be appreciated in the society. Each will work according to his capacity and paid according to his ability. There will be no exploitation of man by the man nor that of natural resources by few individuals for profit making purposes or for their comforts and happiness.

Prof. Ely's Views

As Prof. Ely points out, a collectivist is "a person who looks to society organised in the state for aid in bringing about a more perfect distribution of economic good and an elevation of humanity." Collectivism has following objectives :

1. To abolish private ownership of the means of production.

2. To bring the main industries and services under public control and ownership.

3. To press industry in serving the needs of the community as a whole and not the interests of few.

4. To eliminate the incentive of private profit in favour of the motive of social service.

5. To bring the possession and control of the chief factors of production under the control of democratic authority and not under private capitalists or workers. Nationalised means of production are to be under democratic control. Values in society are created by society and therefore the whole society should have them. This is to ensure better production and better distribution of wealth. There should be a national minimum wage for workers and equal pay for equal work. Collectivists desire to reduce inequality in income by introducing a highly progressive system of income tax. Hence, this type of socialism is called state socialism. It differs from syndicalism and guild socialism.

Methods of Collectivism

The collectivists believe in evolutionary methods and not in revolutionary changes. Gradualness is the key word of the collectivists. Thus, collectivism differs from communism as follows:

1. C.E.M. Joad says "True to the biological conception of society as a social organism, collectivist socialists have insisted that society is capable only of gradual change, and that each change must be conditioned by the nature of the social structure that proceeded it. From this point of view it is essential to start with what exists and allow the present to decide the direction, as well as the rapidity of the steps which are taken in the future."

2. The existing state is not be overthrown but it is to be utilised for making the proposed change.

3. Those who hold collectivist views should disseminate their ideas and try to capture power. They should employ all political, constitutional and educational methods to prepare a ground for an evolutionary change.

4. Collectivists should organize a party of their own which must have a majority in the legislature. It is only if that can form a government and introduce the necessary legislation for making collectivism a reality.

5. Unlike communists the collectivists are for the ballot box and are against the bullets. Thus, they support democratic ideals.

Collectivists have a well planned programme and also definite constructive proposals with regard to the future set up. They stand for the universal enforcement for the national minimum wage. It is the business of the state to prevent unemployment, Not only all the factors of production are to be nationalised, these are also to be put under democratic control.

The state socialists aim at bringing about a revolution in the national income. They stand for a highly progressive system of income tax. All the income will go to the National Fund. It will be spent in a way which is most conducive to the betterment of society and for the welfare of masses.

Collectivists justify their plans on many grounds. Nationalisation of industries is absolutely necessary, if the interests of the public at large are to be safe-guarded. They plead for "the state ownership of land and producer's capital as the means of absorbing for the public, both interest and the various forms of economic rents." There will be no wasteful advertisement of competition.

Justification of Collectivism

1. Under state socialism, all the free gifts of nature will be conserved for the future happiness of men.

2. All collectivist states will be guided by the consideration of service motive.

3. There will be more unity and the principles of social service; social usefulnes, and love of activity will be followed.

4. Changes can be only gradual and not violent.

5. The defect of the prevailing political structure can be got rid of only through collectivism.

6. Collectivism assures the welfare of all, while capitalism provides comforts and conveniences only to a few rich persons, it assures comforts to all.

7. The present political, social and economic structure brings about starvation in the name of the sanctity of private property and contract but actually these things bring untold sufferings on poor persons.

8. Natural gifts should be owned by state to make the best use of them in the interests of all.

9. Industry should be state owned so that it can cater to the needs of all.

10. Under capitalism goods are produced with the profit motive, but under state socialism service motive will replace the profit motive. Thus, they support social welfare instead of private gain.

Criticism of Collectivism

1. The state ownership, management and control of all the factors of production and distribution will result in an authoritarian and bureaucratic state.

2. There is every likelihood of an increase in corruption, intrigue and personal spite. It may give rise to nepotism, red tapism and favouritism.

3. Supporters of state socialism are overoptimistic in thinking that state ownership is the panacea of all the evils. The difficulties of administration will be so many that there is every likelihood of break down of the machinery.

4. State socialism will destory the chief incentive to individual effort and originality.

5. State socialism is inimical to individual liberty. None can dare to oppose those on whose whim depends the livelihood of a person. In state socialism when state will be omnipotent, no one will dare to oppose the state. The individual will be forced to work as a dumb driven cattle according to the wishes of the persons who will be fortunate enough to exercise the power of the state.

6. There may be loss of production under state socialism.

7. State socialism may be capitalism in another form. The monopoly of the state may not be for the good of all.

8. As all the factors of production and distribution will come under the control of the state, the love of wealth will be replaced by the bitter struggle for power.

9. State socialism may bring into existence cliques and bosses who will spend all their resources to capture the machinery of the state and to use them for their own purpose.

10. State socialism may result in cast iron centralisation.

11. Lastly, power corrupts a person and absolute power corrupts absolutely. It is difficult to imagine that the holders of the absolute power of the state will not be corrupt, but will utilize this power for the welfare of all.

Merit of Collectivism

1. It stands for the welfare of all and not for the welfare of few.
2. It desires to make use of the state for the collective good.
3. It believes in evolution and peaceful means.
4. It also favours decentralization.
5. It believes in social welfare.

Demerits of Collectivism

1. Collectivism is synonymous with stateism. The state assumes all power in the name of social welfare.

2. It kills individual initiative and makes man merely a tool and effects adversely so far as production is concerned.

3. The individual will loose its liberty and will become merely a tool or slave.

4. It allows totalitarianism through the back door. Human nature being what it is, a few clever persons will capture the power of Government to do whatever they like.

5. It will create the evils of bribery, corruption, favouritism and red tape.

6. Marxism ultimately favours utopian ideals but it cannot be said about state socialism.

QUESTIONS FOR EXERCISE

1. "Socialism is like a hat which has lost its shape because everybody wears it" — Joad. Discuss.
2. Describe the main principles of Democratic Socialism or Collectivism.
3. Assess the contribution of Democratic Socialism to the development of the concept of freedom in modern times.
4. Write short note on Political Philosophy of Sidney Webb.
5. Describe in brief the main propositions of the collectivist theory of the state.
6. How and where does collectivist theory discard the Marxian tenets?
7. What are the methods of collectivists for achieving their objects? What arguments have been advanced in favour or against it?

14

Karl Marx (1818—1883)

Karl Marx was born to Heinrich and Henrietta Marx, in 1818 in Germany. At the age of 17 in 1835 he entered the University of Bonn to study. In 1841 at the age of 23 he received the doctorate degree from the university of Jena for his thesis entitled, "*On the Difference between the Natural Philosophy of Democritus and Epicurus.*" He was very much influenced by his stay in Paris from 1843 to 1845. Most significant was his friendship with Engels who was his co-author in the development of his social thought. Both of them published *The Communist Manifesto* in 1848. In August 1849, Marx was presented an ultimatum by the French government to leave the country. He migrated to London and produced such works as *The Class Struggles in France* (1850). *The 18th Brumaire of Louis Bonaparte* (1852), and *Contributions to a Critique of Political Economy* (1859). The first youthful period of his writings was between 1842 and 1848. Among the writings of this stage, some were published during Marx's life time; short articles or essays like *The Introduction to the Critique of Hegel's Philosophy of Law* or *The Essays on The Jewish Question*. Among the more important works of this period which were known for some time are *The Holy Family* and a polemic against Proudhon entitled *The Poverty of Philosophy*, a reply to Proudhon's book *The Philosophy of Poverty*. The other writings of this period were not published until long after Marx's death, because publication of the whole body of his work dates from 1931. In 1844 was published *Economic and Philosophic Manuscripts. The German Ideology* was the last work of this period. In the second period of his life was published *A Contribution to the Critique of Political Economy* in 1859. His magnum opus *Das Capital* was published in three volumes in 1867, 1885, 1894 respectively. Some important books summarising the social thought of Karl Marx are *Karl Marx : Selected Writings in Sociology and Social Philosophy*, Edited By T.B. Bottomore and Maxmillien Ruble, NY : 1964, With Friedrick Engles *The Communist Manifesto*, Chicago; Regenery, 1969 (Orig. 1848), *The Marx-Engels Reader*, Edited by Robert C. Tucker NY : Norton, 1972.

VARIOUS INTERPRETATIONS OF MARXIST THOUGHT

According to Raymond Aron, "Marx was, first and foremost, the sociologist and economist of capitalist regime."[1] His thought, however, has been subject to so many interpretations both by his followers and critics. This variety of interpretations is due to the following causes :

1. Official ideology. Marxism has been declared the official ideology of USSR, China, Poland and other states. Therefore, his thought has been interpreted in the interest of the government of these states.

2. Prolific writings. Marx wrote so many articles and books running into hundreds of pages. Therefore, it was not difficult for the interpreters to lay emphasis upon his contradictory statements here and there.

3. Diversity of subjects. Marx wrote on sociology theory, economic theory, history and so many other subjects. Therefore, his thought has been interpreted from a diversity of viewpoints.

4. Diversity of periods. In different periods of his life Karl Marx was influenced by different thinkers and incidents. Therefore, there is no dearth of contradictory statements in his works written in different periods.

5. Many schools. For over a century many schools of interpretation of Marxist thought have developed in different countries giving rise to so many interpretations.

KARL MARX AND AUGUSTE COMTE

The social thought of Karl Marx and August Comte was concerend with the analysis of human society, racing its development, diagnosing its crisis and suggesting solutions. In spite of this similarity about the fundamental problems the two giants differed as follows :

1. While Comte developed a theory of industrial society Karl Marx analysed modern societies.

2. While Comte distinguished three phases of human evolution, Karl Marx identified four stages of human history.

3. While Comte's distinction was based upon the differences concerning ways of thinking, Marx distinguished stages of human history on the basis of modes of production.

4. While Comte pointed out conflicts between labour and management of marginal phenomena, Karl Marx gave them central place in his analysis.

DECISIVE INFLUENCES

According to Frederick Engels, the social thought of Karl Marx was the result of decisive influences of German philosophy, English economics and French history. According to the German philosophers historical process is the central reality. German philosophy reached its apex in the philosophy of Hegel.

1. Raymond Aron, *Main Currents in Sociological Thought*, Vol. I, 1981, p. 111.

In spite of its contradictory position, the philosophy of Karl Marx was very much influenced by the phillosophy of Hegel.

Marx studied English economy and adopted some of their theories, such as the labour theory of value or the law of the falling tendency of the rate of profit. He considered the concepts and theories of English economists to be scientific. The idea of class struggle was borrowed by Karl Marx from French historians.

MARX AND HEGEL

But the most important influence upon Marx was that of Hegel. Hegel dominated the German intellectual horizon 1770-1831. At the University of Berlin, Karl Marx was a young Hegelian. Hegel "was a liberal, after the German fashion," explain Collins and Makowski, "which meant that he believed in the rule of law rather than the arbitrary rule of men and hence supported the Prussian state. Hegel's philosophy culminated in the idealist tradition that began with Kant; it held that the essence of reality is Reason, but that the spirit of Reason manifests itself only gradually, revealing more and more facets of itself during the course of time."[2] The German philosophy was everywhere influenced by historicism of Hegel. According to Hegel, "History is the growth of Reason to consciousness of itself, and the constitutional legalistic state is the culmination of history." This historicism was borrowed by Karl Marx from Hegel. The iedalistic approach to history by Hegel was, however, transformed into materialism by Karl Marx. Thus, while Hegelian system was dialectical idealism, Karl Marx presented what is known as dialectical materialism. This has been called, "Turning upside down," or "standing Hegel on his head." As Marx puts it, "In direct contrast to German philosophy which descends from heaven to earth, here we ascend from earth to heaven. That is to say, we do not set out from what men say, imagine, conceive, nor from men as narrated, thought of, imagined, conceived, in order to arrive at men in the flesh. We set out from real, active men, and on the basis of their real life-process we demonstrate the development of the ideological reflexes and echoes of this life-process — morality, religion, metaphysiscs, all the rest of ideology and their corresponding forms of consciousness, thus no longer retain the semblance of independence...Life is not determined by consciousness, but consciousness by life."[3] In sipite of this materialistic emphisis it is agreed that the central method of dialectics was borrowed by Karl Marx from Hegel. Explaining the dialectical method of Hegel and therefore, of Marx, Timasheff wrote, "According to Hegel each statement of truth, or thesis, has its opposite statement, or antithesis, which is also true. The thesis and antithesis may be reconciled on a higher level of synthesis, but this is not the end for the dialectical process

---

2. Randall Collins and Michael Makowski, *The Discovery of Society*, New York, Random House, 1972, p. 34.
3. Karl Marx, "German Ideology," pp. 197-216 in Erich Fromm, *Marx's Concept of Man*, New York, Frederick Ungar, 1961, p. 198.

then continues as the synthesis becomes a new thesis with its antithesis and so on."[4] On the basis of dialectical method Karl Marx explained progressive evolution in history. This evolution, according to Hegel, was the evolution of idea. According to Marx, however, it was a material process, in which the material conditions were more important than ideas. He, however, did not deny the reality of subjective consciousness or its significance in social change.

Like Feuerbach, a young Hegelian, Marx substituted spirit-centred or God-centred world by the material world. These Young Hegelians were more concerned with the social relationships in which men were enmeshed rather than the world of ideas and the spirit. The most fundamental thing in human life and human society is survival, the development of materialistic circumstances influencing the social life. Thus, like Ludwig Feuerbach, Karl Marx turned, "for the spirit-centred or God-centred world (as found in Hegelianism) to the analysis of those unhappy social conditions which had led men to find consolation in a world of religious entities of their own creation..."[5] With the British economists Marx believed that the motivating factor in human existence was survival, a materialistic realism. Survival required the production of means of subsistence. "The first historical act," wrote Marx, "is the production of material life itself. This is indeed a historical act, a fundamental condition of all history."[6] Society is an arena of conflicts and strikes between groups of people. The human groups compete for survival. This improves livelihood and generates social change. Thus, the social advancement of community does not depend on peace and cooperation but on strife and competition, struggle and contention.

As has been already pointed out, Karl Marx borrowed the value of history in human existence from Hegel. Human history is made by men themselves. According to Karl Marx, "Men begin to distinguish themselves from animals as soon as they begin to produce their means of subsistence...In producing their means of subsistence men indirectly produce their actual material life."[7] Marx identified four stages of human history on the basis of modes of production: primitive communism, ancient slave production, feudalism and capitalism. The present society is capitalist. The future society will be a classless society with no private property and therefore no exploitation. "Therein," Timasheff comments, "may be seen the inherent notion of historical progess and utopianism in Marx's thought, for human history is treated as an inevitable succession of stages culminating in the best possible social order."[8]

---

4. Nickolas Timasheff and George Theodorson, *Sociological Theory*, New York, Random House 1976, pp. 57-8.
5. Lewis A. Coser, *Masters of Sociological Thought*, New York, Harcourt Brace Javanovich, 1971, pp. 74-75.
6. Karl Marx, *Selected Writings in Sociology and Social Philosophy*, London, McGraw-Hill, 1964, p. 60.
7. Karl Marx and Friedrich Engels, *Selected Works*, 2 Vols., Moscow, Foreign Langauge Publishing House, 1962, p. 488.
8. Timasheff and Theodorson, *Sociological Theory*, p. 61.

According to Raymond Aron, "There is an easy way to produce a Hegelian Marx — which is to present a Marxist Hegel."[9] Both Marx and Hegel have been interpreted differently by different scholars. M. Gurvitch presents Hegel as an idealist philosopher who thinks historical evolution as the evolution of mind. From this viewpoint Karl Marx was anti-Hegelian and Hegelian heritage was minimal. On the other hand, Alexandre Kojeves in his book *Introudction a la Lecture de Hegel* demonstrates that Hegelian philosophy was not different from that of Marx. In this controversy the best thing is to maintain a middle position since both pro- and anti-Hegelian interpretations and Marxist heritage are one-sided. The fundamental idea of his doctoral dissertation that philosophy is complete and nothing remains but to realise it, was borrowed by Marx from Hegel. He also borrowed the idea of progress when he said that philosophers have conceived the world differently 'the time has come to transform it'. The historical movement has a fundamental meaning, this idea was clearly Hegelian borrowed by Marx. As Fromm has pointed out, Marx also borrowed from Hegel the concepts of universal man, total man and alienation. In his book *Introduction to the Critique of Hegel's Philosophy of Law,* Karl Marx accepts Hegelian ideas of the opposition between the particular and the universal, the civil society and the state, the worker and the employer. The notion of alienation had a central place in society. It was philosophical and metaphysical. Karl Marx borrowed it from Hegel but made it sociological. In the words of Raymond Aron, "Alienation sociologically interpreted, is at once a historical, moral and sociological critique of the present social order. In the capitalist regime, men are alienated; they are themselves lost in the collectivity; and the root of the alienation is economic alienation."[10]

PHILOSOPHICAL PRESUPPOSITIONS

Before the exposition of the social thought of Karl Marx we shall briefly summarise the philosophical presuppositions underlying it. The pre-Marxist philosophy was characterised by a struggle between materialism and idealism. The conditions of the rise of Marxist philosophy were socio-economic. Karl Marx brought a revolution in philosophy by changing the role of philosophy and the philosophers. He laid emphasis upon change rather than thought. His philosophy was characterised by a consistent defence of the interests of the proletariat.

Marxist philosophy is dialectical materalism. Reality consists of matter and the forms of its existence. Motion is a form of existence of matter. Consciousness is a product of the development of matter. Dialectics is the doctrine of development and universal connection. The materialistic dialectics is governed by the following three laws :

---

9. Raymond Aron, *Main Currents in Sociological Thought*, Vol. 1.

10. *Ibid.*, p. 148.

1. The Law of the Unity and Struggle of Opposite.
2. The Law of the Passage of Quantitative into Qualitative Changes.
3. The Law of the Negation of the Negation.

1. The Law of the Unity and Struggle of Opposite. According to this law, the existence of all objects is inclusive in each other. None exists separately. In the same way, even in the different states of the same thing the preceding states are assimilated in succeeding. Thus, objects and their states are both inseparable from each other. In social philosophy, the result of this law is the welfare of any one person is not separated from that of other people. Social welfare and indiviudal welfare have no distinctions. In the same way, all activities of men admit of reciprocal relations. According to Marxism, the economic or wealth producing activities predominate in us. Thus, economic activities and social welfare are intimately related.

2. The Law of the Passage of Quantitative into Qualitative Changes. It is not only quantity from quantity and quality from quality but new qualities are also created from quantity. Consciousness is created out of matter although matter completely lacks consciousness. Man is not a mere conglomeration of hands, legs, etc. In him is consciousness, completely differing in nature from the body. Like the Carvakas, Marx treats consciousness as a new quality and the result of combination of parts of the body. Thus, his social philosophy is not only materialism. The evolution of both body and consciousness is necessary because the two are separate.

3. The Law of Negation of the Negation. In the progress of dialectical evoultion every new step produces qualities differing from the preceding step. Thus, these two are called thesis and antithesis. Their conflict is settled in another step called the synthesis. In the field of social philosophy, this law creates relativism. Social laws are not unchangable and eternal; their evolution also is in accordance with this dialectical justice. The following social norms negate the preceding social thoughts and eliminate the internal conflict. The Marxist social philosophy is the synthesis of ancient and medieval moral approaches.

Novelty of Marxist Philosophy

"The discovery of Marx and Engels represents the end of the old philosophy, *i.e.* the end of that philosophy which claimed to give a universal explanation of the world", said A.A. Zhdanov.

"With the appearance of Marxism as the scientific world outlook of hte proletariat there ends the old period in the history of philosophy, when philosophy was the occupation of isolated individuals, the possession of philosophical schools consisting of a small number of philosophers and their disciples, detached from life and the people, and alien to the people.

"Marxism is not such a philosophical school. On the contrary, it supersedes the old philosophy — the philosophy that was the property of a small elite, the aristocracy of the intellect. It marked the beginning of a completely new period in the history of philosophy, when it became a scientific weapon in the hands of the proletarian masses in their struggle for emancipation from capitalism."

"Marxist philosophy, as distinguished from preceding philosophical systems, is not a science above other sciences; rather, it is an instrument of scientific investigation, a method penetrating all natural and social sciences, enriching itself with their attainments in the course of their development. In this sense, Marxist philosophy is the most complete and decisive negation of all preceding philosophy. But to negate, as Engels emphasised, does not mean merely to say `no'. Negation includes continuity, signifies absorption, the critical reforming and unification in a new and higher syntheis of everything advanced and progressive that has been achieved in the history of human thought.'[11]

COMMUNIST MANIFESTO

Communist Manifesto is one of those rare documents that have changed the course of history. It can be compared with the Sermon on the Mount of the Christ and preaching of Lord Buddha at Sarnath. It has become a sort of Bible for the Communists. It is a call to action and "has become a battery to a large portion of the world." It begins with the word that "A sceptre is haunting Europe...The sceptre of Communism." "The history of all hitherto existing society is the history of class struggle." This thesis of class war can be proved through historical facts. In Greece, there were two classes of slaves and slave owners and same was the fate of Roman Empire. During the middle ages serfs were exploited by the feudal lords. From the serfs arose the chartered burgesses and from these burgesses arose bourgeoisie class. With the discovery of India and America and spread of European civilization and industry new capitalist class came into existence. This bourgeoisie class put an end to feudal class and conception of natural superiors in which priest class was regarded with respect "and has left no other nexus between man and man than naked self-interest, than callous" cash payment. "It has converted the physician, the lawyer, the priest, the poet, the man of science, into its wage labourers the bourgeoisie has torn away from the family its sentimental veil, and has reduced the family relation to mere money relation., *i.e.* neither father nor brother are great but greatest relation is of money."

Demand of Communist Manifesto

1. Abolition of property in land and application of all rents of land to public purpose.
2. A heavy progressive or graduated income tax.
3. Abolition of all rights of inheritance.
4. Confiscation of the property of all emigrants and rebels.
5. Concentration of credit in the hands of the state by means of a national bank with state capital and on exclusive monopoly.

---

11. A.A. Zhdanov : *Speech at Philosophical Workers' Conference.*

6. Centralization of means of communication and transport in the hands of the state.

7. Extension of factories and instruments of production owned by the state; the bringing into cultivation of waste lands and the improvement of the soil generally in accordance with a common plan.

8. Equal liability of all to labour. Establishment of industrial armies, especially for agriculture.

9. Combination of agriculture with manufacturing industries between town and country by a more equitable distribution of the population over the country.

10. Free education for all children in public schools. Abolition of children in factory labour in its present form. Combination of education with industrial production etc.

Political power means the organized power of one class for oppressing another, but class supremacy will be abolished if proletariats come in power. There shall be an association in which the free development of each is the condition for the free development of all. Thus, Marx favours classless society in which everybody will work according to ability and capacity and will get according to needs and the state will wither away.

Communist Manifesto ends by declaring "their ends can be attained only by the forcible overthrow of all existing social conditions. Let the ruling classes tremble at a communistic revolution. The proletarians have nothing to lose but their chains. They have a world to win."

"Working men of all countries, unite."

Evaluation

Thus Communist Manifesto throw light on the development of modern production and the rise of bourgeoisie society and proletarian class who come in conflict. It believes in the final victory of proletarian class. It aims at a classless society in which state, the instruments of class rule withers away. To achieve this end it calls workers of the world to make united effort to bring an end to exploitation.

It describes the evolution of bourgeoisie society and calls for revolutionary programme to establish classless state. Communists are both evolutionary and revolutionary with more emphasis on revolution. Communist Manifesto throws light on class war and interprets history as a class war between slaves and their owners, serfs and feudal lords and worker that is proletarian class and capitalists. It desires abolition of bourgeoisie property which is the instrument of exploitation of the workers but property right has been accepted as fundamental rights all over the world. According to Prof. J.J. Laski, the manifesto "gave direction and a philosophy to what had been before a little more than an incholate protest against injustice. According to Laidler, "It was at once an inspiration of the role of the working class in past and future history clarion call to labour to unite for the purpose of securing its emancipation and through that emancipation freedom for all." According to Bertrand Russel, the "Communist Manifesto is the best contribution that Karl Marx made to the History of Political Thought as longer events in our political life are determined by interaction of material conditions and human aspirations."

BASIC POLITICAL IDEAS OF KARL MARX

Communist philosophies and dogmas as expounded by Marx were rational. Even his greatest opponents could not simply dismiss them. They had mass appeal and were read, appreciated and followed by many with great care and interest. Briefly these were as follows :

1. Scientific Theory. Marxian political philosophy took past historical facts into consideration before he arrived at any decision. He did not dismiss past as merely the ghost of events which had no bearing on future. On the other hand, he felt that history was a lesson and it should be studied with all care and interest. Its lessons should be learnt and remembered for future guidance. Marx took historical facts to their logical conclusion and made them applicable to all. He did not confine the lessons of history to a particular area but gave them a universal character.

2. Historical Materialism. Marx borrowed from Hegel the conception of 'historical materialism' or 'materialistic conception of history'. He applied this conception to social and economic conditions of life. This conception became the basis of his subsequent political philosophy. Marx believed that the character of man was formulated by the way in which he earned money. The basis of economic system is the system of production and exchange of products. It is a regular and continuous process and also historical fact which cannot be denied.

3. Class Warfare. According to Marx, the history of hitherto existing society is nothing but that of class struggle or class warfare. In this struggle the poor are always fighting for their very existence. They are not properly rewarded. They are not even paid for the work which they do. The rich are exploiting the poor by keeping with them what should reasonably go to the workers. This exploitation is not of recent origin. It has been continuing since times immemorial. The poor are struggling for their very existence in this world. This is bound to go on as long as the classes exist in this world.

4. Surplus Value. According to this theory the working classes are not paid as much as they produce. They are paid only for their very existence so that they should work and always depend upon the capitalists. The capitalists have a tendency to save something from the labour of every labourer which they claim as their legitimate rights. This is technically known as profit. This surplus makes the rich richer and the poor, poorer. Monopolistic tendencies develop through this surplus value. Each capitalist tries to capture either one market or the other on monopolistic lines.

5. Dictatorship of Proletariat. Marx was of the opinion that under the present conditions capitalism was bound to wither away. In this system the rich will continue to become richer and the poor, poorer. With the passage of time small capitalists will disappear as they shall not be in a position to compete with the rich. Gradually the number of proletariats will increase and the whole trade and industry will be controlled by only a few capitalists on monopolistic basis. These monopolists will create so much trouble for the proletariats that life will become miserable for them. They will have no alternative but to rise in revolt against capitalist. The revolt of the working classes will be very powerful. It is bound to become a success. Accordingly, the rich will be crushed and the proletariats will establish their rule. The rule of the working classes will be extensive and widespread. Finally, working classes shall be in a position to establish their dictatorship. In such a society the interests of the rich will not be injured whereas those of the poor will be safeguarded.

6. Classless Society. A classless society is the ultimate object or end of communism. The ideal society is one in which there was neither class distinction nor disparity between the rich and the poor. It was a society in which all will get according to their needs. Since power corrupted man and even created an unhealthy society, there might be a tendency on the part of the proletariat to misuse their power. But once the means of production were controlled by the working classes, it could safely be presumed that class distinction had disappeared and by the large a classless society had come to stay. Thus, the criteria for judging whether a classless society had or had not been achieved is whether the means of prodcuction had or had not been fully controlled.

REVOLUTION AND EVOLUTION

1. Rise of capitalism. Karl Marx based his political philosophy on economic struggle which was going on between the rich and the poor. It was a struggle in which the rich were exploiting the poor and getting richer because of the labour of the millions of workers. The rich had wealth by which they controlled the means of production. The poor had labour which was a perishable commodity and could not be preserved. The labourer is always in urgent need of selling his labour whereas the capitalist wishes to utilise it for his own selfish ends. The capitalist pays far less to the labourer than what is due to him and terms this surplus value as his profit. He goes on accumulating his profits and becomes a monopolist.

2. Communism will gradually destroy itself. Karl Marx also believed that communism was sowing the seeds of its own destruction and that it will die its own death. In the words of Coker, "Although capitalism proceeds naturally to its own destruction, it does not create socialism. In other words, capitalism inevitably prepares the way for, but does not inevitably lead into socialism. Deliberate, intelligent and informed action is needed for the achievement of socialism."

4. Socialist programme. Under the existing system the capitalists were controlling private rents, interests and profits and decided about the line of action. These should be used in such a fashion that means of exploitation did not go in the hands of any particular class. Coker has said, "The function of a socialist programme, Marx held, is to show wage workers how to convert their potential into an actual superiority or how to prepare themselves for transforming an automatic struggle into a consciously designed political struggle."

5. Communists Revolution : (i) *Peaceful Means.* Marx opines that in order to control the means of production it was essential that the working classes should first of all try to win the existing battle of democracy. He suggested that working classes in all countries should form a group and try to come to power. Once they have come to power by peaceful means they should then try to settle themselves permanently and should make themselves secure in their seats.

(ii) *Socializing Capital.* Once the working classes have found themselves secure then they should embark upon the task of socializing capital. The process should be gradual but the working classes will have to face initial difficulties and in certain cases will have to use force also. It requires use of both intellect and force to use capitalistic owned means of production for the whole community. To quote Coker again, "The particular steps cannot be the same in all states. For the most advanced countries the immediate measures, according to the programme of Communist Manifesto, are the following : abolition of private ownership of land, centralisation of means of the state; establishment of state monopoly of credit and banking; abrogation of right of inheritance, heavily progressive income taxation; prohibition of child labour in factories; enforcement of an equal liability of all to work. These measures are to be followed by a gradual extension of public ownership in other fields of production.

(iii) *No Definite Programme.* Marx, subsequently believed that it was not essential to altogether overthrow the laws passed by the capitalists. He believed that all these laws which made workers politically and economically strong should be retained. He, however, strongly believed that no definite programme could be given because programmes hampered action. He himself said, "Every step of real movement is more important than a dozen programmes."

(iv) *Violent Revolution.* Marx believed that the capitalists will not be willing to hand over the power easily. They will try to stick to it firmly and strongly. They willl put serious obstacles in the way of working classes. In such circumstances the working classes shall have to use force for the overthrow of the capitalism. In his *Communist Manifesto* Marx has said, "Communists openly declare that their ends can be attained only by the forcible overthrow of all existing conditions. Let the ruling classes tremble at the communist revolution"

(v) *Use of Force.* Force is a necessary instrument for bringing about a revolution. Coker has said, "He generally recognised that means of securing political power might differ at different times and in different countries, the method might be direct economic action at one time and place, and a revolution and slow achievement of political predominance at another. His attitude was generally pragmatic. The method of forcible rebellion is permissible where the circumstances are such as to make that method necessary and probably successful."

6. Both Evolution and Revolution. Thus, Marx's method of overthrow of capitalist classes by working classes was both evolutionary as well as revolutionary. He was not concerned with the methods but with the ends of the struggle. For a lasting peace and permanent achievement, however, it is not the ends of the struggle. For a lasting peace and permanent achievement, however, it is not the end that matters but what matters in the method by which these ends are actually achieved.

Criticism of Marxist Theory

1. Never Ending Struggle. Marx's method of overthrowing one social system and its replacement by another is dangerous to the extent that it has never paved way for enduring stability. Capitalists in turn are bound to overthrow the workers. This will be a never ending circle which is unwanted for nation's economic progress and cultural advancement.

2. Oversimplification. Marx has made the problem rather too simple. He has maintained that workers' overthrow of capitalist system is natural and without any serious complications. This is misleading both for the workers and their sympathisers.

3. Set back to Working Classes. Marx failed in bringing about the practical difficulties to the notice of working classes. He has thus done injustice to the workers for whom he had struggled so hard. If his philosophy is taken on its face value then it might give a set back to the cause of working classes which might not be ready to face the hard realities of struggle.

DIALECTICAL MATERIALISM

The concept of history of Karl Marx is known as dialectical materialism or historical materialism. "To Marx" explains Larson, "matter is not a product of mind: on the contrary, mind is simply the most advanced product of matter. Though Marx rejected Hegel's content orientation, he retained his dialectical structure."[12] Historical materialism is the Marxist theory of society. This is clear in a detailed passage in the Preface to *A Contribution to the Critique of Political Economy.* The general conclusion at which I arrived and which once obtained, served to conclusion at which I arrived and which, once obtained, served to guide me in my studies, may be summarized as follows. In the social production which men carry on they enter into definite relations that are indispensable and independent of their will; these relations of production correspond to definite stage of development of their material powers of production. The sum total of these relations of production constitutes the economic structure of society — the real foundation on which rise legal and political superstructures and to which correspond definite forms of social consciousness. The mode of production in material life determines the general character of the

12. Calvin J. Larson, *Major Themes in Sociological Theory* (New York, David McKay, 1973), p. 40.

social, political and spiritual processes of life. It is not the consciousness of men that determines their existence, but on the contrary, their social existence determines their consciousness. At a certain stage of their development, the material forces of production in society come into conflict with the existing relations of production, or — what is but a level expression for the same thing — with the property relations within which they had been at work. From forms of develoopment of the forces of productiuon, these relations turn into their fetters. Then comes the period of social revolution. With the change of the economic foundation the entire immense superstructure is more or less rapidly transformed. In considering such tranformation the distinction should always be made between the material transformation of the economic conditions of production which can be determined with the precision of natural science, and the legal, political, religious, aesthetic or philosophic — in short ideological — forms in which men become conscious of this conflict and fight it out. Just as our opinion of an individual is not based on what he thinks of himself, so we cannot judge of such a period of transformation by its own consciousness; on the contrary this consciousness must rather be explained from the contradictions of material life, from the existing conflict beween the social forces of production and the relations of production. No social order ever disappears before all the productive forces, for which there is room in it, have been developed, and the new higher relations of production never appear before the material conditions of their existence have matured in the womb of the old society. Therefore, mankind always takes up only such problems as it can solve; since, looking at the matter more closely, we will always find that the problem itself arises only when the material conditions necessary for its solution already exist or are at least in the process of formation. In broad outlines we can designate the Asiatic, the ancient, the feudal, and the modern bourgeois methods of production as so many epochs in the progress of the economic formation of society. The bourgeois relations of production are the last antagonistic form of the social process of production — antagonistic not in the sense of individual antagonism, but of one arising from conditions surrounding the life of individuals in society; at the same time the productive forces developing the womb of bourgeois society create the material conditions for the solution of that antagonism. This social formation constitutes, therefore, the closing chapter of the prehistoric stage of human society.[13]

The above passage expresses all the essential ideas of Marxist economic interpretation of history. These essential ideas are as follows :

1. Men enter into definite relations by the force of economic circumstances such as the forces, and relations of production. Thus, historical processes are determined by economic forces.

2. The infrastructure of a society includes forces and relations of production. On this is based the superstructure of legal and political institutions as well as ways of thinking.

---

13. Raymond Aron, *Main Currents in Sociological Thought*, Garden City, Doubleday, 1970, p. 154.

3. The mechanism of the historical movement is the contradiction between the forces and relations of production.

4. This contradiction leads to class struggle which, according to Karl Marx, is the main factor in historical evolution.

5. The dialectics of the forces of relations of production implies a theory of revolution.

6. Social reality governs consciousness and not *vice-versa*.

7. The stages of human history may be distinguished on the basis of their economic mode of production. These stages are : the Asiatic, the ancient, the feudal, and the bourgeois. These four modes are again classified into the ancient and the modern. Asiatic mode of production does not constitute a stage in the history of Western society.

To sum up "Science and society's experience throughout history refutes the views of bourgeois sociologists and demonstrates that the development of society is forward, natural, historical process which follows objective laws independent of man. The history of society is an endless chain of development, revolutionary transitions from the simpler, lower formations to more complex, higher ones. Social progress depends on the development and improvement of material production. Production has developed from the simplest tools, the sticks and stones man used in his struggle for life, to the latest automatic machines and equipments driven by electric power and atomic energy. As production advances, the other spheres of social life also develop."[14]

STAGES OF HUMAN HISTORY

The last theme contained in Karl Marx's *The Communist Manifesto* is the stages of human history. Just as Auguste Comtee differentiated moments of human evolution on the basis of ways of thinking, so Karl Marx differentiated stages of human history on the basis of their economic regimes, and he distinguished four of these or in his terminology four modes of production which he called the Asiatic, the Ancient, the Feudal and the Bourgeoise.

Being a materialist, Karl Marx looks upon thoughts as based on facts. According to Marx, "It is not the consciousness of men that determines their existence, but on the contrary, it is their social existence that determines their consciousness." In this way, social laws change along with the history of social and economic evolution. In these changes; the three foregoing laws apply. There have always been conflicting classes in society. From historical evidence, these conflicting classes have three major forms : (1) Society of slave tradition; (2) Aristocratic society; and (3) Capitalist society. According to Marx, it is only a communist society which can resolve this conflict.

Even the economic basis of social evolution has two parts — (1) means of production; (2) economic relations. The first comprises machines and second, ownership and ways of distribution etc. The order of society underwent a

14. J. Riordan (Ed.) *Marxist Philosophy*, Moscow, Foreign Languages Publishing House, p. 194.

change with the development of the chaos. With the development of agricultural implements, it entered into a state of agriculture. Industrial age was conceived with the discovery of industrial machinery. In the same way society underwent important changes with the entry of banks and currency into the medium of distribution.

MODES OF PRODUCTION

Thus, the history of society is the history of the development and the law governed succession of the modes of production. This succession passes through five stages or five consecutive modes of production : Primitive Communal, Slave, Feudal, Capitalist and Socialist.

1. Primitive Society. This was the first and the lowest form of organisation of people. It existed for thousands of years. In this stage men utilised primitive implements. By these they improved their work. The relations of production and the productive forces were on a lower level. Everything was done on communal basis. The people tilled the communal land together with common tools and living in a common dwelling, sharing products equally. The productive forces developed slowly. With the growth of the labour productivity the clan began to break into families. The family became the owner of the means of production. Thus, arose private property and with it social inequality. This resulted into the first antagonistic classes, masters and slaves.

2. Slave Society. In the earlier stages of human society, called primitive communism by Marx, it was a community in society. People were few. People did not have the craving of accumulation. But when man started using the result of one day's labour over a number of days, the tendency to accumulation increased. This was the beginning of the institution of wealth.

Ownership over objects spread to ownership over men because slaves helped to increase the inflow of objects. In this way slave and master classes came into being in society and consequently, it assumed the form of master and slave morality. Slave morality was service of masters. There was a vast gulf between the lives of the two. This increased dissatisfaction which, in its turn, led to class conflict. Slaves revolted against the masters for equal rights.

3. Feudal Society. As time passed the masters did concede some rights to slaves. They possessed some ownership over land but a major portion of the yield still went to the master. It was the inception of lordship society. In this society, too, there were two conflicting classes -- serfs and lords. This society became more and more complex. Lords were superseded by lords and these by kings or emperors. The serfs laboured to the authority of kings and lords, religion was resorted to.

In this way, religious ethics was born. Heaven and hell were imagined. God was recognised as the religious emperor under whom were many gods and goddesses. The serf was taught to pray to this God and to rest satisfied with his lot, which was allocated to him by God. It was God Who had vested authority in the king. There were lords authorised by the king. Thus, to obey their orders was the duty of the public. There was a vast difference in the status of the ruler and the ruled.

4. Capitalist Society. Thus, the conflict became more grave. This conflict rooted out the lordship system. On the other side, steam was discovered in the forces of production, and factories worked on steam engines. This created the labour class. The lords abandoned their dukedoms and entered the industrial field. They created the capitalist or owner class. They joined hands with businessmen and white collared middle class people. Thus, society was again stratified into two layers or classes — the bourgeois and the proletariat or labour class. This is the present state of society. In the burgeois and proletariat morality too, there is a tremendous conflict as in all conflicting classes. The policy of the bourgeois is one of exploitation. They have nothing to do with the problems of the proletariat. Resorting to secular orders, laws of action and religion, they preach lessons of humility and patience to the labourers.

5. Communist Society. The fifth and the last mode of production, according to Karl Marx, is socialist. The socialist mode of production, in contrast to the capitalist, is based on social ownership. The productive forces and production relations are governed by socialist ownership characterised by cooperation and mutual assistance. In socialist society relations of production conform to the character of the productive forces. However, contradictions in socialism are only removed in communism which requires better forces of social production. This is the society aimed at after revolutionary overthrow of the capitalist society. It will be marked by the most perfect relations between free people of high intelligence and alround development. Rational distribution of the productive forces will be done on full scale. The cultural and technical level of the workers will rise. This communist society, according to Marx, is the future society aimed at by all development and revolution. This is best defined by the Party Programme in USSR in these words, "Communism is a classless social system with one form of public ownership of the means of production and full social equality of all members of society under it, the alround development of people will be accompanied by the growth of the productive forces through continuous progress in science and technology; all the springs of cooperative wealth will flow more abundantly, and the greast principle "From each according to his ability, to each according to his needs" will be implemented. Communism is a highly organised society of free, socially conscious working people in which public self-government will be established, a society in which labour for the good of society will become life's prime want of everyone, a necessity recognised by one and all, and the ability of each person will be employed to the greatest benefit of the people."[15]

In this way, according to Karl Marx, the social ideals of an age depend upon its social and economic circumstances. Means of production and means of distribution undergo change and with them changes the social order, as well

15. J. Riordam (Ed.) *Marxist Philosophy*, Moscow, p. 230.

as the form of the conflicting classes and even the nature of morality. The only true morality is exemplified by the exploited class because it gravitates us towards the ideal society, a communist order. In the history of social evolution we discern that the exploiters of society were always conflicting whereas the exploited were always friendly and loving. This conflict can be resolved only in a classless society. Capitalism will vanish effortlessly in time and the age of the proletariat will come. According to Marx the social order of such an age has two states — socialism and communism. In socialism every worker will get wages according to the work he does and in communism according to his needs. In the communist state the class struggle will come to an end. The disparity between mental and physical labour will lose recognition and the government and religion will be destroyed. Only then will true morality be conceived. As Engles expresses it, "A really human morality which transcends class antagoism and their legacies in thought becomes transcends class antagoism and their legacies in thought becomes possible only at a stage of society which has not only overcome class antagonism but has been forgotten them in practical life."

DIALECTICAL METHOD

Like that of Hegel Marxist methodology is also known as dialectical. Distinguishing it from the dialectical method of Hegel, Marx said, "My dialectic method is not only different from the Hegelian, but is its direct opposite. To Hegel, the life-process of the human brain, *i.e.*, the process of thinking, which under the name of 'the idea', he even transforms into an independent subject, is the demi-urge of the real world, and the real world is only the external, phenomenal form of 'the idea'. With me, on the contrary, the ideal is nothing else than the material world reflected by the human mind and translated into forms of thought."[16] The basic postulates of the dialectical method of Marx, as outlined by Larson are as follows :[16a]

1. All the phenomena of nature are part of an integrated whole.

2. Nature is in a continuous state of movement and change.

3. The developmental process is a produce of quantitative advances which culminate in abrupt qualitative changes.

4. Contradictions are inherent in all realms of nature — but particularly human society."

Explaining the functioning of the dialectical method Stalin said, "The dialectical method holds that the process of development should be understood not as movement in a circle, not as a simple repetition of what has already occurred, but as on onward and upward movement, as transition from an old qualitative state to a new qualitative state from the lower to the higher."[17]

---

16. David Caute (ed.), *Essential Writings of Karl Marx* (New York, Macmillan, 1976), p. 32.

16a. Calvin J. Larson, *Major Themes in Sociological Theory* (New York, David McKay, 1973), p. 42.

17. As quoted by Jerome Balmuth in *Marxist Social Thought* (New York, Harcourt, Brace and World, 1968), pp. 7-11.

The categories of materialistic dialectics of Karl Marx are : The individual and the universal, content and form, essence and phenomenon, cause and effect, necessity and chance, Possibility and Reality. Every society is governed by dialectical progression in its movements. Dialectical method proceeds through class struggle. The dialectics is found within the interaction of society under the influence of materialism. According to Lenin, "Materialism in general recongizes objectively real being (matter) as independent of consciousness, sensation, experience....Consciousness is only the reflection of being, at best an approximately true (adequate, ideal) reflection of it."[18] "Marx's philosophical materialism," Stalin explains, "holds that the world is by its very nature material, that the multifold phenomena of the world constitute different forms of matter in motion, that interconnection and interdependence of phenomena, as established by the dialectical method, are a law of the development of moving matter, and that the world develops in accordance with the laws of movement in matter and stands in no need of a 'universal spirit'."[19]

ECONOMIC DETERMINISM

The economic background of Marxist social thought is of great importance. Marx has recognised a dialectical relation between economic and social problems. This is also called economic determinism. The prevailing mode of economic production and exchange is the basis upon which is built up and from which alone can be explained, the political and intellectual history of that epoch. According to Engels, "...The production of immediate material, means of subsistence, and consequently, the degree of economic development attained by a given people or during a given epoch, form the foundation upon which the state institutions, the legal conceptions, the ideas on art, and even on religion of the people concerned have been evolved."[20]

In the context of moral importance of economic activities and relations, Marx discovered the two following major principles :

1. Labour Theory of Value. According to this theory value is the outcome of labour. The actual price of a commodity is determined by the labour expended in its production. Although here is an element of labour in exchange, the activity still increases the value of the commodity. It is wrong to classify men on the basis of labour. Mental and physical labour should not be distinguished. Society depends upon labour, without labour no one having the right to live. Thus, this law bitterly derides those people, like capitalists, king, lords etc., who want to avoid labour.

2. Theory of Surplus Value. The value created by the labour of one worker is much greater than the value of wages given to him. This is the surplus value which the exploiters pocket. A labour working 12 hours, can and

18. *Ibid.*, p. xxi.

19. *Ibid.*, pp. 7-11.

20. Karl Marx, *Selected Works*, Vol. II, p. 51.

does work enough for his salary in only 4 to 6 hours. He does not get any remuneration for the remaining hours. This is the surplus profit of the capitalists. Exploitation can be destroyed only by giving this surplus profit to the labourer.

From the moral viewpoint, the appropriation of the surplus value is extremely unfair and incorrect. It is the looting of the wealth of the labourers. Communism is very much opposed to exploitation and profiteering. Man should maintain personal property only to the extent of his needs. It is necessary to have social control over accumulation of wealth. Economic disparity is the basis of social problems. Germs of sin breed in poverty. It hinders the development of personality. Thus, an equitable distribution of wealth is the first condition for an appropriate development of the members of society.

Thus, according to Karl Marx, "The political, legal, philosophical, literary, and artistic development rests on the economic base. But they all react upon one another and upon the economic base. It is not that the economic situation is the sole active cause and that everything else is merely a passive effect, there is, rather a reciprocity within a field of economic necessity which, in the last instance, always asserts itself."[21] Elsewhere Marx wrote, "Legal relations as well as the form of state are to be grasped neither from themselves nor from the so-called general development of the human mind, but rather have their roots in the material conditions of life, the sum total of which Hegel...combines under the name of 'civil society'...The anatomy of civil society is to be sought in political economy."[22]

Thus, human thought, awareness, consciousness and relationships are determined by economic circumstances. This theory of economic determinism turns Hegel upside down since as Marx said, "It is not the unfolding of ideas that explains the historical development of society but the development of the social structure in response to changing material conditions that explains the emergence of new ideas."[23] Marx warned that we will fail to understand the historical process "if ...we detach the ideas of ruling class from the ruling class itself and attribute to them an independent existence, if we confine ourselves to saying that in a particular age these or those ideas were dominant, without paying attention to the conditions of production and the producers of these, and if we thus ignore the individuals and the world conditions which are the source of these ideas."[24] This is due to the fact that the ideas of the ruling class are, in every age, the ruling ideas; *i.e.*, the class which is the dominant material force in society is at the same time its dominant intellectual force. The class which has the means of material production at its disposal, has control at the same time over the means of mental production."[25]

---

21. Karl Marx, *Selected Works*, Vol. I. p. 51.
22. *Ibid.*, p. 362.
23. Doyle P. Johnson, *Sociological Theory* (New York, John Wiley and Sons, 1981), p. 79-80.
24. Karl Marx, *Selected Writings*, pp. 79-80.
25. Karl Marx, *Selected Writings*, p. 223.

THEORY OF CLASS

According to Reinhard Bendix and Seymour Martin Lipset "A social class in Marx's terms is any aggregate of persons who perform the same function in the organization of production."[26] Bendix and Lipset have identified five variables that determine a class in the Marxian sense:[27]

1. Conflicts over the distribution of economic rewards between the classes;
2. Easy communication between the individuals in the same class positions so that ideas and action programmes are readily disseminated;
3. Growth of class consciousness in the sense that the members of the class have a feeling of solidarity and understanding of their historical role;
4. Profound dissatisfaction of the lower class over its inability to control the economic structure of which it feels itself to be the exploited victim;
5. Establishment of a political organization resulting from the economic structure, the historical situation and maturation of class-consciousness.

Marx's sociology is, in fact, a sociology of class struggle. Modern society, according to Marx, is an antagonistic society. Classes are the principal actors in the historical drama of capitalism in particular and of history in general. The class struggle is the moving power of history and leads to a revolution which will mark the end of prehistory, and the appearance of non-antagonistic society.

Towards the end of his life, Marx himself wrote that he had found the idea of class and class struggle in the bourgeois historians, especially in the French ones, but that his own contribution to the theory of classes consisted of the following three propositions :

1. The existence of classes is connected only with certain historical phases in the development of production.

2. The class struggle leads inevitably to the dictatorship of the proletariat.

3. This dictatorship is, in turn, merely a transitional struggle in the abolition of all class, in the realisation of the classless society.

The development of social class does not depend only on the organisation of production. It requires a concentration of masses of people and the distinction of their interests and modes of life from other groups. In the words of Marx, "In so far as millions of families live under economic conditions of existence that divide their mode of life, their interests and their cutlure from those of other classes, and put them into hostile contrast to the latter they form a class. In so far as there is merely a local interconnection among these small peasants, and the identity of their interests begets no unity, no national union, and no political organization, they do not form a class."[28] The second category of

26. Reinhard Bendix and Seymour Martin Lipset, *Class, Status, and Power* (New York, Free Press, 1966), p. 7.

27. *Ibid.*, p. 8.

28. *Ibid.*, p. 11.

Marx's texts relating to classes consists of his historical studies, most of which are admirable, such as the study of the German Revolution of 1818 or his study of Louis Bonaparte's *Coup d' etat* of the 18th Century. In his historical studies, Marx utilised the notion of the class, but without developing it into a systematic theory. For example in "Revolution of Counter-Revolution in Germany" he distinguished the following classes : the feudal, nobility, the bourgeois, the petite bourgeois, the upper and the middle peasantry, the free lower peasantry, the slave peasantry, the agricultural labourers and the industrial workers. In "*The Class Struggle of France*" he talks of the list as follows : financial bourgeois, the industrial bourgeois, the petite bourgeois, peasant class; prolatarian class and finally the sub-proletariat.

A social class, according to Karl Marx, is that which occupies a fixed place in the process of production. This implies a place in the technical mode of production and a place in the legal process superimposed upon the technical one. The owner of the means of product on, the capitalist is at the same time master of the organisation of labour, master in the technical propcess and also because of his legal position, the one who takes the surplus value from the associated producers. Marx distinguished three classes, related to the three sources of income; 1. *Salaried workers* — Owners of simple labour power, 2. *Captalists* — Owners of capital, and 3. *Land Owners* — whose respective sources of income are wages, profit and ground rent. Hence, salaried workers, capitalists and landowners form the three great classes of modern society based on the capitalistic mode of production.

Class relationships, according to Karl Marx, tend to become simpler with the development of captalism. Indeed, if there are only two sources of income, aside from ground rent whose value diminishes with industrialisation there are only two classes, the proletariat, consisting of those who possess only their labour power, and the capitalists who appropriate a portion of the surplus value.

In his *Capital* Marx said "Here individuals are dealt with only in so far as they are personifications of economic categories, embodiments of particular class-relations and class-interests." "The individual is a social being" Marx insisted, "The manifestation of his life even when it does not appear directly in the form of social manifestation, accomplished in association with other men is, therefore, a manifestation and affirmation of social life."

A class, according to Karl Marx, does not constitute a unity simply because from the point of view of economic analysis its income has a single and identical source from all appearances, there must also be a certain psychological community and possibly a certain sense of unity or even a desire for common action. This observation brings us to the third category of Marxist texts which carries an explanation why a large group of men do not necessarily represent a social class even if they share the same economic activity and the same style of life. The idea, a very important one, is that community of activity, way of thinking and mode of life is a necessary but insufficient condition for the reality of a social class. For there to be a social class, there must be a consciousness of unity, a feeling of separation from other social classes, and even a feeling of hostility towards other social classes. Marx made a distinction between "class in itself" and "class for itself" to reflect the movement from a class potential self-awareness to actual self-awarness. Only when the "common struggle" as point of consciousness appears within a class does that class actually emerge as a potential power force. "Self-conscious classes", Coser explains, "arise only if and when there exists a convergence of what Max Weber later called 'deal' and 'material' interests, that is the combination of economic and political demands with moral and ideological quests."[29]

CLASS CONFLICT

Establishing his theory of social classes Karl Marx went to point out that there has always been class conflict among different classes. "The history of all hitherto existing societies is the history of class struggles. Free men and slaves, patrician and plebian, lord and serf, guildmaster and journeyman, in a word, oppressor and oppressed, stood in constant opposition to one another, carried on an uninterrupted, now hidden, now open fight, a fight that each time ended either in a revolutionary reconstitution of society at large or in the common ruin of the contending classes."[30]

Marx's original idea was that there is a fundamental contradiction between wage earners and capitalists. He was convinced moreover, that this fundamental opposition of interests dominated all of capitalistic society and would assume an increasingly simplified form in the course of historical development. From another point of view, an excellent observer of historical reality, Marx was aware of the plurality of social groups, a plurality, reducible to two large groups is capitalists and proletariat. However, a capitalistic society did exhibit these two features which should not be confused with social groups. In the case of the workers *versus* the owners of the means of production, the various inertia which may be invented or observed are identified.

Accepting the difference between the conflict among classes in ancient societies and the modern and the difference between the nature of exploitation Karl Marx admitted, "The fact that modern workers are formally 'free' to sell their labour while being existentially constrained to do so makes their condition historically specific and functionally distinct from that of earlier exploited classes."[31]

The industrial workers have a determined mode of existence which depends on the lot they are assigned in capitalistic society. They are conscious of their solidarity, they are becoming conscious of their antagonism towards other social groups hence a "social class" in the true sense of the term. The proletariat will plan it in fundamental opposition to the capitalists. There are sub-groups within each of these classes and also groups which are not yet identified into the camp of one or the other of the two chief actors in the drama of history.

29. Lewis Coser, *op. cit.*, p. 49.

30. Karl Marx and Friedrich Engels, "The Class Struggle," in Amitai Etzioni and Eva Etzioni-Halevy (eds.) *Social Change* (New York, Basic Books, 1913), p. 102.

31. Lewis A. Coser, *Masters of Sociological Thought*, p. 44.

But these exterior or marginal groups will gradually, in the course of historical evolution, be obliged to join one or the other of the two existing camps, of the proletariat or the camp of capitalists.

Marxist theory of class conflict requires the understanding of the development of the proletariat, the importance of property, the identification of economic and political power, the identification of authority, polarisation of classes, theory of surplus value, pauperization, alienization, class solidarity and antagonism, revolution, the dictatorship of proletariat and finally the inauguration of the communist society. The class conflict starts with the development of proletariat, the importance of property and the polarisation of classes. It is a result of exploitation of the proletariat by the capitalists and their consequent pauperization. Exploitation leads to alienation. Class solidarity and antagonism lead to revolution. Revolution eliminates capitalism and establishes dictatorship of the proletariat. The Class conflict ends in the inauguration of the communist society. In fact, the most significant part of the social thought of Karl Marx is the theory of class conflict. Therefore, we shall examine the above mentioned steps of the process in more details. The above mentioned factors may be classified in three groups : the development of social classes, the class conflict and finally the revolution.

Development of social classes

Class conflict presupposes the development of social classes. The following are the important steps in this direction :

1. Importance of property. Classes are determined on the basis of the relation of the individual to the means of production. As the importance of property increases so increases the distance between different classes.

2. Theory of surplus value. Surplus value refers to the extra value produced by the worker by means of his labour. In fact, this is the share of the worker usurped by the capitalists resulting in exploiation.

3. Polarization. Exploitation results in polarization. In the words of Ralf Dahrendorf, "The whole society breaks up more and more into two great hostile camps, two great directly antagonistic classes: bourgeoisie and proletariat."[32]

4. Proletarianization. According to Raymond Aron, "The rise of proletarian results is proletarianisation which means that, along with the development of the capitalist's regime, the intermediate state between capitalists and proletarians will be worn thin and that an increasing number of the representatives of these intermediate strata will be absorbed by the proletariat."[33] Marx described the process of development of the proletariat as follows :

"The first attempts of the workers to associate among themselves always take place in the form of combinations (unions). Large scale industry concentrates in one place, a crowd of people unknown to one another. Competition divides

32. Ralf Dahrendorf, *Class and Class Conflict in Industrial Society*, Chapts. I and IV.

33. Raymond Aron, *Main Currents in Sociological Thought*, Part I, p. 174.

their interest. But the maintenance of wages, this common interest which they have against their boss, unites them in a common thought of resistance-combination. Thus, combination always has a double aim, that of stopping the competition among themselves, in order to bring about a general competition with the capitalists."[34]

5. The rise of political authority. In the words of Raymond Aron, "Political power, properly so-called, is merely the organised power of one class for oppressing another."[35] The political power is embodied in the state. In the capitalist society the sate is an instrument of economic exploitation and the consolidation of the interest of the capitalist. This is the identification of economic and political power. This intensifies class conflict which ultimately leads to revolution.

6. Pauperisation. The exploitation of the proletariat by the capitalist leads to pauperisation of the masses. In the words of Raymond Aron, "Pauperisation is the process by which the proletarians tend to grow poorer and poorer as the forces of production are developed."[36] It follows that in every mode of production which involves the exploitation of man by man, the social production which involves the exploitation of man by man, the social product is so distributed that the majority of people, who labour, are condemned to toil for no more than the barest necessities of life. Sometimes favourable circumstances arise when they can win more, but more often they get the barest minimum, and at times not even that. On the other hand, a minority, the owners of means of production, the property owners, enjoy leisure and luxury. Society is divided into rich and poor."[37]

7. Alienation. Economic exploitation and the inhuman working conditions in capitalist society lead to alienation of men. Due to alienation the man becomes one-sided. It is an impediment in the ideal of total man. Explaining the process of increase of alienation of man Karl Marx has said, "...Within the capitalist system all methods for raising the social productiveness of labour are brought about at the cost of the individual labourer; all means for the development of production transform themselves into means of domination over and exploitation of the producers; they mutilate the labourer into a fragment of a man, degrade him to the level of an appendage of a machine, destroy every remnant of charm in his work and turn it into hated toil; they estrange from him the intellectual potentialities of the labour-process in the same proportion as science is incorporated in it as an independent power; they distort the conditions under which he works, subject him during the labour-process to a despotism, the more hateful for its meanness; they transform his life-time into working-time and drag his wife and child under the wheels of the juggernaut

34. Reinhard Bendix and Seymour Martin Lipset, *Class, Status and Power*, p. 9.

35. Raymond Aron, *op. cit.* p. 152.

36. *Ibid.*, p. 137.

37. Maurice Cornforth, *Historical Materialism* (New York, International Publishers, 1954), pp. 58-9.

of capital. But all methods for the accumulation of surplus value are at the same time methods of accumulation; and every extension of accumulation becomes again a means for the development of those methods. It follows, therefore, that in proportion as capital accumulates, the lot of the labourer, be his payments high or low, must grow worse."[38]

8. Class Conflict. Tracing the process of class conflict in the capitalist society, characterised by proletarisation, pauperization and alienation Karl Marx said, "With the development of industry, the proletariat not only increases in number, it becomes concentrated in greater masses, its strength grows, and it feels that strength more. The various interests and conditions of life within the ranks of the proletariat are more and more equalized, in proportion as machinery obliterates all distinctions of labour and nearly everywhere reduces wages to the same low level. The growing competition among the bourgeoisie and the resulting commercial crises make the wages of the workers ever more fluctuated. The increasing improvement of machinery, ever more rapidly developing, makes their livelihood more and more precarious: the collisions between individual workmen and individual bourgeoisie take more and more the character of collisions between two classes. Thereupon the workers begin to form combination (trade unions) against the bourgeoisie; they club together in order to keep up the rate of wages; they found permanent associations in order to make provisions beforehand for these occasional revolts. Here and there the contest breaks out into riots."[39]

9. The Social Revolution. According to Karl Marx the social revolution is a law of development of an antagonistic class society. In his preface to *A Contribution to The Critique of Political Economy,* Marx wrote that at a certain stage of their development, the material productive forces of society come in conflict with the existing relations of production within which they have been at work hitherto. From forms of development of the productive forces these relations turn into their fetters. Then begins an epoch of social revolution. To quote Marx : "Finally, in times when the class struggle nears the decisive hour, the process of dissolution going on within the ruling class, in fact within the whole range of old society, assumes such a violent, glaring character, that a small section of the ruling class cuts itself adrift and joins the revolutionary class, the class that holds the future in its hands. Just as therefore, at an earlier period, a section of the nobility went over to the bourgeoisie, so now a portion of the bourgeois ideologists who have raised themselves to the level of comprehending theoretically.

10. The Dictatorship of the Proletariat. Between capitalism and socialism "lies the period of the revolutionary transformation of the one into the other. There corresponds to this a political transition period in which the state can be nothing but the revolutionary dictatorship of the proletariat".[40] The dictatorship

38. Marx and Engels in Etzioni and Eva Etzioni-Halevy, *Social Change*, pp. 36-37.

39. Mark and Engles, in Etzioni, *op. cit.*, pp. 36-7.

40. *Ibid.*, pp. 37-8.

of the proletariat is a qualitatively new type of state. It is coercive, determined and ruthless. It is constructive and educative. It is the highest type of democracy. It takes various forms in transition from capitalism to communism. The Marxist party in USSR took the leading role in the dictatorship of the proletariat. However, the concept of social dictatorship gradually became controversial among the Marxists. As Irving Howe observes : "By now almost all socialists have abandoned the treacherous phrase 'dictatorship of the proletariat', both because it is open to obvious misconstruction and because it has acquired, in the Stalinist and post-Stalinist dictatorships, abhorrent connotations. Marx himself had written that he differentiated himself from `those communists who were out to destroy personal liberty and who wish to turn the world into large barrack or into a gigantic warehouse."[41]

11. The Communist Society. In the end class conflict results into victory of the proletariat and establishment of a communist society which abolishes private property and eliminates class. Karl Marx proclaimed that the communist state is the instrument for establishment of communism. After the achievement of this purpose the state withers away.

ALIENATION

The notion of alienation penned by Karl Marx shows it not merely in the result, but also in the process of production, within productive activity itself. The work is external to the worker, that it is not part of his nature, that consequently he does not fulfil himself in his work but denies himself, has a feeling of misery and not of well-being. The worker therefore feels himself at home only during leisure whereas at work he feels homeless. His work is not voluntary but forced labour. It is not the satisfaction of a need but only a means for satisfying other needs. Its alien character is shown by the fact that as soon as there is no physical or other compulsion, it is avoided like a plague. Finally, the alienated character of work for the worker appears in the fact that it is not his work but work for someone else, that in work he does not belong to himself but to another person. Marx made use of three different terms which, in the translations, are often rendered by the same word, 'alienation', although the German terms do not have exactly the same meaning. They are *Entausserung, Verausserung*, and *Entfremdung* The one that most closely corresponds to 'alienation' in French or English is the last, which means to become a stranger to oneself, *fremd* meaning 'stranger'. *Entfremdung* is the activity or process by which someone becomes a stranger to himself. The idea is that under certain circumstances or in certain societies, the conditions imposed on man are such that he becomes a stranger to himself; he no logner recognizes himself in his activity or in his productions.

41. Iriving Howe (ed.), *Essential Works of Socialism* (New York), Holt, Rinehart and Winston, 1971, p. 7.

Marx summarizes the alienation of labour in the following inimitable words :

First, the fact that labour is external to the worker, *i.e.,* it does not belong to his essential being; that in his work, therefore, he does not affirm himself but denies himself, does not feel content but unhappy, does not develop freely his physical and mental energy but mortifies his body and ruins his mind. The worker therefore only feels himself outside his work, and in his work feels outside himself. He is at home when he is not working, and when he is working he is not at home. His labour is therefore not voluntary, but coerced; it is *forced labour*. It is therefore not the satisfaction of a need; it is merely a means to satisfy needs external to it. Its alien character emerges clearly in the fact that as soon as no physical or other compulsion exists, labour is shunned like plague. External labour, labour in which man alienates himself, is a labour of self-sacrifice, of mortification. Lastly, the external character of labour for the worker appears in the fact that it is not his own, but someone else's, that it does not belong to him that in it he belongs, not to himself but to another. Just as in religion the spontaneous activity of the human imagination, of the human brain and the human heart, operates independently of the individual — that is, operates on him as an alien, divine or diabolical activity — in the same way the worker's activity is not spontaneous. It belongs to another; it is the loss of his self.[42]

While universal man and total man are the positive concepts concerning human being, alienation is a negative concept. Man's ideal is to become universal man or total man. He is, however, condemned into alienation. Alienation is not a result but also the process of production. It is the product of labour. Money according to Karl Marx, "is the alienated essence of men's work and existence; the essence dominates him and he worships it."[43] This is the present capitalist society based upon exploitation of man. The material conditions of capitalist society generate alienation in every aspect of life — economic, religious and political. "Objectification is the practice of alienation. Just as man, so long as he is engrossed in religion, can only objectify his essence by an alien and fantastic being, so under the sway of egoistic need, he can only affirm himself and produce objects in practice by subordinating his products and his own activity to the domination of an alien entity, and attributing to them the significance of an alien entity, namely money."[44]

Marx was personally aware of the alienation of the urban industrial workers in capitalist society. Among workers, alienation has four aspects : alienation from the objects produced, alienation from the process of production, alienation from himself and finally alienation from the community of his fellowmen. Of these, the most important is the alienation from the object that he produces. Expressing this type of alienation Karl Marx worte, "This fact expresess merely

42. Richard Schacht, *Alienation* (Garden City, Doubleday, 1970), p. 110.
43. Karl Marx, *Early Writings* (New York, McGraw-Hill, 1964), p. 39.
44. *Ibid.*

that the object which labour produces — labour's product — confronts it as *something alien*, as a power independent of the producer. The product of labour which has been congealed in an object, which has become material is the objectification of labour. Labour's realization is its objectification. In the conditions dealt with by political economy this realization of labour appears as loss of reality for the workers; objectification as loss of the object-bondge, appropriation as estrangement, as alienation.[45]

Alienation results into slavery of the object. It produces deformity, misery and idiocy. The more wealth a worker produces, the more poor he becomes. He is a victim of exploitation. To quote Marx again, "The alienation of the worker in his product means not only that his labour becomes an object, an external existence, but that it exists outside him, independently; as something alien to him, and that it becomes a power on its own confronting him; it means that the life which he has conferred on the object confronts him as something hostile and alien."[46] The two hostile powers leading to alienation are : the other man or the capitalist and the economic system. While the capitalist is a human power, economic system is an inhuman power. The worker finds, "As a worker, I am at the mercy of the other man, who decides what I should make and how I should make it. My product bears no relation to my personality and interest; it ceases to be an expression of my creative powers. Indeed, it never is my product at all; it is an alien object produced at my expense, at the cost of my self-realization and physical well-being, and against my will but at the bidding of "another alien, hostile, powerful and independent man."[47] Referring to the economic system leading to alienation Marx said, "Alienation is apparent not only in the fact that my means of life belong to some one else..., but also that...an inhuman power rules over everything."[48]

The most important type of alienation however, is self-alienation. Explaining this type Schacht writes; "A man is self-alienated for Marx if his true 'human' nature is something alien to him — if his life fails to manifest the characteristics of a truly human life. Therefore, there are three such characteristics of man : indivudality, sociality and cultivated sensibility. Self-alienation thus takes the form of dehumanization in the spheres of life which correspond to them : production, social life, and sensuous life. It my best be understood in terms of dehumanization in each of these areas."[49] Self-alienation leads to so many pathological symptoms. Eric Fromm has very ably presented this form of alienation in the context of American capitalist society in his famous work *The Sane Society*. Private property is the result of self-alienation and the objective alienation. Communist society claims to abolish all types of alienation.

45. Marx and Engels, "On Alienation", in C. Wright Mills (ed.), *Images of Man* (New York, George Braziller, 1960), pp. 498-500.
46. As quoted by Richard Schacht, *Alenation* (Garden City, Doubleday, 1970), p. 95.
47. T.B. Bottomore, "Marxist Sociology," in the *International Encyclopaedia of the Social Sciences* (New York, Macmillan Company, 1968), p. 46.
48. Herbert Marquse, "Re-examination of the Concept of Revolution," in Denisoff, *op. cit.*, p. 319.
49. Charles Wilber (ed.) *The Political Economy of Development and Underdevelopment.*

CRITICAL EVALUATION

Before pointing out appreciation of the political thought of Karl Marx we would like to summarise some criticisms levelled against Marxist political thought. Of these the most important are as follows :

1. Philosophical ideas. The philosophy of Karl Marx has been subject to the following objections:

(1) The dialectics in the philosophy of Karl Marx is neither logically nor philosophically justified. Referring to the use of dialectic to organic and human worlds Raymond Aron wrote "Historically, a certain orthodoxy may combine these different propositions; but logically and philosophically, the economic interpretation of history and the critique of capitalism in terms of the class struggle have nothing to do with the dialectics of nature."[50]

(2) There is no logical or philosophical necessary connection between capitalism and metaphysical materialism.

2. Oversimplification. Marx has tried to make the whole philosophy too simple. According to his philosophy economic factor is the only one which moves the whole world. This suffers from oversimplification.

3. Neglect of role of religion. According to Marx 'religion is the opium of the people'. He has even gone to the extent of saying that 'man created God'. But religion is very deep-rooted in mankind. Religion develops our spiritual feelings which are the basis of modern life.

4. Economic determination. According to Marxian philosophy economic factor is the only one which motivates man. This is economic determinism. This is not correct. Man is not merely an actor but is also a great wire puller. He determines many things including his own economic conditions and also political and social systems.

5. Politics hand-maid of economics. Marxian society is built only on economic basis. He made politics the hand-maid of economics. In actual life however, economics is the hand-maid of politics. Those who enjoy political authority also decide the economic life of the people.

6. State not withering away. Marx believed that 'state will wither away'. But with the passage of time the state has changed its character. Modern state is increasingly getting stronger instead of withering away. Today one cannot imagine a society without a state. The state is being assigned more and more duties and responsibilities. It has now become a welfare state.

7. Undue Stress on Revolution. According to Marxian philosophy revolution is the only method which brings about social changes. But in actual practice, even great changes have come by 'non-violence' and by change of heart. Even the communists are now trying to seize power by democratic means.

8. Possibility of continued struggle. Marx was of the opinion that after the establishment of classless society there will be no struggle. This is not to

50. Raymond Aron, *Main Currents in Sociological Thought*, Vol. I, p. 156.

human nature. A party coming to power after constant use of violence will not abandon violence. One struggle leads to another. In this struggle there will be no idea of reason but of catching power and authority. Thus, the struggle will continue.

9. Utopia. Marx has failed to devise means by which it should be ensured that the working classes will not take revenge on the capitalists for their long oppression. He has not ensured that after being once overthrown, the capitalist classes will not try to recapture power. In so far as the conception of classless society is concerned Marxian philosophy is utopian in nature and character. Though Marx condemned Fourier and Owen for being utopian, yet he himself is no exception to that.

10. Two fatal ambiguities. According to Dunning, "But the theories of Marx which at the first sight seem to be so compact and well provocative of dissension, have two fatal ambiguities which have been provocative of dissensions. The first is that he nowhere describes the general outlines of society which is to spring from the old....Marx moreover expressed the most contradictory statement as to the methods to be pursued. His doctrine of capitalistic development would naturally minimize the importance of active organisation and propaganda save a means of consolidating the proletarian forces for final cataclysm."

VIRTUES OF MARXISM

In spite of above mentioned defects, Marxian philosophy has today appealed not only to thousands but millions of people living around the globe. One-third of the world has accepted his ideas both as a creed as well as a way of life. His philosophy is the only ray of hope for million of the toilers being exploited by the capitalists. His philosophy has laid deep foundations in the minds of men. This is a clear proof that it has many virtues also. Some of these are as follows :

1. Stress on Economic Factor. Marx was the first great thinker who laid stress on the economic factor which had hitherto been ignored. He would have done a still greater service had he not overdressed that.

2. Theory of Class Struggle. Marx logically discussed the theory of class struggle for the first time. His discussion of the class struggle brought class consciousness and thus working classes which had hitherto been ignored, came to light. These classes also began to realise that they have their own role to play and that too a significant and important role, not only in production but also in decididng the methods of production.

3. Call for Workers' Unity. Marx made the depressed classes realise that their problems could not be solved individually but that these shall be solved collectively. He gave the evergreen slogan 'Let the workers of the world unite'.

4. Trade Cycle and Production. Marx has logically discussed the philosophy of trade cycle and the system of production. He discussed for the first time that the capitalist produces keeping in view not the needs of people but his margin of profit.

5. Scientific Socialism. Marx's approach was convincing and appealing. He appealed the heads and hearts of the workers and toiling classes. Even the capitalists began to tremble before his philosophy. In spite of his inaccuracies he tried and respresented the problems in a very rational way. It is, therefore, logical to say that he was a scientific thinker.

Concluding Remarks

Thus, Marx's philosophy is appealing and catching for the common man. His philosophy is even today the only hope for the struggling masses. Marx is still the symbol and prophet of deliverance of the numberless proletariats working under capitalist system. He occupies a very important place among the philosophers of political science. His approach to the problem was scientific and logical.

QUESTIONS FOR EXERCISE

1. "Marxist programme is both revolutionary as well as evolutionary." Discuss.
2. "Marx thinks that socialism can be brought about only by a revolution." Explain and discuss.
3. "The distinguishing feature of communism is not the abolition of property generally but the abolition of bourgeois property" — *Communist Manifesto*. Explain.
4. "The history of all hitherto existing societies is the history of class struggle" — *Communist Manifesto*. Explain.
5. "The dictatorship of the proletariat, the period of transition to communism will, for the first time, create democracy for the people, for the majority, in addition to necessary suppression of the minority....the exploiters" — Lenin. Explain.
6. "Socialism is not reconcilable with the right to property." Explain.
7. "The distinguishing feature of communism is not the abolition of property generally but abolition of bourgeoisie property" — *Communist Manifesto*. Discuss.
8. "In saying that after the establishment of the dictatorship of the proletariat and the communist system of economy, the state withers away and that in a classless society coercive law and use of force will not be necessary, Marx the theorist, Lenin the realist, show themselves to be greater utopians than the early socialists. They do so mercilessly lashed." Examine this statement crtitically.
9. "Marxian programme of action is both revolutionary as well as evolutionary." Discuss.

10. Why is Karl Marx regarded as the founder of scientific socialism? Would you describe him as evolutionary or revolutionary socialist?
11. "Karl Marx found Communism a chaos and left it a movement" — Laski. Comment?
12. Marxism provided the theoretical foundation of the theory and practice of modern Communism; a relationship that Western liberals vigorously deny. What is your understanding of this problem?
13. "The state is an organ of class rule; it cannot conciliate classes" — Marx. Discuss.
14. Describe and examine the Marxian theory that the mechanism of social change is to be found in the idea of class struggle. Do you accept the view that revolution is the indispensable midwife of social changes.
15. "The history of all hitherto existing society is history of struggle" — Marx. Critically examine this thesis.

15

Evolutionary Socialism and Revolutionism

The world today is witnessing the problem of methods of political change. Revolutionary socialists believe that this should be done by violent means. The evolutionaries are of the opinion that the objects should be achieved calmly and peacefully. The concept of revolution is not very clear to the socialists. The term implies sudden overthrow of the existing order as well as achieving of objects through a long period of struggle but by violent means. "Both the evolutionaries, as well as revolutionaries, find the basis of their authority in Marx, who is also the originator of their philosophies. The revolutioanries believe in a revolution in which legitimate majority will overthrow the minority which is at present in absolute control of means of production and distribution. It is a revolution of working classes against the capitalist minority. Marx, therefore, justified revolution. He, however, felt that it should not be violent and that violence should 'sparingly' be used. On the cotnrary, the evolutionaries believe that revolution could not always be justified and it was no solution to many of our problems. The revolution always gives birth to many problems.

JUSTIFICATION OF REVOLUTIONARY SOCIALISM

The revolutioanries feel that the capitalists have all along been enjoying power and it is difficult to believe that they will leave power by persuasion. A violent shock will alone set right the existing order. Without forceful method and use of violence it was not possible to capture power because the capitalists have far more effective resources at their disposal and they shall use all fair or foul means to counter every move of the working classes. The capitalists shall take initiative to defame the working class movement. The workers shall have neither the means nor resources to counteract. Revolutionaries plead that history is a witness that power has never been abandoned simply because of presuasion. Power has been snatched by violent means alone.

1. Value of Force. The revolutionaries justify their action on the ground that force alone can create psychological impression and confidence in the minds of the people. Without the use of force many might not take the revolution very seriously.

2. Essential for Change. Revolution is, therefore, essential for creating an atmosphere for changing an order. The revolutionaries simply ridicule the idea that the immense task of changing the old order and creating a new society or set up could be done by peaceful or evolutionary means.

3. Necessary for New Approach and Standards. The new society will have a new approach and new standards of justice and injustice which can be achieved alone by revolutionaries and not by evolutionaries.

JUSTIFICATION OF EVOLUTIONARY SOCIALISM

1. Improvement of capitalists and state. As the time passed many of Marxian prophesies about capitalism did not come true. The capitalists improved the methods of their working. The conditions of the workers under them considerably improved. The state began to function for collective welfare. It passed legislation by which the working conditions of the industrial workers improved. It was, felt that there was no sense in following violent means for the overthrow of the state.

2. Value of peaceful means of change. A revolution is justified only when it is for common and collective interest and not of a partism character. But the revolution, as contemplated by Marx, was a revolution by a party, *i.e.* the working class, against another party, *i.e.* the capitalists. Both were the organs of the same state and had affiliation to the problems before them. It was, therefore, felt that there was no justification to adopt revolutionary means and methods for changing an order which should preferably be done by peaceful means.

3. Socialism through natural evolution. According to Marxian philosophy socialism is to come naturally. There is no hindrance in the path of socialism coming to power in place of the present state. If it is a natural phenomenon and is bound to come, then why to adopt revolutionary methods?

4. Dislocation by revolution. If the idea of socialism is to gain time, then the disadvantages of dislocations which the revolution is bound to bring with it cannot be underestimated and in fact are many more. They, therefore, plead that for gaining time, revolution is not at all justified and in fact is unwanted.

5. Evolution as first step. Marx said that revolution should not be adopted as the first method for achieving the ends. The working classes should first of all try to follow peaceful means. Violent means should only be adopted when there is no other way out. Evolutionary methods should be tried and these are bound to prove useful if properly used for achieving all objects. Instead of violent means, franchise should be extended and those who are returned to legislature should be persuaded to pass legislation on socialist lines. Sidney Webb was of the opinion that socialism has become part of world constitution. They tried to prove historically that the things are already taking a shape on the lines of socialism. They therefore, pleaded that violent means were not at all justified and that evolution was the only solution to the problem.

6. Revolution unjustified. Revolutionaries quote Marx as saying that a revolution should be carried out by the majority for the welfare of majority. But, according to evolutionaries, revolution in Russia was carried out by working classes who were in minority and also it was not with the approval of the peasants who were in majority. Thus, revolution in Russia was a minority revolution. It was unjustified but every attempt is made not only to justify Russain Revolution but also to characterise it as the glory of socialism and its wonderful achievement. They, therefore, always concluded that revolutionary methods could not be justified.

7. Revolution is nowhere welcome. The revolutionary socialists take it for granted that democratic institutions and parliamentary system of government had failed in achieving their objects. They, therefore, come forward with the idea that revolutionary methods should be adopted. But the very fact that 50 per cent of the world population has adopted democracy as a creed and way of life is sufficient evidence to show that democracy is not a failure and that democratic institutions are very popular and can serve a very useful purpose. Revolution is however welcome, specially when the alternative of attaining the object by democratic means and methods is not available.

8. Revolution morally unjustified. The idea of revolution is morally unjustified. A change brought about by revolution is bound to produce counter-revolutionary tendencies. It is also bound to create hatred and reaction.

CAUSES OF DIFFERENCES

1. Different conditions. The difference is primarily due to the economic, social and political differences in one country and the other. Whereas Russia was a fertile ground for revolution, the Fabians easily checked the advancement of Marxian ideology in England because they had faith in their democratic institutions and parliametary form of Government which was absent in Russia.

2. Economic conditions. Where the economic conditions are somewhat better there the people are not ready to welcome revolution as against the countries where the masses are poverty stricken and are on the verge of starvation.

3. Character of those in power. Character of those in power also brings about a change in approach. In England the democratic institutions were flexible. Seeing the trend of the times they readily agreed to the legitimate demands of the working classes. On the other hand, in Russia the Emperor was not flexible and thus invited revolution.

Choice Between the Two

Use of force is not the indication of a healthy society. All nations of the world should be given a free hand to adopt the form of Government which they like and that too without the use of force. As a method for changing the form of Government, force is everywhere condemned. Even socialist objects can be achieved without the use of force by democratic means as well. Therefore, the general choice is for evolutionary system and not for revolutionary methods.

REVOLUTIONISM

What is Revolution?

1. *Webster's New World Dictionary*. The term revolution has been derived from the term *revolvere*. It means : 1. (a) movement of a body in an orbit or circle, (b) the time taken for a body to go around an orbit, 2. (a) turning motion of a body around its centre or excess; (b) rotation, 3. (a) complete round of events, 4. (a) complete or radical change of any kind, 5. overthrow of a government or social system, with another taking its place. Of these five different meanings of the term revolution, the meaning four and five are relevant for our purpose. Thus, we talk of industrial revolution, economic revolution, managerial revolution, besideş the more famous political revolution and social revolution.

2. *Marx and Engels*. "The mode of production of material life conditions the social, political and intellectual life process in general. It is not the consciousness of men that determines their being, but on the contrary, their social being that determines their consciousness. At a certain stage of their development, the material productive forces of society come in conflict with the existing relations of production, or with the forms of relations within which have been at work hitherto. From forms of development of the productive forces these reactions turn into their fetters, then begins an epoch of social revolution." According to Karl Marx the social revolution is the law of development of an antagonistic class of society. To quote Marx : "Finally, in times when the class struggle nears the decisive hour, the process of dissolution going on within the ruling class, in fact within the whole range of old society, assumes such a violent, glaring character, that a small section of the ruling class cuts itself adrift and joins the revolutionary class, the class that holds the future in its hands. Just as therefore, at an earlier period, a sęction of the nobility went over to the bourgeoisie, so now a portion of the bourgeois ideologists who have raised themselves to the level of comprehencing theoretically."

(i) Some definitions present the concept of revolution as a pure political phenomena. According to this definition revolution is a change in central power or sovereignty.

(ii) Some definitions define revolution as a sudden and violent social change expressed through religious, economic, political and industrial forms.

(iii) Some definitions present the concept of revolution as total and fundamental change in the social system in which are included changes in the material and non-material aspects of culture.

3. *Peter Calvart*. Another type of definition of revolution takes it as change in the attitudes towards fundamental social instiutions. According to this viewpoint changes in economic, political or religious fields are not revolution. On the other hand, revolution involves intense changes in the social attitude towards most important social values. A revolution must include the following four elements :

(i) *Process*. Revolution is a process in which the political structure is considered to be of a lower standard by the people or by an important group. This process may bring about violent or peaceful changes in the government.

(ii) *Event*. In revolution an event is very important which changes the government or encourages fear of change.

(iii) *Programme*. The most important element of revloution is the systematic programme for change in society, politics and other spheres of life. This programme is chalked out by the readers.

(iv) *Myth*. Revolution involves a political myth about the status and actions of the political leaders.

4. *Salvador Giner*. "Revolution may be defined as an intense and rapid societal process of change involving an armed resurrection which results in profound and wide structural transformations." In this definition revolution has been defined as a civil war involving a lot of social conflict which determined types of social changes. Such was the conflagration of 1789 in France in which the government of Bourgeois and Middle class was established and the authority of the king and the church weakened. According to Salvador Giner, revolution points out to a total phenomena which involves every field of society. Social changes include changes in values, laws, religion, power and a new society entirely different from free-revolutionary society. In France the society after revolution was in continuity with the society before revolution. Even Karl Marx has admitted that revolution itself has a seed for the counter-revolution. The revolution has the stamp of the historical age.

5. *Arthar Baur*. Revolutions are changes attempting or achieved by force in the constitution of societies. In this definition revolution involved the following five elements :

(i) Revolution is social change.

(ii) Revolution sometimes succeeds and sometimes fails.

(iii) Revolution involves particualr type of social changes involving violence in some social relationships.

(iv) Revolution is concerned with the social system involving law and justice.

(v) Thus, revolution influences the social existence of the man on a fundamental basis.

6. *Aristotle*. In his book *Politics* Aristotle wrote, "The universal and chief cause of...revolutionary feelings...the desire of equality, when men think that they are equal to others who have more than themselves; or, again the desire of inequality and superiority, when conceiving themselves to be superior they think that they have no more but the same or less than their inferiors; pretensions which may or may not be just." In this definition Aristotle has used the term revolutionary feeling in a very wide sense. It should be remembered here that social changes generally involves economic changes such as found in industrial revolution. The examples of social change through revolution may be found in

France in 1789, USSR in 1917 and China in 1949. Revolutions are not physical phenomena like earthquakes, they involve social activities.

7. *Arnold M. Rose*. "Revolution refers to a radical and far reaching series of changes in a society, usually occurring rapidly but not necessarily with violence."

8. *Wilbert E. Moore*. Revolutions refer to "large scale discontinuous changes in the fabric of society....Polarization is the key indicator of incipient revolution."

9. *Anthony Wallace*. "A deliberate, organized attempt by some members of a society to construct a more satisfying culture by speedy acceptance of a pattern of new ideas."

Besides these definitions Edmund Burk has defined social revolution involving fast social changes. According to P.A. Sorokin revolution involves intense, deep and violent changes in the present social system. Crane Brinton has presented an analysis of revolution and defined it as a type of fever which is a symptom that the society is passing through a crisis.

Stages of the Development of Revolution

Brinton has pointed out the following stages of the development of revolution on the basis of his comparative studies of the revolution of France, USA, England and USSR.

1. Economically speaking the above mentioned four countries were in good condition before revolution. The revolutions were, therefore, due to the extremely repressive politics of the ruler. The revolutionaries were not naked or hungry, repressed or depressed people. The revolution was excited by a new hope based upon optimistic philosophy.

2. These societies exhibited intense class conflict before revolution. This class conflict could be seen in 1640, 1776 and 1789 or 1917. The intense feeling of revolution was found among those people who had sufficient living but who deliberated on the inequalities in the standard of living of the Aristocratic class and the common man. Revolutions occur when a social class feels near to another social class. That is why the untouchables revolted against theocratic aristocrary. It is difficult to say why among equal classes revolutionary feelings are found in one class and not in another.

3. In all the social revolutions there is a common element of detachment of the intellectual.

4. In all the above four societies the government was clearly inefficient and careless and could not realise any social changes. In all these societies one finds new directions of development, new rich classes, new development of the means of transport and communication, new directions of trade and commerce etc. All these new situations created a lot of pressure upon the government machinery which could not bear it.

5. In all these four countries the rulers had lost faith in themselves and faith in the customs and traditions of their class. Some of them developed into intellectuals who adopted humanist viewpoint or favoured the opposite classes.

However, most of them lived an immoral life of luxury and were therefore absolutely useless.

Types of Revolutions

1. View of P.A. Sorokin. According to P.A. Sorokin, "A comparatively sudden, rapid, and violent change of the absolute official law of the group, or of the institutions and systems of values which it represents, may be called a revolutionary change." Pitrim A. Sorokin was well acquainted with the circumstances and causes of the Russian revolution. Therefore, Sorokin has analyzed in detail the sociological aspects of revolution. He has tried to make clear his conception of revolution in his various writings, particularly in his book : *The Sociology of Revolution :.Social and Cultural*. Sorokin categorically terms revolution a crime. The political revolution is nothing but a crime on a large scale. Indeed, there is little difference between crime in general and the crime of revolution. If a revolution is confined to narrow limits it is regarded to be a general crime, while, on the other hand, a general crime on a large scale is regarded revolution. Thus, it is obvious that in the opinion of Sorokin revolution is nothing but criminal act. Sorokin considers revolutionary crime to be the wrath of God. Therefore, he has included revolution in the category of wraths of God such as famine, epidemic, war etc. Revolution is thus inimical to the interests of the society.

Sorokin has pointed out the following six types of revolution :

(i) *Political revolution*. When any revolutionary change aims at overthrow of the political power of a particular group, it is known as political revolution. This includes revolutions to change the kings, the rulers and the government.

(ii) *Economic revolution*. Whenever any revolutionary movement tries to bring radical changes in the economic system of a particular group involving the nature and ownership of property, production, distribution and consumption, we call it an economic revolution.

(iii) *Religious revolution*. Whenever radical changes in the religious values of a group are brought about by a revolutionary movement we call it a religious revolution.

(iv) *Family revolution*. Whenever efforts are made to bring about radical changes in the family or marriage system of a group it is known as family revolution.

(v) *Racial or nationalistic revolutions*. Whenever the institutions, relationships or values involved in radical changes are racial or national, these revolutions are called racial or nationalistic revolutions.

(vi) *Total revolution*. Whenever all the laws aim at radical changes in all the institutions and the entire value system it is called total revolution. In India, Jayaprakash Narayan called his programme of revolution by the name total revolution.

2. View of Karl Marx. Besides the above mentioned types of revolution some other types of revolution have been pointed out by other thinkers. For example, Karl Marx has mentioned the following three types of revolution :

(i) *Anti-slave owning revolutions.* As is clear by the title, these revolutions are anti-slavery. These obviously belong to the early social stage of slaves and masters. The slaves united to oppose the masters and declared themselvees free.

(ii) *Anti-feudal revolutions.* After the anti-slave owning revolutions the society became feudal with the two conflicting classes of landlord and the serfs. Gradually, the serfs rose against the feudal lords to bring about radical changes in the feudal system. These are known as anti-feudal revolutions arising due to the socio-economic consequences of the feudal system itself.

(iii) *Socialist revolutions.* With the change in feudal system arrived the capitalist system in which there were two opposite classes of the capitalists and the labourers. This was the condition of most of the Western societies in 19th century. This aroused socialist revolution opposing the capitalist system or aiming at the elimination of capitalism. The modern revolutions in France, England, USSR and China may be called socialist revolutions.

3. View of Lipset. S.M. Lipset has distinguished between the following three types of revolutions :

(i) *Leftist revolutions.* Communist and Peronist revolutions are known as leftist revolutions since they aim at establishment of a new political system totally replacing the present political system.

(ii) *Rightist revolutions.* Revolutions seeking some necessary modification or reform in the traditional system of authority are known as rightist revolutions.

(iii) *Centralist revolutions.* Revolutions demanding individual liberty on the one hand and trying to establish *status quo* on the other are known as centralist revolutions such as fascism.

Some thinkers have called leftist revolutions as extremist revolutions and rightist recolutions as liberal revolutions.

During 1950-1960 China started a new type of revolution known as cultural revolution. This revolution aimed at eliminating all the symptoms of former bourgeois culture and substituted by the new revolutionary culture of the communist party.

VARIOUS VIEWS ABOUT CAUSES OF REVOLUTION

Sorokin's View

Different thinkers have pointed out various causes of revolutions. Sorokin has described in detail the causes of revolution. According to him contrary forces are always present in a society. There is a conflict among these contrary forces. If there can be no harmony among conflicting elements, revolution results. Sorokin also explains why the harmony is not possible. Like some other psychologists Sorokin believes that the behaviour of man is guided more by sentiment than by reason and that instincts play large part in the life of man. Now, if the natural instincts become corrupted for some reason, man is inclined towards crime and anti-social activity. In this condition social harmony is lost. As soon as social harmony is destroyed there is disorganization in the society and in a disorganized society the criminal tendencies get maximum scope of expression. When revolution comes into force in a society all old values and social laws become extinct. Anarchy rules over everything and peaceful tendencies are subdued. In place of human behaviour animal behaviour becomes the nature of man. In order to substantiate his views Sorokin has referred to a number of revolutions and by analyzing them he has shown that his observations about revolution are valid. According to Sorokin social tensions are the chief causes of social revolution. These social tensions are due to the following causes :

1. Hunger. Poverty, hunger and revolution are closely related. The hungry man loses his faith in the traditional institutions, conventions, ideologies and values. The traditional moral norms cease to be meaningful for him. He has nothing to lose and therefore revolution is full of advantages for him. This was the reason why Karl Marx pointed out to the labourers that they have nothing to lose and a whole world to win. The French revolution was also preceded by widespread hunger in France. Before Russian revolution most of the inhabitants of Moscow were eating only once a day.

2. Property. The sentiment for property leads to a sense of security in property. Therefore, when most of the persons in a society are devoid of property, there is widespread sense of economic insecurity. They lose faith in the present social system. These include unemployed persons and poor farmers who have lost everything to the landlord. All these persons lose faith in the present system and this leads to revolution. With Karl Marx, P.A. Sorokin admits that the main cause of revolution is economic.

3. Self-preservation. Human beings have a natural tendency of self-preservation whose repression leads to revolutionary tendencies. The instinct of self-preservation may be repressed both on the individual and the group level. When most of the persons feel insecurity for their life, revolutionary tendencies are aroused. In some situations not only life of the individuals or some groups but that of the whole nation is in danger. This situation creates acute revolutionary tendencies. Utilising this tendency some rulers wage wars against other countries. Defeat in war also arouses revolutionary tendency since the people feel that the present system is responsible for the defeat. They lose faith in the adequacy, utility and capacity of the present system and find danger for their lives. In order to save their existence most of the people of the defeated country take resort to revolutions. After the First World War the defeated countries including Bulgaria, Turkey, Germany, Hungary and USSR witnessed such revolutions.

4. Sex. According to Sorokin repression of the sex drives in society also leads to revolutionary tendencies. The open sex behaviour, deovid of all moral restraints, in the privileged and rich higher classes creates a deep sense of frustration and reaction towards the present social system among the people. Examples of such behaviour could be found in France and Russia before revolution.

5. Freedom. Repressions of the individual and collective liberties also create background for revolution. The cry for freedom has been the chief slogan of the revolutionaries everywhere. The slogan, "Liberty, Equality and Fraternity" raised during French revolution inspired revolutionaries throughout the world. The ideal of freedom is an ideal of a society free from all exploitation and repression.

6. Equality of opportunity. Repression of the self-expression of the persons having high abilities and capacities also leads to revolutionary tendencies. In a society devoid of equality of opportunity one finds frustration everywhere. When the opportunities for progress are limited to a privileged section of society, other sections become more and more anxious to approve the present social initiations. They want a radical change in the present system of classes, customs, traditions, castes and laws. This leads to revolution.

Theory of Salvador Giner

According to Salvador Giner the following factors are the important causes of revolution :

1. Intense Class Antagonism.
2. Frustrations of Rising Economic Expectations.
3. Frustrations of Rising Status and Power Expectations.
4. Incapacity of the Ruling Classes.
5. A Fraction of the Upper Class Joining the Enemy.
6. Hostility of the Intellectual Community.
7. Revolutionary Myth. According to Peter Calvert, "The genereation of revolutionary energy implies the creation of a rival centre of ideological interpretation."
8. Duality of power between the conservative and the revolutionary.
9. Appropriate International Situation.

VARIOUS CAUSES OF REVOLUTION

1. Psychological Causes. Revolution has its various aspects such as political, economic, social and others, yet fundamentally it is a psychological process. It is this psychological aspect and nature that is analysed and studied by social psychology. According to this science, the following are the main psychological factors at the root of the revolution :

(i) *Explosion of repressed drives*. In the opinion of many psychologists, revolution is the explosion or collective outburst of repressed drives. Most of the modern psychologists hold that the desires and tendencies that the individual represses or suppresses are not completely eliminated from the mind but they rather manifest themselves even more violently as a violent reaction when the right opportunity presents itself. When, in a country, various kinds of desires and tendencies of the people are reepressed and are not allowed the change to manifest and extend themselves, then in most people some sort of reaction takes place. And it is this same reaction that in collective form assumes the proportion of revolution. It is Freud who has specifically explained the reactions of repressed desires. In his *The Sociology of Revolution*, Sorokin has written,

"The immediate cause of revolution is always the growth of 'repression' of the main instincts of majority of society, and the impossibility of obtaining for these instincts the necessary minimum of satisfaction." When the necessary instincts of majority of the population remain dissatisfied, or satisfaction becomes impossible, and repression increases, then the reaction to this suppression expresses itself in the form of revolution.

(ii) *Expression of unconscious and lowly passions*. In order to explain revolution Lebon has given the simile of mob behaviour. Just as in crowd behaviour the unconscious and lowly passions of the people find expression, in the same manner revolution is caused by the same factors. It is often seen that in times of revolution the behaviour of the people is much excited, irrational and emotional as is the case with a crowd. The major constituents of the revolution are derived from the suppressed, tortured and frustrated morals of humanity that form the masses. In a revolution they turn a deaf ear to every one and are prepared to do practically anything. And hence one comes across action done by people which cannot be equalled by any human being possessing his faculties. During the French Revolution even women murdered people and sucked their blood. In this way, in a revolution, extreme cruelty is witnessed and most of the people behave like animals, as if they were reluctant to forget their origin.

(iii) *Expression of unconscious desire*. According to Sigmund Freud, the exploited and tortured beings in society foster feelings of hatred and animosity towards the administrators and upper classes in their unconscious minds. In his infancy the individual hates his father because of latter's tyrannical and strict administration, and later on in life this hatred is transferred to the administration and power. In a revolution it is this same hatred that is collectively manifested and expressed and efforts are made to destroy the power and its representatives.

It is evident from the above description of the various opinions concerning the psychological factors in revolution that the psychological foundations of revolution are formed, particularly of repressed desires and instincts. As L.P. Edwards has written, "People come to feel that their legitimate aspirations and ideals are being repressed or perverted, that their entirely proper desires and ambitions are being hindered and thwarted." What must be kept clearly in view is the fact that psychological causes are not the momentary or immediate causese of revolution but rather the fundamental causes. In other words, the psychological factors create a readiness in the individual for evolution. In the absence of this readiness or psychological preparedness, there can be no revolution because, be the political, social and economic conditions what they will, they are not sufficient to induce the crowd to take any positive action. In the words of Kimball Young, "We may say in fact that no revolution is possible until the psychological moment has arrived. There must be a definite 'readiness' for revolutionary behaviour."

2. Cultural Causes. As has been indicated at an earlier juncture, revolution is caused by factors other than the purely psychological ones. In addition to the psychological there are some cultural factors that help to precipitate a revolution.

These factors are also important cotnributory factors of circumstances in the final result. Ogburn and Nimkoff have written, "Revolution is a rapid change of some magnitude in culture." As and when the existing and traditional institutions, dogmas, customs, mores and traditions, etc., become continuously less capable of satisfying the needs of the people, the society becomes marked with unrest and perturbation and disturbance. The people revolt. And the residents of urban districts have a particular role in this revolt. Because of the more facile availability of the means of suggestions and propaganda in the urban areas in comparison with the rural areas, revolutionary ideas circulate more rapidly among the urban population than they do among the rural population on the whole is more in favour of progress and novelty and opposed to tradition and stagnation. And it is in this class that the revolutionary spark finds the most receptive substance and it easily produces a conflagration. If new notions and thoughts, inventions and novel things find their place in society easily and without resistance and as a matter of course, then the necessity of revolution is avoided. But this does not happen because there are many individuals in society who are opposed to change which adversely affects their vested interests. Hence, revolution becomes necessary and is inevitable. Myth, emotional symbols, legends and stereotypes also have a hand in this. It is the change in them that induces revolution. Kimball Young writes, "The rise of a new social myth means that the desires, beliefs, attitudes and habits of the people have been altered. The new myth is the promise of a new heaven and new earth."

3. Economic Causes. In addition to the cultural causes of revolution there are some economic factors important in this connection. In the opinion of the famous revolutionist, Karl Marx, the main causes of revolution are of an economic nature. According to him, the increase of the disparity between the various social classes and the exploitation of the poor classes by the richer class in society leads to a situation in which revolution becomes inevitable because the exploiters are not prepared to voluntarily relinquish their power. According to Marxist thinking the main factor at the root of revolution is class struggle which is caused by the exploitation of the labourers and the farmers and agriculturists at the hands of the rich classes. The leaders of revolution are these exploited farmers and labourers. What must be kept in view here is that it is not possible to say definitely in exactly which economic condition will a revolution be necessary. Actually, it sometimes happens that a revolution does not take having been subjected to extreme exploitation and continuous poverty and hardship. On the other hand, in 1918, when the German agriculturists revolted against Kaiser their economic conditions was not very poor. Similarly, in the 1917 American revolution the economic conditions of that country was fairly good. The fact of the matter is that even at the root of economic causes, it is the psychological factor that is at work. Whatever may be the condition of economy in the country the people will revolt if they come to believe that it is necessary to improve their economic condition since such belief leads to an increase in the dissatisfaction that is inherent in life. It is not the extent to which the agriculturist and the labourer is exploited that is a determining factor of whether a revolution will take place. It is not the decisive factor. What is also needed is hatred and disgust for the moneyed class and the landlords in the hearts of those who serve them. It is only when these strong emotions are aroused that the revolution can take actual shape. It is for this reason that the revolutionaries pay particular attention to arousing and inflaming these feelings.

4. Political Causes. And, finally, we come to another important aspect of the causes of revolution, the political causes of this phenomenon. In different countries there is continuous conflict between various political parties and leaders for political power. Taking advantage of the opportunities that present themselves, they do their best to persuade the public opinion to support them and to encourage it to denounce their political rival. For example, the communist party always aims at arousing and enraging the labourers and agriculturists in order that the party may be able to gain power. In this manner, revolutions happen and are caused by political interests.

Violence and Revolution

Therefore modern thinkers do not accept the Marxian idea that violence is necessary for revolution. In the words of Arendt Hanna, "Only where change occurs in the sense of a new beginning, where violence is used to constitute an altogether different form of government, to bring about the formation of a new body politic...can we speak of revolution" revolution is fast political change. This change is very comprehensive and multisided. Many a times revolution is violent and therefore, some scholars call peaceful political change not revolution but reformation. In most of the modern societies social change is generally brought about by peaceful means. Reform, however, requires political efficiency since the state has to deal with traditionalists and conservatives on the one hand and the revolutionariese and the extremists on the other. Therefore, the government has to adopt the policy of minimum conflict. Reform is not total change. It requires balance between social and political change. It is not possible if this balance is lost. A more intense change takes towards revolution if balance is lost. A more intense change takes towards revolution rather than reform.

Conditions of Reformation

Communication between the administrator and the administered is necessary for reformation. This requires development of the means of communications so that the rulers may fulfil them before they may give rise to acute discontentment. Reform requires maintenance of the *status quo* on the one hand and satisfaction of the demand on the other. This requires additional means. Therefore, in comparison to the poor countries, social reforms are easier in the rich societies. The reformers believe that the reforms remove social tensions which therefore do not require revolution. But in some cases revolution becomes necessary. This history of the world is full of examples when reforms were made before revolution, but since they did not succeed to fulfil the demands, revolution occurred. The limits to which reformers themselves take towards revolution depend upon several factors.

The nature of reform is an important factor in political change. For example, reform in the field of policies increases the possibility of revolution. On the other hand, reform in leadership diminishes a possibility of revolution. In the event of revolutionary changes in the present government, revolution becomes redundant. Along with the nature of reform, its occasion is also important. If the reforms are available when they are needed revolution does not occur. But if the aim is near mere reform will not do.

Structural Causes

The social structure and the level of aspiration of the groups demanding change is an important factor in political change. Revolution may occur by the efforts of intense reform in the middle class, particularly in the urban society, since they have already a revolutionary attitude. They are not discontented due to physical insufficiency. The important causes of discontent among them are psychological insecurity, individual attention, guilt consciousness and consciousness of identity. They have the sentiments of national dignity, consciousness of progress and national purpose. They want to achieve these values in social reconstruction. However, sometimes these demands cannot be fulfilled by the government. It is also seen that demands go on increasing with the efforts of reformation. On the other hand if the demands of the rural middle class are not particularly concerning the land, agriculture or prices, they may be successfully fulfilled. That is why revolutions are achieved not through the farmers but by the labourers, not through the rural folk but through the urban people.

Revolution occurs due to comprehensive changes in the structure of the society and the state. Widespread changes are made in social values, institutions and leadership. However, political revolution aims at achievement of authority though there may be general consciousness in the society for it. If the political consciousness of revolution becomes widespread, some classes raise political demand which cannot be fulfilled by the existing political system. In order to meet these demands the present political institutions have to be substituted by entirely new political institutions. Sometimes the old monarchy itself crumbles and gives place to a new political system.

Gap Between Social and Political Changes

The main cause of revolutions is the gap between the social and the political changes. As a society becomes more and more complex, new social groups are born which search for the leaders and the means to participate in the political system. If these are not attained, revolutions occur. Political system and institutions sufficient to provide such opportunities do not require revolution. The most important cause of revolution is the rigidity of the political system. Thus, in order to check revolution, social and political demands are met. In less complex social and economic system, demands are never so intense as to require revolution. On the other hand, social and economic complexities go on increasing in modernised societies. This puts pressure upon political initiations and if they do not adapt revolutions occur. Thus, the important cause of revolution is the lagging behind of the political changes from the social change or the incapacity of the political system to accept the new demands.

ROLE OF THE ARMY

The main cause of revolution is the increasing gap and tension, between social and political changes. Dissatisfied groups unite to wage conflict for the achievement of common objectives. As a general rule when the urban middle class is dissatisfied the chances of revolution are high. Dissastisfied farmers and rural people may also struggle for revolution by uniting it with the urban middle class or the labourer class. However, there may be a specific group to lead the revolution change the government and the political system. In many countries this is done by the army since it is a disciplined group having arms and if its commanders seek to assume political leadership, revolution becomes easier. Examples of revolution by army can be seen in so many countries in modern times. But if the general masses do not support political revolution brought about by the army, the new government cannot remain in office and counter-revolution occurs.

However, in comparison to other groups, the army has undoubtedly more power to achieve revolution. Hence, in so many states of Asia and Africa the army has played an important role in bringing about political change. The main factors behind this phenomenon are centralised leadership, hierarchical structure and strict discipline in the organisation. The army is used to fight with the order whatever may be the consequences. This is taught to the soldiers. They cannot even think of challenging the order. They hardly make any gap between order and its fulfilment. The entire army training is geared to achieve this. Again, there are efficient means of communication available to the army by which even far off units may be ordered in no time. Besides, the soldiers have team spirit and a sense of organisation which is created by separate residence, dress, principles, history and traditions. In the end, the most important factor in the favour of army is the fact that the means of violence in a political system are not governed by the politicians but by the army generals. Thus, due to the above mentioned factors, armed revolution is easier for the army. It may be remembered here that whenever armed revolution has been successfully suppressed it is also achieved by the loyal soldiers of the army. In both the cases the power of army in politics is clear.

CONSEQUENCES OF REVOLUTION

As is quite clear from the above discussion, all social organisation is disrupted at the time of revolution. All norms of human conduct and thought, all processes of normal life come to an end at the time of revolution. The political fall-out of revolution is that the ruling clique is thoroughly discredited and may even be divested of property or done to death. Of course, the persons in the forefront of revolution try to take a lion's share of it. They act as a rule, like a band of cirminals. The men of peace are at a disadvantage in revolution and anti-social elements enjoy all the benefits. P.A. Sorokin has summarised the social consequences of revolution as follows :

1. Cycle of Revolution. Every revolution exhibits two stages : one in which the revolution destroys social institutions and cultural values, not only those which are outmoded but also which are creative and revolutionary. In the second stage important social and institutional values arise again and develop and throw back the destructive forces of revolution.

2. Law of Polarisation. This is connected with the various elements of population. Ordinarily, the majority of people are neither bad nor good, neither social nor anti-social, neither religious nor irreligious. Revolution polarises the population into opposite group of saints and sinners, altruists and egoists. This polarisation may be found in all the social and cultural areas.

3. Changes in Vital Processes. Revolutions take the form of civil war. After some months the birth rate begins to fall. In the end of the destructive stage it again starts rising and keeps the momentum for several years. Similarly the death rate also rises and falls and so also the rate of marriages and divorces as well as suicide.

4. Changes in Psychology and Behaviour. These are as follows :

(i) Breakdown of personality structure.

(ii) Effect on overt behaviour.

(iii) Speech reactions and corresponding ideologies.

(iv) Effect on property relations.

(v) Effect on sexual behaviour and relationships.

(vi) Effect on ethical and religious conduct.

5. Change in Social and Cultural Processess. In the first stage the economic life is distintegrated, standard of living falls, poverty, unemployment and hunger increase. Political life becomes uncertain, revolution has its influence on every field of culture including science and philosophy, religion and morality, literature and art, politics and law etc. Cultural values change absolutely.

POSITIVE FORCES OF REVOLUTION

At the root of revolution are the following positive forces :

1. Widespread provocation. Deep frustration against the present conditions and the provocating activities of the government encourage active elements of revolution. The repressed desire becomes active due to widespread provocation.

2. Public opinion. Revolution is a group activity. Therefore, unless anti-government public opinion is formed and takes the form of collective anger, revolution is not possible.

3. Programme of reform. The programme of revolution should be a programme of reform of the present evils presented by the leaders before the people. This required successful leadership. The people cannot choose their programme as was wrongly supposed by Jayaprakash Narayan in his attempt at total revolution. The examples of the great revolution in France, China and Vietnam speak volumes about their leaders.

4. Trusted leadership. Thus, without a Mao Tse Tung, a Fidel Castro, a Ho Chi Minh and a Lenin or a Stalin, revolution is not possible. It is needless to say that total revolution envisaged in India did not have such a leader. The explosion in the form of revolution does not require a leader. But after explosion only trusted leadership may lead the revolution successfully to realise its aim. In its absence, the government easily suppresses the revolution.

5. Weakness of conservation. Revolution involves a direct conflict between the rulers and the repressed class. Naturally, whichever group is more powerful succeeds in defeating the other group. Therefore, in order to succeed revolution requires that the rulers should be weaker than the ruled. As Lenin has pointed out, revolution happens only when the old class is unable to maintain the old system and the lower class is not prepared to maintain it.

THE PROCESS OF REVOLUTION

L.P. Edwards has pointed out the following stages in the naturally history of the process of revolution :

1. Unrest. Revolution starts with general unrest. People feel that the present system is wrong and evil. They are restless but do not know the remedies. This was evident before the revolutions of France, Russia and China. A symptom of general unrest is the increase in seasonal mobility. For example, before Russian revolution, so many intellectuals left the country for Western countries. The internal and external migration increases social disorganisation since the migrated persons are free from traditional social control. People have no fear of police in this stage. The social evils like immoral behaviour, corruption, prostitution, adultery, theft and dacoity increase at an unprecedented rate. The whole society is in a state of shock and utter disorganisation.

2. Defection of the intellectuals. In the second stage of revolution the intellectuals including the teachers, the editors, the lawyers and the writers exhibit fast changes in their beliefs and faiths. Earlier, the intellectuals have sympathy with the rulers and appreciated the circumstances helping in their earning of their livelihood. But, as the circumstances change, the sympathies and loyalties also change. Now, the intellectuals only apparently support the government since they depend on it for their livelihood, but secretly they are against the government and incite the people against the rulers.

3. Emergence of economic incentive and social myth. In the third stage the repressed masses feel that if they make effort they can get rid of pitiable condition. They start dreaming of a future life of comfort and progress.

4. Outbreak of revolution. The secret unrest and dissatisfaction erupts in the sudden and dramatic outbreak of revolution at any time on an apparently very ordinary pretext. It is only after some time that people understand the importance of the initial incidence. Those who are active during revolution, do not know that they are creating new history of the country. After the initial revolution the people realise that the government of which they were so much fearful is so weak that it can be openly opposed. Now the revolutionary activities become more widespread and acute. Those people who are detached also now participate in revolutionary activities. Thus, the number of active revolutionaries increases very fast. The outbreak of revolution is initiated by few and often an unorganised people. But their success exposes the weakness of the government and therefore increase the number of revolutionaries. Thus, an important cause of revolution is the internal weakness of the rulers.

5. Rule of the liberals. For an indefinite period the political power and authority after revolution, remains in the hands of liberals and reformists, those who follow a middle road between the leftists and rightists, the revolutionaries and the conservatives. This is due to the fact that no extremist group becomes powerful in the early days of revolution. However, as the extremist groups attain power, the situation changes.

6. The reign of terror. As the political authority passes from the hands of the liberals into the hands of the extremists, a reign of terror is let loose. The extremists have two fronts, internal and external. As they win, the revolution establishes but most often only after a counter-revolution.

QUESTIONS FOR EXERCISE

1. Explain and discuss Evolutionary and Revolutionary Socialism.
2. What is revolution? Discuss its elements.
3. What are the stages of revolution? Explain its types.
4. Discuss the causes of revolution according to different thinkers.
5. What is the role of army in revolution? Explain the consequences of revolution.
6. Explain the positive forces of revolution and analyse its forces.

16

Vladimir Ilyich Lenin (1870—1924)

Vladimir Ilyich Ulyanov was born on April 10 (22), 1870, in the town of Simbirsk (now Ulyanovsk), situated on the banks of the Volga. During the period of his exile from May 1897 to January 1900 in Siberia, he was known by the pseudonym of Lenin.

Lenin dedicated himself to the cause of the revolution, of the working class from his early youth. His family upbringing, the progressive Russian literature that he read and his observation of the life around him — all these influeced and shaped the character and views of the young Lenin. In Russia in those days the masses were suffering from an appalling poverty. The tyrannical rule of the Tsarist government, landowner and capitalist oppression and the down-trodden position of the poverty-stricken workers and peasants aroused in Lenin a burning hatred for the exploiters and sympathy for the exploited. While Lenin was still at school these revolutionary sentiments were in evidence.

Lenin's elder brother Alexander, a young man of strong will and high principles, exercised a great influence over him. When asked how he would act in a given situation, he invariably answered : "Like Alexander." Alexander was a student at St. Petersburg University. He could have become a brilliant scientist, but he chose to dedicate his life to the revolutionary struggle against the Tsarist autocracy in the hope of winning a better life for the people. Vladimir Lenin first learned about Marxist literature from his elder brother.

When Lenin was still very young, his father died suddenly in 1886. In March 1887 Alexander was arrested in St. Petersburg on a charge of being involved in an attempt to assassinate Alexander III, he was executed in the Schlusselburg Forress in May of the same year.

This was a stunning blow to Lenin. It strengthened him in his resolve to dedicate his life to the cause of revolution. But Lenin was convinced that in the fight against the autocracy, assassination of individual government officials or even of the Tsar himself was a wrong course that could achieve no purpose. Hence, Lenin began his search for a different road to liberation for the working people.

Political Work

Early in December 1887 Lenin was expelled from the University of Kazan and placed under police surveillance. While studying for the bar at the University of Petersburg, he worked in the trade union movement, often defying the police. He later edited *Labor's Work* and *Iskra* (the *Spark*), both underground journals aimed at fomenting revolution among the urban working classes. From 1903 onward he fought against half-way measures advocated by more moderate socialist elements. Arriving late from Switzerland where he had been in exile, he missed the revolution of 1905, which was brutally suppressed by the Tsarist government.

October Revolution 1917

Except for a short time during the revolution of 1905 (in Russia), Lenin lived in Western Europe for most of the period between 1900 and 1917 as an agent of the Social Democratic Party of Russia. On his return to Russia in April 1917 he took up the command of the Bolshevik faction and prepared the ground for the October Revolution. His first action was to issue his *April Theses,* calling on Bolsheviks not to support the floundering provisional government which had taken over after the February Revolt. Instead he called for 'peace, liberty, bread and land' for the workers and peasants. Sensing that conditions were ripe for a second revolt, he proclaimed in October that it was now or never! During the night of October 24, the Bolsheviks surrounded the Winter Palace and other government buildings. On the morning of October 25. members of the provisional government were placed under arrest. The October Revolution of 1917 was thus successfully over.

Leader of Communist Party

Lenin's life was inseparable from the life and struggle of the Communist Party from the time of its inception. He was the organizer and leader of the revolutionary Marxist Party of Russia's proletariat.

"Give us an organization of revolutionaries, and we will overturn Russia!" was Lenin's impassioned appeal Headed by Lenin, the Bolshevik Party, 'the intelligence, the honour and the conscience of our era', led the working class of Russia to victory in the Great October Socialist Revolution. Lenin and the Leninist Party created by the working class of Russia showed mankind the way to socialism and communism both in theory and practice.

DEVELOPMENT OF MARX

Lenin developed Marx's revolutionary theory, which he brought into line with the conditions of the new era of imperialism and proletarian revolutions, of mankind's transition from capitalism to socialism, and the building of a communist society. Marxism is inseparable from Leninism. Marxism-Leninism is now a generally accepted term. It is a great internationalist doctrine whose correctness is being more and more confirmed by the course of world history. The three components of Marxism — philosophy, political economy and scientific communism — were further developed, enriched and specified in Lenin's works.

Lenin waged an unrelenting battle against all kinds of deviations from the revolutionary course of Marxism, from class positions of the proletariat, and against revisionism of reformism. He vigorously combatted all attempts to turn Marxism into a collection of dry and rigid dogmas or formulas, divorced from reality, from practice. He repeatedly said that Marxism was not a dogma but a guide to action.

As a true and faithful disciple of Karl Marx, Lenin accpted everything that his Master postulated. In Lenin's view, the philosophy of Marxism is materialism. But Lenin asserts, Marx did not stop at the materialism of the eighteenth century. Marx enriched it with the acquistition of German classical philosophy, especially of Hegelian system, which in its turn led to the materialism of Feuerbach. The chief of these acquisitions is dialectics. The latest discoveries of natural science have remarkably confirmed Marx's dialectical materialism. Lenin regarded Marx's historical materialism as one of the greatest achievements of scientific thought.

MATERIALISTIC INTERPRETATION OF SOCIAL PROCESS

Like Marx, Lenin pleads that all the ideas, whether individual or social, are the result of reactions to material objects in sense organs. Hence, a true analysis of social process depends upon a thorough understanding of the underlying material forces, which are mainly economic. According to Lenin, the dialectics of historical materialism is not only the greatest contribution of Marx to social thought but it also helps us to interpret and understand correctly his own (Marx's) system of economic and political thought. Appreciating and confirming Marx's views, Lenin says that the former was convinced of the necessity of "bringing the science of society...into harmony with the materialist foundation, and of reconstructing it thereupon."[1] Since materialism regards consciousness as the outcome of being materialism as applied to the social life of mankind has to explain social consciousness as the outcome of social being.

Advance over Earlier Theories

Lenin believed that the discovery of the materialist conception of history removed two of the chief defects of the earlier historical theories :

1. The earlier historical theories examined only the human motives of the historical activity, without investigating what produced these motives, but the materialist conception of history, while going deeper into and analysing the process of history, explains the underlying material forces which prompt the ideological motives of human beings.

2. The earlier theories failed to cover the activites of the masses of the population, whereas historical materialism made it possible to study the social conditions of the life of the masses and the changes in these conditions with the accuracy of natural sciences.

According to Lenin, all the changes in human society are brought about by material forces, but these changes are made possible only when the human beings become conscious of the necessity of a change. Lenin, therefore, advised

1. Engels, F. : *Ludwig Feuerbach*, Eng. ed., 1946, p. 34.

the proletariat first to be sure of the favourable situation for a social and economic change in the society and then to act in accordance with the material realities of the time, never going beyond the limits that the given circumstances would permit. While the whole theory of Marx is "an application of the theory of evolution,"[2] Lenin argued that a successful proletarian revolution would not merely depend on the evolution, but it would be conducted and fought according to a calculated programme of action as indicated by Marx.

SUPPORT TO MARX'S THEORY OF CLASS STRUGGLE

Lenin fully supported Marx's theory of the class struggle. Marx wrote in the *Communist Manifesto* (1848) that the "history of all hitherto existing society is the history of class struggle." Lenin remarks : "That in any given society the strivings of some of its members conflict with the strivings of others, that social life is full of contradictions, that history discloses a struggle within nations and societies as well as between nations and societies, and, in addition, an alternation of periods of revolution and reaction, peace and war, stagnation and rapid progress or decline — are facts that are generally known."[3] Like Marx, Lenin also believed that the modern bourgeois society has not done away with class antagonism. But it has simplified the class antagonisms, as the modern capitalist society has been split up into two clear-cut hostile camps — bourgeoisie and proletariat.

Transformation into Socialist Society

In complete agreement with Marx's thesis of the inevitability of transformation of capitalist society into socialist society, Lenin writes that "the socialization of labour, which is advancing ever more rapidly in thousands of forms, and which has manifested itself very strikingly during the half-century that has elapsed since the death of Marx in the growth of large-scale production, capitalist cartels, syndicates and trusts, as well as in the gigantic increase in the dimensions and power of financial capital, forms the chief material foundation for the inevitable coming of socialism."[4] The socialization of production is bound to lead to the conversion of the means of production into the property of society, to the 'expropriation of the expropriators'. In the process of transformation of the capitalist society into socialist society, the interference of the state power in social relations becomes superfluous in one sphere after another, and then ceases of itself. The government of persons is replaced by the administration of things and the direction of the process of production. The state is not abolished, *it withers away.*[5] Lenin thus corroborates, Marxism on the theoretical plane.

Adaptation of Marxism to Russia

Lenin tried to adapt Marxism to the state of affairs in Russia, as a leader

2. Cf. Burns. E. (ed.) : *A Handbook of Marxism*, New York, International, 1935, p. 740.
3. Lenin, V. I. : *Marx, Engels and Marxism*, Moscow Publication, 1947, p. 27.
4. Lenin, V. I. : *op. cit.*, p. 41.
5. Engels, F. : *Anti-Duhring*, p. 315.

of the Marxist Party. Most of what he wrote was concerned with the Russian Revolution. As a realist and a practical politician, Lenin laboured to bring Marx down to date, taking account of the further evolution of capitalist society and reformulating the tactics of Marxism in the light of new developments in Russia.

Lenin was a realist, and a utopian. His *The State and the Revolution* (1917) consists of quotations from Marx and Engels put together and explaiend to justify the revolutionary Marxism of the Bolsheviks. Against the German Social Democrats Lenin's pamphlet purports to prove that Marx and Engels never ceased to be revolutionary socialists.

Marx produced two doctrines of the state, but he did not explain how they were connected. He said that the state is an instrument of class oppression, that it is often a parasitic growth on society, making class oppression possible even when the government is not the agent of any class. Lenin accepted both these doctrines without noticing that they were incompatible. He also accepted the theory of Engels that the state emerges as soon as there arise in society classes with irreconcilable interests, like Engels, Lenin never thought it necessary to explain how it is that the peace cannot be kept except by sacrificing the interests of all classes in the interest of only one class. Nor did he explain how the keeping of peace within society differs from the conciliation of interests : Repeating Engels, Lenin said, that the function of the state is to maintain peace between 'irreconcilable' classes, and to keep it in the interest of only one class among them.

ORTHODOX MARXISM

On the basis of the theory of state, as advanced by Marx and Engels, Lenin sought to establish as orthodox Marxism two propositions neglected or denied by the German Majority Socialists : (1) that the bourgeois state and all its instruments must be destoryed by the proletariat, and (2) that it is the 'dictatorship of the proletariat' which is destined to wither away. The dictatorship of the proletariat, is not a growing parasite whose function is to maintain the social conditions of class exploitation : It is the instrument of the workers and peasants, of the great majority, who use it to destroy the last traces of class exploitation. It will, therefore, wither away. The workers' state is strongest at the moment of its birth, and must gradually weaken until it dies. Lenin called it a 'half state', becuse its function is not to perpetuate the conditions of its own life but to destroy them. It is repressive and therefore a state; but it is also the instrument of great majority. The organizations, which the workers use, are democartically controlled. They gradually disappear as the work of suppression is completed.

When Lenin wrote *The State and the Revolution*, he had no administrative experience. He had never taken even a subordinate part in the government. Only a few months before the Bolshevik Revolution he stated, that "the great majority of functions of the old state power have been so simplified and can be reduced to such simple operations of registration, filing and checking, that they can be easily performed by every literate person." Lenin believed that capitalism makes the tasks of government easier. But the parasite has fed on its host and is swollen with its blood. This was the simple answer that satisfied Lenin in 1917.

DEVIATION FROM MARXIST ULTIMATE GOAL

Without realizing the falsity of his earlier assumptions Lenin, after the Bolshevik Revolution was obliged to establish highly centralized administrative machine in Russia. He found that he could not govern the society without a strong state. In one of his articles, written in 1923, he told his party men : "The proletarian state is the chief instrument for the building of socialism." The constitution of the new Bolshevik State was federal, but that federalism was a mere pretence; all real power belonged to the well-disciplined Communist Party. Most of the old departments of state were revived under new names. The political police became soon more active than they had been under the Tsars. Even after more than half a century, neither the dictatorship of the proletariat nor the workers' state had withered away, and the Soviet Russia is still governed by a strong centralized machinery.

A Revolutionary Genius

Lenin was a great revolutionary, whose chief aim was to adapt Marxism to the special conditions in Russia. In his book *The Development of Capitalism in Russia*, published in 1899, he showed that capitalism in Russia was making progress not only in industry, but in agriculture as well. This book dealt death blow to Narodism. In it Lenin showed how the working class, the grave-digger of capitalism and builder of a new socialist society, was growing and maturing within the capitalist society. Although compared to the rest of the population the Russian working class was proportionately small. Lenin saw in it a great force and revealed the leading role it was destined to play in the revolutionary movement. He stressed the need for alliance between the proletariat and the peasantry, without which there could be no victory in the coming revolution.

After regaining his freedom Lenin went ahead cautiously and patiently with his plan of organizing a truly revolutionary proletarian party capable of organizing and leading the working class of Russia to the assult of the Tsarist autocracy ad capitalism. In order to lead the workers' movement, to become its guiding force, the Party had to be armed with advanced revolutionary theory, the theory of Marxism. Lenin assessed the role of revolutionary theory by saying. "Without a revolutionary theory there can be no revolutionary movement,"

IMPERIALISM, THE HIGHEST STAGE OF CAPITALISM

Lenin gave the following definition of the substance of imperialism: "Imperialism is capitalism at that stage of development at which the dominance of monopolies and finance capital is established; in which the export of capital has acquired pronounced importance; in which the division of the world among the international trusts has begun; in which the division of all territories of the globe among the biggest capitalist powers has been completed."[6]

In the summer of 1916, Lenin completed his *Imperialism, the Highest Stage of Capitalism*. It is regarded by the Marxists as an outstanding contribution to the treasure-store of creative Marxism. In it Lenin made a comprehensive investigation of imperialism. He traced the development of world capitalism over the course of half a century after the publication of Marx's *Capital*. Basing himself on the laws of the emergence, development and decline of capitalism, discovered by Marx and Engels, Lenin was the first to give a profound scientific analysis of the economic and political substance of imperialism as a *special*, the *highest*, and at the same time, *last stage of capitalism*. He showed that under imperialism all the contradictions of capitalist society inevitably become aggravated. He characterized imperialism as monopoly imperialism and as parasitical, decaying and dying capitalism, disclosing the conditions that will bring on its end and demonostrating that capitalism will inevitably and necessarily be superseded by socialism.

Monopoly rule, Lenin explained signifies a sharp intensification of the exploitation of the working class and an exacerbation of the contradiction between labour and capital, of the contradictions leading to the proletarian revolution. It worsens the condition of the working class and leads to the ruin of the bulk of the peasants and the urban petite bourgeoisie, to increased dissatisfaction among them. This creates the objective conditions for cementing the alliance between the working class and the labouring peasants. That alliance is the principal force in the struggle against the imperialist bourgeoisie.

Furthermore, subjection of all the nations to a handful of 'Great Powers', the sharp intensification of colonial oppression, the brutal exploitation of the hundreds of millions in the colonial and dependent countries must inevitably result in the growth of the national liberation movements and make for a united front of struggle of the proletariat of the capitalist countries and the colonial and dependent peoples against imperialism. Lenin's scientific analysis of the contradictions of capitalism at its last stage brought him round to the conclusion that *imperialism is the eye of the socialist revolution*.

In the Party Programme, drawn up in the period of the Second R.S.D.L.P. Congress, Lenin formulated a damning indictment of Russian capitalism. During the First World War he formulated, an indictment of world imperialism, which was dragging mankind into the abyss of new devastating wars and economic disaster. Lenin's *Imperialism, the Highest Stage of Capitalism* represents a new Leninist stage of the development of Marxian economic theory.

On this basis of his (own) study of imperialism Lenin further developed the Marxist *theory of socialist revolution*, its content, its motive forces and conditions and forms of development, in the new epoch. He proved that the war had

6. Lenin, V. I. : *Collected Works*, Vol. 22, pp. 266-67.

accelerated the growth of the requisites for revolution and that the world capitalist system as a whole had matured for the transition to socialism.

Lenin did remarkable service to communism in creatively developing the teachings of Marx and Engels in the new historical conditions. In the epoch of imperialism, he came to the key conclusion that socialism can be victorious first in one country that does not necessarily have to be at a high level of economic development. He arrived at this conclusion on the basis of the law of the uneven economic and political development of capitalism in the imperialist era, inevitably leading to the uneven maturing of the socialist revolution in different countries. Lenin first formulated this conclusion in August 1915 in the article "On the Slogan for a United States of Europe".

Theory of the Revolutionary Situation

Lenin showed that revolution cannot be 'made to order', that it grows out of objectively maturing crisis. And these crises he called revolutionary situations. In the years of the imperialist war Lenin continued to develop his *theory of the revolutionary situation*. It proved to be of immense significance for the practical activities of the Marxist parties. Popular revolutions do not take place at the whim of one or another party. The masses rise to struggle under the influence of factors deeply rooted in their objective conditions of life. Capitalism itself creates the conditions that make mass revolutionary action inevitable. Thus, capitalist development impels the masses to struggle.

Estimate of Lenin

Lenin's theory and expectation that proletarian revolution will grow successfully in other countries also and become general in due course of time have proved to be incorrect. The fact that the socialist revolution was brought about in Russia which was not so industrially developed as several other countries of the West also falsifies the basic Marxian thesis that only a predominantly industrial country is best suited to a socialist revolution.

Lenin was not much concerned with the precision of his ideas or theories. He also did not care much to follow exactly what Marx and Engels had stated. His main objective was to guide the Bolshevik Revolution with firmness and insight. His enormous power lay in his capacity of organizing a revolutionary party in Russia. He is thus universally acclaimed as a great revolutionary and builder of a first Socialist State in the world. His revolutionary genius paved the way for socialist revolutions in other countries.

QUESTIONS FOR EXERCISE

1. What is meant by living Marxism, according to Lenin? Examine and explain Lenin's conception of the socialist society.
2. Discuss the essential principles of Marxism and how Lenin re-interpreted them?

3. "While the State exists there is no freedom; when the freedom exists there is no state" — Lenin. Comment. How far do you agree with Lenin that the state is the production and manifestation of class antagonism?
4. "The substitution of proletarian for capitalist state is impossible without a violent revolution" — Lenin. Comment.
5. "The essence of Leninism lies in the stress upon the dynamic and revolutionary elements in Marx." Discuss this statement.
6. "Leninism is the theory and practice of the proletarian revolutiion in general and theory and tactics of the dictatorship of the proletariat in particular." Discuss.
7. "Imperialism is the highest stage of capitalism" — Lenin. Comment.
8. Explain the Theory of State as expounded by Karl Marx. In what respects has it been modified by Lenin?

17

Nikita Sergeyevich Khrushchev (1894—1971)

Nikita Sergeyevich Khrushchev was born on April 17, 1894, in a mine worker's family in the village of Kalinovka in the Kursk province. When he was only a child he worked as a herdsman and then as a metal worker in the factories and mines of the Donbass.

Until Khrushchev's visit to America, serious students of Soviet affairs refrained from writing anything about his marriages and his children. On the eve of his departure, the foreign journalists in Moscow reported that he was "married for the first time in 1920, 1921, 1922 and for the second time in 1938." In September, 1959, in Washingtom, Mme. Nina Petrovna Khrushchev gave a press conference and revealed that Khrushchev's first wife died "during the famine", and that she herself married him in 1924, when his two children by his first wife were six and eight years old.

The Khrushchev-story has to begin with his 'Party-birth', when he was chosen to become a member of Stalin's apparatus. Khrushchev's rise in the hierarchy had been uncommonly, unbelievably swift. He had joined the party only in 1918, when he was twenty-four. He had stepped on to the lowest rung of the hierarchical ladder of the Party apparatus as late as 1925, when thirty-one years old. In 1934, he reached the uppermost region of Soviet power by becoming first secretary of the Moscow City Party Committee. On the anniversary of the revolution he stood on the top of the Lenin Mausoleum in Red Square, among the 'great leaders' of the Party and government headed by Stalin.

Khrushchev was a product of Stalin's apparatus. Although only four years younger than Molotov and roughly of the same generation as many of the 'old' Bolsheviks who took part in the conspiratory struggles before the revolution, Khrushchev was not one of the fathers but a child of the Bolshevik revolution. The fathers of the revolution, Lenin, Trotsky, Bukharin and the others, were European revolutionary intellectuals, shaped by the revolutionary heritage of the nineteenth century. Khrushchev had nothing of the intellectual-emotional background of the fathers of the revolution. He learnt to think from the party and knew no other system than the Soviet one. Khrushchev, the functionary, grew up together with the Party apparatus. As the member of the Communist Party, he did not belong to the class of intellectuals who had the interest and the will-power to go on studying and learning. An uneducated and an uncouth man, Khrushchev had no intellectual habits to boast of. His complete acceptance of Marxist theory was not coloured by a previous cultural background.

Khrushchev was to learn words and sentences explaining the scientific laws, by heart. "It is not the consciousness of men that determines their being, but on the contrary, their social being that determines their consciousness." The activity of the Bolshevik Party must not be based on the good wishes of 'outstanding individuals', not on the dictates of 'reason', 'universal morals' etc., but on the laws of development of society and on the study of these laws." During his training in Party schools, he was told that the real meaning of democracy is dictatorship. "Democracy is a state which recognizes the subordination of the minority to the majority, *i.e.*, an organization for the systematic use of violence by one class against the other, by one section of the population against the other."[1] And again :

> "Soviet Socialist Democraticism does not in any way contradict one-man management and dictatorship; the will of the class is sometimes given effect by a dictator who sometimes does more alone and often is more necessary."[2]

After finishing the workers' faculty, N.S. Khrushchev was in leading party-work in the Donbass and then in Kiev. In 1929, he began to study in the J.V. Stalin Industrial Academy in Moscow where he was elected secretary of the party committee. From January 1931. Khrushchev was secretary of the Baumann and then the Krasnopresnenski *raion* Party Committee of Moscow. During 1932-34 he worked at first as second, and then as first secretary of the Moscow city and as the second secretary of the Moscow oblast and city committees of the party where he worked until 1938.

In January 1938, Khrushchev was elected First Secretary of the Central Committee of the Communist Party of the Ukraine. In 1939, he was elected as a member of the Politbureau. During the Great Fatherland War of 1941-45, Khrushchev was with the army in the field, but he simultaneously completed his work at all other fronts — social, economic and political. He conducted work of great magnitude in the organization of all-peoples partisan movement in the Ukraine, against the German Fascist invaders. As political head of the Ukraine, as member of the Soviet Politbureau and as one of the leaders of the local military council, Khrushchev was directly involved in all political, economic and military operations. He was incharge of economic mobilization, of plans for evacuation of industries and of population. The quick evacuation of hundreds of factories, of equipment, supplies, livestock, was one of the sensastions of this period of the great war. It was praised by Soviet and Western observers alike and even German commentators expressed a grudging admiration. Thus, Khrushchev's administrative and organizational talents were fully vindicated.

From December 1949, until Stalin's death in 1953, Khrushchev worked in

1. Lenin : *Selected Works*, Lawrence & Wishart, London, 1937, Vol. IX, p. 70.
2. Lenin : *Works*, 4th Russian edition, Vol. XXX, p. 444.

daily contact with Stalin. On Stalin's 70th birthday, Khrushchev wrote a pamphlet praising Stalin's genius. The day Stalin died, Khrushchev was a member of the Presidium and one of the secretaries of the Central Committee. He was ranked as Number Five in the leadership. He became the actual head of the apparatus on March 14, when Malenkov had to relinquish his first secretaryship.

After ousting Malenkov and Bulganin and defeating all his opponents Khrushchev became Prime Minister of the Soviet Union in 1958. Like many others he had a deep-rooted hatred for Stalin and for those who had an unshakable faith in Stalin's policies, although he worked with Stalin and praised him during the latter's regime. He tactfully dealt with the situation and foiled the attempts of Malenkov and Mikoyan group and of the Molotov-Kaganovitch faction to demote him entirely in the Spring of 1957. When the campaign for a summit meeting was on, Khrushchev had to convince the Central Committee that the real head of the Soviet Union must be the Premier, since otherwise the figurehead, Bulganin, would have to negotiate with President Eisenhower and the other Western leaders. A few days before the end of the March session of the Supreme Soviet, Mikoyan told Western reporters at an Embassy reception in Moscow that they should not expect any 'Government changes' at this session. But at the March 27 Session Voroshilov, as Chairman of the Supreme Soviet Presidium, proposed that 'dear Nikita Khrushchev' should be elected Prime Minister in succession to Bulganin. Voroshilov spoke at length about Khrushchev's 'outstanding personality'. Supreme Soviet voted him into Premiership. Upon that Khrushchev expressed his sentiments : "By your decision, you have just expressed great confidence in me and have done me a great honour. I shall do everything to justify your confidence and shall not spare health, strength or life to serve you."

On the 25the February 1956, Khrushchev delivered a long speech making an all-round exposure of Stalin's mass-murders. He said : "Stalin originated the concept, 'enemy of the people'. This term automatically rendered it unnecesary that the ideological errors of a man or men engaged in a controversy be proven : this term made possible the usage of the most cruel repression, violating all norms of revolutionary legality, against anyone who in any way disagreed with Stalin, against those who were only suspected of hostile intent, against those who had high reputations. This concept, 'enemy of the people', actually eliminated the possibility of any kind of ideological fight or the making of one's views known on this or that issue, even those of a practical character...

> "This led to glaring violations of revolutionary legality, and to the fact that many entirely innocent persons, who in the past had defended the Party line, became victims. We must assert that in regard to those persons who in their time had opposed the party line, there were often no sufficiently serious reasons for their physical annihilation. The formula 'enemy of the people' was specifically introduced for the purpose of physically annihilating such individuals."

REVISION OF MARXIST-LENINIST THESIS

Khrushchev was against the concept of one-man dictatorship. He believed that majority principle to decide policies in the party meeting should be adopted. He insisted that war was not inevitable to defeat capitalism. In his television interview to the Columbia Broadcasting System on June 2, 1957 he stated : "With regard to the ideology of capitalist and socialist countries, we have never concealed that there will be a struggle in this field, an ideological struggle....Some people reproach me for allegedly changing my point of view, since I once said that if an atomic war came about it would be capitalism that would perish in that war. This I repeat today. But we think that *capitalism* should be destroyed not by means of war....but through an ideological and economic struggle...." Thus, Khrushchev appeared as a revisionist of the old Marxist-Leninist theses.

SEVEN-YEAR PLAN

Keeping in view his policy of peace, Khrushchev placed a programme of seven-year plan before the Twenty-first Party Congress at the end of January 1959, for the building of communism, which was finally approved by the Congress. His theses and report on the seven-year plan described its main task as follows :

1. The creation of the material and technical basis of communism.
2. The full satisfaction of the material and cultural needs of the Soviet people.
3. The consolidation of the economic and defence power of the USSR.
4. Ensuring the victory of the USSR in the peaceful economic competition with the capitalist countries of the West.

Khrushchev claimed that United States economic power would be equalled by the USSR in 1970, five years after the end of the seven-year plan. He said, "If we calculate per head of the population, another five years will probably be needed after the fulfilment of the seven year plan to catch up and outstrip the United States industrial output. Thus, by that time, or perhaps even sooner, the Soviet Union will advance to the first place in the world both in the absolute volume of production and in production per head of the population. This will be a historical world victory for Socialism in peaceful competition with capitalism in the international area."[3]

Khrushchev pointed out that in this peacefui competition with the United States, they were to rely on political as well as economic factors. Among these Khrushchev attributed a great deal of importance to the 'scientific laws' about the 'inevitable crisis' and inherent contradictions of the capitalist-imperialist system. These 'laws', promulgated by Marx and Engels and based on mid-nineteenth century experience, and those derived by Lenin from the world situation in the first two decades of the twentieth century are, according to Khrushchev, still valid in the second part of the twentieth century. "Capitalism,"

3. Khrushchev's Speech, January 27, 1959.

he emphasized, "is incapable of freeing itself from the death grip of its own contradictions."

Two other important political factors, according to Khrushchev, were :

1. The plan "will arouse to an unparalleled degree the force of attraction of communist ideas," especially in the less developed countries of the world.
2. The economic progress of the entire Socialist camp, including China, would lead to the consolidation of its strength and unity under Soviet leadership.

THESES ON THE TRANSITION TO COMMUNISM

Theses on the transition to communism contained Khrushchev's very severe attack on Mao and the Chinese leadership. He did not name them. He accused Mao of inflicting damage on the building of communism and of having distorted and compromised the communist cause.

Khrushchev tried to base his theory, policy and action on the real situation of the present world and not on dogmatic generalizations based on the situation in the last century. He fully realised that nuclear warfare by its very nature would prove exceedingly dangerous, particularly for dictatorsships. If A- or H-bombs were dropped on the principal cities of the Soviet and satellite empire, thereby cutting off or annihilating central direction of the organs of repression, MVD, KGB, police etc., popular revolts could break out everywhere. All this experience since Stalin's death had shown to Khrushchev and the apparatus that populations, armies, students, workers, even communists "are not to be trusted". Wherever the system of oppression appeared to be weakened, small and large scale revolts followed. The general disorder and disorganization following a nuclear attack would not turn the British or American population against their regimes. "Nuclear war would entail for the free world many dangers, but not the danger of revolts against the British or American 'systems'. In Soviet Russia the regime itself would be in the greatest of dangers." A regime, which in the last analysis depends on the party apparatus (less than half a per cent of the population) and its secret police, cannot risk breaks in the 'monolithic unity' and strength of the entire machinery of oppression.

Khrushchev knew that his country had not yet got over the after effects of the Stalin era and of the World War II. A third war could dangerously reduce the proportion of Russians within the USSR to that of the non-Russian majority of the inhabitants. And a third atomic war could annihilate the total population of the USSR.

PRAGMATIST IN MARXISM-LENINISM

Khrushchev was a pragmatist in Marxism-Leninism. Marxist 'theses', and the dogmatic approach were used by him only on occasions when it suited his aims. In foreign affairs his approach was often non-ideological and peaceful. He felt that today there were mighty social and political forces possessing formidable means "to prevent the imperialists from unleashing war and, if they actually try to start it, to give a crushing rebuff to the aggressors and frustrate their adventurist plans."[4] To be able to do this, all anti-war forces must be vigilant and prepared, must act as a united front and never relax their efforts in the battle for peace.

Peaceful Ideological War

Thus, Khrushchev dismissed the idea for waging a physical war against the capitalist countries. But the war of men's minds remains. And this 'peaceful, ideological war', according to Khrushchev, must be waged on both sides.

QUESTIONS FOR EXERCISE

1. Give an estimate of N.S. Khrushchev's contribution to Marxism-Leninism
2. Write short note on the part Khrushchev played in Russian politics.

18

Mao-Tse-Tung (1893—1977)

Mao-Tse-Tung came under the influence of Marxism at very early stages. He plunged himself in the struggle for China's freedom. He devoted himself to the cause of propagation of Communism in China. He gave serious thought to Asian version of Communism and got considerable success in that. He gave a new approach and outlook to principles of Leninism and Stalinism in so far as China was concerned. Maoism is considered as Chinese version of Marxism today.

CHINA'S COMMUNISM

Chinese Communism is based on four main ideologies :

1. Marxism. These include the theory of 'Surplus value'; 'Dictatorship of the Proletariats; 'Theory of class struggle' and 'Dialectical materialism'. These principles were seriously studied in China. They found their due place in Mao's philosophy.

2. Leninism. Lenin modified Marxism to suit his own times. He was of the view that imperialism forms a stage of capitalism. In the struggle against Capitalism the position and importance of colonies and semi-colonies cannot be underestimated. While thinking of world revolution, opposition to imperialism cannot be avoided and is inescapable. Lenin recognised the role of the agriculturists in bringing about revolution. He said that Communism will pass through bourgeoise democracy before coming to developing nations.

3. Stalinism. Which stream of ideology to Chinese Communism came from the philosophy of Stalin. Stalin laid stress on respectable behaviour with the minorities.

4. Maoism. But the most important stream of ideas came from Mao-Tse-Tung. He moulded whole ideology and philosophy of Communism in China and it began to be known as Maoism. Some of the main political ideas of Mao-Tse-Tung may briefly be discussed as under.

POLITICAL IDEAS OF MAO-TSE-TUNG

According to Mao, Marxian philosophy was interpreted to suit Chinese conditions. Communism could not find roots in the country. He was, not a blind follower of either Leninism or Stalinism. He interpreted Communism in such a way that even Communism of Russian type was challenged. He made

Communism a living philosophy. He exposed that in such a manner that the people began to consider him as God. He was considered as the most progressive leader of the world.

1. Revolution. Mao felt that armed revolution was as necessary today as it was when Marx or Lenin pleaded for it. According to Mao the working classes were the backbone of all revolutionary activities. Therefore, they should be well trained in guerilla activites. The revolutionaries should create an atmosphere by which civil wars are encouraged. They should try to dominate after the civil war had broken out. No revolution could be a success unless agriculturists and cultivators were association with that. The leadership will however always vest in the hands of worker. Untrained and ill-equipped agriculturists will always need leadership. Without leadership there could be no real revolution. Mao identified revolution with peasantry. He pronounced that every aggression on peasantry was an offence against revolution. He stressed the role of peasants in revolution. In the words of Franz Schurman, "As Mao Tse Tung said in 1927 in the Hills of Hunan, and revolution is not a dinner party, or writing an essay....But let us remember that revolution grew out of China's soil, that a hundred years of rebellion and suppression, of revolution and counter-revolutions had so brutilized China that massive violence was inevitable."

2. Stress on Peasantry. Marx, Lenin and Stalin had laid stress on working classes. But Mao felt that the peasants should be accepted as the leaders of the revolution. "They alone are the real backbone for overthrow of feudal forces. Mao said, "The gigantic struggles of the peasants — the peasants uprisings and wars — alone formed the real motive force of historical development in China's feudal society." Assessing the importance of peasantry in China, Sabine said, "Whether Mao's stress on peasantry was heresy or enlightened application of Marxist-Leninist thought, it certainly had its roots in Chinese situation."

3. Opposition to Capitalism. Mao is also opposed to capitalism, like Marxism, Leninism and Stalinism. Capitalism is definitely denigrating. The two world wars have given a very serious blow to capitalism. It only needed one strong blow. It is the foremost duty of communist countries that they should hasten that. These countries should ensure that capitalist countries which were regularly engaged in war be so engaged that these could not find time to suppress anti-capitalist activities at home. These countries should encourage civil wars and guerilla activities as well.

4. Stress on Villages. Mao laid stress on villages. The villages should be well organised so that the workers and the peasants who hail from the villages, are well organised to face the aggression, which usually comes from the cities. In the words of Sabine, Mao believed that, "Where the revolutionary forces were still weak, it was necessary to build the backward villages into advanced, consolidated base areas, into great military, political, economic and cultural revolutionary bastions so that they can fight the fierce enemy who utilises the cities to attack the rural districts." Due to advancement and concentration of wealth in cities for some time it might be possible that rural areas do not achieve their object, but ultimately revolutionary forces operating from the villages are bound to be a success.

5. Philosophy of Power. Mao-Tse-Tung supported philosophy of power. Everybody's thinking and approach can be changed by political power through political power even all social institutions can be controlled and managed in the way one liked. Economic conditions alone do not mould human thinking and institution. Ideas make the society. After ideas only military strength is most important. Political and military powers are closely associated with each other. Military strength is created with the help of gun. With gun each and everything can be done conveniently. In Mao's own words, "The world can be moulded only with the gun. Whoever wants to seize the political power of the state and to maintain it must have strong army." In the words of Sabine. "Few political thinkers, and indeed few communist leaders, have attributed such great significance to war and to military power."

6. Stress on War. Mao had no love for peace. Peace is nothing else but continuation of present system of capitalism. It is war which can bring the end of capitalism and install communism in its place. The outcome of First World War was Russian Revolution. Revolution in China was accomplished as a result of Second World War. Third World War is bound to end capitalism and in its place sow the seeds of communism. Therefore, Mao favoured war over peace.

7. Neutral States. According to Mao, there is nothing like neutral state. Every state in the world must follow either capitalist or socialist policies. There can be no third policy. Therefore, Mao did not recognise any neutral state or group of states.

8. The State. In the philosophy of Mao state is a means and method for crushing one group by the other. Those who manage to come to power in the state make every effort to crush the opponents. The state should ruthlessly crush those who are working against working classes. Once the communists manage to come to power in the state, they should use their power to end the capitalists. State should be used as a means for crushing the capitalists and anti-communist elements in the state.

9. Personality Cult. Mao believed in personality cult. He believed in the worship of one individual, who should be considered above everything else. His words should be accepted as law. In China, Mao had created this position for himself. His words were accepted fully well to China. He was worshipped as God. His ideas about the cultural revolution are on the lips of every Chinese. Every Chinese considers it his foremost duty to propagate Mao's idea and not to question them. Due to personality cult Mao's authority is not being questioned in China.

10. Politicisation of Army. According to Mao, the army should be thoroughly politicised. It should be made to realise that they are defending a particular cause and they should serve the army as long as they are capable of defending that.

11. The Policy of Fight and Talk. Mao had initiated the policy of fight and talk. The capitalists were at present in a dominant position in the world. They do not like any challenge to their authorty. Any challenge is intolerable for them. Therefore, first of all the capitalists should be engaged in war. This can be an open war or guerilla warfare method of it can also be civil war. All that is wanted is that in the war the enemy should be kept fully engaged and exhausted. An effort should be made to bring him on the table for talks, after he has been exhausted. The communist states however, should be very careful that they are not serious in making the talks a success. They should, therefore, put such conditions which are absolutely unacceptable to the capitalists. The talks should be prolonged. In the meanwhile, if need be some minor concessions should also be given to the other party. In the end an atmosphere should be created by which the enemy is alleged to be non-serious in his talks and charged with the breach of peace. This charge should be widely propagated. The world should be convinced about the failure of the enemy to seriously discuss the problem at the negotiation table. Meanwhile the time gained in talks should be used for military preparations and suddenly the enemy should be attacked. His territories should be captured and he should be forced to sign on the terms and conditions acceptable to the communist counntries.

12. Development of Politics after Revolution. Mao spent time on the development of politics after revolution. In the words of Sabine, "Mao, however, is quite explicit about an open ended, ever continuing dialectical process...Mao's explicit advocacy of a more open ended and flexible understanding of the dialectic is elaborately intertwined with his problem of adopting a Western theory to the peculiarities of Chinese situation." As a practical solution to post-revolution politicfs, Mao also gave the concept of 'New Democarcy'.

13. People's War. According to Mao imperialism and feudalism go hand in hand. Unless the former was ended in the latter it could not come to an end. People were more important than the weapons in winning a war. The people weapons were a decisive factor, people's war was based on the broadest of possible common front of the masses. For power structure in China Mao wanted to establish four power blocs namely those of workers, peasants, petty bourgeoisise and national bourgeoisie. He wanted to have a limited front of masses to fight imperialism. He said that the peasants were capable of bringing revolution independently. The revolution should start from the rural areas before it spreaded out to the cities. Success in revolution must depend on masses, their enthusiasm and creativity. A good leader must come from the masses and struggle for them alone. This leader should take his ideas from the masses. The people should be involved in the task of national regeneration and also in all revolutionary process. Revolution should not aim at merely capturing power but using that for the transformation of society.

14. Permanent Revolution. According to Mao permanent revolution can come only that has roots in the masses. If revolution was to last long it was essential that distinction between the leaders and masses, the government and society and various sections of society should be brought to an end. Mao did not agree with Marx that permanent revolution could be brought only by working classes. Such a revolution could be brought only by working classes in Asian peasantry. A permanent revolution was possible only when all class struggle and class distinctions were removed.

15. Value of Knowledge. In this theory of knowledge Mao laid stress on practice rather than knowledge. He felt that maximum knowledge could be obtained with the help of personal participation in activities rather than their mere knowledge. To quote his own words, "If a man wants to know certain things or certain kinds of things directly, it is only through personal participation in the practical struggle to change reality, to change those things or those kinds of things, that he can come in contact, with the phenomena of things."

16. Hundred Flowers Policy. It was wrong to think that in any society there should be only one ideology or only one state. Mao believed that each thinking was a flower and in China let such hundred flowers blossom and grow. It is only then that the society will come to know which are rotten and out-dated ideas and that which are fresh and acceptable ideas. Terror should not be used in checking the ideas and not allowing the flowers to blossom and spread their smell.

CULTURAL REVOLUTION

Mao launched Grand Proletarian Cultural Revolution in 1966. Masses of Red Guards were organised to propagate this revolution and made to work against well established sectors of Chinese society. Cultural Revolution was planned because Mao was disturbed by growing deviation from his teachings. He, therefore, thought of extensive cultural transformation and political purge. The main targets of Cultural Revolution were handful of party persons in authority who were taking capitalist roads. These people stood against masses of workers, peasants and soldiers. According to Mao, Red Guards were required to completely overthrow them. In the words of Sabine, "The cultural revolution seems designed to preserve Mao's Chinese Marxist Society from being overwhelmed by industrialisation and consequent bureaucratization of life that has characterised the modern West and is increasingly characteristic of Soviet Union as well."

Aims and Objectives

The main aim of Cultural Revolution was the anxiety of Mao, because the people were deviating from his political ideas. He wanted that the people should accept his philosophy more vigorously and closely. Accordingly there was no denial that the masses were the source of all power and authority in so far as political life was concerned. In the words of Stuart Z. Schram, "In essence Mao's Cultural Revolution aims to go beyond the humbling of the existing bureaucratic and technocratic elite, and to extirpate the very roots of any stratification which might emerge in the future, by destroying respect for special status of the party member or the special knowledge of the expert." The same authority, while discussing the causes of revolution has said, 'It makes clear and explicit Mao's growing anxiety lest the right wing deviations in the party which he had described as widespread in 1955, lead to emergence of full blown revisionist tendencies such as he perceived in the Soviet Union, thereby ultimately jeopardising the very survival of the revolutionary movement to which he had devoted himself for over forty years."

Main Ideas of Cultural Revolution

Mao had given the following ideas about Cultrual Revoluton :

1. Marriage. About marriage Mao said that under feudal domination marriage is barbaric and inhuman institution. To quote his words "The whole feudal system of marriage, including power of parent to arrange marriage for their children, to exercise compulsion, and all purchase and sale in marraige contracts shall henceforth be abolished."

3. Children. Children are the masters of new society.

4. Women. The women of China are vast reserve of labour power.

5. Cooperatives. There should be collective produciton, through cooperatives. Therefore the Cooperative should be encouraged.

6. Companion. The best companion is one, who is politically most important and dependable as well as cooperative.

7. Feudalism. Feudalism is the ally of imperialism and bureaucrat capitalism and the foundation of their rule.

8. Peasants. Only the poor peasants can and must be the basic force to be relied upon in the land reform.

9. Agrarian Reform. The work of agrarian reform should be carried forward by state and in an orderly manner.

10. Economic Planning. Blindness and anarchy in the economic field should be gradually eliminated in line with principle of unified planning and of considering the interests of all sections of society.

11. Conclusion. To conclude with Sabine, "It is too early to tell whether Mao was able with the Cultural Revolution to breathe new life into this doctrines and thus to establish for them a wider validity, or whether they will over time come to be seen only as out-dated and peculiarly Chinese response to the problems of the industrialising world."

QUESTIONS FOR EXERCISE

1. Discuss some of the significant political ideas of Mao-Tse-Tung.
2. Give Chinese Version of Marxism, as given by Mao-Tse-Tung.
3. What are the significant features of Cultural Revolution, as expounded by Mao-Tse-Tung?

19

Utopian Socialism and its Thinkers

Utopian socialist is a term applied particularly to St. Simon, Charles Fourier in France and Robert Owen in England. Utopian socialists believed that political ills would he removed by the removal of social evils. They agreed that property was a great social evil. They were against economic individualism. They denounced fair competition in commerce and industry, unearned increments and the existing capitalist system as the chief cause of the prevalent property. French Socialism began with an attack on the economic evils brought by *laissez faire* policy of the state.

SIMONDI

In 1819, Simondi published his *New Principles* as criticism of the *laissez faire* doctrine. It makes the beginning of humanitarian economics later on developed by Christian socialists. He pleaded for abolition of child labour, limitation of working period to 12 hours a day and one day rest in a week.

ST. SIMON

He was a noble man who joined the army in 1777 and took part in U.S.A.'s War of Independence of (1776-1783). He pleaded for the regulation of society on the basis of productive capacity. He realised that private property is exploitation unless it is a result of effort *i.e.* labour. His ideas were as follows:

1. Society should be reorganised and there should be cooperation instead of conflict between capital and labour.

2. Payment for work should depend on capacity and occupation.

3. A positive government of scientists and not of philosophers should be established.

5. He was against functionless property and inheritance of property. He advocated establishment of indusrial and productive farms. He was in favour of monarchical form of government having parliament containing their houses for proposing, passing, and executing laws. He was in favour of giving to only police functions. He emphasized cooperation of labour and capital but was unable to give it practical shape.

CHARLES FOURIER (1742—1837)

Unlike Simon, the French socialist Fourier came from a common family.

He witnessed the injustices of his times which provoked his thought. He focused his attention on the problems of industrialised society and provided food for socialist thought. According to him passion rather than reason is the basis of every kind of association, particularly a productive association. He pleaded for phalanges representing a communal life. The phalanges was decentralised separated community which consisted of 400 families, each family containing four persons. These 1600 persons were to form a self-sufficing community on the basis of integral cooperation. It would govern itself through its own elected leaders. It would be related to other communities on a federal basis. It will not be an industrial federation but agricultural federation with headquarters at Constantinople. The labour could not be made attractive unless the wage earner could be transformed into a capitalist and disagreeable tasks were rewarded. The phalanges was to consist of capitalists, labourers and men of creative genius. Maxey calls St. Simon as "one of the formative influences of 19th century political thought."

ROBERT OWEN

A minimum return was guaranteed to all workers for family support. Each worker was to have the right of mark, in occupation of his choice and capacity. Phalanges would abolish property, bring happiness and liberty and stop coercive activities of the state. He pleaded for women's participation in industry and for their emanciapation and suggested cooperative living for reorganisation of children's education. According to Grey, Robert Owen (1771-1858), a Welshman, son of a saddler was a practical idealist. G.D.H. Cole describes him as "shop boy and manufacturer, factory reformer and educationist, socialist and cooperative pioneer, trade union leader and secularist, founder of ideal communities and practical man of business. He unsuccessfully established a cooperative society 'Colony of New Harmony' in Indiana in North America as an experiment. His outlook was explained through Committee for the Relief of Manufacturing Poor in 1817 and in his book, *The Book of the New View of Society.*" He also made many suggestions in his *The Book of the New Moral World."* His socialist ideas were as follows :

1. The end of Government is to make governed and governors happy.

2. Man is influenced by his surroundings. Crime and degradation arise out of human surroundings.

3. The best governed state will be that which shall possess the best national system of education.

4. There is misery owing to false concepts and false activities.

5. Evils can be wiped out through love and fellowship, with the cooperation of the government, parliament, the church and the people.

6. A good social system can be developed through harmony and cooperation.

7. It is better to look to society than to government for changes.

8. Profit can be earned by giving labourers high wages.

Owen's idea were Utopian but he provided a source of socialist current of thought in 19th century. He has been rightly hailed as father of democratic socialism. Some have called him "forerunner of Karl Marx." According to Maxey, "He did more to fight the evils of industrialism than any other man of his generation."

CHRISTIAN SOCIALISTS

Other notable Utopian socialist thinkers of England were Dr. Hall, William Thompson, Thomas Hodgskin, John Grey and John Francis Bray. In 1850, a society for promoting working men's association was started in England, entitled Christian Socialists. Harles Kingsley, F.D. Maurice and J.M. Ludlow were the leaders of Christian socialism. They aimed at securing more liberal legislation in favour of the working class and at getting legal recognition for cooperative association etc.

BLANCE AND PROUDHAN

In France Louis Blance and Proudhan 1809-65 were other notable thinkers. Louis Blance advocated labour and democracy and enunciated principle of everyone lending his best to the society getting reward from the society according to his needs. Proudhan said 'property is a theft'. He aimed at classless society. He was a prominent socialist thinker.

With the emergence of Marxist ideas these ideas were eclipsed. After Marx, Fabian Socialism, Syndicalism, Guild Socialism, Democratic Socialism and State Socialism gained prominence.

QUESTION FOR EXERCISE

1. Give in brief political philosophy of Utopian Socialist thinkers particularly of Robert Owen, Saint Simon ad Charles Fourier etc.

20

Anarchism

The term 'Anarchism' has been derived from the Greek word 'anarchial' which literally means 'no rule'. Anarchists believe in complete abolition of state authority. It is abolished all at once. As long as the institutions of state and private property exist there is exploitation in society.

In the words of Coker, "Anarchism is the doctrine that political authority, in any of its forms, is unnecesary and undesirable. In recent anarchism, theoretical opposition to the state has usually been associated with opposition to the institution of private property and also with the hostility to organised religious authority." It was also preached by ancient Greek philosophers and Christian missionaries. The theory found expression in the writings of persons like Tolstoy in Russia, Godwin and Hodgskin in England and Tucker in U.S.A.

"There is a Left which lies to the left", wrote Barker, "even of the Socialism of the Left; and this extreme Left has its own conception of liberty. In its Russian form, and as preached by Bakunin and Kropotkin, the philosophy of the extreme Left is a philosophy of Anarchism. Its idea is the absolutely free individual who lives by his own free will in a spontaneous adjustment to some self-acting society which needs and imposes no rules. For the Anarchist there is no civil liberty, because such liberty implies law, and law, in any form and under whatever limits, is a coercive thing, there is no political liberty, because such liberty implies organisation, and organisation, in any form and however democratic, is compulsion. There is only liberty in itself, pure, absolute and unqualified."[1]

Anarchism has been defined by Kropotkin as a "principle of theory of life and conduct under which society is conceived without government — harmony in such a society being obtained not by submission to law, or by obedience to any authority, but by free agreements concluded between the various groups, territorial and professional, freely constituted for the sake of production and consumption, as also for the satisfaction of the infinite variety of needs and aspirations of a civilized being."[2] According to Russell, Anarchism is the theory which is opposed to every kind of forcible government. Liberty is the supreme goal to the Anarchist creed, and Liberty is sought by the direct road

1. Barker, E., *Reflections on Government*, p. 6.

2. Quoted by Joad in *Modern Political Theory*, pp. 100-101

of abolishing all forcible control over the individual by the community."[3] Thus, anarchism is opposed to political authority in any and every form. It was a revolt against every type of authority — political, social, religious and economic. Its aim was to free man politically from the tyranny of the state, economically from the tyranny of the capitalist and morally from the tyranny of priest or church.

INDIVIDUAL PHILOSOPHICAL ANARCHISTS

William Godwin

The first modern anarchist to think strongly against the authority of the state was William Godwin. According to him, the state prevents the individual from acting in a just and reasonable way by upholding injustice and inequity with the help of its authority. He held that all evils in society are the result of government and the instituion of private property. Government is an evil as it is based on violence and property. It creates vanity and depravity among the possessors of property and it creates servility and immorality among propertyless people. So both these institutions should be abolished.

Thomas Hodgskin

Another Utopian anarchist Thomas Hodgskin believed that since the whole universe is regulated by permanent and invariable laws, and man is a part of the universe, there is no need whatsoever for legislation or for planning. The pre-established harmony of self-interest achieves itself when man is left unhindered. Hodgskin was an extreme individualist.

Joseph Proudhon

Joseph Proudhon was the father of Anarchism. He championed the cause of liberty and freedom and condemned the government of man by man. In his book *Philosophy of Poverty* he said, "Government of man by man in every form is oppression and the highest perfection of society is found in the union of order and anarchy." Governments were scourage of God. State was against reason, justice and understanding. State authority must make way for the rise of mutualism. Proudhon advocated the establishment of a Bank of the people for eliminating all private capital. He condemned property as theft and advocated its equal rights for all. He was opposed to communism. To him communism meant privation everywhere and always. Every person should have three acres of land and a cow.

Josiah Warren

Josiah Warren was an American anarchist. According to him, man's need for governmental protection arises from evils originating not in his own nature but in the unfortunate errors committed by his forefathers in setting up the institutions of property and coercive government. Workers should give up all interest in political affairs and confine their activities to voluntary, cooperative

3. Russell, Bertrand, : *Roads to Freedom* (Allen & Unwin London), p. 50.

efforts. If that was done, profits and poverty would gradually get eliminated and the need for government would disappear.

Benjamin Trucker

Benjamin Trucker advocated Anarchism in his book *A Fragmentary Exposition of Philosophical Anarchism*. According to him, man's natural self-interest led logically to a society in which all men were prevailingly free. Liberty was an instrument for bringing happiness and order. The authority of the state must be done away with as it was opposed to liberty. It should be substituted by the associations formed by individuals freely contracting among themselves. These associations were to have the right of enforcing discipline among its members, levy taxes, etc. There was to be no compulsion for joining these associations.

PACIFIC ANARCHISTS

All the above thinkers recommended only gradual elimination of the authority of state by peaceful methods, enlightening and educating the people in the principles of anarchy.

Henry Thoreau

Henry Thoreau advised the people to ignore the state altogether and not to pay any taxes to it. According to him, authority exercised by government was always wrong and unjust. He said : "That government is the best which governs not at all." He advocated passive and active resistance to government. "He preferred the carefree labouring man whose only concern is with the virtue of cheerfulness.[4] He used to say 'Live your life, do your work, then take your hat." The conventional standards of society had no significance for him and he rejected them with contempt. His *Essay on Civil Disobedience* has become a classic in the literature of non-violence. He said, 'If that government in relatively best which governs least then that government is absolutely best which does not govern at all.' Thoreau gave man the right of revolution. This right was to be exercised when actions of government became tyrannical beyond endurance. Man needs no protection from the state. True freedom comes from within oneself. Thoreau was opposed to not only organised government, but also to organised Christianity. He stood for development of one's inner spirit which meant opposition to all law, all external restraints or discipline.

Count Leo Tolsoi

Tolstoi was a pacific anarchist. His advocacy of anarchism was free from violence. It may be called Christian anarchism. He held that both the state and private property were incompatible with true Christianity. As the state is based on force and executes its will through force, so it violates Christ's command 'not to resist evil by force'. Under private property a few prosper at the *expense* of money. This is against Christ's principle of charity and human brotherhood.

4. Blau, Joseph, L. : *Men and Govements in American Philosophy*, p. 135.

But Tolstoi had no clear vision of future anarchist society. He said, "The future....will only be what men and circumstances make it."[5] His teachings had considerable effect because they combined faith in religion with dispassionate observation of facts and regard for truth. He said, "Awaken the consciences of the people; live according to the principles of love and equality; practise passive resistence; refuse obedience to the clearly un-Christian commands of a government; and, where practicable, refuse to pay taxes or to serve on juries."[6]

REVOLUTIONARY ANARCHISTS

Anarchist ideas of menacing nature appeared in the wirtings of Kasper Schmidt, Max Stiner, Bakunin and Prince Kropotkin of which only the last two are noteworthy.

MICHAEL BAKUNIN (1814—76)

Concept of Liberty

Bakunin was a great antagonist of Karl Marx and one of the outstanding leaders of modern anarchism. He was a man difficult to understand. According to Cole, "Liberty he always proclaimed as the great principle of living; and assuredly no one ever lived with more liberty on so little money that was his own."[7] He was the most inconvenient man. "He remained a chaotic figure," wrote Gray, "chaotic in his life, chaotic in his thought, chaotic in his writings — thoroughly impractical and destitute of common sense, as becomes an anarchist, yet with something about him of a likable but rather spoiled child, mingling the real with the imaginary and playing at make-believe conspiracies, with all the paraphernalia of codes and cyphers desinged to be used in communication with possible non-existent correspondents."[8]

Abolition of State

Bakunin's social theory began, and almost ended with liberty. He condemned every institution and every belief found inconsistent with liberty. He made a distinction between society and state, he accepted society as natural to man and the state as an artificial institution *created* by some *men* for the exercise of power over others, either by force or by democractic fraud. Bakunin was against any authority claiming power of command or which restricted liberty in any manner. The state and God were two such authorites. If these were repudiated and overthrown, there would be no one to issue commands and more would enter on a blessed era of liberty. Bakunin regarded these as two tyrants as melting into one. According to him, the state was an evil which degraded and demoralised people. It functioned with the help of force. Whatever form of government it might have, it was an evil. Power had corrupting influence on

5. Tolstoi, *The Kingdom of God Within You*, p. 326.

6. Coker, F.W., *Recent Political Thought*, p. 224.

7. Cole, G.D.H., *A History of Socialist Thought* , Vol. II (1850-1893), p. 218.

8. Gray, Alexander, *op. cit.*, p. 352.

all the rulers as well as the ruled. So the state must be ended. Rousseau's social contract was both historically and morally wrong as it justified the tyranny of man over man. According to anarchists, "The state is morally debasing to all members of a civilised community — to those who govern as well as to those who are governed, for it acts by compulsion rather than by enlightenment and persuasion...Morality and intelligence in human conduct consist solely in performing good and reasonable acts that are approved as good or recognised as reasonable by the doer. As act done under dictation is wholly lacking in moral on rational quality. Thus, the inevitable tendency of state action is to degrade the oral and intellectual levels of those subject to its authority. Political authority also demoralises those who participate in its exercise. To occupy a position of political power engenders attitudes of superiority quite out of relation to any actual distribution in merit...Thus, the state makes tyrants or egoists out of the few and servants or dependents of out of the many."[9] He wrote about the state thus : "The state is not society, it is only an historical form of it, as brutal it is abstract. It was born historically in all countries of the marriage of violence, rapine pillage, in a world war and conquest, with the gods successively created by the theological fantasy of nations. It has been from its origin, and it remains still at present, the divine sanction of brutal force and triumphant inequality."[10]

Against Private Property

With similar vehemence Bakunin attacked the institution of private property which he regarded both the ground of existence and the consequence of the state. Private property was responsible for all kinds of physical and moral evils in society. For millions of workers it brought economic dependence, laborious toil, ignorance, misery and social and spiritual immobility, whereas for a few wealthy persons it brought superfluous luxury, special opportunities for physical pleasure and artistic and intellectual enjoyment.

Atheism

Bakunin detested the very idea of God. In his view anarchism and atheism are almost interchangeable terms. According to him, the Church and the state owed their origin to the same causes. The state was rather the younger brother of Church. Religion taught dependence and subjection and it undermined the dignity of man. So it was an evil. The idea of God's existence arose out of a confusion of thought. It was because men had not understood nature. So they had invoked the notion of God to explain it. The Church always supported the state against which the people had no right to rebel. Religion had always acted as the handmaid of the rich people to maintain their stronghold over the people. Bakunin said, "Of all despotisms that of the doctrinaires or inspired religionists is the worst."

---

9. Coker, F.W., *op. cit.*, p. 204.

10. Russell, Bertrand, *Roads to Freedom* , p. 63.

Federal Society

Bakunin's philosophy had no place for state, private property and Church. In his scheme of things, state, property and Church would get elimitnated but society would remain, which provided the natural home for man. His society was called federal implying the spontaneous and voluntary formation of associations. His aim was "to organise society in such a manner that every individual, man or woman, coming into life, should find approximately equal means for the development of his different faculties and for their utilisation by his work; to organise a society which, making the exploitation of one by another forever impossible, should allow each one to participate in the enjoyment of social riches (which are never in fact produced by anything but labour) only to the extent to which he will have directly contributed to the production of this wealth by his own labour."[11] His federalism was "the free federation of the individuals in the communes, of the communes in the provinces, of the provinces in the nations, and finally of those nations in the United States, first of all of Europe, and later of the whole".

Methods of Change

Bakunin advocated both evolutionary and revolutionary methods. According to him, anarchism had both a scientific and an insurrectionary technique. According to him, "The current of events and facts flows automatically towards the anarchist goal. The task of *anarchist* is to eliminate the impediments to that current, both by removing ignorance of the natural laws of social evolution and by demolishing the institutions which interfere with the evolution."[12] But the work of demolition could not be carried out by peaceful means. It required some measures of violence. It would involve the forcible dissolution of churches, the army, the courts, police, legislatures, administrative officers and the titles to property. The whole process was to be carefully organised and planned. The load was to be taken by small secret societies of faithful anarchists. The anarchist revolution would not mean establishment of dictatorship of the proletariat. It would be followed by the emergence of the anarchist society. Bakunin's methods both evolutionary and revolutionary were based on education, violence and intrigue.

PRINCE KROPOTKIN (1842—1921)

Kropotkin was the most representative, the most attractive and engaging, of the modern anarchists. He was a gifted writer. His important works are : *The Conquest of Bread; Anarchism : Its Philosophy and Ideal; The State: Its Part in History, Fields, Factories and Workshops; Modern Science and Anarchism.*

Kropotkin had an anarchist ideal before him for achieving which he advocated the destruction of all those institutions which stood in its way — the State, the God and the Property. His ideal was : "The anarchists conceive a

11. Gray, Alexander, *op. cit.*, p. 205 — Quoted.

12. Coker, F.W., *op. cit.*, p. 205.

society in which all the mutual relations of its members are regulated, not by laws, not by authority, whether self-imposed or elected, but by mutual agreements between the members of that society, and by a sum of social customs and habits — not petrified by law, routine, or superstition, but continually developing and continually readjusted, in accordance with the ever-growing requirements of a free life, stimulated by the progress of science, invention and the steady growth of higher ideals. No ruling authorites, then, no government of man by man; no crystalisation and immobility but a continual evolution — such as we see in nature. Free play for the individual for the full development of his individual gifts — for his individualisation. In other words, no actions are imposed upon the individual by a fear of punishment, none is required from him by society but those which received his free acceptance. In a society of equals this would be quite sufficient for preventing those unsociable actions that might be harmful to other individuals and to society itself, and for favouring the steady growth of that society."[13] In this future society mutual aid and not struggle was the secret of progress. There would be no authority of any kind. There would be only voluntary association for every kind of work. Poeple were to join groups of their own free will and according to their tastes. The mutual disputes were to be settled by courts of arbitration set up by the people themselves. There would be destruction between goods of production and goods of consumption. Every person was to work according to his bent of mind. According to Kropotkin. "In a system where men choose their labours in response to natural, creative impulses rather than under the goad of wage slavery, men will work more skilfully and more diligently."[14]

No Justification for State

Prince Kropotkin found no justification for state. History showed that people lived amicably for centuries without any political authority. The state was of later origin. The laws of the state were superfluous or hamrful. They were mostly obeyed because they were old customs and which were equally obeyed when they were not legally enacted. They were obeyed because of the fear of the state and not because the people approved them. The state did not serve any useful purpose. It rather added to the miseries and sufferings of the people. Most of its functions could be done in a better way and more efficiently by the voluntary associations. The courts and the prisons were the cause of increase of vice. The people were in a better position to defend themselves than the mercenary armies. According to the Kropotkin, the state was responsible for facilitating and instigating the exploitation of man by man. He defined state as "a society of mutual assurance between the landlord, the military commander, the judge, the priest, and later on capitalist in order to support each other's authority over the people, and for exploiting the poverty of the masses and getting rich themselves."[15] He held that the state had always acted on the side of capitalists. So it must be replaced by a society of voluntary associations.

---

13. Kropotkin, *Modern Science and Anarchism*, p. 45.

14. Kropotkin, *The Conquest of Bread*, p. 182.

15. Kropotkin, *Modern Science and Anarchism*, p. 81.

Opposed to Private Property

Kropotkin was opposed to the institution of private property. He called it the greatest enemy of cooperation. It was the main reason of strife and discord which kept men away from working together harmoniously in the conquest of nature and the building of a better world. According to Kropotkin as the goods of this world were the product of the joint labour of individuals, so no one could by right claim personal ownership of anything. He said, "Individual ownership is neither just nor useful, everything belongs to everyone, since everyone has need of it and since it is practically impossible to determine the part that belongs to each in the actual creation of riches. Everything belongs to everyone, and provided each man contributes his quota of labour he is entitled to his portion of what had been produced by everyone."[16] The institution of private property was responsible for all misery in the world. It led to prodigality, ostentation and idleness among the rich. It encouraged war and made its upholders immoral. With its abolition all the members of society would enjoy life and no one would suffer privation.

Opposed to Religion and Church

Kropotkin was opposed to religion and the Church. Religion had resulted in injustice to the poor. It had enabled the rich to maintain their states. It had always sided with the political and economic oppression. But Kropotkin was not opposed to social morality which evolves unconsciously in society and as a consequence of which men respect one another's interests and rely upon one another's words. Such a morality is exterior to and independent of formal religious creeds. Only such a morality endures while religions fade away.

Support to Revolution

Kropotkin believed that the social evolution was inevitable moving towards the anarchist goal. But he did not think that the goal could be reached through a wholly gradual and peaceful process. The evolution must culminate in a revolution. An uprising in one coutnry would spread into a kind of general European revolution. This revolution would be destructive and violent in its first phase. According to Kropotkin, "A frightful storm is needed to sweep away all this rottenness, to vivify torpid souls with its breath, and to restore to humanity the devotion, self-denial and heroism without which a society becomes senile and discrepit, and crumbles away. But such a revolution would mean not much of bloodshed. After the basic instrments of coercive authority had been forcibly removed, the people would proceed to expropriate private property, peasants expelling land owners, workers expelling factory owners and those having no homes expelling those who had surplus space."[17] Kropotkin had faith in the reasonableness of man. The work of reconstructing society would be peaceful done by voluntary groups.

16. Quoted by Lancaster, L.W., *Masters of Political Thought*, Vol. III, pp. 253-254.

17. Quoted by Coker, *op. cit.*, p. 214.

Anarchism does not mean chaos or confusion. It means hostility to the state and to peculiar social relations which the state sustains. Coker is right when he says, "In all that Kropotkin was to be placed emphasis upon man's sense of social responsibility, his feeling of human brotherhood, and his disposition to engage in labours that satisfy both on impulse to create and desire to see commodities produced in amounts sufficient to meet the needs of his fellow men."[18]

CHARACTERISTICS OF ANARCHISM

1. Condemnation of state. This is following :

(i) *Evils of the State.* According to Anarchists the present society is class-ridden and class-divided. In it constant struggle is going on between the 'haves' and 'have nots'. In this struggle the state always sides with the rich. It uses its force and authority for crushing the poor. It is in itself the child of force. It is interested in the retention of private property. It wants to perpetuate this institution which is based on injustice.

(ii) *State refuses freedom of the individual.* The state is based on force and injstice. It can claim no moral right to get the support of the masses. Joad has thus described Anarchist view about state, "The record of state in guaranteeing security to the individual is no better. So far from protection is the citizen from ill-disposed persons that it creates them."

(iii) *Superfluous.* The state is responsible for crushing individual freedom. State is superfluous. If the state is abolished no harm will be done to the society and community. State's authority is unnecessary. Spontaneous agencies undoubtedly and unquestioningly prove better checks against every invasion than the paid soldiers.

(iv) *Not necessary for law and order.* The state is not necessary for maintaining law and order. In some cases the state itself promotes crimes. In a stateless society, everything will be just. The society in itself forms association which will promote justice. In the words of Kropotkin, "Harmony in such a society is to be obtained not by submission to law, or by any obedience to any authority, but by free agreements concluded between the various groups, territorial and professional, freely constituted for the sake of consumption and production as also for the satisfaction of the infinite variety of needs and aspirations of a civilised being".

(v) *Abolition of state authority.* The state authority should entirely be abolished. From individualists, Anarchists have derived the idea of individual initiative. From socialists they borrowed the idea that the private property was an evil and root cause of exploitation by the rich of the poor. According to Anarchists it should be left to the individuals to join or not to join the state. The Government should be of the type of which the people have given their consent. Modern state is corrupt. It has been retained by privileged classes to

18. Coker, *op. cit.*, p. 217.

protect their interests. No association has any right or authority to rule over the individuals without their approval.

(iv) *Elimination of State by force.* As state is existing since ages and privileged classes are there to protect it, it cannot be overthrown by peaceful means but only by violence of force. The revolutionary anarchists preach complete destruction of state. Philosophical anarchists believe that state should be gradually weakened and finally got rid of by peaceful means. While the philosophical anarchists are evolutionary the revolutionaries are radicals and extremists.

(vii) *Alternatives to state authorty.* As an alternative to state authority Anarchists favour the idea of formation of free societies and associations to deal with various aspects of life. The men should join these on their own with absolute freedom to withdraw at any stage. These associations shall perform the functions which at present are being performed by the state. The system of voluntary associations is far better than that of state because in these associations there is no coercive authority and obedience is not based on force.

2. Opposition to Representative System. The Anarchists oppose the present representative system. It is a defective system because none can represent the other. It is a fallacy to believe that whatsoever the representative do should be treated as correct and imposed on the electorates as expression of their will.

3. Opposition to Religion. According to Kropotkin religion is a great hindrance in the progress of society. Indirectly, it even promotes evil institutions. It helps in the exploitation of the poor by the rich. In inculcates in them the spirit of following things blindly. It promotes the idea that their wretched life is the will of God. It also preaches the philosophy of contentment and thus discourages the poor from struggling against the rich. It also divides the loyalties in many ways and thus divides the attention of the individuals which is quite injurious to the society. Anarchists argue that the religion should be dispensed with because it acts as an opium to the people. It provides them unnecessary and undesirable escape from struggle of life.

4. Opposition to Private Property. To the anarchists the institution of private property is the root cause of many social evils. It is a great weapon in the hands of the capitalists to squeeze the blood of the workers. It promotes selfish interests of the capitalists who do not produce goods as required by the society but to gain maximum profit. Needs of the society are ignored for earning more and more profits. Only a small section of the society takes advantage of means of production. Majority is hoodwinked for the sake of minority. Thus, private property is an agency for the exploitation of many by the few. It creates anarchy in production. It should be abolished for the sake of common welfare.

5. The Anarchist Society. It has the following characterists :

(i) *Stateless Society.* To anarchist the best society will be one which will be stateless. In it the means of production and distribution shall not be in the hands of only a few persons but under collective control. It shall be used for the sake of welfare of all and not in the interest of only a few. Classes like wage-earners and employers will disappear. There will be no class struggle. Everybody will put in maximum labour and in turn will get what he needs.

(ii) *No Coercive Authority.* In anarchist society there will be no coercive authority. The majority, *i.e.*, the consumers shall be free from the yoke of producers. There will be no mystical authority of religion and no awe-inspiring authority of the state against its citizens. It will be a free atmosphere in which the individual will be given maximum liberty to develop his potentialities. Both the systems of production and distribution will be carried out on a voluntary basis. There will be no compulsion and command. Everybody will work on his own accord.

(iii) *Mutual Trust and Cooperation.* In anarchist society there will be mutual trust and cooperation. Economically, everybody will be quite well off. Banking associations will advance credit for increasing production. All means of production will be utilised for social good and welfare.

(iv) *Abolition of Private Property.* In anarchist society the institution of private property shall be absolutely abolished. Free associations will organise productive activities. Every individual shall belong either to one association or the other. These associations shall be responsible for looking after his needs.

(v) *Provision for Arbitration.* In anarchist society there shall be no courts of justice. All disputes shall be decided by arbitration. The arbitration shall be appointed on an *ad hoc* basis by the society. There shall be no distinction between mental and manual labour. Working hours shall be gradually reduced.

(vi) *Utilisation of Human Energies.* In anarchist society there will be maximum scope and outlet for utilisation of human energies. Each trade and industry will have its system of administration and recruitment provided such a system does not interfere with the overall social order.

(vii) *Equality for All.* In anarchist society, the association replacing state will do every work. These will be organised either on territorial basis or vocational basis. The society will have no privileged class. All shall be equal. Such a system will run on cooperative basis. According to Gettell, "They deny the right of any person or of any association to rule over any individual against his will. They aim at justice and freedom and believe that the exercise of forcible authority by the state is never justified."

6. Methods of Struggle. The Anarchists are not very clear and unanimous on the method of their struggle against the existing political system. Following methods have been supported:

(i) *Evolutionary Method.* A group headed by Tolstoy believes in evolutionary method such as persuasion and spreading of education of the type in which the people will condemn the state of their own accord. It is by evolutionary methods alone that the best possible results can be achieved.

(ii) *Use of force.* Proudhan and Kropotkin believe in the use of force. Ignorance should be removed by all means, which includes the use of force. But usually they avoid revolution because they fear the disorder which such a revolution will bring about. They also feel that revolutions are headed by a person who will like to become hero and will try to impose his will on the society. The hero at one stage or the other will be replaced by the present state though it might take some time.

(iii) *No Transition Stage.* The Anarchists believe that there will be no transitory stage between the fall of the present state and the final establishment of the society on anarchist lines. The change-over shall be final. The worker shall take over direct at the overthrow or fall of the present state. After taking over the state authority the evil institutions like private property and capitalism will be abolished. These will be taken over by new institutions which will give freedom to the people.

Criticisms

The ideas of anarchism have been subjected to following criticisms :

1. Impractical in modern states. It is impossible to imagine a state in the modern set up in which the governmental authority will not be required. It was an experiment which could be carried out either in the city states or in the primitive states in which the state was required to perform only police functions. It could be imagined then that these duties might be performed by voluntary associations. But it is wrong to think so about modern extensive states.

2. What will happen after abolition of state? The Anarchists wish to establish a state in which the governmental authority shall not be there so as to enable the people to enjoy maximum freedom. But freedom is enjoyed not in the absence of laws but in the protection of laws. If the laws are unhealthy and bad and hinder progress, it does not mean that the state should be abolished. What shall happen after abolition of state is not clear.

3. Vague methods of struggle. The Anarchists are vague in the methods of their struggle. Simple persuasion can yield frutitful results but that will take quite a long time and the Anarchists are not willing to have any transitory stage. They are not willing to force revolution because they feel that the leaders will resume powers of the state. They do not want regime of one hero but only that of workers.

4. Wrong assessment of human nature. The Anarchists have wrongly assessed human nature. They feel that the human beings are perfect and once the authority is removed and free atmosphere is given they will develop without hindering each other's progress. But in normal practice this is nòt true. Human beings are always selfish. The society can change the extent of their elimination of selfishness but nothing abolish man's selfish nature altogether.

5. Low production. Anarchists believe that in a classless and stateless society there will be no authority to compel the people to work. However, in such a society many persons will not like to work of their own. This will result in low production and the society on the whole will suffer.

6. No absence of authority. The Anarchists argue that in ideal society there shall not be absence of order but only absence of coercive authority. In actual practice, the logical conclusion should be absence of order and prevalence of chaos and disorder.

7. Disruption of Work. Communists argue that the anarchists philosophy is bourgeois socialism which aims at nothing else but disruption in the work which will do more harm than good to the society.

To conclude with Gettel, "In so far as the Anarchists point out evils in the present political organisations of the world their theory is valuable, but their own doctrines are based on the false assumptions, and the solution they propose would be ineffective and impossible."

ANARCHISM, NIHILISM AND COMMUNISM

Nihilism rose in the ninth century in Russia, it was the gospel of terrorism. It advocated the destruciton of present society by violent methods. Bomb-throwing, shooting, poisoning, murder, arson, etc., were their common means for liquidating the present system. For them the end justified the means fair or foul. Like the nihilists the revolutionary anarchists also spread hatred, bitterness, fanaticism and class prejudice. They accepted the communist idea of a stateless and classless society. Anarchists aim to abolish the state all of a sudden. Their revolution is not to be followed by any interim period such as the period of 'Dictatorship of the Proletariat' which is likely to result in the emergence of state capitalism. However, both the anarchists and communists are anti-state, anti-capitalism and anti-religion.

Anarchism and Syndicalism

Anarchism and syndicalism are similar in many respects. The syndicalists advocate the use of violent methods for the destruction of the state and capitalism. They support establishment of workers, associations. Like the anarchists, they also want to abolish the state all of a sudden. But syndicalists place all power into the hands of workers while anarchists stand for a society in which the interests of all the persons are to be safeguarded and harmonised. Thus, anarchism, nihilism, communism and syndicalism are akin to one another in many ways, though they also differ in some respects.

CRITICISM OF ANARCHISM

1. Violent Methods. Though there is lot of truth in what anarchists say but their methods are violent and their picture of society is hazy.

2. Impractical. Anarchist scheme of society can hardly be achieved. It is too mush to believe that society can be built on a voluntary and cooperative basis without any need of authority. It is a vision which can bring only chaos. It is impossible to think that all men shall become gods all of a sudden. It is difficult to curb the cirminal tendencies of individuals. Authority in some form is very necessary. Otherwise there will be complete anarchy and the law of the jungle shall prevail. According to Russell, "The state, in spite of what anarchists urge, seems a necessary institution for certain purposes. Peace and war, tariffs, regulaiton of sanitary conditions and of the sale of noxious drugs, the preservation of a just system of distribution, those, among others, are functions which could hardly be performed in a community in which there is no central government.... the state, though at present a source of much evil, is also a means to certain good things, and will be needed so long as violent and destructive impulses remain common. But it is merely a means, and a means which needs to be very carefully and sparingly used if it is not to do more harm than good."[19] The state is neither wholly evil nor superfluous. It is rather a necessary factor in civilising man. It is not true that in all states the individual has no freedom. Modern states are wedded to the concept of welfare state.

3. Utopian Society. The anarchist society is utopian and, therefore, impossible to realise in practice. According to Lancaster, "It is extremely difficult, if not impossible, to deal critically with anarchist thought. This is true because anarchists are so unrealistic that it is not possible to take them quite seriously. Anarchism as a social system is in fact inconceivable unless the ordinary human passions become so tepid as to make quarrelling impossible, and men so sweetly reasonable that they will cease wanting to do things in their own way."[20] Gray calls anarchists "race of highly intelligent and imaginative children, who nevertheless can scarcely be trusted to look after themselves outside the necessary pen."[21]

4. Paradoxical. Anarchists are accused of spreading hatred, fanaticism and violence. it is really paradoxical that they aim to build a stateless and classless society based on love and cooperation through the means of destruction and murder.

VALUE OF ANARCHISM.

Anarchism may be impracticable but it is not without value. Its significance lies in highlighting the dangers of overgrowth of political power. Power must be pulverised and decentralised. Small layers of authority, territorial and functional, should be set up. Through his membership of a small group man shall become aware of his role in society. It will help in recovering the lost hertiage of freedom. About Anarchism Gettell said, "It taught that liberty without socialism resulted in special privilege, and that socialism without liberty led to autocracy and slavery."[22] As a movement anarchism is now practically dead, but as a philosophy it is still the source of inspiration to many philosophers and reformers.

QUESTIONS FOR EXERCISE

1. "The state is without any natural or historical justification. It is opposed to man's natural co-operative instincts". Examine in the light of this statement the Anarchist view about the futility of hte state and its conception of stateless society.

19. Russell, Bertrand, *Roads to Freedom*, pp. 144-145.
20. Lancaster, L.W., *op. cit.*, p. 262-63.
21. Gray, Alexander, *op. cit.*, p. 380.
22. Gettell R.G., *History of Political Thought*, p. 476.

2. 'Anarchism is not a school of philosophy, it is an exaggerated and superficial protest'. Comment.
3. "Anarchists and socialsits have the same goal, a classless and stateless society. But their roads diverge sharply." — Coker. Examine the above statement.
4. "Anarchism is a principle or theory of life and conduct under which society is conceived without Government." Examine this statement.

21

Count Leo Tolstoy (1828—1910)

Inner Turmoil and Search for the Purpose of Life

Count Leo Nikolaevich Tolstoy was born in an ancient and noble family at his ancestral home of Yasnaya Polyana, Russia on September 9, 1828. He had everything with him that one could suppose necessary for a happy life. He was healthy, physically strong, intellectually vigorous and artistically fresh. As the master of a great estate he had no material worries. He enjoyed reputation as a descendant of one of the most aristocratic noble families. He was among the greatest writers in the Russian tongue, and a novelist famous throughout the globe. His family life was harmonious. He had wife and children, and no outward cause for discontentment with life.

Though an earth-bound man of this world, who had seen and felt the sensuous side of the life Tolstoy had no inclination towards metaphysics and speculative thinking. At fifty he received a blow from somewhere out in the dark, an inward shock. "Life came to a standstill, and turned sinister." There was sudden melancholy, and spells of terror. Nothing pleased or moved him any more. Work revolted him, his wife became a stranger, his children left him indifferent. A disgust of life possessed him. He locked his sporting gun away lest in despair he should turn it upon himself. He described his condition in a self-portrait, the Levine of *Anna Karenina*. "At that time he first clearly realized that every living being, and he too, had nothing to look forward to but suffering, death and eternal decay; and so he had decided that he could not go on living like this; either he must find an explanation of life, or he would shoot himself."

Tolstoy listed the six unknown questions which he had to answer :

1. Why am I living?
2. What is the cause for my existence and that of everyone else?
3. What purpose has my existence or any other?
4. What does the division which I feel within me into good and evil signify, and for what purpose is it there?
5. How must I live?
6. What is death — how can I save myself?

For the next thirty years the answering of these questions was the meaning and purpose of Tolstoy's life.

Tolstoy began to study all types of philosophic books, Schopenhauer and Plato, Kant and Pascal. Tolstoy found that the opinions of these wise men were only "clear and exact where they do not deal with the direct question of life," but that they wholly evaded answering when asked for decisive advice and help; and that none of them could explain the only thing he himself thought important: "What temporal, causal and spatial meaning has my life?" So he shifted from philosophy to religion. "Give me a faith, O Lord, and let me help others to find it." In his book *My Confession* Tolstoy writes :

> "When I had come to this conclusion, I understood that it was useless to seek an answer to my question from knowlege founded on reason, and that the answer given by this form of knowledge is only an indication that no answer can be obtained till the question is put differently — till the question be made to include the relation between the finite and the infinite. I also understand that, however unreasonable and monstrous the answers given by faith, they have the advantage of bringing into every question the relation of the finite to the infinite, without which there can be no answer."[1]

CONDEMNATION OF PROPERTY

As Tolstoy became firm in his belief that property is the root cause of inequality and suffering in society, he started his attack on property more bitterly than Karl Marx and Proudhon. He said, "Today possessions are the root of all evil. They cause the suffering of those who possess and of those who do not possess. And the danger of collision is unavoidable between those who have too much and those who live in poverty." All evil begins with property, so long as the state still recognizes the principle of property, it is both un-Christian and unsocial and becomes one of the chief guilty parties. In the words of Tolstoy "States and governments intrigue and go to war for property, now for the banks of the Rhine, the lands of Africa, now for China and the Balkans; bankers, traders, manufacturers and land-owners work, plant and torment themselves and others, only for property. Officials fight, cheat, oppress and suffer, all for the sake of property alone. Our courts, our police defend property. Our penal colonies and prisons, all the horrors of our so-called suppression of crime exist entirely to protect property."

CONDEMNATION OF STATE AND ITS LAWS

At the present time very act of our lives is under the supervision of the state, a man marries and is divorced, rears his children, and in some countries accepts the religion it prescribes in accordance with its dictates. Do men believe in it? Tolstoy's answer was : "Not at all." In most cases men recognize its injustice, despise it, and yet obey it. It was fit, Tolstoy writes, that "the ancients should obey their law," as they sincerely believed it to be the only true law, to which all men owed obedience. But "We cannot refuse to acknowledge that

1. Tolstoy, Leo, *My Confession* (1882).

the law of our state is not the eternal law, but only one of the many laws of many states, all equally imperfect, and frequently wholly false and unjust — a law that has been openly discussed in all its aspects by the public press."[2] Men have realised today that there is no sense in obeying a law whose honesty is doubtful. They suffer when they still conform to it, though privately denying its prerogative. When a man's whole life is held in bondage by laws, whose injustice, cruetly and artificiality he discerns, he must suffer; it cannot be otherwise.

State Shields Injustice

In Tolstoy's opinion the state shields the injustice of present-day society. It was invented to protect property. For this purpose it set up its many-meshed system of force, with laws, prosecuting attorneys, prisons, judges, policemen, and armies. But the most frightful and Godless misdemeanour of the state was universal military duty. Nothing was such a provocation to the Christian man to betray the precepts of Christ and the Commandments of the Gospels as his yielding to a state's order, allowing a tool of murder to be forced into his hand to kill some perfect stranger for the sake of a change catchword — Fatherland, Freedom, the State. These catchwords have no purpose but to protect prorperty that does not belong to him, and forcibly to raise the idea of property to that of a higher moral law. If men submit to authority, it is only because they fear that if they were to resist, they would be subjected to violence. All the requisitions of the state, such as the payment of taxes and the fulfilment of public duties, the submission to penalties in the form of exile, fines, etc., to which men seem to yield voluntarily, are always enforced by the physical threat or the reality of physical punishment.

Physical Violence as the Basis of Authority

Tolstoy regarded physical violencfe as the basis of authority. The military organization makes it possible to inflict physical violence, it is the organization wherein the entire armed force acts as one man, obeying a single will. The assemblage of armed men, submitting to one will, forms what is called an army. The army has ever been and still is the basis of an authority, vested in the commanding generals. The most engrossing interest of every sovereign, from the Roman Caesars, to the Russian and German Emperors, has always been to protect and flatter the army, for they realize that when the army is on their side, power is also in their hands. We are told that the government and its armies are necessary for our defence against the neighbouring states which might subject us. All the governments say this. As every European nation professes the same principles of liberty and fraternity, and therefore needs no defence against its neighbour. Hence, no man who reflects on the significance of the state, can escape the conviction that there is no longer any reasonable ground for such sacrifice. Tolstoy writes : "The Christian nations of the present-day are in a position no less cruel than that of pagan times. In many respects,

2. From *The Kingdom of God.*

especially in the matter of oppression, their position has grown worse. In the former the external aspect of cruelty and slavery corresponded with the inner consciousness of men, a conformity which only increased as time went on; in the latter the external condition of cruelty and salvery is in utter contradiction which grows more and more striking every year."[3]

RADICAL ANARCHISM

Thus, Tolstoy turned to radical anarchism. He came to the conclusion that it was the duty of every intelligently moral person to resist the state if it demanded something 'un-Christian', such as military service. This should be done not by force but by non-resistance. In addition, he must voluntarily give up every activity which depends on exploiting the work of others. Honourable men must think and act not patriotically but humanely. It is the holiest right of the individual, to be refractory to every pronouncement of the state which they do not recognize as moral. The Christian man should evade all arrangements and institutions as much as possible, not to appear in courts of law and to accept no offices, in order to keep his soul pure. The individual should not be intimidated by the false, the anti-moral principle of force, even if it calls itself the force of law and order. The state in its present form is itself the defender, lawyer and bailiff of a latent injustice. Even anarchical crimes of individuals do not seem to Tolstoy so morally corrupting as the apparently well-ordered and humanly acting institutions of state. He said, "Thieves, robbers, murderers, swindlers are an example of what one must not do, and they inspire in men's minds a horror of wrong-doing. But men who commit acts of theft, of robbery, of murder, of chastisement, and gild them with some religious, scientific or liberal justification — who do it as land-owners, merchants or manufacturers — appeal to others to intimate their acts; they injure not only those who suffer under it, but thousands and millions of men whose morals they ruin by destroying the distinction between good and evil in those men's minds....A single sentence of death carried out by men who are not under the influence of passion, by prosperous, educated persons with the encouragement and assistance of Christian clergymen, corrupts and brutalizes mankind more than hundreds and thousands of murders committed by uneducated working-men, usually in an access of passion...Every war, even the shortest, with all its accompanying losses, thefts, tolerated excesses, robberies, murders, with the supposed justification of its necessity and justice, with the praise and glorification of war-like deeds, with prayers for the flag and the Fatherland and the hypocritical anxiety for the wounded, corrupts men more in one year than millions of robberies, arsons and murders committed by individuals under the influence of passion in the course of hundreds of years." Thus, the state, according to Tolstoy, is the chief criminal, the true Anti-Christ, the personification of evil.

Thus, it was the natural duty of a Christian to withdraw himself both from the demands and the temptations of this devilish spectre. The free Christian

3. *Ibid.*

must be just as indifferent to Russia as a state as he is to France or England. He must think not in terms of nations but on a universal human basis. Tolstoy withdrew from the state as he had from the orthodox Church, declaring : "I cannot recognize states or nations, nor take part in quarrels betwen them, either by writing on the subject or by serving a single state. I can take no part in anything which rests on the difference between states, like custom houses, tax collection, the manufacture of explosives and arms, or any war-like preparations." The 'Christian man' in Tolstoy's sense must deny the state. He must live morally outside this immoral institution. Tolstoy said, "The Christian who contemplates that law of love implanted in every human soul, and quickened by Christ, the only guide for all mankind, is set free from human authority."[4] This wholly passive, wholly negative, apathetic attitude, willingly accepting any suffering, distinguishes Tolstoy from the political revolutionary, who hates the state instead of ignoring it.

THE FREEDOM OF THE CHRISTIAN MAN

This 'anti-state doctrine' of Tolstoy's is in itself splendidly direct and forceful. The flaw within the system appears only when Tolstoy attempts to turn his demand for self-determination into a positive theory of the state. Instead of a stable, unifrom state structure with authorities and laws and executive organs, he recommends simply 'love', 'brotherhood', 'faith', 'life in Christ' as a means of cementing all contradictory interests. According to Tolstoy the vast abyss existing today between the property-owning classes, spoiled children of culture, and the pauper classes can be spanned only if the property-owning classes voluntarily given up their privileges, and cease to make such great demands upon life. Let the rich man create his works with a view solely to intelligibility for the masses, let everyone live wholly by his own work, receiving no more for it than he needs for this primitive form of life. Social levelling must be accomplished not from below, as the revolutionists demand, by forcibly taking all property from the owners, but from above, by a spontaneous concession from the propertied classes.

THE REAL KINGDOM OF GOD ON EARTH

Tolstoy realized that once equal needs or rather simplicity of needs have restored unity among men, the evil instincts of envy and hatred can find no further objects of attack. Now, it will be superfluous to create special authorities and to use force in maintaining them. The real kingdom of God on earth will began as soon as all social exaltations and subordinations are done away with, and people have once more learned to form a single brotherly community.

THESIS ON SOCIETY

So powerful as Tolstoy's authority in his time and so attractive was his thesis on society that many people desired to realize his theory of society in practice. But, these attempts ended in disappointment. Tolstoy did not succeed

4. *Ibid.*

in establishing the basic principles of Tolstoyism even in his own house and family. For years he tried to harmonize his private life with his theories, he gave up his beloved hunting so as not to kill animals. He avoided using the railroad, he turned over the income from his writings to his family or to charitable purposes. He refused to eat meat because it required the forcible death of living creatures. He ploughed in the fields himself, went about in a coarse peasant coat, and nailed the soles of his shoes with his own hands. But all this could not change the hearts of the members of his family. His wife became estranged, his children could not understand why they must be brought up like milk-maids and peasant boys for the sake of their father's theories. His secretaries and translators brawled like drunken coachmen over the property in Tolstoy's writings. Not a single soul around him accepted the life of this splendid pagan as a truly Christian one. In the end he himself knew as his diary shows, that his intellectuality and his pride unsuited him more than anyone to fulfil the imperiously propagated ideal. The eighty-three year old man, when death came upon him, fled out of his house by night, and dies in a little railroad station, lonely and disappointed in his holiest purpose.

CRITICAL EVALUATION

Tolstoy's principles were greatly ridiculed during his own life time, and he died a tragic death. But not one of his contemporary thinkers, Karl Marx or Nietzche, produced equal emotion in millions and millions of people as Tolstoy did. None of the nineteenth-century Russian revolutionists paved the path so much for Lenin and Trotsky as Tolstoy, who was the first to defy the Tsar, and who had left the Church, who had shattered all existing authority with hammer blows, and who demanded social reconciliation as the necessary condition for a new and better world. Forbidden by the censors, his works were copied by hand, and reached a hundred thousand readers, making common knowledge of his demand for the abolition of property at a time when the wildest of the social revolutionists were still modestly satisfied with liberalistic palliatives and reforms. Nothing could make Russia as radical as Tolstoy's radicalism. As Rousseau was the ancestor of the French Revolution, so Tolstoy was the promoter, the true ancestor of the Russian world revolution. It is always "an exquisite delight when we can regard a towering artist as a moral example also, as a man who, instead of ruling by his celebrity, makes himself the servant of humanity, and in his struggle for a true ethos submits to only one out of all the authorities on earth — his own incorruptible conscience."[5]

QUESTIONS FOR EXERCISE

1. Discuss Radicalism of Leo Tolstoy.
2. Describe and evaluate Tolstoy's views about the state, private property and the church.

5. Zweig, Stefan, *Tolstoy* (Cassell & Co. Ltd., London, 4th ed., 1948), p. 19.

22

Revisionism : Bernstein (1850—1903)

Like Fabians, Revisionists also criticised Marx. They also differed from him in many details. The chief exponent of this philosophy is Bernstein who severly criticised Marx in his book '*Evolutionary Socialism*'. He tried to establish that whatsoever Marx had prophesied was not proving true and much to the contrary was being seen everywhere. He called Marx an utopian who tried to simplify the transitionary period from the overthrow of existing capitalist society to the establishment of proletariat society. For Bernstein the process was neither so simple nor so quick as protrayed by Marx.

REVISIONISM *Vs.* MARXISM

1. No faith in revolution. Marxian prophecy was neither correct nor could be justified that a revolution was very soon bound to come and that the working class should not work under the existing arrangements. Revisionists felt that the revolution was not in sight nor the capitalist system was going to wither. They felt that it was criminal to hinder that the revolution was soon coming and that soon there would be rule of proletariats or working classes.

2. Rise of middle class. Revisionists criticised Marx about his prophecy that the middle classes will gradually join the ranks of prolatariats. Berstein felt that the middle class had now definitely emerged as a separate class and was a block in itself. In the words of Coker, "In short, the proleteriat is not becoming the homogeneous and united group that the orthodox Marxians visualised. Diversities in interests, sharp contrast in economic and social status, significant differences in political ideas are found among the various groups that make up the great unprivileged majority in any modern country."

3. Rejection of Marxist theory of value. The revisionists did not agree with Marx that the value of a commodity was exclusively to be determined by the useful labour of labourers put in it. For them it was wrong that surplus value absorbed by the capitalists was measured only by the excess produced by a labourer. Coker has said, "Revisionists in general followed Bernstein in rejecting Marx's theory of value — in so far as theory involves the principle that exchange value of commodities is measured solely by the effors of wage earners and that the surplus absorbed by the capitalists is measureable only by the excess of value of what labourers produced over what they receive."

4. Rejection of Marxian theory of surplus value. Revisionists rejected Marxian theory of surplus value as mere intellectual and imaginary rather than real and true to life. Their theory had neither any bearing on the idea of exploitation nor working classes struggle.

5. Increase in purchasing power of workers. The Revisionists criticised Marx on the ground that purchasing power of workers would gradually come down. For them this had also not come true. All available statistics showed that the purchasing power of working classes had considerably increased and that they were now consuming more commodities.

6. Working classes do have homeland. The Revisionists criticised Marx for the idea that the working classes have no homeland. They definitely have their homelands as well as enjoyed political rights. In all emergencies working classes had shown their loyalities to their governments. Therefore, to believe that working classes had no homeland was absolutely wrong and confusing.

SIMILARITY BETWEEN REVISIONISM AND MARXISM

1. Anti-capitalism. Revisionists agree with Marx that capitalist system was based on naked exploitation. It was bound to live on the earnings of others. In order to do away with economic inequality it was essential that the capitalist system should be uprooted.

2. Proletariat socialist society for democracy. Revisionists believe that there must be a proletariat socialist society in every state if democracy was to work satisfactorily and successfully.

3. Unity of working classes. The Revisionists agree that it was essential for the working classes that they should unite for the bringing about a change in existing agencies. They also believed that democracy and socialism were not against each other but if properly utilised they were helpful and complementary to each other.

4. Revolutionary line of action. The Revisionists like Marxists were not in favour of following evolutionary methods. The workers should proceed on a general strike and bring about revolution if they felt that their purpose could not be served by democratic institutions and methods. It was the duty of the state to restrict private capitalism to all possible extents. Revisionists demanded reforms like universal suffrage, progressive taxation and regularisation of industry etc. It was advisable that the socialists for the present should co-operate with those at least who were willing to give maximum benefits to proletariats. Revosionists favoured acceptance of offices in such cabinets which promoted labour welfare programmes and also were sympathetic to their demands.

CRITICISM OF REVISIONISM

1. Gain is not the essential motive. Revisionists believe that the people work for the sake of gains only. They forget that gains are not the only factor in man's life. We do many things in which gains have nothing to do. We love our children not with the idea of gaining anything but because of our natural instinct of love and affection for them.

2. Man is not a commercial being. The Revisionists also feel that man is only commercial being and he weighs everything in terms of internal and external commercialisation. But commercialisation does not always dominate man's life. For example, human instinct for sympathy has no concern for commercialisation. Sympathy is a natural instinct while commercialisation is artificial. As such both are at different ends.

3. Collective production not always better. The Revisionists believe that collective production can bring better results because it avoids wastage. But it is the individual production which has changed deserts into green fields. Collective production has ruined the fruits of individual production. Therefore, the drastic statement that collective production is always better than the individual production has no justification. Both have their own advantages and disadvantages and do prefer one over the other is rather a partial attitude and cannot be justified.

POLITICAL IDEAS OF BERNSTEIN (1850—1903)

Edward Bernstein, a German political thinker was the chief exponent of Revisionist political philosophy. While in exile in England he came in close contact with the Fabians and also Engels and their contact considerably influenced him. His ideas first appeared in the form of a book entitled "*Problem-des-Socialismus.*" In 1899, he brought out his '*Voraus Setzungen des-Socialismus*' through which he tried to prove that many of Marxian ideas were not at all correct and that Marx's prophecies had not come true.

1. Difference from Marx : (i) *Theory of value.* Bernstein was basically of the opinion that Marx was wrong in his theory of 'value' or 'surplus value'.

(ii) *Self-destruction by capitalism.* Bernstein differed with Marx that capitalism was sowing the seeds of its own destruction.

(iii) *Living standard of working class.* He also condemned the idea that gradually the living standard of working classes would come down and that would only be because the working classes were paid only for basic and bare necessities of life.

(iv) *Materialistic interpretation of history.* He also criticised Marx's materalistic interpretation of history. In the words of Maxey, "After exposing the contradictions between Marx's earlier and later writings on the subject of value, Bernstein endeavoured to prove that Marx was unscientific in trying to make a case against capitalism on the theory that the degree of profit to the capitalist and injustice to the worker varies with the quantum of surplus value wrested from the latter."

2. Political Ideas : (i) *Theory of Values.* Against Marxist theory of value Bernstein said, "We meet ideed today the best placed workers just in those trades with a very high rate of surplus value, the most infamously ground down workers in those with a very low rate. A scientific basis for socialism or communism cannot be supported on the fact only that the wage worker does not receive the full value of the produce of his work."

(ii) *Interpretation of History.* He did not agree with Marx's theory of materialistic interpretation of history. Agaist Marx, Bernstein maintained that the history was not natural, and that the history was not moving in a specific direction of its own. As the time passes the individuals and nations acquire more and more knowledge and also sense of freedom which helps in changing the course of history. There were certain co-ordinating factors. Intellectual and economic factors helped in this regard. Both Marx and Engels have given secondary position to economic and intellectual factors which shows that they are narrow in their outlook. He also criticised Marx for ignorning the value of interdependence which is very vital and gradually increasing. In his own words, "The interdependence of cause and effect between technological economic evolution and evolution of other social tendencies is continually becoming more indirect; and accordingly the necessities of the former are doing much in their power to dictate the form of the latter."

(iii) *Capitalism.* Bernstein did not agree with Marx that capitalism was sowing the seeds of its own destruction. As against Marxian philosophy he tried to prove that small scale industries were rapidly increasing and "that concentration into large industries through the corporate form of organization tends to diffuse rather than concentrate ownership of wealth." He refuted the argument that the small capitalists would gradually disappear and shall join the ranks of the working classes. On the contrary, he tried to show that the number of capitalists was gradually increasing.

(iv) *Workers' condition.* Bernstein did not agree that with the passage of time the workers will undergo miseries and that their purchasing power will be reduced. He felt that per capita income of the workers was considerably going up and the conditions of workers were improving. There were now more commercial credits and improved banking facilities whereby the workers could get loans. The workers are now becoming homogenous and emerging as united.

(v) *Anti-revolution.* It was wrong to believe that the workers should force a revolution or try to establish their dictatorship by revolutionary methods. The workers should try to satisfy themselves by accepting what was extended by the democratic institutions. They should try to acquire a capacity for economic and political supremacy. In the words of Maxey, "The capitalist system said he, was becoming constantly stronger and more stable, centring around wealth; and the number of bourgeoise in proportion to the proletariats was steadily increasing. Therefore, capitalism had a good chance of becoming permanent and reducing the proletariat to lasting servitude.

(vi) *Democracy.* Bernstein did not agree with Marx that modern democratic institutions were only meant for the capitalists. He did not favour the idea that proletariat dictatorship was a solution to the problem. There was no justification for proletarian rule if the workers were hostile to the capitalists. If the capitalists' rule was intolerable for the workers *vice versa* could also be possible.

(vii) *Homeland.* Bernstein did not agree with Marx that the workers had no homeland. He believed that the workers have a homeland. Each worker has now a right to vote. He has share in the making and unmaking of government.

He has all responsibility in developing the wealth of the nation and seeing that the prestige of his nation is not lowered in any way.

(viii) *Capitalist society.* Capitalist society was based on naked exploitation of a vast majority of people. The capitalist produced goods which the majority could hardly purchase. Hence, class antagonism gradually develops. In the words of Coker, "Under a system of private ownership, for majority of the workers to reach the position of luxury and ease flaunted by the wealthy minority and the improved economic conditon of working men generally tends to strengthen, not weaken, both their desire to achieve their full rights and their ability to work effectively for that achievement whether through revolution or through peaceful means."

Conclusion

Thus, as a Revisionist, Bernstein did not see eye to eye with Marx on many points. For him Marxian philosophy was unscientific and much of it had not come true. He refuted Marx on his basic principles and to give a rude shock to orthodox Marxists. He was of the view that prophecies of Marx had not come true in so far as industrial world was concerned.

ACHIEVEMENTS OF REVISIONISTS

Revisionists were not in agreement with many of the Marxian principles. According to them, Marxian philosophy was not scientific. Many of Marxian prophecies had not come true. It was wrong to believe that as long as the present state existed the interests of the working classes shall be ignored. Revolution was not the way out for solving our problems. Democracy should be considered as a necessary complement for socialism. They accepted class character of socialism. Socialism was a movement which aimed at improving material and social conditions of the workers. The society was divided into classes mainly between the workers and those who were living on the labour of others. The socialists should aim at breaking this type of supremacy of one class over the other. In their own words, "It is not by the collapse of capitalist bourgeoisie but by the invigoration of the proleteriat, that the communist order will gradually instal itself in our society." For them modern democratic movement is part of socialist movement. Restriction on private capitalism could either be by way of setting up of state ownership instesad of private ownership or in the form of governmental interference. As long as the socialists could form their ministries they should co-operate with the governments which were willing to extend some rights and privileges to the workers. The socialists should support progressive governments. They believed in the policy of co-operation and compromise. In their own words, "All our reforms must have got as their revolutionary object, the emancipation of the oppressed and exploited labour. But you must realise that the socialism must accomplish immediate reforms."

CRITICAL ESTIMATE

Considerable Influence

The Revisionists had considerable influence in Europe upto the outbreak of World War I, which gave a great set back to the socialist movement as a whole. Second International Socialist Political parties were founded in Germany, France and Italy under their influence and control. Many of the European countries were obliged to extend concessions to their workers and labourers. In the words of Maxey, "In several countries they gained strength enough to hold the balance of power and occassionally slipped into office. A number of top flight statesmen of modern Europe came from their ranks."

Nationalism above Socialism

The Revisionists realised the need of the time. They decided to place nation even above the creed, *i.e.* socialism after the close of First World War. In the words of Coker, "The Socialists should work for popular control of foreign policy and for international conciliation; but they may defend national rights, and they may under the proper conditions, even support colonial expansion — in order to strengthen pacific and democratic against autocratic and imperialistic nations. Jaures, accepting the national democratic state as an indispensable agency in the attainment of socialism proclaimed, on several occasions, the loyalty of French Socialists to the French Republic."

Demands in France

In France, under the leadership of Jaures, Revisionists demanded "Universal adult franchise and proportional representation, the initiative referendum and recall, secularization of schools, removal of the legal disabilities of women, progressive taxation, social insurance, protection of labour, regulation of industry and international peace." They stood for compulsory arbitration of trade disputes. They tried to control municipalities wherever that could. They tried to encourage co-operative system in the trade, establishment of co-operative stores and the formation of trade unions.

The Revisionists, however, got a set back from the orthodox Marxists after the Russian Revolution. Maxey has said that, "They organised the Third International to serve as a sclid international forum for uncompromising Marxian communists and encouraged and aided the formation of communist parties all over the world. The Second International survived in an emaciated state which faithfully reflected the feebleness of the social democratic movement it represented."

Middle Course

The Revisionists followed a middle course between democratic reformists and exclusively revolutionary socialists. They believed that political democracy alone could not eliminate class antagonisms and that the solution to many problems was in compromise. To conclude with Coker, "The ultimate goal of the revisionists is that of all socialists; but just because the completed changes which its attainments involved are so sweeping, complex and remote that the only effective plan for socialists today is to work for the partial change that can be introduced as economic and political conditions permit."

QUESTIONS FOR EXERCISE

1. Discuss and criticise the ideas of 'Revisionists'.
2. "Revisionists as well as the stricter Marxists, regarded Socialism as mainly a doctrine and programme for the working class. Both sought to find the policy that would serve best the interest of working men in improving physical, economic and cultural well-beings and stregthening their political position" — Coker. Discuss.
3. Discuss the main political ideas of Bernstein.
4. Write a critical estimate of the achievements of Revisionists.

23
Fabianism

Origin of Fabian Society

Fabian society established in 1882 when a dozen persons met in London under Thomas Davidson. In the initial stages they believed that moral standards were necessary for self-reforms. Generally they realised their mistake. They felt that the aid of legislative authority was indispensable if they were really interested in bringing about reforms. A society was accordingly established in 1884. According to Coker the members of this new society were highly educated men and women, widely read in the works of classical political economy and the recent literatrue of land taxation and socialism. They were influenced particularly by the doctrines of Henry George and the various British interpretation of Marx, and the developing collectivism in John Stuart Mill's exposition of his individualistic doctirne." Men like George Bernard Shaw and Sidney Webb joined the society in 1884 and 1855 respectively. England was the nerve-centre of this society. The members had no contacts with the working class as they were highly intellectual. They brought a critical outlook to the then existing socialistic philosophy. They were theorists rather than the practical politicans or political scientists.

Difference From Marxism

The members of the Fabian society had thoroughly studied Karl Marx, Proudhon, Robert Owen, Ricardo and Mill. They had come to realise that for social welfare it was absolutely essential that means of production must be in the hands of community at large. They believed that ownership of land and industrial capital be gradually transferred to society. This transfer would give society more representative value.

1. Surplus value. They did not agree with Marxian theory of 'Surplus Value'.

2. Class struggle. They did not agree with the conception that the history of hitherto existing society was that of class struggle.

3. Evolution not the only means of change. Henry Webb believed that the struggle was always due to change in human mind. He believed that historically all changes came through parliamentary system. G.B. Shaw also contributed to this idea when he said that "Fabians agreed to give up delightful ease of revolutionary heroics and to take to the hard work of practical reforms on ordinary parliamentary lines." Thus, Fabians did not believe in Marxian thoery that changes could only be brought through revolution and by dislocating the whole social and economic system. They believed that changes should be brought gradually and peacefully. They also believed that the methods for bringing about the changes should be dignified and not such as are considered immoral by the people. Sidney Webb was of the opinion that socialism would be built only after the development of existing society. He set forth in some detail the Fabian idea about the irresistible progress of democracy and almost the continuous progress of democracy.

4. Rejection of economic determination. Fabians believe that history was a constant process. Economics was not the only factor which dominated society. "History, they maintained, supplies an explanation for the socialism of today, not by proving that economic conditions dominate everything but by revealing a steady movement towards democracy and socialism, in both practice and theory."

5. Rejection of labour theory of value. Fabians believed that the value of the commodities was not always based on the labourer but society created values. Coker has said that "They showed that under the unregulated competitive system a capitalist in manufacture of trade as well as in land, retains the superior yield of his capital, which is not due to his superior ability or services but due to the location of his business, the general increase in population, or the growing prosperity of the people." They pointed out that unearned increments in the values of land and industry were due to the pouring in of more population. It was wrong to believe that the value of goods was determined only by socially useful labour put in. It was also because of social and economic needs of the society. These things were leading us to an unconscious revolution.

6. Minimising class distinctions. According to Fabians land and capital should be transferred from the individuals to the society so that the whole community was benefited by that. They were, therefore, opposed to private property and wanted to end that. In their own words, "The society accordingly works to the extinction of private property in land and of the consequent individual appropriation in the form of rent of price paid for permission to use the earth, as well as for the advantage of superior soil and site."

The Fabian Socialists, however, believed that the difference between the division of classes was too wide. The ratio of profit between these two organs of production should be minimum. The profit was earned because of social conditions, environments and efforts and as such it should not go to one individual but to the society as a whole. They also pleaded that the profit thus earned should be used for the welfare of the society as a whole.

7. Different methods. The Fabian school of thought never agreed with Marxian philosophy that aim and object of social changes could only be achieved through revolution. They agreed that overall dislocation of the existing system would do more harm than good to the society. The minds and thoughts of the people should be brought in tune with the new philosophy. With this end in view the Fabian Socialists used the methods of lecturing, propaganda and issusing pamphlets. The Fabian essays contributed by Shaw, Webb, Graham Wallas and Mrs. Annie Besant are still read with profound interest. In 1906 was founded a Summer School in Fabian Socialism for teaching the workers. In 1912, a research project for collective produciton and distribution was undertaken. The Fabian Socialists were also asked to join existing political insitutions and work there as political cells on Fabian lines.

8. Workers are not a separate class. The Fabians never agreed that working people constitute a separate class, they were also part of society. In the words of Coker they said, "We have never advanced the pretension to represent the working classes of this country, the society 'steadfastly discountenances all schemes for securing to any person, or any group of persons, the entire product of their labour. Its object is to transfer ownership, not to the workers, but to society'."

9. Effectiveness of state. Fabians were fully confident that the existing state was fair and effective. Changes should, however, be brought in making franchise broad-based. Civil services should be trained for spreading education among the people. Fabians believed in social legislation, public ownership of property and taxation on inheritances, etc.

VALUE OF FABIANISM

1. Reformed Socialism. Fabianism is one of the reformed ideologies of communism as expounded and preached by Karl Marx. Marx had given certain doctrines like the one that "the history of hitherto existing society is the history of class struggle" or that "revolution is the only way of changing the present set-up" and so on which he proclaimed as always true and suited to all circumstances.

2. Flexibility. The Fabians showed more sense of reality saying that no philosophy in this world is true and applicable for all times to come. Every doctrine is subject to change. What is correct today may not be correct tomorrow. Thus, fabians turned socialistic doctrines from rigidity to flexibility.

3. Intellectual. Fabianism made socialistic philosophy applicable and acceptable to intellectuals. Hitherto Marxian philosophy was appealing only to the working classes who were disillusioned by the lucidity of Marx. Finding the overthrow of capitalist society very simple, they embraced that philosophy but it was not acceptable to intellectuals who found glaring defects in that. However, Fabians made their doctrines acceptable to intellectuals. Fabians were a society of the intellectuals who began to embrace the socialistic doctrines.

4. Wide-based Doctrine. Marxian philosophy had made socialism applicable for the working classes alone. Fabians openly declared that they did not represent the working classes nor their organisation is of the working classes alone. They made their organisation suited to the working classes and the capitalist. They deliberately avoided the terms 'Proletariats' or the 'Bourgeois' which had by now become very narrow in outlook.

Thus, Fabianism was broader in outlook and ideas than Marxian Socialism. It made valuable improvements in original Marxian philosophy. In the words of Maxey, "It is not going too for, however, to give the Fabian movement credit for a larger part of the vast quantity of legislation which has been enacted in England since the 1880s."

HISTORY OF FABIANISM

A group of German academicians who were un-Marxian and known as 'Socialists of the Chair' were the organisers of Fabianism. Fabian Society was founded in England in 1884. It was somewhat similar to the Academic Socialists of Germany. Democratic Federation was founded in England in 1881. It was named as 'Social Democratic Federation' in 1884. H.M. Hyndman, William Morris, Edward Avaling etc. are a few such names which can be quoted as early associates. But it was neither an influential nor effective organisation. Hence, it could not make any substantial progress. In 1884, Socialist League was founded by Morris Box and others who were associated with Socialisι Democratic Federation. Unfortunately there was disunity among the League as some of its members were Parliamentarians while the others were Anarchists. Morris, the founder was of the opinion that the League should only confine itself to making propaganda till sufficient supporters of new ideologies were available. They also started a journal entitled 'Common Weal' which was discontinued in 1894. Both these parties were the main source of Fabian movement in England. Their contribution primarily lies in the fact that they placed the interests of workers above everything else. By and large their members held political views of the liberal party. As the time passed the trade unionists felt the need and necessity of a separate labour organisation on socialist lines. It was only in 1893 that the idea materialised and an independent labour party was founded. Among its early members were J. Keir Hardie, J. Bruce Glasier, J. Ramsay Macdonald and Philip Snowden. Coker has described the characteristic of this party as less doctrinaire and more disposed to compromise than the earlier socialist organisations but more aggressively socialist than the Fabian Society. In 1900 this very organisaiton provided material for Labour Party and also for Fabian Society.

Fabian Society

According to Maxey, "The Fabian Society was formed in 1884 by a number of British intellectuals who agreed with Marx on many points, but objected to his revolutionism." It was a highbrow movement from the start and had little direct contact with proletarianism until after 1900. Because of its revolutionary objectives, orthodox Marxism had difficulty in gaining a foothold in Great Britain. About the members of this society Coker has said, "They were influenced particularly by the doctrines of Henry George, the various British interpretations of Marx, and developing collectivism in John Stuart Mill's exposition of his individual doctrine. George Bernard Shaw joined the society in September 1884 and Sidney Webb the following year; these two became the most active and the most influential members of the Society."

Objects of the Fabian Socialists

1. Propagation. The Fabian Socialists were fully aware of the problems created by the industrial advancement and also exploitation of man by man. They were also fully alive to the poor working conditions of the workers and the need and necessity of improving them. They wanted to propagate socialist doctrines among the middle class and to put their doctrine into actual practice gradually.

2. Education. Maxey has outlined the objects of Fabian Socialists, by saying that "Their chief aims were to educate the electorate along socialist lines and work for the victory of one small socialist reform after another until finally the whole campaign should be won."

3. Spreading socialism. Coker says, "The objects of Fabians have been to spread the socialist doctrine, as they understand it throughout the educated middle class and to persude the national and local Government of Great Britain to put the doctrine gradually into practical operation."

4. Reform through parliamentary methods. They did not favour direct battle or violent revolution but persuasion and propaganda. In their own words, "The members of the society assert that the competitive system assures the happines and comfort of a few that the expense of the suffering of the many and the society must be reconstituted in such a manner as to secure the general welfare and happiness." George Bernard Shaw used to say that, "The state should compete with all its might in every department of production." They wanted to achieve their object of practical reforms on ordinary parliamentary lines.

5. Reorganisation of society for collective ownership. The Fabians aimed at reorganisation of society from individual to collective ownership. They wanted to extinct private property. In 1887, they said that "The society, further works for the transfer to the community of the administration of such industrial capital as can conveniently be managed socially. For, owing to the monopoly of means of production in the past, industrial inventions and transformation of surplus income into capital have mainly enriched the proprietary class, the worker being now dependant on that class for leave to earn a living. The idle class living on the labour of others should disappear. There should be practical equality of opportunity."

FABIANISM *Vs.* MARXISM

Differences

Some of the differences between the two were on the following points :

1. Revolution. As Maxey has said "But they refused to deduce from this the Marxian conclusion that the emancipation of the working classes could come through revolution followed by transitional dictatorship of the proletariat."

2. Democracy. To quote Maxey again, "Economic evolution, as they analysed it, was not only dispossessing the working class but tending also to eliminate the capitalist as owner and entrepreneur. Individualism was disappearing on both sides of the equation, and the contest in the future would be between collectivized labour and collectivized capital. The advantages of collectivized capital were so great that society could not afford to destroy it. Therefore, in a democratic state, the inevitable trend would be to subject it to increasing government regulation and control and ultimately to take over a large part of it as the proper possession of society."

3. Capitalism. Fabians did not agree with Marx that capitalism was theft and that it was a social evil. They did not agree with him also that under capitalism the working classes shall certainly suffer and that there were no chances for their rise. They also did not support the idea that capitalism was sowing the seeds of its destruction and that a stage had come when capitalism was bound to shape itself on monopolistic lines.

4. Theory of value. Maxey says that for them "value was a social product and it was the duty of the society to distribute the resulting income fairly among all members of society. The state should be deemed as the representative and trustee of all the people for the execution of this duty." For Fabians value was the creation of society and that was to be determined by the requirements of the society as a whole. In the words of Coker, "They showed that under the unregulated competitive system a capitalist, in manufacture of trade as well as in land, retains the superior yield of his capital, which is not due to his superior ability or service, but to the location of his business, the general increase in population, or the growing property of the people."

5. Class struggle. It is the basic idea of Marxian philosophy which said that the history of hitherto existing struggle was that of class struggle. They believed that the working classes alone could achieve socialism. On the contrary, The Fabians believed that socialism could be brought about by the middle classes and not by the working classes. They did not contribute to the idea of class struggle which for them was basically wrong. Till 1889, they did not care for working class movement in England.

6. Natrue of conflict. They agreed to the extent that investment alone was no jsutification or could not be a valid reason for retaining extra income. But beyond that they differed from each other. For fabians the present conflict was not between the employer and the employees but between the community on the one hand and those who intend to grow rich through investment, on the other. Coker has quoted to say from "*English Progress Towards Social Democracy*" in the following passage : "The individuals or classes who passess social power have at all times, consciously or unconsciously, made use of that power in such a way as to leave the great majority of their fellows practically nothing beyond the means of subsistence according to the current living standard. The additional product, determined by the relative differnce in productive efficiency of the different sites, soils, capitals and forms of skill above the margin of cultivation, have gone to those exercising control over these valuable but scarce factors. This struggle to secure surplus of economic rent is the key to the economic history of European progress and he underlying unconscious motive of all revolutions."

7. State. Marx had thoroughly condemned the state and tried to prove that the state always sided with the rich. For him the state was an agency and instrument which was used by the landed and propertied class for their self ends. He preached that with the passage of time the state was bound to wither away. But the Fabians held quite an opposite view. The state was fair and effective agency for solving our problems. The state continues to be both the representative and trustee of the people. The existing state should be made trustworthy by introducing gradual changes. One of the effective instrument was extension of suffrage, which if properly utilised, could set state machinery in order. Therefore, state was not an evil and not bound to wither away.

Agreements between Fabians and Marxists

1. Communism. Both agreed in principle that as long as means of production were under the control of an individual or a few individuals social welfare could not be achieved. For social welfare common ownership of means of production was most essential.

2. Common Basis in Economics and History. Both found their basis in economics and history though the basis of development and understanding were quite different from each other. Maxey has said about the influence of Marx on Fabianism saying that "Fabian thought, though stridently anti-Marxian in some respects, was much affected by various Marxian concepts and actually followed Marx more largely that is often supposed. The Fabians adopted Marx's historical method and generally accepted his theory of economic determinism, but arrived at different conclusions as to the direction and meaning of economic evolution."

ACHIEVEMENTS OF FABIAN SOCIALISTS

1. Influence on government. In England, where Fabian school developed, these thinkers and philosophers very much influenced the activities of their government.

3. Changes in local self-government. From 1894 through their efforts, many important changes were introduced in the field of local self-government.

4. Help in election. They helped the socialists in the election to local councils and through them got their politics promoted.

5. Labour political philosophy. The Fabians supplied the basis for the political philosophy of the labour party in 1883 which had till then no clear cut policy. Their ideas also influenced the pending legislation before the parliament.

6. Influence on Labour Party. Sidney Webb, who was a renowned socialist, prepared a new constitution of Labour Party in 1918. Sydney Webb and Sydney Oliver were the members of the first British Labour Cabinet and both of them were the authors of '*Socialist Esssay*'. In the words of Coker, "In fact Labour

Party has committed itself so thoroughly to the Fabian programme, that the activities of the society appear now to be devoted more preponderantly than ever before to factual research and theoretical discussion."

7. Contribution to practice. The Fabians have contributed more to practice than to theory. They provided their government with useful data, facts and figures. They developed themselves into a semi-proletariat movement. They discouraged class feelings and opposed revolution.

8. Advanced liberal intellectuals. W. Ebenstein has said that "The Artist brand of Socialism was represented by Fabian Society with a very mild programme of distant change. The Fabians had nothing to do with the workers. The were advanced liberal intellectuals."

9. Semi-proletarian movement. Maxey has said, "Fabianism thus developed into semi-proletarian movement, but it opposed revolutionism almost as vigourously as capitalism, discharged class feelings, made room in its ranks for bourgeoisie as well as proletarians, and thus alienated the most radical elements of the working class. It is not going too far, however, to give the Fabian Movement credit for a large part of the vast quantity of the social legislation which has been enacted in England since 1880s."

10. Contribution in Great Britain. Coker has said, "It may be said generally that the Fabian Socialists have contributed more to practice than to theory. The diligence and intelligence with which they have assembled and explained facts about the economic and social conditions of Great Britain have contributed substantially to the success which national and local governments in that country have gradually and cautiously put into actual operation a very moderate sort of socialism.

QUESTIONS FOR EXERCISE

1. "A democratic state cannot become a social democratic state, unless it has in every centre of local population a local governing body as thoroughly democratic in its constituion as the Central Parliament" — G.B. Shaw. In the light of the above statement, examine the basic policy of Fabian Socialism.
2. The members of the society assert that the competitive system assures the happiness and comfort of the few at the expense of the suffering of many and that society must be reconstituted in such a manner as to secure the general welfare and happiness" — Coker. Discuss.
3. Discuss briefly the tactics and ideals of Fabianism and trace its influence on British Policy.
4. Give an account of genesis of the Fabian Society in England and the content of the Fabian Essays.

24

Guild Socialism

Introduction

Guild socialism which has been described by Rockow as "The intellectual Child of English Fabianism and French Syndicalism"[1] is a purely English political theory. To Barker it is that theory which unites "The medieval craft with the French Syndicalism"[2] and it arose an eloquent protest against prevalent capitalism and emerging state socialism. To others it is syndicalism mellowed by pragmatism of British politics. According to Gray, It may be regarded as a fairly typical example of Anglo-Saxon compromise and of the national instinct to excessive theory, when it becomes too obviously and blatantly impracticable."[3] There is a lot of truth in these statements. Guild Socialists attempt to take bright side of both Syndicalism and Collectivism and avoid their dark side as according to them none of these two on its own can remove the evils of capitalism.

Origin of Guild Socialism

Like Fabian Socialism, this school of thought also had a fertile ground in England. The chief exponents of this philosophy were G.D.H. Cole, A.R. Orage, R.H. Tawney, S.G. Hobson and A.J. Penty, who all believed, as Maxey has said, *"that gradual reforms would transform capitalists' society into socialism which could not be realised under a centralised political system"*. Basic principles of this philosophy first of all appeared in A.J. Penty's '*The Restoration of Guild System*' which appeared in 1906. In his publication he expressed his hatred for the then existing industrial system which was not conducive to the interests of the labour as well as consumers. For him, the industrial system destroyed all initiative and incentive in the workers and made their life boring, dull and joyless. The labourers who are one of the real forces in production and consumption do not have any share and choice in industry or produciton. In the words of Coker, Penty believed that "*large scale industry, whether in public or private hands, is concerned with producing and distributing saleable goods and ignores all considerations of beauty and craftsmanship. Penty, therefore, advocated a return to medieval conditions of production,*

1. Rockow, *Contemporary Political Thought in England*, p. 150.
2. Barker, *Political Thought in England* (1848-1914), p. 201.
3. Gray, Alexander, *op. cit.*, p. 433 (The Socialist Tradition).

under which artisans, in small local groups, controlled the work of these crafts."

Samuel George Hobson, another exponent of this philosophy tried to adjust the philosophy of Penty to suit modern conditions. But this philosophy was further developed by A.R. Orage who contributed articles about this philosophy in his weekly 'New Age' and which were subsequently presented in a book form entitled '*National Guilds, an enquiry into the wage system and the way out'*. It was here that he pleaded that "*The foundation of social life was labour, hence it followed that the conditions that governed the labour were evil, the whole way of life must need be evil and that the real emancipation consisted in replacing those conditions by a new scheme of labour. The conditions that had been governing labour formed the wage system or wagery, which was one of the species of genus slavery."* According to him, the workers shall remain under this wage slavery as long as the present capitalist system, which dominates whole of our economic life, is not replaced. He, thereofre, pleaded for a system under which the workeres should also have a hand in the produciton. He stood in favour of industrial democracy in which the workers should have sufficient strength. He also did not very much favour the idea of parliamentary institutions helping the workers in coming out of their wage slavery. He could not reconcile himself to the idea that state could efficiently run industry. Hobson however, wanted to retain the authority of state because in his opinion it was state alone which represented the community as a whole. He however, very clearly said that the state should keep away from all clashes between the guilds except when public interest warranted that. In the words of Dunnings, "*We remain socialists, says Mr. Hobson, because we believe that in the final analysis the state as representing the community must be the final arbiter."*

G.D.H. Cole, another chief exponent of the theory, pleaded in his 'Social Theory and Self-Government in Industry' that the present system of mal-distribution of wealth was bound to continue as long as capitalist system prevailed. The state should control the means of production and there should be nationalisation of all industries. The workers should have a rightful share in what they produced, *i.e.* the national wealth. They should control every industry becaue the state was most unsuitable to manage the affairs of an industry. He, however, believed that the state should manage consumption but should have no hand in production. He also condemned the wage slavery in which the workers were suffering. He stood for the abolition of such a system. According to Maxey, "*The more consistently pluralistic, whose leading spokesman was perhaps Cole, held that sovereignty should be entirely extinguished and reduced to the position of a co-ordiante functional group is the only power necessary to perform its particular social function."*

In 1915, W. Walter along with others organised National Guilds League which became the main source of socialist propaganda. It also published a monthly magazine which subsequently came to be known as 'Guild Socialist'. It did useful work and was active during its existence. Coker says, "*The*

League, though small in membership, was active and influential during the six years of its existence. It found receptive audiences in seversal sections of the British labour movement, where similar trends of opinion had been developing independently." In the words of Hoover, "*Like the Fabian Society, from which it drew some of its numbers, it created an intellectual ferment quite out of proportions of its members. The experience of both organisations shows that a very small group with brains and the gift of expression can influence an entire nation and even the whole of the literature world.*"

WHAT IS GUILD SOCIALISM

Guild socialism as stated above is the mid-way method between Syndicalists' direct action and collectivists' appeals for political reforms, thus, an analytical understanding makes it clear that Guild Socialism is "permeated with the 'self-government' in industry although it retains the idea of nationalism." Its emphasis is that modern capitalism subjects the workers under the most unwanted and cruel wage slavery system. Hence, guild socialists are opposed to capitalism. If capitalism is allowed to flourish the system of wage slavery cannot be brought to an end. They wish to organise a new society in which the ultimate power and authority shall be in the hands of Guilds which shall be set up in all industries. In the words of Maxey, "Hence, the guild socialists argued that the state should be deprived of its sovereignty and reduced to a status of equality with guilds but they were unable to agree among themselves on the role of state in the Guild System." Economic power should be shifted from the capitalists to the workers. The owners have no right to determine working of workers. Coker has said, "Marxian socialism and revolutionary anarchism are proletarian doctines, each standing for an absolute power over economic and social life, to be exercised either through a territorially organised, workers controlled state or through the severally organised occupational groups of workers. Guild socialism would like to withdraw from owners of capital both the power to determine the conditions under which the labourers work and the right to derive profits out of what labourers produce."

According to C.M. Joad, "The Guild Socialists may best be described as a small body of intellectual theorists working within the Labour movement with the object of converting the influential men of the movement to their views but not as a general rule making any direct appeal for the support of the masses."[4]

HALF WAY HOUSE BETWEEN SYNDICALISM AND FABIANISM

Guild socialism was half way back between syndicalism and fabianism. Traditionally, England is opposed to revolutions due to dislocations which are bound to come with that. The syndicalist abolition of state, myth of general strike, policy of sabotage and destruction of machinery by the workers or adopting underhand means for lowering down production in key industries were not acceptable to the British people. At the same time the British

4. Joad, C.M., *Modern Political Theory*, p. 75.

intellectuals like G.B. Shaw and otherse, expounded the basic ideas of Fabian Socialism. Their hold on the Labour Party of England was immense. But the Guild Socialists could not adjust themselves with the Fabians more particularly on the role of State. As against Fabians' idea that the state should be retained, the Guild Socialists believed that the State Sovereignty should be dispensed with.

Guild socialism is an intellectual child of English Fabianism and French syndicalism. It is an attempt to reconcile the syndicalist idea of special producer's interests with the political idea of general or public interests. Guild socialists make a traditonal socialist attack on the present set up of society where the destinies of men are controlled by the owners of capital. Like syndicalism and unlike collectivism, Guild socialism is averse to all doctrines that make productive activity dependent upon political authority and tends to give the workers the control of production so that the control over the conditions of work should rest neither with the capitalists nor with the organised community but with the workers organised into guilds. But at the same time like collectivism and unlike syndicalism and anarchism it would retain the state, the representative of citizens, though limiting its functions to non-economic civil and political matters. Their slogan is that "state should own the means of production and guild should control the work of production".

Even as regards their programme of action they adopt method of 'encroaching control' and 'collective control' — a mid-way method between syndicalist direct action and collectivist appeals for political reform. Thus, Guild socialism has a typical English character. It is a *via media* between traditional collectivism and traditional syndicalism.

Marxian socialism and anarchism are proletarian doctrines. They stand for absolute power of workers over the economic and social life of the society. Like these doctrines, guild socialism also wants to withdraw from the capitalists both the power to determine the conditions under which the workers labour and the right to derive the profit out of what the workers produce. But unlike Marxian doctrine, early guild socialists like Penty believed the machinery has dehumanising influence and the modern industrial system has killed the aesthetic and creative talent in the workers. He arrived at the conclusion that the socialists had no solution of the problem because they had no plan to restore the creative activity of workers which has been destroyed by the capitalist system. Penty, therefore, advocated a return to medieval conditions of production under which the artisans controlled their crafts and had full opportunity to exhibit their aesthetic taste. But Orage, Hobson and later on G.D.H. Cole emancipated guild socialism from the medievalist influence and set it closer to the needs of socialist ideology.

Guild socialist support the Marxian doctrine of surplus value. According to this theory the exchange value of the commodities depend on labour but the worker is paid merely the cost of his subsistence and surplus value of labour goes to land owners and capitalists. Moreover the increase in production does not ensure increase in wages of the worker. This fact weakens the incentive to productive efforts and strikes and reluctant drudgery become a rule.

The guild socialists also attack the institution of private property. They do not admit that the property exists for the sake of the owner without any relation to a social purpose and that the state should guarantee this right even if it serves no useful social purpose. They contend that the present economic life is based upon the unsound principle of acquisition and not performance.

Like Marxists and Syndicalists, the Guild socialists also want to put the workers into power. They assail the present system of political democracy which at best guarantees to ordinary people the opportunity not to govern themselves but to choose their governors and that too in the political field only. Even the method of electing representatives is essentially undemocratic. Political democracy in capitalist society protects the political and economic interests of the landowners and capitalists and does not guarantee to workers any substantial participation in determining the conditions under which they have to work. They contend that society will not be completely democratic until it is organised on functional basis. Man is a jumble of interests which are represented in different associations. Therefore, man must have as many votes as he has interests and functions — one vote for one function. Each industry and each technical cultural service should be organised into guild. A guild is defined "a self-governing association of mutually dependent people organisation for the responsible discharge of a particular function of society. It must include all workers who take part in a particular service whether their work is skilled, unskilled, manual, technical, clerical, administrative or managerial.

Guild socialists agree with syndicalists that transformation cannot be achieved through political methods. Both stress the importance of economic means. But guild socialists are opposed to the revolutionary methods of direct action and strike. Here they are found to agree with the collectivists that socialism can be secured through peaceful means. But unlike them, they do not believe that workers can capture state machinery by means of election. In a capitalist society, they contend, it is not possible to consolidate the workers in such a way as to enable them to obtain the control of a political government. The state, according to the guild socialists, is not a fit instrument for making the changes they desired.

The policy recommended by guild socialists for the achievement of their aim is 'encroaching control' *i.e.,* snatching bit by bit the economic power from the hands of capitalists by a steady transference of functions and rights from nominees of the capitalists to the representatives of the working class. This can be best achieved by enlarging and strengthening the trade unions, by organising all the skilled, unskilled, clerical, technical and managerial workers. 'Encroaching control' policy is a middle path between the revolutionary policy of Syndicalism and peaceful policy of Fabians.

Guild socialism is like early French syndicalism in its opposition to the doctrine that makes economic activity dependnt on political authority. It would protect the worker not only against exploitation of the capitalists but also the bureaucrats of the industry controlled by the state. But unlike syndicaslists it would not eliminate state from society. It is an attempt to reconcile the syndicalist idea of producers' interests with the political idea of public interests. It feels the importance of both the territorial and professional grouping in the society.

So far as the position and sphere of the state is concerned there is a difference of opinion among guild socialists. Some of the guld socialists were of the view that national guild congress would be the final authority in all purely political affairs. But Hobson and Cole did not find this generalisation as adequate as it did not solve the problem of the place and status of state. Hobson regarded the state as representative of community at large. Thus, state remains supreme and source of all authority though it may delegate many of its functions to other associations.

But Cole's conception of state was more pluralistic than socialistic. He attempted to place the state on level with other guilds and did not assign supreme authority to state. It would not be the source of all authority but like any other association it would have as much power as would be necessary to perform its peculiar functions. Cole tries to harmonize the right of producers to control the production with the right of consumers to control the consumption. While the guilds constituted on the basis of functions represent the producers, an association organised on the basis of territorial representation is fit to represent the citizens as consumers. State, according to Cole, shall have political duties to perform *e.g.*, defence of the community, protection and education of children, care of invalid persons, prevetnion of crime etc. But even in this limited sphere state shall not be sovereign. There is every possibility of conflict between the guilds and state and to solve this conflict some superior authority is needed. Cole suggests a joint body representing all the associations — 'Democratic Supreme Court of Functional Equity'. It will act as a court of appeal and not as a legislative or administrative body. Thus, like pluralists Cole regards state as one of the association with no absolute sovereignty and like Marxists expects that state will 'wither away' to a very great extent.

Like other socialists, guild socialists advocated the 'public' ownership of principal resources of production and distribution but instead of allowing the state to manage these activities, they would like to entrust their operation to the worker associates in several guilds. Moreover, they would not prevent the private owner of capital to hire out capital at interest but he would not be allowed to derive the profit therefrom. The private economic enterprise must be controlled by state or commune through taxation and regulations of prices, wages and working conditions.

Like other socialist doctrines, guild socialism wants to end to the present relation of workers and capitalist in society. Like Marxian and Fabian socialism it reatains the state as representative of community. But, on the other hand, it strictly limits the functions of the state. it is nearer to anarchism and syndicalism in its idea that control over the conditions of work should be vested neither in the hands of capitalists, nor in the hands of the state but in the hands of workers themselves. The body of the workers will be organised not on the territorial basis but on professional or functional basis.

Trade unionionists, socialists, post-war syndicalists have accepted the guild socialists doctrine for the administration of natioanlised industries and control of private enterprise. It has also influenced the pluralist doctrine that freedom and equality can be secured by a democratic state but by partitioning power among autonomous groups.

HISTORY OF GUILD SOCIALIST MOVEMENT

1. A.J. Penty. Basic principles of guild socialism first of all appeared in A.J. Penty's *The Restoration of Guild System* in 1886. Penty expressed his hatred for the then existing industrial system which was not conducive to the interests of the consumers. This industrial system destroyed all initiative and incentive in the workers. It made their life boring, dull and joyless. The labourers did not have any share and choice in industry or produciton. To quote Coker, Penty believed that "large scale industry, whether in public or private hands, is concerned with producing and distributing saleable goods and ignores all considerations of beauty and craftsmanship. Penty, therefore, advocated a return to medieval conditions of production, under which artisans, in small local groups, controlled the work of these crafts."

2. A.R. Orage. This philosophy was further developed by A.R. Orage who contributed articles about this philosophy in his weekly '*New age.*" These were subsequently presented in a book form entitled '*National Guides, an enquiry into the wage system and the way out.*" It was here that he pleaded that "the foundaiton of social life was labour, hence, it followed that if the conditions that governed the labour were evil, the whole way of life must need be evil and that the real emancipation consisted in replacing those conditions by a new scheme of labour. The conditions that had been governing labour formed the wage system or waggery, which was one of the species of genus slavery." According to Orage the workers shall remains under wage slavery as long as the present capitalist system is not repalced. He therefore, pleaded for a system under which the workers have a hand in the production. He stood in favour of industrial democracy in which the workers should have sufficient strength. He also did not favour the idea of parliamentary institutions to help the workers in coming out of their wage slavery. He could not reconcile himself to the idea.

3. Samuel George Hobson. Hobson tried to adjust the philosophy of Penty to suit modern conditions. State cannot run industry efficiently. He wanted to retain the authority of the state. In his opinion it was state alone which represented the community as a whole. He, however, clearly said that the state should keep away from all clashes between the guilds except when public interest warranted that. In the words of Dunning, "We remain socialists, says Mr. Hobson, because we believe that in the final analysis the state as representing the community must be the final arbiter."

4. G.D.H. Cole. In his *Social Theory and Self Government in Industry* Cole pleaded that the present system of maldistribution of wealth shall continue as long as papalist system prevaliled. The state should live as long as papalist system prevailed. The state should control the means of production. There should be nationalisation of all industries. The workers should have a rightful share in the national wealth. They should control every industry. The state is unsuitable to manage the affairs of an industry. It should manage consumption but no production. The wage slavery should be abolished. According to Maxey, "The more consistent pluralists, whose leading spokesman was perhaps Cole, held that sovereignty should be entirely extinguished and reduced to the position of a co-ordinate functional group with only power necessary to perform its particular social function."

5. National Guild League. W. Malter, along with others, organised 'National Guilds League in 1915. It became the main source of socialist propaganda. It also published a monthly magazine known as '*Guild Socialist.*" Coker says, "The League, though small in membership, was active and influential during the six years of its existence. It found receptive audiences in several sections of the British labour movement, where similar trends of opinion had been developed independently," In the words of Hoover, "Like the Fabian Society, from which it drew some of its numbers, it created an intellectual ferment quite out of proportion to its members. The experience of both organisations show that a very small group with brains and the gift of expression can influence an entire nation and even the whole of the literate world."

6. Spread of the Movement. The Guild socialists found an opportunity to put their philosophy into action in 1919. It was an occasion of acute shortage of dwelling houses. The Government had failed to solve the problem with the aid of private enterprise. In 1920 the representatives of several buildings trade unions, decided to form of builder's guild under the secretaryship of S.G. Hobson. Subsequently, the organisation established branches in all important cities of England and Wales. A National Buildings Guild was founded. The Government sided the Guild in the initial stages and decided to withdraw its support in 1921. In the words of Coker, "Meanwhile the whole organized movement of the Guild socialists was declining and the National Guilds League was finally dissolved in 1925. Cole has repudiated most of his Guild Socialism and others have turned their attention to other matters."

BASIC PRINCIPLES OF GUILD SOCIALISM

The Guild Socialists defined a guild, "as self-governing association of mutually dependent people organised for the responsible discharge of a particular function of society." The basic principles of guild socialism were as follows :

1. Modification of state. The Guild Socialists were not in favour of retaining the present character of state. However, the state should be retained as the respresentative of the community though it might delegate some of its function. It should remain fountain-head of all power and authority. It shall also finance various guilds. It shall be responsible for formulating and enforcing all criminal laws. It should have the obligation to supply military protection. It should be responsible for controlling internationl economic relations.

As against the above views of Hobson, Cole believed that the state is at par with other guilds and it is neither sovereign nor omnipotent. It is not indispensable but a coordinating organisation of various groups enjoying co-equal powers. Cole did not wish to assign any important function to the state. Coker says, "Cole thus expected that the states would 'wither away' to a very considerable extent, it would ultimately disappear altogether either after a frontal attack or by atrophy following upon dispossession of its vital powers."

2. Public functions of the state. According to Guild Socialists, there are certain public functions which cannot be performed by the guilds. Therefore, the state may be denied of some functions with some necessary changes. They, therefore, were not as much hostile to the state as the Syndicalists. Maxey has said about Guild socialists views on the state that 'Even if the state were democratic, said the Guild Socialists, the socialist programme could not succeed under State Socialism, because state ownership and operation of the means of production and distribution would throw everything into the hands of professionals and politicians and bureaucrats who, as ruling class, would exploit the masses as unconsciously as their former capitalist master." Guild Socialists differed from syndicalists to the extent that they did not like the idea of their revolution.

3. Present society is undemocratic. The Guild Socialists believed that the present society was based on principles which were not favourable to workers. They wished to change the very principles on which the profits were being distributed. The traditional system of production in the society can no longer be justified. They did not like the present system of large scale industry in which no worker was in a position to produce finished goods. Coker says, "They have indeed learned to expect that in many cases limitation rather than enlargement of produciton is the most effective guarantee for an increased return for labour." To quote Coker again, they believed that, "Thus our society is fundamentally undemocratic because the democratic principle does not extend beyond the state and because it operates only partially within the state."

4. Condemnation of wage slavery. According to C.E.M. Joad, Guild Socialism stands for "the abolition of the wage system and establishment of self-government in industry through a democratic system of National Guilds, working in conjuction with other democratic functional organisations in the community."[5]

The Guild Socialists believe that under the present system, the capitalists are in full and overall control of means of production with the result that the workers have no share in the industry. Workers have neither any incentive, nor initiative nor interest in the goods they produce. This results in decrease in production which requires socialization of industries. The main problem is not of improving the working conditions of the labourers but of giving them a share in the national wealth. The present system of wage slavery is inhuman. The workers should be in control of the industry. Unless that is done, it shall not be possible to produce goods, according to social needs. In the socialist society the industry shall be controlled by the guilds, wherein the sense of responsibility

---

5. Joad, C.E.M., *op. cit.*, p. 75.

shall be infused among the workers. The workers shall be relieved from the present wage slavery. They shall have incentive, initiative and security. The existing state and so-called democratic institutions perpetuate wage slavery. These should be replaced by autonomous groups or guilds. These organisations will determine the wages and prices. They will control all industrial matters and they will have the charge of the national income, paying to the state a certain sum to enable it to perform its duties.

G.D.H. Cole says that "the state should own the means of produciton, the guild should control the work of produciton."

5. Opposition of large scale industry. In the present large scale industry the prestige of the workers is very low. Medieval small scale decentralised industry was much better than the present machine age industry. In the present system the lablourer is suppressed and craftsmanship is not stimulated. Guild socialists wish to restore medieval craft spirit. Their sole aim is to make the workers feel proud in the nature and quality of their work. Coker says, "They protest against the dehumanising consequences of the machine system, under which the processes of production are so minutely distributed that the working life of each labourer consists wholly of routine repetition of automatic responses and no worker is able to discern his workmanship in finished product." Guild socialists favoured small scale industry because that promoted close relationship of the worker with the goods produced. The worker feels joyous only in such a system. He also develops informal contacts. In machine system each worker is concerned only with one phase and not all phases. Hence, there is no identificaiton with work.

6. Functional democracy. According to C.E.M. Joad, "The theory of functional democracy.....advocates devolution of powers and functions to a number of different bodies which will, it is hoped, adequately express all the varied interests of man in the complex of modern society."[6] Cole used to say that it is wrong to believe that democracy is in any way a useful institution or that one indiviudal could represent the other. It is equally wrong to believe that political democracy is possible without economic democracy and that political and economic democracy could be separate from each other. The consumers and producers must go hand in hand. Against the centralisation of state authority they plead for decentralisation. They were convinced that once the industries were organised on democratic basis everything else would follow. This theory of functional democracy was applied to social, economic and political fields and also to local and national governments. In the words of C.E.M. Joad, "The Guild Socialist who applies his theory of functional democracy to the industrial sphere does not mean that it is inapplicable in the political and social sphere, he contends on the contrary that the principles of functional democracy should be extended to lcoal and national government and proposes to extend it after if has been applied in industry." With Marx they believed that in the long run it were the economic factors which play a decisive role.

6. Joad, C.E.M., *op cit.*, p. 78.

7. Wages to be determined by producers and consumers. It is wrong to say that a worker got wages since he got only payment for his work. An unemployed worker should also get payment when he is sick or otherwise unable to work. For him uniformity of payment is unrealisable. The prices of goods should be fixed by the national guilds. While deciding or revising the prices, consumer and producer councils should always be consulted. This should also be decided, if necessary, by supreme joint committee, consisting of equal number of consumers and producers. Wages and payments as well as the prices should be determined both by the producers as well as consumers.

8. Territorial but functional representation. Guild socialists believed that the present system of territorial representation was most unwanted. It was wrong to believe that a person living in a territory could represent various profesisons and divergent interests. On the contrary, persons with the same vocation alone can have uniform interests no matter whether they were living in the same constituency or not. Guild socialists, therefore, favoured functional rather than territorial system of representation. According to Gettell, "Guild Socialists believe that industry, church, educations, and other essential activities should each have its own organisation and control its own affairs, and that the state should interfere only as a last resort, or should stand on a par with other natural groups, with final authority to adjust dispute resting in a body that represents all essential interests."[7]

Guild *Vs.* Trade Unions

Whereas trade union is organised for militant purpose and in a hostile society, Guild is organised for a friendly purpose and in a peaceful society. Trade union is organised for peace and production while guild aims at service of the workers in industry and community as a whole. In the words of C.E.M. Joad, "The Guild is modelled on the existing trade union but differs from it in two important respects. In the first place it would include all the workers by hand and brain, from the errand boy to the manager, who are concerned in a particular industry. In the second place its chief function would be not to protect the interest of its members but to carry on the industry." To conclude, Guild Socialists wanted to have a society based on guilds, which shall be in a position to deliver the goods. According to C.E.M. Joad, "The trade union is organised for military purposes in a hostile society, while the Guild will be organised for peaceful purposes in a friendly society."[8]

GUILD SOCIALIST SOCIETY

1. Society Under Guilds. The guild socialists wanted to have a society without regimentation. Each industry will have a guild which will protect the interests of the workers. The state will be gradually replaced by guilds. Changes should be brought by evolutionary means and methods. According to Maxey, "Their ideal society was a federation of self-governing associations of persons

7. Gettell, R.G., *History of Political Thought,* p. 481-82.
8. C.E.M. Joad, *op. cit.*, p. 80.

mutually involved in the performance of related social functions. This concept was a reaction agaist the overweaning regimentation of state socialism." In this society there shall be no concentration of power. Each major activity will be in the hands of autonomous guilds. It will be a society based on functional representation. Each industry as well as technical and cultural service will be properly looked after and administered by a co-operative organisation, a guild which will include all types of persons, whether skilled, unskilled or semi-skilled. Coker says, "The guild must, moreover, be self-governing to the fullest extent compatible with the fulfilment of its obligations to the community whose needs it exists to supply, it is thus an autonomous but not absolutely free group."

He further says, "For Guild socialists, the main economic problem is to find a way of restoring the spirit of craft, to devise a system that develop in workers not nearly skilled but also pride in their work and an interest not primarily in the amount they earn but in the form and quality of what they make."[9] Thus, Guild socialists want a society in which their concept of human welfare workers and consumers put together could be achieved.

2. Organisation of Guilds. Guild socialists favoured local autonomy with strong national organisaitons. The extent of centralisation was to be decided in accordance with the merits of each industry. Though there will be a national guild organisation yet much will be left to the discretion of local guilds. These guild associations would be so organised as to secure, on the one had, the necessary unification and co-ordination of production on a national scale and on the other hand, protection of valid differences among localities and crafts and the encouragement of individual initiative and self-expression. The workers will have the choice of selecting the officer under whom they desired to work.

Cole outlines the nature and functions of Guilds in very clear terms, he writes, "It would serve as a representation of the producers outlook in negotiating with the representatives of the consumers in makers of importance to the community as a whole"[10] On this aspect Cole's views need special reference, he writes : "Orage and Hobson wanted the guilds to be 'chartered' corporations, acting under licence from the state; whereas others, of whom I was one, were social pluralists, and believed that the sovereign state should in due course be replaced by some form of federal authority, resting on a partnership between 'producers' and 'consumers' and other 'functional' representatives."

3. Supreme Court of Functional Equity. Guild socialists foresaw the possibility of conflict over jurisdictions between state and autonomous guilds. Therefore, they felt the necessity of a superior co-ordinating authority named as 'Democratic Court of Functional Equity'. To quote Coker again, "This Democratic Court of Functional Equity will deal with matters common to all associations and it will possess supreme power of coercion maintaining ultimate control over the whole paraphernalia of law and police." "Such a scheme of

9. Coker, C.W., *Recent Political Thought*, pp. 265-66.

10. Cole, G.D.H., *Guild Socialism Restated.*, p. 71.

social organisation eliminates the sovereign state but it retains both the state and sovereignty, ascribing the latter to a body higher than the state."

4. Replacement of State by Communes. In the guild society the state shall be gradually replaced by communes based on functional representation and co-ordinating organisation in the society. Maxey says, "Under such a guild system the political state would survive only as an interlocking and adjusting organ as between the several guilds." These communes shall have very important duties. They shall largely control the national finances. They shall also allocate and fix prices and decide disputes among various functional groups. They will also decide jurisdictions of functional groups. They will be responsible for all constitutional amendments and interpretations of laws. These communes shall declare war or conclude peace, regulate foreign relations and decide boundary disputes. In the guild society there shall be no need for use of force because everybody shall be most willing to perform his duties.

5. Collective Control. In a guild society the means of production and distribution shall be under collective control. The owner of machinery shall be entitled only to interest and not to profit. About a commune, Coker says that "It will make war and decide upon peace, it will determine international political relations, it will allocate capital and labour power among the different economic guilds, ratify their budgets (including salary items), assess taxes upon them, control their credit issues and on appeal, fix prices : it will define the spheres of competence of the various guilds and settle disputes of policy between them finally, it will define and punish crimes and exercise a general police power."

6. Methods of Social Change. The Guild socialists were essentially evolutionaries. At the same time they did not favour the present parliamentary system of government. According to them the objects could be achieved by economic and not by political means. Political authority was bound to depend on economic power. Based on the system of territorial representation the present political system was unscientific and slow. They are opposed to direct action as a method for capturing power as propagated by syndicalists. They, however, do not absolutely rule out the possibility of using force if necessary. The capitalists could not be removed from authority all of a sudden but only gradually. Trade union movement will be organised on the basis of industry. Union should be internally autonomous and should try to monopolise them. There may be big and small trade unions. In the words of Joad, the new structure should "along the lines of vertical as opposed to horizontal organisation. A horizontal organisation would embrace all the workers in a particular industry from top to bottom."

7. Gradual Control of Workers. The Guild Socialists believed in the policy of providing gradual control of workers over economic power. The workers should demand right of electing their technical and non-technical officers, in the industry. Officers who were not liked by them should be removed. There should be a system of collective contract under which the trade unions will provide all the necessary labour etc. In turn, they shall get a lumpsum from the capitalists to be divided among the workers. Control of industry might take some time. Under the joint control the workers shall have some say in the affairs of the industry. Guild socialists' system of getting power by gradual transfer was very much advantageous. Through it the ultimate control could be achieved by least dislocation either in the industry or in the social life of the community.

GUILD SOCIALISM *Vs.* STATE SOCIALISM

Both are very close to each other in some respects but at the same time both also differ in some other respects. Both, for example, believe that capital is a theft and the institution of private property is mainly responsible for present social injustice. They also believe that capitalist system has divided the society. Both believe that in existing society and a social system should be created in which there should be social justice, equality and respect for work.

But both differ in details in bringing about that change. The State Socialists believe that the state should continue to enjoy its present authority but should be reformed. The people should be persuaded, educated, and there should be vast propaganda against the evils which the existing state.and allied intitutions are generating. But the Guild Socialists believe that the State should be deprived of its authority because as long as that is not weakened there can be no chances of social improvement.

In brief similarities and differences between Guild Socialism and State Socialism are as follows.

Similarities

1. Both believe that the capital is a theft and the institutions of private property is mainly responsible for the present social injustice.

2. Both believe that the capitalist system has divided the society.

3. Both believe that a social system should be created in which there should be social justice, equality and respect for work.

Differences

1. Both differ in details in bringing about social change.

2. The State Socialists believe that the state should continue to enjoy its present authority but should be reformed. But the guild socialists believe that the state should be deprived of its authority because as long as that is not weakened there can be no chances of social improvement.

GUILD SOCIALISM *Vs.* SYNDICALISM

Both believe that state authority is an evil and it is protecting private property at all costs. It is squeezing the blood of the poor. The workers are not getting adequate wages and the capital which is a theft is being given all due and undue protection. They both also agree that industrial control should be in the hands of those who work in that industry by way of forming syndicates or trade unions. They have unanimity of view that there should be two parliaments — one economic and the other political.

But both differ in many respects as well. First, the Syndicalists are very extremists and preach negative philosophy. On the other hand, Guild Socialists are midway between Collectivists and Syndicalists. Secondly, the Syndicalists stand for stateless society whereas the Guild Socialists wish to retain authority in a reformed way. Thirdly, the Syndicalists look after the interests of producers only whereas the Guild Socialists look after the interests of the producers as well as consumers. In the words of Dunnings, "*Guild Socialism is a half way house between Syndicalism and Collectivism. It attempts to rehabilitate the doctrine of Syndicalism by seeking to reconcile the doctrine of producers control with the rights and functions of the consumer or public.*"

In brief similarities and diffences between Guild Socialism and syndicalism are as follows :

Similarities

1. Both believe that the state authority is an evil and it is protecting private property at all costs. It is squeezing the blood of the poor.

2. Both believe that the workers are not getting adequate wages. The capital is a theft which is being given all due and undue protection.

3. Both agree that the industrial control should be in the hands of those who work in that industry by way of forming syndicates or trade unions.

4. Both agree that there should be two parliaments, one economic and the other political.

Differences

1. The Syndicalists are extremists and preach negative philosophy. On the other hand, Guild Socialists are midway between Collectivists and Syndicalists.

2. The Syndicalists stand for stateless society whereas the Guild Socialists wish to retain authority in a reformed way.

3. The Syndicalists look after the interests of the producers as well as consumers. To conclude in the words of Dunning, "Guild Socialism is a half way house between syndicalism and collectivism. It attempts to rehabilitate the doctrine of syndicalism by seeking to reconcile the doctrine of producer's control with the rights and functions of the consumer or public."

GUILD SOCIALISM *Vs.* PLURALISM

According to Guild Socialists the state is a clearing house of all communities and interests. It embraces all life. On the other hand, the Pluralists believe that since society is divided the authority must also be divided. They do not distinguish between the ruler and the ruled. In thier opinion the ruler at one stage is ruled at another.

GUILD SOCIALISM *Vs.* COLLECTIVISM

Guild Socialists are near to Collectivists because they concern themselves more with the group of workers as the guilds rather than the individuals. Thus, their political unit is something collective. But they are not all collectivists because they do not vest supreme economic power in the society as a whole. They concentrate power in the hands of few workers. They exclude the moneyed people and classes. Thus, whereas on the one hand they are somewhat collectivists on the other they are not so.

CAUSES OF FAILURE OF GUILD SOCIALISM

1. No common ideology. The chief exponents of this theory lacked co-ordination in their political ideology and co-operation in their working. All these thinkers differed from each other on basic principles with the result that they could not present a united philosophy to the people.

2. Industrial philosophy unacceptable. Guild socialists preached the organisation of industrial system on the basis of medieval guild system. They criticise modern industrial system as inhuman. It did not associate the worker with the commodities he produced. They saw many advantages in the small scale industrial system. They preached against the introduction of machine in an age of industrialisation which was most unacceptable to the people of England.

3. Labour control over industry unconvincing. The Guild Socialists tried to establish that it is morally and economically desirable that the workers should control the industry. This was unconvincing. The Guild Socialists wanted to make the workers a partner in profit and not in loss. This was not convincing.

4. Narrow outlook about representative system. Guild Socialists did not believe in the system of territorial representation on the plea that a person could not represent all interests of his constituency. They, therefore, favoured functional representation against territorial representation. The theory about functional representation, however, appears to be narrow. They forget that a representative in parliament is to represent the nation and not a vocation. If a parliament is constituted on the basis of vocations there is every possibility that it will lose its national character.

5. Common guild of officers and workers not possible. The Guild Socialists propose that in each factory there should be a guild consisting of all the high and low paid staff including all those who are doing manual and mental labour. They propose that officials and officers should form only one guild. But this is both impossible and impracticable. All those who are highly paid and managing the industry on behalf of the owners will always side with the capitalists rather than the workers. If the capitalist finds that his managerial staff is not siding with him, he will try to give it incentives and attract it by other methods.

6. No practical suggestions for state reform. Guild Socialists have taken a very optimistic view about human nature. They assure that there will be no disputes among the workers. All this is too optimistic a view of human nature.

8. Two parliaments system not workable. The Guild Socialists propose that there should be two parliaments namely Political Parliament and Economic Parliament. Each Parliament shall legislate on the subject falling in its sphere of activity. But this is not practicable in actual life because there is no aspect of human life which is either exclusively political or purely economical. Even elections, which one fought on political grounds, have a great leaning on economic life. Political parties win or lose on how they handle economic situation. Trade unions and strikes etc. are neither exclusively political nor economic institutions.

9. Limitations of functional representation. Guild Socialists plead for functional representation. If adopted it will destroy national unity. The parliament which looks after the interest of all will become an organisation for the few.

10. Complicated administration system. The system of administration envisaged by the Guild Socialists consisting of committees and joint committees is very complicated. It can work successfully only when the people have a high standard of intelligence and wisdom. Ordinary citizens have neither wisdom nor capacity to follow this complicated system. it is, therefore, difficult to put the proposal in practice.

11. Supreme Court undemocratic. The Guild Socialists provide that a Supreme Court shall be constituted to decide between the two parliaments. This Supreme Court shall be final authority though this is an undemocratic institution.

12. No proper representation for big industries. Guild Socialists have not laid down any basis under which major industries may get more representation in the Economic Parliament. They feel that all industries have equal importance. This is basically wrong. If they think that there should be some sort of distribution which they have not provided for, that is avoiding a hard reality.

ACHIEVEMENTS OF GUILD SOCIALISTS

The Guild Socialists had their influence for a very short while. Even Cole left it after the dissolution of National Guilds League in 1925. During its short stay, the movement had its influence on contemporary political philosophy.

1. Champion of workers' cause. They championed the cause of workers. They pleaded that they should be given a share in the administration. A worker should feel himself associated with the work which he was doing.

2. Nationalisation. They pleaded for the nationalisation of industries which has been a better accepted alternative to private control.

3. Encouragement to trade unions. Their philosophy encouraged trade union movement. It was under their influence that many governments were obliged to think about having effective control over hours of work and wages of the workers.

4. Influence on other thinker. In the words of Coker, "The guild socialist writers have direclty influenced certain theorists — particularly by suggesting or endorsing the 'pluralist' doctrine that freedom and equality, under the conditions of modern industry, can be secured not by substituting a collectivist democratic region for an aristocracy or plutocracy as the autocrat of society, but only the extensively partitioning power among a variety of generally autonomous working groups, each associated on the basis of source specific economic or cultural function in the service of the community.

QUESTIONS FOR EXERCISE

1. "The Guild Socialist School of thought was a resultant of political and industrial situation and of various other factors" — Laidlser. Examine this statement and discuss the factors that led to the rise of Guild Socialism as a movement in Great Britain.
2. What are the main features of Guild Socialism and how does it differ from Fabian Socialism?
3. Discuss in general the fundamental principles of Guild Socialism and state to what extent these principles may be applicable to the modern state of India where a Socialist Pattern of Society is reported to be in the making.
4. But although Guild Socialism represents an attempt between two equally legitimate points of view, its impulse and force are derived from what it has taken over from Syndicalism?" — Bertrand Russell. Explain.
5. Briefly discuss the type of society of the Guild Socialists. What methods do they wish to follow to establish that ? Differentiate between Guild Socialism and State Socialism.

25

G.D.H. Cole (1889—1958)

G.D.H. Cole, called Guild Socialism, "a half-way house between Syndicalism and Collectivism."[1] Out of the most important exponents of Guild Socialism, G.D.H. Cole was the most important exponents of Guild Socialism, G.D.H. Cole was the most active and most consistent apostle of this new ferment. He was the *infant prodigy* of Guild Socialism. He joined the Fabian society while he was merely an under-graduate. In 1912, he organized the Fabian Research Department for the purpose of studying labour problems. In 1913, he became a Guild Socialist, and was soon recognized as the most active propagandist of the movement.

Cole was originally a Fabian, but the danger of government by 'a man behind a window' made him join the new movement. William Morris was his patron-saint. Like most revolutionaries, Cole desired a restoration of the medieval society of societies. He gave the fullest expression to the demand for a federal structure of the state. The title of the book in which Cole presents the philosophic foundation of his society is *Social Theory* (1920). In his *Guild Socialism Restated* (1920), he formulates the more detailed structure of a Guild-commonwealth.

GENERAL PHILOSOPHY

Expressing the general philosophy of guildsmen, G.D.H. Cole says that "the state should own the means of production, the guild should control the work of production."[2] The paramount evil in present-day society is the complete ordering of the working life of man by the owners of capital. This slavery, or 'wagery' as S.G. Hobson terms it, is far worse than poverty, for "poverty is the symptom and slavery is the disease. The many are not enslaved because they are poor, they are poor because they are enslaved"[3]

ATTACK ON THE ULTIMATE SOVEREIGNTY OF STATE

Cole rejected the point of view of Hobson that "in the final analysis the state as representing the community at large must be the final arbiter." Cole attacked the ultimate sovereignty of the territorial state. He refuted the idea that

1. *A History of Political Theories* (Recent Times), ed. by C.E. Marriam and H.E. Barnes (The Macmillan Co., New York, 1935), p. 227.
2. *Self-Government in Industry* (first edition), p. 109.
3. *Op. cit.*, p. 110.

the state is the centre of social and political unity. The widest sphere of social unity is the community. It is a centre of feeling, a self-contained, inclusive region of associative life. Society is its organized aspect. It is a complex of associations, but cannot include the whole of the lives of individuals since the best elements of individuality escape organization. The principle underlying all associations is the principle of function. Individuals organize associations in order to fulfil a purpose which requires co-operative action for its attainment. "Social purposes are, thus, the raw material of social functions, and social functions, are social purposes selected and placed in coherent relationship."[4] Of all associations the civic and economic associations of both producers and consumers are the most essential. Functions, and not an external source, give rights to associations.

SLAVERY, THE CURSE OF CAPITALISM

According to Cole, the present state, carries with it the marks of its perversion by capitalism. Our present feeble attempts, Cole explains in his book *Social Theory*, to inaugurate democracy in politics are frustrated by the existence of a system approaching slavery in industry. Not poverty of the masses, but slavery is the curse of capitalism. Capitalism and democracy go together. Cole was opposed to the democratic system of government as it worked in actual practice. He attacked the system of territorial representation. A person who represents his locality cannot be expected to decide questions relating to the relationship between the producers and the consumers. Hence, Cole advocated the reorganization of society on a functional basis. When society is organized as a federation of functional organizations, each one democratically controlled, there will be no place for the present state organization. In a guild society the functions, which an all-inclusive association may properly be taken over by co-ordinating bodies more in harmony with the principles of freedom and function which will actuate that society. Cole writes : "It is impossible to represent human beings as persons or centres of consciousness; it is quite possible to represent, though with an inevitable element of distortion which must always be recognized, as much of human beings as they themselves put into associated effort for a specific purpose."[5]

FUNCTIONS OF THE STATE

Regarding the functions of the state Cole's position did not remain constant. In his earlier work *Self-Government and Industry* (1917), he regarded the state as an association of dwellers in a common neighbourhood. Such an association, however, should be only one of many, and ought not to be dominant over other associations which represent men in their capacity as producers, fellow-worshippers, common believers etc. The state, however, should be preserved as the representative of the consumers and should stand opposite the guilds. At

4. Cole, G.D.H., *Social Theory* (1920), p. 54.
5. *Ibid.*, pp. 105-06.

the top there would be Parliament, representing the consumers, and the Central Guilds Congress representing the National Guilds. Cole said, "Neither Parliament nor the Guild Congress can claim to be ultimately sovereign : the one is the supreme territorial association, the other, the supreme professional association."[6] If a dispute between the two were to arise "the final decision of such a quarrel ought to rest with a body representative of all the organized consumers and all the organized producers. The ultimate authority or sovereignty in industrial matters would seem properly to belong to some joint body representative equally of Parliament and of the Guild Congress. Otherwise, the scales must be weighted unfairly in favour of either consumers or producers"[7]

As a result of Mr. Hobson's attack upon the idea that the state represented the consumer, Cole in his later works[8] changed his position in two respects : (1) He advocated the formation of other associations than the state to serve as the representatives of the consumer. (2) He shifted his emphasis from a national to a local co-ordination of production and consumption.

Cole came to believe that the state represented the complex of the separate interests within the territorial unit, and not the consuming interest exclusively. But no group can represent all the interests of men. Each interest or 'function' must have separate representation.

PRINCIPLE OF FUNCTIONAL REPRESENTATION

According to the principle of functional representation, each person must have one vote for each functional association, that he joins. "Instead of 'one vote, one man', we must say 'one man, as many votes as interests', but only one vote in relation to each interest."[9] Each association will have power to regulate its own life, and make rules binding its own members in its own special sphere. Each will also have the power of coercion to a limited degree. Society will present a union of co-ordinated functional democracies.

In accordance, with the principle of functional democracy, each industry in a guild society will be organized into a national guild and administered on behalf of society by the workers, including the managerial and technical force. The management of each guild will be decentralized, with the factory as the unit of organization. The leaders will be chosen by the workers, although, choice may be limited to those who have acquired a certain proficiency. The expert advisers will not be directly elected. The managers of wider units of organization, such as, the district, or region, or nation, will be chosen indirectly. These managers will have the power of supervision and of representing the interest of the producers in conference with the representatives of the consumers. In order to avoid centralization, their power should be kept down as much as

6. *Self-Government in Industry* (third edition), p. 135.

7. *Ibid.*, pp. 135-36.

8. Particularly *Social Theory, Guild Socialism Restated, and The Reorganization of Local Government.*

9. *Social Theory*, p. 106.

possible. Contracts between guilds will be maintained by mutual conference, by interlocking directorates. A Guild Congress will represent the interest of all guilds. It will be highly decentralized into local and regional bodies. It will regulate the disputes between guilds, confer with representatives of consumers, adjust pay of different kinds of workers — which pay need not be equal, at least at first. Each member of a guild will be assured full pay as long as he is connected with that guild.

The consumers, too, will be organized. The consumers must be differentiated into classes. Thus, in "personal and domestic consumption there is differentiation between consumers while in the collective consumption" of, for instance, a commodity like water, the interests of all consumers are alike. There must, therefore, be appropriate councils to represent each respective group of consumers. These councils will also be decentralized with local and regional divisions. The councils existing in every locality will meet with the representatives of the guilds.

The Church will not participate in such a co-ordinating structure. It may co-operate with other bodies. It must have freedom to live its own spiritual life. It cannot conflict with other bodies, since its life is purely spiritual, while that of the others is material.

COMMUNES, THE CO-ORDINATING CENTRE OF THE GUILD SOCIETY

The co-ordinating centre of the guild society will be the communes. The communes will be composed of the representatives of the consumers' councils and of the guilds. The local communes will include representatives of the local consumer's councils and of the local guilds, the regional communes, of the regional councils and of the regional guilds, the national communes, of the national councils and of the national guilds. In addition, representatives of the regional communes, will also include some territorial representation. Wide decentralization will prevent the rise of a bureaucracy. As the representatives of the whole society, the local, regional or national commune will possess the powers of co-ordinating various functional organizations and also such duties which no other authority can exercise. Under the first type of powers will come, a host of financial duties. Thus, it will review the budget of the guilds, supervise pay of guild members, income, price, allocation of capital, the banking system, and allotment of taxation to the various guilds. To it will belong the surplus profits of the guilds. As a co-ordinating body it will act as the final court of appeal in disputes between functional bodies, and pass constitutional laws demarcating the respective spheres of such bodies. Appointed by the commune from qualified members of the legal guild there will be judges to interpret the laws but their decisions on disputed points must be subordinated to the declarations of the commune. Under the second type of powers will come authority over questions of war and peace, colonies, boundaries, personal conduct, and property. International questions of a civic and commercial nature, will be dealt with by the appropriate functional bodies.

Disputes over prices between consumer and producer will be settled by the commune. If goods were sold above or below cost, the commune would make the decision as to how the surplus should be used or the loss borne. The relative amount of energy to be allocated to the product of consumers' goods, productive capital, and non-economic services would be similarly determined upon together with the allowance to be made to each industry or service. The various guilds would present budgets to the communal council after consultation with their corresponding councils of consumers and with each other. After examination, these budgets would be passed upon by the commune. This would involve criticism of and control over the salary scale of the various guilds. The commune will also control the amount of credit to be issued, although it would not necessarily operate the banks.

The commune will also control the coercive machinery and exercise the ultimate power of coercion over individuals and groups. Thus, economic boycott may be applied against a recalcitrant group. But the mutual confidence and consultation which a functional society will stimulate will make the application of coercion infrequent. The guild society will see a wide extension of decisions reached by mutual negotiation. The coercion of individuals is provided for as a last resort but it is to be sparingly invoked. As for the coercion of functional groups, it is much better policy to trust them than to attempt to coerce them. But "trust does not and cannot involve the abandonment of all powers in the last resort." One is left in doubt, however, as to the precise form this ultimate coercion will take since the right of striking is upheld by Cole, as by all guildsmen, and the economic boycott has previously been declared "to be possible but not desirable."

THEORY OF LIBERTY AS APPLIED TO INDUSTRY

Cole presented the most forcible enunciation of the theory of liberty as applied to industry. His doctrine is that of radical socialism, which recognizes the trade union world as an organ of revolt against capitalism and as the most effective means of attaining its ultimate goal of workers.

However, it should be pointed out that while Cole denied the sovereignty of the state, he did not deny the necessity of retaining unity in society. His guild commonwealth is co-ordinated. It is highly decentralized, both territorially and functionally, but its unity is preserved by vesting ultimate authority in the commune. The commune, we may recall, possesses the power to act as an ultimate court of appeal in disputes between functional bodies, to pass constitutional laws, and to control the coercive authority. The essence of a common authority is power to act in capacity of ultimate jurisdiction; the guild society has such authority.

THE STATE ON AN EQUAL FOOTING WITH GUILDS

Cole did not give the state, the same authority which was given by Hobson. He attempted to put the state on an equal footing with the guilds. The state, is to be an association like any other association. Its functions are to be proportionate to the duties to be performed by it. The guilds are to control and manage the whole of production. The state is to perform such functions as the regulation of marriages and divorce, education of children, prevention and punishment of crimes, defence of the country etc. In cases of conflict between the guilds and the state, the institution known as the Supreme Court of Functional Equity is to have the final word. It is also to possess the supreme power of coercion. It is, in this way that the sovereignty of the state is to be taken away from it.

Cole, did not content himself with this role of the state. He went a step further in minimizing the importance of the state. He came to the conclusion that the state could be allowed to wither away and ultimately disappear altogether "either after a frontal attack or by atrophy following upon dispossession of its vital power."[10]

CRITICAL EVALUATION

The above scheme of Cole appears to be very attractive. It attempts to abolish slavery from the industry in order to establishing true democracy in its fuller sense. However, it is not free from certain defects. There is always a likelihood of conflicts. The representatives of the consumers and the producers will come to its session not for the purpose of deliberation, but as delegates of a fraction of the community, to represent its special and private will. Questions that concern the community as a whole can best be dealt with by the representatives of citizens.

The principle underlying the organization of Cole's guild society is the principle of function. It is true that in some respects the workers in a particular industry or service have an immediate interest; but then, it is to be noted, in other respects, other groups have a special interest. If that be true, the logical conclusion is to place socialized industry in the hands of the state under a system which will allow wide decentralization and the active participation of the workers.

QUESTIONS FOR EXERCISE

1. Examine and discuss the doctrine of Guild Socialism as expounded by G.D.H. Cole.
2. Bring out the salient features of the contribution of G.D.H. Cole to the political thought.
3. "The state should own the means of production, the Guild should control the work of production." Discuss.
4. "The Theory of representative Government, which is based upon the idea that the individual can be represented as a whole, is a false theory, destructive of personal rights and social well being" — Cole. What is true representation according to Cole? How far are his ideas workable?

10. *A History of Socialist Thought*, Vol. IV, Part I (1914-31), Macmillan & Co. Ltd., London (1958), p. 454.

26

Syndicalism

The Syndicalists do not like institution of state or that of private property. They hate both and wish to end them by violent means. They favour violent methods of sabotage and destruction. They ask that the workers should be participants in the management of production and distribution. They wish to achieve their ends through the means of general strike. Each strike should be important and must have educative value. Unless violent means are followed there are no chances of social, economic and political problems being solved. The state shall be replaced by syndicates which shall be formed in each industry. The interests of workers and employees as well as those of producers and consumers small be protected. These syndicates shall only manage the industries. All property shall belong to the society as a whole. The labourers should not cooperate with the state authorities. Syndicalists do not favour the retention of parliamentary form of government. A new society will be built up on the debris of present state which will promote collective good. Syndicalist movement had deep influence on the labour movement of France. It was subsequently challenged by many other socialist schools of thought.

Syndicalist moverment was a spontaneous outcome of working class struggles. No prominent intellectual or philosopher associated himself with the movement in the beginning. In this movement theory followed action. There was no specific theory which provided guidelines to the workers. The exponents of this theory learnt much from the working classes. Workers' activities were the laboratories and libraries for them. The basic principles of syndicalism were revisionists or even the Anarchists. They tried to revive the Marxian philosophy. Syndicalist philosophy combined both Anarchism as well as Marxism.

Origin of the Movement

Syndicalist movement originated in France. Its name was derived from the French word 'Syndicate', which is used for ordinary labour movement or labour union in the country. The movement was controlled by workers in France. By the last decade of the present century it divided into 'Reformist Syndicalism' and 'Revolutionary Syndicalism.' It was the latter which subsequently controlled the labour movement.

Definitions and Aims

1. *C.E.M. Joad*. "Syndicalism is the name given both to a body of social

doctrines or theory of social organisation, and to a plan of action. The plan of action is a particular phase of what Marx called struggle and its object is to bring a syndicalist organisation of society."

2. *Coker*. "Syndicalism, loosely defined, holds that the workers alone must control the conditions under which they work and live : the soical changes then can be achieved only by their own efforts, by direct actions and through means suited to their particular need." "Syndicalism is that form of social theory which regards the trade union organisation as at once foundations of the new society and the instrument whereby it is to be brought into being."

3. *Maxey*. Syndicalism aims "(i) that workers must unite not simply to get better working conditions, but to become proprietors and masters of industrial system; (ii) that they must organise as a class without reference to craft lines and must keep their organisation separate from all other political, economic, and social movements etc."

Syndicalist movement aims at giving vast powers to the workers. They alone should control their working conditions and for that they should make personal efforts. They should themselves be the final judges to decide the method of achieving their ends.

BASIC PRINCIPLES OF SYNDICALIST PHILOSOPHY

1. Abolition of property and state. The syndicalists are of the opinion that the institutions of private property and state are evil. These must be abolished. In their place worker unions should control both the means of production as well as those of distribution.

2. Revolutionary means. The workers should adopt the policy of direct action and sabotage to achieve their ends. They should bycott the present institutions based on injustice.

3, Abolition of profit system. There should be no compromise with the present profit system in which the capitalist is keeping the profit with himself. All efforts should be made to see that the system is brought to an end.

4. Creation of new society. Each syndicate should represent the new age. It should have the double task of ending the old order which is based on injustice as it should aim at establishing a new order. Each labour union should be a cell for the development of new society.

5. Workers as proprietors. It is the foremsot duty of each trade union to see that its workers do not satisfy themselves with having a share in the profit earned by the capitalist but aim at becoming the proprietors of the industry in which they are working. The syndicalists also preach that the workers should aim at forming a class in themselves.

DEVELOPMENT OF MOVEMENT IN FRANCE

1. Emotional. According to some syndicalism developed because it had an emotional appeal to the sentiments of the people.

2. Adverse Labour Laws. Syndicalism developed because the trade union meethods available at that time were not sufficient to solve labour problems. The French law was strict enough to foribid the formation of trade unions and also did not allow people to pursue Marxian principles. The French trade union movement willingly embraced violent methods prached by the syndicalists and trade unions became revolutionaries in Frence.

3. Labour Exchange 1887. In 1887 in Paris a Labour Exchange was set up which became a cell for the development of syndicalist movement. Subsequently these cells were established in other towns as well. They worked as agencies for providing employment to the workers and to educate them. In the words of Coker, "Soon they became centres of viogrous activity not only in these services of mutual aid and education but also in organising the workers for their conflicts and supplying moral and practical support in time of strikes."

4. L.G.T. In 1883 a federation of these 'Labour Exchanges' was set up and two years later 'General Federation of Labour' or 'L.G.T.' was set up. The influence of socialists had by now considerably increased.

5. Seat in Cabinet. In 1899, for the first time, an independent socialist, Alexander Miller, was offered a seat in the Cabinet. It was due to his efforts that an attempt was made to make trade unions as body corporate which could sue as well be sued.

6. Labours of Theorists. Ultimately however, triumph of Revolutionary syndicalism was due to the labours of theorists like 'Fernand Relloutier and George Sorel.

BASIC PRINCIPLES OF REVOLUTIONARY SYNDICALISM

1. Ideal Society. The present society is one in which the propertied class is ruling. It can only be reformed through working man's asociations. These associations, however, should not only aim at protecting material interests of the persons but should also try to educate the people. They should try to secure higher wages with less hours of work. The working classes should have dignity as well as independence. A society will be ideal in which the workers will not be forced to work for fear of the employers but where they shall feel like working themselves. Coker has said, "When the workshop is free, society will be free, and the workers' sense of dignity and spirit of independence will be revived. They preached the idea of free work in a free society. For him the present society can be changed by proper organisation of unions, labour exchanges, confederations of federastions. They believed that the society was the organisation of the consumers. They do not favour the idea that the new society will emerge with the aid and assistance of any other institution especially the government but the workers shall work independently without any aid or assistance."

2. The state. It is wrong to believe that at any stage the state could bring about social unity, because the society consists of different people and classes which have different and sometimes quite opposite interests. For example, the interests of the propertied classes are absolutely different from those of propertyless. The interests of the capitalists are quite different from those of the workers. Many a time these clashing interests cannot be reconciled. The state protects the capitalists who control the means of production. The state protects the property of the rich at the cost of the poor. The capitalist coerce the worker with the help of the state. There are no indications to believe that the state is in any way willing to leave its present character of its own unless the workers become powerful and force the state to shed away its present character. No amount of reform can set the state right.

Since the state has been purposely designed to suit the convenience of the capitalists it is futile to expect that it can be made an agency to suit the conveniences of the working classes. The state officials cannot understand the difficulties and problems of those engaged in production. History is a witness that state officials are quite unsympathetic towards the working classes. Joad has said, "A central organisation tends to uniformity, to routine, to lack of imagination and initiative, and to distrust of loyal development and enterprise. Even a benevolent state, therefore, would, if left in control of industry, be inimical to progress. It is not the middle class civil servant, but the manual worker who knows what the manual worker wants, and it is to the manual worker, therefore, in his industrial organisation, that it shall fail to describe accordingly."

The sate is an institution which protects the interests of the consumers and not those of the producers. For syndicalists it is basically wrong to believe that any institution can do good to all on uniform basis. Therefore, the very concept of democracy is wrong. It cannot work for collective welfare. Workers are miserably mistaken if they feel that they can get the assistance of parliametary institutions. Similarly, constitutional agitations cannot help the workers.

3. Conclusion. Therefore, Syndicalists are bitterly opposed to state which is responsible for the exploitation of workers. They wish to do away with state and establish a new society. For this purpose they adopt the methods of strikes and non-cooperation.

METHODS OF SYNDICALISTS

1. Strike. According to Syndicalists one of the most important and effective methods for achieving the object was that of general strike. Every strike trains the workers and makes them realise the need and necessity of discipline. It arouses a sentiment of solidarity and class consciousness. It is the only method for bringing the capitalists down to their knees. It is through it that workers will come face to face with the employers and will be morally encouraged. It is necessary for regeneration of the societv. Democratic devices cannot set the capitalists right. A representative elected on territorial basis cannot represent the cause of all professions and vocations in the same constituency. For a successful strike there should be revolutionary spirit with an appreciation of leadership. Every strike is good in itself and a step towards achieving the ultiamte objective. It has great educational value. It creates spirit as well as enthusiasm among the workers.

2. General strike. A general strike can be the only solution for bringing about far-reaching changes. It will be welcome everywhere and for all wage earners. It shall overthrow the capitalist order. About general strike, Coker has said, "It is primarily a demonstration of the talent and social power of wage earners by simultaneously quiting work in essential industries. They can paralyze the whole economic and social life of the community and thus force privileged groups to yield to their demands." Strikes in small industries shall prepare the nation for general strike. A strike in a few of the key industries can dislocate the whole of national industrial set-up and thus lead to general strike.

The syndicalists knew that it is difficult to arrange simultaneous strikes in all key industries and also to counteract the reaction of the capitalists to their activities. But they did not wish to solve the mystery of General Strike. They wanted to keep it as a myth. As Coker has said, "General strike of syndicalists is different also from the ordinary political strike used as a means of unsetting an oppressive political regime or of intimidating a government into granting political concessions."

The idea of general strike put forth by the syndicalists was not a new one. It was known to the leaders of labour movements in France and England in the 19th century. It was discussed by many socialist organisaitons as a method for overthrowing reactionary governments. Arstit de Briand, in France and others preached and propagated this idea in the later 19th century. These people had clear notions about the general strike. The syndicalists, on the other hand, wanted to keep it a myth and this was done purposely. To quote Coker again, "The masses of men are stripped into preserving an action not by practical and scientific demonstration of some rational desirable goal but only by appeals to imaginations."

3. Sabotage. According to the syndicalists it was most appropriate and reasonable to sabotage the present industrial system. This sabotage could either be in the form of delayed work or by adopting a go-slow policy by absenting themselves at intervals from the work or by destroying the machines. Thus, sabotage could be violent as well as non-violent. Useful devices of sabotage include bungling and producing goods of low quality, to produce goods at such a rate that the cost of production unusually goes up and to propagate among the consumers in a manner that sale considerably goes down. Violent means include injuring property of the owner, damaging machines and tools and to destroy everything that is helpful in production. Sabotage is the natural culmination of the principle of general strike which implies retarding of production and to create hatred in the minds of consumers for those who control the means of production.

4. Boycott. The syndicalists preach boycott of goods produced by those who have means of production in their hands and produce goods in which they have maximum margin of profit instead of producing goods which are required by the society. The people should be persuaded to purchase only such goods which bear the label that the goods have been produced by the labour union. All those goods should be boycotted which do not carry such a label. The workers should not hesitate to give to the public all trade secrets so that they develop hatred for the producers. The workers may even spread all sorts of false rumours.

5. Non-cooperation. The syndicalists plead that there should be complete non-coopesation with socialists or other political parties. The syndicalists did not cooperate in any election campaign. The individuals might attempt at getting favourable legislation for workers from their governments but collectively they should not make any asttempt in getting the favours of their illegally constituted governments. Coker has said, "Moreover, the syndicaslists have agreed that, secured by aggressive act which intimidate the government into the actions desired, then the government's concession could be accepted, since it had been obtained by direct action of the workers."

6. Creation of a new society. The syndicalists did not discuss much about the shape of society which was likely to merge after the establishment of syndicalist society. According to Joad, "While, however, the syndicalist plan of action is direct, vigorous and well defined, the state of society which it seeks to realise is extremely nebulous. The general outlines are indicated, though even these are hazy, but the details are awaited. There is reason for this vagueness, a vagueness which is often deliberate, as we shall see when we come to consider the peculiar philosophy which is alleged to have influenced the syndicalist leaders." There will be no class struggle and also no exploitation of the poor in an syndicalist society. The administration shall not be over-centralised. The workers will organise themselves into various syndicates and each one of them will look after its allotted work. Each industry shall be self-sufficient and shall ultiamtely replace the state. Means of produciton shall be syndicates only.

7. Federalisation of syndicates. There shall also the federation of syndicates which will not only control the local syndicates but also perform nation-wide service. It will also co-ordinate the activities of local syndicates and help them in providing technical knowledge. The federation will follow a uniform national policy.

8. Abolition of private property. Syndicalists want that private property shall be altogether abolished. The syndicates shall manage the industry but not own it. The proerpty shall belong to society as a whole. Society shall decide about the means of production and distribution.

9. Abolition of elections. The present system of elections and imparting justice was most defective and should be scrapped altogether. The existing system of electing representatives should be abolished since in it an elected representative had neither any knowledge of the people whom he represented nor any sympathies with them.

10. Abolition of police force and army. According to syndicalists there was no need to maintain police or army. These have stood to defend the capitalists and not the nation. History is a witness that the armies have never come forward to champion the cause of the workers. According to Coker, "The syndicalists contended that the army's essential task appeared to be that of defending not the national but the capitalist groups within the nation; in war the army served the imperialistic designs of international financies; in peace it suppressed strikes; it was never used in the cause of the workers."

11. Abolition of present legal system and discipline. There shall be no need or necessity for maintaining discipline by the state because such a discipline could better be maintained by the syndicates. The system of present laws which is based on force and coercion shall be replaced by laws which shall be willingly obeyed.

12. Social boycott of criminals. The syndicalists proposed social boycott of criminals. Instead of courts of law the syndicates shall decide all disputes. The syndicates shall not make regulations which are by and large not acceptable to the people.

13. Defence of national borders. National borders should be defended by a strong army. In each union there shall be armed troops which shall check all disturbances. Having made their work free the people will have the commonsense to arm themselves in order to protect their hard won liberty.

14. Abolition of state. Finally, the syndicalists plead for abolition of the state as that is the product of oppression and promotes highhandedness. State is not based on justice. Sovereignty vests in the people or in the national association of workers. In the hands of syndicates the industries shall produce goods of better quality and quantity. The goods which are required by the people shall be produced. The state shall not try to promote unity among the people. This shall be accomplished by the syndicates. According to Coker, "Thus, the syndicalists often condemned the political activity not only of reformist socialists with their compromises and alliances with liberal groups, but also of orthodox socialists, who sought to acquire control of a government and use its machinery to construct the whole economic order for the benefit of the workers."

NEW SYNDICALISM

In 1914 as the war broke out and the workers did not go on strike the whole syndicalist philosophy came under review. In 1920, May Day strike failed miserably. The myth of General Strike was thus exploded. Accordingly New Syndicalism came to the forefront.

Causes of Origin of New Syndicalism

1. First World War. The syndicalists did not favour retention of standing and professional armies. Each union shall an armed group which shall check both anti-social and anti-revolutionary activities. But war brought a definite change in this soultion. As the war progressed general confederation of labour was obliged to leave its anti-militarist policy. It found it desirable to join actively with the socialist government in France and making war a success. The confederation was crushed. Anti-war policy was condemned in France. But as the war concluded there were serious post-war problems which brought a division in the ranks of the confederation. The confederaton could not decide as to how pre-war liberties of the workers should be restored and how the government should be asked to give concessions to the workers.

2. The Third International. Third International was convened at Moscow after the First World War. In Paris the syndicalists were obliged to think whether they should affiliate themselves with the International or not. It was felt that such an affiliation was bound to end syndicalist movement which will become only a part of communism. In the broader interests of socialist movement it was essential that the syndicalists should co-operate with the Third International.

3. Failure of May-Day Strike. In May, 1920, the Confederation of Central Labour Exchanges decided to participate with the Railway men in general strike. This strike was a complete failure. The leaders had to concede that every strike was not a success and not in the collective interest of the workers. The myth of strike was exploded. There was division among the workers. They had to consider seriously the desirablity of the method to be followed by the syndicalists.

Growth and Nature of the Movement

The above factors helped in the division among the ranks of the movement. In January 1922 a minority group formed new organisation called 'General Confederation of United Labour'. The new organisation was evolutionary in character. It decided to affiliate itself with the Communist International. According to them such a change is revolution in all walks of life — social, economic and political. Produciton is not simply a mater of hard labour but also of high standard of administration and co-operation from all directly or indirectly concerned with production. According to Coker, "The new syndicalists wish, therefore, to supplant the negative, destructive tactics of the older syndicalism by positive and comprehensive policy."

Industrial Revolution

The syndicalists stand for bringing revolution in industries by an abrupt break from the past. The workers should have high standard of discipline. They should establish that they can be trusted in the management of industry. New syndicalists are against dictatorship of the type desired to be established by the old syndicalists.

Opposed to Violence

New syndicalists did not favour violence preached by old syndicalists. In the words of Coker they believed that, "It is impossible to assign to violence a rationally limited place, for violence is essentially the negation of moderation and reason and the domination of instinct. A dictatorship, like war requires a highly centralised organisation, and an arbitrary authority and iron discipline whereas syndicalism is democratic, federalistic and pacific."

Change in Methods

1. No strikes. New syndicalists believed that producers, users and the public should have a share and effective hand in industry. The workers should not have any right to go on strike if their employers are agreeable to their legitimate demands. One of their chief exponents, Leroy used to say that the strike is "less out of respect for the exercise of a legitimate faculty that to satisfy one of the fundamental beliefs of the working class, which does not consider itself to be actually free except to the extent that it is free to use this particular means."

2. Co-operation with state. New syndicalists extend co-operation to the state. They have faith in political authority of the state. They wish to modify the character of the state and provide for a tribunal to settle all disputes which might arise in the industries. According to them the state is necessary not only to defend national borders but also as Coker has said, "to collaborate in the management of production by selecting representatives of the collective interests and on the other hand, to provide means of education and artistic expressions and also enjoyment for the masses and to encourage intellectual enquiry and technical invention." In a syndicalist society the state will enlighten and guide the society. Instead of coercing the people it shall get their willing co-operation.

Thus, the methods of New Syndicalists are not revolutionary. They have tried to follow more rational and practical lines. They have influenced communist internationals. They have realised that proper ends could be achieved not through negligence of work or non-co-operation of employees with the employers or even by overall destruction of machinery. These were the fundamentals of revolutionary syndicalist philosophy which the new syndicalism rejected.

SYNDICALISM *Vs.* SOCIALISM

Similarities

1. End of capitalism. Both like to end capitalism as according to them that is the sole cause of trouble and the root cause of many evils. Both wish that the power should shift from the capitalists and pass on to the working classes, who should be given a share in the profit.

2. Workers value. Both believe that unless workers value increases there can be no produciton and the question of earning profit would not arise.

3. Modification of state. Both believe that the state should either be altogether dispensed with or alternately its functions should be reduced to the minimum. For them the state is the agency which has always exploited the poor and the working classes. It has only protected the interests of the rich.

4. Anti-democracy. Both believe that democracy in its present form is not in the interests of workers. Workers have neither the resources nor capacity and time to contest elections. The powers, therefore, slip to the elite of the society who enact and legislate for their own interests. Hence, democracy should be replaced by other means and methods of representation.

5. Violence used where required. Both believe that violence should not be feared or necessarily condemned. It should be used as and when need be.

Differences

1. Syndicates *versus* the state control. The syndicalists are of the view that syndicates should have ultimate control over all industries. On the other hand, the socialists believe that the state should have control over the industry.

2. Dispensation of state. According to syndicalists the syndicate should take over all the functions which are now being performed by the state. They wish to have a classless society. They, therefore, wish to dispense with the state as quickly as they can. On the other hand, the socialists are in no hurry to dispense with the state, as according to them, the state is performing some useful functions.

3. Masses *Vs.* classes as owners. Both the syndicalists as well as the socialists feel that property as well as free trade system should come to an end. But with that their similarity ends. For the socialists both these instituions should be brought to an end. In other words, whereas the socialist think of masses the syndicalists plead for a particular class, *i.e.* producers to have ownership of industries.

4. Differences on use of violence. Syndicalists stress on the use of violence in bringing about changes. They feel that no change can come without the use of violence. On the other hand, socialists believe that there should be no use of violence, so long as that is not necessary or unavoidable.

5. Difference of appeal. On the whole the syndicalists appeal to the workers and producers whereas the appeal of the socialists is to the society as a whole except the capitalists and the exploiters.

CONTRIBUTION OF SYNDICALISM

Syndicalist school of thought was very popular among the working classes. The myth of general strike was very popular with them. They found it easy to destroy the machine and sabotage the industry from within. It was very much convincing for the workers that without their work it shall not be possible for the industrialists edither to earn profits or to have any production. They were also convinced that the state was only an instrument for exploiting the poor and protecting the rich. They saw that their interests were being sacrificed for the sake of propertied class.

The syndicalist idea of sabotaging industry and destroying machinery was not confined to France but it spread to other countries of Europe as well. An association named Industrial Workers of the World was founded in U.S.A. under the influence of syndicalism. In England this movement found an apologist in Tom Mann who founded Industrial Syndicalist Educational League and 'The Industrial Syndicalist'. A journal 'New Age' also preached syndicalist philosophy in England. The spread of trade union movement owes much to the movement in France. British trade union leaders drew much inspiration from Sorel and others in France. Britain's love for tradition found its expression in Guild Socialism. The syndicalists also influenced labour movement in Italy and Spain where the labourers used the methods preached by syndicalists to a considerable extent.

CRITICISM OF SYNDICALISM

It has been said that "Syndicalism is anti-democratic, anti-rational and anti-intellectual." It was the last factor which was very much responsible for giving a severe blow to this philosophy. Some of its main defects were the following:

1. Unscientific Theory. As a theory syndicalism was unscientific. It did not lead one to logical conclusions. It was not very convincing and appealling. Put into actual practice it could disappoint a vast majority of workers. It was not based on sound principles like the dialectical materialism or theory of surplus value, etc.

2. Vague Theory. Syndicalist theory was very vague in all respects. It did not tell the method of capturing power or the concept of society, or the form of government after capturing authority. Thus, it leads us nowhere. They had no clear idea even about general strike which was their greatest weapon for the overthrow of the state.

3. Negative Theory. Syndicalist theory was negative in character. It believed in sabotage and destruction of machinery which is national property. They did not allow the workers to participate in parliamentary institutions which, if allowed, might bring about reforms.

4. Opposed to Improved Methods. Under syndicalism the workers did not like to introduce improved means and methods due to the fear of unemployment. Obviously such a policy was bound to result in backwardness of the society. In the words of Dunning, "There is a distinct and serious danger that an organisation of producers will not introduce improved equipment and method lest it throws out of work some of its members."

5. Unhealthy Society. Syndicalism had only taken the interests of producers into a consideration. In a healthy society, on the other hand, the interests of both producers as well as consumers should be taken into consideration. Syndicalism did not take into consideration the interests of consumers which was most undesirable.

6. No Guarantee Against Misuse of Authority. What is the guarantee that in a syndicalist society producers will look after the interests of the consumers honestly and properly? The syndicalists had provided for no such safeguards. There was every danger that the authority might be misused or used by the producers for selfish ends alone.

7. Myth of General Strike. Syndicalist Method of general strike for capturing power appeared to be very optimistic. However, general strike can only be a success when the labourers are self-disciplined and fully aware of their rights and duties. But if the workers are so well disciplined and competent enough to catpure power by means of general strike, they can equally well capture power at the time of elections, by voting their representatives to power. It is said that "a general strike is unnecessary because a general election is never far off. It is most essential that each general strike or even a local strike would be successful. Strikes can also be failures and each failure will demoralise the workers. In addition to this, the working classes usually have no stand-by with the result that they will have to face starvation if a strike prolongs.

8. Creation of Monopoly Conditions. There could be temptation on the part of powerful workers to admit selected workers in key industries, though by creating monopoly conditions. History is a witness that wheresoever these monopoly conditions have been created there has been degeneration. Dunning said that, "danger would be the temptation for given industries and particularly the more favoured ones, rigidly to limit the number that might be admitted to trade and thus maintain monopolistic position."

9. One-sided Philosophy. Syndicalist philosophy was one-sided. It took into consideration the interests of only producers and not of consumers. It had laid stress on economic aspect and had completely ignored political aspects of the problem. A complete transformation of authority could only be possible when economic success was followed by political consolidation.

10. Irrational Philosophy. The philosophy of syndicalism was irrational. Had it not found an apologist in Sorel it would not have been anything beyond a labour movement. There was no rational philosophy beyond this theory. It was because of this lack of rationalism that it had been said that it is anti-rational and anti-intellectual. Syndicalism had preached hatred against capitalism. It has favoured violent means and methods like the sabotage for the overthrow of the capitalist order. But violence and hatred are very vicious and never ending circles. Dunning says, "The hatred and violent passions srirred up by struggle between the classes could not be exercised by a wave of the want but would inevitably lead the men who had surrendered themselves to hatred and violence merely to seek objects for their hatred." Thus, the methods suggtested by the syndcialists provided no solution to the problem.

ASSESSMENT OF SYNDICALISM

1. Bertrand Russell. "Whatever may be thought of the practicability of syndicalism, there is no doubt that the idea it has put into the world has done a great deal to revive the labour movement and to recall to it certain things of fundamental importance which it had been in danger of forgetting."

2. Professor Robson. This philosophy could not become popular due to "slender intellectual equipment of its exponents and the absence of a constructive programme."

3. Coker. "The most important influences of earlier French syndicalism are to be found today in other places. On the one hand, in the revival chiefly in fascist Italy and communist Russia of the Sorelian Philosophy of Violence as an indispensable means of bringing about any fundamental social regeneration; on the other hand, in the national guilds and industrial parliaments of guild socialists, the corporation of the fascists, and the schemes for industrial nationalisation and 'joint control' put forth by various groups of socialists and liberal cllectivists today."

QUESTIONS FOR EXERCISE

1. Explain and examine the philosophy of syndicalism and thfc syndicalist view of state. How far is it relevant to the present age?
2. Give a brief explanation of revolutionary syndicalism both as a scientific theory and a method of action. How does new syndicalism differ from Revolutionary Syndicalism?
3. "Syndicalism is anti-democratic, anti-national and anti-intellectual." How far do you agree with the statement?
4. Write about the concept of general strike and its importance in syndicalism.
5. Briefly but critically discuss the central tenets of syndicalism.
6. Briefly discuss some of the important methods followed by Syndicalists to achieve their objects.
7. Write a short not on 'New Syndicalism'.
8. Differentiate between Syndicalism and Socialism.

27

Georges Sorel (1847—1922)

Sorel was born in Cherbourg in 1847. After he had matriculated in his home town, he attended the Ecole Polytechinque in Paris and became an engineer. For nearly 25 years, he served as a Government Engineer and was busy in building French bridges and roads.

Sorel was much devoted to his wife, who had died childless. She had been his most devoted and faithful comrade. To her memory he dedicated later on the following moving words : "Happy is the man who has met a devoted, energetic, and proud woman who never allows his soul to be contented, who knows how to recall the obligations of his task and who occasionally reveals to him even his own genius."

Sorel's deep moralism — so reminiscent of Proudhon — has 'its roots in his marriage."[1] He himself acknowledged to morally purifying effect of a good and happy marriage. It was here that he had discovered the bulwark against the tendency of levelling down the moral values by the decadent sensualism of his age.

Having reached the age of forty-five, he took retirement from government service. Up to this period he did not make any distinctive mark of his literary career. Only as a mature man he began with his literary work before he died in 1922 Georges Sorel wrote seventeen books, lengthy introductions to eight books, written by others, and published numerous articles and essays in forty-one reviews.

Sorel's spiritual and pollitical development is based on his faith in moral values and his belief in the proletariat, which he developed as a result of his feelings of bitter resentment and contempt against the middle classes in whose contact he came as an officer. His first writings published in 1889, show conservative attitude. He got interested in Marxism and accepted the perspective of the revolutionary cataclysm. In 1899, he gave up socialism for syndicalism. He contributed a series of articles on syndicalist philosophy. Those articles were compiled in the form of his famous book, *Reflexions sur la Violence,* which he published in 1906. With it he became the intellectual leader of French revolutionary syndicalism. During the World War I, Sorel showed his antipathy towards democracy and the middle classes. Later on, he bitterly attacked the

1. *The Third Republic : Political Thought in France* by J.P. Mayer (Routledge & Kegan Paul, London, 1944, Revised ed.).

treaty of Versailles and hailed Lenin as the liberator of the proletariat in a powerful postscript to the fourth edition (1919) of the *Reflexions.*

MARXISM

Sorel was a Marxian, with the conviction that capitalism carries the seeds of its destruciton within its own nature. Marxism could not be understood without syndicalism, and syndicalism was meaningless without a clear apprehension of Marxism. Sorel formulated an anti-state principle and, rejected the state entirely. He did not find any gain from political action even if the workers came to have complete control over it. His main aim was to set up an organization of the working class for industrial self-government. It was to be separate from the state and would part in political affairs. It was not to co-operate with the state in any way. The state was to be destroyed and a new social system consisting of autonomous economic groups was to be established.

SOCIAL CLASSES

Sorel maintained that social classes were differentiated by dissimilarity of cultures and economic distincitons. Every class, developed separately its own peculiar social characteristics, its own ethics and its own mode of action. Every class attempted to impose its own system upon others. The propertied class used the territorial state for that purpose. It gained control over the state and used it to dominate the working class either by military force or by electoral manipulations. It was of no use to the workers to capture the state from the middle classes because the state was entirely unsuited to the proletarian rule. Hence, the state had to be replaced by a new social system adapted to the special qualities of proletarian class, arranged according to the economic functions. Workers in every vocation were to be grouped in syndicates and unions. They were not to fight for higher wages, shorter hours and better working conditions, but also to manage and administer the industry as their own. In the new system, the workers were to act as their own masters and, thus, develop their creative and productive faculties.

SUPPORT OF VIOLENCE

Sorel had bceome an apostle of violence before he professed the pragmatic faith. He had manifested his predilection for it in its generally anti-intellectualistic aspects. He had shown himself an unconscious disciple of the 'will to believe' by his doctrine of social myths, and in particular the myth of the general strike. In syndicalist theory, the general strike has been conceived as the means by which society will pass from capitalism to socialism.

THE 'WILL TO POWER' AND THE CHANGE IN SOCIETY

All political, social, moral and religious revolutions of the past have been made by minorities while the masses have always been passive. The militant Christians forced the edict of Milan and the Jacobins were also a resolved minority. According to Sorel, "The majority of a country cannot generally perform great changes which are based on absolute theories. A society develops itself historically and the masses remain in their traditions."[2] Sorel wrote in 1889 in his book *Le Process de Socrate*, "The 'will to power', not numbers, creates a new social substance. *Elites* of soldiers, officers, and generals have alone won battles, the captains of industry have built up capitalism; Catholicism, too, has been formed by a religious elite." According to Sorel, the elites of the future will be the proletarian elites. The workers, must be as certain of their victory as the martyrs of the first Christian centuries. This may alone give them perserverance in their battles and make them overcome all obstacles which they may meet on their strenuous way. The discipline of elites cannot grow within a political party. The *centre* of the formation of a proletarian elite must be seen in the syndicalist movement. In strikes, the appropriate means for bringing about social and economic changes the leaders of the syndicates try out their social responsibility until the masses in the factories are ripe for the 'myth' of the *general strike*.

THE 'MYTH' OF GENERAL STRIKE

Sorel felt that intimidation by the employers and repression by the government would be rendered impossible because the strike would be general, extending over the entire country, whereas the army would be scattered and dispersed. In common with all the beliefs of a similar nature which have inspired men to sacrifice and even to martyrdom, general strike is mythical in its character. Sorel's principle of general strike announces the birth of a new society which is to follow the period of capitalism. A militant energy, discipline, love of work, purity of morals — these are the virtues of a proletarian elite to be qualified for building a new order of society. As such, Sorel had given a most striking exhortation, in the spirit of his interpretation of the 'will to believe', urging the necessity of creating a heroic 'myth' — the catastrophic regeneration of society through the general strike — a sublime fanaticism of violence to revitalize the sick soul of Europe.

VALUE OF 'SOCIAL MYTHS'

Sorel seized upon the syndicalist doctrine to turn it into a 'myth', a motive force. Man must have faith in order to act. The pragmatic essence of Sorel's thought follows a reasoning which he put in something like the form of James's 'faith-ladder' of inferences, by which men actually proceed to a determination. Sorel himself consistently attempted to avoid the pragmatic test for his myths. He warned his disciples against the querulous effort to test a 'myth' in terms of its actual consequences. In the *Reflexions sur la Violence* he writes, "I do not attach importance to the objections given to the General Strike on the ground of practical considerations. There is no way to be able to forecast the future in a scientific manner or even to discuss the superiority which certain hypothesis can have on other." About the value of 'social myths' he further writes : "Experience proves to us that the constructions of a future, undetermined by time, can be of a greast value and need not have any disadvantages while

2. *Ibid.*, pp. 116-17.

they are of a certain nature; that is to say, while they concern myths in which they find the strongest tendencies of one people, party or class, forces which present themselves to the spirit with the insistence of instincts in all circumstances of life, and which give an aspect of plain reality to the hopes of the next action on which the reform of the will is founded. We know that these social myths prevent no man from knowing how to make profit from all the observations he makes in the course of his life and are no obstacle to the fulfilment of his normal occupations."

PRAGMATIC INTERPRETATION OF A MYTH

For all his pragmatism, Sorel had insisted that the myth was not to be tested in any way. His pragmatic interpretation of the doctrine of myth as 'will to believe', which he mostly drew from William James, is fully in consonance with the pragmatic spirit. About pragmatism William James said, "...an idea is 'true' so long as to believe it is profitable to our lives. That it is *good*, for as much as it profits, you will gladly admit. If what we do by its aid is good, you will allow the idea itself to be good in so far forth, for we are the better for possessing it."[3]

Sorel's main aim was to inspire the working classes to revolt without questioning the efficacy of his method. The philosophy of revolution, as maintained by Sorel, was an attitude of mind, a way of thinking, which he firmly maintained and which suited his special temperament. Sorel's doctrine of myth, which he interpreted as 'will to believe', was to serve as a belief, a motive force to encourage the proletariat to will to revolt. And a 'will to believe' is a pre-requisite condition before a firm action is being taken in any direction. It has a value in itself. The sacrifices of the Napoleonic soldier to the glory, of the glory, of the Roman to the conquest of the world, of the Christian to his other-worldly faith — these are things which no intellectualistic philosophy may explain. History shows such faith rewarded by success, and it is a faith that does not go with intellectualism.

THEORY OF ELITES

Sorel's theory of elites has its roots in his appreciation of the moral forces which are substance and strength of the human being. He was much more influenced by Proudhon than by Karl Marx, Sorel's theory of histroy is deeply indebted to Marx. Yet he was always very conscious of the difficulty, if not of the impossibility, of giving a general and *direct* series of causes inter-relating the economic sphere of societies with the non-economic realm.

THEORY OF HISTORY

Sorel maintained that contingency and human will-power play a decisive role in the historic process. He largely draws on Vico's social philosophy, interpreted in latter's doctrine of the *ricorsi*, the 'repetitions'. But he attempted to transform the doctrine of the *ricorsi* in an original sense. While Vico gave

3. James, William, *Pragmatism* (Longmans, Green & Co., London, 1907), p. 75.

the *ricorsi* a providential meaning, Sorel taught that the *ricorsi* were by no means only a historic division into *epochs.* The 'repetitions'can happen, more frequently in the course of the historic process than Vico assumed. Development and primitivity may occur simultaneously.

Criticism of Democracy

Sorel was a most bitter critic of his own time, a true contemporary for Jacob Burckhardt and Nietzsche. He strongly criticized democracy because it attempts to dish out a cheap happiness to all men, without acknowledging qualitative differentiations or asking for moral energy. During democratic elections only money rule the whole scene.

Criticism of Marrriage

Sorel also criticised the marraige system. Marriage is only an alliance of interests. Look at the divorce statistics of the capitalist countries.

Against Neo-Malthusianism

Sorel was against neo-Malthusianism. He said that we were living in an age of inescapable mediocrity. Here he was deeply influenced by the Caesarism, Louis Napoleon and its consequence on French history.

DOCTRINE OF ACTION

Sorel's political philosophy was a doctrine of action. His activism reveals itself in his theory of knowledge, where he was indebted to Henri Bergson. Although be stood for giving into the hands of the workers all the powers, he refused to give details regarding the syndicalist society. He used Bergsonian irrationalism to justify a revolutionary labour movement having no definite goal. The future of society, according to Sorel, was to be known by intuition. He drew his philosophy of 'intuition' and 'action' directly from Bergson. Bergson said : "There are in truth no things; things and states are only views, taken by our mind, of becoming. There are no things, there are only actions."[4] Under the guidance of intuition, we perceive that "form is only a snapshot view of transition," and the philosopher "will see the material world melt back into as single flux."[5] In the same way, Sorel was of the view that only action is the criterion of truth. There is no monism of thought. The ancient philosophy of unity has finally abdicated : "enough of metaphysics....Let us descend to the level of daily life." The proletarian elites alone can build a new world : they will replace the old static metaphysics by the right and the ethics of the world of the worker.

QUESTIONS FOR EXERCISE

1. Discuss the political ideas of Georges Sorel.
2. Discuss Sorel's view in the Myth of General Strike.

4. Russell, B., *A History of Western Philosophy* (London, 1947), pp. 826-27.
5. *Ibid.*

28

Political Pluralism

The view of state as exercising absolute sovereignty over all citizens and subjects unrestricted by law, has come to be attacked most recently by political pluralists. These include Professor Laski, Lindsay, G.D.H. Cole, MacIver, Barker, Duguit and Krabbe etc.

Meaning of Pluralism

1. *Maxey.* "The pluralist doctrine owes its name to the central contention of its adherents namely, that social authority is not, and from the nature of social institutions and processes cannot be, a unity, but is of a plural character and greatly divided."[1]

2. *Hsiao.* "The pluralistic state is simply a state in which there exists no single source of authority — it is divisible into parts and should be divided."[2] Pluralists hold that life is many-layered and every petal is precious and important. Different associations grow to fulfil the varied needs of man's life. Modern society is a web of associations.

3. *Barker.* "We see the state less as an association of individuals in a common life; we see it more as an association of individuals, already united in various groups for a further and more embracing common purpose."[3] The various associations must have their functional freedom. Their autonomy is the main concern of the pluralists.

4. *Gettell.* "The pluralistic theory of sovereignty, in general, insists on democracy and has a strong tinge of individualism. It is, however, not so much the right of separate individuals that are aimed at, but the rights of the various associations and groups which represent the real interests of man. Pluralism lays great stress on function and believes that the natural organisations and communities within the state should manage their own affairs. It poses a centralised, all powerful state, and urges a division of power along the lines of functional democracy. It rejects the psychology of the general will and the conception of absolute sovereignty as based on a formal and metaphysical rationalism that does not correspond with actual and changing political reality. In this respect, it allies itself so a certain extent with the anti-intellectualism

1. Maxey, *Political Philosophies*, pp. 630-631.
2. Hsiao, *Political Pluralism*, p. 1.
3. Barker, E., *Political Thought in England 1848-1914*, 2nd edition, p. 155.

that characterizes social psychology and the new economics."[4] The pluralists, however, do not want to dispose of the political state altogether. They want to retain the state but merely as a useful social institutions, like so many other useful institutions, at best a *primus inter pares*. The pluralists' view "lays stress on the role of society, as a richly creative matrix of varied behaviour".[5] None of the associations, including the state, can claim moral excellence over other associations.

5. *Lipson.* (1) That the state is one of the numerous social, economic, political and other groupings through which men in society seek to satisfy their numerous needs and promote their welfare; (2) that these different groups or associations are not the creatures of the state but they arise independently of the state and they acquire power and authority not given by the state; (3) that the various associations and the state are at par with each other and the state enjoys no superior value; (4) that the various associations such as trade unions, churches, professional societies, etc., are as necessary and important as the state; (5) that the monist state is not only incapable of wielding absolute authority over such bodies but is also incapable of regulating their affairs intelligently or administering them efficiently; (6) that conception of state sovereignty is moral legal fiction; and that (7) the sooner the conception of state sovereignty is given up, the better it will be for human progress.

MAIN CONTENTIONS OF PLURALISM

History of Political Pluralism

During the middle ages, the state was no longer the predominant social organisations of the community. The Roman Church, Holy Roman Emperor, king, feudal lord, chartered town, guild, etc., were the contending parties for the allegiance of the individual. In the early period, the church was dominant. Then, Coker, points out, "There was no feeling for the state; no common and uniform defendence on a central power; no omni-competent sovereignty; no equal pressure of civil law. In the later middle ages, various factors combined to increase the power of the state was associated with tthe national monarch. It was given legal form first by Jean Bodin and later on by John Austin. The monists held that as an organisation for law within a given territory the state was legally superior to all other groups within that territory."[6]

Origin of the Theory

Political pluralism originated in the writings of Otto V. Gierke and F.W. Maitland in the last quarters of the nineteenth century. According to these writers, various associations which exist within any society are instinctive to man. These associations possess real personalities of their own. Each association has a collective consciousness and will distinct from the wills of its individual

4. Gettell, R.G., *History of Political Thought*, p. 464.

5. Lipson, *The Great Issue of Politics*, p. 149.

6. Quoted by Coker in *Recent Political Thought*, p. 499.

members. Associations have rights and duties as groups. Emile Durkheim put forward the case of the restoration of the ancient occupational association as a definitely recognised public institution. According to him, as Coker writes, "Economic life is too specialised to be reached by the state. The activities of any given occupation can be regulated only by a group near enough to that occupation to be acquainted with its functions and needs. The professional groups must, therefore, be re-established both as bases for political representation and as sources of economic regulation. Geographical divisions have lost their economic and social, and, therefore, their political significance; they must be replaced by vocational divisions which will reflect more accurately the variety of social interests."[7] Paul-Boncour pleaded for the autonomy of economic groups. According to Figgis, "The state did not create the churches; nor even in any real sense can it be said to have created the club or trade unions, nor in the middle ages, the guild or the religious order, hardly even the universities or the colleges within the universities; they have all arisen out of the natural associative instincts of mankind, and should all be treated by the supreme authority as having a life original and guaranteed, to be controlled and directed like persons, but not regarded in their corporate capacity as mere names."[8] Laski argued, "Because society is federal, authority must be federal also."[9] MacIver regarded state as one association among many within the community, although exercising functions of a unique character. Other associations exist apart from and prior to the state's act of recognition. The state, cannot make or unmake them. Against the doctrine of state sovereignty Laski exclaimed: "It would be of lasting benefit to political science if the whole concept of sovereignty were surrendered."[10] Laski regarded the concept of state sovereignty historically absurd and fatal to the well-being of humanity. He declared the concept of state sovereignty a legal fiction, a barren concept, and dangerous to humanity. To Lindsay, the state is simply an organisation of organisations, though it has got a compulsive and comprehensive membership while membership is voluntary and selective in other organisations. But the sate has neither a personality nor a will of its own. Lindsay said, "If we look at the facts, it is clear enough that the theory of sovereign state has broken down."[11] In spite of rejecting the conception of the real personality of groups Ernest Barker agrees with that permanent groups within society have existed prior to the state and each of them has a corporate character and functions of its own. Duguit, the French jurist, thought that the concept of sovereign state was dead. He approved the opinion of Charles Benoist that "the notion of the sovereign state was an antiquated mystical and theological idea, false in its origin, further falsified by history, and all things considered, useless, worse than useless, dangerous" Krabbe, the Dutch jurist, also denied to the state its sovereignty. He admitted

7. Coker, *Recent Political Thought*, p. 506.

8. Figgis, J.M., *Churches in the Modern State*, p. 47.

9. Laski, H., *A Grammar of Politics*, p. 271.

10. *Ibid*, pp. 44-45.

11. Lindsay, "The State in Recent Political Theory", *Political Quarterly*, I (1914), p. 136.

sovereignty of law independent and superior to the state. G.D.H. Cole advocated the concept of co-sovereignty of the groups of producers and consumers. His theory of Guild Socialism is accepted pluralism. In her book *The New State,* the American writer, Miss M.P. Follet, advocated pluralism by saying that the state, the group and the individual were sovereigns at different levels.

Factors for the Growth of Pluralism

Followings factors are responsible for the growth of pluralism :

1. Reaction against absolutism. It grew out of the traditional theory of state sovereignty as developed by political thinkers like Bodin, Grotius, Hobbes, Rousseau and John Austin. Praising the state to mystical heights the idealists, particularly the German idealists of the Hegelian School, described it as the march of God on earth. On the other hand, the pluralists hold that the conception of state as an absolute legal sovereign does not fit in with political practice nowadays. The authority of the state is not infallible.

2. Comparative failure of democracy. This has its concomitant in majority tyranny over economic, political, racial and religious minorities. Guild socialists have condemned territorial representation as unsatisfactory, inadequate to represent diverse interests of society, and harmful to minorities. Hence, they aim to build up a new doctrine of plural sovereignties in place of a monist sovereign.

3. Breakdown of state administration. This was due to expansion and overcentralisation of the functions of the state. As Ward puts it : "There is apoplexy at the centre and anaemia at the extremeties. To remove the congestion at the centre and to increase social efficiency pluralists put forward proposals which aim at decentralisation of authority."

4. Writings of scholars like Gierke and Maitland. These also contributed to the popularity of the pluralistic theory.

5. The development of internationalism. It has also contributed to the strengthening of the doctrine of political pluralism. International peace and security demand certain modifications in the Nationalism, which is required to be briddled and kept under discipline. This can be done only if the conception of state sovereignty is surrendered.

6. State Sovereignty and Group Autonomy. Pluralists attach the traditional concept of state sovereignty from three different angles — the parmanent groups or associations, the law and international relations.

The pluralists hold that the state is neither superior nor inferior to other institutions of society, some of which are older than the state itself. These economic, religious, social or political associations are not creatures of the state. Their growth is spontaneous and their functions are independent of the state. They are, co-sovereign with the state. Here Paul Boncour and Durkheim put forward the cause of professional and economic groups while Figgis advocated the autonomy of the church. G.D.H. Cole advocated functional representation. Laski wants the state to share its sovereignty with the other groups. Lindsay believes that social groups may claim and win greater allegiance of the individual than the state and may serve as better means of coordination than the state. MacIver writes, "If we look again into the rich complexity of human associations, we must see how vain is the project which would place under a single centre of control not only the economic enterprises of individual but also the activities of multitude of economic groups, corporations and monopolies, trade unions and cooperative societies, leagues of manufacturers and of wholesalers and retailers in their myriad forms, circle beyond circle of economic interests, financial and commercial and industrial and agricultural alliances seeking through union, inclusive and exclusive, the particular aims which distinguish them from the rest, to say nothing of the professional and technical objectives, which are reinforced by the sense of a common economic motive."[12]

Thus, political pluralists hold the view that the individual does not belong to the state and state alone. The groups or associations are as important to an individual as the state itself. The loyalties of an individual are many or plural. The state has no claim to the total loyalty of man. A functional democracy with active participation of groups in decision-making processes is the vision of the pluralist thinkers. Functional decentralisation will infuse new life into the administration. It will allow maximum opportunity for free expression of individual needs and experiences. To quote Gettell, "The pluralists also make a timely protest against the rigid and gogmatic legalism associated with the Austinian theory of sovereignty. They emphasize the necessity of studying the actual facts of political life in a rapidly changing social system. In this connection, they point out the growing importance of non-political groups, the danger of overinterference on the part of the state with the proper functions of such groups, and the desirability of giving to such groups greater recognition in the political system. The federal organisation of government and the principle of group representation in legislative assemblies which they propose are unquestionably valuable devices in government."[13] Miss M.P. Follet sums up the merits of pluralism thus : (1) The pluralists prick the bubble of present state's right to supremacy. They see that the state which has been slowly forming since the Middle Ages with its pretences and unfulfilled claims has not won either our regard or respect. (2) They recognise the value of the group and they see that the variety of our group life today has a significance which must be immediately reckoned within political life. (3) They plead for a revivification of local life. (4) They see that the interest of the state is now always indentical with the interests of its parts. (5) Pluralism is the beginning of the disappearance of the crowd. (6) Pluralism contains the prophecy of the future because it has with keenest insight seized upon the problem of identity of association, and of federalism.[14]

DOCTRINES OF POLITICAL PLURALISM

1. Limitations of State Authority. Pluralists believe that the state is one

12. MacIver, R.M., *op. cit.*, pp. 461-62 (*The Modern State).*

13. Gettell, R.G., *op. cit.*, pp. 468-469.

14. Follet, M.P., *The New State*, pp. 315-317.

of the associations. It has no superior position. The authority of the state is being challenged by all other associations and groups. This indicates that the state is not the only authority to demand loyalties. Man requires not only state but also clubs, churches and recreational associations for the expression of human personality. The state authority has been challenged by trade unions and religions. According to Coker, "Man's social nature, they maintain, finds expression in numerous groupings, pursuing various ends : religious, social, economic, professional, political, no one of the groups is superior morally or practically to others." Chief exponents of pluralist philosophy are Dr. J. Nevilli, Figgis, Laski, Lindsay, Barker and Duguit. These people maintain that the state authority can be challenged both on national and international grounds.

2. Concept of Sovereignty. The concept of legal sovereignty is only of recent origin. It was known to the people of ancient Greece. For them the state was not above laws. They desired that the state should obey the dictates of God and also human customary laws. To them the state was the highest of all the associations but other associations were also essential for the existence of the state. During the Middle Ages the state was not the predominant organization. In the words of Coker, "Thus, it has been said, speaking generally of the Middle ages, that there was then no feelings for the state; no common and uniform dependence on a central power; no omni-competent sovereignty; no equal pressure of civil law; no abstract of association in formal and legal rules or at any rate, so far as anything of the sort was present, it was a matter only for the church and in no wise for the state."

(i) *Bodin.* The concept of sovereignty was expounded in modern times by Bodin who believed that the state was an association of families. But Bodin also put sovereignty under certain limitations. State was the highest power over citizens and subjects. The state sovereignty was not absolute like the natural and divine laws.

(ii) *Hobbes.* After Bodin, Hobbes tried to give the conception of absolute sovereignty but he also put limitation on the sovereign authority of the state.

(iii) *Rousseau.* Rousseau tried to create absolute sovereignty through his conception of 'General Will' but he also subjected this sovereign to many limitations. Thus, he also did not give absolute conception of sovereignty.

(iv) *Austin.* In modern times Austin has given a conception of state sovereignty by saying, "If a determinate human superior, not in the habit of obedience to a like superior, receives habitual obedience from the bulk of given society, that determinate human superior is sovereign in that society political and independent." Thus, doctrine has also been put to severe criticism on the grounds that in every state there is some person or group of persons who must share the unlimited legal sovereignty.

(v) *The Pluralists.* The Pluralists also agree with the idea that the state sovereignty is not essential for constituting a state. The idea of absolute and unlimited sovereignty of the state is both legally as well as ethnically wrong. They believe that the state must compete with other associations to justify its existence. In the words of Coker, "The analytical jurist holds merely that state exists to enact and apply law; though the state cannot be subjected to limitation of some character and authorities as those with which it is established and to formulate and execute." But the Pluralists do not agree even with this idea. They go a bit further by saying that the state has no authority even to execute the laws.

3. Basic Principles. Maxey has summed up basic pluralist principles as follows :

(i) The state is but one of the numerous, economic, political and other groupings through which men and society must seek to satisfy their interests and promote their welfare.

(ii) Though these different groupings are not mere creature of the state they arise independently and acquire power and authority not given by state.

(iii) That the functions of such voluntary associations as churches, labour unions, trade organizations, professional societies and the like are as necessary and important as those of the state.

(iv) That the monistic state is not only incapable of wielding absolute authority over such bodies but is incapable of regulating their affairs intelligently or administering them efficiently.

(v) That the monistic concept of sovereignty is a mere legal fiction which not only misses the truth but does incalculable harm in obstructing the evolution of society along more beneficial lines."

4. Trade Unionism. According to the Pluralist, in modern times there is increasing nationalization of industries and with that trade union movement is also increasing. Under trade unions the workers organize themselves. They run parallel adminsitration with the Government. Many a time even the Government is obliged by circumstances. These associations and trade unions have spontaneous growth.

5. State *Vs.* Church. One of the chief exponents of pluralism, Dr. J.V. Figgis used to say that the authority of the state has all along been challenged by the church. The state has never absolutely controlled the church. Many a time Pope has challenged the authority of the state. Prof. A.D. Lindsay used to say, "If we look at the facts it is clear that the theory of the sovereign state has broken down." Prof. Barker has aid, "The state has become more an association of individuals already united in various groups in order to bring harmony in the society." To conclude with Maxey, "This institution need not be all powerful or morally unquestionable, all it really needs are the necessary means, legal and political, to perform its indispensable social function." Therefore, the state is needed for regulation of social, economic and political life. One cannot imagine a society without the authority of the state. Without the state the society will revert to the state of nature and civilisation might get a set back.

POLITICAL PHILOSOPHY OF INDIVIDUALISM

1. Meaning of Individualism. Individualism aims at the non-interference of the state in controlling the activities of the individuals. According to it the happiness and progress of mankind can be achieved only if the people are left to manage their affairs by themselves without any restriction from without. This philosophy gives perfect liberty to individuals.

2. Real Function of the State. The governments by their restraint of services can hardly make any contribution to the welfare of the individuals. On the other hand, they tend to destroy it if they extend their activity beyond the limits of maintaining law and order in the society. The individualists regard the state a necessary evil. The real function of the state is to train and improve the individuals in such a way that they should not feel any necessity for the existence of state. The greatest service that the state can do to mankind is to make itself superfluous.

3. Negative Function of the State. As the exponents of individualism consider the state as an evil, they tend to minimise the sphere of the state activity. The state exists to protect the country from external aggression with the help of army. The army has to maintain internal peace and order with the help of police force. Thus, the function of state is negative in nature and not positive. It simply checks the individuals from violating the law of the state.

4. Power Concepts. The political thinkers have disagreed regarding the extent of control the government should have to regulate the conduct of the individuals. Increase in govenment powers comes into conflict with the rights and liberties of individuals, when unlimited power comes into his hands, a benevolent king is likely to become a tyrant. Intelligent men of aristocracy become intolerant and unwise, when come into power, even democracy has not been able to solve this problem where the majority rule ruthlessly oppresses the minority groups. As Mill pointed out, the self-government of democracy is not the government of each man by himself but the government of each by the rest of the community.

5. Limits of State Control. The existence of state implies that a government should have certain powers to control and guide the conduct of the individuals. Even the individualist cannot deny this fact. What sort of activities should be controlled by the government? What is the sphere of individual's activities in which the government should have no interference at all? The state should safeguard the natural rights of man and should not violate them. But it may be difficult to decide what particular actions of the government tend to infring the natural rights of the individual or when should the government intervene to protect the rights. J.S. Mill has tried to provide a criterion where the state is justified to intervene and restrain the activities of an individual. He divides the action of the individuals into two parts : (i) self-regarding, and (ii) other-regarding. According to Mill, man is sovereign over himself, over his body and mind. "The only purpose," he says "for which power can be rightfully exercised over any number of a civilised community against his will, is to prevent harm to others," In so far as the action affects only the doer, the state has no reason to intervene. It cannot justifiably interfere in the individual's action even if it claims to do so for the good and benefit of the man concerned. It should not assume a paternal role. Once it begins to interfere in the moral conduct of man, it takes liberty to intervene at wrong places as well.

7. Law of Naturally Perfection. Spencer is of the view that natural forces help the society to achieve perfection. The natural laws demand that the state should allow the natural selection to operate in its own way without any interference. Natural selection *i.e.* survival of the fittest and elimination of the weaker is the fundamental law of nature. This law also applies to human society. It helps in its improvement by eliminating the weak and undesirable existence which amount to modify nature. The essential end of the state is to support nature and allow it to function freely on its own way. The state has only two duties to perform : defence against the external aggression and to prevent encroachments reciprocally among the individuals within the state. According to Spencer, "Every man is free to do that which he wills, provided he infringes not upon the equal freedom of any other man."

8. No State Help in Survival of Unfit. Spencer has gone as far as opposing all organised charity, public or private, all state aid to education and all laws regulating the industry. All poor relief, compulsory education, care of public health are of little use. They attempt to hinder the natural progress of society by helping the unfit to survive. It is not the function of state to help the poor, lame, dumb, old and destitute. They should be allowed full freedom to perish soon. The state should not interfere in the industrial competition and there should be no labour laws. It is not justified to operate the mint or post office or erect light houses and life saving stations.

9. Free Trade. In the economic field the individualists advocate free trade. Every individual knew best his own interest and means to procure it. By pursuing his own interest be serves the common interest as well. There should be no restrictions on industries and workers. There should be free competition without any legal restraint. The existing economic differences are the result of natural endowment of chances of fortune. The state should sustain private property and whatever inequalities appear with it.

10. View of Humboldt and Sumner. According to Humboldt, "State should abstain from all solicitude for the positive welfare of the citizens and ought not to proceed a step farther than is necessary for their natural security and protection against foreign enemies." Deeply influenced by thfe biological writings of Darwin and Huxley and application of biological principles to social phenomena by Spencer, Sumner says, "Let it be understood that we cannot go outside of this alternative; liberty, inequality, survival of the fittest; non-liberty, equality, survival of the unfittest. The former carries society forward and favours all its best members; the latter carries society downwards and favours all its worst members."

11. Freedom from State Control. Thus, the individualists contend that the state should not interfere into the affairs of the individual. Man finds scope for development only in perfect liberty. Government action kills the initiative, self-reliance and self-confluence of the individual. It blunts his character. The highest civilisation can develop only under an individualist society. Nature should be given free hand to work in its own way. It will lead to the survival of the fittest. The rule of the rich, wise and intelligent will be established. On the other hand the state help to the poor and weak will lead to the establishment of the rule of ignorant people. In the economic fields the state must allow full scope to free competition. It will stabilise the prices, raise the level of efficiency and result in manufacture of superior type of goods. Most of the state regulations are ridiculous, mischievous, useless and futile. State control leads to inefficiency and corruption.

Criticism

1. State is not a necessary evil. The individualists hold that the state is a necessary evil. But experience shows that mankind has made tremendous progress with the help of state.

2. Contributions of state. The establishment of railways and roads, the compulsory education, regulations for traffic and public health etc. have added to the comforts of man and not retarded his progress.

4. Need of state in modern complicated society. With the progress of civilisation, the activities and responsibilities of the state have also increased. In the modern complicated society of today it is no longer possible for a man to lead life in his own located way without having any regard for others. Of course, when life was very simple and man did not have the amenities provided by the scientific knowledge of today, the scope for state intervention in individual's life was little. As the society gets more complicated, the sphere of state action will increase. Instead of the state becoming superfluous it tends to become more powerful and paramount.

5. Economic individualism is conservative. Today the economic individualism has become the creed of conservative. It is being used as a weapon against socialism and regulations of prices, profit, wages or working conditions. It wants to preserve the *status quo*. It opposes the transfer of private enterprise into the hands of community. It maintains that the state should not interfere between the employees and they should be left free to make the contracts and strike the bargain. This is nothing short of throwing the workers to the wolves. This principle of liberty gives licence to the capitalist to exploit the workers and gives the latter the right to starve to death. The poor worker cannot refuse to work at the wages offered by the employer because refusal means starvation of himself and his family. Therefore, there is a direct need of state intervention to check the exploitation of the large number of masses by a handful of capitalists.

6. Harms of cut-throat competition. The cut-throat competition permitted by individualism is harmful and destructive. It leads to waste of money, dishonesty in business, misleading advertisements and fall in public morals. It creates artificial shortage and overproduction of goods. This system brings about frequent economic crisis resulting into mass employment, famines and starvation.

7. Need of state activities. The individualists hold that the state enterprise is less efficient than the private enterprise. Moreover, state action gives rise to corruption and waste. This allegation may be true ot some extent. But the fault does not lie with the public enterprise. In a society where the pattern of its system is capitalistic and the possession of wealth determines the status of an individual in the society, the state enterprise may not show better results. During the last war individualists amassed huge wealth while the poor masses were starving to death. Huxley has rightly remarked that "State lives in glass house; we see what it tries to do, and all its failures, partial or total, are made the msot of but private enterprise is sheltered under good opaque bricks and mortar. The public rarely knows what it tries to do and its failures when they are gross and patent to the whole world."

8. Consequences of *laissez-faire*. The doctrine of *laissez-faire* has wretched consequences. The living conditions of the worker were horrible. They were ruthlessly exploited by the capitalists. The conscience of the people was aroused and social reformer came forward to mend the society. They rejected the basic assumptions of individualism and regarded social evil as man-made which could be removed by courageous application of moral authority of church and positive assertions of the powers of the state. Michael Salder, William Cobbet and John Fielder agitated for reforms through governmental interference. The appeal to humanitarian sentiments of Christian and civilised nations made by Thomas Arnold, Carlyle and Mrs. Gaskell had much influence in promoting the enactment of labour legislation in England.

Major Postulates of Pluralism

Maxey has been summed up thus : "That the state is but one of numerous social, economic, political and other groupings through which men in society must seek to satisfy their interests and promote their welfare; (2) That these different groupings are not mere creatures of the state but arise independently and acquire power and authority not given by the state; (3) That the functions of such voluntary associations as churches, labour unions, trade organisations, professional societies, and the like are as necessary and important as those of the state; (4) that the monistic state is not only incapable of wielding absolute authority over such bodies but is incapable of regulating their affairs intelligently of administering them efficiently; (5) That the monistic concept of sovereignty is a mere legal fiction which not only misses the truth but does incalculable harm in obstructing the evolution of society along more natural and beneficial lines."[15]

CRITICISM OF THE DOCTRINE OF PLURAL SOVEREIGNTY

1. Anarchistic individualism. If every association is to be placed at par

15. Maxey, : *Philosophies*, pp. 631-632.

with the state and there is no superior agency to co-ordinate and regulate relations between different groups, there is bound to be great confusion and lawlessness in society. To divide sovereignty is to destroy it. The pluralists deny to the state a position of supremacy but give it much power in a veiled manner. Almost all the pluralists deny to the state the function of co-ordination and adjustment. This function, cannot be performed satisfactorily without making the state legally supreme. If the state is an associations of associations, it has to be supreme. It has to see that no association undertakes an activity hostile to the general welfare. No association trespasses into the area of another association. All this means that the state should have the final legal authority.

2. Based on wrong assumptions. It is wrong to assume that the various associations run along parallel lines and that there is no overlapping of functions. Life is so complicated that it cannot be divided into watertight compartments. As society is constituted, there is always a clash of interests and a conflict of loyalties. If there is no central authority, the result will be constant struggle and stoppage of progress. In the absence of central authority, the pluralists cannot assure to each of the proposed functional bodies the security and autonomy necessary to its existence as a separate entity. They cannot provide to various groups attain their own ends but not ends hostile to the welfare of society as a whole. They cannot maintain national independence and carry on foreign relations.

3. Misunderstanding of Monism. The monists of today are not supporters of Hegelian absolutism. They have discarded old metaphysical appendages of sovereignty. Gettell is right when he says that "it is quite possible for the state to recognise moral obligations, to limit the scope of its activities, and to recognize its internal organisation along the lines of local decentralization and representation of group interests without the loss of its ultimate legal sovereignty."[16] This is what pluralists want and this is what monists concede safely.

4. Confusion about state authority. Lindsay admits that the state is unique in so far as it possesses coercive authority and is comprehensive in its membership. But he pleads that this is not enough to make the state sovereign. On the face of it, this argument is devoid of any logic or sense. The state is the one all-inclusive association. It is above all groups. It also possesses coercive authority. It serves the general interests of society. It is the unifying force and not a mere co-ordinating agency.

5. Confused objectives. Pluralists are not clear about what they want. While they deny sovereignty to the state they make it representative of general interests and national solidarity. Even Laski say, "However much we may reduce the direct administrative capacity of the political state, the fact remains that once it is charged with the provision of services of which men stand in common need, it has their interests in trust to a degree with which no other body can, at least in a temporal sense, compete. Even if we abstract from the

16. Gettell, R.G., *op. cit.*, p. 469.

modern state the final control of international affairs, the civic area of internal matters that is left seems, in any casual glance, overwhelming."[17]

6. Harmony in society requires state. The society cannot be organised harmoniously in a peaceful manner without the authority of the state. State performs fundamental functions and occupies a unique position.

7. No valid attack on state supremacy. Pluralism cannot be accepted as a valid attack upon the claim of the state to supremacy over individuals and groups of individuals. The society of today with its multiple pulls of allegiance requires a central focus of organisation and cohesion. Even Laski says, "Legally, no one can deny that there exists in every state some organ whose authority is unlimited."[18]

State Sovereignty and Law

Duguit and Krabbe reject the Austinian conception of law as a command from a superior to an inferior. According to them, the theory of law as a command of the sovereign is a relic of the past. Law, is in reality anterior to, above and more comprehensive than the state. The state does not create law. It is only adopting the already existing rule of law to new sets of facts. Law resides in thfe social forces operating independently of the will of the sovereign. Duguit contends that the extent to which a government may exact obedience from the citizens depends upon the services it renders to them. In the present welfare state, law is the organism of public services. An individual is to observe social discipline and carry out faithfully all rules of conduct resulting from the facts of social life. These laws are obeyed by the people not because of the fear of state penalties but because of social pressure the sense of social solidarity. Following this, Laski writes, "The end of law is the promotion of social solidarity : its growth depends upon the growth of this sentiment."[19] Krabbe removed the political sovereign as a source of law from both legal and political theory. He held that law was prior to and independent of the state. It arose from the sense of right of the people. This view was upheld by Shepard, who defined law as a rule of conduct originating in and sanctioned by the general sense of right of the society.

Criticism of View

It is said that the term 'social solidarity' used by Duguit is misleading and vague. It simply substitutes 'a social monism for political absolutism'. It means the absolutism of the existing social order. The term 'sense of right' used by Krasbbe is in no way better. A legal system presupposes a legal sovereignty. Coker is right is insisting that law is something which is prescribed. Specific laws are given to us by a determinate authority only; it may be of the person or of the legislature. Monists are always willing to concede that legal sovereignty and positive law are not above and against moral law. There are limitations of

17. Laski, H., *A Grammar of Politics*, p. 75.

18. Laski, H., *Foundation of Sovereignty*, p. 236.

19. *Ibid*., p. 273.

natural law and moral law but they do not take away the contents of legal sovereignty.

State Sovereignty and International Law

Internationalists hold that international law is a law in the real sense. It is superior to municipal law and the sovereignty of the state is legally limited by it. International community has come to possess a juristic personality, the liability of one state to another is determined not by municipal law but by international law. Limitations upon state sovereignty, set by the recognised rules of international behaviour, are quite common in recent times. Limitations have been placed on the sovereignty of state by the Charter of the United Nations Organisation in Article 2, paras 4, 6 and 7 and Article 24, para 1. In recent times, there has been a tendency to treat individuals as persons entitled to the protection of international law. The famous Nuremberg Trials marked the beginning of the enforcement of an effective international criminal law. Oppenheimer writes, "It is being increasingly realised that progress in international law, the maintenance of international peace and, with it, of independent national states, are in the long run conditioned by a partial surrender of their sovereignty so as to render possible, within a limited sphere, the process of international legislation and within a necessary unlimited sphere, the securing of the rule of law as ascertained by international tribunals endowed with obligatory jurisdiction."[20]

Criticism of this View

1. International law is not law in the real sense. There is no proper authority to enforce it. Even the decisions of the U.N.O. have been flouted by different states. As a matter of fact, the U.N.O. has become, more or less, a political arena for fighting big bouts between giants. In the absence of a common supreme authority to enforce its decisions, international law cannot be regarded more than mere dictates of moral conduct.

2. Even if a world state with coercive authority comes into existence, it will simply mean sovereignty getting vested in the world state instead of a national state. The state is a growth and the national state may further develop into an international state. Gilchrist writes, "The abolition of national sovereignty would only transfer sovereignty to the world state which could not be a state at all unless it had sovereign power."[21] The principle of federalism, applicable in modern big states, shall also operate in the world state. This, however, does not mean divided sovereignty. Whatever the limitations on sovereignty are, they are self-imposed under pressure of public opinion or common necessity.

CONTRIBUTION OF PLURALISM

1. Political pluralism was a welcome reaction against the ever increasing

20. Oppenheimer, *International Law*, Vol. I, pp. 119-120.

21. Gilchrist, R.N., *Principles of Political Science*, 7th ed., p. 108.

glorification of the state. Though the state stands legally supreme but it is not absolutely free from all its moral obligations to its citizens and to other states.

2. The pluralism has done a lot of service to modern political theory by bringing into importance the reality of group life. Nobody can deny the superior role of the state. It is a co-ordinating and regulating agency for bringing unity in their social life of the community.

3. The pluralists have forced the monists to revise the traditional doctrine and bring it more in accordance with the realities of life. They have now cast away much of the confusion and vagueness which surrounded their old doctirne. The states of today are changed ones; they take full cognizance of social groups within the state and international requirements of civilised life.

4. Pluralism may not be given the name of a doctrine; it may be a new tendency, a new movement for focusing the attention of old monists to new conditions of life. One may conclude Sabine's remark "For my own part, then, I must reserve the right to be a monist when I can and a pluralist when I must."

QUESTIONS FOR EXERCISE

1. "It is clear enough that the theory of the sovereignty of the state has broken down" — Lindsay. Discuss.
2. "It is impossible to make the legal theory of sovereignty valid for political philosophy" — Laski. Comment.
3. Explain and examine the view that "If pluralism is pressed for clarity, it must either accept the doctrine of sovereign state or else Anarchism."
4. Examine the grounds on which modern writers have adopted the orthodox conception of sovereignty.
5. "Society is federal, authority must be federal also." Examine the pluralist attacks on state sovereignty in the light of this statement.
6. "Pluralism bases its theory on a subject disease." Do you agree with this point of view?
7. "Pluralism has influenced theory more than practice." Explain and comment on this statement.
8. Political pluralists disagree with the definitions of sovereignty and law as given by John Austin. Why?
9. "The pluralist political philosophy transforms society into the anarchy of trade unions." Explain and discuss.

29

The Law and the State

Individualism

The attempts to define the limits of state authority have taken three different forms :

1. The theory that man has a definite sphere of private life in which there can be no interference of any kind from the state or government. All the familiar doctrines of individualism and such concepts as the ideas of natural rights, freedom of opinion and freedom of contract and the survival of the fittest are based on this view.

2. The theory that within any normal community are a number of social and economic groups which are at par with the state and that the state is one of the many associations, though an important one. These views constitute the substance of Pluralism.

3. The theory that the state is in fact and by right limited by 'law' and that law is superior and anterior to the state.

Law Above State

It has been known in all ages of political speculation that state decress and law are higher than the state. This was known to the Greeks. Most of the contemporary discussion of the relations of the state to law centres on 'the formal or orthodox or analytical theory of law'. According to this conception, laws are the commands of determinate political authorities. Bentham and Austin were the two principal exponents of this school. But jurists in the early nineteenth century were under the influence of the historical school of jurisprudence founded by German writer Hugo. They rejected the natural law doctrine of absolute, universal and unchangeable rules of law and put forward a new conception of law determined by the characteristics and experiences of particular people. "These laws they maintained", writes Coker, "have their origin neither in a universal and unchanging human reason nor in the decisions of contemporary agencies of government, but in a national will or mind that reveals itself in the orderly practices of a national community. Judges, informed by legal history, find that law and make their decisions accordingly.... Enacted law should be only a formal embodiment of historic law."[1] Thus, all laws are

1. Coker, W.F., *Recent Political Thought*, p. 523.

common law or case law. The ultimate sanctions of law are not the penalties prescribed by the courts or the legislatures but the habits, opinions and emotions of the people. Law is an instrument of human welfare. The rules demanded by the community and area are accompanied by the coercive authority of the government. A transition from the historical to the positivist conception of law in Germany and other countries led to the view that law is independent, superior and anterior to the state. Duguit, Krabbe and Laski placed law above the state and made it independent of the political authority.

The Positivist's Concept of Law

The utilitarians viewed law as simply a command of a determinate human superior or the sovereign whose authority was unlimited. While they did not deny the rational, moral and historical ingredients of law, they simply said that those could be maintained by deliberate political action. Law was only a means towards an end and the end was human welfare. It received its sanction from the compulsive and coercive power of the state. Customs become laws only when they get enacted by a competent political authority. Bentham and John Austin were the two pillars of this school. Karl Friedrich Von Gerber (1823-1891) held that German law is an expression of German juridical consciousness through the acts of tribunals and officials of the state. The sanctions applied by those organs of the state transformed the norms with legal rules. Law had no meaning apart from a system of political agencies which had the power to rule. Paul Laband (1838-1918) held that the authority of the state had no legal limits. The main function of the jurist is to find out what the law of the state is. This may be done by analysing objectively the commands of the legal sovereign. George Jellinek (1851-1911) held that the state is the corporate expression of an established people with an autonomous sovereignty or an autonomous corporation exercising territorial sovereignty. The true state is the supreme agency for realising a great human moral ideal. It does recognise its subservience to its great moral task and so voluntarily submits itself to law. All political organs act under the impulsion of cultural, intellectual and moral forces which determine the actual life and character of a state and influence the content and effectiveness of the law.

The later jurists began to view law as a part in the whole content of human life. These include three German jurists — Rudolf Vol Jhering, Rudolf Stammler and Joseph Kohler. They incorporated the positivist conception into sociological and philosophical theories of law.

RUDOLF VOL JHERING (1818—1892)

Acording to Jhering human institutions are to be explained by their purposes and not by their causes. End provides the key to the ways of human behaviour. Man's purposes may be individual or social. An individual is moved to action by self-interest as well as by a desire to help others. In the state the organisation of human purpose "attains its highest point and takes individual egoism into its service."[2] The state acts through law made for the masses. Law is a means to an end the interest of the society as a whole and not the right of any particular individual. The main object of law is social welfare. Laws are those rules which men apply in society through their political agency for the object of securing conditions necessary for the life and welfare of society. Laws are observed through the coercive authority of the state whereas moral precepts and social conventions need no such authority. The psychological supports of the state power are : "insight into necessity of political order; the sense of right and law; anxiety for the danger threatening persons and property in every disturbance of order; and fear of punishment."[3] Only those rules deserve the name of laws which have coercion. Since the state has the monopoly of coercion, only the rules of the state are laws. Thus, the stae is the only source of law.

RUDOLF STAMMLER

According to Stammler the main function of a jurist is to find out the criterion for right law. The end of law is the perfect community, as the end of moral doctrine is the perfect individual. Ethics inculcates good motives, purity of thought and perfection of the inner life. It makes a distinction between love and hatred, mercy and cruelty, honesty and dishonesty. On the other hand, law is indifferent to motives. It is concerned with the execution of contracts and the prevention of crimes and torts. Ethics operates through instinct and the regulation of intent while law operates through physical rewards and penalties. As Coker puts it, "Justice is the end of the law not because each law has or even is intended to have that end but because, within any community governed by law, there is a general recognition of the fact that law ought generally to tend to that end."[4] Thus, the jurist is directly concerned with the good faith of law. He is concerned not only with the actual law of the country but also with what a law ought to be, what laws should be made by the legislature and how the courts should decide the cases. Law is a social means to a social end. According to Stammler, right law is natural law with a variable content. Law changes infinitely from time to time and from country to country. However, an individual is bound by the law of his land, regardless of his consent. The end of law is not individual freedom, equality, happiness or moral goddness but 'a community of men willing freely.'[5] Law is prior to the state. It is autocratic social regulation.

JOSEPH KOHLER (1849—1919)

According to Kohler, law must be discovered empirically. There is no eternal or universal law. Law is always changing various institutions such as family, property, slavery, etc. Legal institutions are in accordance with the economic and social conditions and intellectual and ethical ideas prevailing at any time. Law is the product of 'totality of human achievements' in knowledge,

2. Jhering, *Law as Means to an End,* Translated by Issac Husk, 1913, p. 32.

3. *Ibid.*, p. 239.

4. Coker, *op. cit.*, p. 529.

5. Stammler, *The Philosophy of Law,* Translated by Adalbert Albrecht, p. 59.

literatrue, art, and religion. A philosophy of law msut set forth how at every stage of development definite legal institutions have embodied the cultural ideas then maintained. A jurist is concerened with the ideal as with the actual content of law. Law is both the product of culture and the means for further promoting it. Law is good or bad according to the measure in which it helps or retards the growth of culture....'the maximum of human knowledge and of creative power'.

According to Kohler the supreme function of the state is to promote culture in all its forms, directly for particular nation and indirectly for all humanity. Kohler gives an exalted position to the state. Defining law he says, "Law is the standard of conduct which, in consequence of the inner impulse which urges men toward a reasonable form of life emanates from the whole, and is forced upon the individual. It is distinguished from morals, customs, and religion as soon as the point is reached at which compulsory standards are separated from those demands that involve merely social amenity."[6] Law is the guardian of cultural values. All the activities of the state have the sanction of law.

LENON DUGUIT (1859—1928)

A great literary scholar, Duguit was an eminent teacher of law. He wrote *Treatise of Constitutional Law.* His book *Transformation of the Theory of the State*, was translated by Laski under the title "Law in the Modern State".

Sociological Standpoint

Duguit took a sociological or 'societal' view of law. Rule of Law is born from the need of social solidarity. Law is simply the name for the rules of conduct actually controlling men who live in society. "Its obligations", writes Coker, "arise not from having been commended expressly or by implication, by any organised authority but solely and directly from the necessities of social life. The obligations are ba ed upon the fact that men live in society and must so live in order to survive and that life in society requires a certain manner of conduct. If the advantages of social life are to be maintained, certain rules must be observed; otherwise society disintegrates. Men are naturally conscious of these rules and are impelled by self-interest to obey them. They are instinctively aware or learn naturally from experience that they have common needs and desires which can be satisfied only by living together; that they have diverse capabilities as a consequence of which their several needs can be satisfied only by an exchange of services; that, in short, they live longer and suffer less in association with other men. These facts constitute social solidarity."[7] Duguit thus condensed the rule of conduct arising out of social solidarity. "Do nothing to diminish social solidarity by similitude, or social solidarity through division of labour. Do everything materially practicable for the individual to increase

6. Kohler, *The : Philosophy of Law*, Translated by Adalbert Albrecht, p. 59.

7. Coker, *op. cit.*, pp. 533-34.

social solidarity in both its forms."[8] According to Ward, "Social solidarity for Duguit is almost metaphysical. It is the source of morals, the logical basis of law and expresses the essential significance of sociological groupings."[9] Laws are the conditions of social solidarity or the interdependence of man. They are the outcome of social living arising out of the nature and needs of human life. They are not enforced by any superior will. They are inherent in society. They are obeyed because they represent the necessary conditions of society and because they are the formal expression of social rules. The sanction behind them is psychological. It rest in each individual's awareness of the social approval or reprobation of his conduct according to its conformity or non-conformity to the fundamental social rules.

Law Prior to State

Duguit holds that law is not a creature of the state but is anterior to it born of the juridical consciousness of the people, it is product of social psychology. The mass of men given a norm a juridical content and make it law. It is not a command of the sovereign. Obligations to obey it arise not from the coercive authority but from the necessities of social life. Breach of law is prevented by the use of collective social force. The state is merely an agency of law. Its content changes from time to time and from place to place. "Law is independent of anterior to, above, and more comprehensive than the state",[10] writes Coker.

Types of Laws

According to Duguit, every law can be explained to some type of service. Laws are of three kinds — organic laws, penal laws and civil laws.

1. *Organic laws*. These provide for the internal organisation of the state such as constitutional and administrative laws.

2. *Penal laws*. These are prohibitive statutes addressed to the public citizens.

3. *Civil laws*. These are concerned with the services of police and justice. It organises the public services of justice.

Nature of the State

Duguit denies an independent personality to the state. The state personality is merely a fiction. The only real persons are human beings, bound together by social interdependence. The state is not sovereign. It is subject to limitations imposed by law, which is superior to the state. Law is obligatory not as the will of the state but because it serves social ends. Public service rather than sovereignty is the essential feature of the state. Like a private person, the state can be held legally responsible for its acts. To Duguit state is a cooperation of public services, organised and controlled by government. The acts of the government are valid to the extent that they conform to the rules of social solidarity. The force of government is justified only if it is employed to sustain law and

8. Duguit, L., *Modern French Legal Philosophy*, p. 296.
9. Ward, J., *Sovereignty*, p. 129.
10. Coker, *op. cit.*, p. 535.

promote social solidarity. The state and government are subject to law. They must not do anything which is injurious to social solidarity. They should do those things which promote social solidarity. As D.K. Bhandari rightly says, "Duguit's denial of sovereignty to the state was influenced by positivism, federalism, decentralization, syndicalism and internationalism."[11]

Limits to the Power of State

According to Duguit, there are both positive and negative jural limits to the power and authority of the state. The state acts unlawfully if its actions violate any of the rules of social solidarity. As the state acts through human agency which can commit faults; so it is liable to its faults. According to Gettell, Duguit "is not primarily interested in the political importance of social groups within the state; his chief interest lies in placing judicial limitations upon administrative action and in developing the theory of state responsibility."[12] His state is a legally limited agent.

Concept of Rights

Duguit did not accept rights as natural and universal. He conceived of rights in terms of duties and functions. Rule of law imposes both government and individuals negative and positive obligations which are essential for the promotion of social solidarity. The so-called rights to work, property and various kinds of freedoms are the functions of the individual.

Authority of Law *Vs.* State

Duguit distinguilshed between the authority of the state and authority of law. Both reflect facts. Both apply to men living in society. Both give rise to commands sustained by sanctions which secure habitual obedience. However, both differ fundamentally. The state represents the fact of a community living in a certain territory in which the stronger element imposes its will on and rules the weaker. Its power is sustained by physical penalties. Its authority is based on force and hence has no connection with law. Law is independent of, anterior to, above and more comprehensive than the state. Actions are lawful if they sustain the rule of law and promote social solidarity. The legal validity of an act depends upon the end which it serves.

Criticism of Duguit's Philosophy

Duguit's philosophy is subject to following criticisms :

1. Social solidarity. It may amount to replacing political absolutism by social monism. It will mean the absolutism of the expecting social order. There is never unanimity of individual wills.

2. Confused meaning of legal sovereignty. Duguit miserably fail to grasp the true meaning of legal sovereignty. He gave a poor view of the state and made the mess of the community the real maker of law. He wanted the state

11. Bhandari, D.R., *History of European Political Philosophy*, 8th ed., p. 522.

12. Gettell, L.G., *History of Political Thought*, p. 561.

to be responsible but forgot that this responsibility can only be political and not juridical.

3. No distinction between government and state. Dugict failed to make a distinction between government and state. For him the state is merely an abstraciton, the only reality is government. This is fundamentally wrong.

4. To refer all law to the notice of public service is meaningless. Law cannot be concerned solely with material needs. There is a sphere of humanitarian, aesthetic and spiritual considerations also with which law has to reckon. Duguit's law did not keep a balance between the individual and the state.

However, Duguit remains one of the most original and stimulating jurists. His enunciation of the principle of responsibility is a remarkable contribution to political thought.

HUGO KRABBE

Krabbe made an attempt to find out an ethical foundation for law. His important books are *The Theory of the Sovereignty of Law* and *The Modern Idea of the State.* He rejected the Austinian concept of state sovereignty and of law as the creature of state. In *The Modern Idea of the State* Krabbe succeeded in assigning sovereignty to law and in making the state its creature and agent. He gives law a source and sanction independent of political authority. He gave no separate authority to the state. The authority of state is the authority of law. Krabbe differed from Duguit who allowed the state a growth on sociological basis alongside law.

Nature of Law

According to Krabbe, law is the expression of one of the many judgments of value which human beings make by virtue of our disposition and nature. Krobbe said, "We obey law because it appears to us just and good and not because of fear of punishment which its disobedience involves." Law is what is just and good from our standard of value and judgment. It is not a matter of external legal authority but an internal human matter. The source of law is not the command of the sovereign, king or parliament, as law is objective and independent of the will of any individual or body of individuals. There is only one course of law and that is the sense of right. Upon this all law is based whether it is positive law or customary or unwritten law in general. Law not based on the sense of right is not law at all, even if it is obeyed voluntarily or by compulsion. Krabbe defined Law as the "totality of rules, general or particular, written or unwritten which spring from men's feeling or sense of right."[13] But it is not the individual's sense of right. Law is the rule of the community. As the community exists for some social end so it postulates unity of legal rule. This is possible only if there is a substantial agreement between members of the community regarding what is right. This agreement is reached by the majority principle. According to Krabbe, "Since there cannot be a single rule

13. Krabbe, H., *The Modern Idea of the State*, p. 39.

except by recognizing the principle of the majority, the communal life, which controls our consciousness and makes the sense of right effective in us, carries with it the obligation to govern our conduct according to the rule approved by the majority."[14] Thus, law is that which is demanded by the sense of right of the right-minded majority. Unity of law is very essential. Law cannot include rules which are mutually contradictory. When there is a representative assembly the sense of right of each of its members has an equal value in law-making. The rule approved by the majority becomes the rule of the community. Nothing is really law except what proceeds from the sense of right. In enacting a law, legislature simply gives a concise form to the sense of right. Members of the rightly constituted legislature are the best judges for determining what the sense of right of the community is. If the legislature is defective in organisation the people may either revolt and disobey such laws or modify laws by unwritten law or customs or by judge and juries. A law which does not embody the social sense of right will encounter social opposition, suffer wide disobedience and thus become inoperative.

Authority of Law

Krabbe accepted no valid authority except that of law. Sovereign disappears as a source of law from both legal and political theory. He assigned sovereignty to law which is independent of the state. The state has come to being and has its authority because of law. The state is a creature of law and subordinate to it. A community becomes a state because the rule of law binds its members together and regulates the relations between its individuals and associations. Every holder of public office is an agent of law. His authority and powers are derived from law. The government is a creature of sovereign law. The state is a legal community with its own body of laws and legal relations. Law and not power is the essential attribute of the state.

International Law

Krabbe held international law as fully valid as national law. Both stand in the same position. The binding force of international law is based upon its spiritual and moral nature. It springs from the sense of right. But while in national law the community is small in internatioal law, the community is world-wide. As the international community is not well organised as yet, so international law lacks the character of real laws. In due course the nation states would overstep their national limits and federate themselves into one state of the world. It is possible only when a world sense of right is created. The sense of right must extend itself to international affairs.

Contribution to Political Thought

Krabbe's point of view is essentially similar to that of Duguit. He tried to separate law and political sovereignty from one another. His sense of right is a universal human impulse which calls forth a specific reaction with respect to

---

14. *Ibid.*, p. 78.

our own behaviour and that of other men. However, his theory of law, suffers from a serious flaw. Law is not merely what a common sense of right demands or what the community demands. It is something which is prescribed. Sense of right is incapable of producing specific laws. There is need for some political authority to give legal shape to rules of conduct. That authority must be backed by coercive power.

"There appears to be nothing essential to conclude with Coker, in the juristic doctrines of Duguit, Krabbe, or Laski that is inconsistent with theories either of the strictly analytical jurists (*e.g.*, Austin and Laband) or of those who adhere to the analyst's definition, yet study broadly the social origins and consequences of the laws. Each group acknowledges the existence and significance of the normative rules, the other calls laws. The anti-positivists recognize explicitly or implicitly, that there are differences of great practical significance between politically supported rules and the rules enforced only by other forms of social pressure. The positivists recognize that law-enacting assemblies or deciding judges act under the impulsions and restraints of opinions and sentiments, current in the community or in its 'most influential part'."[15] No jurist scholar makes the state a general arbiter of right or wrong. All jurists now take law as an instrument for the promotion of human welfare. All recognize the varied social and psychological sources of law. Laws reflect the ideas and wishes of the people — the rulers and the ruled. All the jurists clothe the state with the function of unification and co-ordination and make it comprehensive and compulsive in its membership. Law may not originate in the state, may be independent of it but it receives its sanction from the state.

QUESTIONS FOR EXERCISE

1. Explain the relationship of law and the state.
2. Discuss the views of Duguit about the nature of law.
3. How does Hugo Krabbe explain the authority of law ?

15. Coker, *op. cit.*, p. 539.

30

Harold J. Laski (1893—1950)

Harold Laksi, the second son of Nathan and Sarah Laski, was born in a Jewish community on June 30, 1893. This was the period when different ideologies, such as Utilitarianism, Fabian Socialism and Communism were spreading to reforming the various prevalent conceptions regarding sovereignty, parliamentary democracy and economic and political liberties of the individual. Laski, the product of such a period, imbibed its spirit fully. As a young boy he spent most of his time reading books on science and liberalism. They predisposed him to oppose all orthodox opinions and dogmas regarding the social and political institutions. Right from his birth to death in 1950, Harold J. Laski was concerned mainly with the liberty and rights of the individual. It is interesting to note that the political movements which imposed young Laski in his undergraduate days, and to which he constantly referred in his early articles, were the Women's Suffrage Movement, Trade Union Movement in France and the alliance between Ulster and a section of the Conservative Party to sabotage the Liberals' Home Rule Legislation for Ireland. These movements of the per-war period were rooted in a violent outburst against the spirit of Victorian Liberalism. In this period the belief in the gradual progress in the status of women and the respect for constitutional procedures were rejected by the more violent suffragettes and the radical trade unionists. It seemed as if the orderliness and respectability of the nineteenth century had become such a strain on the feelings of a number of men that they were trying to destroy the liberal world in which they lived. It was at this period that Laski spent his formative years in school and college, and he became a rebel against such an atmosphere. He felt the need to dedicate his life to find out a new world with a view to relieving the down-trodden common man from want, ignorance and misery that were noticed as the common feature of the Victorian era. He took part in Suffragette Movement and helped the strike of chain-makers by collecting money. At this time, though he remained content with constitutional agitation, yet the idea of revolution was agitating his mind. He wrote a short book with the title *The Chosen People* (which remains unpublished) in which he told that we should welcome the ideas of Darwin and Marx in order to get rid of the traditional outlook that had become outworn. Further, he maintained that social truth could only be discovered in an atmosphere of freedom.

Influences on Laski

Laski's first book was a translation of Leon Duguit's book, *Law in the*

Modern State, on political pluralism from French. At the same time, he was greatly influenced by the writings of the late F.W. Maitland while studying history at Oxford. Ernest Barker was mainly responsible for it. Barker, his tutor, himself being interested in the academic revolt against Hegelianism, encouraged him in his study of medieval lawyers. Gierke, Maitland, Figgis had justified the theory of corporate personality as applied to religious and industrial organizations in society. Laski drew inspiration from them, and his earlier writings were devoted to the task of supporting the theory of corporate personality of religious bodies and guilds which were able to maintain their rights and independence against the state in the Middle Ages. He argued that trade unions should have a similar position in the modern society. But his theory of groups was different from that Figgis, Gierke and Maitland. It was purely individualistic in essence, because he maintained it for safeguarding individual liberty. For this purpose he also made a special study of the legal system which protects the rights of associations and free speech in America.

Laski's Scholarship

Professor Harold Joseph Laski ranks as one of the most outstanding political thinkers, teachers and publicists of our times. As a teacher he won great popularity and was highly stimulating. He exercised tremendous influence on a whole generation of students both in America and England. Students from all parts of the world flocked to the London School of Economics and found themselves privileged to study under his guidance. Besides being a reputed political thinker and teacher, Laski was also an effective speaker and a great publicist. He was also active in politics of his country, associated with the Labour Party. In 1945 he became its Chairman. He valued friendship and he had a number of prominent personalities as his personal friends. One of the Chief features of his life was that he was a rebel from his youth. He revolted against his father in marrying Frida Kerry, a Christian girl while he was a Jew. Because of his rebellious tendencies he abandoned Fabianism and moved towards pluralism and socialism of the left. In spite of his being very active in politics he succeeded in writing a very large number of books, some of which have become classics today.

Laski's political ideas underwent modifications and changes as conditions changed from time to time in Europe, America, Asia and elsewhere. At successive stages of his career he was an advocate of Pluralism, Fabianism and Marxian-socialism. It is very difficult to say what he exactly was before his death. But the ideals cherished as a boy, remained the same throughout his life. Deane writes, "Throughout his life the ultimate ideals that Laski cherished remained the same, and he pursued them with great zeal and unusual selfishness. He wanted to see human suffering, ignorance, and poverty alleviated; he wanted every man to have the opportunity to develop his potentialities in man to have the opportunity to develop his potentialities in his own way; and he hoped for the growth of a spirit of sympathy and understanding the men's relationships with their follows. His fundamental goals won the principles of the French Revolution — liberty, equality and fraternity."[1]

Works by Laski

Studies in the Problem of Sovereignty; Authority in the Modern State; Political thought from Locke to Bentham; Foundations of Sovereignty; A Grammar of Politics; Communism; Liberty in the Modern State; The Dangers of Obedience; Where Socialism Stands today; Recovery Through Revolution; Democracy in Crisis; The State in Theory and Practice; The Rise of European Liberalism; An Introduction to Politics; Karl Marx; Parliamentary Government in England; Reflections on the Constitution; Reflections on the Revolution of Our Time; The Socialist Tradition in the French Revolution; Studies in Law and Politics; Where Do We Go From Here; The American Democracy; The American Presidency; Communist Manifesto; Nationalism and *The Future of Civilization; Marx and Today; The Dilemma of our Times.*

Source of Thought

Laski drew his inspiration from many sources. Teachings of Maitland and Barker inspired him for his pluralism. From Morris Cohen's writings he got the inspiration to move from pluralism to new type of social organization in which the truly federal nature of society receives instruction of expression. From Hobhouse he got his theory of ethics and the ethical foundations for his doctrine of federal authority. Liberal tradition, especially the teachings of Locke, Burke, Bentham and J.S. Mill wielded tremendous influence upon Laski. His *Theory of Rights* is Mill restated. Finally, Marx and Lenin brought great change in his thinking. After 1930 he became more and more Marxist. He accepted whatever was good in Marxism-Leninism surplus value, theory of revolution. He rejected whatever was bad theory of class struggle, dialectics and the theory of party. Thus, his was a theory of many mixtures.

Nature of State and Political Power

Laski studied in the *Problem of Sovereignty, Authority in the Modern State* and *Foundation of Sovereignty*. There are implications of Austinian that contain his criticism of the concept of state sovereignty. He attempted to destroy the monistic view of state sovereignty as expounded by Bodin, Hobbes, Austin and many others.

According to Laski, there are three implications of Austin's theory of sovereignty. He writes, "The State for Austin is a legal order in which there is a determinate authority acting as the ultimate source of power. Its authority, secondly, is unlimited. It may act unwisely, or dishonestly, or in an ethical sense, unjustly....command, thirdly, is of the essence of law. You must do certain things: you must not do other things. Failure to fulfil in either direction your obligation is punished by a penalty".[2] As regards the first and second

1. Deane, H.A., *The Political Ideas of Harold J. Laski* (New York, Columbia University Press), p. 340.

2. Laski, H., *A Grammar of Politics*, 4th ed., pp. 50-51.

implications, Laski regarded the Austinian theory as artificial to the point of absurdity. He wrote, "No sovereign has anywhere possessed unlimited power; and the attempt to exert it has always resulted in the establishment of safeguards. Even the Sultan of Turkey in the height of his power was himself bound down by a code of traditional observance, obedience to which was practically compulsory upon him. In law there was no part of the field of social fact he could not alter; his practice be survived by willing not to will those changes which might have proved him the sovereign of Austinian jurisprudence."[3]

Third Implication

As regards the third implication, according to Laski, "To think, more over of law as simply a command, is, even for the jurist, to strain definition to the verge of decency."[4] Uniformity is the chief feature of law. It is the same for both the legislators and the subjects but it is not so with the command. It separates the giver from one who obeys the command. The person who gives the command is not bound by it. It is very difficult to see how the exercise of delegated authority can be brought within the ambit of the Austinian definition.

State Sovereignty Ethically Unsound

Laski found the idea of state sovereignty as ethically unsound. According to him, "The Austinian theory of sovereignty ungenial enough even in its abstract presentation, would as a fact breed simple servility were it capable of practical application."[5] The total obedience to the dictates of the state is likely to stunt the development of each citizen's personality and moral stature. The attempt to magnify the authority of the state, according to Laski, has resulted in "The implicit acceptance of a certain grim Hegelianism which has swept us unprotestingly on into the vortext of a great All which is more than ourselves."[6]

Incompatible

The concept of state sovereignty was regarded by Laski as incompatible with the interests of humanity. He wrote, "The notion of an independent sovereign state is on the international side, fatal to the well-being of humanity. The way in which a state should live its life in relation to other states is clearly not a matter in which that state is entitled to be the sole judge....It is, enough, for the moment, to postulate the disappearance of state sovereignty as the conditions without which the life of reason is impossible in states."[7]

Against Centralisation

Laski had great distrust of power and of those who exercised it. So he desired to prevent its concentration at any single point and this led him to

3. *Ibid.*, p. 51.
4. Laski, H., *A Grammar of Politics*, 4th ed., p. 51.
5. Laski, H., *Studies in the Problem of Sovereignty*, p. 273.
6. *Ibid.*, p. 208.
7. Laski, H., *A Grammar of Politics*, p. 65.

attack the notion of state sovereignty. His aim was "to see power split up, divided, set against itself, and thrown widespread among men by various devices of decentralization, and he wants to be certain that the civil, economic, and social rights of individuals and groups are insured against the encroachments of those who exercise power."[8] According to Laski the good of the governed demands that the state ought to be responsible for its actions. There is no permanent right to power. An unconditional power has always proved disastrous to those over whom it is exercised. Power corrupts and absolute power corrupts absolutely. Laski wrote, "The state is not itself an end, but merely the means to an end, which is realised only in the enrichment of human lives. Its power and the allegiance it can win depend always upon what it achieves for that enrichment....Realisable good means always some happiness won for the lives of persons, or it means nothing. Power, therefore, must seek the widest possible distribution of such happiness."[9]

ALL AUTHORITY IS FEDERAL

From his attack on the theory of state sovereignty Laski developed another doctrine 'All Authority is Federal.' That there is no authority which can claim absolute control over individuals. The state can only exercise a partial control over the lives of individuals. Man's wants may be political, economic, social or religious. In order to fulfil these multifarious wants men join various associations which cater to the satisfaction of these wants. The State can satisfy only the political needs of the people. Each of the associations make only a partial contribution to the development and enrichment of men's personality. Hence, allegiance to various associations must be partial and proportional to its contribution. Rights and powers are relative to functions. As society is essentially federal in nature, it is impossible and unwise to attempt to confine sovereignty to the state or to any of the co-ordinate groups that constitute society. According to Laski, "The group is real in the same sense as the state is real. It has, that is to say, an interest to promote, a function to serve. The state does not call it into being. It is not, outside the categories of law, dependent upon the state. It grows in the whole environment as a natural response to the factors in that environment. It lives and moves as its surrounding circumstances seem to warrant".[10] The group possesses its own personality and it lives, not apart from its members but in and through what they do. According to laski, These groups "Determine, quite loyally, his choice of friends, of opportunities, of a career. They drive roads through life along which a little timidly and dubiously, he makes his way to his goal....They evoke, accordingly a loyalty which, not seldom goes down to the very roots of his being. They give him a feeling that he has found himself a power of recognition that is an invalauble factor in the achievement of personal harmony".[11] The groups are voluntary bodies. They

8. *Ibid.*, p. 17.

9. Laski, H., *A Grammar of Politics*, p. 88.

10. *Ibid.*, 3rd ed., p. 256.

11. Laski, H., *A Grammar of Politics*, pp. 256-57.

lack the coercive power. The authority of any group is based, upon the living and spontaneous trust it can command. The society does not present itself as a unity, authority is found to be federal everywhere. Even in the matter of legislation, the work cannot be given to any single individual. Laski wrote, "Legal right has no meaning for the individual save as he himself makes it have meaning. It has no sanctions save the authority he lends to it by articulating it with his own experience. We are loyal to the demands of the state just to the degree that the articulation accomplished results for us in a satisfied activity....The state, that is to say, must make its law valid, must discover what I have called the legality of law by compounding it from the experiences of its citizens. It can only do so by associating them with the process of law-making".[12] Thus, Laski regarded state as one of the many associations whose function is not the regulation of the whole life of man but of co-ordination only. He said, "No group including the state has total claim upon my loyalty. No group can ignore the wishes of its members."

THE PROBLEM OF OBEDIENCE

On the problem of obedience Laski's view changed as his thought developed from his early liberalism to Marxism of later days. According to Laski in modern society the state and many other groups are engaged in struggle. The will of the state is merely a competitor with the wills of other groups. The expression of the state's will has no pre-eminence over the expression of the will of any other group in society. Laski wrote, "Whenever in a state a group of persons large enough to make its presence felt demands the recognition of certain claims, it will not recognise a law which attempts defiance of them; nor will it accept the authority by which that law is enforced."[13] Thus, Laski rejected the plea of idealists that by its nature and purpose state is morally entitled to the undivided allegience and absolute obedience of the individual. According to Laski, the individual is himself the sole judge whether a given act of the state fulfils its purpose or not, and if his conscience tells him that it does not do so he should refuse obedience to it. Laski accepted Newman's principle: "Man should do that which he deems morally right, and the only obedience he can render is the obedience consonant with his ethical standards."[14] He applied this theory to the state thus: "The only ground for state success is where the purpose of the state is morally superior to that of its opponent. The only ground upon which the individual can give or be asked his support from the state is from the conviction that what it is aiming at is, in each particular action, good. We deny, that is to say, that the general end of the ideal state colours the policy of a given act of a special state. And that denial involves from each member of the state continuous scrutiny of its purpose and methods."[15] All this means, according to Deane, that "each citizen must examine the

12. *Ibid.*, p. 251.

13. Laski, H., *Authority in the Modern State*, p. 44.

14. Laski, H., *Studies in the Problem of Sovereignty*, p. 206.

15. Laski, H., *Authority in the Modern State*, pp. 45-46.

purpose of every action of the state in order to determine whether it is 'morally superior' to other purposes; he should obey the state only if he is convinced that the aim of a given state act is a good, that is, consonant with his ethical standards."[16]

Criticism of Laski's View

Laski's solution of the problem is too individualistic. It makes man not law-abiding but law-breaking. It makes social life impossible. Every individual is not morally or intellectually so strong and advanced as to be able to judge the moral worth of state actions. It will produce a state of anarchy. Laski's doctrine of obedience fraught with great danger. As Deane wrote, "We cannot accept the view that each man must be allowed to act in accordance with his own view of right or justice even though the heavens may fall or the state may perish in the process."[17]

SHIFT IN LASKI'S POSITION

In his *Grammar of Politics* Laski shifted his position and began his analysis of the problem of obedience by considering man not as an isolated being but as a social being. If men are to live in peace, there must be rules to regulate their social relations and a government to enforce the obervance of these rules. Laski wrote, "Man finds himself, in the mordern world, living under the authority of governments : and the obligation to obey their orders arises from the facts of his nature. For he is a community-building animal, driven by inherited instinct to live with his fellows."[18] He further said, "That no effort involved in the peaceful maintenance of a common life does not permit the making of private decisions upon what the society deems essential to its existence. At some points, that is, spontaneity ceases to be practical, and the enforced acceptance of a common way of action becomes the necessary condition of a corporate civilisation."[19] Thus, according to Laski, the state exists for the promotion of common social interests and securing to each individual the enjoyment of rights which are necessary for his self-development. Its actions are right to the degree that they maintain rights. It forfeits its claim, to the allegiance of its members when it is either indifferent about them, or wedded to their limitation. But Laski said "The right of disobedience is, of course, reasonably to be exercised only at the margins of political conduct. No community could hope to fulfil its purpose if rebellion became a settled habit of the population."[20] In the same breath he said, "That no community could hope to fulfil its purpose unless the will of its government were limited in a variety of ways. It must answer at stated periods to those from whom it derives its power."[21]

16. Deane, H.A., *The Political Ideas of Harold Laski*, p. 37.
17. *Ibid.*, p. 40.
18. Laski, H., *A Grammar of Politics*, p. 17.
19. *Ibid.*, p. 18.
20. *Ibid.*, p. 62.
21. *Ibid.*, p. 62

Thus, one finds a lot of confusion in Laski's views on the problem of obedience. But one cannot disagree with him when he said, "The state as it was and is, finds the roots of allegiance in all the complex facts of human nature; and a theory of obedience would have to weigh them differently for each epoch in the history of state if it won to approximate to the truth."[22] By 1931 Laski was shifting the ground of obedience away from the moral adequacy of the state's commands as judged by the individual and making the obligaiton to obey contingent on the ability of the state to provide to each individual at least a minimum of material well-being. As the years passed Laski, under the influence of Marxism, laid emphasis more and more upon the social and economic aspects of man's life.

The Final Phase

The final phase of Laski's doctrine of obedience started from 1932 onward when he adopted the Marxian position. To quote Deane, "His individualistic theory of obedience disappears from his wiritings and the focus of his attention shifts from the individual to the class. He is interested not in the minority that refuses in the name of conscience to obey, but in the conditions under which the great majority, the proletariat, will withdraw their allegiance from the state that exists to protect the interests of their exploiters."[23] Laski was against the present day capitalist democracy which means increasing privation for an ever-expanding proletariat. Laski supported the worker's right to revolt against the system. However, "His adoption of a purely materialistic standard of judgement is a fatal error",[24] writes Deane. Laski's doctrine of obedience is as much full of inconistencies as his doctrine of the state.

THE CONCEPT OF RIGHTS

Nature of Rights

Laski made citizen's duty of allegiance to the state contingent upon the extent to which it succeeds in promoting good life for him. The only way in which it can promote good life is by promoting and maintaining those external conditions of life which are most favourable for the development of the personalities of its citizens. These external conditions are called Rights. As Laski said, "Every state is known by the rights it maintains. Over method of judging its character lies, above all, in the contribution that it makes to the substance of man's happiness."[25] But the state does not create rights. It simply recognises them. Rights do not mean "the reflection of a natural order which lies behind the shifting appearance of contemporary society. For such an order cannot be permanent in a world in which science changes at a pace so rapid as we have come to expect."[26] Rights also do not mean satisfaction of desires

22. Laski, H., *A Grammar of Politics*, p. 22.
23. Deane, H.A., *op.cit.*, p. 172.
24. *Ibid.*, p. 178.
25. Laski, H., *A Grammar of Politics*, p. 89.
26. *Ibid.*, pp. 89-90.

as Hobbes held. Laski rejected Bentham's view of rights. The legal theory of rights will not tell us whether the rights recognised are the rights which need recognition. Rights, according to Laski, "are those conditions of social life without which no man can seek, in general, to be himself at his best."[27] The ends of the state are secured only by maintaining of the rights. Rights are prior to the state in the sense that they are there whether they are recognised or not. They are not natural in the sense that a permanent and unchanging catalogue of them can be prepared. They are historical in the sense that, at some given period and place, they were demanded by the character of civilisation. They are natural in the sense that the facts demand their recognition. According to Laski, "They have a content which changes with time and place. They win their way the more securely they can justify themselves in the facts about them."[28]

Rights and Duties

Rights are rights because they are useful for the purpose of the state. They may be opposed to the existing social, moral, economic and political order in a country. Their validity cannot be challenged because they are necessary for the progress of the people concerned. According to Laski, the individual has rights against the state. He said, "The citizen has claims upon the state. It must observe his rights. It must give him those conditions without which he cannot be that best self that he may be."[29] This does not give the guarantee that his best self will be attained. At the maximum the hindrances to its attainment shall be removed by the state as far as possible. The possession of rights does not mean possession of claims which are empty of all duties. Rights and duties are co-related. Our rights are not independent of society, but inherent in it. Thus, rights are co-relative with functions. Laski wrote, "He who will not perform functions, cannot enjoy rights any more than he who will not work ought to enjoy bread."[30]

Objectives of Rights

It is the duty of the state to secure minimum rights for each of its citizens, without which it is impossible for individuals to live a creative life. Thus, rights are built upon individual personality. The welfare of the community is built upon the happiness of the individual. One cannot have rights against the public welfare. According to Laski, "For any social order which fails consistently to recognise the claims of personality is built upon a foundation of sand. Sooner or later it will provoke the dissent of those whose nature is frustrated by its policy. Its disasters will become their opportunity. For to deny the claims of right is to sacrifice the claim to allegiance. The state can exercise moral authority upon no other basis."

27. *Ibid.*, p. 92.
28. *Ibid.*, p. 93.
29. *Ibid.*, p. 97.
30. *Ibid.*, p. 102.

Safeguarding of Rights

Som people hold that rights are safeguarded if they are embodied in the written constitution. Laski rejected this view. He said, "Musty parchments will doubtless give them greater sanctity; they will not ensure their realisation."[31] The maintenance of rights is much more a question of habit and tradition than of the formality of written enactment. Rights have their best safeguards in the eager spirit of the citizens to safeguard their rights. Eternal vigilance is the price of liberty.

Conditions of Rights

According to Laski, following three general conditions facilitate the task of guaranteeing rights to the people:

1. A decentralised state. The state organs which exercise power must not be concentrated at a single point in the body-politic. Local questions must be settled by local people. There may be central inspection but no dictation from the centre. To concentrate power at any point where it can, is to oepn the door to the abuse of authority.

2. The central government should be surrounded by a number of advisory bodies. It means the organised and prior consultation of all interests which are likely to be affected by a decision it is proposed to take. But consultation must not be selective consultation. A nominated advisory body is of no use. According to Laski, "Consultation means eliciting opinions from representatives nominated by the bodies concerned."[32]

3. No state interference in Associations. The state should refrain from interfering in the internal life of other associations as far as possible. There should be no interference as long as other associations are peaceful and do not indulge in violent activities with the aim to overthrow the government.

Aspect of System of Rights

Any system of rights has three essential aspects : the interest of the individual, the interest of the group and the interest of the community which is the total result of the whole pressure of social forces. Thus, the state must enforce and interpret the common rules concerning the community but it must ensure that both group and individual are safeguarded in their freedom.

Laski's definition of rights changed after 1930. He modified his old concept and declared rights as "condition without which, in the light of the historic experience, the individual lacks assurance that he can attain happiness."[33] But, here he failed to define happiness.

Essential Rights of the Citizen

Laski has discussed only those rights which are absolutely essential for the development of men's personality. They must be possessed by man if he is, in

31. *Ibid.*, p. 103.

32. *Ibid.*, p. 133.

33. *Ibid.*, p. 45.

any creative way, to contribute his share to the common stock of welfare. These rights are the following :

1. The right to work. According to Laski, "The citizen has a right to work. He is born into a world, if rationally organised, he can live only by the sweat of his brow. Society owes him the occasion to perform his function. To leave him without access to the means of existence is to deprive him of that which makes possible the realisation of personality."[34] But this means the right to be occupied in producing some share of those goods and sevices which are useful to society. It means that the state must ensure every body against unemployment.

2. The right to adequate of wages. It means that "a man has not only the right to work. He has the right also to be paid an adequate wage for his labour. By the work that he performs he must be able to secure a return capable for purchasing the standard of living without which creative citizenship is impossible."[35] But it does not mean equality of income. The fixation of adequate wage should be left to an impartial authority, neither to the employer nor to the employee.

3. The right to reasonable hours of work. Laski wrote, "The right to reasonable hours of labour is the right to discover the land of the mind. It is the key to the intellectual heritage of the race."[36] Of course, the term reasonable may means differently with different people in different countries with different productive systems. Forty hours a week has come to be accepted as reasonable.

4. The right to education. "First of all things, I place education. Certainly in the modern world the citizen who lacks it is bound to be the slave of others. He will not be able to convince his fellows. He will not be able to restrain his nature into those paths along which it is best fitted to travel. He will not rise to the full height of his personality. He will go through life a stunted being whose impulses have never been ordered by reason into creative experiment."[37] But this does not mean the right to an identical intellectual training for all citizens. Every individual must be given that minimum of education which is essential for the performance of his duties by him. It means provision of at least elementary education for all and free of cost. Laski wrote, "A citizen must be trained to make judgments. He must learn to weigh evidence. He must learn to choose between the alternatives between which he is called to decide. He must be made to feel that this is a world in which he can by the use of his mind and will shape at once outline and substance."[38]

5. The right to political power. This right means three things, that every body has the right to vote, the right to be elected as a representative and the right to assume office and run the administrative machinery. According Laski,

34. *Ibid.*, p. 106.

35. *Ibid.*, p. 107.

36. *Ibid.*, p. 111.

37. *Ibid.*, p. 114.

38. *Ibid.*, p. 118.

neither sex nor property, neither race, nor creed, ought to prevent the citizen from aiding in the choice of his rulers. This power belongs equally to all. No class is good enough to legislate for the other class. The right to be chosen as a governor implies as well the right to be chosen for political office.

6. The right to freedom of speech. According to Laski, A political system in which the pivot is the right of the citizen to the articulate about his wants clearly requires to safeguard his articulateness. There must be, that is to say, freedom of speech with all that makes freedom of speech effective."[39] But the right of freedom of speech does not mean the right to free scandal-mongering. The exercise of this right will enable man to ventilate his grievances and organise public opinion in its favour. A government must not be afraid of its criticism. Laski wrote, "A government can always learn more from the criticism, of its opponents than from the eulogy of its supporters. To prepage that criticism is — at least ultimately — to propose its own destruction."[40]

7. The right to freedom of association and public meeting. Laski wrote, "Legally to prevent men from associating as communists does not prevent them so associating. It serves only to make the forms of communist activity more difficult to discover. To prohibit a meeting on the ground that the peace may be disturbed is, in fact, to enthrone intimidation in the seat of power."[41] Every government is entitled to ban or even destroy any group that seekes to usurp its authority violently but as Laski worte, "No government ought, in its purely executive aspect to be the sole judge of whether its action is right. It ought always to be compelled to the submission of proof; and it ought always to be compelled to the submission of proof under the fullest judicial safeguards."[42]

8. The right to judicial safeguards. Rights can be maintained only if the citizen is provided with full judicial safeguards. In their absence rights become meaningless. Laski wrote, "There is rarely a better index to the quality of state life that the justice it offers to its citizens. It must be a justice without discrimination. It must not be harder upon the poor than upon the rich. It must organise the fullest means of defence for those charged with the commission of crime. It must not set apart the acts of its officials into a category different from that of other men. It must itself answer in its own courts. The sovereignty of the state must never mean that it is not amenable to law....The judiciary must be able to deal with every complaint of offence without distinction of persons. The rule of law, in brief, is fundamental; and the rule of law means that no person, and no office however exalted, are exceptions to the rule of law."[43] The judiciary must be independent and that there should be no union of the judicial and executive functions.

9. The right to property. According to Laski, "If property must be

39. *Ibid.*, p. 121.

40. *Ibid.*, p. 123.

41. *Ibid.*, p. 122.

42. *Ibid.*, p. 123.

43. *Ibid.*, pp. 128-129.

possessed in order that a man may be his best self, the existence of such a right is clear."[44] One has the right to it to the extent it is desirable for the growth of his personality. So Laski admitted a limited right to property.

CONCEPT OF PROPERTY

Value of Property Rights

According to Laski, "The root instinct of man is self-preservation. Because he must guard himself from danger he has developed an acquisitive faculty which now forms the basis of all Western institutions. The world over, states are divisible into those who, out of that impulse to acquire, possess property which is a foreguard against the wants of the morrow, and those who, lacking that property, are uncertain whether the morrow will give them the means of life."[45] A man of property has security against starvation. He can afford to pursue intellectual and social luxury of choice. He is free from the spectre of fear. The ownership of property involves the control of capital which involves the power to direct the lives of those who depend upon the application of capital to production. In the capitalist society the so-called rights are really the rights of the men of property only. The propertyless man has, as a matter of fact, no rights. According to Laski, "The present system is inadequate from whatever angle it is regarded. It is psychologically inadequate because, for most, by appealing mainly to the emotion of fear, it inhibits the exercise of those qualities which would enable them to live a full life. It is morally inadequate, in part because it confers right upon those who have done nothing to earn them, in past because when such rights are related to effort, this in its turn has no proportionate relevancy to social value....It is economically inadequate because it fails so to distribute the wealth it creates as to offer the necessary conditions of health and security to those who live by its process. In the result, it has lost the allegience of the vast majority of the people."[46]

Justification of the Present System of Property

1. Incentive to Work. It makes people work and work more, thereby resulting in the increased good of the community. But society gains nothing if only harmful things are produced for sake of profit only. The power to acquire property may defeat more incentive that it creates.

2. Ethically sound. It is the return made to the individual for his effort. Whatever man gains on account of his hard labour, rightfully belong to him. But a thing invented or produced may be harmful to society or in its production many hands may have participated with insignificant return for their work.

3. Full of virtues essential to society. Love of one's family, generosity, energy, inventiveness, etc. are not such which cannot be acquired by propertyless

44. *Ibid.*, p. 130.

45. *Ibid.*, p. 173.

46. *Ibid.*, p. 216.

man. There is no connection between the two. Sometimes rich people have no domestic peace whereas poor people live in contentment.

4. Result of supplying effective demand. But demand of every type cannot and should not be met.

5. Historical justification. All progressive societies are those which are built upon the regime of private property and the backward societies are generally built upon collective basis. But such a view is fallacious. Property in slaves was valid in Greece and Rome in ancient times, but no longer valid today. The right to property has never been absolute in any period.

DOCTRINE OF REWARD

Laski divided theories of reward into three classes.

1. Communist case for equality of income. All the distinctions rest upon an arbitrary foundation. It is very difficult to estimate the price of services of a judge or a bricklayer. Laski rejected the theory of equality of income. According to him, "There seems no justice in an equal reward for unequal effort. Nor does it seem just to reward equally where needs are unequal. The miserly bachelor, the church devoted spinster, ought not, surely to receive the same remuneration as the parents who have five or six children to maintain."[47] This theory is built upon sandy foudations.

2. Remuneration should be fixed by the higgling of the market. The operation of the forces of demand and supply should determine the wages of a labourer. This theory is also rejected by Laski. According to him, "Supply and demand would only be a true index to income if there was an equal opportunity to apply for the post applied."[48] Then it is not morally adequate test of worth. The labourers are not in a position to bargain. The theory can always work in the interest of employers who can wait. Then there are services which cannot be paid in money terms, but paid in moral coins.

3. Reward according to needs. Each person should contribute to society according to his powers, and be rewarded by society according to his needs. This doctrine, lacks reality. Needs cannot be the same for all persons. So the theory must be rejected.

Laski's Own Theory

After rejecting all the three theories Laski gave his own doctrine. According to him, "Any principle of reward must satisfy the two complex conditions, that it enables the individual to reach out towards his best self, while, simultaneously, it preserves and develops the necessary functions of society."[49] There is need to reconcile the interests of the individual with that of the community. There must be a primary level in remuneration, a point below which no person can be permitted to fall who is capable of acting as a citizen. No person can be

47. *Ibid.*, pp. 189-90.

48. *Ibid.*, pp. 190-191.

49. *Ibid.*, p. 195.

permitted to secure remuneration except on the condition of performing work recognised as useful. Laski wrote, "Once he perrorms work recognised as necessary he must be entitled to a reward which gives him the means of civic completeness. It must keep him in good wealth. It must give him room for the development of his faculties. It must enable him to build a home and pay such family costs as the community does not provide. Such a reward is inherent in his quality as a human being."[50]

Critical Evaluation

Laski's theory of reward applies equally to a collectivist and a non-collectivist society. It is a general principle of justice. It assumes that all are equally entitled to find the means of full life and that beyond those means differences must be required by the common good of society.

Laski follows the middle course about the view that no man is entitled to wealth he has not earned. Industry should be carried on in the interest of the community and not for making profits. This may take the form of nationalisation or co-operative production. Compensation paid must be to the extent that it guarantees to the person whose property is taken a living according to the same standard as he was living before the acquisition of his property by the state. Of course on the owner's death there is to be reduction in the amount of money to be paid to his family. His children must be enabled to stand on their own legs.

According to Laski the existing institution of property is wrong because, "it is subversive. It is futile because it is ustopian. It is erroneous because it runs counter to the eternal laws of human nature. But the existing rights of property represent, after all, but a moment in historic time. They are not today what they were yesterday, and tomorrow they will again be different."[51] Thus, Laski admitted the right to property but in a modified form. He found nothing inherently wrong in it. He wrote, "There is nothing inherently wrong in the notion of private property. There is a sense in which it may be so held as genuinely to express personality and to contribute to its enrichment. But, so to be held, it must be derived from the personal effort organised in such a way as to involve an addition to the common welfare. It must never be so large in anount that its owner exercises power by reason of its sheer magniture; it must never be so small that its possessor cannot be himself at his best."[52]

CONCEPT OF LIBERTY

Nature of Liberty

Laski rejected the view that liberty means absence of restraint. He defined it as, "the positive and equal opportunity of self-realisation."[53] He agreed with

50. *Ibid.*, p. 196.

51. *Ibid.*, p. 215-216.

52. *Ibid.*, pp. 216-217.

53. Laski, H, *Authority in the Modern State*, p. 37.

the definition given by T.H. Green and Acton as "a positive power of doing or enjoying something worth doing or enjoying, and that too, something that we do or enjoy in common with others, and as the assurance that every man shall be protected in doing what he believes his duty against the influence of authority and majority, custom and opinion." But "while defining liberty as the positive opportunity for self-realization," writes Deane, "he is unsable to implement the definition by analyzing the nature of the self which is the goal of the process of realization."[54] So in the late twenties we find a change in Laski's view of freedom. In 1930 he came to form a new view of liberty. He said, "By liberty I mean the eager maintenance of that atmosphere in which men have the opportunity to be their best selves. Liberty, therefore, is the product of right...without rights there cannot be liberty, because, without rights, men are the subjects of law unrelated to the needs of personality."[55] Liberty, is positive. It is not absence of restraint. It is never real unless the government is called to account and it must be always called to account when it invades rights.

Kinds of Liberty

Laski gave three aspects or kinds of liberty.

1. Private liberty. It means, "the opportunity to exercise freedom of choice in those areas of life where the results of any efforts mainly affect me in that isolation by which at least ultimately, I am always surrounded."[56] Religion is a good exasmple of it. Laski further wrote, "Private liberty is thus that aspect of which the substance is mainly personal to a man's self. It is the chance practically to avail himself of the safegaurds evolved for the maintenance of those relations."[57] Private liberty is infringed if law fails to afford protection to the employment or access to public places on grounds of religion, caste, creed or sex.

2. Political liberty. By it Laski mean the power to be active in affairs of state. It means free access to positions of authority. For political liberty, Laski provided two conditions — education and free press. One must be educated to the point where he can express what he wants to express in a way that is intelligible to others. Laski sought to overhaul the present system of education. As free press is very essential for political liberty. According to Laski, "A people without reliable news is sooner or later, a people without the basis of freedom. For to exercise one's judgment in a miasma of distortion is, ultimately, to go disastrously astray."[58]

3. Economic liberty. It implies democracy in industry. According to Laski, "It means that industrial government is subject to the system of rights which

54. Deane, H.A., *op. cit.*, p. 45.

55. Laski, H., *A Grammar of Politics*, p. 142.

56. *Ibid.*, p. 146.

57. *Ibid.*, p. 146.

58. *Ibid*,, pp. 147-48.

obtain for men as citizens, and it means that industrtial direction msut be of a character that makes it the rule of laws made by cooperation and not by compulsion. In other words, it means that the citizens be free from the constant fear of unemployment and insufficiency. It also means that the workers should have a share in the administration of the productive system. All other freedoms are meaningless in the absence of economic liberty. An economic system based upon fear is incompatible with liberty."[59]

Safeguards of Liberty

1. No special privileges in society. Laski wrote, "Unless I enjoy the same access to power as others, I live in an atmosphere of contingent frustration. It does not matter that I shall probably not desire to take full advantage of that access. Its denial will mean that I accept allotted station as permanent condition of my life; and that, in its turn, is fatal to the spontaneity that is of the essence of freedom."[60] Men who enjoy special privileges regard those outside their own circle as inferior beings. They do not part with their power except when they are compelled to do so by force. They always fight for their status.

2. Rights of some should not depend upon the pleasure of others. Common rules must be binding upon those who exercise power as well as upon those who are the subjects of power. Thus, the ruler and the ruled must be subject to the same laws. This requires the planning of the principles of social action and the absence of those uncertainties from social organisation which ressult in social loss and are deliberately planned by individuals.

3. The unbiased incidence of state action. Rights which are the guarantee of a minimum bias are a security against the use of state power by some few persons in a biased manner.

4. Determination of the people to fight for their freedom. Eternal vigilance is the price of liberty. Pericles said, "The secret of liberty is courage."

CONCEPT OF EQUALITY

According to Laski the concept of equality is the most difficult to understand. If cannot mean identity of treatment so long as men are different in want, capacity and need. It implies a certain levelling process. To quite Laski, "It means that no man shall be so placed in society that he can overreach his neighbour to the extent which constitutes a denial of latter's citizenship."[61] Equality means the absence of special privileges based upon birth or property. It means enjoyment of equal rights by all and equality of all before law. Nobody is denied access to the avenues of authority. That adequte opportunities are laid open to all. Those opportunities should be given to individuals which are considered to be essential for their growth and without which there is all frustration. All individuals must be ensured the minimum of rights. Differences may arise only above that minimum level. Everyone must have those things

59. *Ibid.*, p. 148.

60. *Ibid.*, p. 149.

61. *Ibid.*, p. 153.

without which life is meaningless. There cannot be equality of wages as there is no equality of capacity for work. "Equality, therefore, involves upto the margin of sufficient identity of response to primary needs. And that is what is meant by justice. We are rendering to each man his own by giving him what enables him to be a man. We are, of course, therein protecting the weak and limiting the power of the strong."[62] Inequalities of wealth must be done away with as there cannot be political equality in the absence of economic equality.

Equality of States

Laski holds that the question of equality of states in the international field is meaningless. Small states cannot be put at par with the great powers. Each state should be allowed to have complete freedom in those matters which affect her alone. Laski wrote, "Just as, that is, no individual can find freedom outside the common rules of his society, so also no state can find freedom save by accepting limitations of its sovereignty by the will formed by the common decision of a society of states."[63]

CONCEPT OF LAW

Meaing of Law

According to Laski, the term 'Law' is used in three different senses — the juristic sense, the political sense, and the ethical sense.

1. Juristic sense. In the juristic sense it is no more than a mere announcement, ultimately dependent upon the sovereign authority, of the will to enforce certain decision.

2. Political sense. In it the formal announcement is variegated by the acceptance of it by those to whom it applies.

3. Ethical sense. In it the decision announced ought to be obeyed because it is merely right that what is proposed should be done.

Law is an instrument of satisfying social needs. Life of law is not logic but experience. Laws are obeyed because they satisfy the requirements of the people. Roots of law are found within the individual conscience. The source of law is the individual acting according to his conscience.

Making of Law

All men must have equal right to share in the making of law. According to Laski, men are entitled to disobey a law which ceases to secure their self-realization. There is violation of law only when people don't find another way to redress their grievances except through open definance of law or through a revolution. According to Laski, Individual conscience and willing obedience are its two pillars of strength.

---

62. *Ibid.*, p. 160.
63. *Ibid.*, p. 166.

International Law

Laski refuse to accept the view that international law has the force of law only for those states which agree to accept the same. According to Laski, "This view is as bad as to allow the private citizen to be the judge of his own acts."[64] He held the view that every state is "bound in the rules by the superior rules of the international community to which it belongs. It cannot make or unmake them any more than the individual can make or unmake the law of the state of which he is the subject."[65] International law requires the surrender of state sovereignty.

CAPITALISM AND WAR

Laski was a great critic of capitalism and capitalist society. He said that capitalism means war. In a capitalist society war is inevitable on account of the existence of class relationship. There cannot be real bond between the capitalists and the poor. Capitalism in practice means huge production and that requires both home and foreign markets. Hence, capitalism has always sought the help of the states for penetrating into other countries for economic exploitation. This has always led to war.

According to Prof. Gregory, Cobden and Bright, the era of capitalist supremacy in the nineteenth century was not the richest in armed conflict. There had been wars even before the emergence of capitalism. But Laski refutes them by saying that the history of British occupation of Egypt, South Africa and India demonstrates that capitalism inevitably resulted in wars. The South African war was a struggle for the domination of the gold mines. States have always interfered, to protect the interests of the capitalists which has brought wars. International peace could be established only if the states surrendered their sovereignty which was possible only if capitalism was ended.

Laski opined that capitalism and democracy could never sail together. Only in a period of economic expansion and prosperity they could work side by side. But in the period of economic depression, the capitalists become avowed enemies of democracy and take steps to destroy it. Capitalists have no love for democracy. They will go a long way to welcome even dictatorship to get out of economic depression. If democracy is to flourish, capitalism must go. There is no place in democracy for a class of vested interest.

SOCIALISM AND MARXISM

It is said that Laski started as a pluralist and ended as a Marxist but Laski neither accepted theories of Marx in toto nor deviated from him totally. He never endorsed Marxist doctrine of materialistic interpretation of history and labour theory of value. But, nonetheless, he remained a socialist throughout his

64. Laski H., *Law and the State*, p. 273.

65. *Ibid.*, p. 279.

life. He said "I have, I suppose, been a socialist in some degree since the last years of my school days."[66]

Laski's faith in socialism was hardened by the social bias of his society on account of his belonging to the Jewish community. During his stay at Harvard University, the famous Boston Police strike of 1919 deepened his socialist faith by demonstrating "how the vast machinery of the state is used to crush any movement that questions the authority of those who own economic power."[67] When Laski returned from America he was a confirmed socialist. His early socialism was, however, the result of his experience of injustice. He was nearer to Proudhon than to Marx. About Proudhon he said, "He (Proudhon) seems to me to have anticipated most of Karl Marx and have said it better."[68] At this stage Laski wanted industrial democracy to precede political democracy. He was opposed to Marxists or Fabians who advocated the nationalization of basic industries as the solution of contemporary problems. According to Laski, "The evils implied in a regime of state management are hardly less great than those of the present system. For to surrender to government officials not merely political but also industrial administration is to create a bureaucracy more powerful than the world has ever seen. It is to make a certain kind of paternalism which perhaps above all other systems, would prevent the advent of the kind of individual freedom we desire."[69] Thus, Laski's early socialism was critical of bureaucratic implications of both Marxism and Fabianism.

Laski had full sympathy for Marx though he was not prepared to accept everything Marx had said. He regarded Marx's view of human nature as abstract, materialistic and contradictory of the total facts. He rejected as radically false the Marxian insistence upon an 'economic background as the whole explanation of political phenomena'. He regarded Marxian labour theory of value as inconsistent and inadequate. But as Deane points out, "The main weight of Laski's attack on Marxism is directed against its insistence on the inevitability of a violent revolution in the transition to socialism and the corollary, the belief in the necessity of an iron dictatorship during the period of consolidation."[70] Laski held the view that it is impossible to oust a government by an armed uprising on the part of the proletariat so long as it retained the loyalty of its armed forces. Differences in national background and religion cut across the solidarity of the working class and thus weaken them for effecting a revolution. As Deane says, "Laski's main ground for rejecting the Marxist doctrine, however, is his belief that security and freedom will vanish from the earth if profound belief in any cause is held to be justification for a resort to

66. Quoted in Clifton Fediman; ed. *I Believe : The Personal Philosophies of Certain Eminent Men and Women of Our time*, New York : Simon and Schuster, p. 139.
67. Deane, H.A., *op. cit.*, pp. 53-54.
68. Quoted by Deane, *op. cit.*, p. 55 footnote *Halmos-Laski Letters*, 1916-35 ed. by Mark De Wolfe Howe (2 Vols.), Cambridge, Harvard Uni. Press (1953) I, p. 82, 1917.
69. Laski, H., *Authority in the Modern State*, p. 95.
70. Deane, H.A., *op. cit.*, p. 71.

revolutionary violence."[71] For Laski the good society is one in which there is provision for the fullest possible release of the creative energies of its members and in which intellectual and spiritual goods are valued more highly than material goods. Laski also attacked the doctrine of dictatorship of Proletariat. Laski was opposed to violent revolution as inconsistent with civilized life. But as years rolled by he learnt from experience that no class would abdicate from power voluntarily. He leaned more and more towards Marxism. His ideas on the thesis of materialistic interpretation of history and the use of violence from capturing changed though in his heart of heart he remained a socialist democrat. The great depression of 1931 convinced him that the coming of socialism would be marked by violence and by serious restriction upon individual liberty. Sometimes Laski suggests that it is possible to attain socialism peacefully and sometimes he regards revolution inevitable. His is an attempt to bring the two opposites revolutionary doctrine and democratic socialism, in wedlock. By the year 1946 Laski had less the view that violent revolution was inevitable.

With Marx, Laski believed that the economic factor played an important part both in society and government. He held the view that a change in the economic system necesarily produce a change both in society and state. Changes in the method of production are the most vital factor in the making of changes in all social patterns. They determine changes in social relationship which in turn are interwoven with all the cultural habits of man. Thus, they determine our religion, morals, intellectual pursuits, social relations and political institutions. Economic classes always struggle for capturing control of the sovereign power. But Laski holds that economic factor though most important, is not the only factor for bringing changes. there is also the influence of logic, personality and religion.

Thus, Laski was not a Marxist of the orthodox type. He accepted Marxist views to the extent those were fitting with his democratic socialism. In the words of Kingsley Martin, "His argument might be derived from Marx, but at the final test he was a follower of William Morris rather than of Lenin....like William Morris, he held that socialism and fellowship are the same thing."[72]

AN ESTIMATE OF LASKI

About Laski, Kingsley Martin wrote, "He was a scholar and political philosopher, author and journalist; he was above all, a teacher and a friend. All these aspects of his personality were knit closely together by his conception of the task of an intellectual in society."[73] Kingsley compared Laski to Montesquieu and De Tocqueville. Kinsley thought that since the seventeenth century no other man in Europe or America had such a profound knowledge of democratic thought and institutions. However, critics like Herbert Deane and Carroll Hawkins under-rate Laski's importance. Deane writes, "Our summary and analysis of

71. *Ibid.*, p. 71.

72. Kingsley Martin, : *Harold Laski*, p. 270.

73. Kingsley, Martin, *Harold Laski*, : *A Biographical Memoir*, pp. 256-57.

Laski's writings demonstrate that he never achieved the distinction as a political theorist or as a scholar in the field of political philosophy that was promised by the erudition and brilliance of his early essays."[74]

Deane is most uncharitable to Laski. Though Laski was not a philosopher of the level of Plato or Aristotle but he was not a mere propagandist. He was a great teacher and scholar whose influence was widely felt not only in England and Europe but even in the new emerging nations of the East.

QUESTIONS FOR EXERCISE

1. "For its citizens a state is what it does, it is not justified merely because it is a state" — Laski. Comment.
2. "The structure of social organization must be federal, if it is to be adequate" — Laski. Discuss this statement.
3. "It will be a lasting benefit to political science if whole concept of sovereignty was surrendered" — Laski. Discuss.
4. "Every government must submit itself to the judgment of those who feel the consequences of the acts" — Laski. Comment.
5. "By its very nature the state is simply coercive power used to protect the system of rights and duties of one process of economic relationship from invasion from another class which seeks to change them in the interest of another process" — Laski. In what respect do you consider the above definition of the state inadequate.
6. "No theory of state can pretend to completeness which does not account for effects involved in the existence of international community" — Laski. Examine this statement.
7. "Political equality is never real unless it is accompanied by vitrual economic equality; political power, otherwise, is bound to be the handmaid of economic power" — Laski. Examine the statement.
8. "Rights are not the creatures of law but it is condition precedent. They are that which law is seeking to realise" — Laski. Discuss.
9. "The state briefly, does not create but recognizes rights and its character will be apparent from the rights that at any given period secure recognition" — Laski. Discuss.
10. "Our rights are not independnet of society but inherent in it" — Laski. Discuss.
11. "Every state is known by the rights it maintains" — Laski. Comment.
12. "The present system is inadequate from whatever angle it is regarded" — Laski. Discuss this statement with reference to private property.

---

74. Deane, H.A., *op. cit.*, p. 333.

31

Behaviouralism

Behaviouralism is the ideology or approach which motivates a citizen to achieve power, to sustain it, to influence one self and others and to organise associations or parties. In his famous book on the subject Laswell has defined Behaviourslism as "Politics who gets what, when and how." According to Dall, Behaviouralism aims at describing the political events in terms of observed behaviour of human beings. Behaviouralists seek to develop an applied science which may be utilised to understand man in society in a scientific context in any social research.

POSTULATES OF BEHAVIOURALISM

Kirk Patrik points out that Behaviouralism today, cannot be taken in any aniliquous meaning. Behaviourlism is based on the following postulates :

1. Political research in which behaviour is constituted as a unit in place of political institutions.

2. To admit all social sciences as behaviouristic and to accept that political science is one of the social science.

3. To define the object of political science in the form of a systematic and empirical science.

4. To survey, classify and to arrive at algebraic equations so far as possible for the assessment of purity of facts.

OBJECTIVES OF BEHARIOURALISM

Robert Andel admits that Behaviouralistic revolution is the result of dissatisfaction with the achievements of traditional political science. According to David Easton, we may believe that political life is a system of behaviour which is based in those influences of environment to which political system opens and to which it reacts. Thus, Behaviouralism seeks to establish political science on a scientific foundation.

EVOLUTION OF BEHAVIOURALISM

The evolution of Behaviouralism may be traced through the following three stages:

1. Pre-Behaviouralism or Empiricism.

2. Behaviouralism.

3. Post-Behaviouralism or New Behaviouralism.

1. Pre-Behaviouralism or Empiricism. John Locke is considered to be the founder of Empiricism. He, first of all, presented the parliamentary ideology on the basis of experience. Pluralist thinkers including J.S. Mill and Harold Laski further developed this trend. Max Weber, Karl Marx, Graham Wallace, Durkheim and Bentley developed it further. Chicago school was the main organisation of the Behaviouralists. They achieved force through American Political Science. Association and Social Science Research Council, Capitalists like Lord Cornegie and Rockfeller spent millions of dollars on research in social sciences due to which Behaviouralism came to be accepted everywhere.

2. Behaviouralism. Upto Second World War, political philosophy, comparative government, international relations and national governments were being studied from empirical viewpoint. This tried to develop a systematic discipline and a technical vocabulary for the study of political events. it was, however, not being given much importance so far.

In 1928, a famous American journalist Frank Kent, First of all gave this method the name Behaviour in his book *The Political Behaviour*. Scholars who arrived from Europe made a significant contribution to Behaviouristic revolution. This in turn also influenced methodology of the study of political science in European countries including France, Germany and England. Empiricists in U.S.A. had occasion to witness the political events during Second World War. They studied it closely which resulted in the rise of Behaviouralism out of the work of empiricism.

3. Post-Behaviouralism. This includes development after 1965. The tendency to make political science a science of behaviour may be traced since ancient times. It may be found in Aristotle, Machiavelli, Sophists, Hobbes, Thomas, Montesqueu, Comte, Durkheim, Bagehot, Max Weber and Marx who were very much impressed by the scientific principles and methods of their time.

Neo-Behaviouralism, today, is an independent science. Though Americans are leaders in this approach it is being developed all over the world. However, it has failed to provide definite principles to political science.

SCOPE OF BEHAVIOURALISM

The scope of Behaviouralism is expanding very fast. It has borrowed inter-disciplinary approach, system analysis, functional approach etc. from sociology. Thus, it has become difficult to define its scope. However, the following may be included in the present scope of Behaviouralism :

1. Study of subjects of mutual inter-relations of human being.

2. Individual and collective form of small groups and organisations.

3. Study of political systems and sub-systems including political parties, pressure groups, legislatures etc.

4. Study of subjects of polling behaviour.

5. Concepts like will, power, decisions, processes, groups and structure in politics.
6. Study of action and methods of processes.
7. Study of comparative politics.
8. Study of new methods.
9. Study of policies and values.
10. Study of political theories and ideologies.

EVALUATION OF BEHAVIOURALISM

According to David Easton, Behaviouralism is a new development in a long life of analysis and change in social sciences. Dahl points out that political science has failed to bring together the principles, methodologies, achievements and approaches of modern psychology, sociology and economics. Political science requires a new synthesis, a more comfortable unity and more confident knowledge and behaviour. Through its scientific empiricism Behaviouralism has given new standpoint, new methods, new tools of measurement and new areas to political science.

Behaviouralists claim that they can construct a science of human behaviour, and find out principles of human behaviour which may become sound bases of control and prediction. This however, has not been achieved so far. Behaviouralists have ignored the past. According to Christina, they suffer from prejudice in favour of democracy. To a great extent, they are a political, anti-politics and supporters of *status quo*. They have concentrated their efforts in the study of micro events and have left important questions on individual and collective levels. Separating themselves from immediate and serious issues they have joined the rank of arm chair intellectuals, busy in intellectual adventures and fantasies.

However, Behavioralistic revolution has made significant contribution to change the face of political science. Political science, today, has accepted their scientific methodology and value centred appraoch. This has influenced the form and subject matter of political science. According to Robert Dahl, Behaviouralism has now been accepted in main channel of political science.

POST-BEHAVIOURAL REVOLUTION : DAVID EASTON

1960 saw an anti-behaviouralistic revolution. This was due to the feeling that the limits of Behaviouralistic revolution have made political science aimless. Value-neutral political science was indifferent to actual politic. It did not offer any suggestion to ameliorate human life or to solve its problems. David Easton has pointed out that political science should study contemporary problems and suggest remedies. Presiding over the 65th session of American Political Science Association, David Easton pointed out that Behaviouralistic methodology is leading towards too much factuality to make it a physical science. This is reductionism. David Easton pointed out to the following important issues unsolved in Behaviouralism :

1. Behaviouralistic method should emphasise present serious problems in place of methodology. Even antiquity is better than inconsistent purity.

2. Behaviouralism involves empirical basis and supports *status quo*.

3. As Behaviouralism has crossed the limits of actuality, post-behaviouralism should try to bring it back then alone, it can make significant contribution to evolution of human race.

4. However, social science may make efforts, the researcher can never be absolutely free from personal prejudices and bias. Hence, instead of being value-natural, the researcher should try to develop values creatively. They should in fact, protect human values.

5. Behaviourism should be able to reconstruct society as knowledge does not mean indifference. The intellectual, as a scientist, has an important responsibility to put his knowledge into action. Thus, he must develop an action which may remove the contemporary conflicts of society towards ideals.

6. It is necessary to politicise study of behaviourism. It should concentrate on world problems. For this the intellectuals will have to wage struggle.

Easton has described eight characteristics of Behaviourism of which at least six have been criticised by the traditionalists. During 1920-30 Rice and Harold Lasswell used quantitative methods. Thus, started the first stage of quantitative development. In the second stage of development there was also development of principles particularly by David Easton. Gabriel Almond, Robert Dahl, Harold Lasswell and Karl Dice. Standardisation of principles has started under the inspiration of Lasswell. One finds a synthesis of knowledge, principles and methodology. Today, most of the political scientists are no more confined to Behaviourist methodology. They are using many other methodologies with advantage. This is particularly due to efforts of David Easton. Political science is now being used to improve international relations.

HEROLD D. LASSWELL

In his work Lasswell has admitted that the study of politics is the study of power. It means that it studies the strategies and procedures to attain power in politics. But the study of power cannot be separated from all those factors whose confirmation, opposition or cooperation affect power equilibriums. In due course Lasswell admitted all those factors in the study of political science which enter political field. Thus finally, political science is the study of the influencer and the influenced in the political field.

Study of Power

Lasswell was one of the chief architects of Behaviouralism. He analysed power and authority and its impact. According to him, where there is power, there is its direct or indirect impact. It also influences the progress of history. There are many sources of power in community and society, which may be both political and non-political. This power can be predicted and assessed scientifically. It is carried on politically. The assessment of sources of power in present-day politics gives birth to a political science which may predict about the future trends of national and international politics.

Analyses of Power

Lasswell has divided the analysis of power into two classes : Contemplative Analysis and Manipulative Analysis. Contemplative Analysis has been further divided into Descriptive Analysis and Predictive Analysis. Descriptive Analysis has been further divided into the following :

1. Contemplation and Analysis of various aspects of power on the basis of scientific facts.

2. Prediction of results on the basis of analysis.

3. Control of power and its impact to attain desirable results and study of possibilities of necessary changes on the basis of above two.

Main Questions in Political Life

According to Lasswell the main questions in political life are what, when and how. These have been discussed in his work. *Who Gets What, When and How.* Without answering these quesionss the objective of modern political science cannot be fulfilled. Political processes and power are analysed to seek answer to these questions. Lasswell has called it Configurative analysis whose two factors are : Equilibrium and Development. Equilibrium Analysis further includes factors like political activities, demands, symbols and competitions etc. Political activities include demonstration, strikes, conflicts, lock up, etc. adopted by various factions and groups. There have both direct and indirect effects.

Symbols, Equilibriums and Development

According to Lasswell, symbols represent political power and influence. These also include particular ideologies and philosophies. Many symbols are connected with nations, classes, castes and religions. Lasswell's developmental analysis presents a unique interpretation of history. In this he has studied the forms and repetitions of power in the historical events like Toynbee, Spengler, Comte and Marx. By the analysis of historical facts he has tried to prove that creation is evolving like the proceeds of a dynamic power in which various forms of powers are achieving equilibrium. When this equilibrium is destroyed, the development process loses momentum. By the study and analysis of powers in the society, equilibriums and development may be predicted.

Critical Estimate

1. Lasswell has tried to predict in the political field on the basis of direction of history by accepting man as a thing like brick, stone or metal. Thus, his assessment of human tendencies has been far from successful.

2. There is nothing new in Lasswell's analysis. He has only named the dialectical powers as models of political system or patterning of political forces.

3. Lasswell's study resembles studies of Comte and Karl Marx. His theories cannot give guidance to any political leader in actual politics.

QUESTIONS FOR EXCERCISE

1. What is Behaviouralism? Discuss its evolution and scope. Evaluate its contribution to political thought.
2. What do you know about Post-Behavioural revolution? Discuss its chief characteristics.
3. Discuss the main political ideas of Herold D. Lasswell.
4. Critically examine the political thought of famous Behaviourist Herold D. Lasswell.

32

Fascism

The term fascism is derived from the Latin word faces, which means bundle. In ancient Rome a bundle of rods with an axe was the sign of authority, which included the power of life and death. Fascism emerged in the Twentieth century as a reaction against liberalism and democracy.

Definition of Fascism

1. *Ebenstein*. "Stripped to its essentials, fascism is the totalitarian organisation of government and society by a single party dictatorship, intensely nationalist, socialist, militarist and imperialist."[1]

2. *Barnes*. "Fascism may be defined generally as a political and social movement having as its objects the re-establishment of a political and social order, based upon the main current of traditions that have formed one European civilisation, traditions created by Rome, first by the Empire and subsequently by the Catholic Church. Conversely, fascism may be described as the repudiation of that individualist mentality that found expression first in the Pagan Renaissance, then in the Reformation and later in the French Revolution."[2]

3. *Roucek and others*. Mussolini has declared. "That fascism was an ideology compounded of the teaching of Machiavelli's doctrine of opportunism, Hegel's Political absolutism, Sorel's doctrine of violence and William James' pragmatism. Fascism did not have a dogmatic ideology and adopted its doctrine as the exigencies of the moment required."[3]

4. *Maxey*. "It is a compound of many ingredients which have been blended together with great ingenuity. We may perceive among others borrowings from Machiavelli, Hobbes, Fichte, Hegel, Trietschke, Nietzche, Marx, Sorel, Mosca, Schoperhauer, Bergson, James and Pareto."[4]

5. *Websters New World Dictionary*. Fascism is a system of government characterised by dictatorship, belligerent nationalism, racism, militarism, etc., first instituted in Italy in 1922.

6. *Mussolini*. "Fascism is based on reality, we want to be definite and real. Our programme is action, not talk." Mussolini has explained fascism by saying,

1. Ebenstein, W., *Today's Isms*, 3rd ed., p. 95.
2. Barnes, J.S., *The Universal Aspects of Fascism*, p. 35.
3. Roucek & Others, *Introduction of Political Science* (1954), p. 90.
4. Maxey, *Political Philosophies*, pp. 638-39.

"We Fascists have had the courage to discard all traditional political theories and we are aristocrats and democrats, revolutionaries and reactionaries, proletarians and anti-proletarians, pacifists and anti-pacifists. It is sufficient to have a single fixed point, the Nation, the rest is obvious." Fascism has been called as the Italian variant of totalitarianism just as Nazism is the German variant and Bolshevism is the Russian variant of totalitarianism.

7. *Jawaharlal Nehru*. "Fascism had the unique distinction of having no fixed principles, no ideology, no philosophy behind it, unless the mere opposition to Socialism, Communism and Liberalism might be considered to be a philosophy."

ORIGIN AND GROWTH OF FASCISM

After the first great war the fascist movement began in Italy. Material for this movement and also an opportunity to start it in the right earnest was provided by post-war economic social disorganisation, gross profiteering, inflation, strikes for higher wages, deficit national budget, dissatisfaction among soldiers, adverse course of the peace negotiations and a general distrust in the government and its various institutions. Mussolini described the condition of Italy in these words : "Politicians and philosophers; profiteers and losers, for at least many had lost their illusions; sharks trying to save themselves; promoters of war trying to be pardoned, demagogue seeking popularity; spies and instigators of trouble waiting for the price of their treason; agents paid by foreign money; in a few months threw the nation into an awful spiritual crisis. I saw before me with awe the gathering dusk of our end as a nation and a people."[5] On 23rd of March, 1919 Mussolini founded the *Fascio di Combattimento*. Its aim was "to defend the victory at any price, to maintain in fact the second memory of the dead and the admiration not only for those who fell and for the families of those who were dead, but for the mutilated, for the invalids, for all those who had fought. It was hoped a new Italy would be created that would know how to put value upon victory and to fight with all its strength against treason and corruption, against decay within and intrigue and avarice from without."[6] The new party was chiefly drawn from retiring army officers, jobless, disillusioned youth and land owning families. The party continued to grow in strength and in March 1921 elections it won 34 seats in the Italian Parliament. From now onward both the labourers and the capitalists joined this movement. Mussolini had no love for democracy. He said, Our democracy of yesterday had died: its testament had been read; it had bequeathed us naught but chaos."[7] In October 1922 as a result of march on Rome by the fascist militia, the king of Italy invited Mussolini to form the government which he did. From now onward there started the march of fascism in Italy. The period from 1922 to 1925 was a period of consolidation. Complete fascist dictatorship established after 1925.

5. Mussolini, Benito, *My Autobiography* : Translated by Richard Washburn Child, Hutchison & Co. London, p. 59.

6. *Ibid.*, p. 66.

7. *Ibid.*, p. 103.

Press was placed under censorship, political parties other than fascist party were banned. The Chamber of Deputies was replaced by a Chamber of Fascist Corporations. By 1939 Italy had become completely totalitarian. In the second great war it sided with Hitler, the dictator of Germany. Fascism as a force came to an end after end of second great war and the defeat of Germany, Italy, Japan, but as a philosophy its remnants are still found in many parts of the world.

SOURCES OF FASCISM

The main sources of fascism were Social Darwinism as interpreted by Nietzsche, irrationalism, traditionalism and idealism. Though these sources were full of incompatibilities between them but the fascist were clever enough to combine them into a whole and compact philosophy. According to McGovern, "The fascists have not hesitated to use the arguments and ideas of all four of these schools. When one peers below the surface it would seem that Mussolini himself is primarily affected by irrationalism and social Darwinism but that he sees the value of traditionalism and idealism as 'window-dress' — as means of presenting fascist doctrines in such a way as to appeal to large sections of the populace who would be shocked by the cold-blooded nationalism of the other two schools."[8]

1. The Social Darwinism. The Social Darwinists started with the assumption that all life or at least, all progress, is based upon the struggle for existence, the elimination of the unfit and the survival of the fittest. The struggle or conflict is not only between individuals but also between various groups. In the struggle between an individual and a group, the group always wins. In the struggle between groups it is the more coherent, compact, homogeneous disciplined group that always wins. Mussolini's speeches and writings were full of ideas reminiscent of the early Social Drawinists. He said, "Strife is the origin of all things— strife will always remain at the root of human nature like a supreme fatality and on the whole it is well that it is so. Today strife is possible in war, in economics, in ideas; but the day in which there would be no more strife would be a day of Melancholy, of the end of things, of ruin."[9] Peace is pause in war. Mussolini and the fascists pause in war. Mussolini and the fascists preached a glorification of war, denunciation of peace, and a thoroughgoing nationalism and imperialism. Glorifing war Musolini said : "War alone brings upto its highest tension all human energy and puts their stamp of nobility upon the people who have the courage to meet it." Mussolini accepted Nietzsche's view that life is not merely a struggle for existence but also a struggle for domination and power. Mussolini, an Imperialist, declared, "For fascism the growth of empire, that is to say the expansion of the nation, is an essential manifestation of vitality, and its opposite a sign of decadence. Peoples which are rising again after a period of decadence are always imperialist; any renunciation is a sign of decay and death."[10] Social

8. McGovern, *From Luther to Hitler*, p. 538.

9. Quoted in Schneider, *Making the Fascist State*, p. 276.

10. Mussolini, *Fascism*, Translation in International Conciliation, p. 16.

Darwinism affected Mussolini's views, regarding the organisation of government based upon brutal type of authoritarianism.

2. Irrationalism or Anti-intellectualism. William James, Bergson, Nietzsche, Sorel and Pareto were the great irrationalists who exercised influence upon Mussolini. Irrationalism was a reaction against the philosophy of rationalism. Irrationalists held that reason affords no satisfactory solution of the problems of the universe. It does not give us an absolute standard for judging what is right and what is wrong. Applied to politics it means that man is essentially an irrational animal. All his social and political activity and thinking must be based on this fundamental principle. Man is not all reason, he is also sentiment. He is more governed by instincts than by reason. Fascism supported the superior claims of instincts over reason. For Mussolini abstract thing was of no use, the need of the hour was action. He said : "My programme is action not talk." The fascist thinker Rocco wrote, "It is true that fascism is above all, action and sentiment and that such it must continue to be. Were it otherwise, it could not keep up that immense driving force, that renovating power which it now possesses, and would merely be the solitary meditation of a chosen few."[11] Thus, fascists were in full accord with the irrationalists. The rationalists view that certain doctrines, certain facts and certain scientific laws are absolutely and eternally true, was outright rejected by Mussolini. To irrationalists all standards of value and moral codes were simply weapons in the struggle for power. Mussolini accepted Sorel's idea of the myth and he glorified it. He said, "We have created our myth. The myth is a faith, a passion. It is not necessary that it shall be reality. It is a reality by the fact that it is a goal, a faith that is courage. Our myth is the Nation, our myth is the greatness of the Nation. And to this myth, to this grandeur, that we wish to translate into a complete reality, we subordinate all the rest." He further said, "It is faith that moves mountains, not reason. Reason is a tool but it can never be motive force of the crowd."[12] He rejected all forms of determinism, such as the doctrine of economic determinism of Marx. For fascists 'the economic man does not exist. Man is integral, he is political, he is economic, he is religious, he is saint, he is warrior'. Thus, irrationalism had tremendous influence on Mussolini.

3. Traditionalism. It was advocated by men like Mozzini and Treitschke. Mussolini's going back to tradition was because of his being an ardent nationalist. Natonalism and traditionalism go together. Then Mussolini found in it a valuable ally from the practical, pragmatic point of view. McGovern defined traditionalism as : "The belief that legal and political institutions must have an historical background and must be in accord with specific genius or culutre of the people concerned as shown in their national tradition."[13] Traditionalism as an integral part of fascism was accepted by Mussolini and other fascist leaders and writers.

---

11. Rocco, *The Political Doctrine of Fascism* (1926), p. 10.
12. Quoted in H. Finer, *Mussolini's Italy*, p. 126.
13. McGovern : *op. cit.*, p. 343.

According to them, the nation is "an entity with a unity brought about by common traditions among the people who compose it, traditions formed in the course of time owing to the working of a variety of influences such as.... community of languages, race, culture, religion, laws, customs, history, feelings, and volitions."[14] Traditionalism adopted by the fascists is of the Hegelian type. It believed in progress and evolution. It was compatible with advocacy of violent and bloody revolution.

4. Idealism. Hegel's Philosophy of the state was an important factor in the moulding of Italian nationalism and the fascist doctrine of the state as an ethical entity. Idealism was used to give support to the principles of irrationalism and Social Darwinism defend fascism and attack liberalism. Fascists adopted the old concept of idealism laying stress on duties rather than on rights and the chief function of the state to promote moral welfare of man. Man was primarily a creature of duties rather than of rights and his primary duty was to serve his community and nation. This amounted to even sacrificing one's life, liberty and hapiness for the benefit of the community and the nation. With the idealists the fascists raised the state to mystical heights. Mussolini made clever use of idealistic phrases to hide his authoritarianism. The facists were indebted to the idealists for their conception of freedom. Like idealists they conceived freedom for man only within the state. To Hegel man was free only when he completely subordinated himself to the state. Mussolini also preached such a gospel of freedom. He said, "The fascist state has curtailed useless or harmful liberties while preserving those which are essential. In such matter the individual cannot be the judge, but the state only."[15] The fascists also borrowed the idea of spirit and spiritual from the idealists. According to Mussolini, fascist conception of life was a spiritual one while that of liberalism was materialistic one. The spirit unfolded itself through the state which is the march of God on earth.

Fascists were not eager to formulate a consistent and coherent political doctrine. They had no faith in a fixed theory. They needed justification for their acts. For this they borrowed freely from various sources.

VILFREDO PARETO (1848—1923)

Pareto was the morning star of fascism. His book *The Mind and Society* propounded doctrines which provided the soul to fascist Movement. Its first principle was that men are irrational. Men always have been and always will be unequal in their capacities and potentialities.

Philosophy of Irrationalism

Pareto's philosophy of Irrationalism was the result of his profound study of the motivations underlying human conduct. According to him, the stimulus to activity is not logic or reason but such factors as geographic enviornment and social, historic and economic background. The two basic factors, responsible

14. Quoted in Palmieri, *The Philosophy of Fascism*, p. 123-24.

15. Mussolini, *Fascism : Translation in Fascism, Doctrine and Institutions*, p. 30.

for human action have been given the names of 'Residues and Derivations'. While the first means emotions, instincts and sentiments, the second means the patterns of thought, the *pseudo-rational* 'myths', ideas and ideologies which most men think rational but which are really drived from the residues. Pareto gave a very long list of Residues which McGovern groups into six broad classes:

1. Tendency to form 'combinations', the instructive tendency to combine things and thoughts into a group. The first group consists of those tendencies which aim at the protection of the integrity of the individual.
2. Tendency to worship, defend and protect the combinations which have been made by an earlier generation.
3. Tendency to express sentiments by external acts.
4. The residues of gregariousness or sociability.
5. The tendency in mankind to form groups, desire of mankind to be like every one else.
6. The desire of man to impose their manners, mode of life and belief on other people.

The last group consists of the various manifestations of the sexual instinct. Pareto holds that these residues are found to some extent in all normal human beings and provide the most important factor for motivation of human conduct. The social myths which are derivations serve a very useful prupsoe. Those influence even human history and the residues of a people. The ruling class of each country must make a good study of the residues and derivations and promote those derivations which are in accord with residues and which find wide acceptance. Thus, the derivation of the Nation is more powerful than the derivation of general strike. According to McGovern, "By the use of such derviations the ruling class can keep its control and induce the masses to follow their leadership with a minimum of difficulty and with a minimum use of armed force."[16]

Concept of Elite

Pareto doctrine of inequality of human beings is closely associated with two concepts — the cocnept of the Elite and the concept of the circulation of the Elite. According to the first concept, mankind has always shown an enormous amount of divergence. Some are stronger, others are weaker; some are wiser, others are stupid; some are law-abiding, others are criminally inclined; some are more artistic and literary, others are less artistic and less literary. There are always special groups of persons in every community outstanding in their ability in some particular line. Pareto gives the name of Elite to such groups. Thus, in every community there is an artistic, a sporting and scientific elite and also the governing elite and elite of a small group of persons who dominate the economic and political scene of the country. Each and every country is really

16. McGovern, *op. cit.*, p. 438.

dominated by an elite, whether it is a democracy or any other form of government. Sorokin has paraphrased Pareto thus : "There never has been any social or political system in which equality or real democracy has been realised. What is styled democracy is rather plutocracy, the control of the governed principally through deceit, machinations, and combinations and by demagogues, capitalists, hypocrites, and cynical persons."[17] Pareto believe that there is a real biological difference between the Elite and the masses. The community whatever its formal construction, is always dominated by a small group of Elite at all times and at all places.

Circulation of the Elite

Pareto's concept of the circulation of the Elite, means the fall of creation members from the groups of the Elite to the rank of the masses, and the corresponding rise of certain outstanding members of the masses in the ranks for the Elite. This circulation is sometimes rapid and sometimes slow. A community must always be governed by an Elite but no one fixed group of Elite has a permanent existence. History is the graveyard of aristocracies. No Elite is permanent, though some elites are more enduring, more successful than others, depending upon the methods they use to motivate their integrity and to preserve their domination over the masses. Pareto mentions those special types of Elite : the Elite of the old regime, its circulation is not easy and revolution becomes inevitable, the liberal democratic type which breaks down because of its selfishness, inefficiency and corruption and the fascist Nazi type. Fascist type is advocated by Pareto. It is more stable, more efficient and more successful than the other two types because it is willing to use force which gives to the community a sense of security and enables it to survive for long periods. It is dominated by sentiments of group persistence and the desire to maintain established institutions. It gives importance to the hierarchic principle in government which accounts for both a more stable and a more efficient type of government. It is more honest than democratic-liberal type. It lays more emphasis on vigorous moral codes.

Authoritarianism

Pareto was more or less authoritarian. He wanted all political power to be in the hands of a small vigorous Elite — an elite governing by force rather than by consent. According to McGovern, "Pareto would like to combine political dictatorship with economic liberalism. The aristocrats should control the state, but the state should not interfere with private enterprise in the economic sphere."[18] Preto's importance llies in the fact that he "undertook a systematic presentation of the science of society from the irrationalism point of view."[19]

Gaetano Mosca Government by Minority. According to Gaetano Mosca, another scholar of the school of irrationalism, there are always two classes in

---

17. Sorokin R., *Contemporary Sociological Theories*, p. 56.

18. McGovern, *op. cit.*, p. 448.

19. Maxey, *Political Philosophies*, p. 625.

every society — the rulers and the ruled. The rulers always constitute a small minority. Masses can never govern, they can never be organised. Only minorities can be organised to govern. According to Mosca, the ruling class is seldom united. It is always divided into sections at war with one another for pre-eminence in the state. Groups or individuals attain positions of power in the state through this struggle. The basic motivation force behind this struggle is pre-eminence and power. At the same time each ruling group has a political formula by which it tries to justify its aspiration or its actual exercise of power. This formula may have the form of a popular slogan or an ideal appealing to mass such as divine right, social contract, popular will, democracy, social justice, etc.

Mosca favoured a democratic regime as it enabled the ruling class to be more moderate and altruistic. But by advocating the doctrine of struggle for power between individuals and classes Mosca unconsciously advocated the cause of fascism which was so blatantly upheld by his contemporary Pareto. His doctrine of struggle is the acceptance of the doctrine of Nietzsche who said : "They (living things) seek power for power's sake; not for good, not for evil, not for any reason save to satisfy their insatiate craving for power." Struggle results in dividing the community into two classes — ordinary men and supermen who form the elite. Thus, Mosca supported fascism in an indirect way.

According to Schneider, "The fascists are the gypsies of Italian politics, not being tied down to any fixed principles, they proceed unceasingly towards one goal, the future well-being of the Italian people."[20] The fascist movement came first and its philosophy afterwards. The doctrine was brought to serve the requirements of the main objectives of the fascists. Thus, the fascist theory was a guide to action. Its aims were total reorganization and invigoration of Italian life. It aimed at a restoration of the strength and prestige of Italian governmental authority and winning back ancient Roman glory and raising the standard of life of the people. Mussolini said, "My objective is simple; I want to make Italy great, respected and feared; I want to render my nation worthy of her noble and ancient traditions. I want to accelerate her evolution toward the highest forms of national co-operation, I want to make a greater prosperity always possible for the whole people. I want to create a political organization to express, to guarantee and to safeguard our development..."[21] Thus, for the fascists the glorification of Italy with strong and vigorous government and prosperous people was the chief aim and objective and for it any methods or tactics could be employed.

Rocco described fascism as a 'new conception of civil life', a powerful innovating movement, and the beginning of a new culture. It repudiates democracy, liberalism and socialism of fascism looks to the interests of all. "For fascism", writes Rocco, "Society is the end, individuals the means, and its whole life consists in using individuals as instruments for its ends".[22]

20. Schnieder, H.W., *Making the Fascist State*, p. 67.

21. Mussolini, *My Autobiography*, p. 250-251.

22. Rocco, *Political Doctrine of Fascism*, p. 12.

GENERAL PRINCIPLES OF FASCISM

Fascism had no set principles. Fascists did their work first and then gave some philosophic basis to their work. However, from the beginning they exalted the fighting spirit, military discipline, ruthlessness in actions. They had no consideration for ethical standards. They stood for politics alone. People were to obey the leader blindly. The state was exalted to mystical heights. Man was completely subordinated to the requirements of the Almighty state.

Sociological and Psychological Roots of Fascism

Fascism in Italy was founded on mass support. Failures of democracy gave an opportunity to the fascist adventurists to win the support of the masses. A country with a fairly advanced industrial development provides a rich and fertile ground for fascism to grow. "In its social background", writes Ebenstein, "fascism has particularly appealed to two groups : first, a numerically small group of industrialists and land-owners who are willing to finance fascist movements in the hope of those by getting rid of free labour unions. The second main source of fascist support — and numerically by far the most important — comes from the lower middle classes, mostly in the salaried group. Many persons in this class dread the prospect of joining or (rejoining) the proletariat, and look to fascism for a salvation of their status and prestige."[23] Army provided source of strength to the fascist movement. It was an attraction for military people because of its insistence on discipline and unity. Finally, economic crisis or depression has always been helpful for the growth of fascism. It enables it to secure mass support. As it was present in Italy, fascism grew in strength.

The Fascist Idea of the Nation

Fascism conceived of the nation as the ultimate moral being. It is an organism, evolving through countless generations. Fascists equated nation with society. It represents the ultimate synthesis of all the material and spiritual values of the race. The state is "the legal incarnation of the nation."[24] National state is the ultimate reality, it is more real than the individuals or groups which compose it. It claims the absolute loyalty of all. Individual and group interests must be subordinated to the interests of the nation as it is 'the march of God' on earth which alone can change class conflicts into national co-operation. One can realize himself only through the nation. Glorification of the nation is the first objective of the fascists. Men owe duties to the nation while nation owes duties to none. As nation has the right to exist only if it can successfully compete with other nations in the general struggle for existence. Thus, fascist nationalism is imperialist in character. Fascists say, "Imperialism is the eternal and immutable law of life. At bottom it is but the need, desire, and will for expansion which every individual and every life and virile people have inside

23. Ebenstein, W., *Today's Isms* : 3rd ed., pp. 97-98.

24. Ray, P.N., *Mussolini and the Cult of Italian Youth*, p. 17.

them."[25] The growth of empire was an essential manifestation of vitality for fascism and its opposite a sign of decadence. The fascists stand for the absolute moral and legal sovereignty of the national state. According to Coker, "It is the explicit aim of fascism to displace the enfeebling creeds of individual equality, freedom and right, by its own orderly doctrine of an organic, hierachically constituted nation, whose few virile and discerning citizens hold the multitude of common place individuals in subservience to the realization of destinities more important and permanent than their limited hopes and beliefs can contemplate."[26] The determining factor of the fascist principles of governmental structure and policy is the idea that the nation is superior to all of its members. Hence, fascist conception of authority is aristocratic and autocratic. The nation is the supreme arbiter of the people. It is our duty to serve the national faithfully, honestly and ardently. All must contribute to the growth and enrichment of the power of the nation. All means of propaganda should be used to inculcate this spirit of love for the nation. Nation is the supreme entity and its glorificaiton is the supreme end to be achieved. Rocco said, "For Liberalism the individual is the end and society the means...for Fascism, society is the end, individuals the means, and its whole life consists of using individuals as instruments for its social ends."[27]

Fascist Idea of the State and the Individual

According to fascists, "The state is more than the sum of its individuals of one generation; it has an actual entity of its own, a transcendental existence deriving from the past, from the present and the future."[28] The fascist state consists of individuals grouped in a number of corporations in accordance with their different functions. The fascist state is an organic state with "a varied symmetry and classes organised in syndicates and corporations of syndicates and above all, directed by its hierarches."[29] In controlling and directing the lives of citizens the state is all powerful. The fascist state is totalitarian. Politics, economics, art, literature, education and religion all serve the needs of the state.

According to fascists so-called individual rights are nonsense. Individuals have only duties. Duty, discipline and sacrifice are demanded for them. The state is absolutely sovereign. It must dominate all the existing forces in the country, co-ordinate them, solidify them and direct them to the ends of national life. The state must preside over and direct national activity in every field. The fascists say : "All is in the state and for the state; nothing outside the state, nothing against the state." The fascist state is totalitarian and authoritarian. According to fascists, the state and government have always originated in conquest and not in a voluntary compact. The state can be maintained by force alone rather than by consent.

25. Schneider, " *Making the Fascist State*, p. 18.
26. Coker, *op. cit.*, p. 476.
27. Rocco, *The Political Doctrine of Fascism*, p. 403.
28. Frank Fox, *Italy To-day*, p. 97.
29. Cresswell, G.M., *The Keystone of Fascism*, p. 298.

Fascists reject the old liberal slogan that ultimate sovereignty rests with the people and that government derives its authority from the people. According to Rocco, "Democracy vests sovereignty in the people, that is to say in the mass of human beings. Fascism discovers sovereignty to be inherent in society when it is juridically organized as a state — Fascism rejects the dogma of popular sovereignty and substitutes for it that of state sovereignty."[30] The fascist state is the supreme ethical entity absolute in its authority. The individual is what he is because of his being in the state. There is complete identification between the individual and the state. There is no such thing as inalienable rights of an individual.

To conclude with a quotation from Mussolini : "The state, as conceived of and as created by fascism, is a spiritual and moral fact in itself, since the political, juridical and economic organization of the nation is a concrete thing, and such an organization must be in its origin and development a manifestation of the spirit. The state is the guarantor of security, both internal and external, but it is also the custodian and transmitter of the spirit of the people, as it has grown up through the centuries in language, in customs and in faith.....It represents the imminent spirit of the nation.... It is the state which educates its citizens in civic virtue, gives them a consciousness of their mission and welds them into unity; harmonizing their various interests through justice, and transmitting the future generations the mental conquests of science, of art, of law and the solidarity....When the conception of state declines, and disunifying and centrifugal tendencies prevail, whether of individuals or of particular groups, the nations where such pehnomena appear are in their decline."[31]

LIBERTY UNDER FASCIST STATE

Liberty is an outmoded ideal under fascism, Italy needed law, order and efficiency rather than liberty. Liberty was not a natural endowment of nature but a concession made by the state. Real liberty consisted in subjection to law. According to Gentile, the Italian philosopher, the maximum of liberty coincided with the maximum of state force. Law and state are the supreme manifestation of liberty. The state is the sole judge to determine the nature and extent of freedom to be enjoyed by the people. This fascist interpretation of liberty is entirely differnet from democratic interpretation which accepts the claims of the individuals for freedom of thought, speech, association, faith, etc., as essential for the development of one's personality.

Repudiation of Democracy and Liberalism

Thus, fascists were the arch enemies of both democracy and liberalism. They had no faith in parliamentary form of government. They described democracy as stupid, corrupt, slow moving, visionary, impracticable, inefficient and a decaying corpse. Parliaments are talking shops and the country needed action and not talk. Authoritarianism is better than democracy. It is always

30. Rocco, *The Political Doctrine of Fascism*, p. 405.

31. Mussolini, *The Political and Social Doctrine of Fascism*, pp. 21-22.

better for the wise few to govern than for the foolish many to attempt to do so. True democratic rule is an impossiblity. Mussolini said, "Democracy is a kingless regime infested by many kings, who are sometimes more exclusive, tyrannical and destructive, than one, even though he be a tyrant."[32] According to Rocco, "Fascism therefore proclaims that the great mass of citizens is not a suitable advocate of social interests for the reason that the capacity to ignore private individual interests in favour of the higher demands of society and of history is a very rare gift and the privilege of a chosen few."[33] Mussolini also said, "All is the principal adjective of democracy. It is time to a few and chosen. Democratic equalitarianism, anonymous and grey, which forbade all colour and flattened every peronality is about to die...once there were courtiers who burned incense, before the kings and the Popes; now there is a new breed which burns incense, without sincerity, before the proletariat."[34] The Fascists give up all postulates of democracy such as government rested upon the consent of the governed, sovereignty of the people, universal franchise, equality of all persons, fundamental freedoms, etc. Fascists place all authority in the hands of the leader. The principle of centralised authority is equally applicable to the party machine. The liberal principal of separation of powers has no appeal for the Fascists. The state is unitary. All power is concentrated in a single group, preferably in the hands of a single individual. Control is not to be divided as that would mean chaos and anarchy. There should be no distinction between legislative and executive functions.

In spite of authoritarian character of fascism, it remained a mass movement. Mussolini called it as an organised, centralised, authoritarian democracy. McGovern writes, "The fascist leaders are perfectly willing to use brutal, ruthless force to keep themselves in power, but at the same time they are desperately anxious to have the fascist idea of an authoritarian, totalitarian state voluntarily, enthusiastically, and whole-heartedly accepted by the citizenry".[35]

Repudiation of Socialist Ideas

The fascists were anti-socialist and anti-communist. They rejected socialist doctrine of economic determinism. They believed that besides materialism, religion and patriotism also played a vital role in the lives of the people. Fascists did not believe in the theory of class-struggle. They wanted all classes to cooperate for the glorification of the state. The fascists not only aimed to abolish class-strtuggle but also to remove causes for it. They aimed to bring together both the employers and employees and make them for the glorification of the state. The idea of economic well-being alone would reduce man to the level of animals caring for one thing only to be fat and well-fed. It would degrade humanity to a purely physical existence. Fascists rejected almost all the socialist doctrines — economic determinism, class-struggle, surplus value and

32. Mussolini, *Fascism : Translation in Fascism, Doctrine of Institutions*, p. 21.

33. Rocco, *The Political Doctrine of Fascism*, p. 405.

34. Quoted in *Mussolini's Italy*, p. 208.

35. McGovern, *op. cit.*, p. 583.

internationalism. Fascists believed in holiness and in heroism, in actions not influenced by economic motive, direct or indirect.

FASCISM AND CHURCH

Though in the beginning fascists's attitude towards religion was thsat of hostility but after 1921 it became one of conciliation. This was due to the affiliation of pro-clerical nationalists with the fascists in their struggle for power. Coker gives other reasons thus: "Perhaps more important than this were the intellectual and emotional sympathies between fascism and the Vatican in their common antipathy to liberalism, and also the fascist's realisation that the church was a potential rival, which could be silenced or mollified not by conquest but only through conciliation and a division of authority."[36] As a result of this policy the famous 'Vatican Italian Accord' was reached in Feburary 1929 by which the Pope recognized the validity of the kingdom of Italy under its fascists auspices. The fascist government recognised the temporal authority of the Pope in the city of Vatican. It guaranteed certain judicial privileges to the clergy in Italy such as religious instruction in the Catholic faith for children of Catholic parents. The Pope prohibited all priests from taking part in any political party, though support to fascist candidates was permitted.

THEORY OF EDUCATION

Indoctrination of the people from the cradle was part of the fascist programme. Educaiton was aimed to inculcate the spirit of nationalism and the building of character in the youth. It was fully controlled by the state. According to Coker, "The government use the elementary and secondary schools for fascist propaganda; this use determines the selection of courses and text books and the appointment of teachers."[37] Professors were required to swear to maintain their loyalty to the fascist regime and to inculcate the fascist ideals in the minds of the students. There was complete control of the educational system by the fascist regime.

IMPERIALISM AND RADICALISM

Fascist nationalism was imperialist in nature. According to them, imperialism is the eternal and immutable law of life. They regarded the expression of the nation as an essential manifestation of vitality. According to Ebenstein, "Within the nation, fascist doctrine holds the elite is superior to the rest and may impose its will upon them by force. Similarly, between nations the elite nation is superior to others and is entitled to rule them."[38]

Though the fascists were originally free from race theories but after 1938 they caught the contagion of race superiority from Hitler. They started advocating the theory that the Italians constituted a pure and superior race entitled to rule over the less superior races of the world.

36. Coker, *op. cit.*, p. 471.

37. *Ibid.*, p. 472.

38. Ebestein, W., *op. cit.*, p. 110.

WAR AND INTERNATIONALISM

The logical conclusion of fascist imperialism and racialism was its hostility to International law and order. Instead of peace they advocate war. According to Mussolini, "War alone brings up to their highest tension all human energies and put the stamp of nobility upon the peoples who have the courage to meet it."[39] The principle of elite nation was against internationalism. According to fascists international peace was a coward's dream. It was an absurd fable. A conflict of races and nations had been and shall always there in history.

FASCIST METHODS

According to Coker, in the pursuit of their aims, "The fascists recognize no individual liberties as sacred and rely chiefly upon the methods of moral intimidation, physical compulsion, and official censorship and propaganda. Both in their illegal activities before the seizure of formal power and in their subsequent governmental policy, they have dealt summarily and malevalently with their opponents."[40] Kidnapings, beatings and slayings of opponents were common during the fascist regime. A rigid censorhsip was placed on the press. All non-fascist parties were forcibly dissovled. Local government was suppressed. It was made a crime to criticize the government. Special courts were established for the trial of anti-state offences. Public opinion and educational institutions were totally conrolled by the government. By those methods the Italian state was converted into worst type of dictatorship by the year 1939.

Corporate State of the Fascists

According to McGovern, "By Corporatism is meant the set of institutions through which the state attempts to control the economic life of the nation on a more or less authoritarian basis."[41] The corporate state does not consist of unrelated and disconnected indivduals, but of individuals grouped together according to the functions they discharge in the community. It is an organization of functional groups known as corporations at the higher level. Each individual plays his part in the dynamic life of the state through his corporation only and in and through it he joins others who render the same service to the community. In fascism the control over the economic and social life of the nation lies in the hands of a number of occupational groups, each of which in turn is under governmental supervision and control. It is a system in which divergent interests of employers and employees are co-ordinated and harmonized in the unity of the state. The corporations are "The organs which under the aegis of the state carry out the integral, organic and unitarian regulation of production with a view to the expansion of the wealth, political powers and well-being of the Italian people."[42] Thus, corporatism is a means rather an end. It was determined

39. Quoted by Ebenstein, *Ibid.*, p. 111.

40. Coker, *op. cit.*, pp. 470-71.

41. McGovern, *op. cit.*, p. 584.

42. Palmiere, *The Philosophy of Fascism*, p. 168.

by the Corporation Act of 1934. Maxey describes the system thus, "This plan organized the life of the nation on a politico-economic basis. Local workers were grouped into workers' syndicates and local employers into employers' syndicates; those in turn were linked together in provincial federations of workers' and employers' syndicates, and the provincial federations were finally joined in nation federations and confederations. Those were organised into twentytwo national corporation of workers' and employers' syndicates, each corporation having a council made up of representatives of the component workers' and employers' federations. The twentytwo corporation councils sitting together constituted the national council of corporations, which had vast power in the regulation and control of commerical and industrial matters. The central committee of the National Council included not only federation of representatives but the secretary of the fascist party and all of the fascist ministers of the state. The Head of the government (Mussolini) was also head of the Ministry of Corporations and thus stood at the apex of the organized economic life of the country as well as the head of its political institution."[43]

Thus, corporations were an instrument of rigid governmental control over the entire economic, social and industrial life of the community. They were not independent bodies. They were simply the means to bring glorification of the state and to make life disciplined.

Though these corporations were declared to be autonomous in the eyes of law but in actual practice they were run by the state. According to Barker, "Corporation is not the result of a voluntary trade unions of workers and voluntary associations of employers. It is a state created cramp."[44] Mussolini called the corporativism by the name of a disciplined or a controlled economy. According to Barker, "It was a happy balance of indiviudals, groups, and the state. It left to the individuals private property and individual initiative, it left to the associated groups the right of self-discipline in their several categories; it left to the state the right to intervene."[45] Every corporation was presided over by a minister of the government who was to determine what was to be discussed or not in the council. The decisions of the council required the approval of the central government. According to Mussolini, corporatism ensured a higher social justice for the whole of the Italian people which meant a higher standard of livng, guaranteed work of fair wage and decent house. It also meant participation of workers both in the knowledge of the process of production and in the determination of its discipline. Internally it meant higher production. Eternally, it meant increasing the power of the nation for the purposes of its expansion in the world.

Corporatism provided a new conception of the functions of the state superior both to the *laissez faire* of the liberal individualism and to the state control of socialism. It was independent of the political regime. It could exist under any

43. Maxey, *op. cit.*, p. 645.
44. Barker, E., *Reflections on Government*, p. 348.
45. *Ibid.*, p. 349.

form of government. It provided a new form and structure of state, a new kind of democracy. It brought a new self-discipline in the economic field. In politics it brought a new basis of representations.

Criticism

Though corporations played an important part in shaping the economic life of Italy, they were completely subject to the state and the will of the fascist party. The doctrine did not offer any alternative to parliamentary democracy. As Saline comments, "It was a way of bringing the economy under political control, both management and labour lost their freedom of association and independence of action."[46] The second great war proved the hollowness corporatism. It was a dismal failure. It brought misery for the people in the long run.

FASCISM AND COMMUNISM

Points of Difference

1. Communism is the product of a long course of intellectual development and it formed on the whole, a coherent and carefully developed body of thought. The fascist philosophies on the other hand "were mosaics of ancient prejudices, put together without regard for truth or consistency, to appeal not to common purposes but to common fears and hates."[47]

2. The communists had a theory to follow in the 'Communist Manifesto' but fascists had no theory at all. They simply acted according to the exigencies of action. Its course of action has been less planned, less continuous and more opportunist.

3. While fascists put too much emphasis on state which for them was the supreme reality, an ethical entity, for communists it was an instrument of exploitation and it was to wither away ultimately.

4. The communist ideal was stateless and classless society, whereas for fascists the Nationalist Sate was the highest ideal to be achieved.

5. The communists were avowed enemies of capitalism and imperialism whereas fascists retained both of them. The fascists supported the cause of private property and private enterprise.

6. Communists advocated Internationalism. Marx called upon the workers of the world to unite in struggle against international capitalism, the fascist, on the other hand, regarded internationalism as a figment of imagination. For them nation state was everything.

7. For communists the doctrine of economic determinism and the doctrine of class struggle were all improtrant but for the fascists these doctrines were useless, narrow and fruitless. According to them, man was motivated by myths, fictions, traditions, beliefs and sentiments and not by economic interests.

---

46. Sabine, George, *A History of Political Theory*, 3rd revised ed., p. 920.

47. *Ibid.*, p. 884.

8. Communist was atheist. It stood for the abolition of church and religion. For communists religion was the opium of the people. Fascists made full use of the religious beliefs.

Points of Similarity

1. Both were the result of the post-war conditions in their respective countries. Though fascism collapsed during the second great war but communism became a world-wide force and more than half the world had gone red.

2. Both had faith in totalitarian form of government, relied force and hated democracy and democratic methods. They had close spiritual affinities.

3. Both acquired power through violence and both exalted compulsion as the supreme method of political action.

4. Both did not recognize any individual liberties. Both demolished distinction between the party and the government.

5. Both had aggressive, courageous, skilful and public spirited leaders.

6. Both justified their methods of coercion by the exalted aims they pursued: "freedom, comfort, and elightenment for the Russian massess; unity, power and prestige for the Italian Nation."[48]

7. Both work on the high velocity propaganda — for communists, supremacy of the proletariat and for fascists, the supremacy of the nation. While communists relied on class-struggle, fascists relied on struggle between nations.

8. Both had hatred for democracy and liberalism and both despise parliamentary institutions — parliament, elections, parties, etc. Both stood for one party rule.

Thus, fascist and communist were similar to one another in their methods and attitudes towards the most cherished freedoms which are essential for making the individuality and personality of a human being. Their quarrel was simply over the loot. Ebenstein is right in saying, "The quarrel between communism and fascism results from the inability of burglars to agree over the division of the loot whereas the quarrel between communism and democracy is that between the burglar and the law. The same quarrel exists between fascism and democracy."[49]

CRITICAL ESTIMATE

Achievement

According to Coker, "Where representative institutions and liberal governmental policies fail in vigour of will and action or permit the sacrifice of national to factional interests, then the people are ready to yield to the autocratic domination of any one who, however he gains his power and by whatever methods he rules, keeps order and makes government efficient and respected, at home and abroad."[50] Such a thing happened in Italy. The failure

48. Coker, *op. cit.*, p. 485.

49. Ebenstein, *op. cit.*, p. 120.

of democracy allowed fascism to grow. However, fascists put new life into the dying nation and Italy came to have rebirth. Under them Italians got what they needed most — strong and efficient government, peace at home and glory abroad, harmonious relations between the labour and the capital, higher standards of life and a pride in their nation.

Failures

But in spite of its achievements, fascism could not last long.

1. The Second World War sounded its death-knell because of its many shortcomings. It had no coherent philosophy. It was just a body without a soul, a doctrine full of inconsistencies.

2. As it was anti-everything, it could not make a head-way. It was anti-democracy, anti-liberalism, anti-socialism, anti-internationalism, anti-freedom, anti-labour, anti-idealism and anti-intellectualism.

3. Its insistence on war and violence came to be looked down upon. It destoryed the development of great-learning, literature and art. Lessons from history were a pointer towards the short life of fascism. According to Benedetto Croce, history teaches "That...regimes of force can survive only among decadent peoples; that they can figure only as temporary expedients in nations that are growing and in the ascendant; and that...repressions only produce more violent explosions of the forces they would restrain."[51]

4. Finally, it may be said that dictatorship sows its own seeds of destruction. It cannot live long. Parkinson wrote, "Dictatorship decays by the law which governs its very nature. It could not last for more than a life time in any case. In practice it may not last as long. The dictator believes in his own genius — how otherwise could he have seized power ? — so he resents opposition. He believes in his own vision of the state — so he will listen to no advice. He believes in the need for centralized authority — so he will delegate no power to others. The natural results are that he is surrounded by flattering non-entities; that he is never told the truth; and that he is driven mad by overwork. He is apt to end as a physical wreck, unable even to make the decisions which none else is allowed to make for him."[52] So dictatorships collapsed in Italy and Germany.

Reasons for Survival of Fascism

According to Maxey, the reasons for survival of fascism are not far difficult to find. He wrote, "It sugarcoated raw power with a mystical idealism; it supplied a moral justification for violence; it exploited patriotism to the limit; it subtly rationalized minority rule; it capitalized the widespread fear of communism and the equally widespread dissatisfaction with democracy and *laissez faire*, it offered the masses as new religion with a new god to worship.

50. Coker, *op. cit.*, p. 488.

51. Quoted in *Ibid.*, p. 491.

52. Parkinson, C. Northcote, *The Evolution of Political Thought*, p. 296.

Because of those qualities the fascist cult remains a potent force in the world, notwithstanding the annihilation of fascist states in World War II."[53] Some people believe that the threat from communism can be met only through fascism. Democracy with all its weakness is no match to meet danger from communism. If shortcomings of democracy are not cured at an early date, there is possibility of revival of fascism in some form. Real danger to democracy is from within. Ebenstein wrote, "If there is any fascist threat to democracy today — and there is — it no longer comes from Berlin, Rome and Tokyo. It derives its parasitic strength from the inertness and apathy of the citizens of a democracy, because without such civic disease there can be no support for demagogues and fear-mongers who seek to aggrandise themselves at the expense of the body politic."[54]

Thus, fascism is dead as a movement but as a cult it still survives and it shall continue to do so as long as authoritarian personality is not replaced by democratic personality and people do not learn to live democratically. Strengthening of democratic forces and sharpening of democratic processes are essential for paralysing the fascist cult permanently.

QUESTIONS FOR EXERCISE

1. "There was nothing original or creative in Fascism." Examine this view with reference to the leading idea of Fascism.
2. "Fascism is a primitive anti-intellectual verson of the socialist theory." Examine the view that 'Fascism had no coherent, social or political philosophy and was merely a body of ideas taken from various sources and put together to fit the exigencies of circumstances."
3. "What has passed as Fascist philosophy....is a body of ideas taken from various sources and put together to fit the exigencies of circumstances" — Sabine. Explain and point out the main features of the Fascist philosophy.
4. Discuss the principal elements of fascist doctrine and policy.

53. Maxey, *op cit.*, p. 647.

54. Ebenstein, *op. cit.*, p. 121.

33

Nazism or National Socialism

Fascism and Nazism

Fascism of Italy and Nazism or National Socialism of Germany were like twin brothers, professing the same ideology and following the same tactics or methods. Hence, many people believed that the Nazis were simply the successful initiators of fascism. But the Nazi philosophy was not shaped by the changes in conditions and circumstances. The leaders of this movement had solid foundations. They made practically no change in the Nazi doctrine found in Gottfried Feder's '*The Political and Economic Programme of the National Socialist German Workers Party'*, Hitler's '*Mein Kampf*' and Rosenberg's '*The Myth of the Twentieth Century*'. The Nazi philosophy was more logical, more consistent and more thoroughgoing than the philosophy of fascism.

SOURCES OF NAZISM

The sources of Nazi philosophy were the same as that of fascism — Irrationalism, Social Darwinism, Traditionalism and Idealism. The Nazis, however, laid greater stress on Irraitonalism and social Darwinism, though they quietly took over the basic assumptions of the traditionalists and the idealists also. In *Mein Kampf* Hitler gave a philosophical exposition of traditionalism thus : "The entire human culture, as well as man himself, is only the result of one long single development, during which every generation added to and built in its building stones. The meaning and aim of revolutions is not to wreck the entire building, but rather of take away unsuitable stuff which had been badly filled in and to continue to build on and add to the healthy spot that has been made free."[1]

The Nazi's view of the *volk* or nation as a permanent, supernatural, mystical entity, real beyond the existing totality of all inhabitants and the *volk* as having a soul, mind or will of its own differnt from the wills of its individual was a simple statement of Hegelian principles. The Nazis identified the *volk* with the state and defined it. Idealist moralism of Hegel taken over by the Nazis, it gave the self-serving notion that "man must seek virtue not pleasure; that he must seek to perform his duty rather than secure his rights; that self-sacrifice must take the place of egoistic self-interest."[2] According to the Nazis, true idealism

1. Hitler, Adolf, *Mein Kampf* (Houghton Miffin Co.), p. 358.

2. McGovern, *op.cit.*, p. 622.

was nothing but subjecting the interests of the individuals and his life to the community. It was identified with patriotism. Like irrationalists, Nazism held that a nation could become great and powerful only if her people and leaders were motivated by passionate faith in patriotic glory. The people were emotionally swayed by sentiment, passion, emotion and prejudices and not by reason or logic, had to be suppressed to realize glorious Faith in racial excellence — true Aryan entitlement of German race to overlordship of the universe. So Nazism insisted upon the value of creating a myth to stir the people. To them the doctrine of struggle for existence and the survival of the fittest was a part not only of the laws of nature but also of the laws of God. For them "Nature's will is the continuous improvement of all life and consequently her law is the continuous victory of the stronger over the weaker species, the stronger elements of a stock over the weaker, the stronger race over the weaker race."[3] On this score Nazism rejected all such doctrines as humanitarianism, pacificism, democracy and egalitarianism as they were all opposed to the aristocratic principle writ large in nature.

FACTORS OF RISE OF NAZISM

As in Italy, so in Germany there were present the factors which could give rise to a fascist movement. According to Coker, "There were, in the first place, the unsettled economic and political conditions; extreme economic distress; a restless nationalistic fervour aroused by resentment over the terms of the treaty of Versailles; the inability of the several groups supporting the republic unit in any working agreement; a growing belief in the incompetence of any sort of liberal leadership or even of any reactionary leadership... to find a way out. Secondly, their leader Adolf Hitler was skilful in popular electioneering and impressive, at least to conservative interests, in his promises of valiant action against socialism and communism"[4]

HISTORY OF NAZISM

The Nazi movement was started by Auton Drekler. In 1920 its name was changed from German Workers' Party to National Socialist German Workers' Party. In 1921 Hitler became its leader with dictatorial powers. Under Hitler the party grew in numbers and influence. The attempt to seize power by armed revolution failed in November 1923. Hitler and his colleagues were put in jail and the party was dissolved. The party was however, revived after Hitler's release from jail after nine months. Storm troopers were reorganized and a new Black-shirted Elite guards was created. The great economic depression in 1929 and 1930 made the people rally under the banner of the Nazi party. In the elections of 1932 they secured 230 seats in the Reichstag. But no effective government could be formed to be able to fight the economic crises and danger from the communism. So on January 30, 1933 Hitler was invited by President Heindenburg to form the government and he gladly did so. In the fresh elections

3. Dakeshott, M., *Social and Political Doctrines of Contemporary Europe*, p. 98.

4. Coker, *op. cit.*, p. 486.

the Nazi party secured absolute majority in the Reichstag. In 1934 Hindenburg died and Hitler was elected the President of the Republic. The office of Chancellor and President were combined in Hitler who thus became the Dictator. The Weimer Constitution was superseded. Germany passed under authoritarian and totalitarian rule. All parties other than the National Socialist (Nazi) Party were dissolved. By September 1933 Hitler declared that 'The Natonal Socialist Movement is the German Reich. It is the state'. The federal structure of the state was replaced by unitary structure. There was complete centralization of authority.

The Nazi movement got support from all sides. The labour class was attraced by appeals of patriotism. Peasants were given the promises of establishing socialist society. The upper classes were assured of protection against Marxism and violent trade unionism. The lower middle and middle classes were the great pillars of the movement. True, it is to say that fascism whether of Italian or German brand "looks within all social groups for the great common denomination, frustration, resentment and insecurity. These psychological attitudes can easily be turned into hatred and aggression, against both internal and external enemies."[5] These they got in Germany and succeeded.

The Nazi Ideology

The Nazi ideology was not a well-worked out theory of the state or government. However, it was more coherent and consistent than the theory of Italian fascism, though it also kept itself changing and adjusting according to changed conditions and circumstances.

1. Nature and Functions of the State. To the Nazis the supreme unit was the *volk* which is equivalent to the English word Nation. The *volk* or the nation was not only more important than the individual, it was also more important than the state. It was a sort of metaphysical, supernational entity possessing a spiritual reality apart from the existence of its members. It was an End in itself, state was simply a means to an End. Rosenberg wrote, "National Socialism places nation or race higher than the state in its various forms. It declares that the protection of the nation is more important than the protection of a religious creed, a class, a monarchy, or a republic. It sees in the betrayal of a nation a more serious crime than so-called treason against the state."[6] Hitler expressed the same idea when he said, "The state represents not an end but a means — we must sharply distinguish between the state as a vessel and the race as the content. This vessel has meaning only if it is able to preserve and protect the content."[7]

2. Glorification of the Nation State. The nation state was a thing of veneration for the Nazis. It should not only be obeyed but worshipped. It must have supreme and absolute power over all citizens.

5. Ebenstein, W., *Today's Isms*, p. 100.

6. Quoted by McGovern, *op. cit.*, p. 644.

7. Hitler, Adolf, *op. cit.*, pp. 592 and 595.

3. Subordination of the Individual. The individual had no meaning for the Nazis. It had no separate existence apart from the state. It must always be subordinated and sacrificed for the community, the nation and the nation state. Common interest before self-intereset or the welfare of the individual. The individual was to have no freedom or initiative. He was to find his happiness in obedience to the orders of the state. He was simply to serve the needs and requirements of the state. He could find his true spirit only in the state. Service of the state constituted his freedom. Maxey wrote thus : "Although the Nazis declined to glorify the state as such to the same degree as the Italian Fascists, they demanded the individual just as fully with the dictum of Kant and Fichte that the individual possesses not rights but duties, they ardently agreed. One of their axioms was that true freedom for the individual consists of subordinating himself to the *volk* and working for its welfare."[8]

4. Authoritarianism. Thus, Nazis allowed no sphere of privacy to any one. They controlled every sphere of human life — religion, education, art, literature, architecture, music, science, recreation, drama, theatre, and economic matters and even fashions. Their state was completely authoritarian, absolute in all respects. They followed the fascist slogan 'All is in the state and for the state; nothing outside the state, nothing against the state'. According to Sabine, "Both Italian fascism and German National Socialism were intrinsically efforts to submerge all differences of class and group in the single purpose of imperialist aggrandisement. The myths which constituted their philosophy were designed to further that purpose. Hence, the practical outcome of both, however rationalized was the totalitarian internal organization of the state."[9]

5. Totalitarianism. Totalitarianism is the doctrine according to which the state should dominate each and every phase of the citizen's activity and not merely his political activity. According to Nazis, Sabine writes, "Government may, indeed must, control every act and every interest of every individual or group in order to use it for enhancing national strength; government is not only absolute in its exercise but unlimited in its application. Nothing lies outside its province."[10]

6. Dictatorship. As a principle of political organization totalitarianism meant complete dictatorship. As a consequence all democratic institutions — Parliament, independent judiciary, etc., were destroyed. It was one party dicatorship revolving around a magnetic leader Hitler. It was exactly in line with the view expressed by Carlyle in 1840, when he said "Find in any country the ablest man that exists there; raise him to the supreme place and loyally reverence him: you have a perfect government for that country; no ballot box, parliamentary eloquence, voting, constitution building or other machinery can improve it a whit. It is the perfect state, the ideal community."[11] Such a personality was Herr Hitler for the German nation, its perfect embodiment.

8. Maxey, *op. cit.*, p. 652.

9. Sabine, G.H., *A History of Political Theory* : 3rd revised ed., pp. 915-16.

10. *Ibid.*, p. 916.

11. Carlyle, *Heroes and Hero-Worship*, p. 197.

CRITICISM OF DEMOCRACY

Nazis were against every form of democratic or parliamentary government. Hitler wrote "...At all times it has been the principles of democracy which have brought people to ruin. And if Germany has fallen in the last fourteen years that was only because the representation of the principles of democracy was carried to such lengths that its fathers and its representative in Germany did as a matter of fact stand even below the average of those numbers whose supremacy they preach....Never has any system or any government left its place in a more melancholy, more miserable, more mediocre fashion than did the representatives of the present system."[12] Accordinging to Nazis, democracy was the greatest of all fallacies. They supported the doctrine of government by the political elite. According to them, most human beings are stupid, irrational, seldom guided by intelligent self-interest incapable of governing themselves. According to Hitler, "States are founded through the personality of brilliant leaders and through a people which deserves to have the crown of laurels bound upon its brows."[13]

Thus, like their fascist friends, Nazis were thoroughly anti-democratic and anti-liberal. They espoused the cause of Heroes and Hero-worship. Their slogan was "The Laws of nature demand that authority shall be exercised from above downward, and responsibility from below upward".

ATTACK ON COMMUNISM

Like the Italian fascists the nazis were opposed to communism and all forms of socialism which advocated state ownership and operation of the means of distribution or of production. But they were not in favour of unrestricted right to private property. According to McGovern, "The Nazi economic policy is based upon the private ownership and the private operation of all trade and industry, but on the condition that this private ownership and operation shall, at all times, be subejct to state guidance and control."[14] Maxey writes, "The Nazis had no objection to socialism;...what they could not tolerate was the proletarianism of the communist movement, especially the proletarianism of Russia."[15] The Nazi movement was a middle class movement. It did not tolerate any kind of socialism which was a working class movement and which aimed to disposses all private owners of private property and capitalists.

CONTROL OF ECONOMIC LIFE

Nazis aimed at establishing full political control over the economic forces and economic activities inside Germany. Hence, they created a number of estates which were in a way a rival of old mediaeval guilds. Those estates were the state agencies for the control of all phases of economic life. They were to

12. Hitler, Adolf, *Mein Kampf*, Trans. by James Murphy, London, 1932, p. 256.
13. *The Speeches of Hitler*, edited by Baynes, N.H. (1942-Oxford), Vol. I, p. 81.
14. McGovern, *op. cit.*, p. 658.
15. Maxey, *op. cit.*, p. 660.

carry out the policies of the government in the economic field. The officers of these estates were selected by the government. Each estate consisted of particular interests. Thus, the food estate included both landlords, tenants, farmers and agricultural workers. The labour front included owners of factories and workers both. Thus, the German system was more authoritarian than the Italian system of corporations. Through national economic chamber the government could interfere in any economic concern. There was no conflict between labour and capital. Strikes and lock-outs were prohibited. Disputes were to be settled by the labour trustee. Thus, the Nazis had complete control over economic life.

BELIEF IN THE USE OF FORCE

The Nazis believed in the use of brute force for the achievement of their objectives and for meeting every type of opposition. According to Hitler, "An institution which is no longer determined to defend itself with all weapons practically gives itself up. Every half measure is then the visible symptom of internal decay which will and must be followed, sooner or later, by external collapse."[16] 'Might is Right' was the Nazi principle. Hitler believed that force to be successful must be used ruthlessly and persistently. Their philosophy was the philosophy of sword. As Hitler said : "He, who would live, must fight. He who does not wish to fight in this world has not the right to exist. Such a saying may sound harsh, but that is how the matter stands." Nazis used force both in the internal and external fields, with the aim to establish authoritarian, totalitarian dictatorship internally, and for establishing the supremacy of the German nation externally. War was considered to be the climax of human achievement.

THE ROLE OF PROPAGANDA

The Nazis were great organizers, and expert propagandists. The pulpit, the stage, the cinema, the raido, the press, art, science, literature and school all were made instrument of Nazi propaganda. According to Hitler, writes Lorimer, "It is to the masses that propaganda must be addressed. It must not aim at instruction; the less it is weighed with fact or information the better, for at all costs it must avoid the risk of being above the heads of the hearers. It must work always and wholly on the emotions. No amount of skill in concocting propaganda is of any use if the basic principle is forgotten, *viz.*, that its subject matter must be surely restricted and content must be repeated over and over again. The presentation may be infinitely varied, but the theme must be always the same; the one refrain must eternally recur. The results which can be achieved by this procedure are simply incalculable."[17] Hitler believed in the doctrine of Big Lie. According to him, a definite factor in getting a lie believed was the size of the lie. The broad mass of the people in the primitive simplicity of its heart more readily falls victim to a big lie than to a small one. By telling big lies Hitler made the German people follow him blindly.

---

16. Hitler, Adolf, *Mein Kampf*, p. 336.
17. Lorimer, E.O., *What Hitler Wants* (A Penguin special, 1939), p. 39.

ANTI-JEWISH POLICY

Soon after coming into power Hitler followed a policy of ruthless persecution of the Jews. They were made the scapegoats for all the miseries of the German nation. Hitler was convinced that by devilish skill the Jews had acquired complete control of the banks, the stock-exchange, and the whole German economic system, and used this power for the political disintegration of the country. Schopenhauer called a Jew 'The master of lying'. The Nazis believed that the German armies were never defeated in the battle-field. They were stabbed in the back by the Jewish-Marxist traitors. Nazis regarded the Jew as the greatest misfortune of the German nation and Hitler their greatest saviour. So millions of Jews were thrown into concentration camps and gas chambers and butchered to death, Hitler said, "I believe that I am acting today in accordance with the intention of the Almighty Creator, when I attack the Jew I am fighting for the work of the Lord."[18]

ROLE OF RELIGION AND WOMEN

The Nazis were anti-Catholic and anti-Protestant as both the forms of religion were international in character. Prof. Bergmann wrote : "We of the German religion today turn to this ancient Nordic, Indo-Germanic Light Hero figure and get rid of a false and diseased Christ picture created by the Christian Pope and Church to the heart of humanity. The high priest of the new German paganism is Hitler himself. Hitler is God. Hitler is a new, a greater and a more powerful Jesus Christ." All the Christian Churches in Germany were muzzled and totally gagged. They dared not oppose the regime for fear of being thrown in the concentration camps.

Nazis held conventional views about the role of women. The sole end for which women were meant was to produce children and sending them to war. Von Paper said, "Mothers must exhaust themselves in order to secure the future for their sons." The female education laid emphasis on motherhood. Some writers went to the extent of preaching even sex-immorality if it resulted in the multiplication of thorough-bred Nordic children. Large families were encouraged. Home was considered as the natural and proper place for women.

IMPERIALISM AND INTERNATIONALISM

The Nazis followed a policy of expansion and conquest. They were thoroughly imperialist in their outlook and design. Their foreign policy aimed at three things : the absorption of all 'Germans' into the Reich; the total destruction of France; and the expansion of the Reich. Hitler had no regard for political boundaries. German must have new lands for her expanding population. She was justified in seizing new territories. The world was not made for coward peoples. Hitler aimed to make Germany militarily strong enough to get back her colonies and new land for millions. His policy was not to tolerate the rise

18. Hitler, *Mein Kampf* (Eher Verlag, Munich), p. 70; Quoted in *Ibid.*, p. 56.

of a second military power on Germany's frontiers and prevent it rise even by force. This policy resulted in the second Great World War.

The Nazis were patriots *par excellence*. They loved their fatherland more than anything else. Glorification of Greater Germany was their sole aim. They were enemies of Internationalism and believed in the supremacy of the National state. International peace was coward's dream. Germany withdrew from the League of Nations as force and war were the only vehicles for resolving differences. A nation could progress only by coming into conflict with other nations, showing thereby its strength and supremacy. The Nazis regarded it as their duty and wise policy to wage war whenever a favourable opportunity occurred to expand their territory and subjugate inferior peoples. They had utmost hatred for any kind of international amity and cooperation.

DOCTRINE OF RACIAL SUPREMACY

According to Maxey, "The most prominent feature of Nazi philosophy was its emphasis on race and its insistence that race is the measure of all strength."[19] The Nazis gave full support to the doctrine of Social Darwinism and the eugenic creed which was related to it. The principles of this creed were : (1) Men are naturally and innately unequal; (2) These innate differences are hereditary; (3) The innately superior persons and stocks show a tendency to rise to the top of the social ladder; (4) Under present conditions superior stocks show a tendency to die out while the inferior stocks are gaining ascendency; and (5) Thus, the state must take steps to secure the preservation of the superior stocks and thereby reverse the course of the tendency.

The Nazi leaders accepted all those promises, elaborated, amplified and propagated them. The teachings of Gobineau and Chamberlaine regarding the doctrine of race superiority were fully accepted by the Nazis. As pointed out by Maxey these were[20] "that not only the biological but mental differences of men are the result of natural selection in the struggle for existence; that by this method nature produces superior races and discards inferior ones; that every struggle between peoples furthers this selective process, and takes the superior races further on the road to final perfection and supremacy; and that a mixture of superior with inferior races is dangerous if not wholly had, because it dilutes the superior race, retards perhaps even reverses, the process of evolution. It was also generally believed that the white race was superior to all others, that the Teutons were the best of the white race, and the Germans the best of the Teutons."[21]

The Nazis made racial doctrines more refined and more acceptable to the people of Germany. They converted the doctrine of racialism into a kind of myth which could mobilize the youth. For the Nazis the inequalities were the result of heredity. They were eager to create a new aristocracy of the finest

19. Maxey, *op. cit.*, p. 653.

20. *Ibid.*, p. 654.

21. Lorimer, E.O., *op. cit.*, p. 58.

stock in the country. They aimed to protect the superior stock with the help of the state. They raised the race doctrine to mystical heights. According to Hitler, 'All that is not race in this world is trash'. For Rosenberg the idea of the genuine natural state was born out of the concept of race. As certain family stocks were superior to certain other family stocks, so certain races were innately and externally superior to the other races. Each race had a soul of its own which must found through the recognition of its own supreme value. Nazis laid stress on purity of race.

After surveying the races of the world Hitler came to the conclusion that Aryan Race was really the most important and the superior one of all the races. The purest-Aryan stock was to be found in Germany alone. The Aryan was regarded as the highest image of God. Human civilization and culture were bound up with the existence of the Aryan. All nations were mixed. Only the Aryans were the purest of all races. All those racial doctrines provided Hitler with many excuses to follow his policy of totalitarianism and authoritarianism. According to Lorimer, "To justify his intention to exterminate the Jews, he (Hitler) had to evolve some theory of Race; hence, he created the mythical Aryan. Alternatively, called the Nordi, or more bluntly, the German." The doctrine of race provided the Nazis with an argument to enable them to subordinate ethics to political expediency. Those doctrines helped the Nazis to build up aggressive nationalism. The Nazis aimed to build strong German race which could be able to win the world.

THE NAZI PARTY

Germany under Hitler developed one party system. The Naszi Party, the only party in the country, was the embodiment of the Philosophy of National Socialism. It was the connecting link between the *volk* or the community and the state. The party dominated every aspect of life of the people. It was opposed to every type of democratic thinking and working. It was authoritarian. A belief in the leadership of one man — leader emerging from top and not from bottom. Heroes are born from time to time. Such was Hitler whose word was law. He was head of the state, the government, the nation, the army and the party. "He is the genius or the hero conceived as a man of pure race,"[22] writes Sabine. The programme of the party was to win back ancient glory of Germany, rehabilitate her lost prestige, build a superior culture, serve as a containing vessel for the race and to preserve the purity of German blood. It was to recast the entire economic and educational system to serve the needs of the nation. It aimed to replace the parliamentary system by the elite headed by a leader who was a superman. Its flag represented the Imperial conception of Germany.

CRITICAL ESTIMATE

Nazism was a German version of fascism. Hence, all the shortcomings of Fascism were also its shortcomings. It was hostile to liberty and equality. Life

22. Sabine, *op. cit.*, p. 904.

under Nazi regime was horrible. No private person felt safe. Letters were opened, telephones taped and friendships spied upon. The Second Great War once more brought the defeat of Germany. But the philosophy still persists. According to Maxey, "Nazism is still dynamic and still dangerous because its conglomeration of myticism, half-truth, prejudice, amoralism, and statism is an invitation to destroy any disliked social order."

QUESTIONS FOR EXERCISE

1. Distinguish between Fascism and Nazism.
2. Give a critical estimate of Nazi political thought of Hitler.

34

Democracy

ADVANTAGES OF LIBERAL DEMOCRACY

Historically speaking, the twentieth century political philosophers, aim at providing a theoretical basis for liberal democracy. They supported liberal democracy due to its following advantages :

1. Consensus out of conflict. Its basic institutions are committed to the aim of realising consensus out of conflicts, thus not allowing them to effect the stability of the social system. In fact, according to the political thinkers, conflicts are not injurious to the democratic political process. On the other hand, conflicts preserve the health of the democratic political process. They are the results of the uneven distribution of resources. This uneven distribution of political power leads to the emergence of the elite rule. The rule of the elite is therefore justified by the political philosophers. The non-elitist thinkers and the Marxists maintain elitist rule as a sign of exploitation of the masses by oligarchic rule. These, therefore, do not accept the viewpoint of the political philosophy which has been particularly developed by American philosophers.

2. Political power within limits. Liberal democracy has the virtue of keeping political power within limits. The state in a liberal democracy never becomes absolute. It transforms its power into authority of a rational-legal type. Such an authority is respected by the people. It is again, constantly reinforced by securing the growth of an appropriate political culture and also by encouraging meaningful political participation.

3. Scope for pluralist operation of political power. Liberal democracy provides scope for the pluralist operation of political power. It encourages the formation of political parties and pressure groups which, in their turn, influence the working and direction fo political power. Through these parties and pressure groups, the people voice their opinions. Thus, the government may use the mass approval in the process of decision-making.

4. Dynamic political system. Liberal democracy is a dynamic political system. Therefore, it successfully adjusts with social and political changes and thus avoids violent protests and revolutions. This is particularly done by the development of a mature political culture.

The above discussion does not mean that most of the political philosophers glorify the democratic states. They point out that liberal democracy is by far the best alternative since it derives its legitimacy from the rational-legal sources.

The bureaucracy in a democratic society, tends to be more responsible. Political culture is participant and homogenous. Political participation is more widespread. Political parties and pressure groups serve more useful functions. Revolutions are a distant possibility. Thus, the political process goes on spontaneously and in an orderly and valid fashion. Such an order is widely prevalent among most of the non-communist developed countries. The communist thinkers, on the other hand, lay the charge that this political philosophy aims at vindication of the cause of the capitalist society. This charge is based upon the fact that liberal democracy is against revolution and wide changes, thus supporting the *status quo* so much cherished in a capitalist society. The charge by the communist thinkers is also rooted in historical development of political philosophers. Marxism provides an alternative to the democratic political philosophy. The credentials of both however, will be tested by the future political growth in developed and developing countries.

DEFINITION OF DEMOCRACY

1. *Arabham Lincoln*. Democracy is the government for the people, by the people, of the people. It has been defined in other ways also but this is the most appropriate definition. In democracy it is the public that rules. Generally, the representatives of the public are chosen by adult franchise and the governmental functions are based on liberty, equality and fraternity. Democracy established political, economic and social equality. In it, every individual has the right to express his thoughts, make associations and indulge in all constitutionally permissible activities. The ultimate objective of democracy is not only a successful government but the establishment of an ideal state in which there is the maximum scope for the development of brotherhood. Democracy aims at the evolution of conditions which allow for the maximum possible and the best development of the human personality.

2. *Sir Stafford Cripps*. "By democracy we mean a system of government in which every adult citizen is equally free to express his views and desires, upon all subjects in whatever way he wishes and influences the majority of his fellow citizens to decide according to those view and to implement those desires." As far as a definition of a democratic state is concerned, the above definition is quite appropriate. But, as Dr. Radhakishanan pointed out in his University report, democracy is not merely a political system but a way of life which affords equality to everyone, irrespective of the differnces of race, religion, sex, economic status. The equality implies equal freedom and equal rights. In fact, democracy is a very comprehensive concept which can be interpreted in three ways — political, social and economic. The creation of democracy depends upon the extent to which the ideals of freedom, equality and brotherhood can be concertized in all the three spheres.

BASIC ELEMENTS OF DEMOCRACY

1. Liberty. Liberty is a prerequisite of the success of democracy. John Stuart Mill attached the greatest importance to the liberty of the individual. But liberty does not imply complete wilfulness, for, freedom is not absolute but subject to control imposed by the individual's own conscience. Liberty implies the freedom given to the individual to develop his own abilities as he thinks best, without being conditioned or restricted by any extenal factor. But the freedom of a large number of people is possible only when no single individual has unlimited power and no individual misuses the rights given to him.

2. Equality. If democracy is to be successful it is necessary for every individual to be socially, politically and economically equal. Generally speaking, no privileges or special rights should be given to any class of people in a democracy. But equality also does not imply a deliberate neglect of individual differences between one person and another. State more accurately, equality actually means an equality of purpose, because equality cannot be used as the basis for ignoring differences between individuals. Lord Haldane was quite correct when he said that one cannot make all people equal because nature is far too powerful. While one woman is born beautiful, another is ugly, and this creates great differences. One man is born with remarkable intelligence, while another is remarkable for the lack of it. The concept of equality should be abandoned, for it has governed the minds of people long enough, with little good effect. In democracy it is perfectly practical to give certain privileges to a backward class of people in order to educate the citizens in connection with the elements of communal life at an early age. The practical education concerning democracy is imparted to the citizens when he takes part in democratic institutions, panchayats, municipalities and the elections of union and state legislatures.

Social, political and economic equality is absolutely necessary if democracy is to be a success. As a general rule, no individual or class of individuals should have special privileges over and above those available to the people in general. But equality does not imply that there should be no distinction on the basis of skill and qualities or on any other basis. Actually the real implication of equality is the equality of opportunity. The differences between the individuals cannot be eradicated in the name of equality. Haldane is only too correct in his statement that you cannot make men equal because nature is too powerful.

3. Fraternity. In order that the democracy may be a success and should also be rid its psychological difficulies it is necessary that the ideal of democracy and fraternity should be achieved. The real problem is the establishment of a democratic society and not a democratic government, the later being only a means to the establishment or achievment of the former. The main characteristic of a democratic society is fraternity and cooperation is the main basis of the activity of individuals belonging to a democratic society. Fraternity should be encouraged in all spheres in order to hasten the establishment of a democratic society.

From the foregoing description of the nature, difficulties and the means to the achievement of democracy it is evident that in its progress is comparatively slow but ultimately the most beneficial.

ASPECTS OF DEMOCRACY

The word democracy is derived from the Greek words *demose* and *kratein* of which the former means the people and the later means administration or government. This is borne out by the earlier descriptions of the conditions sought to be created by democracy.

1. Political Democracy. As has already been pointed out earlier, the three ideals of democracy have to be translated into reality in the political, economic and social spheres. It is therefore important to understand these three aspects. In its political aspect, democracy can be defined in the words of Lord Bryce, "Democracy is the form of government in which ruling power of a state is legally vested, not in any particular individual or class but in the members of the community as a whole." In a democracy, legally every individual is equal, because law and justice are the same for everyone. Although a democratic government is the representative of the majority it takes care to protect the rights of the minorities. Every individual has complete right to think as he chooses and to express his opinion. Citizens are not discriminated against on the basis of sex, race, religion or any other ground which distinguishes them from others.

2. Social Democracy. In its social aspect, democracy lies in emphasis upon equality and brotherhood between all individuals. In the words of Dewey, "Such a society must have a type of education which gives individuals a personal interest in social relationship and control, and habits of mind which secure social change without introducing disorder." The social feeling of a democratic society is best expressed in Kant's famous formula, "So act as to treat humanity whether in thine own person or in that of any other, always as an end and never as a means." From this principle Kant derives the practical suggestion that, "Try always to perfect thyself and try to conduce to the happiness of others, by bringing about favourable circumstances, as you cannot make others perfect." The democratic individual, therefore, functions as one member of a special government of ends. And this system of ends is the state of democratic ideals. As Kant puts it, "Act as a member of kingdom of ends." Implicit in this is the notion that one should treat oneself and every other individual as something having inherent value, should act as the member of a state in which every person treats the good of another as no less valuable than his own good. In such a state or country, all the others should also behave so that everyone is not a means but an end. Everyone should endeavour to promote the good of another while trying to achieve his own ends.

3. Economic Democracy. The economic aspect of democracy comprehends the rights of individuals to economic independence and equality. In democratic societies all individuals have the right to earn wealth without interfering in or obstructing the right of the other people. This liberty to earn wealth is limited or restricted by the right to equality because, despite the freedom to earn and accumulate wealth, no individual in a democracy has the right to control the means of production in such a way that his possession may obstruct the economic freedom of other people or his wealth may create a chasm between his position and that of others. In order to maintain the right to equality, all democratic societies enact legislation in order to protect the rights of the working class or backward classes. Democracy is opposed to capitalism and it does not approve of excessive economic differences between individuals. Because it believes in brotherhood, democracy is opposed to any kind of economic exploitation.

DIFFICULTIES OF DEMOCRACY

But while on the one hand democracy has been praised it also on the other hand has been ridiculed and criticised. And Oscar Wilde has gone so far as to say that democracy means no more than the beating with sticks of the people, by the people, for the people. But this criticism of democracy is not logical and is further not supported by facts. And yet there can be no denying the fact that the institution of democray is beset with some fundamental difficulties. Roughly speaking, these difficulties can be put into the following classes :

(A) *Difficulties Concerning Elections.* The following are the difficulties concerning elections that are faced by a democratic institution of government:

1. Political Groupism. In a country governed on the democratic pattern there are more than one political parties all of which constantly indulge in true or false propaganda to further their respective political interests and sometimes do not care even if the public stands to lose by their actions. And sometimes political groupism can even result in storms of violence and bloodshed. In the face of political gain no consideration of the propriety of the means employed worries the parties and recourse is had to the worst means if they further the interests of the party.

2. Forgetfulness of the Objectives of Election. In fact, in democratic countries the various contestants fight for election only in order to gain power and are blissfully unaware of the actual objectives of election. Neither the contestants nor the electing public pay any heed to the aims and objectives that are at the root of the election. On the one hand, the aim of democracy is the establishment of equality and fraternity. But on the other hand, in the days of election one sees a preponderance of mutual hatred, competition, jealousy. Votes are solicited in the name of caste, relationships and friendships and are also cast on these bases by the public. And sometimes even votes are bought by distributing money. Sometimes people are bribed out of their political convictions by offers of subsequent facilities in return for the votes. In this way, the interests of the nation are thrown to the winds while limited and narrow interests of political power and economic liberty rule the roast. Communal tensions are aroused and class struggle are made even more bitter.

3. Evil Effects of Propaganda. In the democratic pattern propaganda is indulged in to give currency to opinions. And propaganda is the best means of educating the public but when at the time of elections the very objectives of elections are forgotten, then the propaganda at that time is hardly calculated to educate the people and is more likely to deceive and mislead them. In these campaigns of propaganda all kinds of falsehood are resorted to in order to turn the public opinion into their own favour. This has the cumulative effect of electing those people who are completely inefficient and corrupted while it also deprives the deserving and deficient person from success. At the time of election the propaganda is calculated to rouse the passions and prejudices of the people rather than to educate the people and to teach them.

4. Misuse of Monetary Power. As has been pointed out before, it often happens that the votes are bought and in this way, the democracy is reduced to being a puppet in the hands of the capitalists and these people exploit the public in order to gain their own interests.

5. More Rejection than Election. In fact, just as H.G. Wells has written, we find more rejection than election in democracy. What happens is that the voter instead of selecting turns more to the rejection of candidates. He does not turn to the consideration of the efficient and able candidate but things in terms of bad qualities, hatred, possibilities of loss because of the election of a particular candidate. In this way, he proceeds from one to the other rejecting each one in turn and ultimately selects the one against whom he can find nothing or from whom he can hope to benefit in some way or the other. In this manner then, there is more rejection than there is election in any electoral campaign in a democracy.

6. Problems of Representation. In addition to the above mentioned difficulties of election there are some difficulties of representation that characterise a democracy. In fact the main difficulty among them is the absence of good and proper representation. Now-a-days the countries are extremely big entities and in a people running into a few millions it is not possible to have direct election and for this reason indirect election is resorted to. And even in this there is the difficulty of it being doubtful as to the extent to which a particular individual can represent the public that has elected him for this very purpose. Evidently in a society some people become the rulers while the rest are only the ruled. Then how can it be called the government of the people? Sometimes it also happens that the leader of the powerful group takes over the administration. In this way, in its practical form democracy does not appear to be very different from aristocracy. It is a matter that needs thought. After all, how can the people be represented at all adequately by an individual who is a leader coming from a higher social strata and who only rarely comes into direct contact with the public except for a short time in the days of election? And even if they do attend to the problems of their electors it is only to provide security for opinions and the vested interests.

(B) *Psychological Difficulties*. As was indicated at an earlier juncture, democracy is also faced with some difficulties of a psychological nature. The main difficulties are the following :

1. Inability of the Public to Understand Public Problems. The public is never so well educated and understnding as to comprehend the public problems with facility. And, unscrupulous interests exploit this situation and further their own interests at the expense of the public. Lincoln has observed that you can fool some people for some time but you cannot fool all people for all time. It is true that no leader can pull the wool across the eyes of the public indefinitely but some people bribe other individuals to do wool pulling for them. This bribe can take almost any form.

2. Lack of Interest in Public Project. The public not only evinces lack of understanding of public projects but also professes lack of interest for them. Most people do not have time to spare for the public projects from the struggle that is their own life. Secondly, they have no direct gain coming to them from the public projects, at least such a contingency cannot be envisaged and even if they do have some gain accruing to them they are not likely to realise it. Hence, most people are prone to ignore public projects. It is only in the few days in which election is held that the people come out of their lethargy and then they again go to sleep till the occasion of the next election.

3. Urge to Power. Alfred Adler, the famous psychologist, has written that the most powerful urge or desire in man is the urge to power. The urge to power is clearly evident in the field of politics whether or not it is so in other spheres. The various parties and the different candidates of these parties are contesting the election only in order to attain power and it is only this that motivates them to compete in the political field. And in this race, all the means are adopted with a surprising impartiality which is not marred by any thoughts of moral or ethical propriety or otherwise.

4. Change in the Established Leaders. At the time that elections are being contested, the candidates of the various parties assume a self-righteous attitude and behave in the most patriotic manner possible and put on the air of humility and servitude that lasts only as long as the elections do. But once they are elected, they are entirely changed individuals.

5. Tendency Towards Hero Worship on the Part of the People. Another psychological difficulty facing democratic societies is the tendency to hero worship of the public. As a result of this tendency the public fails to utilise its democratic rights and blindly accepts all that the leaders tell them. Democracy can be a success only in a country in which most of the citizens are educated, uninhibited and thoughtful, aware of their rights and prepared to make full use of them. In a country in which most of the citizens are uneducated, poor and possessed of a tendency to trustful attitude towards the leaders, democracy does no more than foster aristocracy and dictatorship. India at the moment is faced with a situation that is somewhere in between both these conditions. Although there are many critics of the leaders they are far outnumbered by the blindly faithful and the result is that the leaders do as their fancy dictates them.

SOLUTION OF PROBLEMS OF DEMOCRACY

To some extent, the above mentioned problems of democracy can be sovled. The difficulties of efficient representation can be removed by dividing the areas of election on the basis of efficiency. The difficulties of election can be eliminated by effective education. The time taken in the discussion of problems by the

Parliament can be materially reduced if committees constitued of expert persons are formed for the solution of various problems. The public itself can prevent undesirable changes in the established leadership. Many of the psychological difficulties can be removed by developing the national character and the sense of cooperation.

If a democracy is to be a success, a high level of general education, not literacy, is very essential. The citizens cannot make a success of democracy as long as they do not introduce a high conception of public life. This education can be imparted in two ways — mass education and political education. In mass education what is of particular importance is the newspaper in addition to speeches and the freedom of making associations and communities. The leaders of mass education are independent, knowledgeable and impartial newspapers. It is necessary to educate the citizens in connection with the elements of communal life at an early age. The practical education concerning democracy is imparted to citizen when he takes part in democratic institutions, panchayats, municipalities and the elections of union and state legislatures.

Social, political and economic equality is absolutely necessary if democracy is to be success. As a general rule, no individual or class of individuals should be possessed of special privileges over and above those available to the people in general. But equality does not imply that there should be no distinction on the basis of skill and qualities or on any other basis. Actually the real implication of equality is the equality of opportunity. The differences between the individuals cannot be eradicated in the name of equality.

NEED OF EDUCATION IN DEMOCRACY

Aldous Huxley has remarked, "If your aim is liberty in democracy, then you must teach people the arts of being free and of governing themselves." Democracy can never be successful without education. Whenever democracy has been unsuccessful, it has been because of the lack of education. In a democracy the government is composed of the elected representatives of the people and consequently can never create the right kind of government. In fact, it is impossible even to hope for democracy in the absence of education. It is difficult to expect a citizen to behave responsibly if he is not even aware of his rights and duties. Bertrand Russell has commented, "Democracy in its modern form would be quite impossible in a nation where many men cannot read." The truth of the matter is that education is a prerequisite of democracy. 'Only after proper education should citizen be invested with his democratic rights.' As Fichte, the German philosopher, has commented, 'Only the nation which has first solved in actual practice the problem of educating perfect men will then solve the problem of the perfect state." Although Fichte made this comment in the context of autocratic states, it cannot be doubted that the perfection of even a democratic state can be judged only by the extent to which it contains educated people. As Hetherington puts it, "Democratic government, at least, demands an educated people." Throwing light on the objectives of education in the 1949 meeting of the Universities Commission, S. Radhakrishnan stressed the fact that the democratic state recognises the importance of the individual, and it is the process of development of the individual which is called education. Hence, edcuation is absolutely necessary for establishing a democratic society. Dewey has pointed out that democarcy is inconceivable without education, because education alone can generate and instil the qualities which democracy demands as a prerequisite significance of education. Both Plato and Aristotle laid stress on the importance of education for the success of democracy. Earnest Barker comments, "To Plato education was the most important function of state department which was particularly advocated for producing the philosopher kings to improve the man's minds for becoming virtuous beings." Plato, in his famous text, *Republic,* stressed not only the importance of education for democracy but even formulated a plan for the education of men and women which made all kinds of development — physical, mental, moral and aesthetic — possible. Aristotle was of the opinion that the aim of the state is to make possible the achievement of the highest moral level and this can be reached through education alone. Thus, education is the most important function of the state. From one point of veiw, the state itself is a school in which the individual learns citizenship, for Aristotle suggested that the aim of education was to produce good citizens. These truths were known not only to the Ancient Greeks but also to Indian thinkers of ancient times. India has been the home of democratic ideals and principles since ancient times. Hermitages and places of worship were used as schools in which the sages tried to produce ideal citizens who could become useful members of society. But the modern age needs democratic education far more than was needed in ancient Greece or ancient India because modern democracies are so vast and their problem so complex that the education of citizens is even more imperative today.

FREDOM OF THE PRESS

Need of Freedom of Press

In the modern world, with all the enlightened thought at its disposal all the thinkers of present generation are unanimous in their approval of a free press. The term press is not applied to the printing press but to that medium of the communication of thoughts that employs the printing machines. In this way, then the press is the expression, in printed form, of thoughts, ideals and values. Hence, the phrase freedom of the press, implies the idea that any individual or groups of individuals may present its thoughts, ideas and values to the public in any form it desires. The government cannot interfere in such expression in any overt manner and also cannot restrict it. Even ideas that conflict with those of the government can be published with impunity. In a country that boasts a free press people can propagate all kinds of thoughts and ideas in the public through the medium of the press.

Limited *Vs.* Complete Freedom

In this connection some people are in favour of a complete freedom of the press and are averse to any kind of restrictions being placed upon it. According to this school of thought, the press should be possessed of complete freedom. They are prepared to carry this freedom to the extent that they would not curb the activities of an individual or a group of individuals intent upon publishing thoughts that contradict those which are considered improper and morally deplorable. It is herein contended that every individual has the right to think upon every aspect of life in accordance with his own reason, intelligence and experiences. Man is born free and looks upon life in complete independence. Hence, he should also possess the right whereby he be permitted to manifest and give precise expression to life as he experiences it and as he meditates upon it.

Many difficulties manifest themselves in agreeing to this particular concept of the absolute freedom of the press. There can be no disputing the fact that the individual is free and independent, and every individual has the right to give expression to his thoughts but the problem concerns the source whence he derives this right. Who has provided him with this right? Whatever the right that one may possess and however much it may be considered to be of natural origin is bestowed upon him by society. If an individual elects to take up residence in the forest then he has the right to conduct himself according to his own wishes and comfort himself as his instinct guides him. But so long as he continues to live in society, to each right that he can legitimately claim is attached a corresponding duty. In other words, every right of the individual is limited and circumscribed by the duties. So far as human questions are concerned all the individuals of society will begin with equal and similar rights. Now, the individuals in society having been given the right of free expression of their views, in order to successfully implement this right, it is essential that everyone expresses, his individual right only to the extent to which it does not interfere with the exercise of another's right. If this rule is not observed, even his own rights are endangered since the uncontrolled and unrestricted exercise of one's rights on the part of every individual will result in a situation where it will be impossible for anyone to do so. It is essential to keep in mind this mutual relation between right and duty in discussing the freedom of the press.

Importance of the Press in Democracy

The freedom of the press is a very important element and if the press is deprived of its freedom in the modern world a dangerous situation is precipitated. In countries where the press is controlled and dominated by the government no expression is given to any thoughts that contradict and criticize the government and neither the government nor the public become aware of the presence of the objectionable elements. The result of this is that there is actual valuation of the achievements of the government and this tends to obstruct the progress of the nation. Nowadays, most of the states of the world have democratic government. And in democratic nations there are more than one political parties. The party that takes over the functions of the government is that the members of which stand in majority among all those elected by the people.

And of the remaining political parties those that are in majority lead the opposition in the various legislative assemblies. In the democratic method of government much importance attaches to those opposition groups. This opposition helps to remind the government party of its functioning and to keep it on its toes, besides which it awakens the public to a sense of its rights. If the quantity of ills heap up against the party in power then the opposition wins the support of the public and at the next general election it succeeds in defeating the ruling party and taking the control in its own hand. In this way, the balance of power is maintained to the direct benefit of the nation in as much as it prevents the precipitation of an autocratic state. And in this process, the importance of the freedom of the press is evident and readily apparent. It is a misconception to think of a democracy without any free press. In countries in which the government vigilantly controls the press and shackles it, there can neither be any free and unhindered development of literature nor the independent development of thought. Under such circumstances even education is restricted and inhibited with the result that the future citizens of the country are deprived of the opportunity of developing and manifesting their qualities. A certain school of thought, holds free press the highest or best facility offered by any state. Its absence endangers almost grievously, the possibility of all human welfare, irrespective of the heights attained in the economic sphere in the country. Hence, it is an indisputable and an undisputed fact that the press should be granted freedom.

Press Should not Possess Absolute Freedom

But at the same time there is no gainsaying the fact that this freedom of the press should not be absolute. While each and every unit of the press has the right to free expression, it is also bound by its duty to abstain from intervening in the freedom and independence of the other units. For example, no press can claim to possess such freedom as to warrant its indulgence in immoral and deviate subjects. It should of course have the right to criticise the activities of the government but this right cannot be interpreted to permit the inciting of unpatriotic emotions and feelings of the people. Often many of the communal newspapers encourage communal feelings and interests while many indulge in propaganda that tends to rise to racial and tribal prejudices and questions. Along similar lines today in India many of the newspapers foment regionalism. None has the right to indulge in activities which compromise the interests of the nation. Hence, some control over the press, and some limitations upon it are quite essential.

The question that now remains to be considered is that of the extent to which this curtailment of the press's freedom is to be effected. As a general observation one can say that feats of reason and flow of soul should not be obstructed so long as it does not give rise to any actual danger threatening the sociey or country. If the government did hinder or control the writings of John Milton, such activity on its part is to be contemptuously looked down upon. In the field of literature, it is reasonable and proper to exercise some control upon those expressions and compositions which affect or insult the sensibilities of a national or a people, or of a religious cult or which spread unhealthy interest in the society. Hence, it is that in all civilized and cultured societies of the world all pornographic and other immoral literature is conscientiously banned and suppressed. The necessity for control is also felt in the case of newspapers. For example, no newspaper has the right to inflame the emotions of the people by printing false but sensational material or by making any improper or unjustified comment on current events. In order to maintain an unbiased and unprejudiced appraoch or viewpoint, the least it can do is to express its opinions in such a manner as to avoid injuring the self-respect of any individual or group. Every press has the right to give free expression to its healthy, invigorating and stimulating thoughts. Fair criticism is to be welcomed in spite of any bitterness or bite that it may possess. True news should not be suppressed even if they tend to besmirch the reputation of any individual. But no press has the right to publish and print news and advertisements that are untrue and misleading; steps should be taken to curb any misleading and depraved propaganda and advertisement. Difference in an variety of the non-concurrence of values and ideals is not harmful in any manner. But since the reading of any immoral or depraved thoughts or concepts that contradict the normally accepted norms of social behaviour has an undesirable influence on immature minds, the publishing of such literature can justifiably be prohibited. Briefly, then, the freedom of press should be restricted to the extent to which it can conceivably harm any individual, group or nation. If such a contingency need to be entertained then there is no need for any control of restriction. Secondly, there need be no control on the publication of true and well founded news so long as their concealment does not directly benefit the nation. In India, the Constitution provides for the freedom of the press and recognises it as a fundamental right. But in the light of foregoing discussion, the meagre degree of control exercised by a government upon the press is well justified and need arouse no fears of any autocratic control.

QUESTIONS FOR EXERCISE

1. What is democracy? Explain its elements.
2. Write short note on Aspects of Democracy.
3. "Democracy ensures neither better government nor greater liberty." Examine this statement and discuss the causes of reaction against democracy in recent times.
4. "Democracy is the Government of the cattle, by the cattle and for the cattle." Discuss.
5. "Democracy is, of all forms of state, the most unfriendly to liberty and individuality" — Coker. Discuss.

35

John Dewey (1859—1962)

John Dewey, the third of four sons of a middle-class couple, was born on October 20, 1859, in Burlington, Vermont. He was to become in this country the voice of scientific method, of disciplined inquiry as the chief agency and instrument of freedom in the complex industrial society of our time.

Dewey has been to describe as a maker of twentieth-century America. He is recognized as a peculiarly American philosopher because he caught the voice, accent and temper of the American tradition and the nature of the special contingencies and choices before it in his own era. The expanding forces of technology, the intervolvement of public and private affairs, the rising tides of the labour movement, the revolt against authoritarianism in religion and in education — all of these played a large part in his social thought.

All his life Dewey retained something of the simplicity of the nineteenth-century world of individuality and of fair play, of first-hand respect for first-hand experience that was characteristic of the nineteenth-century Vermonters among whom he grew up. He retained a paramount sense of individual, and the private dignity of the individual, that had been the themes of Thoreau and Emerson in the nineteenth century. He had the slowness of speech and the sharpness of perception of the weathered Vermonter. Nearly all his life he spent in the Universities; yet he early had become aware that schools are a function of society, and he spent not a small part of his own life becoming acquainted with that society outside of schools, in adult education, in labour movements, in what was happening in science and government and industry, among plain people and artists.

Gradually Dewey's fame became world-wide. He was invited to China, where he spent two years following World War I teaching at the University of Peking, and at the Imperial University of Tokyo, where he delivered a series of lectures of which his book entitled *Reconstruction in Philosophy* was a consequence. He also visited Russia, with which, long before a great many other liberals, he became drastically disillusioned. In France a generation ago Dewey's philosophical rather than his educational works were very widely known. But he remained to the end of his life, in his ninety-second year, characterized by both a shrewd simplicity and an acute awareness of the complicated new problems of men and women in the twentieth century. He always "saw around" the academy and felt that philosophy had its obligation to that society in which it emerged and which it expressed, and which it could help intelligently to transform itself, to grow and change in the light of disciplined guiding hypotheses, of which for him philosophy essentially consisted.

John Dewey, greatest of the pragmatists and generally recognized as the most outstanding philosopher, his country has yet produced, made significant contributions to virtually very field of philosophy as well as to such other areas of inquiry as education and psychology. Active for 70 years as a scholar, he was a prolific writer publishing approximately fifty books and more than eight hundred articles. Many of these have been translated into various foreign languages. New volumes are still coming out with more Dewey material, mainly correspondence; and books and articles on him are appearing at a rapidly increasing rate.

Some Dewey material is at present available only in Chinese. In February and March of 1919 he lectured at the Imperial Unviersity of Tokyo, and these lectures were published as *Reconstruction in Philosophy.* While in Japan he was invited to lecture in China also, and he spent from May 1, 1919 to July, 1921 there, finding the developments there of extremely great interest. He lectured extensively in Peking, Nanking, and Shanghai, speaking in English from brief lecture notes; and his lectures were translated and recorded in full on the spot in Chinese by his former students. Dr. Hu Shih, for example, translated his Peking lectures. According to Dr. Hu Shih's account in "John Dewey in China,"[1] Dewey provided the translators and recorders with his typed lecture notes in advance of each lecture so that they could study them and think out suitable Chinese words and phrases before the lecture and its translation. The translation was checked against his notes before publication in newspapers and periodicals or later publication in book form. What was known as "Dewey's Five Major Series of Lectures" in Peking, some 58 lectures on Modern Tendencies in Education, Social and Political Philosophy, Philosophy of Education, Ethics, and Types of Thinking according to Hu Shih, went through ten large reprintings in book form before Dewey left China, and continued to be reprinted for at least three decades before government authorities on the mainland put a stop to them. There were also series on such other topics as Democratic Developments in America, Experimental Logic, History of Philosophy, and (as an introduction to Russell's lectures there in 1920), three Philosophers of the Modern Period, James, Bergson, and Russell.

Fortunately, the Institute for Advanced Projects East-West Centre, University of Hawaii, with Professor Robert W. Clopton as special consultant, has undertaken to translate these materials, and in the fall of 1964 Dr. Tusin-Chen Ou as the first of a team of translators began the work of translation. When this material is available it may well shed significant new light on various areas of Dewey's thought.

The southern Illinois Unviersity Co-operative Research Project on Dewey publications has discovered a number of previously unlisted publications by

1. Charles A. Moore, ed., *Philosophy of Culture* : *East and West* (Honolulu, University of Hawaii Press, 1962); pp. 762-769.

Dewey, and it has assembled the most complete collection in existence of works by and about him. Under the direction of its Editorial Board — Professors George E. Axtelle, Je Ann Boydston, Joe R. Burnett (University of Illinois), S. Mooris, Eames, and Lewis E. Hahn — the project, with the cooperation of a number of other leading Dewey scholars, is planning a definitive edition in forty or more volumes of all his published writings (books and articles).[2] The materials are to be arranged chronologically with careful textual editing but with a minimum of interpretive comment. The editorial and textual work connected with this pioneering venture for a major American philosopher will extend over many years, but it was hoped that the first volumes will be ready from the Southern Illinois University Press in 1967. Accompanying *The Works* was to be a one-volume *Readers' Guide* with interpretive essays by eminent. Dewey scholars on the main subject areas of his thought and writings. It was expected that this volume will be completed by 1967 so that it may be used throughout the publication period of *The Works.*

Further evidence of the contemporary relevance of Dewey, especially in education broadly conceived, may be had in connection with the activities of the John Dewey Society for the Study of the Education and Culture. Organized at Atlantic City in February, 1935, it exists to promote the study of the educational aims and educated methods of a democratic society. Regular meetings are scheduled in connection with the annual meetings of the National Society of College Teachers of Education. Much of the work of the Society is carried on through its Commissions on Meetings and Communications, Monographs in Educational Theory, and Annual John Dewey Lectures. It helped launch the journal, *Educational Theory,* and it has had a distinguished series of year-books going back to 1937 when William H. Kilpatrick edited the first one on *The Teacher and Society.* Among the other editors for this series are Harold D. Alberty, Christian O. Arndt. George E. Axtelle, Harold Benjamin, Theodore Brameld, Bovd H. Bode, John S. Brubaeher, Samuel Everett, Hollis L. Caswell, H. Gordon, Hullfish, Virgil Clift, Archibald Anderson, Ernest O. Melvbv, Harold Rugg, William Van Til, Harold G. Shane, Lindly J. Stiles and William W. Wattennberg. The Annual Dewey Lectures have included Ordway Tead, Oscar Handlin, Seymout Harris, Gardner Murphy, Loren Eiseley, R. Freeman Butts,, and Huston Smith.

PRAGMATIC VIEW OF THE STATE

Dewey's trips abroad played a decisive part in the evolution of his social and political ideas. He discussed the state and its functions in his work, *The Public and Its Problems* (1927). The state can be approached with as little respect for abstractions as state can be approached with as little respect for abstractions as greeted Society and the Individual. The State, seems to be indeed a thing, an entity, a metaphysical essence — at the very least, a causal agency having power to produce action. The state has come to mean the whole

2. The Editorial Board has the assistance of a larger Advisory Committee under the chairmanship of Professor Willis More, Chairman of the Philosophy Department Southern Illinois University.

series of hypostatisations that parade regally through the history of political philosophy. It ranges from the Hegelian capstone of the universal processes to a wicked ogre which is waiting only to be pushed over. But by the pragmatic methods of Dewey the state must be sought in actual happenings and consequences.

Necessity of State

Dewey found the state in the need for regulation of activities. As a pragmatist he stated : "The state is the organization of the public effected through officials for the protection of the interests shared by its members."[3] Thus, the states come into existence as they are required. They grow and develop as they face new and more complicated problems. They are the consequences of specific needs. There is prepotent force which generates a mystical state by fiat or nisus. Neither is there any trick with changeless, permanent states. States are no more all-embracing than they are insignificant. They result from the projection of important consequences which require the establishment of special agencies beyond the direct concern of persons and groups. Therefore, as Dewey said, the formation of states becomes a series of experiements. Publics differ; their needs and demands change. It is able to expect states to be flexible. By their very origin and nature they require constant scrutiny, revision, amendment. It is, thus, futile to talk about the 'best state'. Yet it is equally futile to rely simply upon improvisation. Instead, the *specific* search for the nature of the state directs its attention to problems that are real and soluble. In pragmate approach is included a deliberate accounting of the actual characteristic which states do possess.

These characteristics are worked out in Chapter II of Dewey's book *The Public and Its Problems.* They include such traits as localization of the state somewhere between associations which are narrow and intimate, and those which are remote and disconnected; concern of the state peculiarly with long-time interests which are channelized and standardized by means of law; functions of the state in dealing with irreparable conditions, *e.g.*, those of inferiority of age or capacity, and the like.

Nature of State

As the state is a functioning arm of public it can be experimented with. States are plural. They can be manipulated and directed. State is not a totalitarian idol changeless, untouchable and awe-provoking. State must be regarded as neutral in predeteremining the extension of powers. States expand when the indirect and far-reaching consequences of private action expand. They contract when intimate, face-to-face relations dominate. As the indirect and far-reaching consequences have expanded prodigiously since the industrial revolution; the powers of the state have expanded. Yet to label the state collectivistic or total in its essence is as prejudicial to the understanding of political function as falling back upon *laissez faire* or limited police powers.

3. Dewey, John : *The Public and Its Problems*, p. 33.

DEMOCRACY AND FAITH IN HUMAN NATURE

Too often pragmatism, has been decried as blined expediency or as resigned acceptance of whatever happens to be 'working' at the moment. It has been accused of being responsible at the same time for both the fumbling and pointless efforts of liberalism, and the ostensible efficiency of fascism. But neutral does not mean indifferent. It does not mean refusal to allow concepts and symbols which have been obviously weighted one way or the other to determine antecedently what kind of state must be supported by political philosophy. Instead, the purpose of political philosophy is precisely "the creation of methods such that experimentation may go on less blindly, less at the mercy of accident, more intelligently, so that man may learn from their errors and profit by their successes."[4] Dewey said, "It seems unnecessary to add that the political set up for such experimentation requires a democratic state. This mention of the democratic state will not be a stimulus for discussing his historical or political democracy."[5] That would involve material which is both too familiar and too tricky; besides, it would not be exactly the point in question. For the connotations of Dewey here are those of method. "The prime condition of a democratically organized public is a kind of knowledge and insight which does not yet exist. In its abesence, it would be the height of absurdity to try to tell what it would like if it existed. But some of the conditions which must be fulfilled if it is to exist can be indicated....An obvious requirement is freedom of social inquiry and of distribution of its conclusions."[6]

As a personal, an individual, way of life Democracy involves nothing fundamentally new. But when applied it puts a new practical meaning in old ideas. Powerful present enemies of democracy can be successfully met only by the creation of personal attitudes in individual human beings. We must get over our tendency to think that its defence can be found in any external means whatever, whether military or civil, if they are separated from individual attitudes so deep-seated as to constitute personal character.

Democracy is a way of life controlled by a working faith in the possibilities of human nature. Belief in the Common Man is a familiar article in the democratic creed. That belief is without basis and significance save as it means faith in the potentialities of human nature as that nature is exhibited in every human being irrespective of race, colour, sex, birth and family, of material or cultural wealth. This faith may be enacted in statutes, but it is only on paper unless it is put in force in the attitudes which human beings display to one another in all the incidents and relations of daily life. The foundation of democracy, according to Dewey, is faith in the capacities of human nature; faith in human intelligence and in the power of pooled and co-operative experience. It is not belief that these things are complete but that, they will grow and be able to generate progressively the knowledge and wisdom needed

4. *Op. cit.*, p. 34.

5. *Ibid.*, Chaps. III & V.

6. *Ibid.*, p. 160.

to guide collective action. Dewey remarked that "the keynote of democracy as a way of life may be expressed, it seems to me, as the necessity for the participation of every mature human beings in formation of the values that regulate the living of men together : which is necessary from the standpoint of both the general social welfare and the full development of human beings as individuals."[7] Dewey firmly maintained that mankind was always subject to passion, dogma, self-interest, partisanship and propaganda. But these causes have lost "whatever frnak, stout downrightness they once possessed....They find entrance into the mind invested with a protective are in fashion."[8] A society of free individuals in which all, through their own work, contribute to the liberation and enrichment of the lives of others, is the only environment in which any individual can really grow normally to his full stature. To profess democracy as an ultimate ideal in a country that has anything of a genuine democratic spirit in its traditions, it signifies desire for possession and retention of power by a class, whether that class be called Fascist or Proletarian. Dewey was not happy with a state which tries to curtail reasonable freedom, although he never supported the idea of freedom as a licence to do whatever one likes without being considerate to others. He firmly asserted that our state is founded on freedom, but when we train the state of tommorrow, we allow it just as little freedom as possible. He remarked : "No government by experts in which the masses do not have the chance to inform the experts as to their needs can be anything but an oligarchy managed in the interest of the few. And the enlightenment much proceed in ways which force the administrative specialists to take account of the needs. The world has suffered more from leaders and authorities than from the masses."[9] Dewey strongly believed in human equality. He denounced those persons who condemned Nazism for intolerance, cruelty and stimulation of hatred while their own actions were moved by racial, colour, or other class prejudice. The democratic faith in human equality is the belief that every human being, independent of the quantity or range of his personal endowment, has the right to equal opportunity with every other person for development of whatever gifts he has. According to John Dewey the democratic belief in the principle of leadership, is a generous one. It is belief in the capacity of every person to lead his own life free from coercion and imposition by others provided right conditions are supplied.

DEMOCRACY AS A WAY OF PERSONAL LIFE

Thus, democray is a way of personal life controlled not merely by faith in human nature in general, but by faith in the capacity of human beings for intelligent judgment and action if proper conditions are furnished. Dewey stated : "I have been accused more than once and from opposed quarters of an undue, an utopian faith in the possibilities of intelligence and in education as

7. Dewey, *Problems of Men*, New York, The Philosophical Library, 1946, p. 58.
8. Dewey, *Education Today*, New York, G.K. Putnam's Sons, 1940, p. 185.
9. *The Public and Its Problems*, New York, Henry Holt & Co., 1927, p. 208.

a correlate of intelligence. At all events, I did not invent this faith. I acquired it from my surroundings as far as those surroundings were animated by the democratic spirit. For what is the faith of democracy in the role of consultation, of conference, of persuasion, of discussion, in formation of public opinion which in the long run is self-corrective, except faith in the capacity of the intelligence of the common man to respond with common sense to the free inquiry, free assembly, and free communication? I am willing to leave to upholders of totalitarian states of the right and the left the view that faith in the capacities of intelligence is utopian. For the faith is so deeply embedded in the methods which are intrinsic to democracy that when a professed democrat denies the faith he convicts himself of treachery to his profession."[10]

The final guarantee of democracy is in free gatherings of neighbours on the street corner to discuss back and forth what is read in uncensored news of the day, and in gatherings of friends in the living rooms of houses and apartments to converse freely with one another. Intolerance, abuse, calling of names because of differences of opinion about religion or politics or business, as well as becase of differences of race, colour, wealth, or degree of culture, are treason to the democratic way of life. Everything which bars freedom and fullness of communications sets up barriers that divide human beings into sets and cliques, into antagonistic sects and factions, and thereby undermines the democratic way of life. Legal guarantees of civil liberties of free belief, free expression, free assembly are of little avail if in daily life freedom of communication, the give and take of ideas, facts, experiences, is choked by mutual suspicion, by abuse, by fear and hatred. These things destroy the essential condition of the democratic way of living.

FUNCTIONING OF DEMOCRACY

Democracy as a way of life is controlled by personal day-by-day working together with others. Democracy is the belief that even when needs and ends or consequences are different for each individual, the habit of amicable co-operation is itself a priceless addition to life. To take as far as possible every conflict which arises out of the atmosphere and medium of force, of violence as a means of settlement, into that of discussion and intelligence, is to treat those who disagree with us as those from whom we may learn, and in so far, as friends. A genuinely democratic faith in peace is the possibility of conducting disputes, controversies, and conflicts as co-operative undertakings in which both parties learn by giving the other a chance to express itself, instead of having one party conquer by forceful suppression of the other. This suppression is one of violence when it takes place by psychological means of ridicule, abuse, intimidation, instead of by overt imprisonment or in concentration camps. To co-operate by giving differences a chance to show themselves because "of the belief that the expression of difference is not only a right of the other persons but is a means of enriching one's own life experience, is inherent in the

10. Quoted from the speech of Dewey given in *John Dewey* by Irwin Edman (The Bobbs-Merrill Company, Inc., New York, 1955), pp. 311-12.

democratic perseonal way of life."[11] While elaborating his standpoint regarding the functioning of democracy Dewey said that "to get rid of the habit of thinking of democracy as something institutional and external and to acquire the habit of treating it as a way of personal life is to realize that democracy is a moral ideal and so far as it becomes a fact is a moral fact. It is to realize that democracy is a reality only as it is indeed a commonplace of living."[12]

Thus, as compared with other ways of life, democracy according to Dewey, is the sole way of living which believes wholeheartedly in the process of experience as end and as means. It is that which is capable of generating the science which is the sole dependable authority for the direction of further experience and which releases emotions, needs and desires so as to call into being the things that have not existed in the past. Every way of life that fails in democracy, limits the contacts, the exchanges, the communications, the interactions by which experience is steadied while it is also enlarged and enriched. The task of this release and enrichment is one that has to be carried on day-by-day. It is one that can have no end till experience itself comes to an end. Hence, the task of democracy is the creation of a freer and more humane experience in which all share and to which all contribute. Political or economic democracy is thus the setting for experimental method in social thinking. That alone is sufficient reason for cherishing it. Given that will follow all the implications about democracy making possible the realization of individuality amid co-operation. Granted that, liberalism will assume a new and richer significance.

ATTACK ON LIBERALISM

The historical fate of the liberal movement exemplifies the bankruptcy of political concepts. Dewey has particularly addressed himself to this problem.[13] He has undertaken so complete a reformulation of neo-liberalism that at least a mention of the liberal movement is necessary.

According to Dewey, truly liberal programmes of any period must have a similarity of purpose — a commitment to the principle that the mass of individuals should possess actual, not merely legal liberty. This 'liberty' does not mean being let alone. It does mean that the individual be given full opportunity to develop the potentialities and talents that alone make him an individual. But unless it be elaborated with great particularity that purpose will remain empty, and indeed as abstract as any platform that has only nobility to recommend it. Dewey complained that the liberal is so often found either to fall back upon the most vague and vicious abstractionism dealing with individualism, *laissez faire,* free competition, and the rest; or to give his programme content

11. *Ibid.*, p. 313.

12. *The Philosopher of the Common Man* (New York, G.P. Putnam's Sons, 1940) (Refer address of John Dewey in it).

13. See particularly his *Individualism — Old and New* (1930); and *Liberalism and Social Action* (1935).

in terms of the historical liberalism of the eighteenth and nineteenth centuries, the liberalism, that is, of the commercial, the pre-industrial, revolution.

Dewey's whole approach was introduced by his attack upon both of these brands of 'latter-day' liberalism. He pleaded that liberalism should become the truly radical, the subversive reform that once upon a time evoked energies directed to fundamental social change. It must undergo basic readjustment. Its principle of providing a soil for the complete growth of personality must be so adopted to economic and political life that direction and relevance can be achieved. This requires recognition of the power of organized society, which alone can insure the conditions in which individuals may function fully. Here is where Dewey broke cleanly with *laissez faire* or individualistic liberalism. Individualistic liberalism is bankrupt because it refuses to accept the corporate civilization which has made so many of its premises unreal and downright ghostly. It refuses to accept the need for co-operative control and organized social planning.

The study of particular social needs and the construction of special social machinery, the planned social employment of the resources of scientific knowledge and of the forces of produciton — these cannot be carried through by the uncoordinated acts of individuals, and they must not be stopped by platitudes of an older liberalism which is anarchy of natural laws and personal liberty. Traditional liberalism has lagged far behind the shattering consequences of the industrial revolution, just as the folklore of capitalism has lagged behind the transformation of a scarcity into an abundance economy. Both have been sufficiently impressed by the realization that economic insecurity is now instituional and not 'natural', just as both have failed to appreciate that 'socialism' must come — of it is not here already. Whether the socialistic, the corporate, state be public or capitalistic — that is the specific problem that must be met. But liberalism can never meet it by closing its eyes and wishing for the salad days.

Dewey was a liberal instead of a socialist for the same reason that men like Max Lerner perfer the phrase 'democratic collectivism'. Socialism and communism are terms which are indissolubly connected with the name of Marx. There is much in Marxism of which Dewey not only approved, but which, in real sense, he had actually helped put into operation. For example, the economic interpretation of history had been used by Dewey himself to explain many sections of the history of philosophy. Dewey did not quarrel with Marx over the very questionable intelligence and effectiveness of the capitalistic state, or over the values of a socialized society. Nor did the quarrel lie in any suspicion of the proletariat. "The world has suffered more from leaders and authorities than from the masses."[14] Dewey was definitely suspicious of an elite class, even of experts whose investigations he cherished. Experts can discover and make known the facts, but that fundamental social change has relevance but only as an embodied intelligence raises the entire level of a society.

14. *The Public and Its Problems*, p. 208.

DEWEY'S REJECTION OF THE PHILOSOPHY OF MARX

Dewey's refusal to follow the philosophy of Marx was refusal to accept metaphysical explanation for social and political problems. For Dewey, the Marxian dialetic, the class struggle, the labour theory of value are as abstract and as essentially meaningless as any of the Hegelianisms or economic classicisms from which they derive. There is no cosmic reason why capitalism must give rise to communism via socialism, why collectivism must be achieved by means of a revolutionary technique, why surplus value must arise, why any abstract sequence must appear. Marxism is as much 'a logic of general notions' as the individualistic liberalism it despises. Both rely on a metaphysic of general principles. What does happen, what can happen — these are realistic and instrumental problems; not what must happen.

QUESTIONS FOR EXERCISE

1. Explain Dewey's concept of State.
2. What is Democracy? How can it be realised according to Dewey?

36

Bertrand Russell (1872—1969)

Bertrand Arthur William Russell belonged to one of the oldest and most famous families in England, a grandfather, Lord John Russell, was a great liberal Prime Minister who fought an unyielding battle fo free trade, for universal free education, for the emancipation of the Jews, for liberty in every field. His father, Viscount Amberley, was a free thinker, who did not overburden his son with the hereditary theology of the West. He was heir presumptive to the Second Earl Russell but he rejected the institution of inheritance, and proudly earned his own living. When Cambridge dismissed him for his pacifism he became a travelling Sophist, whom the world supported gladly.

Russell was one of the top-most philosophers of the world. Described by many as anti-Christ and philosopher of immorality, he was a great intellect who was awarded Nobel Prize for Literature in 1950. He was one of the greatest writers of the modern age and he has written more than five hundred books, pamphlets and articles. His political ideas can be found from his many books such as *German Social Democracy, The Problems of Philosophy; War, the Off-spring of Fear; Principles of Social Reconstruction; Roads to Freedom; The Practice and Theory of Bolshevism; The Analysis of Mind; The Problem of China; Marriages and Morals; The Conquest of Happiness; Freedom and Organisation; Power, a New Social Analysis; A History of Western Philosophy; Authority and Individual; Wisdom of the West; Justice in War Time; The Scientific Outlook; Human Knowledge, Its Scope and Limits,* etc. Russell identified himself completely with the peace movement in the world, lived and died espousing its cause.

Philosophy Before the War

1. Emphasis on Logic and Science. In *Mysticism and Logic* Russell attacks the illogicality of mysticism and glorifies the scientific method. He puts emphasis on logic and regards mathematics as divine. In his heart he usually thinks of philosophy as an inferior pursuit compared with mathematics and science. One of the most often repeated notes in his writings is the continued refrain at 'the philosophers' for being too lazy to undertake the study of mathematics, or too stupid to understand it.[1] He expressed regret more than once that he had not been a scientist instead of a philosopher.

1. For example, in *Principles of Mathematics* (Passion), *Mysticism and Logic*, p. 80, and *Sceptical Essays*, p. 72.

Russell's philosophy is essentially a by-product. To treat it as though it were an end in itself, is liable to render it meaningless. But in fact there is a sense in which any worthwhile philosophy is a by-product. As Russell himself wrote, "A philosophy which is to have any value should be built upon a wide and firm foundation of knowledege that is not specifically philosophical."[2]

2. Primary objectives. Russell's primary objects were to establish the turth of religion, the truths of mathematics, and the truth of science. He himself said, "I hoped to find religious satisfaction in philosophy...."[3] "...I came to philosophy through mathematics, or rather through the wish to find some reason to believe in the truth of mathemactis." In 1914 Russell impressed one as cold-blooded, as a temporarily animated abstraction, a formula with legs. He never saw a motion-picture till he read Bergson's cinematography analogy for the intellect; then he reconciled himself to one performance, merely as a task in philosophy. Bergson's vivid sense of time and motion, his feeling that all things were alive with a vital impetus, made no impression on Russell : It seemed to him a pretty poem and nothing more; for his part he would have no other god than mathematics. He had no liking for the classics. He argued vigorously, for more science in education. The world's woes, he felt, were largely due to mysticism, to culpable obscurity of thought. The first law of morality should be, to think straight. Russell said, "Better the world should perish than that I, or any other human being, should believe a life;....that is the religion of thought, in whose scorching flames the dross of the world is being burnt away."[4]

3. Philosophy Through Mathematics. Russell's passion for clarity drove him inevitably to mathematics. He was almost thrilled at the calm precision of this aristocratic science. He said, "Mathematics, rightly viewed, possesses not only truth but supreme beauty, a beauty cold and austere, like that of sculpture, without appeal to any part of our weaker nature, without the gorgeous trappings of painting or music yet sublimely pure, and capable of a stern perfection such as only the greatest art can show."[5] He believed that the progress of mathematics was the finest feature of the nineteenth century; specifically, "the solution of the difficulties which formerly surrounded the mathematical infinite it probably the greatest achievement of which our age can boast." In one century the old geometry which had held the fortress of mathematics for two thousand years was almost entirely destroyed; and Euclid's text, the oldest schoolbook in the world, was at last superseded. "It is nothing less than a scandal that he should still be taught to boys in England."[6] What drew Russell to mathematics is its rigid impersonality and objectivity; these *a priori* theorems are the 'Ideas' of Plato, the 'eternal order' of Spinoza, the substance of the world. In an early article Russell described how, in the greatest mathematical works, "unity and

---

2. Review of Urmson's *Philosophical Analysis in The Hibbert Journal*, July 1956.
3. *Philosophy of Bertrand Russell* ('My Mental Development').
4. *Mysticism and Logic* (London, 1919), p. 241.
5. *Ibid.*, p. 60.
6. *Ibid.*, p. 95.

inevitability are felt as in the unfolding of a drama....The love of system, of interconnection... is perhaps the inmost essence of the intellectual impulse." Russell was later forced to the conclusion that the love of system was the greatest barrier to honest thinking in philosophy; just as he decided that "the demand for certainty is one which is natural to man, but is nevertheless vice."

Russell put his conclusions in their most extreme form when he wrote in 1931 : "Academic philosophers, ever since the time of Parmendies, have believed that the world is a unity....The most fundamental of my intellectual beliefs is that this is rubbish. I think the universe is all spots and jumps, without unity, without continuity, without coherence or orderliness or any of the other properties that governesses love. Indeed, there is little but prejudice and habit to be said for the view that there is a world at all...."[7] "The external world may be an illusion, but if it exists, it consists of events, short, small and haphazard. Order, unity, and continuity are human inventions, just as truly as are catalogues and encyclopaedias."[8]

According to Russell, the aim of philosophy should be to equal the perfection of mathematics by confining itself to statements similarly exact, and similarly true before all experience. Russell's ambition was to reduce all philosophy to a rigid mathematical form, to take all specific content out of it, to compress it into mathematics.

"People have discovered how to make reasoning symbolic, as it is in algebra, so that dedcuctions can be effected by mathematical rules....Pure mathematics consists entirely of assetions to the effect that if such a proposition is true of anything, then such and such a proposition is ture of that thing. It is essential not to discuss whether the first proposition is really true, and not to mention what the anything is of which it is supposed to be true....Thus, mathematics may be defined as the subject in which we never know what we are talking about nor whether what we are saying is true..."[9]

4. Agnosticism. Bertrand Russell was almost fated to pass into agnosticism. He found so much in Christianity that could not be reconciled to science that he abandoned it all except its moral code. He was scornful of a civilization that persecutes men who deny Christianity and imprisons those who take it seriously.[10] He could find no God in such a contradictory world. He followed Spencer in his vision of the end of the world, and rose to eloquence in describing the Stoic's resignation to the ultimate defeat of every individual and every species. We talk of evolution and progress; but progress is an egotistical phrase and evolution is but half of an amoral cycle of events terminating in dissolution and death. "Organic life, we are told, has developed gradually from the protozoan to the philosopher; and this development, we are assured, is indubitably an advance. Unfortunately, it is the philosopher, not the protozoan, who gives us

7. *The Scientific Outlook*, p. 98.
8. *Ibid.*, p. 101.
9. *Mysticism and Logic*, pp. 75-76.
10. *Why Men Fight* (New York, 1917), p. 45.

this assurance."[11] The 'free man' cannot comfort himself with childish hopes and anthropomorphic gods. He has to keep his courage up even though he knows that in the end he too must die, that all things must die. Nevertheless, he will not surrender. If he cannot win, he can at least enjoy the fight, by the knowledge that foresees his own defect he stands superior to the blind forces that will destory him. His worship will go not to these brute powers without, that by their aimless persistence conquer him, and tear down every home and every civilization that he builds, but to those creative powers within him that struggle on in the face of failure, and raise for at least some centuries the frail beauty of carved and pictured things, and the majestic ruins of the Parthenon.

COMMITMENT TO COMMUNISM

Bertrand Russell, who had remained unknown to the world for many years, suddenly burst forth like a liberated flame, a man of great courage and a passionate lover of humanity. Out of the recesses of his formulae the scholar stepped forth, and poured out upon the most exalted statesmen of his country a flood of polemic that did not stop even when they ousted him from his chair at the University, and isolated him, like another Galileo, in a narrow quarter of London. Men who doubted his wisdom admitted his sincerity; but despite his most respectable origins this embattled pacifist was outlawed from society, and denounced as a traitor to the country which had nourished him and whose very existence seemed to be threatened by the maelstrom of the war. He was horrified by the war, and he tried to find out its causes. His conclusion was that private property was the cause and communism was the only cure.

COMPENSATION OF PRIVATE PROPERTY

All property, Russell pointed out, in his genial way, had its origin in violence and theft; in the Kimberley diamond mines and the Rand gold mines the transition of robbery into property was going on under the nose of the world. "No good to the community of any sort or kind, results from the private ownership of land. If men were reasonable they would decree that it should cease tomorrow, with no compensation beyond a moderate life-income to the present holders."[12] As private property is protected by the state, and the roberies that make proerpty are sanctioned by legislation and enforced by arms and war, the state is a great evil. Most of its functions must be taken over by co-operatives and producers' syndicates. Personality and individuality are curshed into a rote enformity by our societies; only the greater safety and orderlines of modern life can reconcile us to the state.

SAFEGUARDS OF LAW AND CUSTOM

In his famous book *Power* (1938), Russell stressed the psychological as distinct from the environmental forces in politics. He bought himself into

11. *Mysticism and Logic*, p. 75-76.

12. *Why Men Fight*, p. 134.

general line with the Chicago School by asserting a 'power interpretation' of politics. He admitted the need for coercive power against crime. But he concluded that the lust for power is natural in humanity and that it must be controlled. In his book *Power,* Russell wrote "Most of the great abominations in human history are connected with naked power — not only those associated with war, but others equally terrible if less spectacular. Slavery and the slave trade, the exploitation of the Congo, the horrors of early industrialism, cruetly to children, judicial torture, the cirminal law, prisons, work-houses, religious persecution, the atrocious treatment of the Jews, the merciless frivolities of despots, the unbelievable iniquity of the treatment of political opponents in Germany and Russia at the present-day — all these are examples of the use of naked power against defenceless victims."[13]

There must be power, either that of governments, or that of anarchic adventurers. There must even be naked power, as long as there are rebels against governments, or even ordinary cirminals. But if human life is to be anything better than a dull misery punctuated with moments of sharp horror, there must be as little naked power as possible. Russell remarked that the exercise of power, if it is to be something better than the infliction of wanton torture, must be hedged round by safeguards of law and custom, permitted only after due deliberation, entrusted to men who are closely supervised in the interests of those who are subjected to them.

It is useless to trust in the virtue of some individual or set of individuals. The philosopher king was dismissed long ago as an idle dream, but the philosopher party, though equally fallacious, is hailed as a great discovery. No real solution of the problem of power is to be found in irresponsible government by a minority, or in any other short cut. The permanent political solution of the problem of power is co-operation, not domination. The immediate individual duty is the unintimidated statement of permanent ethical values against Marxist or Fascist fanaticism and, if necessary, through pacifist non-violent resistance.

POLITICS IS THE STUDY OF POWER

According to Russell, politics is the study of power. Violence is the enemy of reason. Man is too sensitive to the allurements of power to be trusted, save with the utmost pragmatic caution to use violence to repel it. According to Russell, the use of force is permissible sometimes where there is the minimum possibility of illusion; crusading never above particular interests and sectional ideologies. Russell was hostile to every kind of force, which is being used for the coercion of the individual or individuals. And the state which mostly bases its authority on force did not find favour with Russell. He was hostile to the state more than Laski.

THEORY OF POLITICS : CREATIVE AND POSSESSIVE IMPULSES

Russell approached the theory of politics from a psychological point of

13. *Power* (Unwin Books, 1960), pp. 70-71.

view. Impulses, not conscious purpose, determine man's conduct. Man holds those beliefs that accord with his impulses. The reasons which he offers are quasi-rational. Man's conduct is normally governed by attempts to satisfy his impulses. His acts are directed not to the results which his innate tendencies involve but to the mere satisfaction of these tendencies themselves. According to Russell, there are two kinds of impulses : the creative and the possessive. The creative impulses are concerend with art and knowledge, of which there can be no exclusive ownership. The possessive, impulses are concerned with the acquisition of exclusive ownership. Material goods alone can be exclusively possessed; spiritual goods cannot. The possessive impulses involve taking things away from others; the creative impulses involve adding new things for all. Impulses should not be crushed. It is the task of social institutions to direct impulses to healthy channels. Russell wrote that "the supreme principles, both in politics and in private life, should be to promote all that is creative and so to distinguish the impulses and desires that centre round possession."[14]

THE INDIVIDUAL AND THE STATE AUTHORITY

According to Bertrand Russell, the state is not at all suited for the purpose of creative freedom. Its essence is power. Its basis is authority and tradition. It is thus unfit for the promotion of liberty. "The state and property are the great embodiments of possessiveness; it is for this reason that they are against life, and that they issue in war." In external affairs the state uses its power for purposes of exploitation. It is limited only by fear of defeat in war. Its very efficiency as a power encourages international anarchy. It is primarily an organization for killing foreigners that is its main purpose. There are, of course, other things it does. It does a certain amount of educating, but in the course of educating it tries very hard to make the young think that it is a grand thing to kill foreigners. Russell stated: "I mean, take for instance, that verse in the national anthem which they don't sing as often as they did when I was young, where it says, 'Confound their ravish tricks, frustrate their politics and make them fall.' We all used to sing that with great gusto about every foreigner."[15] A national state is based on tribal feeling, which is the root of patriotism. Patriotism is a false religion since it lacks universality. The state attempts to confine human obligation to one segment of humanity. Our love for our own nation must be supplemented by justice for all peoples. The power of the state is limited by the fear of rebellion or by the organized opposition of a strong group. Men obey the state because they fear anarchy within and aggression from outside.

Freedom is the supreme good; for without it personality is impossible. Life and knowledge are so complex, that only by free discussion can we pick our way through errors and prejudices to that total perspective which is truth. Let even teachers, differ and debate. Out of such diverse opinions will come an

14. *Principles of Social Reconstruction,* p. 236.

15. *Bertrand Russell Speaks His Mind* (Arthur Barker Ltd., London, second ed., Jan. 1961), p. 100.

intelligent relativity of belief which will not readily fly to arms. Hatred and war come largely of fixed ideas or dogmatic faith. Freedom of thought and speech would go like a cleansing draught through the neuroses and superstitions of the 'modern' mind.

EDUCATION : A SCIENTIFIC HABIT OF MIND

Russell Commented that we are not so educated as we think; we are but beginning the great experiment of Universal Schooling; and it has not had time to affect profoundly our ways of thinking and our public life. We are building the equipment, but we are still primitive in methods and technique. We think of education as the transmission of a certain body of settled knowledge, when it should be rather the development of a scientific habit of mind. The distinctive feature of the unintelligent man is the hastiness and absoluteness of his opinions; The scientist is slow to believe, and never speaks without modification. The larger use of science, and of scientific method, in education, would provide a measure of that intellectual conscience which believes only up to the evidence in hand, and is always ready to concede that it may be wrong. With such methods, education may prove the great solvent of our ills : It may even make of our children's children the new men and women who must come before the new society can appear. According to Russell, "The instinctive part of our character is very malleable. It may be changed by beliefs, by material circumstances, by social circumstances, and by instituions." It is now quite conceivable, that education could mould opinion to admire art more than wealth, as in the days of the Renaissance, and could guide itself by the resolution "to promote all that is creative, and so to diminish the impulses and desires that centre round possession." This is the principle of growth, whose corollaries would be the two great commandments of a new and natural morality: first, the Principle of Reverence, that "the vitality of individuals and communities is to be promoted as far as possible"; and second, the Principle of Tolerance, that "the growth of one individual or one community is to be as little as possible at the expense of another."[16]

If our splendid organization of schools and universities were properly developed and properly manned, and directed intelligently to the reconstruction of human character there is nothing that man might not do. Each individual has a distinct principle of growth which when distorted by governmental regimentation, makes the life of the individual flabby, dull, and exhausting. The impulsive actions of the individual, which are injurious to others, are mainly the result of attempts to block individual growth. Men should aim at harmony through differentiation, and not through mere aping of a uniform pattern. Russell states that "if human life is not to become dusty and uninteresting, it is important to realize that there are things that have a value which is quite independent of utility. What is useful is useful because it is a

---

16. *Why Men Fight*, pp. 101, 248, 256 : *Mysticism and Logic*, p. 108.

means to something else and the something else, if it is not in turn merely a means, must be valued for its own sake, for otherwise the usefulness is illusory."[17]

The sphere of individual action is not to be regarded as ethically inferior to that of social duty. On the contrary, some of the best human activities are rather personal than social. Prophets, mystics, poets, scientific discoverers are men whose lives are dominated by a vision while they are essentially solitary men. When their dominant impulse is strong, they feel that they cannot obey authority if it runs counter to what they profoundly believe to be good. Although, they are often persecuted in their own day, on this account, they are apt to be, of all men, those to whom posterity pays the highest honour. Such men put into the world the things that we must value, not only in religion, in art, and in science, but also in our way of feeling towards our neighbour. Improvements in the sense of social obligation, as in everything else, have been largely due to solitary men whose thoughts and emotions were not subject to the dominion of the herd.

SCORN OF DOGMATIC POLITICAL CREEDS

Russell felt that the world had become the victim of dogmatic political creeds, of which, the most powerful were capitalism and communism. He wrote: "I do not believe that either, in a dogmatic and unmitigated form, offers a cure for preventible evils. Capitalism gives opportunity of intiative to a few; communism could (though it does not in fact) provide a servile kind of security for all. But if people can rid themselves of the influence of unduly simple theories and the strife that they engender, it will be possible, by a wise use of scientific technique, to provide both opportunity for all and security for all. Unfortunately our political theories are less intelligent than our science, and we have not yet learnt how to make use of our knowledge and our skill in the ways that will do most to make life happy and even glorious. It is only experience and the fear of war that oppresses mankind, though this is perhaps the greatest of all the evils of our time. We are oppressed also by the greatest of all the evils of our time. We are oppressed also by the great impersonal forces that govern our daily life, making us still slaves of circumstance that no longer slaves in law. This need not be the case. It has come about through the worship of false gods. Energetic men have worshipped power rather than simple happiness and friendliness; men of less energy have acquiesced, or have been deceived by a wrong diagnosis of the sources of sorrow."[18]

Russell stood for a simple and unsophisticated life. He praised China for its faith in simple life when he went for a year to teach there. He felt that there was less mechanism, and a slower pace; one could sit down and reason, and life would stand while one dissected it. He, remarked : "I have come to realize that the white race is not as important as I used to think it was. If Europe and America kill themselves off in war it will not necessarily mean the destruction

17. *Authority and Individual* (second impression 1955, George Allen & Unwin Ltd., London), p. 113.

18. *Ibid., pp.* 120-21.

of the human species, nor even an end to civilization. There still will be a considerable number of Chinese left; and in many ways China is the greatest country I have ever seen. It is not only the greatest numerically but the greatest culturally. It seems to me the greatest nation intellectually. I know of no other civilization where there is such open-mindedness, such realism, such a willingness to face the facts as they are, instead of trying to distort them into a particular pattern."[19]

But as the situation completely changed in Communist China, Russell regarded it as great a threat to world peace and humanity.[20]

CAPITALISM, COMMUNISM AND SOCIALISM

Russell thought that in oder to serve the purpose of individual freedom a reconstruction of institution was fundamental. The capitalist autocracy in industry must be abolished. In this connection Russell remarked that socialism is not only inevitable, but desirable. Care must be taken, however, not to substitute the dictatorship of the administrator for the dictatorship of the capitalist. Russell praised communism and had high hopes from it, but when he visited Russia, he was disappointed to find out that the Russian government did not tolerate liberalism, freedom and democracy. Russell was so angered by the suppression of free speech and free press, and by the resolute monoply and systematic use of Russian people; the ability to read being, in this age of subsidized newspapers, an impediment to the acquisition of truth. Russell was shocked to find that nationalization of the land had been forced to yield to private ownership. It dawned upon him that men, as made today, will not properly till and husband their holdings unless they can rely on transmitting them, and the improvements which they put into them, to their children. "Russia seems on the way to becoming a greater France, a great nation of peasant proprietors. The old feudalism has disappeared," Russell observed. He began to understand that this dramatic overturn with all its sacrifices and all its heroism, was only Russia's 1789. Hence, it is necessary that a regenerated society, must see an end to the evils of property and also to the evils of power. Equalization of power must follow equalization of wealth. A social system, must not only secure economic justice, but also the greatest possible development of the creative impulses. A vast dispersion of power by functional and territorial federalism is necessary.

DECENTRALIZATION OF POWER

Decentralization provides new opportunities for hopefulness and for individual activities that embody hopes. If our political thoughts are all concerned with vast problems and dangers of world catastrophe, it is easy to become despairing. Fear of war, fear of revolution, fear of reaction, may obsess you according to your temperament and your party bias. Russell said, "Unless you are one of a very small number of powerful individuals, you are likely to feel that you cannot do much about these great issues. But in relation to smaller

19. Interview in *New York World*, May 4, 1924.

20. *Bertrand Russell Speaks His Mind* (Arthur Barker Ltd., London, second imp., Jan 1961), p. 56.

problems — those of your town, or your trade union, or the local branch of your political party, for example — you can hope to have a successful influence."[21] This will engender a hopeful spirit, which is most needed if a way is to be found of dealing successfully with the larger problems. War shortages and financial stringency have caused almost universal fatigue. These have made hopefulness seem shallow and insincere. Success is the best cure for this mood of pessimistic weariness. For most people, success means breaking up our problems, and being free to concentrate on those that are not too desperately large.

FUNCTION OF THE STATE IN INDUSTRY

Russell supported the principle of self-government in industry. The interests of the consumers can best be represented by *ad hoc* organizations. The state cannot represent consumers, since when industry is concentrated in different sections the representatives of these districts in the government really represent the producers. The state should retain ownership of land and industrial capital, determine prices and quantity needed of each commodity. It should also have power to prevent any particular organization from acting in hostility to the interests of the community. It may also have the power of making war and peace, tariffs, and foreign policy. But international questions like movement of population and apportionment of raw material can best be settled by special functional organizations. Both producers and consumers may use strikes and boycotts to enforce their demands. With the abolition of capitalism the state will be neutral in disputes between organizations. It may, therefore, demand arbitration, and then offer its decisions for the guidance of public opinion. The principle of organization should be self-government for each organization in those activities that concern it alone, and regulation by a neutral authority of those activities that also concern others.

DEMAND FOR INDIVIDUAL FREEDOM

Bertrand Russell demanded individual freedom which is a characteristic aspect of contemporary thought. The state is no logner a glorified policeman, but is becoming virtually a national householder. It participates in industry, education, sanitation, and sometimes alone manages innumerable industrial undertakings, like other individualists. Russell conceived the state as an external force.

When Russell accussed the collectivists of not being conscious of the dangers of concentration of power; he had in mind the collectivism of the older type. In order to avoid the evils of power, the Webbs stressed individuality, decentralization, publicity, participation of workers. Older variety collectivism was undoubtedly an enemy of liberty. With liberal socialists, Russell recognize the necessity of protecting and encouraging variation and growth. The issue,

21. *Ibid.*, pp. 119-20.

between Russell and Webbs was not whether liberty was desirable, but by what means it could best be attained. Russell's suggestions for self-government in industry and for the organization of functional associations are realizable only after a long and gradual transition. He wrote in *Practice and Theory of Bolshevism* (1920): "When I suggested that whatever is possible in England can be achieved without bloodshed, he (Lenin) waved aside the suggestion as fantastic idea except in time of national misfortune. It is by slower and less showy methods that new world must be built." Therefore, for more immediate purposes, a greater participation by the workers in industry and a greater decentralization of the functions of the present state is important.

CRITICAL ESTIMATE

Wide experience from England to America, and then to Russia, and then to India and China, convinced Bertrand Russell that it was too big for his formulae. One found him in the last decade of his life "an older and a wiser man," mellowed by time and a varied life; as wide-awake as ever to all the ills that flesh is heir to and yet matured into the moderation that knows the difficulties of social change. Russell was a very lovable man; capable of the profoundest metaphysics and the subtlest mathematics, and yet always speaking with the clarity which comes only to those who are sincere. He was a scholar and a gentleman, and a better Christian than many who consider themselves true heir to Christianity and religion. Throughout his life he fought for the cause of world peace.

QUESTIONS FOR EXERCISE

1. Estimate briefly the contribution of Bertrand Russell to political thought.
2. "If mankind succeeds in abolishing war it should not be difficult to find other outlets for the love of adventure and risk" — Bertrand Russell. Discuss.
3. "But although Guild Socialism respresents an attempt between two equally legitimate points of view, its impulse and force are derived from what it has taken over from syndicalism" — Bertrand Russell. Explain.

U-96- 1193372/L